Microprocessor-based Systems
Level IV

Units in this series

Microprocessor-based Systems

Level IV

A. Potton

Department of Technology, Mathematics and Computing, Dorset Institute of Higher Education

TECHNICIAN EDUCATION COUNCIL
in association with
HUTCHINSON
London Melbourne Sydney Auckland Johannesburg

Hutchinson Education

An imprint of Century Hutchinson Limited

62-65 Chandos Place, London WC2N 4NW

Century Hutchinson Australia Pty Ltd
PO Box 496, 16-22 Church Street,
Hawthorn, Melbourne, Victoria 3122, Australia

Century Hutchinson New Zealand Limited
PO Box 40-086, Glenfield, Auckland 10, New Zealand

Century Hutchinson South Africa (Pty) Ltd
PO Box 337, Bergvlei 2012, South Africa

First published 1983
Reprinted 1984, 1986

Set in Times

Printed and bound in Great Britain by
Anchor Brendon Ltd, Tiptree, Essex

British Library Cataloguing in Publication Data
Microprocessor-based systems Level IV.
   1. Microprocessors
   2. Technician Education Council
621.3819′5835   TK7895.M5

ISBN 0 09 148911 3

Contents

Appendices

Preface

This book is one of a series on microelectronics/microprocessors published by Hutchinson on behalf of the Technician Education Council. The books in the series are designed for use with units associated with Technician Education Council programmes.

In June 1978 the United Kingdom Prime Minister expressed anxiety about the effect to be expected from the introduction of microprocessors on the pattern of employment in specific industries. From this stemmed an initiative through the Department of Industry and the National Enterprise Board to encourage the use and development of microprocessor technology.

An important aspect of such a development programme was seen as being the education and training of personnel for both the research, development and manufacture of microelectronics material and equipment, and the application of these in other industries. In 1979 a project was established by the Technician Education Council for the development of technician education programme units (a unit is a specification of the objectives to be attained by a student) and associated learning packages, this project being funded by the Department of Industry and managed on their behalf by the National Computing Centre Ltd.

TEC established a committee involving industry, both as producers and users of microelectronics, and educationists. In addition widespread consultations took place. Programme units were developed for technicians and technician engineers concerned with the design, manufacture and servicing aspects incorporating microelectronic devices. Five units were produced:

Microelectronic Systems	Level I
Microelectronic Systems	Level II
Microelectronic Systems	Level III
Microprocessor-based Systems	Level IV
Microprocessor-based Systems	Level V

Units were also produced for those technicians who required a general understanding of the range of applications of microelectronic devices and their potential:

Microprocessor Appreciation	Level III
Microprocessor Principles	Level IV

This phase was then followed by the development of the learning packages, involving three writing teams, the key people in these teams being:

Microelectronic Systems I, II, III — P. Cooke
Microprocessor-based Systems IV — A. Potton
Microprocessor-based Systems V — M. J. Morse
Microprocessor Appreciation III — G. Martin
Microprocessor Principles IV   — G. Martin

The project director during the unit specification stage was N. Bonnett, assisted by R. Bertie. Mr Bonnett continued as consultant during the writing stage. The project manager was W. Bolton, assisted by K. Snape.

Self-learning

As an aid to self-learning, questions are included in every chapter. These appear at the end of the chapters with references in the margin of the chapter text (for example Q1.2), indicating the most appropriate position for self-learning use. Answers to each question are given at the back of the book.

The books in this series have therefore been developed for use in either the classroom teaching situation or for self-learning.

Introduction

This book, which is written to the objectives specified in the TEC Unit Microprocessor-based Systems U80/674, is intended for readers with some basic knowledge of the architecture and instruction set of a microprocessor. The material in the book builds on this initial knowledge to give a deeper and broader understanding of microprocessors themselves and the way they function in systems.

A major section of the text describes methods of designing and developing microprocessor-based systems. Particular emphasis is placed on planning and the use of well established formal design procedures for both hardware and software. Top-down structured methods are advocated for software design. In most cases, program examples are given in three versions for the 8080, Z80 and M6800 microprocessors. The role of special-purpose microprocessor development systems to assist the design and debugging of hardware and software is investigated in some depth.

To broaden the reader's knowledge, the features of a range of different microprocessors are compared and contrasted. Devices used as examples range from a simple 4-bit single-chip microcomputer to one of the new powerful 16-bit microprocessors. The characteristics of a variety of compatible support devices are also described. This development of comparison procedures is extended to microprocessor systems.

The later stages of the book introduce the principles of fault location in microprocessor systems. Methods of fault location using traditional instruments such as oscilloscopes and multimeters are described. A major part of this section, however, relates to the use of special-purpose equipment such as microprocessor development systems, logic analysers and signature analysers. Also included in this later part of the book is a description of EPROMs and their use in microprocessor systems together with EPROM programming methods.

Since the book is mainly concerned with real semiconductor devices, brief manufacturers' data for a range of devices is included in appendices. For reasons of space and cost, this is necessarily restricted; the reader is advised to obtain the complete data sheets from the manufacturers concerned.

Acknowledgement

I would like to thank my wife, Dorothy, not only for her expert typing of the manuscript but also for her forebearance during the book's gestation period.

Bournemouth, November 1982   A. POTTON

Chapter 1 Assemblers and assembly language

Objectives of the chapter *When you have completed studying this chapter you should be able to:*

1 *Describe the process by which object code is assembled from the source program.*
2 *State that a function of an editor is to prepare an assembly language source program.*
3 *Interpret the information provided by the assembly listing.*
4 *State the function of pseudo-ops.*
5 *Identify the essential difference between pseudo-ops and executable instructions.*
6 *State how a relocatable program differs from an absolute program.*
7 *Describe the function of a locator/relocator.*
8 *Describe the function of a linker.*
9 *Explain the need for global variables in linked programs.*

1.1 Computer language

Today, an increasing number of people of all kinds are learning how to program computers; the teaching of computer programming is now common in many primary and secondary schools in this country, for example. Depending on the type of computing task, students will be initially taught to program using one of two different approaches. These are:

1 Writing programs in a high-level language such as BASIC, FORTRAN, PASCAL, etc. These languages are efficient in the use of programmer's time in that programs to perform quite complicated tasks can be produced relatively quickly. When writing programs in these languages, the student does not need to understand any of the internal operations within the computing system he is using. High-level languages are by far the best approach to the vast majority of general-purpose computing tasks.
2 Writing programs in machine-code form. With this approach, programs to perform even simple tasks can take quite a long time to develop. It is therefore inefficient in the use of programmer's time. To be successful in writing machine-code programs, the programmer must have a good understanding of the internal structure and fundamental instruction set of the computer being

used. For this reason, potential designers of circuits or systems that include microprocessors will normally learn machine-code programming methods. In this text, we assume that readers have had some exposure to machine-code programming.

Although machine code and assembly language programs take far too long to develop for general-purpose computing tasks, they are of vital importance to the designer of computer circuits and systems. This is because machine-code instructions allow the programmer a much more direct and immediate control over circuit and system hardware than is the case with high-level language statements.

It is not the purpose of this text to act as an assembly language programming manual for any particular microprocessor. Instead, the reader is referred to the manuals provided with the computing system he is using. In this chapter, the aim is to provide a general background to some of the more important aspects of assemblers and assembly language. This material is included at the beginning of the book since assembly language mnemonic source code is usually the most convenient means of describing microprocessor operations at the machine-code level and is so used throughout later chapters. A more fundamental treatment of formal programming methods is deferred until Chapter 8.

1.2   Assemblers

When writing programs for a microprocessor in machine code, the program is first written down in the form of standard instruction mnemonics such as MOV, LDA, etc. The programmer then looks up the codes for the various instructions in a table included in the microprocessor data sheet. Programs written in this way can be loaded into memory using the very simplest type of computing system.

The process of converting the mnemonic instructions to code form, usually written in hexadecimal format, is called hand assembly. Most simple microcomputers allow hexadecimal code to be entered directly via a keyboard which converts it to binary form and stores it in memory. Examples of microcomputers that operate at this level are the Motorola MEK6800D2, Nascom 1, Kim, and the Intel SDK80 and SDK85. No doubt many readers will have experience in the use of a system of this kind.

1.3   Hexadecimal number representation

Instruction codes and numbers within a digital computer are essentially binary in form since conventional digital electronic devices manipulate data in the form of ones and zeros. Hexadecimal representation is a convenient way of describing binary numbers as shown below:

1100	1001	0001	1111	Binary
C	9	1	F	Hexadecimal

It is assumed that the reader is familiar with the use of hexadecimal numbers in this way.

The different assemblers described in this chapter require the user to identify hexadecimal numbers in a variety of ways. Rather than adopting the standard used by any one assembler, the following rule is observed:

Unless otherwise stated, all addresses and machine code are in hexadecimal form

No special appendage is used with hexadecimal numbers. Wherever ambiguity can occur, numbers are identified explicitly by writing the number type in brackets after the digits as shown below:

   10 (dec)
   103 (hex)
   1101 (binary)

1.4   Different assemblers

In texts in which assembly language is the primary vehicle for developing programming techniques, it is common to restrict the treatment to one microprocessor and one assembler. This has the admirable result of ensuring consistency and giving the least cause for confusion in the mind of the reader. One of the objectives of this text, however, is to broaden the reader's understanding of different types of microprocessor, allowing, among other things, proper methods of comparison to be established. To meet this broadening objective therefore, programs are presented throughout the text which have been developed using a variety of different microcomputer systems incorporating a variety of microprocessors.

In general the majority of programming examples will be given with code for three different microprocessors: the 8080, M6800 and Z80. From time to time, program code for other microprocessors will also be included. In the preparation of program examples, the following microprocessor systems were used (the final version of program listing has normally been produced using the Futuredata system):

1   GR Futuredata universal microprocessor development system supporting assemblers for 8080, Z80 and M6800 microprocessors.
2   North Star Horizon supporting standard CP/M 8080 assembler ASM.
3   Nascom 2 supporting Z80 'ZEAP' assembler.
4   SWTP 6800 system supporting 6800 assembler ASMB.

5 Zilog system supporting Z8002 assembler.

In addition to illustrating the facilities available with different systems, it is hoped that providing program code for different microprocessors will make the text relevant to the systems actually available to as wide a range of readers as possible. The majority of program examples are produced using the Futuredata system. Apart from its general efficiency, this system supports assemblers for the M6800, 8080 and Z80 and provides some measure of consistency of format, number representation, etc., in the assembly listings. Differences between the assemblers offered by the various systems will be identified as the various general features are described in the following sections.

Object
program   *Source*
(hex)   *program*

```
3E 04       MVI   A,X'04'
06 3F       MVI   B,X'3F'
87          ADD   A
32 00 01    STA   X'0100'
```

Figure 1.1

In the discussion that follows, a program written using the manufacturer's instruction mnemonics for a particular microprocessor will be called the source program. The assembler converts this source program into machine-code form. The resulting machine code is called the object program. The process of converting the source program into the object program is called assembly. Machine code and data may be represented in hexadecimal format.

A mnemonic source program with the corresponding machine-code object program is shown in Figure 1.1.

1.5   Mnemonic translation

At its most fundamental level, an assembler program acts as a translator to convert instruction mnemonics into the corresponding machine code. Consider the following instruction mnemonic for the 8080 microprocessor.

    INX   B

The code for this instruction is

    00000100 (binary) = 04

This is the code that must be placed in memory in the correct location together with the codes for any other instructions of a program before the program can be executed. Once the instruction codes are in memory, the program can be executed. One function of an assembler for 8080 mnemonics is therefore to convert INX B into 04.

Digital computers manipulate data in binary form. To perform translation of mnemonics, it is therefore necessary to present them to the computer in binary form. This is normally done by the console device of the microprocessor development system. The console will typically consist of a video display terminal (VDT) incorporating a keyboard rather like that of a typewriter. When a key is depressed, a code corresponding to the letter or number on the key is transmitted to the

> See note in Preface about questions

Q1.2

computer. An input program running at the time stores the character code in memory.

Various internationally agreed codes are in existence to represent numbers, letters, punctuation marks, etc. One of the most common is the American Standard Code for Information Interchange (ASCII) given in Appendix R.

The program that takes in ASCII code characters from the VDT keyboard will normally echo characters back for display on the VDT screen. This is a useful check for the operator. In addition, the program may provide facilities for the easy correction of mistakes in the text characters entered. The program would be described as an editor in this case. Editors are discussed in Section 7.3.

Q1.3

Suppose that a particular editor program stores character codes in memory starting at location 1000. Table 1.1 shows the contents of this area of memory when the following two lines of the program have been entered:

```
MVI   A,03
ADD   B
```

Note that character codes for space and control functions, carriage return and line feed are also included.

Q1.1

When the characters for a complete source program have been stored in this way, the assembler program is then executed. The assembler scans the area of memory containing the coded program, searching for combinations of text characters which represent instruction mnemonics. When a combination such as ADD B is recognised, the assembler then forms the byte 80 which is the corresponding machine instruction code.

It should be obvious from the discussion up to this point that the assembly language particular to one microprocessor cannot be used for another microprocessor unless the instruction sets are identical. Even where compatibility apparently exists, assembly languages may not be interchangeable between microprocessors. For example, the instruction set of the 8080 microprocessor is a subset of the Z80 instruction set. It might therefore be thought that a Z80 assembler could be used to produce machine-code programs for an 8080 provided that instructions are restricted to those appropriate to the 8080. In fact, different mnemonics are used by the manufacturers of the 8080 (Intel) and the Z80 (Zilog), even for identical instructions. Thus the machine-code instruction 04 is described by the mnemonic INX B for the 8080 and INC BC for the Z80. To use the Z80 assembler for 8080 programs, the programmer would therefore need to convert his programs to Z80 mnemonic form.

The description, given above, relating to the mnemonic translation

Table 1.1

Character	Address	Contents (ASCII)
M	1000	4D
V	1001	56
I	1002	49
SP	1003	20
A	1004	41
,	1005	2C
0	1006	30
3	1007	33
CR	1008	0D
LF	1009	0A
A	100A	41
D	100B	44
D	100C	44
SP	100D	20
B	100E	42

process is somewhat simplified. Many instructions consist not only of operation codes (*opcodes*) but will also include operands. The instruction for the 8080 microprocessor MVI A,03 for example, when executed, causes 03 to be loaded into register A. The code for this instruction occupies two bytes. The first byte is the opcode 3E, the second the operand 03. Operations performed by the assembler in this case include the translation of the ASCII code characters for 03 to the corresponding binary number. Fortunately, it is not necessary to understand the internal workings of an assembler in great detail in order to become an effective assembly language programmer.

1.6   The assembly listing

During the process of assembling a machine-code object program from the mnemonic source program, the assembler produces an assembly listing. This is essentially a copy of the source program with the machine code produced by each mnemonic instruction. Figure 1.2 shows the listing for an 8080 assembly language program. An indication of the information contained in the listing has been added.

The assembly listing is a valuable item of program documentation and serves a vital function in assisting program debugging. A further advantage is the facility for introducing comments in the listing as discussed in Section 1.8. For documentation purposes, a microprocessor development system will normally include a printer which is used for making a permanent copy of the listing.

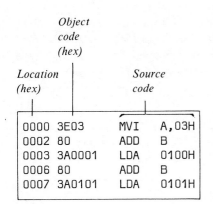

Figure 1.2 Information contained in the assembly listing

1.7   Symbolic addresses

When writing programs in machine code, it is necessary for the programmer to keep track of the locations in which the individual instruction codes will be ultimately stored. This is because some instruction codes are dependent on the locations in memory at which other instruction codes are stored.

Consider the program listing shown in Figure 1.3. The JNZ conditional jump instruction at the end of the program has an operand 0103 which is the address of the next instruction to be executed if the jump condition is met. The code word for the instruction as a whole therefore depends on the location of the MOV A,M instruction, currently at location 0103 which is the destination address for the JNZ instruction.

Suppose now that an error is found in the program requiring the insertion of additional instructions near the beginning. Let us assume that we wish the first instruction of the program to be at 0100 as before and that we wish the destination of the JNZ operation to be the MOV A,M as before. In this case, the operand of the JNZ instruction

```
                                                          PAGE    1
-- 8080/85 ASSEMBLER V01 --------------------- FUTUREDATA -

0000                         ORG     X'0100'
0100 210012                  LXI     H,X'1200'
0103 7E                      MOV     A,M
0104 C605                    ADI     5
0106 77                      MOV     M,A
0107 23                      INX     H
0108 05                      DCR     B
0109 C20301                  JNZ     X'0103'
010C                         END
```

Q1.4   *Figure 1.3*

```
                                                          PAGE    1
-- 8080/85 ASSEMBLER V01 --------------------- FUTUREDATA -

0000                         ORG     X'0100'
0100 210012                  LXI     H,X'1200'
0103 060A                    MVI     B,10
0105 110001                  LXI     D,X'0100'
0108 7E                      MOV     A,M
0109 C605                    ADI     5
010B 77                      MOV     M,A
010C E1                      POP     H
010D 23                      INX     H
010E 05                      DCR     B
010F C20801                  JNZ     X'0108'
0112                         END
```

Figure 1.4

must be changed to 0108 as shown in the listing in Figure 1.4. Any program modifications that involve the insertion or removal of instructions must therefore be carried out with care. When using numerical addresses, a detailed check should be made on any modifications required to the destination addresses for jump or branch instructions. The problem exists for both absolute and relative jumps and branches.

Assemblers allow a label to be included at the beginning of a line of the source program. The label then becomes the symbolic address at which the instruction code assembled from the same line is subsequently stored. This symbolic address can then be used as an operand in other instructions. Figures 1.5 and 1.6 show the same

```
                                                          PAGE    1
-- 8080/85 ASSEMBLER V01 --------------------- FUTUREDATA -

0000                         ORG     X'0100'
0100 210012                  LXI     H,X'1200'
0103 7E        AGAIN         MOV     A,M
0104 C605                    ADI     5
0106 77                      MOV     M,A
0107 23                      INX     H
0108 05                      DCR     B
0109 C20301                  JNZ     AGAIN
010C                         END
```

Figure 1.5

```
-- 8080/85 ASSEMBLER V01 --------------------- PAGE   1
                                                 FUTUREDATA
0000                          ORG     X'0100'
0100 210012                  LXI     H,X'1200'
0103 060A                    MVI     B,10
0105 110001                  LXI     D,X'0100'
0108 7E          AGAIN       MOV     A,M
0109 C605                    ADI     5
010B 77                      MOV     M,A
010C E1                      POP     H
010D 23                      INX     H
010E 05                      DCR     B
010F C20801                  JNZ     AGAIN
0112                         END
```

Figure 1.6

programs as Figures 1.3 and 1.4 but using a symbolic address as the operand of the JNZ instruction. It will be seen that the assembler automatically inserts the correct numerical value for the jump destination address.

The use of symbolic addressing can be extended to identify any memory location, whether or not it contains an instruction code. This is convenient since it allows locations used to store data to be referred to symbolically. A full description of this facility requires an understanding of pseudo-ops and is therefore deferred until Section 1.10.

Labels and symbolic addresses if carefully chosen can help to improve the 'readability' of the assembly listing. In Figures 1.5 and 1.6, for example, the destination address for the JNZ instruction is, of course, the beginning of a loop structure. The choice of the symbolic address, AGAIN, helps to remind the reader that a loop is involved. This may appear trivial but is important. One of the major problems with assembly language programs is that unless they are carefully presented and documented it is very difficult for anyone but the programmer to interpret them. An imaginative choice of symbolic addresses is one feature of good program documentation.

For the 8080 assembler used to generate the majority of the listings in this chapter, the number of characters in a label must not exceed sixteen. Characters may be alphanumeric (letters or numbers), but the first character must always be a letter.

1.8   Comments

As a further aid to make the assembly listing more readable, assemblers allow the programmer to insert comments at appropriate points in the source program. Figure 1.8 shows a listing for a program with the same code as that of Figure 1.7, but with comments added. If comments are written with care, they can describe the program structure and also present a 'running commentary' on operations performed by the program.

From Figure 1.8 it will be seen that the 8080 assembler used in the

```
                                                                    PAGE   1
        -- 8080/85 ASSEMBLER V01 --------------------- FUTUREDATA -

        0000                        ORG     X'0100'
        0100 210012                 LXI     H,X'1200'
        0103 222801                 SHLD    PTR1
        0106 210013                 LXI     H,X'1300'
        0109 222A01                 SHLD    PTR2
        010C 060A                   MVI     B,10
        010E 2A2801     AGAIN       LHLD    PTR1
        0111 7E                     MOV     A,M
        0112 C605                   ADI     5
        0114 2A2A01                 LHLD    PTR2
        0117 77                     MOV     M,A
        0118 23                     INX     H
        0119 222A01                 SHLD    PTR2
        011C 2A2801                 LHLD    PTR1
        011F 23                     INX     H
        0120 222801                 SHLD    PTR1
        0123 05                     DCR     B
        0124 C20E01                 JNZ     AGAIN
        0127 00                     NOP
        0128            PTR1         DS      2
        012A            PTR2         DS      2
        012C                         END
```

Figure 1.7 Uncommented program

```
                                                         PAGE   1
    -------- 8080/85 ASSEMBLER V01 ---------------------------- FUTUREDATA --------

                *********************************************************
                *THIS PROGRAM ADDS 5(DECIMAL) TO EACH NUMBER IN A       *
                *LIST                                                   *
                *RESULTS ARE STORED IN A NEW LIST                       *
                *THE OLD LIST CONTAINS TEN ENTRIES AND STARTS AT        *
                *1200.                                                  *
                *THE NEW LIST STARTS AT 1300                            *
                *                                                       *
                *                    STRUCTURE                          *
                *                    *********                          *
                *POINTER1 = X'1000'                                     *
                *POINTER2 = X'1300'                                     *
                *LOOP = 10                                              *
                *DO UNTIL LOOP = 0                                      *
                *    GET NUMBER POINTED BY POINTER1                     *
                *    NUMBER = NUMBER + 5                                *
                *    STORE NUMBER IN ADDRESS POINTED BY POINTER2        *
                *    POINTER2 = POINTER2 + 1                            *
                *    POINTER1 = POINTER1 + 1                            *
                *    LOOP = LOOP - 1                                    *
                *END DO                                                 *
                *********************************************************
                *
0000                                ORG     X'0100'
0100 210012                         LXI     H,X'1200'
0103 222801                         SHLD    PTR1            POINTER1 = X'1200'
0106 210013                         LXI     H,X'1300'
0109 222A01                         SHLD    PTR2            POINTER2 = X'1300'
010C 060A                           MVI     B,10            B = 10(DECIMAL) = LOOP
010E 2A2801     AGAIN               LHLD    PTR1            GET POINTER1 IN HL
0111 7E                             MOV     A,M             GET POINTED NUMBER
0112 C605                           ADI     5               NUMBER = NUMBER + 5
0114 2A2A01                         LHLD    PTR2            GET POINTER2 IN HL
0117 77                             MOV     M,A             STORE NUMBER IN POINTED ADDRESS
0118 23                             INX     H               POINTER2 = POINTER2 + 1
0119 222A01                         SHLD    PTR2            SAVE POINTER2
011C 2A2801                         LHLD    PTR1            GET POINTER1 IN HL
011F 23                             INX     H               POINTER1 = POINTER1 + 1
0120 222801                         SHLD    PTR1            SAVE POINTER1
0123 05                             DCR     B               LOOP = LOOP - 1
0124 C20E01                         JNZ     AGAIN           END DO?
0127 00                             NOP
                *
                *
0128            PTR1                 DS      2               POINTER1
012A            PTR2                 DS      2               POINTER2
012C                                 END
```

Figure 1.8

example allows comments to follow the operand in a line containing an instruction mnemonic. Comments may also occupy whole lines of the source program. In this case, the comment line must start with an asterisk. The details of how comments are identified vary, depending on the particular assembler used. Some assemblers require a semi-colon (;) to precede comments, for example.

Comments affect only the assembly listing. They do not affect the assembled machine-code program.

1.9   Data constant representation

We have said in Section 1.3 that, throughout this text, numbers identifying program code or addresses are assumed to be hexadecimal unless otherwise stated. Hexadecimal numbers are not therefore distinguished in any special way. In most assembly language source programs, however, it is necessary to identify hexadecimal numbers in a way that distinguishes them from decimal numbers. With all of the assemblers used here to generate program listings, a number appearing with no extra identification in the source program is interpreted as being decimal. Table 1.2 shows the way hexadecimal numbers must be identified with the different assemblers.

Table 1.2

Assembler	Decimal number	Hexadecimal number
Futuredata 8080	nn	X'nn'
Futuredata Z80	nn	X'nn'
Futuredata 6800	nn	X'nn'
CP/M 8080 ASM	nn	nnH
Nascom Z80 ZEAP	nn	nnH
SWTP 6800 ASMB	nn	$nn
Zilog Z8000 PLZ/ASM	nn	%nn

Table 1.3

Assembler	Instruction	
Futuredata 8080	MVI	A,X'F3'
Futuredata Z80	LD	A,X'F3'
Futuredata 6800	LDAA	#X'F3'
CP/M 8080 ASM	MVI	A,0F3H
Nascom Z80 ZEAP	LD	A,0F3H
SWTP 6800 ASMB	LDAA	#$F3

A list of source code instructions for the different assemblers is given in Table 1.3. Each of the instructions causes register A of the microprocessor concerned to be loaded with F3. Note that in the case of CP/M8080 ASM and Nascom Z80 ZEAP, hexadecimal numbers must not have a first digit consisting of a letter. Thus F3 must be written as 0F3H. Note also that the '#' character in the SWTP 6800 ASMB Futuredata 6800 examples is not part of the hexadecimal number format but indicates that the immediate mode of addressing is specified.

Some assemblers also allow the programmer to specify numbers in binary and octal form by appending appropriate characters. The CP/M 8080 assembler, for example, accepts binary and octal numbers as shown in the program in Figure 1.9. The letter 'B' appended to a number identifies it as binary whereas 'O' implies octal. With decimal numbers the appended letter 'D' is optional. Note that this assembler requires hexadecimal numbers to start with a numeric character. Thus F3 must be expanded to 0F3.

```
0000  0EB3     MVI    C,10110011B
0002  061F     MVI    B,037O
0004  018303   LXI    B,899D
0007  3AC23F   LDA    3FC2H
000A  3E41     MVI    A,'A'
000C  21335A   LXI    H,'3Z'
```

Figure 1.9   Constant representation using CP/M 8080 assembler

The last two lines of Figure 1.9 show how ASCII-coded characters can be used in the source program by enclosing them in quotes. Taking the instruction MVI A,'A' for example, we note that it assembles to the two-byte code 3E 41. Now 3E is the opcode for MVI and 41 is the ASCII-code representation of A. The ability of the assembler to convert text strings to ASCII code form is very convenient when writing programs which put out messages to a printer or VDT.

1.10   Pseudo-ops

It will be recalled that during the process of assembling a program, the assembler scans the coded characters of the source program in a search for valid instruction mnemonics. Pseudo-ops are mnemonics that are not part of the microprocessor instruction set, but are recognised by the assembler. Since they are not part of the mnemonic instruction set, pseudo-ops are not assembled into executable instructions. They are a means by which the programmer passes information to the assembler for use during the assembly process.

Q1.5, 1.6

```
                                                             PAGE   1
 -------- 8080/85 ASSEMBLER V01 ----------------------------- FUTUREDATA --------

              ****************************************************
              *THIS PROGRAM TAKES IN FIFTY NUMBERS VIA PORT 1F AND *
              *CONVERTS THEM TO ASCII CODE FORM.                 *
              *THE CODE CHARACTERS ARE STORED IN A LIST STARTING AT*
              *1F00                                              *
              *STATUS WORD IS INPUT VIA PORT 1E                  *
              *NUMBER SOURCE NOT READY IN STATUS WORD = 0        *
              *                                                  *
              *                  STRUCTURE                       *
              *                  ********                        *
              *LOOP = 50(DECIMAL)                                *
              *POINTER = X'1F00'                                 *
              *DO UNTIL LOOP = 0                                 *
              *    DO UNTIL STATUS = READY                       *
              *       SCAN STATUS WORD                           *
              *    END DO                                        *
              *    INPUT NUMBER                                  *
              *    CONVERT TO ASCII                              *
              *    STORE IN POINTED ADDRESS                      *
              *    POINTER = POINTER + 1                         *
              *    LOOP = LOOP - 1                               *
              *    END DO                                        *
              ****************************************************
              *
 0000                    ORG     X'1000'
 1000 0632               MVI     B,50                 LOOP = 50
 1002 21001F             LXI     H,LIST               POINTER = LIST = H
 1005 DB1E    NEXTIN     IN      X'1E'                INPUT STATUS
 1007 CA0510             JZ      NEXTIN
 100A DB1F               IN      X'1F'                INPUT NUMBER
 100C 0E30               MVI     C,X'30'
 100E B1                 ORA     C                    CONVERT TO ASCII
 100F 77                 MOV     M,A                  STORE IN LIST
 1010 23                 INX     H                    POINTER = POINTER + 1
 1011 05                 DCR     B                    LOOP = LOOP - 1
 1012 C20510             JNZ     NEXTIN
              *
 1015                    ORG     X'1F00'
 1F00         LIST       DS      50                   RESERVE 50(DECIMAL) LOCATIONS
 1F32                    END
```

Figure 1.10

Figure 1.10 is an assembly listing for a program which includes pseudo-ops, the first of which is ORG. This pseudo-op is used twice. On the first occasion, it occurs in the following line of the source program

```
ORG  X'1000'
```

Q1.8 When the program is assembled, the assembler interprets this line as meaning that the machine code for the next executable instruction of the program will be stored starting at location 1000. Thus the MVI B,50 mnemonic on the next lines assembles as the two-byte code 06,32 which is assumed to be ultimately stored in locations 1000 and 1001. It should be emphasised that these machine-code instructions are not actually stored in memory at this point. The assembler simply uses the information when assembling address operands for instructions in which location is important. The JNZ instruction in Figure 1.10 is a typical example. From the fact that the first instruction will be stored at location 1000, the assembler determines that the three-byte code for the line labelled NEXTIN is to be stored at 1005, 1006 and 1007. It therefore assembles the JNZ NEXTIN instruction with the operand 1005.

Pseudo-ops also occur in the last two lines of the program. The DS pseudo-op identifies an area of memory, the first location of which can be referred to by a symbolic address. The ORG and DS pseudo-ops in the last two lines of Figure 1.10 identify fifty memory locations starting at 1F00. The first location, i.e. 1F00, can be referred to in the program using the symbolic address LIST.

Note that the symbolic address LIST can be used to store the contents of register A in location 1F00 using direct addressing.

Thus the following instruction would be perfectly valid.

```
STA  LIST
```

LIST can also be used as an operand in the immediate addressing mode. The following instruction when executed loads register pair H,L with the *value* of LIST, i.e. 1F00:

```
LHLD  LIST
```

Q1.7 Pseudo-ops vary from assembler to assembler. The intention here is to identify their function in general with the help of a few examples. The reader is referred to the manual for the particular assembler he is using to obtain more details of the pseudo-ops available. Where important pseudo-ops are used in programs later in the book, their function is described as they arise.

1.11   Syntax rules and error messages

This section discussed the format of an assembly language source program. When the assembler is initially conceived, rules are established for the layout or format of lines of source code. If these rules are not adhered to, the assembler will not assemble the desired machine-code instructions.

The reader will by now be familiar with the line format for the Future-data assembler which is used for many of the examples in this chapter. The source code line is conceptually divided as four fields. These are the label, opcode, operand and comment fields. A typical line of a program with these fields identified is

Label	*Opcode*	*Operand*	*Comment*
START	OUT	35H	DUPLICATE LABEL

As will be seen from the many examples in this chapter, not all fields

```
*ERROR DEMONSTRATION
START       MV          B,A
*
            MVI         A,X'31FD'
*
            OUT         B,X'35'
*
START       OUT         X'35'
*
            LDA         DATA
*
            JP          START
*
            END
```

Figure 1.11

are necessarily occupied in every line of the source program. When fields are occupied, however, certain rules must be followed. The fields must always occur in the correct order is one such rule. These syntax rules are defined in the user's manual for the assembler. Syntax rules are broadly similar for different assemblers but may differ in detail.

During the assembly process, the assembler program checks the source program for syntax errors. Lines containing errors of this kind are identified on the assembly listing. Some indication as to the type of error is also usually given.

Figure 1.11 shows an 8080 assembly language program, written for the Futuredata assembler with deliberately introduced errors. Figure 1.12 shows the assembly listing. It will be seen that syntax errors are clearly identified. Figure 1.13 shows the same program, this time written for the CP/M8080 assembler ASM. The errors are again identified but in a much less sophisticated manner. In this case a letter against the offending instruction in the listing identifies the position of the error. To show the type of syntax error, the letter identifies an entry in a list of error types in the assembly language manual. Thus the V at the start of the listing for the second instruction is the code for a data error. The operand of 31FD for the MVI A instruction is inappropriate since this instruction demands an operand of not more than two hexadecimal digits.

By comparing Figures 1.11 and 1.13 the reader will notice other minor differences between the two assemblers. Both allow comments to be introduced in the source program. These comments are ignored during the assembly process, but provide valuable assistance in the

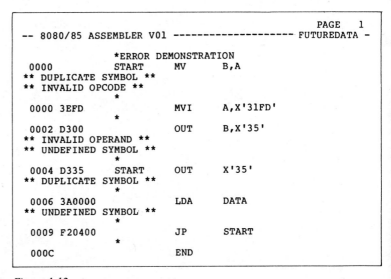

```
                                                        PAGE   1
-- 8080/85 ASSEMBLER V01 -------------------- FUTUREDATA -

                    *ERROR DEMONSTRATION
    0000            START       MV      B,A
** DUPLICATE SYMBOL **
** INVALID OPCODE **
                        *
    0000 3EFD                   MVI     A,X'31FD'
                        *
    0002 D300                   OUT     B,X'35'
** INVALID OPERAND **
** UNDEFINED SYMBOL **
                        *
    0004 D335       START       OUT     X'35'
** DUPLICATE SYMBOL **
                        *
    0006 3A0000                 LDA     DATA
** UNDEFINED SYMBOL **
                        *
    0009 F20400                 JP      START
                        *
    000C                        END
```

Figure 1.12

```
                                       ;      ERROR DEMONSTRATION
                                       ;
                     L                 START    MV     B,A
                                       ;
             V0000 3EFD                         MVI    A,31FDH
                                       ;
             S0002 D300                         OUT    B,35H
                                       ;
             0004 D335                 START    OUT    35H
                                       ;
             U0006 3A0000                       LDA    DATA
                                       ;
             0009 F20400                         JP    START
```

Figure 1.13

interpretation of the assembly listing. It is the way the comments are identified that differs in the two assemblers. A full comment line for the Futuredata assembler must start with an asterisk whereas the CP/M 8080 ASM requires a semi-colon as described in Section 1.8. Comments on the comment field of an instruction for the Futuredata assembler need no initial identifying character but the CP/M 8080 ASM still requires the initial semi-colon. The reader should have no difficulty in accommodating these minor differences.

1.12 Absolute programs

The program listing shown in Figure 1.14 is an example of an absolute program for the M6800. When writing this type of program, the programmer identifies, within the program, the locations at which the instructions are stored when the program is executed. This

```
                                                              PAGE   1
       -------- 6800/02 ASSEMBLER V01 ---------------------------- FUTUREDATA --------

                     ****************************************************
                     *M6800 LIST SEARCH FOR CHARACTER 'Z'             *
                     *THIS PROGRAM SEARCHES MEMORY LOCATIONS 1000 - 17FF*
                     *FOR THE FIRST OCCURENCE OF THE ASCII CODE FOR 'Z' *
                     *ON EXIT, THE ADDRESS AT WHICH 'Z' IS FOUND IS    *
                     *STORED IN 2000                                  *
                     *IF 'Z' IS NOT FOUND, 2000,2001 CONTAINS 1800 ON  *
                     *EXIT                                            *
                     ****************************************************
                     *
     0000                       ORG     X'3000'
     3000 CE1000       SERCH     LDX     #X'1000'        INITIALISE INDEX REGISTER
     3003 A600         SERCH1    LDAA    0,X             GET NEXT CHARACTER
     3005 815A                   CMPA    #'Z'            IS IT 'Z'?
     3007 2706                   BEQ     SERCH2          BRANCH IF YES
     3009 08                     INX                     INCREMENT POINTER
     300A 8C1800                 CPX     #X'1800'        END OF LIST?
     300D 26F4                   BNE     SERCH1          DO AGAIN IF NOT
     300F FF2000       SERCH2    STX     X'2000'         STORE ADDRESS
     3012 39                     RTS                     EXIT
     3013                        END
```

Figure 1.14 M6800 absolute program

is normally done by means of an ORG or similar pseudo-op. Absolute programs have the advantage of simplicity and are satisfactory when the size of the program is not too great.

Modern programming methods strongly favour the writing of large programs in modular form. This involves splitting the total programming task into a number of smaller sub-tasks. Each sub-task is then approached as a programming task in its own right. Sub-programs are written and debugged as independent program modules. If necessary at this stage, sub-programming tasks can be split down further. When all sub-programs have been written, debugged and fully tested, they must be combined in some way to form the complete program.

Bringing together separate sub-programs to form one larger program presents a number of problems. Ideally, the separate sub-programs should be stored in memory, before execution, in an economical way but avoiding overlap. This can be achieved by keeping a careful record of the memory space occupied by each sub-program and proper use of ORG pseudo-ops.

Figures 1.15 and 1.16 show listings for sub-programs associated with an overall programming task to put out ten characters from output

```
                                                        PAGE   1
      -------- 8080/85 ASSEMBLER V01 --------------------------- FUTUREDATA --------
                         *                OPMSG
                         *************************************************
                         *THIS SUBROUTINE PUTS OUT A MESSAGE OF TEN  *
                         *DATA BYTES VIA PORT X'7D'                  *
                         *DATA IS STORED IN MEMORY STARTING AT       *
                         *LOCATION X'2000'                           *
                         *                                           *
                         *                STRUCTURE                  *
                         *                *********                  *
                         *LOOP = 10                                  *
                         *NEXTADDRESS = X'2000'                      *
                         *DO UNTIL LOOP = 0                          *
                         *        OUTPUT BYTE FROM NEXTADDRESS       *
                         *        NEXTADDRESS = NEXTADDRESS + 1      *
                         *        LOOP = LOOP - 1                    *
                         *END DO                                     *
                         *************************************************
                         *
      0000                       ORG    X'1009'
      1009 060A   OPMSG          MVI    B,10              LOOP = 10
      100B 210020                LXI    H,DATA            SET POINTER
      100E CD0010 NEXTCH         CALL   X'1000'           CALL OPCH
      1011 23                    INX    H                 INCREMENT POINTER
      1012 05                    DCR    B                 LOOP = LOOP - 1
      1013 C20E10                JNZ    NEXTCH
      1016 C9                    RET
                         *
      1017                       ORG    X'2000'
      2000         DATA          DS     10
      200A                       END
```

Figure 1.15 Absolute subroutine

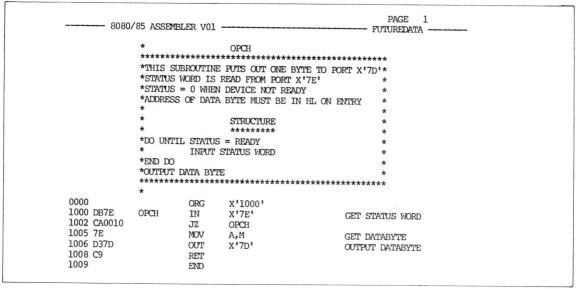

```
--------- 8080/85 ASSEMBLER V01 ---------------------------  PAGE   1
                                                            FUTUREDATA ---------

                        *                 OPCH
                        ***************************************************
                        *THIS SUBROUTINE PUTS OUT ONE BYTE TO PORT X'7D'*
                        *STATUS WORD IS READ FROM PORT X'7E'            *
                        *STATUS = 0 WHEN DEVICE NOT READY               *
                        *ADDRESS OF DATA BYTE MUST BE IN HL ON ENTRY    *
                        *                                               *
                        *                 STRUCTURE                     *
                        *                 *********                      *
                        *DO UNTIL STATUS = READY                        *
                        *          INPUT STATUS WORD                    *
                        *END DO                                         *
                        *OUTPUT DATA BYTE                               *
                        ***************************************************
                        *
        0000                    ORG     X'1000'
        1000 DB7E       OPCH    IN      X'7E'           GET STATUS WORD
        1002 CA0010             JZ      OPCH
        1005 7E                 MOV     A,M             GET DATABYTE
        1006 D37D              OUT     X'7D'           OUTPUT DATABYTE
        1008 C9                 RET
        1009                    END
```

Figure 1.16 Absolute subroutine

port 7D. The output operation involves handshaking with status information taken in from the status port address 7E. The peripheral device is assumed to be not ready for data if the status word is zero. The reader need not have a detailed understanding of the program at this stage.

The subroutines whose listings are shown in Figure 1.15 and 1.16 can be debugged and tested separately. In the case of the OPMSG routine, debugging and testing will require the use of a dummy subroutine which substitutes for 0PCH. This dummy subroutine might consist simply of a single RET instruction. During this development phase, provided that a subroutine is self-contained, the programmer can use an ORG pseudo-op to locate the program in any convenient area of memory. It is only when two or more subroutines or other programs are required to be resident in memory at the same time that care must be taken to locate them correctly. At this point, the programmer must review ORG pseudo-ops to ensure that programs are economically packed in memory without overlap.

Although it is possible to successfully write programs in modular form, even using absolute assembly, the degree of inconvenience increases as the size and number of program modules increase. The root of the difficulty lies in the fact that with absolute assembly, the location in memory of the machine-code object program must be defined by the programmer with an ORG pseudo-op in the source program.

1.13   Relocatable programs

To avoid the problems associated with absolute programs discussed in Section 1.12, assemblers are available which allow the programmer to write position-independent source programs. With these relocatable programs, the programmer does not define, in the source program, the location at which the machine-code object program will ultimately be stored. The ORG pseudo-op is therefore not used. Assembly takes place as though the object program is to be stored starting at location 0000. The decision as to where the program will actually be stored before execution is deferred until later.

Figure 1.17 shows a listing for the OPCH routine discussed in Section 1.12. In Figure 1.17, the assembly is for a relocatable program however. No ORG pseudo-op is included and the listing shows object code as if it is to be stored starting at location 0000. The listing in Figure 1.18 is for the subroutine OPMSG and is in partly relocatable form. The executable instruction code is relocatable but the data storage area DATA is still defined absolutely as 2000 by means of the ORG and DS pseudo-ops at the end of the program. Relocatable assemblers normally allow sections of absolute code in a relocatable program.

In the assembly of a relocatable program, symbolic addresses of instructions are defined relative to the address of the first instruction of the program. In the listing shown for OPMSG in Figure 1.18, the address of the instruction assembled from the line labelled NEXTCH is therefore identified as 0005. This will not be the absolute address but is simply the distance from code for MVI B,10 which is the first executable instruction of the program.

Q1.9

1.14   Locators and relocating loaders

Before an assembled relocatable program can be executed, the program machine code must be placed in memory by some form of loader program. At this point a decision must be made as to where in memory the program code is to reside. When this is known, all position-dependent operands in the program code must be modified accordingly.

Suppose that we wish to relocate the OPCH routine of Figure 1.17 to location 5000. This will involve changing the code for the JZ OPCH instruction from CA0000 to CA0050 since the destination address for the conditional jump is now 5000. This is of course the address of the first byte of the IN instruction, which is the first executable instruction of the program.

Programs are available that take the code for a relocatable program and modify it to form absolute code at a specific location. These

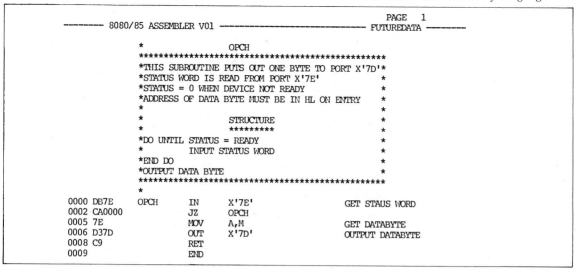

```
         -------- 8080/85 ASSEMBLER V01 --------                          PAGE   1
                                             ----------------------- FUTUREDATA --------
              *                    OPCH
              ***************************************************
              *THIS SUBROUTINE PUTS OUT ONE BYTE TO PORT X'7D'*
              *STATUS WORD IS READ FROM PORT X'7E'             *
              *STATUS = 0 WHEN DEVICE NOT READY                *
              *ADDRESS OF DATA BYTE MUST BE IN HL ON ENTRY     *
              *                                                *
              *                    STRUCTURE                   *
              *                    *********                   *
              *DO UNTIL STATUS = READY                         *
              *       INPUT STATUS WORD                        *
              *END DO                                          *
              *OUTPUT DATA BYTE                                *
              ***************************************************
              *
0000 DB7E     OPCH       IN      X'7E'              GET STAUS WORD
0002 CA0000              JZ      OPCH
0005 7E                  MOV     A,M                GET DATABYTE
0006 D37D               OUT     X'7D'               OUTPUT DATABYTE
0008 C9                  RET
0009                     END
```

Figure 1.17   Relocatable subroutine

Q1.10   programs are known as locators. Relocating loaders perform the same function but, in addition, the relocated code is loaded into memory at the defined location.

1.15   Linkers and linking loaders

In Section 1.12 we discussed the problems involved in combining two or more program modules to form a single larger program. Writing program modules in relocatable form overcomes many of the problems. Some assemblers also define special pseudo-ops which provide additional facilities for linking program modules. The GLBL mnemonic which appears in Figure 1.18 is one such pseudo-op.

The GLBL pseudo-op allows references to be made in a program module to symbolic addresses which are not directly defined in that module. The symbolic address can be defined in another, quite separate, program module to which the first module is later linked. Symbolic addresses which are defined in one program module and appear in other modules are said to be global symbols. In the listing for OPMSG in Figure 1.18, the line GLBL OPCH identifies OPCH as a global symbol which means that it is defined in another program module. The programmer is then permitted to include instructions such as CALL OPCH in the source program module, even though OPCH is not defined in OPMSG in the normal way. If OPCH is not declared as a global symbol, the CALL OPCH instruction would be flagged in the assembly listing as an undefined variable. Figure 1.19 shows precisely this situation.

Since global symbols are often not directly defined within the

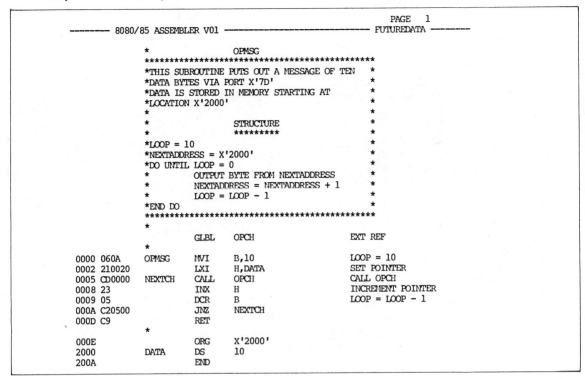

```
                                                             PAGE   1
 --------- 8080/85 ASSEMBLER V01 ------------------------------- FUTUREDATA ---------

                    *                   OPMSG
                    *************************************************
                    *THIS SUBROUTINE PUTS OUT A MESSAGE OF TEN   *
                    *DATA BYTES VIA PORT X'7D'                    *
                    *DATA IS STORED IN MEMORY STARTING AT         *
                    *LOCATION X'2000'                             *
                    *                                             *
                    *                   STRUCTURE                 *
                    *                   ********                   *
                    *LOOP = 10                                    *
                    *NEXTADDRESS = X'2000'                        *
                    *DO UNTIL LOOP = 0                            *
                    *       OUTPUT BYTE FROM NEXTADDRESS          *
                    *       NEXTADDRESS = NEXTADDRESS + 1         *
                    *       LOOP = LOOP - 1                       *
                    *END DO                                       *
                    *************************************************
                    *
                               GLBL    OPCH                  EXT REF
                    *
 0000 060A     OPMSG     MVI     B,10                  LOOP = 10
 0002 210020             LXI     H,DATA                SET POINTER
 0005 CD0000   NEXTCH    CALL    OPCH                  CALL OPCH
 0008 23                 INX     H                     INCREMENT POINTER
 0009 05                 DCR     B                     LOOP = LOOP - 1
 000A C20500             JNZ     NEXTCH
 000D C9                 RET
                    *
 000E                    ORG     X'2000'
 2000          DATA      DS      10
 200A                    END
```

Figure 1.18   Relocatable subroutine with global symbol

program module in which they are used, operands which include these symbols cannot be generated by the assembler. In Figure 1.18 it will be seen that the operand for the CALL OPCH instruction is assembled as 0000 since the assembler has no way of knowing, at assembly time, the absolute or relative value of the address referred to symbolically as OPCH. This information does not become available until the location at which the OPCH module is to be loaded is known. The locators and relocating loaders described in Section 1.14 are not adequate to deal with this situation.

Programs known as linkers perform the operations necessary to link program modules together. To function in this way the linker must be supplied with the address at which the first module of a linked set is stored. The linker scans all modules to be linked, establishes the absolute values of global symbols, and inserts the values as the operand code for instructions making use of these global symbols.

1.16   Operating procedures for assemblers

Until low-cost magnetic floppy disk stores became widely available, assembly language program development was often carried out using punched paper tape as the secondary storage medium. The process of

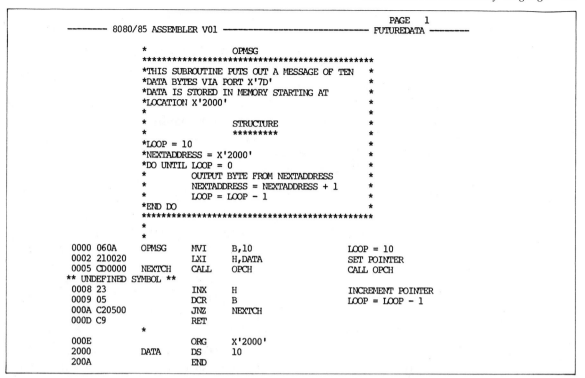

```
                                                          PAGE   1
--------- 8080/85 ASSEMBLER V01 --------------------------- FUTUREDATA ---------

            *               OPMSG
            **************************************************
            *THIS SUBROUTINE PUTS OUT A MESSAGE OF TEN   *
            *DATA BYTES VIA PORT X'7D'                    *
            *DATA IS STORED IN MEMORY STARTING AT         *
            *LOCATION X'2000'                             *
            *                                             *
            *               STRUCTURE                     *
            *               ********                      *
            *LOOP = 10                                    *
            *NEXTADDRESS = X'2000'                        *
            *DO UNTIL LOOP = 0                            *
            *          OUTPUT BYTE FROM NEXTADDRESS       *
            *          NEXTADDRESS = NEXTADDRESS + 1      *
            *          LOOP = LOOP - 1                    *
            *END DO                                       *
            **************************************************
            *
            *
0000 060A   OPMSG       MVI     B,10            LOOP = 10
0002 210020             LXI     H,DATA          SET POINTER
0005 CD0000 NEXTCH      CALL    OPCH            CALL OPCH
** UNDEFINED SYMBOL **
0008 23                 INX     H               INCREMENT POINTER
0009 05                 DCR     B               LOOP = LOOP - 1
000A C20500             JNZ     NEXTCH
000D C9                 RET
            *
000E                    ORG     X'2000'
2000        DATA        DS      10
200A                    END
```

Figure 1.19   Undefined symbols as a result of non-declaration of global symbols

editing, assembly, linking and loading was very slow. This was mainly due to the time taken to punch and read paper tape at each stage of the operation. Although today punched paper tape is seldom used in this way, a few systems can be found which support assembly language program development using audio-cassette tape as the secondary storage medium. The vast majority of professional assembly language programmers, however, have access to a disk-based computing system. This section assumes the use of a hard or floppy disk secondary store.

One feature of a system which includes a magnetic-disk-based secondary store is that it is normally provided with a disk-operating system (DOS). This is a program which organises the transfer of programs and data between RAM and the disk. The user communicates with the DOS by issuing commands via the system console keyboard. From the user's point of view, the most important feature of a DOS is that data and programs are stored on the disk in files which are identified by name. This section assumes the use of a conventional DOS of this type.

The first stage in the assembly language programming cycle is to prepare the source program using an editor program. The editor allows easy manipulation of the source program text which is entered via the VDT console keyboard. When the source program is in the desired form it can be stored on disk in the source file. Details of editor operations vary greatly from system to system.

After the source program file has been prepared, the assembler operates on this file to generate the object program which is then stored on disk in the object file. Generally, the assembler is stored on disk in such a way that it can be transferred to RAM and execution commenced by means of a single command. It may be necessary to include the name of the source file in this command. A typical DOS command of this kind is:

```
ASM   SFILE
```

where SFILE is the name chosen by the programmer for the file containing the source program. This type of command is used by the well established CP/M operating system. An alternative adopted by some assemblers is for the command to simply invoke the assembler. The assembler then puts out a message to the console requesting the name of the source file. The user enters the file name via the console keyboard. The Futuredata universal microprocessor development system operates in this way.

Before the process of assembly commences, the user can normally choose certain options. One such option is the direction of the assembly listing to a printer in addition to the console display. Another option is the suppression of the assembly listing apart from those lines containing errors. This is particularly useful at the stage when syntax errors are being eliminated from a long source program since it reduces the print-out time during each assembly run. Again, the details of assembly procedures and the way they are specified by the user depend on the particular assembler used.

Operations required after the assembler has stored the object program on disk will depend on the type of assembler used. With a simple absolute assembler, it may be possible to transfer the machine-code object program to RAM using a DOS LOAD command. The object program can then be executed. If the program is relocatable, a locator or relocating loader must be used. When the locator or linking loader is invoked, the user will enter the address at which the object program is to be stored in RAM.

Assemblers that allow program modules to be linked vary greatly in the details of their operation. Probably the most common are those assemblers which facilitate the linkage of object program modules. The source program modules are assembled into separate object files. The contents of the object files are then linked using a linker program which creates a single object code load file. A relocating loader then transfers the contents of the load file to RAM. Alternative schemes also exist in which linkage of source code modules is possible. A

Q1.12 combined source program is then assembled and loaded using a relocating loader.

References and bibliography

1.1 L.A. Leventhal, *6800 Assembly Language Programming*, Osborne and Associates Inc, USA (1978).

1.2 A. R. Miller, *8080/Z80 Assembly Language*, John Wiley (1981).

Questions

1.1 In what form is a source program stored in RAM prior to assembly?

1.2 What is the essential function of an assembler?

1.3 State the name of a program which assists the programmer in creating the source program text.

1.4 In the listing shown in Figure 1.4, identify the various types of information by name.

1.5 State the general function of pseudo-ops in an assembly language program.

1.6 Explain how pseudo-ops differ from executable instructions.

1.7 Identify the pseudo-ops in Figure 1.18.

1.8 Give the mnemonic for a pseudo-op which defines the address of the first instruction of an absolute program.

1.9 State the essential difference between absolute and relocatable assembly language programs.

1.10 Describe the function of a locator/relocator.

1.11 Describe the function of a linker.

1.12 Modify one of the programs shown in Figure 8.12, 8.13 or 8.14 so that it is compatible with an assembler to which you have access. Use an editor to prepare the source text. Assemble, link and load the program in memory. Run the program with the help of the system monitor/debugger.

Chapter 2 Choosing a microprocessor

Objectives of this chapter *When you have completed studying this chapter you should be able to:*

1 *Analyse, with the help of manufacturers' data sheets, some of the important physical features of a microprocessor as being:*
   (a) Word length/data bus length.
   (b) Speed of operation of typical instructions.
   (c) Size and facilities of the instruction set.
   (d) Versatility of addressing modes.
   (e) Size of address bus.
2 *Explain the use of bench marks for comparing different micro-processors.*

2.1   How do we choose a microprocessor?

The broad aim of this chapter is to give the reader a feel for some of the physical characteristics that are important when choosing a microprocessor for a particular application. At the time of writing, over fifty different microprocessors are produced by more than ten major manufacturers. Other manufacturers act as 'second sources' for the more popular devices. The fact that so many different microprocessors are currently available might seem to suggest that the first task of the design engineer at the beginning of each project is to sit down and choose, on technical grounds, the most suitable device for the particular application. In fact, this is a situation that does not often arise.

The choice of microprocessor is usually influenced by factors that are not purely technical. One of the chief of these will be the background experience of the designer or design team. If this experience related mainly to the M6800 family of devices, there will be a predisposition to continue using this range. This is a sensible approach since it is obviously better to build on past experience and avoid problems associated with the peculiarities of an unfamiliar microprocessor unless the reasons for change are very powerful. As a result, an experienced design team may well persist in the use of one microprocessor, even when other, apparently more suitable, devices are available. The background of the firm or organisation employing the designer or design team will also affect the choice of micro-processor. Development systems that assist the design of hardware and software are discussed in Chapter 7. They are expensive items and often support only one type of microprocessor. A firm that has invested heavily in equipment to support the 8080 microprocessor is unlikely to be sympathetic to an engineer wishing to use an M6800 device unless the justification is strong.

Having said this, it is still important for the engineer to understand those features of a microprocessor which are advantageous or disadvantageous in a given application. This will at least avoid the use of a particular microprocessor in an application for which it is patently unsuited. At the end of the day, however, in the vast majority of cases, the skill and experience of the hardware and software designers are far more important than the choice of microprocessor. Put in another way, it is the way a microprocessor is used, rather than the choice of microprocessor, which most often governs the success or failure of a project.

2.2 Computing power

As we have seen in Section 2.1, the choice of microprocessor used in a system is governed by many factors both technical and non-technical. However we arrive at this choice, a fundamental requirement is that the system must contain sufficient computing power to perform the desired computation within the available time. It is obviously important for the engineer to be capable of assessing whether a given microprocessor has this required computing power. Unfortunately computing power is a property which does not lend itself to the same sort of unambiguous definition as, say, electrical power. Some meaningful comparisons of the computing power of different microprocessors are, however, possible. We might, for example, compare the performance of two different microprocessors by finding the time each device takes to execute a program which transfers 100 bytes of data from one area of memory to another. If one microprocessor completes the task twice as quickly as the other, this would undoubtedly be significant if the envisaged application requires rapid and frequent movement of blocks of data within the memory.

The reader should avoid bestowing too much significance on single comparisons of this kind. A microprocessor that can perform one kind of operation very efficiently may well be rather unimpressive in other situations. The processor described above which can move data about memory very rapidly could also be very slow when arithmetic operations are required. Much of the remainder of this chapter is concerned with the way we can compare the computing power of different microprocessors.

Although in some cases the question of computing power can be a critical factor in the choice of microprocessor, in others it is not an issue. This is because non-technical factors, such as available development support, have determined the choice of a microprocessor which has far more computing power than is required for the particular application. Computing 'overkill' of this kind is quite common. A few years ago, the use of a processor with much more computing power than is necessary would have been regarded as bad design practice. Historically, computing power was very directly related to cost. Although a link still exists between computing power and cost, it is much less direct in the case of microprocessors. In particular, the central processing unit, i.e. the microprocessor itself, is often one of the lowest cost components of a system. The engineer's major concern is therefore to ensure that sufficient computing power is available without worrying too much if the power appears excessive.

Our discussion so far implies the use of only one microprocessor in a system. This again reflects the traditional approach when the cost of the central processing unit was a significant proportion of the overall system cost. Bearing in mind the current situation of the central processing unit as one of the cheapest system components, it is perfectly acceptable, and often desirable, to use two or more microprocessors in a system rather than a single device of greater computing power. This is one example of the way that the low cost of microprocessors changes the approach to computer systems design.

2.3   Some real microprocessors

In order to illustrate the features that are important when comparing microprocessors, we shall take some real devices as examples. This section introduces these devices and describes how they are connected in microcomputer systems. The microprocessors described are listed in Table 2.1 and data sheets will be found in Appendices A–E.

Of these processors, the COP420L must be treated somewhat differently to the others. The 8080, M6800, Z80 and Z8000 could most properly be described as central processing units or CPUs. This implies that to make a computing system incorporating one of these microprocessors, we need to add memory, I/O interface circuits and

Table 2.1

Microprocessor	*Major manufacturer*	*Word length*
COP420L	National	4
8080	Intel	8
M6800	Motorola	8
Z80	Zilog	8
Z8000	Zilog	16

peripheral devices to communicate with the outside world. The COP420L, however, is an example of a rather different type of device. In this case, memory and I/O interface circuits are included on the chip together with the CPU. To make a computing system incorporating a COP420L we need only add a power supply and whatever peripheral devices we might need. Devices such as the COP420L are referred to as single-chip microcontrollers or single-chip microcomputers.

Q2.1

Microprocessors that consist of a CPU only are flexible and expandable. They can be used for a wide range of general-purpose computing tasks. Systems incorporating single-chip microcontrollers on the other hand have a more rigidly defined configuration. Single-chip microcontrollers are normally used for fixed or dedicated computing tasks. The distinction between general-purpose and dedicated computers is explored fully in Chapter 5.

Setting aside the special case of single-chip microcontrollers, it is possible to identify common requirements in a microcomputing system. An example of this is the need for an exchange of information between the CPU chip and other system components, e.g. memory and I/O circuits. Figure 2.1 separates the various connections between the CPU and system in terms of their functions. The precise

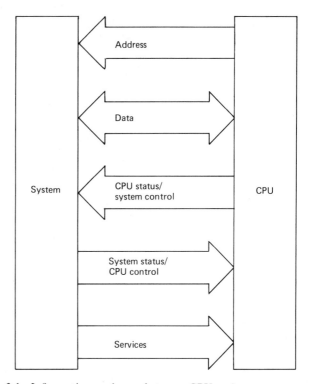

Figure 2.1 Information exchange between CPU and system

nature and function of the various CPU–system interconnecting lines is one of the distinguishing features of a microprocessor. We shall use Figure 2.1 as a model to illustrate the special features of the microprocessors we are describing.

The data bus consists of *n* parallel connections where *n* is equal to the microprocessor word length. This bus carries instruction codes and computational operands between the system memory and the microprocessor. It will also transmit data between I/O circuits and the microprocessor. The address bus carries addresses which identify the locations of data in memory during memory read or write operations. It may also carry an address which identifies a particular port during an input or output operation.

Lines labelled as 'CPU status/system control' carry signals which provide information relating to the internal activity of the microprocessor. A typical example of this is the R/$\overline{\text{W}}$ line of the M6800 device. This line is high when the M6800 is performing a memory read operation and low when a write operation is taking place. It could therefore be regarded as a status line which informs the system when the read or write operation occurs. Looking at R/$\overline{\text{W}}$ from the point of view of the system, however, it is obviously important that whenever the line is high, the memory must place the contents of the address's location on the address bus. If this does not happen, the read operation will not be successful. As far as the system is concerned therefore, R/$\overline{\text{W}}$ could be regarded as a command or control line which initiates some specific activity.

Complementing the CPU status/system control function, we have lines such as INT of the 8080 microprocessor. From the point of view of the system, INT can be regarded as a status line which informs the microprocessor that, for example, a peripheral device such as a printer is ready for some attention. As far as the microprocessor is concerned however, INT is very definitely a control line which suspends normal program activity and transfers control to an **Q2.2**   interrupt service routine.

Finally, we have those functions labelled 'Services' in Figure 2.1. Under this heading we include d.c. supply requirements which vary considerably between different microprocessors. Many microprocessors also require the provision of one or more external a.c. clock waveforms and these are included in the services category.

Figure 2.1 implies that all of the lines connecting the CPU with the rest of the system are distinct in that they perform one function only. In practice, this is not always the case. The reason for this lies in the desire of microprocessor designers to minimise the number of pins on the microprocessor package since this reduces production costs. The result is that not enough pins are available to provide the desired functions. To overcome this difficulty, some signals are multiplexed.

Q2.4 This means that some lines perform different functions during different parts of the computing cycle.

A typical example of signal multiplexing is provided by the eight lines of the 8080 microprocessor whose major function is that of a data bus. For a period during the first two clock intervals of each instruction cycle, these lines carry eight CPU status/system control signals instead of a data byte. Although this saves eight extra pins on the 8080 package, there are obvious hardware complications. Special registers are required, external to the microprocessor, to 'catch' data or status signals at the time they appear.

The 8080

Although the 8080 was one of the first 8-bit microprocessors, at the time of writing it is still one of the most widely used. Figure 2.2 shows the pins of the 8080 identified in functional groups rather than the direct physical configuration shown in Appendix A. As a result of

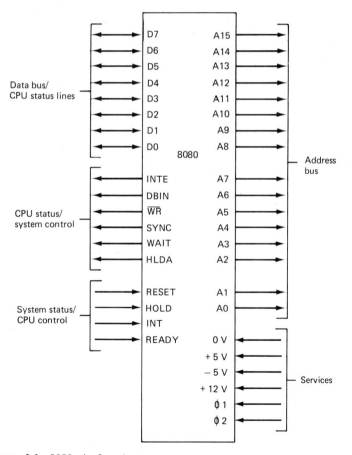

Figure 2.2   8080 pin functions

being one of the earlier 8-bit microprocessors, the 8080 is somewhat less convenient for the user than some more recently developed devices. It will be seen for example that the 8080 requires no less than three d.c. supplies. A two-phase clock is also demanded by the 8080.

As we have said earlier in this section, the 8080 has a multiplexed data bus. For part of each computing cycle, the lines D0–D7 carry status signals informing the rest of the system of activity within the micro-processor. During the time these status signals are on lines D0–D7, the microprocessor holds the SYNC line high. When data is present on D0–D7, the DBIN line is high. These two signals can be used by external circuits to capture status signals and data bytes. Special-purpose integrated circuits are produced specifically to perform this function.

Q2.5

The M6800

Figure 2.3 shows the signals on the pins of the M6800 identified in functional groups. Like the 8080, the 6800 requires a two-phase clock but, unlike the 8080, requires only a single 5 V supply. No multiplexing of any of the signals on any of the pins takes place in the

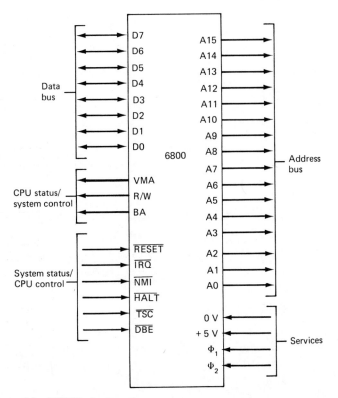

Figure 2.3   M6800 pin functions

M6800. The precise function of status and control signals is defined in Appendix C.

The Z80

Although the Z80 and 8080 microprocessors have many common instructions, comparison of Figures 2.2 and 2.4 shows that the way the two devices are connected to the rest of the computing system must be very different. The exact functions of control and status lines is defined in Appendix B. A major hardware difference between the Z80 and 8080 is that no multiplexing of signals on the data bus occurs with the Z80. It will also be noted that, unlike the 8080, a single 5 V supply only is required. Unlike both the 8080 and 6800, the Z80 requires only a single-phase clock.

The Z8000

The title Z8000 identifies not one but a family of microprocessors. Devices in this family are by far the most powerful of the micro-

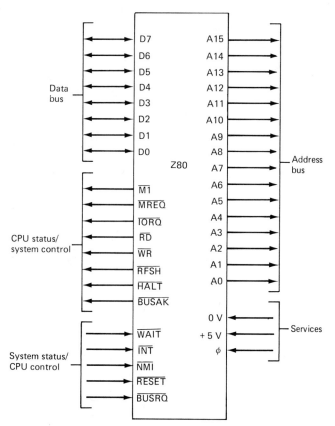

Figure 2.4   Z80 pin functions

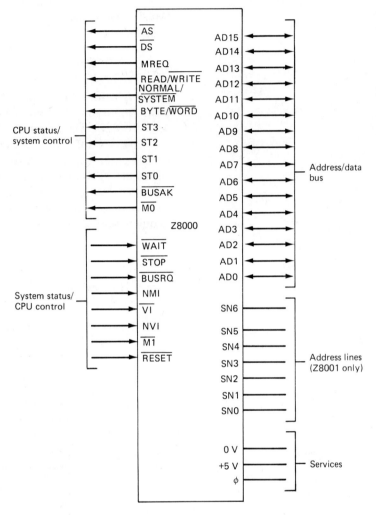

Figure 2.5   Z8000 pin functions

processors considered here. Two family members are the Z8001 and the Z8002. Figure 2.5 shows the pin connections for the Z8001 and Z8002 identified in functional groups. A more complete description of the Z8002 is given in Appendix D.

Microprocessors in the Z8000 family operate mainly with units of data containing 16 bits. This implies the availability of a 16-line data bus. To keep the number of pins on the Z8000 package within reasonable limits, the designers therefore chose to multiplex data and address signals. Lines identified as AD0–AD15 therefore carry an address during one part of the computing cycle and data during another part.

Figure 2.5 also reveals that the major difference between the Z8001 and Z8002 lies in the width or number of lines of the address bus. The Z8001 has seven additional address lines compared with the Z8002. These lines form the most significant part of an enhanced address bus. The Z8002 can therefore directly address $2^{16} = 65,536$ memory locations, the same number as the 8080, 6800 and Z80. With the extra address lines, the Z8001 has direct access to $2^{23} = 8,388,608$ locations. This ability to access large amounts of memory can be very important **Q2.6** for some applications as discussed in Section 2.8.

The COP420L

Unlike the other microprocessors described in this section, the COP420L does not allow the user access to the data bus or the address bus. This is because memory and I/O circuits are contained within the microprocessor chip. The division of CPU–system connections into functional groups therefore has no relevance as far as this device is concerned.

Appendix E indicates that the COP420L is one of a family of single-chip microcontrollers. Members of the family differ in the provision of memory, I/O facilities and speed of operation. From Appendix E it will be seen that the COP420L contains $1K \times 8$ ROM and $64K \times 4$ RAM. The ROM is of the mask-programmed variety which means that the program and data is inprinted during the manufacturing process. The implications of this are discussed more fully in Chapter 5.

2.4 Word length

The term word length when applied to a microprocessor defines the number of bits of data that are normally manipulated during the execution of arithmetic, logic, data transfer and I/O instructions. Within the microprocessor, data are transferred between the various functional units along a parallel data bus. The number of parallel lines in this main data bus is equal to the word length in most microprocessors. The number of I/O lines is also normally equal to the word length as is the size of the majority of internal working registers.

At the time of writing, a large proportion of available microprocessors have a word length of 8 bits. Microprocessors are also available with word lengths of 32, 16, 12, 4 and even 1 bits. Perhaps the most clearly defined 8-bit microprocessor is the Motorola M6800. The microprocessor contains two main working registers identified as A and B. Each stores 8 bits of data. The main data bus which carries data between the memory and working registers is 8 bits wide, i.e. consists of 8 lines. This same bus is also used for I/O operations. Each memory location in an M6800 system will store 8 bits of data.

The 6800 has been described as a classical 8-bit machine, which probably means that it conforms, more than most microprocessors, to the traditional ideas of the internal structure of a computer CPU. Even with such a straightforward architecture and an instruction set which identifies the vast majority of data manipulations in 8-bit terms, other units of data are possible however. Within the internal structure of the 6800 are several 16-bit registers. These include the index, stack pointer and program counter registers, each of which is accessible to the programmer. This means that within the instruction set there are instructions which cause the data stored in these registers to change. Thus, in an 8-bit microprocessor, we have some 16-bit registers and some instructions which operate on 16-bit data words.

Q2.8

If we investigate further it will be found that the instruction set also contains instructions which operate on individual bits of a data word and are therefore manipulating units of data consisting of one bit. The point of this discussion is to emphasise that no microprocessor currently available operates exclusively with one word length. It would indeed be most inconvenient to make use of such a device in the unlikely event of it becoming available. In fact the trend is in the opposite direction. The more recently developed microprocessor families gain extra flexibility and computing power from their ability to manipulate different units of data.

If the M6800 is an example of the classical computer architecture, we may take the Z8002 as an example of the new generation of microprocessors. From Appendix D it will be seen that the Z8002 is described as a 16-bit microprocessor which means that the most common unit of data to be manipulated is 16 bits. The internal structure of this device includes a number of general-purpose working registers which can be described in various ways. The most straightforward and common description is that the Z8002 contains 16 general-purpose working registers, each capable of storing 16 bits of data. These registers are identified as R0–R15. The Z8002 instruction set includes instructions which move and manipulate 16-bit data words contained in these registers. Also included are instructions which move and manipulate data in the form of 8-bit words. For these instructions, each of the eight registers R0–R7 is treated as two registers of 8 bits. The programmer therefore has access to, effectively, 16 general-purpose 8-bit registers. The flexibility of word length does not end there. Instructions are available which manipulate data in the form of 32-bit words. For these instructions, the 16 registers R0–R15 are combined in pairs to give the programmer effective access to 8 general-purpose 32-bit registers.

With some of the newer microprocessors, the flexibility is such that it is difficult to identify a characteristic word length. The Motorola 6809 and Intel 8088 are two such microprocessors. They are often described as 8-bit devices and indeed data is taken in and put out from these microprocessors in units of 8 bits. In each case, however, many of the internal data transfers and manipulations might be more properly regarded as characteristic of a 16-bit processor. This point relating to the M6809 is expanded further in Ref. 2.6.

Having identified some of the subtleties of word-length definition, we now consider how this parameter affects the suitability or otherwise of a microprocessor for a given application. At first sight, the relationship between word length and computing power is obvious. If a microprocessor can perform a given operation on an 8-bit operand during the execution of one instruction, it is processing data at twice the speed of a device that can perform the operation only on a 4-bit word, all other things being equal. When a shortage of computing power becomes evident during the system design process, one possible solution is to move to a microprocessor with a greater word length. In some applications, however, the resulting higher rate of data processing may not be useable.

Consider an application in which a frequent requirement is to find the largest entry in a list of 4-bit numbers, stored in memory. Any of the common 4-bit microprocessors would be capable of this operation with a suitable program. Suppose, however, that none of the available 4-bit devices is capable of performing this sorting operation in a sufficiently short time. Various options are open for consideration by the system designer. One possibility is to provide more computing power by using an 8-bit microprocessor. To exploit the 8-bit capability, we must pack two of the 4-bit numbers in one 8-bit word. Simply storing each 4-bit number as the least significant half of an 8-bit word would mean that the microprocessor is manipulating data 4 bits at a time, which leaves us no better off. The snag to all this is that the complexity of the sorting program is likely to be considerably increased if the numbers are stacked two in an 8-bit word. This will almost certainly nullify the theoretical advantage of the 8-bit device used in this way. In fact the 8-bit microprocessor would probably take longer to perform the search using this technique than would the 4-bit device, all other things being equal. The greater computing power of the 8-bit microprocessor is simply not accessible in this situation.

As with most situations in life, the comparison is not quite as straightforward as this. In practice, it is complicated by the fact that by moving from a 4-bit to an 8-bit microprocessor, we are likely to gain access to a much more powerful instruction set. Compare the instruction set of the COP420L with that of any 8-bit microprocessor described in the appendices to see what this means. The more powerful instruction set of the 8-bit device may be just as important, or even more important, in improving the speed of computation than greater word length. This is discussed in more detail in Section 2.6.

2.5   Microprocessor architecture

When we describe the internal structure of a microprocessor or indeed the central processor of any computer, the term architecture is commonly used. Within the integrated circuit which is a microprocessor are contained a complex collection of component units: registers, counters, arithmetic circuits, logic circuits, memory elements, etc. A description of the architecture will often only include those components which are of direct interest to the programmer and applications engineer. These are the registers and other units whose contents or behaviour can be directly changed by the execution of an instruction. When the description of the microprocessor is simplified in this way, it is called the programmer's model.

Manufacturers' data sheets will include a description of the microprocessor architecture. The amount of detail varies depending on the manufacturer. Figure 2.6 shows the architecture of the 8080 microprocessor and is taken from an Intel data sheet. Figures 2.7 and 2.8 show programmer's models for the Z80 and M6800 microprocessors taken from Zilog and Motorola data sheets.

Q2.9, 2.10

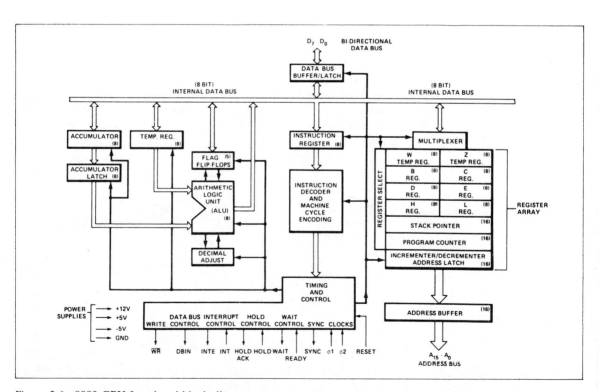

Figure 2.6   8080 CPU functional block diagram

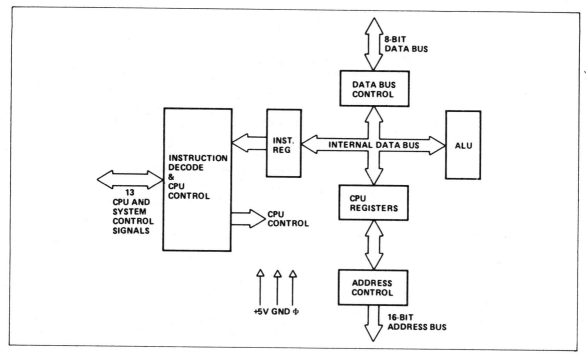

Figure 2.7   Z80 CPU functional block diagram

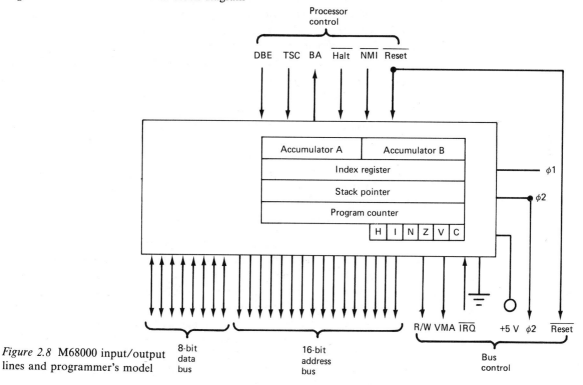

Figure 2.8 M68000 input/output
lines and programmer's model

2.6   Instruction sets

General

Probably the most difficult comparison to make between different microprocessors relates to their instruction sets. This is because each type of microprocessor has its own particular strengths and weaknesses which may not compare directly with those of another device. Common features do exist, of course. All microprocessors will have instructions which allow the transfer of data between one or more of the working registers and memory. Instructions that perform arithmetic or logical operations are another obviously common feature, as are I/O instructions. As we shall see, however, even apparently similar arithmetic operations, for example, may not be directly comparable in different types of microprocessor.

Even a brief exposure to the subject of instruction sets will soon reveal that it cannot be divorced from processor architecture. The instruction set and architecture of a microprocessor are two complementary and equally important aspects of its total description. Instructions can only be specified if they relate to the manipulation of data stored in some component part of the architecture, such as a register. Thus, the instruction ADD B from the 8080 instruction set implies the existence of registers A and B within the system architecture since the definition of the instruction states that it causes the contents of registers A and B to be added with the result left in register A. An instruction ADD W would be meaningless in the context of the 8080 since the device does not contain a register identified as W. One conclusion from this might be that a microprocessor with a complex architecture containing many registers might be expected to have a more comprehensive instruction set than a simple device with perhaps only one or two registers. This is generally, although not universally, true if only because the existence of a register available to the programmer implies one or more associated instructions. Examine the instruction sets and architectures of the M6800 and Z8002 microprocessors in Appendices C and D to see how the size of an instruction set relates to the complexity of the microprocessor architecture.

To compare the numbers of instructions available to perform a particular class of operations in different microprocessors, it is important to note that different manufacturers may define instructions in different ways. Consider the number of instructions for performing a logical AND operation as an example. First look at the M6800 instruction set in Appendix C. This shows quite clearly that two instructions AND A and AND B are available for performing the operation. The 8080 instruction set in Appendix A on the other hand lists three instructions: ANA r, ANA M and ANI. In the case of ANA r, however, this could legitimately be regarded as a general definition for no less than seven instructions since the 'r' in the mnemonic can mean any one of the registers A, B, C, D, E, H or L. The mnemonic form of these instructions is:

```
ANA   A
ANA   B
ANA   C
ANA   D
ANA   E
ANA   H
ANA   L
```

Register- and memory-oriented microprocessors

The instruction set of a microprocessor also reflects its design philosophy in a very fundamental way. Look again at the instruction set of the M6800 in Appendix C. This microprocessor is often described as memory-oriented since the majority of instructions for logical, arithmetic and other operations involving two operands, require that one of these operands is stored in memory. Typical examples of this are the two subtract instructions in mnemonic form:

```
SUBA   xxxx
SUBB   xxxx
```

Here xxxx is a four-digit hexadecimal address. When executed, the instructions subtract the contents of the addressed memory location from register A or B as the case may be. The following instruction, for example, subtracts the contents of the hexadecimal address 1000 from the contents of register B, leaving the result in register B:

Mnemonic	*Machine code*
SUBB X'1000'	F0 10 00

An alternative philosophy is adopted for the 8080 and Z80 families of microprocessors. These devices are said to be register-oriented. In the majority of instructions involving two operands, both are required to reside in the working registers. There is, therefore, no direct equivalent to the M6800 SUBB instruction. The available 8080 instructions for subtraction all require one operand to be in register A with the other in one of the working registers A, B, C, D, E, H or L. To exactly duplicate the effect of the M6800 SUBA instruction involves several separate operations since, before subtraction can take place, the contents of the specified memory location must be transferred to register B. This results in the two-stage process shown below:

1   Transfer the contents of memory location to B.
2   Subtract the contents of register B from register A.

A further complication arises, however, since the 8080 only allows single-byte transfers of data from memory into register A. In this case, register A initially contains one of the operands. The following procedure overcomes this problem:

1 Save contents of register A in register C.
2 Load A with contents of memory location.
3 Transfer contents of register A to register B.
4 Transfer contents of register C to register A.
5 Subtract contents of register B from register A.

Figure 2.9 shows a program for performing this operation.

```
MOV   C,A       Save A in C
LD    A,1000H   Get number
MOV   B,A       Transfer A to B
MOV   A,C       Transfer C to A
SUB   B         Subtract B from A
```

Figure 2.9 8080 subtraction program

From this example we might conclude that subtraction is less convenient with the 8080 than with the M6800. In fact, the only conclusion which is correct is that we are trying to use the 8080 in a very unsuitable and inefficient way. Attempting to copy the exact function of the M6800 SUBA instruction with the 8080 is a futile activity. Instead, the programmer should write programs which exploit the register-oriented architecture of the 8080. Before a sequence of arithmetic or logical instructions are to be executed, the numbers involved should be transferred to the working registers A, B, C, D, E, H and L where they are conveniently placed for use as operands in 8080 arithmetic or logical instructions. The register-oriented instruction set of the 8080 is reflected in the architecture which includes seven working registers accessible to the programmer compared with the two of the M6800. Even this comparison must be qualified since the functions of the registers in the two processors are **Q2.11** also different in many ways.

2.7 Addressing

Addressing modes

With a few exceptions, instructions for a microprocessor or indeed any computer will identify

1 An operation such as load, store, shift, or add.
2 Data on which this operation is performed.

The addressing mode of an instruction determines the way the data are identified. A wide range of addressing modes is as important to the programmer as a comprehensive instruction set. In this section we shall define the addressing modes most commonly available to microprocessor programmers. Most manufacturers use the same names when referring to the various addressing modes. Discrepancies can be found, however, and we shall identify some of these. When an unfamiliar microprocessor is encountered, it is always a wise precaution to check the manufacturer's literature for the precise definition of the various addressing modes available.

Implied addressing

In implied addressing, the operation code itself defines the location of the data to be used as an operand. This contrasts with other addressing modes which require two parts to the instruction, an operation code or opcode and an address which defines the data or the location of the data. A typical example of the implied addressing mode is the ABA instruction for the M6800 microprocessor. When executed, ABA causes the contents of registers A and B to be added, leaving the result in A. In 8-bit microprocessors, instructions with implied addressing may often be defined by a single-byte code since no further information is necessary to specify the operand(s). All 8-bit microprocessors have some instructions with this mode of addressing. Some examples are given below:

1 *8080*   XCHG means exchange the contents of register pair D,E and H,L.
2 *Z80*   LD SP,IY means load the stack pointer register SP with the contents of register IY.

With 16-bit microprocessors, the definition of implied addressing may become somewhat different. This is mainly because these devices have a much more complex architecture, with many more working registers than the 8-bit microprocessors. Compare the programmer's models for the Z80 and Z8000 in Figure 2.7 and Appendix D. The Z8000 contains sixteen general-purpose registers compared with seven in the Z80. The instruction set of the Z8000 is also said to be regular. This means, among other things, that an instruction which uses the contents of one particular register as an operand should also work with any other register. An instruction is available, defined by the mnemonic NEG R3, which replaces the contents of register 3 by the twos complement negative value. Using the criterion that the opcode identifies the location of the data, this could be said to be an example of implied addressing. The NEG R3 instruction, however, is only one of a group of sixteen instructions NEG xx, where xx can specify any one of the sixteen working registers R0–R15. For this reason, the term implied addressing is replaced by register addressing in this case. Register addressing is also the name some writers use in place of implied addressing for the Z80 and 8080 microprocessor families. To add further confusion, the term implied addressing is used in Z8000 manufacturer's data but the definition is totally different to that given here and by most other manufacturers. Pages 3–32 of Ref. 2.2 gives more details of this addressing mode.

Immediate addressing

The immediate addressing mode requires a two-part instruction consisting of the opcode and the data which constitutes the operand. In an 8-bit microprocessor, the operand will occupy one or two bytes, depending on the particular instruction. An example of this addressing mode with a one-byte operand is:

```
MVI  X'F0'   code 3E F0
```

This is an 8080 instruction which loads register A with F0. The instruction shown below is for the Z80 and loads register pair H,L with the 16-bit operand 10F0:

```
LD  HL,X'10F0'   code B6 F0 10
```

Direct addressing

With this addressing mode, the instruction is clearly divided into two sections: the opcode and the address. Note the distinction between this mode and immediate addressing. With immediate addressing, the data are provided as part of the instruction. With direct addressing, the address of the data is part of the instruction. In microprocessors with a 16-line address bus, this address will consist of 16 bits. For a typical 8-bit microprocessor such as the 8080, Z80 or M6800, therefore, an instruction employing the direct addressing mode would consist of three bytes, a single-byte opcode and a two-byte address. An example of this is the Z80 instruction

```
LD  A,X'2F00'   code 3A 00 2F
```

which loads register A with the contents of memory location 2F00. This is shown schematically in Figure 2.10. The result of executing the instruction at 1000 would be to load A with 1F.

An important difference exists in the definition of direct addressing in literature relating to the M6800. In M6800 manufacturers' data, two forms of direct addressing are defined. The first type requires only the least significant byte of the address in the instruction word. When the instruction is executed the most significant byte of the address is assumed to be zero. An example of an instruction using this addressing mode is:

```
LDA A X'F3'   code 96 F3
```

When executed, this instruction loads register A with the contents of memory location 00F3. This addressing mode offers the advantages of faster execution and less memory occupancy than the more common form of direct addressing but has the disadvantage that only addresses in the range 0000 to 00FF are accessible. It would normally be used for frequently used operands which would be purposely stored in the lower part of memory. Figure 2.11 shows this modified form of direct addressing which would load register A with 3C when executed.

The more common form of direct addressing is called extended addressing in M6800 literature. This mode requires a two-byte address and allows access to the full address space 0000 to FFFF. An example of this is:

```
LDA A X'10F3'  code B6 10 F3
```

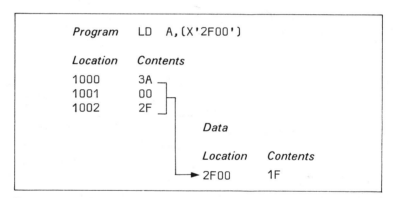

Figure 2.10 Direct addressing of location 2F00

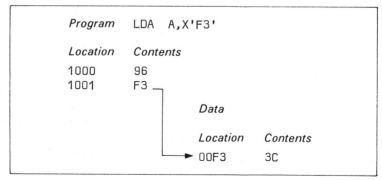

Figure 2.11 Modified direct addressing with M6800

Register indirect addressing

This addressing mode is supported by the 8080, 8085, Z80 and Z8000 families, among others, but not in the same form by the M6800 family. In an instruction employing an indirect address, the instruction word identifies a register or register pair which contains the address of the operand. The register pair is often referred to as an address pointer. The Z8000 instruction shown below, for example, loads register R8 from an address which is found in register R1:

```
LD R8,qr1   code 2F 18
```

Here, QR1 is used to specify register indirect addressing. This is a standard assembly language format for the Z8000. It is, of course, the responsibility of the programmer to ensure that the pointer register(s) is loaded with the correct address before an instruction using indirect addressing is executed. This example of register indirect addressing is shown schematically in Figure 2.12. Another example of register indirect addressing is shown below, this time for the 8080 micro-processor. The instruction adds the contents of the address found in register pair H,L, to register A:

```
ADD M   code 86
```

Indexed addressing

Indexed addressing may be regarded as an extension of the register indirect mode which allows the addition of an offset to the indirect address pointer. If an instruction specifies indexed addressing, the instruction code will include an offset. When the instruction is executed, the processor forms an effective address by adding this offset to the contents of an index register. The indexed addressing mode is not supported by the 8080/8085 family of devices but can be implemented by the 6800, Z80 and Z8000.

The M6800 architecture contains a single index register as shown by the programmer's model in Figure 2.8. It is the responsibility of the programmer to load the index register with the correct 'base address' so that when the offset is added, the desired data address is formed. Suppose that this has been done and the 16-bit index regiser X contains, say, 2000. The assembler format for an M6800 memory reference instruction with indexed addressing is:

```
LDA B X'30',X
```

Here, the X'30' indicates a hexadecimal number as usual with the Futuredata assembler. The second 'X' implies indexed addressing. To form the effective address therefore, we add 30 to the contents of the index register which have previously set to 2000. The effective address is therefore 2030 and register B is loaded with the contents of

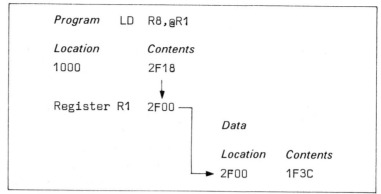

Figure 2.12 Register indirect addressing with Z8000

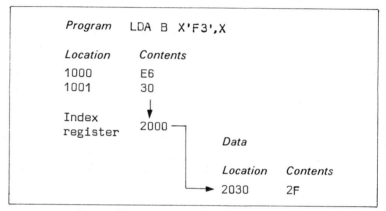

Figure 2.13 Indexed addressing with M6800

this location or 2F after execution. Figure 2.13 shows this situation in diagram form.

The availability of the indexed mode of addressing is a very powerful weapon for the efficient implementation of programs. More recently developed microprocessors have architectures that extend this facility. The Z80 for example includes two index registers IX and IY as shown in Figure 2.7. A further development of this trend is shown by the Z8000 in which no less than fifteen of the general-purpose registers can also be used for address indexation. The sophisticated architecture of the Z8000 in fact allows several addressing modes which do not fit the 'classical' definitions given in this section.

Q2.12, 2.13

2.8 A programming problem

We said at the beginning of this section that every processor has its own particular strengths and weaknesses. To demonstrate this, we shall examine a typical computing task implemented by three

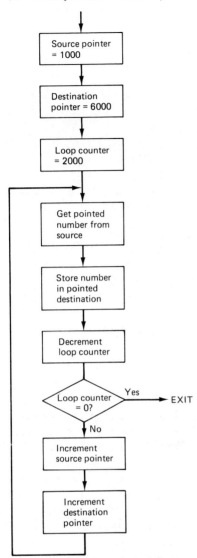

Figure 2.14 Data transfer program flowchart

different microprocessors. The processors are the 8080, Z80 and M6800, all of which are 8-bit devices. The task is to move a block of 2000 (hexadecimal) bytes of data from the source memory area 1000–2FFF to the destination area 6000–7FFF. Speed of execution, number of bytes of machine code required and the ease with which a standard algorithm can be implemented will be the criteria we shall use to compare the three microprocessors.

Figure 2.14 shows a flowchart for the algorithm to be used. The method is a standard one that uses two address pointers, one of which holds the next address in the source area from which the data byte is obtained. The other pointer holds the next address in the destination area in which the data byte will be stored. A loop counter is used to ensure the transfer of the correct number of bytes. After each data transfer is complete, the loop counter is decremented and checked for zero. If zero is not detected, source and destination pointers are incremented and the next data transfer takes place. The procedure stops when the loop counter contains zero.

It will be seen from the flowchart in Figure 2.14 that the program divides naturally into an initialisation segment and a data transfer segment. In the initialisation segment, the source pointer, destination pointer and loop counter are all set to their initial values. The time taken to execute this segment is a small proportion of the total execution time since it is only executed once the data transfer segment on the other hand is executed 2000 (hexadecimal) times.

The 8080 solution

Let us first look at the problem confronting the programmer of the 8080 microprocessor for this operation. A suitable program in machine-code mnemonics is shown below:

```
START   LXI   H,X'1000'
        LXI   D,X'6000'
        LXI   B,X'2000'      Initialisation completed

AGAIN   MOV   A,M
        STAX  D               Byte transfer completed

        DCX   B
        MVI   A,0
        CMP   C
        JNZ   NOTDON
        CMP   B
        JZ    FINISH          Loop counter decremented
                              and checked for zero
```

(continued)

```
NOTDON   INX   X
         INX   D          Pointers incremented

         JMP   AGAIN
FINISH   RET
```

An assembly listing for the program is given in Figure 2.15. With the 8080, the only way of implementing an address pointer is by making use of indirect addressing. The initialisation procedure therefore sets up the source address pointer by loading the H,L register pair with 1000, the first address in the source area. In the destination area, the first address is 6000 and this number is loaded into the D,E register pair. Register pair B,C is loaded with 2000, the hexadecimal number of bytes to be transferred, and acts as a loop counter.

In the data transfer loop, the MOV A,M instruction loads register A with the contents of the memory location whose address is found in register pair H,L. This is an example of indirect addressing. The STAX D instruction, which follows, stores the data byte in A in the memory location whose address is found in register pair D,E – indirect addressing again. The transfer of one byte from source to destination is now complete.

At this point, the loop counter must be decremented and the result checked for zero. This is done in the program by a conditional jump instruction, JZ, which implements a jump only if the Z(zero) flag is set. Now we are using register pair B,C as a 16-bit loop counter since a single register would not hold 2000, the number of bytes to be transferred. An instruction DCX B is available in the 8080 instruction set which decrements the contents of this register pair. The instruction, however, has the restriction that its execution has no

```
 -------- 8080/85 ASSEMBLER V01 ----------------------------- PAGE    1
                                                    FUTUREDATA --------
            ****************************************************************
            *8080 BLOCK DATA TRANSFER PROGRAM                             *
            *THIS PROGRAM TRANSFERS A BLOCK OF 2000(HEX) BYTES FROM       *
            *1000-2FFF TO 6000-7FFF                                       *
            ****************************************************************
 0000 210010  START   LXI   H,X'1000'          SOURCE POINTER
 0003 110060          LXI   D,X'6000'          DESTINATION POINTER
 0006 010020          LXI   B,X'2000'          LOOP COUNTER
            *INITIALISATION COMPLETE
            *
 0009 7E     AGAIN    MOV   A,M                GET POINTED WORD
 000A 12              STAX  D                  STORE IN DESTINATION
 000B 0B              DCX   B                  DEC LOOP COUNTER
 000C 3E00            MVI   A,0
 000E B9              CMP   C                  LSB = 0?
 000F C21600          JNZ   NOTDON             JUMP IF NO
 0012 B8              CMP   B                  MSB = 0?
 0013 CA1B00          JZ    FINISH             DONE
 0016 23     NOTDON   INX   H                  INC SOURCE POINTER
 0017 13              INX   D                  INCT DEST POINTER
 0018 C30900          JMP   AGAIN              DO IT AGAIN
 001B C9     FINISH   RET
 001C                 END
```

Figure 2.15 8080 block data transfer program

effect on the condition flags. This is a crucial limitation since the effectiveness of the 'jump if zero' instruction, JZ, depends on the setting of the Z flag by the preceding instruction.

To overcome this difficulty, register A is loaded with zero and compared with registers C and B in turn. The compare instruction, CMP, unlike DCX, does affect the Z flag and can therefore be followed by an effective conditional jump. When the loop counter decrementation does not result in zero, the address pointer register pairs, D,E and H,L are incremented and an unconditional jump is made to the beginning of the loop. The program is written in the form of a subroutine and exit is via the subroutine return instruction, RET.

One indication of the convenienve of the 8080 instruction set for this programming task is the time it takes the program to execute. To determine this, the numbers of clock cycles required to execute the various instructions in the program are listed. The 8080 instruction set summary, included as part of Appendix A, shows the number of clock cycles required to execute each instruction in the set. From this, the total number of clock cycles required to execute the whole program can be calculated. Execution time is fixed by the number of clock cycles and the clock period. In an attempt to make some sort of meaningful comparison between the different microprocessors, we shall assume the maximum clock frequency of the 'standard' version of each device. High-speed versions of most microprocessors are now available, in addition to the standard versions.

In the initialising segment of the 8080 program, the three LXI instructions require 10 clock cycles each, making a total of 30 cycles for this part of the program. In fact, the contribution of the initialisation to program execution time is minimal and included only for completeness. During each excursion round the data transfer loop, the sequence of instructions executed will not always be the same. This is due to the fact that the conditional jump instructions sometimes initiate jumps and sometimes do not. The time taken to execute a conditional jump also varies depending on whether or not the jump actually occurs. There are three possible routes through the instructions in the data transfer loop. These are shown below as A, B and C with the number of clock cycles indicated. Conditional jump instructions which cause the jump to occur are indicated with an asterisk.

		Instruction		*Clock cycles*	
Route A	AGAIN	MOV	A,M	7	
		STAX	D	7	
		DCX	B	5	
		MVI	A,0	7	
		CMP	C	4	
		*JNZ	NOTDON	10	*(continued)*

```
          NOTDON   INX    H          5
                   INX    D          5
                   JMP    AGAIN      10
                                     ──
                                     60
```

Route B
```
          AGAIN    MOV    A,M        7
                   STAX   D          7
                   DCX    B          5
                   MVI    A,0        7
                   CMP    C          4
                   JNZ    NOTDON     7
                   CMP    B          4
                   JZ     FINISH     7
                   INX    H          5
                   INX    D          5
                   JMP    AGAIN      10
                                     ──
                                     68
```

Route C
```
          AGAIN    MOV    A,M        7
                   STAX   D          7
                   DCX    B          5
                   MVI    A,0        7
                   CMP    C          4
                   JNZ    NOTDON     7
                   CMP    B          4
                 *JZ      FINISH     10
          FINISH   RET               10
                                     ──
                                     61
```

Note that in the above all numbers of clock cycles are in decimal form.

Now the total number of loop excursions is 2000, or 8,192 (decimal). Of these, C will occur only once since it terminates the loop. B will occur when the loop count is 0100, 0200, 0300–1F00, i.e. 1F or 31 (decimal) times. The total number of clock cycles, N, is

$$(1 \times 61) + (31 \times 68) + (8{,}160 \times 60)$$
$$= 491{,}769 \text{ (decimal)}$$

To this must be added the 30 cycles taken for initialisation, giving a grand total of 491,799 (decimal). The minimum clock period for the 8080 is 320 ns. The execution time is therefore

$$516{,}464 \times 320 \text{ ns} = 157.37 \text{ ms}$$

The M6800 solution

A program which implements the data transfer algorithm with the M6800 microprocessor is shown below in machine-code mnemonic form, with a full assembly listing in Figure 2.16.

```
START    LDX     #X'1000'
         STX     SPOINT
         LDX     #X'6000'
         STX     DPOINT
         LDX     #X'2000'
         STX     NCOUNT          Initialisation completed

AGAIN    LDX     SPOINT
         LDAA    0,X
         LDX     DPOINT
         STAA    0,X             Byte transfer completed

         LDX     NCOUNT
         DEX
         BEQ     FINISH          Loop counter decremented
         STX     NCOUNT          and checked for zero

         LDX     SPOINT
         INX
         STX     SPOINT
         LDX     DPOINT
         INX
         STX     DPOINT          Pointers incremented

         BRA     AGAIN
FINISH   RTS
```

The M6800 does not allow the indirect mode of addressing. In this case, address pointing is achieved by making use of the indexed mode of addressing. A memory reference instruction using the indexed addressing mode will include an 8-bit address offset as part of the instruction code. When the instruction is executed, the processor forms an effective address by adding the 8-bit offset to the contents of the 16-bit index register, X. The format for load and store instructions with indexed addressing is:

```
LDAA    d,X
STAA    d,X
```

where 'd' is the offset or displacement. The corresponding instructions in the program of Figure 2.16 are

```
LDAA    0,X
STAA    0,X
```

```
               PAGE  1
-------- 6800/02 ASSEMBLER V01 ---------------------------- FUTUREDATA --------

                 ****************************************************
                 *M6800 BLOCK DATA TRANSFER PROGRAM                 *
                 *THIS PROGRAM TRANSFERS A BLOCK OF 2000(HEX) BYTES *
                 *FROM 1000-2FFF TO 6000-7FFF                       *
                 ****************************************************
0000 CE1000  START     LDX     #X'1000'
0003 FF0037            STX     SPOINT              SOURCE POINTER
0006 CE6000            LDX     #X'6000'
0009 FF0035            STX     DPOINT              DESTINATION POINTER
000C CE2000            LDX     #X'2000'
000F FF0039            STX     NCOUNT              LOOP COUNTER
             *INITIALISATION COMPLETE
             *
0012 FE0037  AGAIN     LDX     SPOINT              GET SOURCE POINTER
0015 A600              LDAA    0,X                 GET POINTED WORD
0017 FE0035            LDX     DPOINT              GET DEST POINTER
001A A700              STAA    0,X                 STORE IN DESTINATION
001C FE0039            LDX     NCOUNT              GET LOOP COUNTER
001F 09                DEX                         DEC LOOP COUNTER
0020 2719              BEQ     FINISH              DONE?
0022 FF0039            STX     NCOUNT              SAVE LOOP COUNTER
0025 FE0037            LDX     SPOINT
0028 08                INX                         INC SOURCE POINTER
0029 FF0037            STX     SPOINT              SAVE SOURCE POINTER
002C FE0035            LDX     DPOINT
002F 08                INX                         INC DEST POINTER
0030 FF0035            STX     DPOINT              SAVE DEST POINTER
0033 20DD              BRA     AGAIN               DO IT AGAIN
             *
0035         DPOINT    DS      2
0037         SPOINT    DS      2                   SOURCE POINTER
0039         NCOUNT    DS      2                   LOOP COUNTER
             *
003B 39      FINISH    RTS
003C                   END
```

Figure 2.16   M6800 block data transfer program 1

In the program shown in Figure 2.16, the index register in fact plays the same role as the 8080 register pairs H,L and D,E in the previous example since the offset is zero in every case.

For programming problems such as the one we are considering here, the use of indexed addressing with the M6800 has two limitations. The first is the fact that the address offset has a maximum value of FF which renders the offset facility valueless for this application. This point is discussed in more detail in Section 2.7 which covers addressing modes. The second limitation is that the M6800 architecture includes only one register which can be used for address indexation. The algorithm shown in Figure 2.14 requires two address pointers, one each for the source and destination addresses. A further problem lies in the necessity for a 16-bit loop counter as discussed in Section 2.6. Only two 16-bit registers are accessible to the programmer in the M6800. These are S, the stack pointer, and X, the index register. The stack pointer can be used as a loop counter. It also plays an important role in storing subroutine return addresses and processor status data during interrupt servicing. In view of this, great care is necessary when using it for other purposes. The program shown in Figure 2.16 avoids using the stack pointer as a loop counter by employing register X.

Register X performs three separate functions in this program. These are:

a A source address pointer.
b A destination address pointer.
c A loop counter.

To perform these three functions, the current values of the three variables, source address, destination address and loop count are stored in memory. They are then loaded into register X when required and returned to memory after modification.

In the initialisation segment of the program, register X is loaded with 1000, the first source address. This 16-bit value is then stored in two memory locations, the first of which is identified by the symbolic address SPOINT. The single STX instruction accomplishes this. Initialisation of the destination pointer and loop counter is then performed in a similar manner.

The data transfer loop follows the flowchart shown in Figure 2.14 exactly. Comments in the assembly listing should make this self-explanatory. Note that the current values of the source address, destination address and loop count are loaded from memory into X before they are used by the program.

Although the program shown in Figure 2.16 implements the algorithm described by the flowchart in Figure 2.14, it could be argued that this is really a rather inefficient program for the M6800. Examination of the instruction set reveals a simple program modification which allows the program to execute more rapidly and occupy less space in memory. This modified program is:

```
START    LDX     #X'1000'
         STX     SPOINT
         LDX     #X'6000'
         STX     DPOINT       Initialisation completed

AGAIN    LDX     SPOINT
         LDAA    0,X
         INX
         STX     SPOINT
         LDX     DPOINT
         STAA    0,X          Byte transfer completed

         INX
         CPX     #X'8000'
         BEQ     FINISH
         STX     DPOINT       Pointers incremented

         BRA     AGAIN
FINISH   RTS
```

It will be seen that the use of a separate loop counter is avoided by employing the compare X instruction, CPX. After the destination address pointer has been incremented in register X during the data transfer loop, the contents of X are compared with 8000. This is the limiting value of the destination address. If a match is found, the data transfer is obviously complete and the Z bit of the condition code (flag) register is set to 1. The following conditional branch on zero instruction, BEQ, causes the program to exit via the subroutine return, RTS.

This modified program does not correspond exactly with the flow-chart of Figure 2.14. A modified flowchart is shown in Figure 2.17.

```
                                                             PAGE   1
     -------- 6800/02 ASSEMBLER V01 --------------------------- FUTUREDATA --------

                    **********************************************************
                    *M6800 BLOCK DATA TRANSFER PROGRAM(MODIFIED)        *
                    *THIS PROGRAM TRANSFERS A BLOCK OF 2000(HEX) BYTES  *
                    *FROM 1000-2FFF TO 6000-7FFF                        *
                    **********************************************************
     0000 CE1000    START     LDX     #X'1000'
     0003 FF0027              STX     SPOINT             SOURCE POINTER
     0006 CE6000              LDX     #X'6000'
     0009 FF0025              STX     DPOINT             DESTINATION POINTER
                    *INITIALISATION COMPLETE
                    *
     000C FE0027    AGAIN     LDX     SPOINT             GET SOURCE POINTER
     000F A600                LDAA    0,X                GET POINTED WORD
     0011 08                  INX                        INCREMENT SPOINTER
     0012 FF0027              STX     SPOINT             SAVE SPOINTER
     0015 FE0025              LDX     DPOINT             GET DEST POINTER
     0018 A700                STAA    0,X                STORE WORD IN DESTINATION
     001A 08                  INX                        INCREMENT SOURCE POINTER
     001B 8C8000              CPX     #X'8000'           FINISHED?
     001E 2709                BEQ     FINISH
     0020 FF0025              STX     DPOINT             SAVE DPOINTER
     0023 20E7                BRA     AGAIN              DO IT AGAIN
                    *
     0025           DPOINT    DS      2                  DESTINATION POINTER
     0027           SPOINT    DS      2                  SOURCE POINTER
                    *
     0029 39        FINISH    RTS
     002A                     END
```

Figure 2.17 M6800 block data transfer program 2

An experienced M6800 programmer would, of course, be aware of the use of the CPX instruction in situations such as this and design the algorithm with this in mind from the start. This is a good example of the way a detailed knowledge of an instruction set helps the programmer to design program structures which exploit the strengths of the particular microprocessor.

In calculating the execution time, we shall use the more efficient version of the program. The number of clock cycles (in decimal form) required by the initialising instructions is shown below.

Instruction	Clock cycles
LDX #X'1000'	3
STX SPOINT	6
LDX #X'6000'	3
STX DPOINT	6
	18

Two alternative routes exist round the data transfer loop, shown as A and B.

	Instruction			Clock cycles
Route A	AGAIN	LDX	SPOINT	5
		LDAA	0,X	5
		INX		4
		STX	SPOINT	6
		LDX	DPOINT	5
		STAA	0,X	6
		INX		4
		CPX	#X'8000'	3
		BEQ	FINISH	4
		STX	DPOINT	6
		BRA	AGAIN	4
				52

	Instruction			Clock cycles
Route B	AGAIN	LDX	SPOINT	5
		LDAA	0,X	5
		INX		4
		STX	SPOINT	6
		LDX	DPOINT	5
		STAA	0,X	6
		INX		4
		CPX	#X,'8000'	3
	*BEQ	FINISH	4
	FINISH	RTS		5
				47

During a program run, the initialising instructions are executed once, B is executed once and A is executed 8,191 (decimal) times. The total number of clock cycles, N, is thus

$$18 + 47 + (8{,}191 \times 52) = 425{,}997 \text{ (decimal)}$$

The minimum clock period for the standard M6800 is 1,000 ns. The execution time is, therefore,

$$425,997 \times 1,000 \text{ ns} = 426 \text{ ms}$$

The Z80 solution

With the Z80, we return to a register-oriented architecture very similar to that of the 8080. The instruction set of the Z80 duplicates the vast majority of 8080 instructions. A substantial number of additional instructions are also available. Given this information, we might expect that the Z80 program would look similar to the 8080 program. The listing in Figure 2.18 and the program below show that this is not the case.

```
START    LD      DE,X'6000'
         LD      HL,X'1000'
         LD      BC,X'2000'    Initialisation completed

         LDIR
         RET
```

The reason for the difference between the 8080 and Z80 programs lies in the use of the LDIR instruction in the latter case. This is a powerful data transfer instruction which is not present in the 8080 instruction set. When the LDIR instruction is executed, the contents of the address pointed by register pair H,L are transferred to the address pointed by register pair D,E. The contents of register pairs H,L and D,E are then incremented and the contents of pair B,C decremented. If B,C contains zero after this operation, the next instruction in sequence is executed, otherwise the data transfer is repeated with the new pointer values.

From the above description of LDIR, it will be seen that this single instruction implements the complete data transfer segment of the flowchart in Figure 2.14. This has an obvious and dramatic effect on the length of the program.

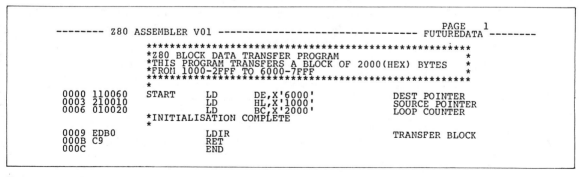

Figure 2.18 Z80 block data transfer program

Execution time calculations are straightforward for this program. The three 16-bit load instructions required for initialisation require 10 clock cycles each for execution. Two routes only are possible for the remainder of the program. These are shown below (with, again, the clock cycles in decimal form).

	Instruction	*Clock cycles*
Route A	LDIR	16
		16
Route B	LDIR	21
	RET	10
		31

B is executed once only since it terminates the routine and the initialising instructions are executed once only. A is executed 8,191 (decimal) times, so the total number of clock cycles, N, is

$$30 + 31 + (8{,}191 \times 16) = 131{,}103 \text{ (decimal)}$$

The minimum clock period for the Z80 is 400 ns. The execution time is, therefore,

$$131{,}103 \times 400 \text{ ns} = 52.44 \text{ ms}$$

Some conclusions

In the above sections we have looked at the way the different instruction sets and associated architectures of three microprocessors affect the approach to a particular programming task. The task itself is by no means uncommon. Manipulation of blocks or strings of data is required quite frequently in many different types of program. We have been investigating the efficiency and convenience of the three microprocessors in one aspect of string manipulation.

In assessing the power and convenience of the instruction sets of the three microprocessors for the specified programming task, program execution time and memory occupancy are a useful guide. The results of the exercise are tabulated in Table 2.2.

Table 2.2

Processor	*Execution time*	*Program memory*
8080	165 ms	25 bytes
M6800	426 ms	42 bytes
Z80	52 ms	12 bytes

Minor modifications to the programs in the nature of 'fine tuning' could perhaps reduce execution times and memory occupancy marginally. In the 8080 program, for example, use of the conditional subroutine return, RZ, in place of the conditional jump, JZ, followed by RET would save one clock cycle per loop excursion. This minor improvement would not change our conclusions significantly.

It is quite clear when looking at these results that when a block of 2000 bytes of data is to be transferred from the source area of memory at 1000 to the destination at 6000, the Z80 offers shorter execution time and less occupancy of memory by the program than does the 8080. The 8080 in turn shows a similar advantage over the M6800. The results relating to a single programming task should not, however, be extended automatically to a general conclusion that the Z80 has an overall superiority compared with the 8080, which in turn is superior to the M6800. We have investigated only one aspect of the instruction sets of the three microprocessors. Other computing tasks might well produce different results. Rather than prove any point concerning the superiority of one type of microprocessor over another, the object has been to demonstrate the methods of comparison and emphasise the importance of the instruction set in determining microprocessor performance.

Certain specific points relating to the three microprocessors have emerged, however. Perhaps the most important is the effect that special string handling instructions can have in programs performing this type of operation. The good performance of the Z80 in this exercise results from the availability of the LDIR instruction. The reader should examine the Z80 instruction set in Appendix B and note other instructions for manipulating strings of data.

A limitation of the 8080 in handling 16-bit operands has also emerged from this exercise. Although the program is concerned with the transfer of data, 8 bits at a time, many of the variables used as operands in the program are 16-bit numbers. These include the addresses themselves and the number of data bytes to be transferred. The inability of the 8080 16-bit decrement instructions, such as DCX B, to affect the Z flag must be regarded as an inconvenience in this context.

The major problem with the M6800 in this exercise is an architecture which includes only one 16-bit register which can be used as an address pointer. As we have seen, a minimum of two such registers is necessary to implement the data transfer algorithm conveniently. The M6800 does, however, allow us to perform the logical compare operation between two 16-bit operands, one of which is in the address pointer register X. In the program shown in Figure 2.17 this is used to avoid the necessity for a separate loop counter. The availability of the indexed mode of addressing is another advantage although it could not be exploited in this exercise.

Although in this section we have concentrated on the effect of the instruction set on speed of execution and program memory occupancy, other factors are often more important. Programmers are increasingly aware of the importance of writing clear, well structured programs which are easy to follow and easy to modify. The ability of an instruction set to support the writing of assembly language programs with these characteristics should be an important consideration. The subject of program structure is discussed in more detail in Chapter 6.

For more complex computing tasks, it is now generally realised that programs can be developed more easily and economically using high-level languages such as PASCAL, CORAL, FORTRAN and ADA in place of assembly language or machine code. Some of the more recently introduced microprocessors such as the M6800 and Z8000 have instruction sets that lay special emphasis on the support of high-level languages. A detailed study of this aspect of instruction sets is outside the scope of this text, but the reader may expect to see it becoming increasingly important in the future. Ref. 2.1 is a good introduction to this aspect of instruction sets.

2.9   Bench marks

In Section 2.8 we have seen how different microprocessors can be compared by implementing a simple computing task. In the example given, only one aspect of computing performance was investigated, relating to the movement of data blocks in memory. To provide a meaningful overall computing power, it would be necessary to complete a whole range of similar exercises, covering a variety of different types of computation.

When attempting to choose the best microprocessor for a particular application, one approach involves the design of a set of special test programs for each of the microprocessors under consideration. These programs cover the major tasks expected of the microprocessor in the particular application. The efficiency of the microprocessor in terms of the memory occupancy of the programs and speed of execution can then be assessed. The term *bench marks* is often used for tests of this kind. Bench marks are also used for comparing all aspects of micro-
Q2.14   processor system performance.

References and bibliography

2.1   S. Davis, '16-bit microprocessors – special report', *Electronic Design News*, pp 71–85 (5 August 1979).
2.2   *Z80 – Assembly Language Programming Manual*, Zilog (1978).
2.3   W. Barden, *The Z80 Microcomputer Handbook*, Howard W. Sams & Co., Inc (1978).

2.4 *M6800 Microprocessor Programming Manual*, Motorola Semi-conductor Products Inc. (1975).

2.5 L. A. Leventhal, A. Osborne and C. Collins, *Z8000 Assembly Language Programming*, Osborne/McGraw-Hill (1980).

2.6 M. Gooze, 'How a 16-bit microprocessor makes it in an 8-bit world (6809 development)', *Electronics*, Vol. 52 (20), pp 122–5 (27 September 1979).

Questions

2.1 How does the COP420L device differ in concept from micropro-cessors such as the 8080, Z80 and M6800?

2.2 Using Appendix B as a guide, state whether the Z80 $\overline{\text{HALT}}$ line could be regarded as a status or a control line from the point of view of:
(a) The microprocessor
(b) The associated system

2.3 List the number of clock phases required by the following micro-processors:
(a) 8080
(b) Z80
(c) 6800
(d) Z8002

2.4 Explain why some designers of microprocessor chips choose to multi-plex status with other signals.

2.5 Give an example of two microprocessors that feature multiplexed status signals.

2.6 How does the address bus of the Z8001 microprocessor differ from that of the Z8002?

2.7 What is the maximum number of memory locations that can be addressed by the following microprocessors:
(a) M6800
(b) Z80
(c) Z8001

2.8 Give two examples of 8080 instructions that manipulate data in the form of 16-bit words.

2.9 Explain what is means by the architecture of a microprocessor.

2.10 Sketch a diagram describing the architecture of any microprocessor with which you are familiar.

2.11 Explain the distinction between memory-oriented and register-oriented microprocessors.

2.12   State the normal definition of the following terms:
  (a)   Implied addressing
  (b)   Direct addressing
  (c)   Immediate addressing
  (d)   Register indirect addressing
  (e)   Indexed addressing

2.13   Register indirect and indexed are two important addressing modes. Which of these modes is not available
  (a)   With the 8080?
  (b)   With the M6800 microprocessor?

2.14   Explain what is meant by a bench mark.

2.15   Using the instruction sets given in Appendices A, B and C, write programs for the 8080, Z80 and M6800 which add the contents of two addresses, leaving the result in a third address. Compare the number of bytes required to store each program. Assuming that the M6800, 8080 and Z80 operate with clock frequencies of 1, 1 and 2 MHz, respectively, compare the speed of execution of the three programs.

Chapter 3 Further considerations in choosing a microprocessor

Objectives of this chapter *When you have completed studying this chapter you should be able to analyse, with the help of manufacturers' data sheets, the following important features of a microprocessor: (i) I/O facilities; (ii) power requirements.*

3.1 Microprocessor I/O facilities

Every computing system must have facilities for transferring data to and from the CPU. This is because the essential function of the CPU is to manipulate, in some way, data with which it is presented in order to produce some desired form of output. The input may originate from a keyboard, transducer, switch or any one of a wide variety of information sources. The output may consist of numerical results which must be displayed or printed. It may, on the other hand, be non-visible signals which control electronic or electromechanical devices.

Taking an overview of the whole field of computing systems, therefore, the type of external device to which we may wish to connect a CPU can vary widely. The simplest devices will require only a single line connection. Among these devices are indicator lamps, relays and switches. For devices such as lamps or relays, the CPU must change the logical state of a single output line. Substantial amplification of this output signal may be necessary if the output device absorbs a significant amount of power. Devices such as switches are connected in a simple circuit to generate a CPU input signal which is high or low depending on whether the switch is in the on or off position.

More complex I/O devices, e.g. printers, numerical indicators, keyboards and ADCs, will transmit or receive information in coded form. A printer for example will accept code characters of, say, 8 bits each. Each code character represents a letter, number or punctuation character. Appendix R shows a typical code of this type. An ADC will generate a code character which represents the magnitude of the analogue input. For these more complex devices therefore, I/O operations involve the transfer of information in the form of characters or words, each containing several bits of data.

An important distinction must be introduced at this point between serial and parallel data transfer. Parallel transfer of an *n*-bit data character between two points requires a connecting path of *n* lines together with a ground return. Each bit of the character is conveyed along a separate line. Serial data transfer on the other hand involves only a single line connection together with a ground return. With this serial mode, individual data bits are transferred one at a time along the single line. Each method of data transfer has its own advantages and disadvantages which are discussed in Chapter 4. Both serial and parallel data transfer are widely employed in microcomputer systems for transferring data to and from different types of peripheral devices.

Designers of microprocessors tend to adopt one of three possible approaches to the provision of I/O facilities. These can be described as:

1   The single-chip microcomputer approach.
2   The I/O port approach.
3   The memory-mapped I/O approach.

Of course, each microprocessor manufacturer produces convincing arguments as to why the approach adopted for his products is by far the best. As usual, each approach has its own advantages and disadvantages.

Single-chip microcomputer I/O

With a single-chip microcomputer, the need for special I/O interface circuitry may be minimal or non-existant. The COP420L described in Appendix E provides us with a good example of this. It will be seen from this appendix that a total of 23 I/O lines of different types are available with this processor. These allow serial and parallel data transfer between the microprocessor and the outside world. An obvious potential difficulty with this approach is lack of versatility. Since the I/O facilities are totally determined by the microprocessor manufacturer, it is easy to conceive of a situation in which a user's particular I/O requirements are not met. It is also possible that for a very simple system, the I/O facilities may be far in excess of the requirements of the user. Compare this with the situation of users of CPU-type microprocessors. Here, the user tailors the I/O facilities exactly to the requirements of the system. To provide similar flexibility with the single-chip approach would require a specially designed microprocessor for each application.

To overcome this problem of flexibility, manufacturers of single-chip microcomputers adopt two approaches. The first is to manufacture families of microcomputers rather than single isolated devices. These families comprise devices with broadly similar characteristics in terms of architecture and instruction sets. Individual members of a family may differ in the amount of memory available and perhaps

I/O facilities. The potential user is therefore able to choose from a family the device most suited to his requirements.

Some manufacturers also have a second approach to the problem of flexibility by allowing certain I/O options for each member of a single-chip microcomputer family. The COP420L is an example of this approach. Various options for the characteristics of I/O lines are listed in Appendix E. We note for example that one option is for a set of I/O lines capable of providing sufficient current to activate the segments of an LED numerical display. The microcomputer could therefore present numerical data by connecting these lines directly to an LED numerical display device. No additional circuitry is required.

The I/O port approach

The provision of ports through which input and output data passes is the most common approach to I/O operations with microprocessors. An essential feature of the facility is the availability of special-purpose I/O instructions in the instruction repertoire. Different microprocessors identify these instructions in different ways but we shall use the general-purpose mnemonics, IN and OUT, for this purpose. When an IN or OUT instruction is executed, the CPU places a port address on the address bus. Data are then put out or taken in from the data bus. It is the responsibility of the peripheral interface circuit (PIC) to ensure that the peripheral device is ready to accept or generate data at this time.

I/O data are normally conveyed to and from peripheral devices via the data bus in microprocessor systems. Some minicomputers have separate buses for input and output data, but luxury of this kind is precluded by the limited number of pins on a microprocessor package. The system data bus therefore conveys I/O data in addition to data to and from memory. Although the fundamental objective is the transfer of data to and from peripheral devices, most I/O operations also involve the exchange of status and control information. This is because, in the majority of I/O operations, it is necessary to synchronise the activity of the peripheral device with the internal CPU operations. Section 3.2 investigates this in detail.

To successfully perform an input or output operation the CPU must have some way of informing all peripheral devices that an I/O operation is taking place. A typical way of doing this is by a signal from the CPU on a line which we shall call IORQ. The CPU must also identify which peripheral device is to be involved in the input or output operation. It does this by placing on the address bus, the port address allocated to the particular peripheral device.

Since the system data bus is bidirectional, it is necessary for the CPU to identify the direction of data flow. This is true not only for I/O

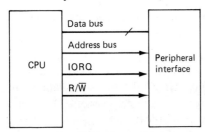

Figure 3.1 Connections between CPU and peripheral interface

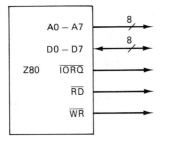

Figure 3.2 Z80 I/O lines

operations but also for memory read and write operations. Indication of data flow is important if only because any buffers associated with the data bus must be enabled to allow the data to pass in the appropriate direction. We shall use the signal identification R/W̄ as the data direction indicator.

A general view of I/O lines is shown in Figure 3.1. This identifies the signals necessary for successful implementation of I/O ports. This does not mean that every microprocessor using the I/O port approach is provided with a line uniquely allocated to, say, the IORQ signal. It does mean, however, that it must be possible to derive a signal that performs the IORQ function from CPU status information. As we shall see, of the three microprocessors considered in this section, only the Z80 has a line uniquely allocated to the IORQ function.

The Z80 microprocessor provides a straightforward example of the I/O port approach. Figure 3.2 shows the lines involved in I/O operations. The line IORQ goes low when an IN or OUT instruction is executed. The port address appears on the 8 least significant lines of the address bus and data are put out or taken in on the 8-line data bus. The timing of the various signals together with the range of I/O instructions will be found in Appendix B.

Like the Z80, the 8080 uses the I/O port approach. In this case, however, interfacing is complicated by the fact that there is no line specifically carrying an IORQ signal. Instead, status signals appear on the lines of the data bus during part of each instruction cycle. Table 3.1 shows the function of these status signals. To make use of the status signals, the status byte may be 'caught' in a register at the time it appears on the data bus. The 8080 generates a signal, SYNC, which can be used for register latching in this situation as described in Section 4.3. More information relating to the timing of 8080 I/O

Table 3.1 *8080 status byte*

Symbol	Data bus bit	Function
INTA	D0	Acknowledge signal for interrupt request
W̄O	D1	Memory write or output operation (when high indicates a memory read or input operation)
STACK	D2	Indicates that the address bus carries the stack address
HLTA	D3	Acknowledge signal for HALT instruction
OUT	D4	Output operation
M1	D5	Indicates that CPU is in the instruction fetch phase
INP	D6	Input operation
MEMR	D7	Memory read operation

Q3.9

operations is given in Appendix A. A circuit showing how the status byte is captured is shown in Section 4.3.

Yet another variation of the I/O port approach is provided by the Z8000. Like the 8080, the Z8000 does not have a uniquely identified IORQ line to indicate when an I/O instruction is being executed. Instead, status information is provided by a code which appears on lines ST0, ST1, ST2 and ST3 at certain times during each instruction cycle. Table 3.2 shows the codes allocated to different operations. From Table 3.2 it will be seen that code 0010 or 0011 indicates that an I/O operation is taking place. Like the status byte of the 8080, the Z8000 status code may be captured in a register at the time it appears.

Table 3.2 *Z8000 status codes*

Code				Type of operation
ST_0	ST_1	ST_2	ST_3	
0	0	0	0	Internal operation
0	0	0	1	Memory refresh
0	0	1	0	Normal I/O transaction
0	0	1	1	Special I/O transaction
0	1	0	0	Reserved
0	1	0	1	Non-maskable interrupt acknowledge
0	1	1	0	Non-vectored interrupt acknowledge
0	1	1	1	Vectored interrupt acknowledge
1	0	0	0	Memory transaction for operand
1	0	0	1	Memory transaction for stack
1	0	1	0	Reserved
1	0	1	1	Reserved
1	1	0	0	Memory transaction for second fetch
1	1	0	1	Memory transaction for first fetch
1	1	1	0	Reserved
1	1	1	1	Reserved

A further complication of I/O operations exists with the Z8000. From Section 2.2 it will be recalled that the 16-bit data format together with the desire to limit the number of pins of the integrated circuit package makes multiplexing of data and addresses necessary. When a Z8000 IN or OUT instruction is executed, therefore, at one part of the instruction cycle the multiplexed bus carries the 16-bit port address. The input or output data are carried by the bus during a later part of the cycle. In fact if we take the complete fetch–execute cycle, four types of information appear on the multiplexed 16-line bus at different times. These are

1 The address of the instruction. This appears on the bus during the instruction fetch phase.

2   The instruction code.

3   The port address allocated to the I/O device.

4   The data being transferred to or from the peripheral device.

As with the 8080, signal multiplexing leads to additional complications in circuitry external to the CPU. One other slightly unusual feature of the Z8000 is the provision of two sets of similar I/O instructions. This results in 'normal' and 'special' I/O operations. During I/O operations, the Z8000 also puts out a 16-bit port address unlike the 8080 and Z80 which only allow 8-bit port addresses. The Z8000 can therefore service a total of $2^{16} = 65,536$ normal ports and an equal number of special ports with the two sets of I/O instructions. Since the Z80 and 8080 are limited to 8-bit port addresses and a single set of I/O operations, the maximum number of ports available with these microprocessors is $2^8 = 256$.

Q3.10

Memory-mapped I/O

The major alternative to the provision of I/O facilities directly is to employ a memory-mapped I/O system. Of the microprocessor families offering only memory-mapped I/O, the M6800 and 6502 are the most important. The technique tends to make the design of the microprocessor itself more straightforward, but complicates the external circuitry needed in peripheral device interfaces.

One feature of microprocessors offering only memory-mapped I/O is the absence from the instruction set of special-purpose input and output instructions. Examine the instruction set for the M6800 in Appendix C. It will be seen that there is no equivalent to the 8080 and Z80 IN and OUT instructions. If the definitions of the M6800 status lines are also examined, it will be seen that there are no signals such as IORQ which are dedicated to I/O operations. At first sight, it might appear that the M6800 has no provision for data input or output.

The apparent absence of I/O facilities is a result of the fact that microprocessors using memory-mapped I/O make no distinction between input operations and memory read operations. Similarly, data output operations are treated in exactly the same way as memory write operations. To interface primary memory with the M6800, the VMA, R/W and $\phi2$ lines are used to carry status information. These same lines are used by peripheral interface circuits during I/O operations. An important consequence of this is that peripheral interface circuits must be designed to behave just like primary memory cells to the CPU.

The similarity between I/O and memory read/write operations is not confined to hardware. Data are read from primary memory in a M6800 system by an LDAA or LDAB instruction together with the address of the appropriate location. The same instructions are used for data input operations. Similarly, STAA and STAB are used to implement both memory write and data output. It is a characteristic of memory-mapped systems that any memory reference instructions can also be used to manipulate I/O data.

To simplify the design of interface circuits for systems using memory-mapped I/O, special-purpose integrated circuits are available. A range of such devices is available which are compatible with the M6800 and 6502 microprocessor families. For parallel I/O operations, the interfacing circuits are called peripheral interface adaptors or PIAs. We shall describe PIAs in more detail in Chapter 4. To compare the hardware requirements for I/O port and memory-mapped systems, it could be said that whereas a parallel interface for, say, a Z80 microprocessor will often consist simply of an 8-bit latch together with a few gates, a similar interface of a M6800 is very much more likely to involve a PIA. Even so, special-purpose I/O interface integrated circuits that are compatible with the Z80 are available although less commonly employed than M6800-compatible PIAs.

It will not have escaped the attention of the more observant reader that memory-mapped I/O can be implemented with any microprocessor that allows access to the system address and data buses. Memory-mapped I/O can therefore be used with the 8080, Z80 and Z8000. It is not commonly used, however, if I/O port facilities are also available. Where memory-mapped I/O is used it should not be forgotten that addresses allocated for I/O purposes share the same address space as primary memory. In other words, an address allocated to an I/O device is not available for a memory location and *vice versa*. This fact must be remembered when the partitioning of memory is considered during the design phase of a microprocessor **Q3.7, 3.8, 3.11** system.

3.2 Synchronisation of I/O operations

In a computing system, the CPU and peripheral devices normally operate asynchronously. Thus there is no mechanism by which the speed of operation of, say, an output printer is directly tied to that of the CPU. It would be undesirable if completely synchronous operation were imposed on the system at all times since the CPU is capable of operating much more rapidly than the printer. To impose synchronism when the computer is undertaking tasks not concerned with the printer would simply slow the whole system down to an unacceptable degree.

If we accept that completely synchronous operation between the CPU and peripheral devices at all times is undesirable, this leaves the problem of synchronisation between the two parts of the system when data transfer is required. The problem can be demonstrated by using a printer again as an example. Let us consider a very simple printer which accepts a single character code and prints the corresponding character. Most printers nowadays do not use this 'one character at a time' approach, but the synchronisation problems still remain in a slightly more complex form.

We shall assume that our hypothetical printer is capable of printing a maximum of 100 characters/sec (cps). The synchronisation problem arises because any CPU will be capable of supplying the printer with character codes very much more rapidly than this. Taking the 8080 as an example, the code for the character 'A' will be put out to port address FF by executing the following instructions

```
MVI  A,X'41'  ;Load A with ASCII code for 'A'
OUT  X'FF'    ;Output to port FF
```

Executing these two instructions requires a total of 17 clock cycles or 17 µs if the 8080 is operating with a clock frequency of 1 MHz. Simply sending character codes to the printer at the rate of one every 17 µs will not be very fruitful if the maximum printing rate is 100 cps. This is the crux of the synchronisation problem.

Two methods are available for overcoming the synchronisation problem described above. Both involve two-way communication between the CPU and the peripheral device. The first method we shall refer to as busy scan or handshaking and requires that the peripheral device should generate a 'busy' status signal which is active when the device is unable to take in or put out data from or to the CPU. Thus, the printer described above would be provided with a busy line which is active while a character is being printed. When printing is complete, the busy line becomes inactive indicating that the printer can accept a new character code.

When employing the handshaking synchronisation technique, the status of the busy line is checked by the CPU before an I/O operation is implemented. Figure 3.3 shows a flowchart for the procedure employed. In addition to the data output port which transfers the character to the printer, one line of an input port is used to carry the busy signal. Figure 3.4 shows a generalised schematic diagram of this. A strobe line is also shown in Figure 3.3. This carries a pulse put out from the microprocessor to inform the printer that a new character code is present on the data lines.

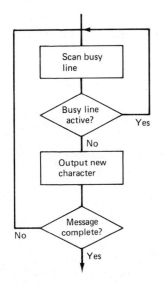

Figure 3.3 Printer handshaking flowchart

The problem with the straightforward handshaking method of I/O is that the CPU is occupied in checking the status of the busy line for long periods when useful computing tasks might otherwise be performed. In the case of the printer described above, only 17 µs in each 10 ms are devoted to the output of data. The remainder of the time is occupied by the processor repeatedly checking the busy status.

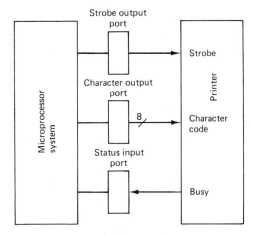

Figure 3.4 Schematic representation of printer interface lines

Often this is of no consequence, particularly if there are no computing tasks which can be usefully performed during this 'wasted' time. If this is the case the handshake technique is almost always simpler and more economically implemented than alternative methods.

Synchronisation by simple handshaking only becomes a liability when there are other pressing demands for computation during the time spent checking busy status. This is particularly the case in a system with several input and output devices which may be competing for attention by the CPU. In this situation it is necessary to move away from program-initiated handshake I/O to input or output operations that are initiated by the peripheral device themselves.

To allow a peripheral device to claim the attention of a CPU and initiate an I/O operation requires that the CPU should be capable of being interrupted. Facilities for interrupts vary greatly from processor to processor. The basic principle is common, however, in that a peripheral is able to initiate a sequence of events resulting in the suspension of a currently running program followed by a jump to a program which puts out to, or takes in data from, the interrupting device. Returning to the printer described above, the busy line would then not be scanned by the CPU but could instead be used to generate an interrupt at the end of each print operation. The CPU would then suspend whatever else it was doing and put out a new character code to the printer, returning afterwards to its previous activity.

Q3.1, 3.2

3.3 Interrupts

An interrupt is essentially a means by which a program, running in a CPU, can be suspended in an orderly fashion and control transferred to another program called the interrupt service routine. The current program is suspended in such a way that it can be resumed at some later stage with as little disruption as possible. An interrupt is initiated when the processor interrupt line is taken to its active state. In the case of the M6800, Z80 and Z8000 microprocessors this involves taking the interrupt line to the low state. The 8080 interrupt is active high.

To gain some idea of the way an interrupt can function in a real time situation, consider the use of a microprocessor to monitor and control the environment inside a building. The microprocessor has a routine or background task which involves checking the digitised outputs of temperature transducers in each room and adjusting the heat input to maintain the temperature constant. Each room is monitored in turn. In addition to a temperature transducer, each room is fitted with a smoke detector whose output initiates an interrupt when smoke is detected. Therefore, when an interrupt occurs, control is transferred from the background program to a program which turns on sprinklers and sounds an alarm in the affected room. After dealing with this situation, a reset switch allows the microprocessor to return to the background program. The program flow is shown symbolically in Figure 3.5.

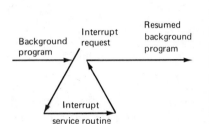

Figure 3.5   Interrupt response

This example describes a situation in which an interrupt can result from any one of a variety of different sources. In the event of an interrupt occurring, the processor must have some means of identifying its origin in order to turn on the sprinkler in the correct room. To explain the significance of this and other factors in the provision of interrupt facilities, a few definitions are required.

Maskable and non-maskable interrupts It is sometimes advantageous to be able to 'switch off' an interrupt capability. A maskable interrupt line allows us to do this by inserting a special instruction at an appropriate point in the program. Non-maskable interrupts can never be disabled.

Vectored and non-vectored interrupts In the case of multiple interrupts, it is often important to be able to identify the origin of an interrupt. With a vectored interrupt system the interrupting device also supplies the CPU with an identifying code or address. This allows the CPU to enter the appropriate interrupt service routine as quickly as possible. With non-vectored interrupts, the CPU must scan or poll each potential interrupting device one at a time until the originator of the interrupt is identified.

Q3.5

In many microprocessors using interrupts, as we have said, it is convenient for the interrupt facility to be switched off or disabled from time to time. There are other situations however in which it may be quite dangerous to disable an interrupt. These would be situations in which an interrupt indicates the occurrence of an extremely important event which requires the immediate attention of the processor. In a chemical process system controlled by a microprocessor, an interrupt indicating that the plant is about to explode might be considered a good example of this. These very important events are used to generate non-maskable interrupts. Unless there are strong reasons for using a non-maskable interrupt, maskable interrupts should be used wherever possible.

Non-maskable interrupts are particularly important in protecting computer systems from the consequences of electrical power failure. When a power failure causes the mains voltage to fall, reservoir capacitance in the circuit power supply will hold the low voltage supplies to the microprocessor system above the minimum required value for a finite time. Provided that the reservoir capacitance is sufficiently large, this can allow time for the orderly shut down of the system controlled by the microprocessor. The microprocessor will continue executing instructions to effect this shut down until the supplies fall below the critical value. Failure to shut down, in an orderly manner, systems such as large machines or chemical plant can have important safety risks. Implementation of a power fail interrupt facility of the type described above is quite straightforward. Figure 3.6 shows how a voltage comparator monitors the mains supply. When this voltage falls below the reference level, a non-maskable interrupt is generated.

Q3.12

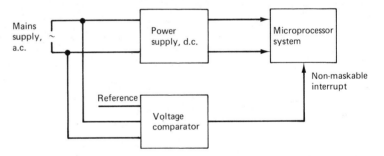

Figure 3.6 Power fail interrupt

With power fail interrupts, we have introduced the idea that some interrupts might be more important than others. When several interrupt sources are present in a system we may wish to extend this idea to allocate a priority rating to each interrupting device. In multiple interrupt situations, the problem arises of conflicting demands for service. Whilst it is unlikely that two interrupts will occur at exactly the same instant of time, it is quite likely that an interrupt from one source will occur during the servicing of an interrupt from another source. Allocation of priorities allows servicing of the new interrupt to take place or be deferred depending on its priority.

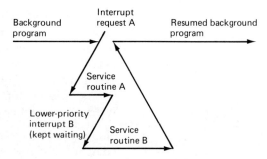

Figure 3.7   Lower-priority interrupt occurring during servicing of higher-priority interrupt

Figure 3.7 shows the program flow when a lower-priority interrupt occurs during a higher-priority service routine. The system takes no action on the lower priority interrupt until servicing of the higher-priority interrupt is complete. The alternative situation is shown in Figure 3.8. Here, servicing of a lower-priority interrupt is suspended by the occurrence of a higher-priority interrupt.

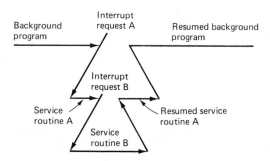

Figure 3.8   Higher-priority interrupt occurring during servicing of lower-priority interrupt

The ability to allocate priorities to interrupts (apart from the special case of a non-maskable interrupt) is not normally an inbuilt facility with microprocessors. For some applications it is a necessary capability and must therefore be provided for by circuitry external to the microprocessor. Some microprocessors have devices in the same **Q3.3, 3.4**   family which allow implementation of an interrupt priority system.

M6800 interrupt facilities

The M6800 has the most straightforward interrupt facilities of the microprocessors described here. Maskable and non-maskable interrupt lines are shown on the pin assignment in Appendix C. These lines are identified by the mnemonics $\overline{IRQ}$ and $\overline{NMI}$, respectively, which indicates that the signals are active low. To enable the maskable interrupt, a 'clear interrupt mask' instruction, CLI, must be executed. Disabling of the interrupt occurs when a 'set interrupt mask' instruction, SEI, is executed. These instructions also cause the resetting or setting of the interrupt mask bit of the condition code or flag register. The state of this bit can be used to check whether or not the non-maskable interrupt is enabled.

Assuming that a program is being executed by the processor and that the interrupt mask is not set, when $\overline{\text{IRQ}}$ is taken low, the following sequence of events occurs:

1 Execution of the current instruction is completed. Further interrupts are disabled.
2 The contents of the index register, program counter, register A, register B and condition code register are saved on the stack.
3 A program jump occurs to the address found in the interrupt vector.

The interrupt vector is a pair of dedicated memory locations, FFF8 and FFF9, which are used to hold the address of the first instruction of the interrupt service routine. It is the responsibility of the programmer to ensure that the interrupt vector contains the correct address before the interrupt occurs. If the service routine starts at 1000, the programmer would ensure that FFF8 is loaded with 10 and FFF9 is loaded with 00.

The interrupt service routine should normally terminate with a 'return from interrupt' instruction, RTI. Execution of this instruction causes the contents of the program counter, index register, register A, register B and condition code register to be loaded with data popped from the stack. This restores all working registers to the values they had when the interrupt occurred. A jump therefore occurs to the instruction in the background program which would have been executed had the interrupt not occurred. Interrupts are also automatically re-enabled.

The M6800 response to a non-maskable interrupt is exactly the same as that for a maskable interrupt, but with a different interrupt vector. In this case, the address of the first instruction of the service routine must be stored in addresses FFFC and FFFD. Although not described as an interrupt, the $\overline{\text{RESET}}$ signal behaves in much the same way. When $\overline{\text{RESET}}$ is taken low, a program jump occurs to an address which is stored in the reset vector FFFE, and FFFF. The major difference in this case is that the contents of working registers are not saved on the stack as is the case with the maskable and non-maskable interrupts.

An interesting feature of the M6800 is the provision of a software interrupt. In the M6800 instruction set is a 'software interrupt' instruction, SWI. When this instruction is executed, the processor behaves exactly as if an interrupt had occurred. The software interrupt vector in this case is FFFA,FFFB. Software interrupts have a variety of uses, one of which is to allow easy termination of a program. Some readers will be familiar with the Motorola MEK6800D2 evaluation system which makes use of the SWI instruction for this purpose. In the software interrupt vector, the entry point of the system monitor JBUG is stored. The user terminates his program with a software interrupt instruction, SWI. When this instruction is executed the system monitor program is entered, providing the user with facilities to check the successful execution of the program.

The main characteristic of the M6800 interrupt facilities is simplicity. A maskable or non-maskable interrupt from a single source can be implemented with little or no circuitry external to the microprocessor. It should also be noted, however, that the processor gives no assistance in the vectoring of interrupts in the multiple interrupt situation. This must all be done by a combination of software and external hardware. In common with other micro-processors described here, the M6800 also makes no internal provision for allocating priorities in multiple interrupt situations.

8080 interrupt facilities

Interrupt handling with the 8080 is a good deal different to that of the 6800. The 8080 supports a single interrupt facility which is maskable. Three signals are associated with interrupt handling and are identified as follows:

INT   An active high interrupt request input.
INTE   An active high interrupt enable output.
INTA   An interrupt acknowledge signal which appears on the multiplexed data/status bus.

Within the 8080, the state of interrupt line INT is sampled during the final clock cycle of each instruction cycle. If the interrupt facility is enabled, this causes an internal latch to be set, but the current instruction execution continues to completion. The setting of the interrupt latch forces an interrupt cycle in place of the normal next instruction cycle. From the interrupt timing diagram shown in Appendix A it will be seen that the INTA interrupt acknowledge signal appears on the multiplexed data/status bus line D0, synchronised by the SYNC signal during clock intervals T1 and T2 of the interrupt cycle. The interface circuit of the I/O device originating the interrupt must detect the active INTA signal and 'jam' or force an instruction code on to the data/status bus during clock interval T3. A synchronising signal DBIN becomes active during T3 and can also be used by the peripheral interface circuit.

The code jammed on to the data bus during the interrupt acknowledge is usually that for a restart instruction, RST. Because that instruction is so important in the 8080 interrupt response, we shall describe it in some detail. The 8080 instruction set includes eight restart instructions, RST0–RST7. Each of these instructions when executed causes the contents of the program counter to be saved on the stack and implements a jump. Eight jump destinations are defined, one for each of the restart instructions, as shown in Table 3.3. From this table, we can deduce that if a peripheral interface generates an interrupt and responds to the interrupt acknowledge by jamming, say, DF on to the data/status bus then the contents of the program counter will be saved on the stack and a jump to 0018 will occur. At location 0018 we can place the first instruction of the interrupt service routine or, more usually, a jump instruction to a routine in another part of memory. Since the return address is stored on the stack, a 'subroutine return' instruction, RET, will allow a return to the main program just as if a subroutine were being executed.

Table 3.3

Instruction	Code	Jump destination
RST 0	C7	0000
RST 1	CF	0008
RST 2	D7	0010
RST 3	DF	0018
RST 4	E7	0020
RST 5	EF	0028
RST 6	F7	0030
RST 7	FF	0038

The reader will note that, unlike the 6800, the 8080 does not automatically save the contents of all working registers as part of its response to an interrupt. Only the program counter contents are saved. This means that the first few instructions of the interrupt service routine will be concerned with storing the contents of registers on the stack or in dedicated memory locations. These registers must be restored to their original state at the end of the service routine.

The requirement for the peripheral interface to supply a restart instruction code when the 8080 acknowledges an interrupt adds to the complexity of the interface circuit. It does however have an advantage compared with, say, the 6800 in that it makes it easier to implement a limited vectored interrupt system. Up to eight interrupting devices can each be allocated a different restart instruction. The particular code that an interface jams on the data/status bus will then direct the processor to the appropriate service routine. Of course, precautions must be taken to prevent two interrupting devices from attempting to jam different codes on to the bus at the same time.

Q3.6

Z80 interrupt facilities

Compared with the M6800 and 8080, the Z80 offers much more comprehensive interrupt facilities. Two interrupt lines are provided. These are identified as $\overline{\text{INT}}$ and $\overline{\text{NMI}}$ for maskable and non-maskable interrupts, respectively, both of which are active low. When the $\overline{\text{NMI}}$ line is taken low, the following sequence of events occurs:

1 Execution of the current instruction is completed.
2 The contents of the program counter are pushed on the stack.
3 A jump to location 0066 instruction is executed.

The way the Z80 responds to a maskable interrupt can be in any one of three possible modes, 0, 1 or 2. Instructions IM0, IM1 and IM2, when executed, set the response mode to 0, 1 or 2, respectively. It is therefore the responsibility of the programmer to establish the correct interrupt response mode by inserting the appropriate instruction in the system initialising program. After reset, the Z80 will be in mode 0, irrespective of its previous state.

When the Z80 is in mode 0, the response to an interrupt is similar to that of the 8080. The interrupting device must jam on to the data bus the code for the next instruction to be executed. In practical terms, the major difference between the 8080 and the Z80 in mode 0 lies in the fact that the Z80 data bus does not also carry multiplexed data signals such as the 8080 INTA. Like the 8080, the Z80 samples the level of the maskable interrupt line $\overline{IRQ}$ during the final two clock cycles of each instruction cycle. After completion of the instruction, the processor enters an interrupt cycle if $\overline{IRQ}$ is detected as being low. A distinguishing feature of the interrupt cycle compared with a normal cycle is that $\overline{IORQ}$ and $\overline{M1}$ become active, i.e. low, simultaneously. This is the only situation in which this occurs. Within the peripheral interface the detection of $\overline{IORQ}$ and $\overline{M1}$ simultaneously low provides the interrupt acknowledge equivalent to the 8080 INTA signal.

Mode 1 is rather more straightforward than mode 0. The response to a maskable interrupt in this case is quite similar to that for a non-maskable interrupt. After $\overline{IRQ}$ is taken low in mode 1, the following sequence of events occurs:

1 Execution of the current instruction is completed.
2 The current contents of the program counter are saved on the stack.
3 A jump is forced to location 0038.

Location 0038 could contain the first instruction of the non-maskable interrupt service routine or alternatively the code for a jump or call to the service routine. It will be seen that the only difference between the mode 1 and non-maskable interrupt response lies in the destination address of the jump instruction. If vectoring of interrupts is not required, mode 1 allows the simplest interrupt interface circuit.

When a vectored interrupt system is required, mode 2 gives the Z80 a very powerful capability compared with the 8080 and M6800. To employ this mode, a look-up table must be stored in memory. This table contains the starting addresses of the service routine for all of the interrupting devices. Taking line $\overline{\text{IRQ}}$ low when in mode 2 initiates the following sequence of events:

1   Execution of the current instruction is completed.
2   The processor forms a 16-bit address pointer. The eight most significant bits are taken from the internal I register. The eight least significant bits are taken from the data bus where they have been placed by the interrupting device. In fact, the interrupting device need only provide 7 bits since the processor will always assume that the least significant bit is 0.
3   The current contents of the program counter are pushed on to the stack.
4   A jump instruction is executed. The destination address for the jump is recovered from memory at the address given by the pointer generated in (2).

This all sounds, and is, rather complicated. We can, however, identify some general points. The first is that vectored interrupts involve complications in both hardware and software. Hardware complications are involved in the peripheral interface of the interrupting device. The circuit is required to identify the simultaneous low logic level on $\overline{\text{MI}}$ and $\overline{\text{IRQ}}$, which constitutes the interrupt acknowledge, and jam the least significant part of the vector pointer address on the data bus. Software complication arises from the fact that the programmer must ensure that the memory contains the interrupt service routine look-up table. It is also the responsibility of the programmer to load the interrupt register with the most significant byte of the look-up table pointer. The LDI,A instruction is provided for this purpose. As with all Z80 interrupts, interrupt response does not include automatic saving of the contents of the working registers which is again the responsibility of the programmer.

Z8000 interrupt response

As befits its position of the most powerful and recently developed microprocessor of those considered here, the Z8000 also offers the most comprehensive interrupt handling facilities. Indeed, to fully describe these facilities would require a whole chapter to itself. We shall therefore describe the Z8000 interrupt capability only in sufficient detail to allow a meaningful comparison with other microprocessors.

In order to describe the way interrupts are handled by the Z8000, it is necessary to have some preliminary background relating to the processor architecture and instruction set. Crucial to the operation of the interrupt system is the concept of the program status area. This is an area of memory maintained by the programmer, which has some similarity with the interrupt vector table used by the Z80 in mode 2. In the case of the Z8000, however, the program status area stores other information in addition to interrupt vector addresses.

The location of the Z8000 program status area is determined by the programmer when writing the system initialisation routine.

This routine will include instructions that load the program status area pointer register PSAP as shown below:

```
LD      R2,#%1000
LDCTL   PSAP,R2
```

The first instruction loads 16-bit register R2 with the hexadecimal number 1000. This number is then transferred to register PSAP by the LDCTL instruction. Execution of these two instructions causes the start of the program status area to be at 1000.

A further concept that is important in the understanding of Z8000 interrupts is that of the processor status word which can be defined at any point in the execution of a program and is shown in Figure 3.9. It is a 32-bit word, the first 16 bits of which consist of the current contents of the flag and control word register FCW. The Z8002 FCW register can be compared with the M6800 condition code register, CCR, or the Z80/8080 flag register. Functions of the various bits of the FCW register are listed in Appendix D. The second 16 bits of the processor status word consist of the current contents of the program counter.

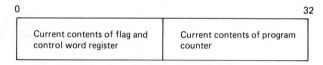

Figure 3.9   Z8000 program status word

It will be recalled from Section 2.3 that the Z8000 family at the time of writing comprises two members, the Z8001 and Z8002. We shall consider here interrupt facilities with the simpler Z8002. In addition to hardware interrupts, the Z8002 provides for software interrupts similar to the SWI facility of the M6800. A further feature is the provision of a form of interrupt called a software trap. The response of the Z8002 is similar for all types of hardware interrupts, software interrupt and software traps. The interrupt facilities available with this microprocessor are summarised in the list below:

1 Maskable, non-vectored hardware interrupt. $\overline{\text{NVI}}$ line is active low.
2 Maskable vectored hardware interrupt. $\overline{\text{VI}}$ line is active low.
3 Non-maskable, non-vectored, hardware interrupt. $\overline{\text{NMI}}$ line is active low.

4 Software interrupt initiated by the execution of a 'system call' instruction, SC.
5 Software traps initiated by the attempted execution of certain instructions in situations which are not allowed by the Z8002. Software traps and software interrupts both have higher priority than maskable hardware interrupts.

When a Z8000 interrupt or trap occurs, the following sequence of events occurs:

a Execution of the current instruction is completed.
b The processor enters an interrupt acknowledge cycle. During this cycle, the interrupting device must send to the processor a 16-bit interrupt identifier word.
c The interrupt identifier is pushed on to the stack followed by the processor status word that is the contents of the FCW register and program counter.
d A new processor status word is extracted from the program status area and loaded into the FCW register and program counter. This causes an automatic jump to the instruction at the address contained in the program counter.

From this sequence of events it will be seen that, since the programmer fills the program status area, the destination address for the program jump is determined during system initialisation. Since various types of hardware and software interrupts must be differentiated, different areas of the program status areas are allocated to these different types of event. Assuming that we have initialised the program status area pointer register to 1000 as described above, Figure 3.10 shows a map of the resulting program

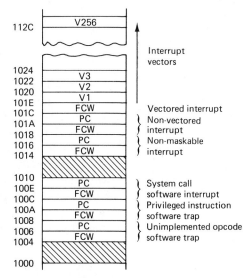

Figure 3.10 Z8002 program status area with (PSAP) = 1000

status area. In interpreting this map, remember that although the Z8002 is a 16-bit microprocessor, the memory is organised in 8-bit bytes. Thus, to store, for example, the contents of the 16-bit FCW register, two memory locations are required.

To help clarify the function of the program status area, we shall consider a specific example. Assume that a Z8002 system has been initialised with the contents of the program status area pointer = 1000. During this initialisation, memory locations 1016 and 1017 have been loaded with 0000 and locations 1018 and 1019 with F800. From Figure 3.10 it will be seen that these locations are the part of the program status area associated with non-vectored interrupts.

Now suppose that a program is running and the Z8002 is currently executing the following instruction whose 4-byte instruction code is stored in addresses 2000–2003:

Mnemonic	*Code*
LD R4,#%0FFF	21,04,0F,FF

If the $\overline{\text{NVI}}$ line is taken low during the execution of this instruction, the non-vectored interrupt response is initiated. The instruction currently being executed is first completed. The Z8002 then enters an interrupt acknowledge cycle. This can be detected by the peripheral device generating the interrupt since the four Z8002 status lines, ST3–ST0, carry the non-vectored interrupt acknowledge code 0110 as described in Table 3.2. On detecting this status code, the peripheral interface places on the multiplexed address/data bus a 16-bit interrupt identifier. In the case of non-maskable interrupts, the function of this identifier can be defined by the user. It may contain a code which identifies the origin of the interrupt for example. Alternatively it may consist of numerical data which is used during the interrupt service routine.

After taking in the interrupt identifier, it is then pushed on to the stack by the processor. The processor status word consists of the current contents of the FCW register and the program counter. The program counter contains 2004 at this stage, of course. This processor status word is also stored on the stack. A new processor status word is then extracted from addresses 1016–1019. These locations, it will be recalled, have been loaded with 0000,F800 during initialisation. The FCW register is therefore loaded with 0000 and the program counter with F800. A program jump to location F800 therefore takes place automatically. Note that if it is required to save the contents of other working registers, this must be done in the initial stages of the interrupt service routine which starts at address F800.

Although the user can choose to use the interrupt identifier in any desired way in the above example, this is not always the case. For other types of interrupt the identifier has specifically identified functions. In the case of vectored interrupt, the identifier supplies part of the information required to direct the processor to the service routine for the interrupting device. For a system with PSAP initialised to 1000 as before, at the end of the interrupt response sequence, the Z8002 loads the program counter with the contents of location $101E + (2 \times VV)$. In this expression, 101E is the start of the vector area of the program status area as shown in Figure 2.12. The 8-bit number VV is supplied by the interrupting device as the least significant byte of the interrupt identifier.

As an example of a vectored interrupt response, consider a peripheral device which takes $\overline{VI}$ low and then responds to the resulting 0111 (binary) status code on ST3–ST0 by putting the identifier word 0006 on the address/data bus. After saving the identifier and processor status word on the stack, the processor loads FCW with the number found in address 1014 and loads PC with the number found in address 102A since:

$$VV = 06$$
$$2 \times VV = 2 \times 06 = 0C$$
$$101E + 0C = 102A$$

(*Note:* all arithmetic in hexadecimal.)

This section does not form a user's guide to Z8000 interrupt facilities. The object has been to give the reader some insight into the power and versatility of these facilities.

Comparing interrupt facilities

Whether or not interrupt facilities are an important consideration when choosing a microprocessor depends on the number and nature of I/O devices in the system. In general, unless performance requirements demand the use of interrupt initiated I/O, simple handshaking with repetitive scanning of a busy signal is easier to implement. If it is possible to service all I/O devices in this way, within the time available, interrupt facilities are of no importance.

Q3.2

In our study of interrupt facilities of microprocessors we have seen that they can vary from the very simple such as those of the M6800 to the highly complex as is the case with the Z8000. The more sophisticated interrupt facilities will tend to pay off where the system involves a multiplicity of I/O devices combined with a requirement to respond rapidly to the demands of individual devices. An efficient method of interrupt vectoring is very important in this situation.

Of the microprocessors we have considered, the M6800 has the least complex interrupt system. It has the great advantage of simplicity from the point of view of hardware and software requirements. Peripheral interface requirements are particularly simple, requiring the peripheral to do little more than activate the interrupt line in addition to normal I/O operations. The straightforward interrupt response sequence makes software demands straightforward, even the saving of working registers being performed automatically.

The 8080 is, in many ways, the least satisfactory of the microprocessors considered from the point of view of interrupt handling. Undoubtedly, the requirement for the peripheral interface to jam the next instruction code on the bus leads to greater hardware complexity compared with other microprocessors. One possible advantage of this approach over that of the M6800, however, is that simple interrupt vectoring can be easily implemented.

Of the 8-bit microprocessors considered, the interrupt facilities of the Z80 are the most comprehensive. Mode 0 gives complete compatibility with the 8080 interrupt facility. Mode 1 provides a simple interrupt response, similar in many ways to that of the M6800. Mode 2 offers the advantage of a true vectored interrupt capability.

The Z8000 microprocessor offers a very comprehensive system of hardware interrupts, software interrupts and software traps. It has obviously been designed with an eye to the more powerful type of microprocessor system probably involving a disk secondary store and an operating system of the type previously found in much larger computing systems. In systems such as this, techniques lean towards those used in minicomputer and even mainframe computer systems where efficient interrupt handling is very important.

3.4   Microprocessor power requirements

To operate properly, all microprocessors must be supplied with a constant or direct current at a voltage which is, at least nominally, constant. This current is normally supplied from the a.c. mains via a transformer, rectifier, reservoir capacitor and, possibly, a voltage stabiliser. Alternatively, the power may be supplied by a battery.

The power supply requirement is a parameter that is sometimes ignored when selecting a microprocessor for a particular application. Voltage and current supplies required for different types of microprocessors do, however, vary considerably. For some applications the voltage and current required can be the single most important characteristic of a microprocessor. Some applications that will involve careful consideration of power supply requirements are:

1   Systems in which component cost must be as low as possible.
2   Systems that are required to operate all or part of the time from batteries.
3   Systems that must operate in a confined space or in a high-temperature environment.

Before discussing the requirements of specific microprocessors, we shall consider some general points relating to power supplies, most of which are relevant to all digital system elements. As a first and non-controversial point, few designers would dispute the premise that the fewer the number of supply voltages required the better. Purely from the point of view of power supply requirement, therefore, the 8080 which requires three voltage rails is a less desirable microprocessor than, say, the M6800 which requires only a single +5 V supply. It should not be forgotten, however, that it is pointless choosing a microprocessor specifically because it needs only one supply voltage if we combine it with system elements, such as certain memory chips, which require multiple supplies.

Another statement with which most would agree is that the lower the current requirement of a device the better. There are various reasons for this. The cost of the power supply circuit increases more or less linearly with the current supplied. High current consumption implies high power dissipation which in turn leads to higher operating temperatures. Since reliability decreases as temperature increases, it may be necessary to resort to cooling fans, etc., if high current consumption is a feature of a system.

Less widely appreciated is the fact that in digital systems devices consuming large amounts of current make the physical layout of a circuit much more critical. With most digital integrated circuits, including microprocessors, the current consumption is not constant. As individual logic gates within the integrated circuit switch on and off, current demands fluctuate abruptly. A system may therefore effectively demand pulses of current from a power supply. These pulses may often require a rapid rise time of the order of nanoseconds or less which must be taken into account when designing the power supply circuit. The reader may care to contemplate the design of a circuit capable of generating pulses of 100 mA amplitude with rise times of 1 ns, although this perhaps overstates the problem slightly.

Fourier analysis tells us that pulsed waveforms with rapid rise times contain very high frequency components. We should therefore regard the voltage supply lines in a microprocessor circuit as constituting transmission lines carrying signals with very high frequency components. This is why well designed printed circuit boards for microprocessor systems follow similar rules to those used for VHF analogue circuits. These rules include the use of ground planes, conductors of adequate dimensions, and adequate decoupling of power supply lines at regular intervals. All of these layout problems tend to become worse as the current consumption of individual devices increases.

Comparing power supply requirements

The amount of power consumed by a microprocessor depends on the particular process by which it is manufactured. Although manufacturing technology is developing constantly, at the time of writing, two processes and their variants are dominant in the production of microprocessors. These are described as

1 NMOS: N-channel complementary metal oxide semiconductor.
2 CMOS: complementary metal oxide semiconductor.

It is not the intention here to describe these processes. We shall concentrate only on the characteristics of the resulting microprocessors.

All microprocessors introduced up to this point are NMOS devices. These are the 8080, Z80, M6800, Z8002 and COP420. We initially exclude the rather specialised COP420 and concentrate on the remaining general-purpose devices. All consume power at the rate of 0.5 to 1.5 W. Typical supply requirements are 5 V at 300 mA for the Z8002 and 5 V at 200 mA for the M6800. This may sound substantial but the reader should note that in a medium or large system, power requirements of the microprocessor chip may constitute only a small proportion of the total power needed. High-speed digital elements, particularly arrays of memory chips, are notorious power consumers. An overall power consumption of 10 A at 5 V is by no means uncommon for a microprocessor system. We may also note in passing that the cost of power supply components such as the transformer and reservoir capacitors can easily be many times that of the microprocessor chip itself.

When designing microprocessor systems of medium or high speed and computing power, the relatively high current consumption must normally be tolerated. In other systems where low production and component cost or perhaps battery operation is required, we cannot allow high power consumption. This will involve the choice of a different type of microprocessor. When making a choice like this, we must, as with most digital electronic components, exchange low power consumption for speed of operation. Microprocessors with low power consumption tend to operate at lower speeds and hence offer less computing power than higher power consuming devices although this is not a universal rule.

The COP420 is an example of a microprocessor of modest performance with a relatively low power requirement. Although utilising NMOS technology like the other microprocessors described here, the power requirement is only 6 mA at 4.5–9.5 V. In addition to the low current requirement, the ability to tolerate wide variations in supply allows the use of very cheap power supply circuits. The same characteristics allow operation from a relatively small battery. For continuous operation from battery supplies, however, the COP420C from the same family as the COP402L is more suitable.

The COP420C device, although having many similarities to the COP420L, is manufactured using the CMOS process. One characteristic of this technology is very low power consumption. When operating at the same 16-μs instruction time as the COP420L, the COP420C requires only 600 μA at 5 V. Slowing down the clock frequency reduces the power required even further. When operating at its minimum speed, the COP420C will function with a power supply of as little as 25 μA at 2.4 V. The instruction cycle time in this case is 244 μs.

Manufacturers of microprocessors are, of course, aware of the desirability of low power consumption. At the time of writing, low-power CMOS microprocessors with similar characteristics to the M6800 and Z80 have been introduced. We may expect this type of development to continue, but for the highest possible speed and computing power it is likely that we shall continue to pay the price of high power consumption in the foreseeable future.

Q3.13, 3.14

Questions

3.1 Explain what is meant by 'handshaking' in connection with micro-processor I/O operations.

3.2 What major advantage does interrupt-initiated I/O have compared with the busy scan method?

3.3 With the help of a diagram, describe the program flow when a high-priority interrupt occurs during the servicing of a lower-priority interrupt.

3.4 With the help of a diagram, describe the program flow when a low-priority interrupt occurs during the servicing of a higher-priority interrupt.

3.5 Explain the difference between vectored and non-vectored interrupts.

3.6 State the major advantage of vectored interrupts compared with non-vectored interrupts and describe the sequence of events that occurs after an interrupt with the following microprocessors:
(a) 8080
(b) M6800

3.7 State the three alternative approaches to I/O provision found with different microprocessors.

3.8 Explain the distinction between the port approach to I/O and memory-mapped I/O. Give examples of microprocessors using these methods of I/O.

3.9 In a Z80 microprocessor system, define the signal which is used by a peripheral interface circuit to indicate that an I/O instruction is being executed.

3.10 Explain how the status word is used by a peripheral interface in a Z8000 system to indicate that an I/O instruction is being executed.

3.11 State the maximum number of I/O devices that could be theoretically addressed in systems based on the following microprocessors:
 (a) 8080
 (b) Z80
 (c) M6800
 (d) Z8000

3.12 Describe an application that requires the use of a non-maskable interrupt rather than a maskable interrupt.

3.13 State the number of separate d.c. supply lines required by the following devices
 (a) 8080
 (b) M6800
 (c) Z80
 (d) Z8000
 (e) COP420L

3.14 Two manufacturer's processes commonly used for the production result in devices which are described as NMOS and CMOS. Which of these two is the most suitable for battery-operated devices?

Chapter 4 Microprocessor support devices

Objectives of this chapter *When you have completed studying this chapter you should be able to identify, with the help of manufacturers' data sheets, the function and characteristics of typical examples of the following functional elements in a microprocessor system:*

1   *The CPU chip set.*
2   *Bus buffers.*
3   *Parallel I/O devices and circuits.*
4   *Serial I/O devices.*
5   *Address decoders.*
6   *Bus demultiplexers.*
7   *Clock circuit.*
8   *Static and dynamic primary RAM.*
9   *ROM and EPROM.*

4.1   Introduction

In Chapters 2 and 3 we explained that some microprocessors are specifically designed to require the minimum of additional circuitry to perform their computing function effectively. These are the so-called single-chip microcomputers. Other devices, which we have referred to as CPU-type microprocessors, constitute only one part of the microcomputer system. The single-chip microcomputer offers an advantage in terms of cost. The CPU-type microprocessor usually has the advantage of greater potential computing power. More significantly, the user can choose the support circuitry to tailor the computing capability to the needs of a specific task. Flexibility and versatility are therefore much greater than is the case with single-chip systems.

The need for additional circuitry to support CPU-type microprocessors has engendered the production of a variety of special-purpose integrated circuits. We shall examine some of these devices in this chapter. They can vary from the conceptually simple such as buffers and latches to highly complex serial and parallel interface devices. The level of complexity of some of these devices matches that of the simpler microprocessor chips.

Figure 4.1 shows a block diagram for a computing system based on a

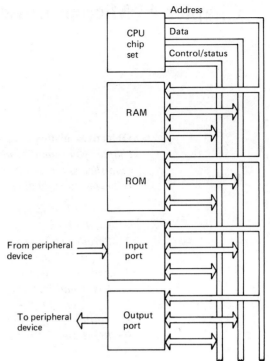

Figure 4.1 Microcomputer structure

CPU-type microprocessor. The system consists essentially of functional units such as CPU, RAM, ROM, I/O ports, etc., linked by parallel data communication channels called buses. In Figure 4.1, we show an address bus, a data bus and a control/status bus. Without being too precise, we could say that the data bus carries data and instruction codes, used during a computation, between the CPU and other functional units. The address bus carries an address which identifies the functional unit involved in a data transaction.

The status/control bus is less clearly defined. It will contain input and output lines to and from the microprocessor. The actual function and number of lines will depend on the system requirements and the particular microprocessor used. Typical lines in this bus are IORQ and INT. The IORQ signal when active is used by I/O ports to indicate that the CPU is executing an I/O instruction. INT carries a signal from a peripheral device which initiates the interrupt sequence in the microprocessor.

Q4.1, 4.2

Figure 4.2 which is taken from Ref. 4.1 shows a much less general, but more practical, system block diagram. In this system which is based on the 16-bit Z8000 microprocessor, the functional blocks are less clearly defined than in the more general system shown in Figure 4.1. In spite of this, the division of the function of system bus lines into data, address and control/status is still quite clear.

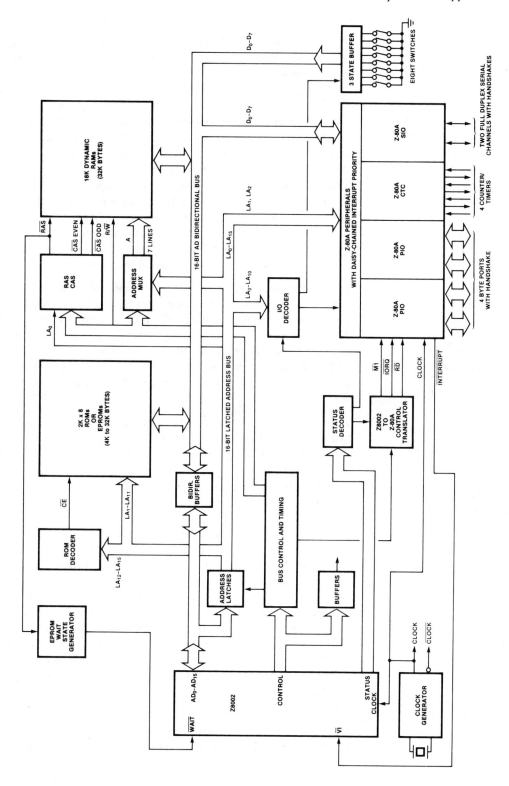

Figure 4.2 Z8000 microprocessor system

4.2 The need for buffering

Before the widespread development of integrated circuits based on field effect devices, the vast majority of digital systems employed devices manufactured using transistor–transistor logic (TTL) technology. The TTL family of logic devices is still the most popular and offers by far the widest range of available functions. As a result of this, designers of microprocessor systems find it convenient to be able to mix TTL components with those from the microprocessor family which will normally employ NMOS or perhaps CMOS technology. With the very early microprocessors, this caused a great deal of inconvenience since the current and voltage logic levels of the microprocessor differed greatly from TTL logic levels. Whenever an interface between the two types of device was required, it was necessary to interpose a special-purpose integrated circuit that converted the current and voltage levels as required. Conversion circuits of this kind are called shifting buffers.

Today, the situation is rather more convenient. Most integrated circuits in microprocessor families are said to be TTL-compatible. This means that they can usually be connected directly to TTL devices and can successfully exchange logic signals. It does not mean however that the current/voltage I/O characteristics of say an NMOS microprocessor will be identical to TTL components. The difference lies mainly in the amount of output current the devices can provide.

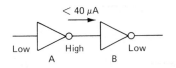

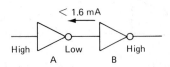

Figure 4.3 Current sourcing and sinking with TTL

TTL logic elements are said to be 'current sinking'. Figure 4.3 shows two gates of a 7404 hex inverter chip connected in series. When the output of gate A is high, only a very small current of less than 40 μA flows into gate B. The effective input resistance of gate B is high in this situation. If we cause the output of gate A to become low, then current flows out of gate B input into gate A output. Gate A is said to be sinking current from gate B. This current can be as high as 1.6 mA with standard TTL devices. In fact, to be absolutely sure that the correct logic levels are maintained, gate A must be capable of sinking the required maximum current of 1.6 mA from gate B. If more than one gate is to be driven as shown in Figure 4.4, then gate A must be able to sink 1.6 mA for each gate input connected. Standard TTL gates of this kind can sink a minimum of 16 mA which means that a gate output is capable of driving 10 inputs. For use in microprocessor systems, it is more common to use the low-power Schotky or LS variant of TTL. In this case, the maximum low-level input current is 0.36 mA and the maximum current which can be sunk at the output is 8 mA which implies that each gate output is capable of driving 8/0.36 = 22 inputs.

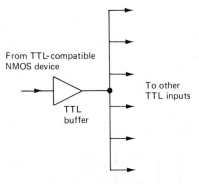

Figure 4.4 TTL buffer gate to improve drive capability

When we examine the current sinking capability of the output lines of a typical NMOS microprocessor it is normally found to be much less

Q4.3, 4.4 than that of TTL circuits. Taking the M6800 as an example, data and address lines can sink current from not more than one standard TTL gate. Therefore, if it is required to drive more than one TTL input from these lines, a buffer gate must be used as shown in Figure 4.4.

So far we have only considered the problem of sinking sufficient current to maintain logic levels within required limits on TTL inputs. A more subtle, but equally important, problem is that of maintaining adequate rise and fall times and delay of the pulsed waveforms which of necessity must occur on the bus lines. This problem arises not only when driving TTL from NMOS devices, but also when connecting two NMOS devices via a bus. To appreciate this problem, it is necessary to understand that the conductor connecting a device output to another device input appears as a largely capacitive load to the driving device. The input impedance of the driven device will also appear partly capacitive. Now to change the voltage at the input of the driven device, we are therefore effectively changing the voltage across a capacitor.

The voltage across a capacitor of capacitance with charge Q is given by

$$V = Q/C$$

To change the voltage involves a transfer of charge. The maximum rate at which charge can be transferred therefore determines the minimum rise and fall times and delay of the voltage waveforms. This provides another limiting factor to the number of inputs that can be driven from one output since each input, whether TTL or MOS, adds additional capacitance. Because of the static and dynamic considerations outlined here, M6800 lines can drive a maximum of 1 TTL load and 8 NMOS devices from the M6800 family. The maximum capacitive loading on any line must not exceed 130 pF which includes the stray capacitance of interconnecting wires and capacitance of devices connected to the bus line.

Q4.5, 4.6 From the above discussion, the reader should be able to appreciate two points. The first is that buffer devices are a necessity for all but the simplest systems. A good general rule for designing hardware is to always include buffers if in doubt. The second point is that a good layout which minimises stray capacitance is as important for high-speed digital circuits as it is for high-frequency analogue circuits.

Three-state bus drivers

In any system that includes a bus, there is an inherent requirement for the output lines of many different devices to be connected together via the lines of the bus. This is evident from Figures 4.1 and 4.2. In the system shown, the ROM, RAM and input port will all at some time wish to place data on the data bus for transfer to the CPU. As a result of this requirement, certain restrictions are placed on the output circuits of these devices. To understand these restrictions, consider what would happen if the outputs of two standard TTL gates were connected to a bus line. Standard TTL employs the totem pole output circuit shown in Figure 4.5. When the output is high, the upper transistor in the totem pole is ON with the lower transistor OFF. The opposite situation prevails when the output is low. Figure 4.4 shows one consequence of connecting the outputs of two gates together. The ON upper transistor of totem pole B and the ON lower transistor of totem pole A provide a low impedance path between V_{cc} and ground. Surprisingly, this does not always destroy the output circuit. It does however always prevent either gate working in the proper manner.

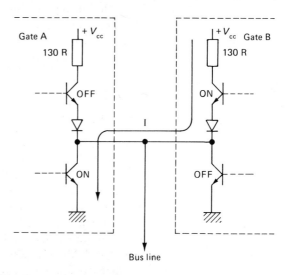

Figure 4.5   Connection of totem pole outputs

For putting out data from the functional units of a computing system on to a system bus, special output circuits known as tristate or three-state gates are normally employed. The term *tristate* is used by the National Semicondictor Corporation and is a registered trade name subject to copyright. Other manufacturers may employ the term *three-state* to describe the same type of circuit.

Three-state gates are provided with an 'enable' input in addition to the normal gate inputs. When this enable line is not active it has the effect of turning OFF both transistors in a totem pole output circuit. This effectively leaves the output floating at an indeterminate voltage with a very high resistance to ground, almost an open circuit in fact. The circuit therefore has three possible output states – high, low and disabled. Functionally, the circuit behaves rather like the gate and switch shown in Figure 4.6.

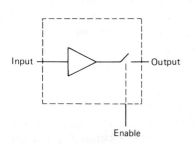

Figure 4.6   Functional description of three-state gate

The difference between the normal totem pole output circuit and the three-state arrangement shown in Figure 4.6 is that we may safely connect the outputs of as many three-state gates together as we wish provided that only one gate is enabled at any one time. Appendix H shows a range of buffer gates with three-state outputs, specifically designed for use in bus-oriented systems. The majority of micro-processor support integrated circuits described in this chapter have three-state output circuits built in.

Q4.7

Open-collector bus drivers

An alternative to three-state buffers is provided by the use of open-collector circuits at the output of bus driving devices. Before three-state circuits became available, the open collector technique was widely used. Currently, however, the three-state approach is favoured by most designers.

As the name implies, the output circuit of an open-collector gate is a single transistor with no collector load resistor. The collector load resistor must be connected externally. Figure 4.7 shows the output circuits of two open-collector gates connected to a common bus line.

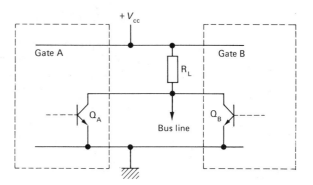

Figure 4.7 Open-collector gates

The bus line is connected to V_{cc} via a resistor R_L which provides a collector load for each output transistor. We note that when the output of either gate is high, the output transistor is OFF. A low output from either gate implies that the output transistor is in the ON condition.

Now suppose that in Figure 4.7, the output transistor of gate A is OFF. The common output line will now follow the output of gate B. When Q_B is ON, the output is low. When Q_B is OFF, the output is high. An essential feature of the open-collector approach is that all inactive gates must be in the normally high output state with the output transistor in the OFF condition. The common output line will

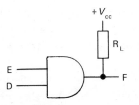

Figure 4.8 Open-collector AND gate with collector load resistor

E	D	F
0	0	0
0	1	0
1	0	0
1	1	1

Figure 4.9   AND truth table

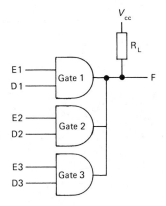

Q4.8 *Figure 4.10* Open-collector AND bus drivers

then follow the normal output of the active gate. Naturally, only one gate is allowed to be active at once.

An AND configuration is convenient for open-collector buffers. Figure 4.8 shows such a gate with the truth table given in Figure 4.9. A TTL type 7409 integrated circuit contains four open-collector gates of this kind. From the truth table, it can be seen that when the E input is high, the output F always follows the D input. When the D input is low, for a single gate as shown, the output F is always low. In circuit terms this means that the output transistor is in the OFF state which effectively releases the output line for control by any other open-collector gate to which it is connected.

Figure 4.10 shows three open-collector AND gates driving a single bus line. Suppose we hold E2 and E3 low. This puts the output transistors of gates 2 and 3 in the OFF condition, drawing little or no current through R_L. Now if E1 is high, the logic level on the bus will always follow the logic level on D1. The E inputs to the gates are therefore enabling lines which allow a given gate to take control of the bus. The reason why only one E input may be high at any given time should be obvious.

4.3   The CPU chip set

In Chapter 1 we described devices such as the 8080, Z80, 6800 and Z8000 as CPU-type microprocessors, implying that they are by themselves capable of performing the function of the CPU in a microprocessor system. This is not exactly true. Each of these microprocessors requires additional support circuitry to perform the CPU function. This support is usually in the form of specialised integrated circuits although discrete component support circuits are sometimes used. We shall use the term 'CPU chip set' to describe the collection of devices or circuits which together perform the CPU function.

Clock requirements

All microprocessors require some form of clock oscillator to lay the basis for the timing of the interval events which occur during the fetching and execution of an instruction. Some early microprocessors required a total of four clock waveforms of identical frequency but displaced in time relative to each other. Today, this so called four-phase clock requirement would be regarded as an unacceptable complication by most system designers. Of the microprocessors described in Appendices A–E, the 8080 and M6800 each require a two-phase clock. The Z80 and Z8000 require only one clock waveform, i.e. a single-phase clock. An increasingly common clock provision is demonstrated by the COP420L which has most of the circuit for a clock oscillator included within the chip. The user must simply connect a crystal or resonant circuit between appropriate pins to satisfy the clock requirements of the device.

For microprocessors such as the Z80 and Z8000 which require a single-phase clock, it is common to use discrete component clock generator circuits since it is not usually possible to make the circuit successfully using TTL gates only as the active devices. This is because the standard TTL gate with its totem pole output circuit has a very limited current sourcing ability although, as we have seen, it has a good current sinking capability. Open-collector TTL gates have an improved current sourcing capability, but even with these devices it is difficult to obtain the rise time required for most microprocessor clock waveforms.

Figure 4.11 shows how the limitations of TTL can be overcome by using a transistor as an active pull-up for a standard TTL gate. The circuit shown is used with minor variations to provide a clock in several commercial microprocessor systems based on the Z80. Clock

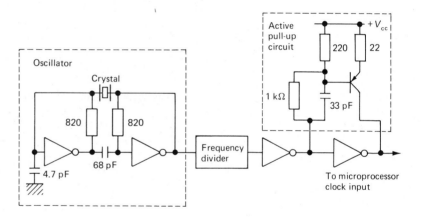

Figure 4.11 Single-phase clock generator circuit

frequency is determined by the crystal frequency and the frequency division ratio. Any suitable TTL frequency divider may be employed. In some cases, the oscillator frequency is identical to that of the required clock in which case the frequency divider may be omitted. The transistor used in the active pull-up must be able to provide the required rise time of the clock waveform, 2N3906 being a popular choice.

Figure 4.12 shows a clock generator circuit recommended for use with the Z8000 microprocessor (Ref. 4.1). In this case, the clock waveform requirements are met by a discrete component totem pole configuration drive circuit.

When two or more phases of the clock are required by a micro-

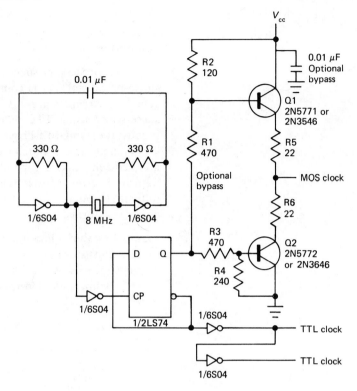

Figure 4.12 Z8000 clock oscillator and driver circuit

processor, it is almost always worth employing a special-purpose integrated circuit for generation of the clock waveforms. Figure 4.13 shows an 8224 clock generator forming part of the 8080 CPU chip set. The 8224 is described in Appendix F.

Within the 8224 is an oscillator circuit and a scale-of-9 frequency divider. In a typical system, an 18 MHz crystal with a value of C of 10 pF would generate a 2 MHz clock. Both phases of the clock are generated by the 8224. The 8224 is more than a clock generator since it performs additional timing functions. The SYNC signal from the 8080 is taken in by the 8224 and used to generate a timing strobe for the 8228 bus controller whose function is described below. Other functions performed by the 8224 relate to the reset function and the RDYIN signal which allows the 8080 to wait during read and write operations with very slow memory devices.

Q4.9, 4.10

Bus controllers and demultiplexers

Of the CPU-type microprocessors used here as examples, only the Z80 and M6800 do not employ multiplexing of the address and/or data bus(es). For these two devices, the microprocessor together with

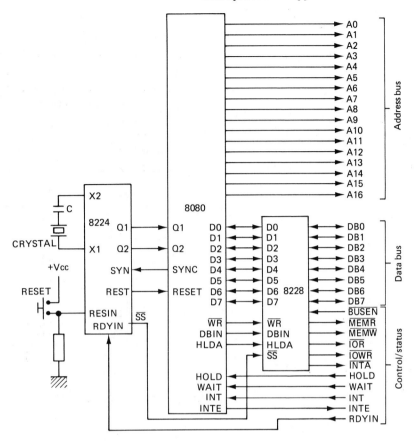

Figure 4.13 8080 CPU chip set

a clock generator constitute the CPU chip set. The 8080 however multiplexes status and data signals on one 8-bit bus. These must be separated or demultiplexed to provide distinct data and control/ status buses as shown in Figure 4.1. The integrated circuits required to perform this demultiplexing form part of the CPU chip set. In the case of the Z8000, addresses and data are multiplexed on a single 16-line bus. Again, demultiplexing is required if the microprocessor is to be used in a conventional structure like that of Figure 4.1.

The complete 8080 CPU chip set is shown in Figure 4.13. Here the 8228 bus controller is used to provide distinct data and control/ status buses. The 8228 is described in Appendix G. Typical status lines provided by the 8228 are $\overline{\text{MEMR}}$ and $\overline{\text{IOWR}}$. The $\overline{\text{MEMR}}$ signal is active when a memory read operation is being performed. This signal is used together with the address, by the system memory devices when memory read operations are implemented. Similarly, $\overline{\text{IOWR}}$ is active when an OUT instruction is executed to write data to an output port. This signal is, of course, made use of by the output

Q4.11 port circuit. Some control signals such as HOLD, WAIT, etc., are not multiplexed and can therefore go directly to the 8080 itself.

With the Z8000 microprocessor the derivation of distinct control/ status bus lines presents a slightly different problem. It will be recalled that status information for this microprocessor is carried in coded form on four lines ST0–ST3 as shown in Table 3.2. To generate discrete status signals, this code must be decoded. Figure 4.14 shows how a 74154 TTL 4 line to 16 line decoder performs this function. Readers not familiar with decoders may care to skip ahead to Section 4.4 and refer to Appendix Q at this point.

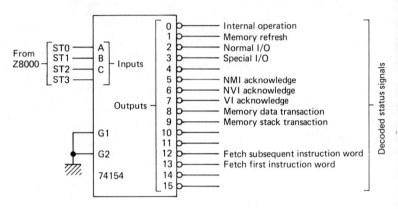

Figure 4.14   Decoding Z8000 status signals

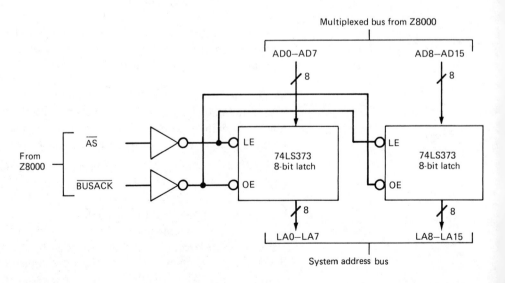

Figure 4.15

The Z8000 also differs from the 8-bit microprocessors described in that it employs a multiplexed 16-line address/data bus. One function of the CPU chip set must therefore be to demultiplex or separate the address and data lines. In the system shown in Figure 4.2 this is achieved by 'catching' an address in a 16-bit latch when it appears on the multiplexed bus. The Z8000 generates a timing signal $\overline{AS}$ which is specifically for this purpose. Figure 4.15 shows a suitable arrangement. Note that the latch outputs to the address bus are three state. The signal $\overline{BUSACK}$ is active whenever the Z8000 wishes to relinquish control of the address/status bus. If this happens, the three-state outputs of the latch are disabled.

Q4.13

In the system shown in Figure 4.2 the data bus is derived by simply buffering the multiplexed bus. This does lead to a potential conflict between addresses and data. Memory and I/O ports must therefore be designed in such a way that they never attempt to place data on the bus in the time interval when an address is already present.

4.4   Address decoders

One of the more useful features of many integrated circuits designed for use in microprocessor systems is the provision of a control line called chip select (CS) or chip enable (CE). When the chip select line is not active, no communication with system buses can take place. In this state, the device does not exist as far as the system is concerned. With simple devices, which do not have a chip select line as such, the same effect can be achieved by disabling the three-state buffers that drive the system data bus.

With a microprocessor such as the 8080 or Z80, I/O instructions define a port address which is placed by the microprocessor on the least significant eight lines of the address bus during execution of the instruction. To convert the port address into an enabling signal for the port circuit an address decoder is used. Appendix Q shows a data sheet describing a TTL 4 line to 16 line decoder. This 74154 device takes in a 4-bit code and activates one of the 16 outputs depending on the code value.

As an example of the use of the 74154, consider the design of an 8080-based microprocessor system which requires 16 input ports of 4 lines each. For each port, we shall use a simple three-state buffer type 8T97 described in Appendix H. Only four of the six gates of each 8T97 will be used. From Appendix H it will be seen that the three-state enable line for the 8T97 is active low. It is in fact described in the truth table as an active high disable line DIS4 which comes to the same thing. Employing only gates 1–4, we shall use the symbol in Figure 4.16 to describe the device.

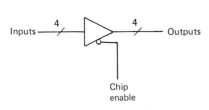

Figure 4.16 Symbolic representation of gates 1–4 of 8T97 buffer

Figure 4.17 shows the method of selecting a particular port during the

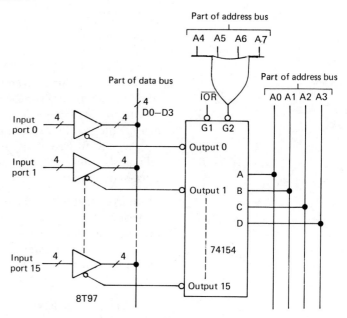

Figure 4.17   The 74154 as a port address decoder

execution of an IN operation. A bus structure is assumed similar to that generated by the 8080 CPU chip set shown in Figure 4.13. Port addresses are 00–0F. The 74154 is only enabled when $\overline{\text{IOR}}$ becomes low when A3–A6 are also low, i.e. during an input operation when the four most significant bits of the 8-bit address are 0. If this condition is not met, none of the ports shown in Figure 4.17 is enabled since all outputs of the 74154 will be high as shown by the truth table in Appendix Q. During an input operation with a port address 00–0F, A4–A7 are all low which makes G2 low and $\overline{\text{IOR}}$ is low which makes G1 low. The 74154 is therefore enabled. Only one output of the 74154 will be low in accordance with the device truth table and the corresponding three-state input port gate is enabled thus allowing the data on to the system data bus.

Enabling I/O ports is only one application of address decoders in microprocessor systems. Other applications include enabling memory chips in a memory array and decoding control/status signals **Q4.14** as described in Section 4.3.

4.5   I/O devices

We have seen in Section 4.3 that the CPU ship set provides the system designer with data, address and control/status buses. Data to or from external devices are transferred from or to the microprocessor via the data bus. In order to ensure that the timing of data transactions is correct and to allow the CPU to identify the external device with which it wishes to communicate, special-purpose I/O circuits are required. The nature and complexity of these I/O circuits will depend on the microprocessor used and the external device that is receiving or sending the data. Of course, in the case of single-chip micro-controllers, I/O circuits are contained within the single chip. For other microprocessors such as the 8080, Z80, M6800 and Z8000, it is the job of the system designer to specify the I/O circuit configuration.

We will first consider the 8080, Z80 and Z8000. In Section 3.1 we said that these microprocessors differ from the M6800 in that their instruction sets contain specific instructions for data input and output operations. Associated with this is the presence in the control/ status bus of lines that carry signals of direct use to I/O circuits. These may be generated directly by the microprocessor, $\overline{\text{IORQ}}$ of the Z80, for example. They may alternatively be derived by other devices in the chip set such as the 8228 shown in the 8080 system of Figure 4.13. This device derives $\overline{\text{IOR}}$ and $\overline{\text{IOWR}}$ signals. Similarly, the Z8000 system employs a decoder to derive 'normal' I/O and special I/O status lines as shown in Figure 4.14.

With the availability of I/O control/status signals, I/O circuits can often be quite simple. We have already seen (Section 4.4) that an input circuit may consist simply of a set of three-state buffers. Figure 4.17 shows how the 8080 $\overline{\text{IOR}}$ signal is used to enable the port address decoder. This in turn enables the three-state gates when an IN instruction with the appropriate port address is executed.

The use of a simple buffer gate described above for input operations is not usually adequate for output operations. This is because data is only present on the system data bus for part of the instruction cycle when the OUT instruction is executed. Any output circuit must therefore catch the output data when it appears on the bus. For this purpose, a simple latch may be adequate. Appendix I shows a suitable TTL octal latch. The data sheet shows the F or high-speed variant of the standard TTL 74373 circuit.

An output circuit for a Z80 system is shown in Figure 4.18. When LE is low, the latch is transparent. Referring to the I/O timing diagram for the Z80 in Appendix B, it will be seen that $\overline{\text{IORQ}}$ and $\overline{\text{WR}}$ are low during the executiuon of an OUT operation. At the same time, the port address is on the address bus and the data bus carries the output data. This data is still present on the bus when $\overline{\text{IORQ}}$ and $\overline{\text{WR}}$ go high, thus latching it into the 74373.

The 74373 is sometimes used as an input buffer in much the same way as the 8T97 shown in Figure 4.17. This is possible since the latches can be made transparent with LE low. Three-state control is provided by $\overline{\text{OE}}$ and the circuit can therefore behave exactly like an octal three-state buffer.

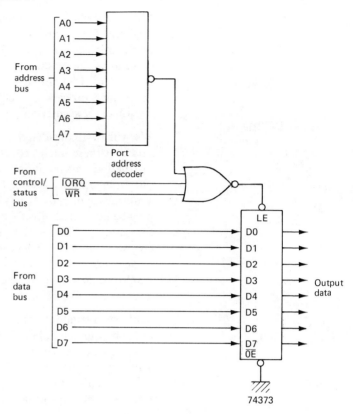

Figure 4.18   The 74373 as output data latch in Z80 system

Simple register and buffer I/O circuits can provide a low component cost solution to the problem of I/O. An alternative approach is to make use of special-purpose integrated circuits. A wide range of integrated circuits is currently available covering I/O requirements for most types of microprocessor. Two situations in which it is almost always preferable to employ specialised I/O integrated circuits are:

1   When the microprocessor employs memory-mapped I/O.
2   When serial data I/O is required.

Q4.15

Many designers also choose the convenience of special-purpose integrated circuits even when simple buffer/register circuits would be adequate.

PIAs and PIOs

Integrated circuits for implementing parallel I/O operations are known by a variety of names, peripheral interface adaptor (PIA) and parallel I/O (PIO) being the most common. Appendix J describes a typical example, the M6820 PIA which is a member of the M6800

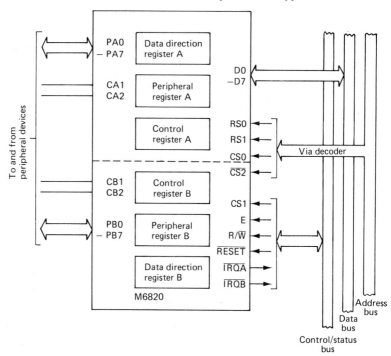

Figure 4.19   M6820 internal structure and external connections

family. The M6800 employs memory-mapped I/O which is the main reason why almost all systems based on this microprocessor use devices such as the M6820 for parallel I/O.

Like the majority of special-purpose I/O chips, the 6820 is programmable and is capable of operating in a variety of different ways. The user must program the M6820 to behave in the required manner before attempting to perform I/O operations. In common with other devices of this kind, programming is performed by storing, in registers within the PIA, codes that identify the desired operating mode. This process, which is implemented with a program executed by the M6800 microprocessor, is called initialisation.

Figure 4.19 shows the internal structure and external connections of the M6820 PIA. It will be seen that the device provides effectively 16 lines which can be inputs or outputs in any combination. The choice of which lines are inputs and which are outputs is fixed by a bit pattern stored in the two data direction registers during initialisation. Lines CA1 and CB1 can carry interrupt signals which may be passed on to the CPU if the M6820 has been programmed to allow this. Lines CA2 and CB2 can also carry interrupt signals but may also act as **Q4.16** outputs again depending on how the system is initialised.

The M6820 is designed for use with memory-mapped I/O and

therefore employs the same control/status lines as memory devices in the system. To the M6800 CPU, the M6820 appears as four memory locations which can be read from or written into using load and store instructions. A description of the M6820 is given in Appendix J.

UARTs and USARTs

The I/O techniques we have discussed so far have all involved parallel data transfer. For an 8-bit microprocessor this involves the simultaneous transfer of all 8 bits of an I/O word via 8 connecting wires. Many items of peripheral equipment by contrast transmit and receive data in serial form, i.e. one digit at a time. The connection in this case consists of a single wire together with an earth return. Video display terminals (VDTs) and printers are common examples of devices that may require serial data transfer. Within the microprocessor system, data are carried in parallel along the system data bus. An I/O circuit which acts as an interface to a serial data source or sink must therefore convert data from parallel to serial form and back again.

From the brief introduction given above, the serial interfacing problem sounds straightforward. After all, a simple shift register can convert data from parallel to serial form and *vice versa*. In fact, before the arrival of special-purpose integrated circuits, the circuitry required to implement a serial interface was far from trivial. This is mainly due to the problem of synchronisation between sending and receiving devices when transferring serial data.

One such problem relates to bit synchronisation. Figure 4.20 shows a very simple serial data communication system in which an 8-bit word is loaded in parallel into the transmit register. The contents of the transmit register are then shifted one at a time into the serial communication channel at a rate determined by the transmit clock. Digits are shifted into the serial-in receive register at a rate determined by the receive clock. The receive register is effectively sampling the serial data waveform at instants fixed by the occurrence of a receive clock pulse.

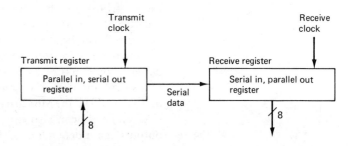

Figure 4.20   Serial data transmission

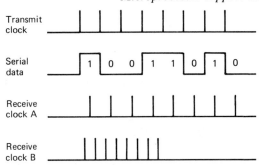

Figure 4.21 The problem of bit synchronisation

Figure 4.21 shows the situation when the 8-bit data word 10011010 is transmitted. When the receive clock A is of exactly the same frequency as the transmit clock, the correct word is shifted into the receive register. This is the case even if the receive clock pulses are shifted in time with respect to the transmit clock pulses. In the case of receive clock B, however, the waveform is sampled at twice the correct frequency resulting in the word 11000011 being left in the receive register.

Figure 4.21 may appear to overstate the problem of bit synchronisation since it is not difficult to design transmit and receive clock oscillators which have nominally equal frequencies to a high degree of precision. This does not help us however since *any* difference between transmit and receive clock frequencies will, over a sufficiently long period of time, cause errors if serial data words are being transmitted in succession. Consider the situation, for example, if the transmit clock oscillator generates 1,000 clock pulses in the same time interval as the receive clock oscillator generates 999 pulses.

The second major timing problem when transferring data serially relates to word synchronisation. Let us suppose that we have in some way overcome the bit synchronisation problem with the simple system shown in Figure 4.20 and that a continuous succession of 8-bit words is being transmitted serially from the transmit to the receiver register. The data waveform will consist of a continuous bit stream. Should the receiver now 'hiccup' and miss a single received digit, the system will enter a state of permanent error since words collected by the receive register will not be the same as transmitted words. Instead, received words will consist of the last seven digits of one transmitted word together with the first digit of the next word.

There are two approaches to the synchronisation of serial data. The first employs asynchronous data transfer. Using this technique, data words are transmitted using a standard format identified by the sending and receiving circuits. Figure 4.22 shows one form of an internationally agreed format known as RS232. It will be seen that the

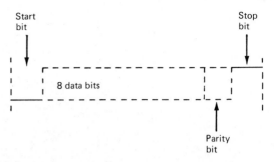

Figure 4.22 RS232 asynchronous serial data format

data bits are framed by a start bit, which is always low and a stop bit which is always high. The start of a data word is therefore identified by a high–low transition. After the start bit come the 8 data bits followed by an optional parity bit.

The parity bit provides a means by which the receiving circuit can check whether the serial data has suffered corruption. Parity checks can be defined as odd or even. Assuming that an even parity check has been assumed by transmitting and receiving circuits, at the transmitter, the number of ones in the data word are counted. A parity bit of 1 or 0 is then inserted to make the total number of ones an even number as shown in the two examples below:

Data word	*Parity bit*
11010011	1
01100110	0

The importance of the parity bit is that if a single digit is corrupted in the transmitted word, it must convert a 1 to a 0 or a 0 to a 1. This either adds or subtracts 1 from the total number of ones thus converting this number of ones in the whole word (data + parity) from an even to an odd number. To detect this the receiving circuit simply counts the number of ones in the received word. An odd parity check works in the same way but, in this case, the parity bit makes the total number of ones an odd number. Figure 4.23 shows the RS232 format for the data word 46 with even parity.

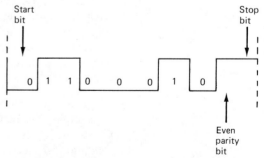

Figure 4.23 RS232 format for 46 with even parity

In an asynchronous serial data transmission system, the receiving device commences by scanning the serial input, waiting for the first high–low transmission. When this transition is detected, it is used as a timing reference to fix the instants of time when sampling of the received word will occur. This effectively resynchronises the receiver at the beginning of each word which overcomes the problem of bit synchronisation if the transmit and receive clock frequencies are at least roughly equal.

To implement asynchronous serial data transmission, the hardware will obviously need to be a good deal more sophisticated than the shift registers of Figure 4.20. Special-purpose integrated circuits known as universal asynchronous receiver/transmitters (UARTs) are available for use in serial data communication systems. They can be used as special-purpose I/O devices performing the function of serial data transmitters and receivers. A more detailed description of a specific example of this type of device is given later in this section.

The alternative to asynchronous serial data communication is provided by the synchronous technique. In this case, bit synchronisation is achieved by simply transmitting a clock waveform along with the data waveform. The physical communication link therefore requires an extra conductor compared with an asynchronous system. At the receiver, the clock identifies the position of each digit in the received bit stream exactly.

Synchronous serial communication removes the problem of bit synchronisation but the problem of word synchronisation remains. This is overcome by organising the transmitted words into blocks in a defined format. Blocks of data start with an agreed synchronising word and are separated by redundant words which do not carry any data. Figure 4.24 shows a typical format of this kind. Synchronous methods are normally used when the amount of data to be transmitted is large and/or when the highest speed of transmission is required. Because of the block format employed (as shown in Figure 4.24), it would not be sensible to transmit say one or two data words at a time by the synchronous method. In this case, the asynchronous technique would be much more appropriate.

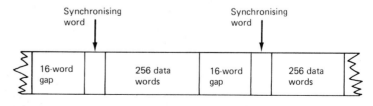

Figure 4.24 Typical synchronous serial data format

To implement synchronous data communication, the hardware is different but no less complex than is required for asynchronous communication. As might be expected, special-purpose integrated circuits are also available for this purpose. They are referred to by various titles. The M6850 synchronous serial data adaptor (SSDA) being typical. This device is from the M6800 family and is compatible with the memory-mapped I/O philosophy of this microprocessor.

As a specific example of a serial interface device, the 8251 is described in Appendix K. This device is known as a universal synchronous/asynchronous receiver/transmitter (USART). As the name implies, a USART can be used to implement either asynchronous or synchronous data communication. USARTs are obviously programmable devices and must therefore be initialised to operate in the desired manner, synchronous or asynchronous. As with other programmable integrated circuits, initialisation is performed by loading registers within the USART with the appropriate programming codes.

When operating a transmitter in the asynchronous mode, the 8251 offers the user a variety of options. The number of data bits in a transmitted word may vary between 5 and 8. Figure 4.22 shows the word ending with a high logic level of 1-bit interval. The 8251 allows this to be extended to 1½- or 2-bit intervals if the user wishes. Parity checks may be implemented or not as the user wishes.

As an asynchronous receiver, the USART must obviously be initialised to recognise the same word format as the transmitting device. In addition to converting the received word to parallel form, the USART performs various checks. These include:

1   Parity check, if implemented.
2   Framing error check. The USART checks whether correct stop bit(s) occur in the expected place in each received word.
3   Overrun error check. The receiving USART assembles a parallel word which it presents to the microprocessor. If the microprocessor fails to take in this word before the next parallel word is assembled, an overrun error has been detected.

In the asynchronous mode of operation formatting of data words is performed automatically by the USART. The programmer simply ensures that the correct data word is put out to the USART via the port allocated for this purpose. Start bit, stop bit(s) and a parity bit are inserted and the formatted word is then put out in serial form from the USART. At the receiver, the serial is taken in, start, stop and parity bits are stripped and a parallel data word is presented to the receiving system. A status line informs the receiving system that the received word is available. Detected errors cause the setting of flags in a status register within the USART which may be read by the receiving device.

When the USART is operating in the synchronous mode, data format is the responsibility of the programmer to a much greater degree than is the case with the asynchronous mode. If the programmer wishes the USART to put out a serial stream of 16 all-zero words forming the gap shown in Figure 4.24, the program must be written to put out 16 all-zero words from the microprocessor to the USART. The chosen synchronisation word and subsequent data words must similarly be put out from the microprocessor to the USART in the correct order.

As a synchronous receiver, the USART can operate in a 'hunt' mode. In this mode, the received bit stream is scanned, searching for a specified synchronising word. When the word is found, a flag is set in the status register or alternatively an interrupt may be generated. It is also possible to initialise USARTs to implement a synchronising scheme which requires the recognition of two successive synchronising words. In addition to implementing the usual serial-to-

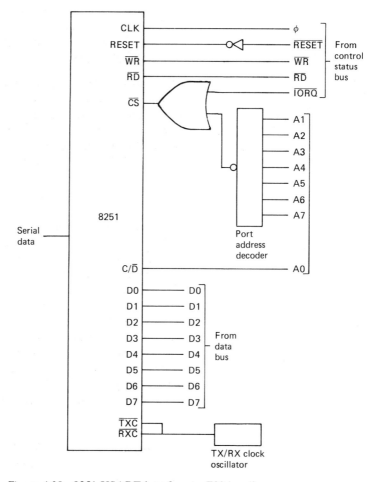

Figure 4.25   8251 USART interface to Z80 bus lines

parallel conversion of received data words, a receiving USART also performs a parity check for the detection of errors.

Appendix K shows how the 8251 USART can be used as an I/O device in an 8080 system which features the standard bus structure described in Figure 4.13. It may also be used with other types of microprocessor. Figure 4.25 shows an 8251 interfaced to the Z80 bus structure. Minor modifications may be required to these interface connections in some practical situations. Figure 4.25, for example, implies that no interrupts are used; this may not, however, be the case for all systems.

Q4.17–4.21

4.6 Memory devices

Memory is an inherent and essential requirement in any computing system. The provision of a memory adequate in size and performance is therefore an important task of the computer systems designer. In this section we review the general characteristics of different types of memory currently available to the systems designer. We also examine some specific memory devices in more detail.

The range of memory devices and technologies available to the computer systems designer is ever increasing, but this section concentrates on one particular data storage requirement, that of primary memory. In most systems this primary memory is composed of monolithic integrated circuits of various types. Secondary memory characteristics are discussed in Chapter 5.

Types of memory

Primary memory   Sometimes also called high-speed memory. This refers to memory that is directly accessible via a microcomputer address and data bus. It is primary memory which is read from or written into during the execution of a memory reference instruction. The primary memory also stores the instruction codes of programs being executed.

Secondary memory   Also referred to as backing storage. This is memory not directly accessible via the microcomputer address and data bus. Typical secondary memory media are magnetic disks and tapes. Programs and data stored in secondary memory must be transferred to primary memory before they can be used by the microprocessor.

Random-access memory (RAM)   A type of memory in which the time taken to perform read or write operations is the same for all locations. Although not strictly accurate, the term RAM is commonly used to describe primary memory which can be written into and read from in contrast to ROM which can only operate in the read mode.

Sequential-access memory (SAM) A type of memory in which the physical location of a memory location affects the time taken to read or write data. To reach a particular address it is necessary to sequence through all address locations until the desired address is reached. Typical sequential-access memory devices are magnetic tape, disk and bubble memories. Sequential access storage is hardly ever used in primary memory.

Read-only memory (ROM) Generally used nowadays to refer to semiconductor devices in which data is permanently stored during the manufacturing process. Sometimes the term is also used to include devices in which the user can store data permanently or semi-permanently (*see* PROM, EPROM, EAROM).

Programmable read-only memory (PROM) A semiconductor memory device in which the user can store data by a process which may be irreversible. A typical example of this type of device involves the selective blowing of fusible links within an integrated circuit to store data. PROM is sometimes used as a general term to include erasable devices (*see* EPROM, EAROM).

Erasable programmable read-only memory (EPROM) This refers to a semiconductor memory device in which the user can store data by a reversible process. The most common types of EPROM store data as packets of charge on capacitors within an integrated circuit. This charge can be dissipated and the data erased by exposing the circuit to ultra-violet light for a period of time. EPROMs are sometimes called read-mostly memories (RMM).

Electrically alterable read-only memory (EAROM) Sometimes also called electrically erasable read-only memory (EEROM). This is a type of EPROM in which the erasure process is effected by applying appropriate voltages to the integrated circuit.

Access time and cost per bit

The two most important parameters of memory for the designer are access time and cost. Access time is the time between the memory read signal becoming active and the data becoming available on the memory output lines. Memories operating with microprocessors are normally required to have an access time less than a defined maximum value. Some microprocessors also have a wait facility which allows its operation to be temporarily suspended while waiting for data from a slow memory. The 8080 READY line and the

Z80/Z8000 WAIT line are examples of control inputs for this purpose.

The price we pay for a memory is usually given in terms of cost per bit of information stored. When calculating this figure it is important to remember that not only the cost of the memory device(s) themselves is involved. A memory made up of monolithic integrated circuits will require a variety of support, from printed circuit board provision to d.c. power supplies. The cost of this support may easily exceed that of the integrated circuit memory elements.

Static RAM

Our discussion of memory devices starts with the static RAM. This is the name normally used for one type of monolithic integrated circuit read/write memory device. At the time of writing a very popular integrated circuit of this kind is the 2114. Appendix L contains data sheets for this chip. It will be seen that each 2114 can store 1,024 words of 4 bits. In an 8-bit microprocessor system each 1K block of memory would therefore be composed of two type 2114 integrated circuits, one storing the four least significant bits of each word, the other the four most significant bits. Address lines would be common for the two chips, of course. The chip is enabled by taking $\overline{CS}$ low and data are then read from or written into the addressed location, depending on the state of $\overline{WE}$. A 1,024 x 8-bit unit of memory composed of type 2114 chips is shown in Figure 4.26. Larger units of memory are formed in the usual way by decoding higher-order address lines to select units of memory as shown in Figure 4.27.

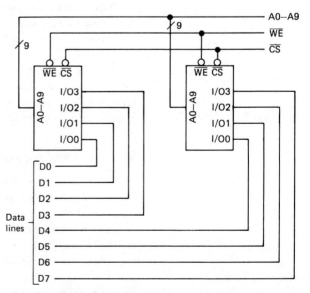

Figure 4.26 Two 2114s forming a 1,024 × 8-bit unit of memory

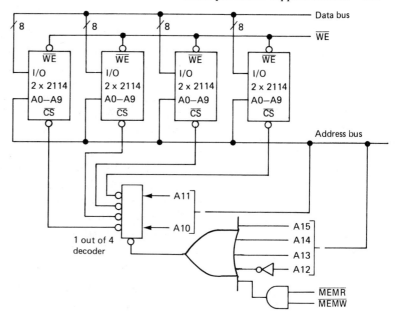

Figure 4.27 1,024 × 8 static memory addressed 1000-13FF

Dynamic RAM

The method described above of connecting individual memory chips together to form larger units of memory is also employed with dynamic memory integrated circuits. Various complications arise however. One of the attractive features of dynamic memory is that it is possible to pack more of it on a single integrated circuit than is the case with static devices. The greater the number of memory locations within one integrated circuit, however, the greater the number of pins must be devoted to address lines. This conflicts with the constant desire of integrated circuit manufacturers to keep the number of pins on each package as low as possible for reasons of cost. A solution increasingly adopted is to multiplex address lines.

Appendix M contains data sheets for a typical dynamic memory device which features multiplexed address lines. The 4116 contains 16,384 individual memory locations. To identify an individual address therefore requires a 14-bit address since $16,384 = 2^{14}$. Within the 4116, as in most integrated circuit memory devices, individual memory cells are arranged in a matrix. The address identifies the position of the cell in the matrix and can therefore be conventionally split into two parts, a row address and a column address.

To use the 4116, the 7-bit row and column addresses must be presented at different times on the 7 address lines. The row address is first placed on the address lines and the row address strobe $\overline{RAS}$ is activated. Within the 4116 chips, $\overline{RAS}$ latches the row address into a register. The column address is placed on the address lines and the column address strobe line $\overline{\text{CAS}}$ is activated. After a suitable delay to allow latching of the column address, data is read from or written to the addressed memory location, depending on the status of the $\overline{\text{WRITE}}$ line. The timing of these operations is, of course, vitally important and is shown in the read/modify/write cycle timing diagram in Appendix K. Page 11 of Ref. 4.5 discusses multiplexed addressing of dynamic RAM in more detail.

As a result of the need for row and column strobes, the 4116 can dispense with a chip select line thus saving one pin connection. The chip is effectively selected by applying the row and column strobe pulses. A disadvantage of multiplexed address lines is the necessity for external circuitry to provide $\overline{\text{RAS}}$ and $\overline{\text{CAS}}$ at the correct time. A circuit that performs the chip select function then directs these strobes to the selected chip(s).

Figure 4.28 demonstrates the principles of the control circuit required for a memory involving multiplexed row/column addressing. The circuit operation is initiated by a Z80 $\overline{\text{MREQ}}$ signal, but most microprocessor systems will have available a status line of the same kind indicating that a memory read/write operation is required. To understand the circuit operation, the reader will need to refer to the timing diagrams for the Z80 and 4116 read/write operations given in Appendices B and M, respectively. Initially, $\overline{\text{MREQ}}$ is high which multiplexes address bits A0–A6 on to the row/column address lines of the memory. When $\overline{\text{MREQ}}$ goes low, this provides the column address strobe thus latching the column address A0–A6. After delay period *A*, the MUX control line goes low thus multiplexing address bits A7–A13 on to the row/column address lines. After a further delay period *B*, $\overline{\text{RAS}}$ goes low, thus latching the row address.

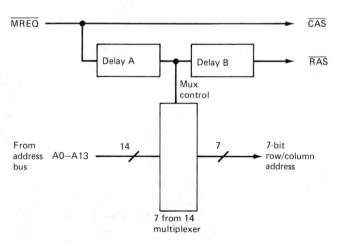

Figure 4.28   Multiplexed address control circuit

The circuits generating delay periods A and B are critical to the successful operation of this circuit. A variety of practical address multiplexing circuits will be found in Sections I and II of Ref. 4.5.

The major difference between static and dynamic RAM relates to the refresh requirement. In dynamic RAMs, data is stored as packets of charge on capacitors. Since this charge leaks away naturally, it must be replenished at regular intervals. For the 4116, which is typical, this interval must not exceed 2 ms. Refreshing is accomplished by accessing each memory location in turn. For devices with multiplexed addressing, simply addressing a row will refresh all addresses in that row; this simplifies and speeds up the operation. In practical terms, a refresh counter must be provided external to the memory which cycles through all row addresses as it counts up. For each state of the refresh counter, a refresh operation is performed by activating the $\overline{\text{RAS}}$ line.

The major practical difficulty with refreshing is that the refresh operation must be integrated with the normal memory read and write operation. This can be done in two ways. Asynchronous refresh is achieved by disabling normal read/write operations at regular intervals during the execution of a program to allow the refresh operation to take place. Many microprocessors are provided with a control, such as the 8080 HOLD, that suspends the computing process for memory refresh operations. Asynchronous refresh has the advantage that it permits the design of standard memories which can be used with a variety of microprocessors since its operation does not depend on the timing of the computing cycle of a particular device. It has the disadvantage that the timing of the running of a program is distorted by the regular interruptions caused by memory refresh.

Synchronous refresh of dynamic memory interleaves the refresh operation with the activity of the microprocessor during the execution of each instruction. Typically, the refresh circuit uses the microprocessor status signals to detect those clock cycles during the execution of an instruction when data transfers to or from the CPU are not taking place. During these clock cycles, a refresh operation is performed. If we take the M6800 as an example, no data transfers occur during the $\phi 1$ clock period. Any memory refresh operations during the $\phi 1$ clock period will therefore appear completely transparent to the user. Interfacing dynamic memory with the M6800 is discussed in Section 4–2.5 of Ref. 4.2. Synchronous refresh has obvious attractions since it does not interfere with the normal operation of the microprocessor when executing a program. It has the disadvantage, however, that it depends on the characteristics of a particular microprocessor; this means that a dynamic memory designed for one system cannot be used in another system with a different CPU.

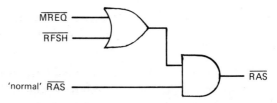

Figure   4.29   Z80   memory   refresh   circuit

Synchronous refresh is much more easily implemented with some microprocessors, e.g. the Z80 and Z8000. This is because much of the refresh circuitry is contained within the microprocessor chip and refresh operations are automatically interleaved within the normal computing cycle. From the instruction OPCODE fetch timing diagram (Appendix B) it will be seen that the $\overline{\text{RFSH}}$ line becomes active during clock cycles T3 and T4 of the M1 or FETCH cycle. At the same time, the Z80 places on the address bus the output of a refresh address counter contained within the Z80 chip. To use this facility with the 4116-based memory requires only the addition of the circuit shown in Figure 4.29 to the 'normal' $\overline{\text{RAS}}$ generator circuit.

In a description of monolithic static and dynamic RAM devices it is useful to conclude with a brief discussion of practical considerations. Designing with static RAM has the attraction of simplicity at the expense of increased memory chip count and greater power consumption. Dynamic RAM involves a smaller number of memory chips, but may require external circuitry for refresh purposes. Power consumption is typically a good deal less than is the case with static devices. For large memories, the relative overhead of the refresh circuit is less of a problem since it is provided only once for the whole memory. It must also be said, however, that dynamic RAM has in the past had an (often deserved) reputation of being 'tricky' from the point of view of circuit layout. The reader is cautioned that building a successul dynamic RAM is not just a case of stringing together a few integrated circuits. Proper layout, adequate power supply rails, decoupled at regular intervals, and avoidance of crosstalk between adjacent conductors are all of great importance. It must also be remembered that many dynamic RAM devices require multiple power supplies and that different supply voltages may often need switching on in a particular sequence. This is the case with the 4116 as may be seen from Appendix M.

Appendix P shows a recently introduced memory chip and gives an indication of one way that memories will develop in the future. The 6132 is a quasi-static RAM – a dynamic RAM with all refresh circuitry contained within the chip. It may thus be said to offer many of the advantages of both static and dynamic RAM. Although the chip stores 32,768 bits, the need for a multiplexed address has been avoided by its organisation in 4,096 8-bit words. Low power consumption and a single supply voltage are other obvious attractions of this device.

Interfacing the various types of ROM, PROM and EPROM to a microprocessor bus generally presents few problems. They are normally static devices and thus present no refresh problems. Appendix N describes a popular EPROM, the 2716. When the $\overline{CS}$ line is activated, the 2716 places the contents of the addressed location on the output data lines. The reader should note that the 2716 is a good deal slower in its operation than the RAM chips we have considered earlier. This may require the use of the wait facility with some microprocessors (as discussed in Section 4.7). Of course, a read-only device should never be enabled if any other system element is attempting to place data on the bus at the same time.

Q4.22–4.25

4.7 Counter-timers

In later chapters we shall see that counting pulses and generating timing intervals are very common requirements in microprocessor systems. This is particularly the case if the system is functioning as a real-time controller which must respond rapidly to events in the controlled system. Appendix O shows an example of a special-purpose counter-timer circuit or CTC.

The 3882 CTC shown in Appendix O contains four channels which may be operated as either counters of input pulses or timers which generate given time intervals from the system clock. Like the USART and PIA described earlier, the 3882 CTC is a programmable device. Programming or initialisation is performed in the usual manner for programmable devices by loading registers within the CTC with bit patterns appropriate to the required mode of operation.

An added advantage of the 3882 is its ability to generate interrupts. When used with the Z80 microprocessor, the 3882 is also capable of implementing an interrupt priority scheme by connecting more than one CTC in a daisy chain configuration.

4.8 A near-minimal 8080 system

Figure 4.30 shows an 8080-based microcomputer system which incorporates some of the devices described in this chapter. The system includes 2K of EPROM and 1K of RAM, together with serial and parallel I/O ports. Since only a small part of the total memory and I/O port address space is occupied, address decoding can be very simple. The $\overline{CS}$ line of the 2716 EPROM for example is energised when $\overline{MEMR}$ and A15 are simultaneously low. Therefore, whatever logic levels are on A11–A14, the contents of an EPROM location will be read. Thus the lowest EPROM address could be designated 0000,

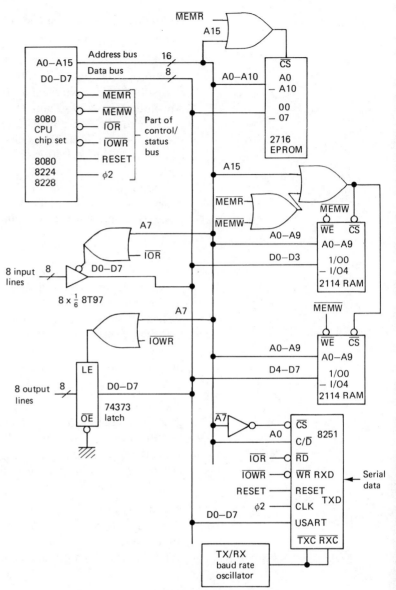

Figure 4.30   Near-minimal 8080 system

0800, 1000, 1800, etc., . . . , 7800. This is perfectly acceptable since no other memory element is allocated addresses in this area.

RAM in the system shown in Figure 4.30 is allocated a 1K block in the address space 8000–FFFF. This could be 8000–83FF, 8400–87FF, 8800–8BFF, etc. Similarly, the 8-bit parallel output port could be addressed as 00, 01, 02, . . . , 1F, and this is also true of the input port. The serial port is addressed as 80, 81, . . . , FF.

References and bibliography

4.1 P. Alfke, *A Small Z8000 System*, Zilog application note (August 1979).

4.2 *M6800 Microprocessor Applications Manual*, Motorola.

4.3 W. Barden Jr, *The Z80 Microcomputer Handbook*, Howard W. Sams & Co., Inc. (1978).

4.4 *MCS-80 Users Manual*, Intel.

4.5 D. Bursky (Editor), *Memory Systems Design and Applications*, Hayden Book Company (1980).

Questions

4.1 State briefly the functions of the address and data buses in a microprocessor system.

4.2 Give two examples of typical CPU control/status lines in a microprocessor system.

4.3 Explain why TTL logic gates are said to be 'current sinking'.

4.4 How does the current-sinking capability of a typical NMOS microprocessor output line compare with that of a TTL gate.

4.5 Explain how line capacitance and input capacitance affects the rise times of pulses in microprocessor systems.

4.6 Explain how the use of buffers can improve pulse rise times in microprocessor systems.

4.7 Describe the possible output states of a three-state buffer.

4.8 Sketch a circuit showing how the outputs of four open-collector, two-input AND gates are connected to a common bus line.

4.9 With the help of Appendix F, calculate the resonant frequency of the crystal used with an 8224 clock generator in an 8080 system if the required clock frequency is 1 MHz.

4.10 Identify two functions performed by the 8224 in addition to the generation of the 8080 microprocessor clocks.

4.11 State the function of the 8228 in an 8080-based microprocessor system.

4.12 Sketch a circuit showing how status signals can be derived from lines ST0–ST3 in a Z8000 microprocessor system.

4.13 Explain the function of the AS signal generated by the Z8000 microprocessor.

4.14 Sketch a circuit similar to Figure 4.17 showing how 8T97 buffers and a 74154 decoder could be used to implement 16 input ports with addresses F0–FF.

4.15   Describe two types of I/O operation which almost always involve the use of special-purpose integrated circuits.

4.16   State how input and output lines are defined when using an M6820 PIA for I/O operations.

4.17   What is the function performed by a UART?

4.18   Explain the distinction between synchronous and asynchronous serial data communication.

4.19   By means of a waveform sketch, describe the RS232 serial data format.

4.20   Explain how word and bit synchronisation are achieved in synchronous and asynchronous serial data communication.

4.21   Describe the error checks made by the 8251 USART when operating asynchronously.

4.22   State one advantage and one disadvantage of static RAM devices compared with dynamic RAM devices.

4.23   Explain the distinction between synchronous and asynchronous refresh of dynamic RAM.

4.24   What particular advantage is possessed by the Z80 and Z8000 microprocessors for the use of dynamic RAM.

4.25   Explain the reasons why designers of dynamic RAM chips often choose to multiplex row and column addresses.

Chapter 5 Typical microprocessor systems

Objectives of this chapter *When you have completed studying this chapter you should be able to analyse different microprocessor systems in the following typical applications:*

1 A washing-machine controller as an example of a small dedicated system.
2 A word processor as an example of a medium-size semi-dedicated system.
3 A microprocessor development system (MDS) as an example of a general-purpose system with reference to:
   (a) Appropriate device technology.
   (b) Average chip count.
   (c) Total cost.
   (d) Predicted production volume.

5.1 Dedicated and general-purpose systems

In this chapter we investigate the way in which the amount and variety of computation required in a microprocessor-based system affects the choice of microprocessor and other system elements. We shall also consider the system configuration. This is a term used to describe the components of a system and the general way they are interconnected. Our investigation will range from the highly specialised or dedicated to much more general-purpose systems. Particularly in this section, much of what is said is of a general nature and applies to most computer-based systems, whether or not the computer happens to be a microprocessor. We therefore use computer as a general name to apply to microprocessors, mini-computers and other larger machines.

A large computer of the traditional type is a good example of a general-purpose computing system. A system of this kind is commonly required to carry out a wide variety of computing tasks. These may include executing special-purpose programs relating to business, commerce, science, statistics, etc, in addition to compiling and assembling new programs written by the users themselves. Users of large general-purpose computing systems communicate with the computer in a sophisticated and often complex way in order to specify the particular computation required.

Operator communication

Compared with general-purpose machines, dedicated computers are specialised and can perform only a very limited range of computing tasks. A microprocessor controlling a domestic appliance is an example of this. Because the range of computing activities is limited, the user normally has a restricted choice when specifying a particular computing task. The level of communication between the user and computer is therefore much lower than is the case with general-purpose systems. It is possible that with a computing system designed to perform only one specific task, the only intervention from the user is operation of the on–off switch. In other cases, selection of the desired computing function is by means of a simple front panel switch. It is not even necessary for the user to be aware that the system contains a computing device.

Peripheral devices

When a computer is dedicated to one or a few computing tasks, this restricts the range of peripheral devices to those associated with these tasks. This in turn means that the input and output facilities required in the computing system are defined very precisely. A general-purpose computing system on the other hand may need to be much more flexible. A wider range of peripheral devices may well be required to accommodate the many different computing activities. The peripheral devices may also change from time to time as the demands on the computing system change.

Program storage

Probably the single most significant difference between dedicated and general-purpose computing systems lies in the way the program is stored in memory. By definition, a truly dedicated system always executes the same program since its purpose in life is totally pre-determined. The program is therefore normally stored permanently in read-only memory (ROM). With a general-purpose computing system, some very fundamental programs concerned with the control of the system may be stored in ROM, but other programs are stored in a non-volatile secondary store such as a magnetic disk or tape memory. When it is required to execute a particular program, it is first transferred from the secondary store to the primary random-access memory (RAM). Because the programs run by a general-purpose computing system may be quite large, a primary RAM of substantial size is a common feature. The RAM requirement in dedicated systems by contrast is usually quite small, being restricted to the provision of a stack area and temporary storage of computed data.

System characteristics

The main characteristics of dedicated and general-purpose computing systems are summarised in Table 5.1. This table should not be regarded as a way of rigidly defining a system as being dedicated or general-purpose. Many systems are, in fact, operated in a way which is partly dedicated and partly general-purpose as we shall see when we consider some specific examples.

Table 5.1 *Computer system characteristics*

Dedicated	General-purpose
Single or very few fixed computing tasks	Many different computing tasks including execution of programs written by user
Program stored permanently in ROM	Programs stored in secondary memory and transferred to RAM before execution
RAM usually quite small	RAM relatively large
Fixed I/O facilities	Flexible I/O facilities
Low level of communication with user	High level of communication with user

Q5.1, 5.3

5.2 A microprocessor-controlled washing machine

A washing-machine controller is an example of a highly dedicated microprocessor system. Figure 5.1 shows a typical configuration in schematic form. In this system the computing function of the micro-processor is restricted to the generation of control signals to implement the different washing programs available with the machine. The user selects a particular washing program and the microprocessor then executes a stored program which generates the required

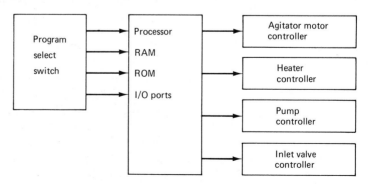

Figure 5.1 Washing-machine controller

sequence of control signals to activate the pump, agitator, heater, etc., at the appropriate times.

At first sight, it may appear from Figure 5.1 that a large number of input and output ports are required. In fact, the requirements are quite modest. The four outputs controlling the water pump, water inlet valve, agitator motor and heater are single lines carrying logic levels which implement on/off operation of these devices. These logic levels are used to activate relays or more sophisticated electronic power switches. A fifth output line could be provided if a high-speed spinning operation were required. The heater control is likely also to be of the simple on/off variety since the low precision required does not merit a sophisticated proportional temperature control system.

The number of input lines associated with the switches on the front panel will depend on the degree of choice of washing program offered to the user. If a choice of 16 programs is available, the output of the control switches could be converted into a 4-bit binary code. Since the accuracy required of the temperature control system is not high, a sophisticated temperature transducer is not necessary. One technique is to use one or more switches which close when the temperature reaches a predetermined value, thus causing a change in the logic level on one of the microprocessor input lines.

System characteristics

Analysing the computing demands made on the microprocessor in this system, we note that the program is fixed and also simple. This means that it will be stored in a ROM of modest size. A very small RAM will also be required to use as a stack and as a temporary store during the execution of the ROM-resident program. Since no complex calculations are required and since washing machines operate relatively slowly, it is likely that even the slowest microprocessor will be able to provide sufficient computing power. As we have seen, the microprocessor I/O requirements are also modest. Eight input and eight output lines would be more than adequate for the majority of controllers of this type.

Production costs

Low production cost is perhaps the single most important requirement of a microprocessor system used in consumer products such as washing machines. To be economically viable, the microprocessor-based system should be able to implement a given range of washing programs and cost less to produce than a controller based on, say, a motorised switch. The production volume of consumer products is normally high which means that development costs are likely to be less important than production costs. This is because the total development cost can be spread over a large number of units; thus the resulting contribution to the individual cost of the item is relatively small. Production costs do have a much greater and direct effect on the price of each item.

In the production of electronic systems, the cost is often largely determined by the number of integrated circuits in the system. This is because the area of the printed circuit board, size of power supply, assembly cost, etc., all depend on the number of integrated circuits. This establishes a clear link between the number of integrated circuits and the production cost of each system. The choice of microprocessor used in the washing-machine controller will be greatly influenced by the need to keep the integrated circuit count as low as possible.

Summary

Summarising the factors outlined above, it is apparent that a strong preference must be for a microprocessor system of modest performance containing the minimum number of integrated circuits. This points directly to the use of one of the so called 'single-chip' microprocessors such as the COP420L described in Chapter 2. The conclusion is not surprising since these single-chip devices are designed specifically for applications such as the washing-machine controller described here. They contain a central processor, ROM, RAM and I/O ports within one integrated circuit package. Programs are stored in ROM during the integrated circuit manufacturing process and the washing-machine manufacturer therefore buys 'customised' versions of the microprocessor. When buying single-chip microprocessors, the purchaser is required to pay a 'masking' charge which covers the cost of modifying the ROM so that it contains the purchaser's own program. Once this initial charge has been paid, the unit cost of each microprocessor is often very low. At the time of writing, the masking charge can be from around £500 upwards. Thereafter, the cost per device may be less than £2. This unit cost can be expected to decrease in the future. In 1979, the world market for single-chip microprocessors of the type described here was

Q5.5 estimated to be in excess of 50 million units.

The following list shows some of the wide range of single-chip microprocessors available at the time of writing:

Rockwell PPS – 4/1 family
Western Digital 1872/2272
Texas TMS1000 family
AMI S2000/S2150/S2200/S2300
National COP400 family
Oki MSM5840
NEC uCOM-42/43/44/45
NEC uPD75XX

The list includes only those devices which manipulate data 4 bits at a time. This results in a restricted performance but lower cost when compared with the more powerful 8-bit single-chip microprocessors. For applications such as the washing-machine controller, a 4-bit microprocessor provides more than adequate computing power.

For applications in which the production volume does not merit the use of a mask-programmed single-chip microprocessor, low cost alternatives exist. Microprocessors that incorporate erasable programmable read-only memory within a single chip are available. These offer the advantage of being programmable by the system designer although they cost considerably more than mask-programmed chips when purchased in large quantities. For small or medium quantities, the large masking charge for mask-programmed chips may make programmable devices a lower-cost alternative.

5.3   A word processor

Word processors are computing systems designed to manipulate data in the form of text characters. These text characters are the letters of the alphabet and the numbers 0–9 together with punctuation and other special characters such as £, $, @ , etc. The operator enters the text characters using a keyboard, similar to that of a typewriter. As they are entered, the characters are displayed on a video display screen. Once the text has been entered, the operator can then manipulate it in various ways by issuing commands via the keyboard. When the layout of the text is satisfactory a command from the keyboard causes it to be printed on a hard copy device.

Figure 5.2 shows an example of one form of text manipulation possible with a word processor. The first paragraph is a passage of text as entered by the operator. The second paragraph shows the

```
     This is a demonstration of the way a word processor can be
used to manipulate data in the form of text. The first paragraph
shows the text as it is entered from the keyboard by the operator
The second paragraph shows the text after the
execution of a right justify command. Note that the word
processor automatically retains the paragraph structure

     This is a demonstration of the way a word  processor   can  be
used to manipulate data in the form of text.  The first paragraph
shows the text as it is entered from the keyboard by the operator
The  second  paragraph  shows  the  text after  the execution of a
right  justify  command.   Note   that   the   word   processor
automatically retains the paragraph structure
```

Figure 5.2

same passage after the execution of a 'right justify' command. The spaces between words on each line are adjusted so that each line extends to the right hand margin thus giving a neater appearance to the finished text.

When the operator enters a text character in coded form via the keyboard, it is stored in an area of memory commonly called the text buffer. The video display shows the text stored in that part of the buffer currently being examined. Manipulating the displayed text therefore really involves the microprocessor manipulating the coded text characters in the text buffer area of memory. In the case of the 'right justify' command described above, the codes for the text characters are moved about in the text buffer by inserting additional 'space' codes between words.

Operating characteristics

Although the word processor could be said to have a single function only, that of manipulating textual data, it is less of a dedicated system than the washing-machine controller described in Section 5.1. This is because the number of different operations required is much greater than is the case with the washing machine. A particular, popular, word processor, for example, has a repertoire of over 90 commands available to the operator. This requires a much greater degree of control by the operator using a keyboard rather than the simple switch operation by the user of the washing machine. Perhaps a word processor could best be described as a semi-dedicated computing system.

Memory requirements

Figure 5.3 shows the major components of a word-processing system in schematic form. When comparing this system with the washing-machine controlled analysed in Section 5.1, we might note a much

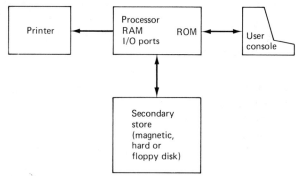

Q5.7   *Figure 5.3*   Word processor

greater size of RAM in the word processor. Each text character, consisting of a letter, number, punctuation mark, etc., is represented by a code occupying one 8-bit byte, normally stored in one memory location. The characters forming a single page of text might well require around 5,000 memory locations. It is not unreasonable to store this amount of data in RAM. However, for larger documents of perhaps several hundred pages, it becomes unrealistic to contemplate holding the whole of the coded text in RAM. In any case, only a limited amount of text can be viewed on the screen of the VDU at any one time. In most word-processing systems, an efficient secondary store, often a floppy disk system, is required. Disk secondary stores allow rapid transfer of large amounts of data to and from the primary RAM. The code for a limited amount of text, usually one page, is therefore held in primary RAM. When it is desired to examine a different page of text, the code is transferred from secondary memory to RAM. It should be noted here, however, that an excessive reliance on secondary storage can impair the performance of a word processor. Consider the situation in which an insertion is made near the beginning of a large passage of text part of which is in RAM with the remainder stored on a floppy disk. The whole of the text following the insertion will need rearranging. This involves manipulation which can only be performed on the text in RAM. The procedure will therefore involve many transfers of blocks of text between RAM and the floppy disk, the number of such transfers depending on the maximum size of the block of text held in RAM at any one time. If this block size is too small, the time spent in transferring text to and from disk may be unacceptable to the user.

Also stored in RAM will be the program that interprets the commands issued via the keyboard and modifies the text in the required manner. This is a major program which will itself occupy a substantial area of memory. To complete the software, a disk operating system program is also required. A disk operating program organises the transfer of data between primary and secondary memory. At least part of the disk operating system program is normally in RAM at all times.

A satisfactory word-processing system of modest capability can be implemented using one of the popular 8-bit microprocessors such as the 8080, Z80 or 6800. The size of RAM would normally lie in the range 32–64K. Since these 8-bit microprocessors have 16-line address busses, the maximum number of memory locations which can be directly addressed is 64K. For the more sophisticated word processor, this limit will be inadequate, pointing to the use of a powerful microprocessor such as the 8086, Z8000 or 68000 families, all of which have the ability to directly address a larger area of memory than the 8-bit devices. With a memory management support device, the Z8001 can, for example, address 8 Mbytes of memory, which may offer significant advantages for fast response.

Q5.6

Peripheral devices

From the description of the operations performed by a word processor it is evident that the type of I/O device is predetermined. The operator obviously needs to communicate with the processor and normally uses a keyboard input device for this purpose. The processor communicates with the user by displaying text and other messages using a video display screen as an output device. Finally, the word processor is usually required to produce a hard copy output for which a printer is required. Printers that produce an output of the quality required for, say, business correspondence are expensive items; this may contribute significantly to the overall system cost.

Development costs

Although a manufacturer producing a word processor would hope to sell a substantial number of systems, the production volume is unlikely to match that of the microprocessor-controlled washing machine described in Section 5.1. Development costs can therefore be expected to contribute significantly to the final selling price of the system. In any case the selling price is likely to be at least an order of magnitude greater than that of the washing machine.

Currently, the cost of a word processor varies between several thousand and several tens of thousands of pounds. Of this selling price, a significant proportion is related to the non-electronic parts such as disk drives, printer, etc. A further significant proportion will relate to the cost of developing the programs for the system. It is not unusual for software development costs to contribute well over 50% of the total cost of development.

From this discussion it can be seen that the factors affecting the final selling price of the word processor differ from those relating to the microprocessor-controlled washing machine. In the case of the word processor the designer does not have the very high priority of reducing chip count to a minimum, although good design practice would imply this wherever possible. On the other hand, it is very important that the word-processor software should be efficient and reliable with development costs as low as possible.

The above analysis is correct at the time of writing. There are many indicators, however, that the potential market for word-processing equipment is very large indeed. Many people believe that the conventional typewriter will become extinct, replaced by small, powerful word processors with printers attached. When this happens, the pressures on designers of word processors will direct their efforts along the same lines as the washing-machine designer. Chip counts will be sharply reduced and a much greater emphasis will be placed on production costs as opposed to development costs. Similar pressures apply to the designers of the mechanical and electromechanical parts of a word-processing system. We may note as an example of this that, over the last few years, the number of printers sold has risen rapidly with a corresponding sharp fall in the cost.

Component count

The number of integrated circuits in a typical word-processing system lies in the range 100–300, depending on the size of RAM. Average chip count figures such as these will tend to decrease in the future. This is the result of trends, which have now been underway for several years, for manufacturers to produce specialised integrated circuits for applications such as word processing. One of these specialised integrated circuits can often replace a substantial number of the more general types. The other continuing trend is for manufacturers to pack more and more components into each integrated circuit, thus reducing the total number of integrated circuits required to perform a given function.

5.4   A microprocessor development system

Microprocessor development systems were originally devised as tools to assist engineers designing hardware and software for microprocessor-based systems. A team developing a microprocessor-controlled washing, for example, might reasonably expect to have access to a development system supporting the particular microprocessor used. The software support provided should assist the rapid and economical design and debugging of programs for the chosen microprocessor. Support may also be provided for hardware development in the form of 'in-circuit emulation' which is described in detail in later chapters.

Some microprocessor development systems are referred to as 'universal', which in practice means that they can support several different microprocessors. Other systems, usually produced by the microprocessor manufacturer, can support only one such device. In this section, we shall concentrate on an analysis of microprocessor development systems that support only one microprocessor, leaving a discussion of universal types until later.

Memory requirements

Unlike a word processor, which is required to run only the program associated with its text-manipulating function, a microprocessor development system will normally be required to run a wide range of different programs. These will include software support packages in addition to programs devised by the user for the system being developed. Many of these programs are of substantial size and do not normally reside in RAM. For this reason, an efficient and rapid-access secondary store is a necessity in a comprehensive microprocessor development system. As with the word-processing system described in Section 5.3, the secondary memory is a magnetic disk store in the vast majority of systems. The most popular of these is the floppy disk of either 8 or $5\frac{1}{4}$ inches diameter. The provision of secondary storage of this kind implies the need for a disk operating system to allow convenient exchange of data and programs between the disk and primary RAM. This will also provide the user with the convenience of being able to organise programs and data as named files stored on the disk.

To support the disk operating system and the various other activities of a microprocessor development system, a primary RAM of substantial size is required. Typical development systems currently operate with between 32 and 64 Kbytes of RAM. This is substantial in the context of microprocessor systems. In the case of, say, a large mainframe computer, a RAM of this size would be regarded as quite modest.

Peripheral devices

Figure 5.4 shows the components of a typical microprocessor development system in schematic form. The system includes a video display terminal or console with a keyboard which allows the user to communicate with the central processor. A printer is necessary to provide a 'hard copy' of program listings, etc., although the user may accept a print quality which is not as high as that produced by a word processor. In addition to these standard peripherals, the role of the system in supporting hardware and software development may

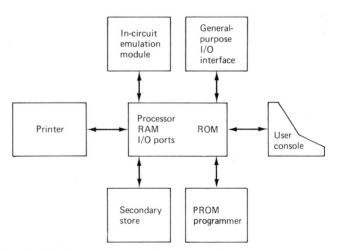

Figure 5.4 Microprocessor development system

require other more specialised peripheral devices. A PROM programmer and 'in-circuit-emulator' (ICE) commonly form part of a microprocessor development system. The function of these sub-systems is described in Chapter 7.

Component count

The total number of integrated circuits used in a microprocessor development will be relatively high, probably several hundreds. The substantial RAM requirement contributes to this. In addition, a variety of special facilities such as in-circuit emulation. PROM programming and general-purpose serial/parallel interfaces will involve additional circuitry. Associated with the substantial integrated circuit count and special-purpose circuitry is a relatively high development cost for the system. Compared with consumer products or even moderately successful word processors, production quantities of microprocessor development systems are likely to be relatively low. The high development costs for this type of system are therefore reflected directly in its selling price.

Support software

The usefulness of a microprocessor development system is highly dependent on the quality of the support software supplied with the system. This support software (described in more detail in Chapter 8) will include at least an editor/assembler/debugger package. Other facilities may include interpreters or compilers for one or more high-level languages such as BASIC, PASCAL, etc. Programs will also be provided to support any special hardware features such as in-circuit emulation or PROM programming.

Since some, if not all, of the software supplied with the micro-processor development system is written specifically for the system, the cost of software development will significantly affect the selling price. This again results from the relatively small production numbers.

System costs

A typical microprocessor development system is that produced by Zilog to support their Z80 microprocessor. Facilities include 64 Kbytes of RAM and a secondary store consisting of two 8-inch floppy disk drives. The system allows in-circuit emulation of the Z80 micro-processor and is also provided with general-purpose serial and parallel input/output interfaces. A wide variety of video display terminals can be used with the system.

A count of the number of integrated circuits in the Zilog system reveals approximately 250 in the central processor, RAM and secondary memory controller. Included in this number are the in-circuit emulator and serial/parallel interfaces. Excluded are integrated circuits in the video display terminal and printer which might total between 30 and 100, depending on the complexity of these items of equipment.

At the time of writing, a development system of this type would cost approximately £10,000. In general, microprocessor development systems can vary from less than £5,000, for software support only, to an upper limit in excess of £30,000 for a sophisticated system with full in-circuit emulation capability and powerful support software.

Choice of microprocessor

The central processor in a microprocessor development system of the type described here is normally the same microprocessor as that supported by the system. Thus a development system designed to support engineers working, say, with Intel 8080 microprocessors would itself normally contain an 8080 as the processor. This is not a rigid rule, however, since it is possible to produce machine code for an 8080 microprocessor using a different type of computer by means of programs called cross-assemblers and cross-compilers. It is even possible to run and debug programs written for the 8080 on a different computer using a special program which causes the computer to simulate the behaviour of the 8080. If only one micro-processor is supported by the system, however, it is usually more convenient to assemble, run and debug programs using the micro-

Q5.2, 5.4, 5.8   processor for which the programs have been written.

Questions

5.1 State whether the following systems could be described as dedicated, semi-dedicated or general-purpose:

(a) A computer used for calculating wages and controlling stock in a large firm.

(b) A computer-aided diagnosis system used by a doctor.

(c) A computer-controlled point-of-sale terminal (cash register).

(d) A video game in an amusement arcade.

5.2 For the following systems, state, with reasons, which would be the more important, development or production costs:

(a) A dedicated microprocessor system controlling a large machine-tool system of which only three are to be manufactured.

(b) A hand-held personal microcomputer capable of running simple BASIC programs.

    (c) A microprocessor controlling the fuel system to a jet aircraft engine which has expected sales of 5,000 units over a 20-year period.

5.3 Explain how a dedicated computing system differs from a general-purpose system in the way the program is stored.

5.4 How does the number of integrated circuits in a typical dedicated computing system compare with the number in a typical general-purpose system?

5.5 Explain what is meant by the term 'masking charge' relating to a single-chip microcomputer.

5.6 Explain why a word processor requires a large RAM if it is to operate efficiently.

5.7 Sketch a block diagram showing the component units of a typical word-processing system.

5.8 Explain how development costs affect the selling price of a micro-processor system:
    (a) When only a few systems are to be made.
    (b) When a large number are to be produced.

Chapter 6 **Planning microprocessor systems**

Objectives of this chapter   *When you have completed studying this chapter you should be able to:*

1   Show, by means of a flow diagram, the typical stages of a system design/development programme.

2   Understand that an accurate system specification is an important prerequisite for successful microprocessor system design.

3   Derive a system specification from end-user requirements in a typical case.

4   Choose the most cost-effective method of solving a typical design problem where two or more alternatives exist.

5   Analyse the procedure for partitioning the system tasks between hardware and software.

6.1   Design and development

This chapter is concerned with the planning of design and development programmes for systems that incorporate one or more microprocessors. Careful planning should, of course, be a feature of all engineering design and development programmes. The incorporation of any sort of computer in a system, however, brings with it special planning problems over and above those expected for other electronic systems.

In an electronic system not involving a microprocessor, two main features affect the performance. The first is the choice of components – resistors, capacitors, integrated circuits, etc. The second is the circuit describing the way these components are interconnected. These features remain just as important when the system includes a microprocessor. An additional factor now affects the way the system behaves however. This is the stored program executed by the microprocessor. In a dedicated microprocessor system the program is stored in read-only memory (ROM) and is referred to as firmware. With more versatile, general-purpose systems, the program is transferred to random-access memory (RAM) when execution is required. It would then be called software. We shall use the term software to mean either software or firmware in this chapter.

In conventional electronic systems, the circuit configuration and choice of components are interdependent. Changing the circuit configuration may well involve a different choice of components and *vice versa*. When developing a microprocessor-based system, three interdependent factors must be considered. These are:

1 The choice of components.
2 The circuit and system configuration.
3 The software.

Changing any one of these is likely to involve changes in the other two. The additional complication of software in a microprocessor-based system makes the planning of the design/development programme particularly important. Making correct decisions at the planning stage can vitally affect development and production costs. The extent to which the finished system meets the required specification will also depend on planning decisions.

Q6.1

6.2 Stages in development

Figure 6.1 shows the various stages in the development of a microprocessor-based product from the initial definition to manufacture. It will be seen that some hardware and software development can take place in parallel. For final testing and debugging, however, it is necessary to bring together hardware and software. The reader should appreciate that the flowchart shown in Figure 6.1 presents a somewhat idealised picture of most development programmes. In a practical programme, iterations or repetitions of various stages are often necessary. When the hardware and software are brought together, for example, design faults in either may come to light for the first time. At worst this could lead to fundamental revisions in the specification of hardware or software, or both. Proper attention to the planning of the development programme will do much to avoid situations of this kind.

Q6.3

6.3 System specification

In order to plan a development programme it is important to have available an accurate and unambiguous specification of the product or system being developed. In the first instance, this will consist of the product definition or external specification. This external specification defines the system outputs and behaviour for all possible inputs. As the name implies, it is a description of the system viewed externally. The behaviour expected when inputs fall outside the normal limits should also be defined.

Microprocessors operating as controlling devices often implement sequential operations. The microprocessor-based control of washing-machine programmes described in Chapter 4 is a good example of this. Sequential behaviour must also be defined in the

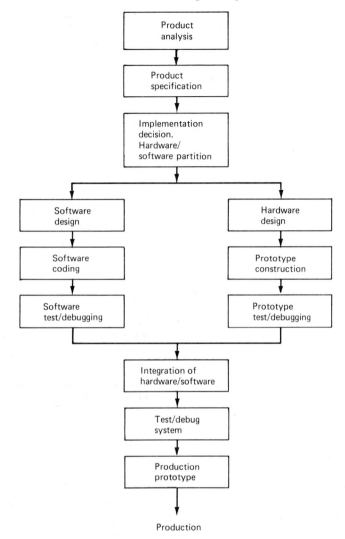

Q6.2 *Figure 6.1* Stages in microprocessor system development program

specification of the system. For this purpose, flowcharts often provide the most effective form of description.

Consider, as an example, a requirement for a small data logging system. The logger is required to sample the temperature at four measuring points once every hour and print the resulting measurements. Figure 6.2 shows the system viewed externally with no internal details of the microprocessor system itself. The specification for the system is shown below.

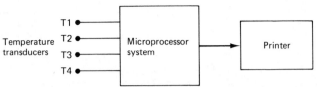

Figure 6.2   Temperature logging system schematic

Data Logging Specifications

Number of measuring points	4
Measured variable	Temperature
Normal limits:	
T1	85–110°C
T2	0–220°C
T3	50–150°C
T4	50–150°C
Maximum absolute error	± 2 degC
Maximum full-scale incremental error	± 1 degC
Resolution	1 degC
Sampling rate per channel	1 sample/hr
Maximum short-term sample time error	0.1 s/hr
Maximum long-term sample time error	1 s/day
Power source (mains) frequency	50 Hz

```
DAY 1              09.00 HR

TEMPERATURES
T1 = 105 DEGREES
T2 =  16 DEGREES
T3 = 102 DEGREES
T4 =  56 DEGREES


DAY 1              10.00 HR

TEMPERATURES
T1 = 111 DEGREES
T2 =  18 DEGREES
T3 = 155 DEGREES
T4 =  60 DEGREES


!WARNING! T1 OUTSIDE LIMITS
!WARNING! T3 OUTSIDE LIMITS
```

Figure 6.3   Temperature logger print output format

It will be seen from the specification that the temperatures are to be printed with an error message included if the value falls outside the normal range. Figure 6.3 shows the format for the printed output.

From the external specification shown above some of the internal features of the logger can be established immediately. For example, one or more analogue-to-digital converters (ADCs) will be required to change the analogue output from temperature transducers to digital form. The system specification also allows us to establish certain parameters relating to the particular ADCs to be used. We note initially that a temperature resolution of 1 degC is required. This is important since it implies that the ADC output must contain at least 8 bits as shown below.

The resolution of a measuring system is the smallest detectable change in output. For the data logger, this means that the printed output is required to register changes as low as 1 degC. Since the maximum temperature variation expected at any measuring point is 220 degC, the system must resolve 1 in 220. An 8-bit binary word can represent numbers 0–255 and this number of bits therefore provides adequate resolution.

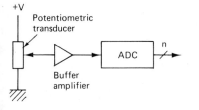

Figure 6.4 Digital measurement of shaft angular position

Worked example

A precision potentiometric transducer is used in a microprocessor system to measure the angular position of a shaft. The output of the transducer provides the input to an ADC as shown in Figure 5.4. The maximum total angular rotation of the shaft is 200° and the system in which the transducer is used requires a resolution of 0.5°. If the ADC output is in binary form, estimate the minimum number of bits required.

Solution   Resolution is 0.5° in a total travel of 200°, i.e. 1 in 400. The output of the ADC must therefore contain a minimum of 9 bits since the largest unsigned 8-bit binary number is 255 which does not give sufficient resolution. The largest 9-bits unsigned binary number is 511 which is adequate for the purpose.

Other parameters such as the accuracy of the temperature transducer/ADC combination can also be specified at this point. In the main, however, initial decisions must be made concerning the system configuration before the majority of system elements can be specified.

Q6.4, 6.5

6.4   Measures of cost-effectiveness

When considering the way in which a design/development programme is carried through, one should realise that it is very seldom that a designer can find only one solution to a problem of implementation. In most cases, the designer must choose one of several strategies, each of which, when implemented, is capable of satisfying the system specification. Faced with this situation and assuming that the various possibilities all meet the required performance criteria, the designer must realistically base his choice on the question of cost.

An estimate of the cost of implementing a particular design strategy should take into account all factors that will affect the selling price of the manufactured product or system. This will involve design, development, production and component cost. The contribution made by design and development to the selling price of the final product depends, of course, on the total number produced. Excluding profit, we can estimate the cost per unit as

$$\text{Cost} = C + P + (D/N)$$

where C is the total component cost per unit, P the production cost per unit, D the total cost of design/development programme and N the number of items produced.

The cost of developing software must be included in the total cost of

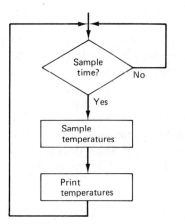

Figure 6.5 Initial flowchart for temperature logger

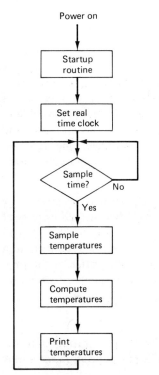

Figure 6.6 Expanded flowchart for temperature logger

the design/development programme. It is not unusual for software development costs to exceed 50% of the total design/development budget and figures of 80–90% are by no means impossible.

An example of the way the cost of two alternative designs is estimated is given in Section 6.8. The accuracy of cost estimations will depend on the skill and expertise of the project planners in the judgement of the time and facilities required to develop hardware and software. Inexperience almost always results in an underestimate of hardware and software development costs, often by a very wide margin.

6.5 The system flowchart

We have said in Section 6.3 that a flowchart is often the most suitable method of describing the sequential type of operation characteristic of many microprocessor-controlled systems. In fact, a number of flowcharts will be constructed during the planning of the development programme. The amount of detail in these flowcharts will increase as the proposed system design emerges.

A flowchart that describes the behaviour, viewed externally, of the data logger introduced in Section 6.3 is shown in Figure 6.5. This flowchart is expanded in Figure 6.6 to include more detail. In Figure 6.6 certain previously undefined features of the system are identified. We note for example that the digital temperature measurements taken in from the ADC must be processed before they are suitable for presenting to a printer to produce the required data message. The amount and nature of this processing of data may well effect the choice of hardware components such as the type of microprocessor used.

Another feature of Figure 6.6 that does not appear in Figure 6.5 relates to the start-up procedures. Figure 6.6 recognises that at some stage power is switched on and the system must then start operating in the desired fashion. The logger can be described as a 'real time' system because the times at which the temperatures are sampled are recorded. To synchronise the microprocessor internal timing system, whatever it is, with 'real time', some way of setting this internal clock is required. The fact is recognised in Figure 6.6. Although these start-up or initialisation procedures are not described further at this point, other examples are given later in the text which expand the methods used in greater detail.

6.6 Initial hardware decisions

At this stage in the development program, initial decisions are made relating to the selection of the electronic devices to be used in the system. The microprocessor itself, peripheral devices and interface components are all initially specified at this point. As with the system flowchart described in Section 6.5, this is an evolutionary process with components being considered and possibly discarded later. The system flowchart will also expand to incorporate more detail as the behaviour of the chosen system components is clarified. This phase of the development program necessarily goes hand in hand with a consideration of the hardware/software partition discussed in the next section. As we have said in Section 6.1, hardware choices affect software and *vice versa*.

Figure 6.7 shows how the internal configuration of the system might first be specified during this stage. Only those components related to I/O operations are shown in Figure 6.7. Memory in the form of RAM and ROM will obviously be necessary, in addition to the components

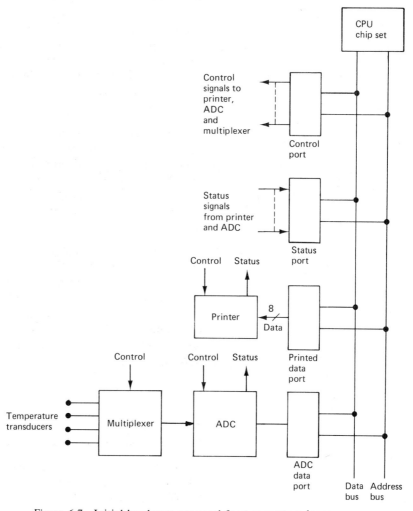

Figure 6.7 Initial hardware proposal for temperature logger

shown. The system shown in Figure 6.7 uses one ADC with a multiplexer to allow the four temperature transducers to be sampled in turn. An obvious alternative to this scheme is to use one ADC for each temperature transducer. In producing a system diagram such as Figure 6.7, the designer has made certain decisions regarding system components. An experienced designer would have analysed the costs associated with the two alternatives in coming to a decision to use a single ADC with a multiplexer rather than four ADCs. An example of the way decisions such as this are reached is given in Section 6.7.

One important decision involving both hardware and software is the choice of microprocessor. Many factors are involved in this, including the amount of processing of logged data required. This subject is discussed in detail in Chapters 2 and 3. Perhaps more important than the choice of microprocessor is the decision as to whether or not to become involved in the design of circuitry associated with the CPU. The alternative to designing this hardware is to employ an off-the-shelf single-board computer. These boards come in various configurations but normally include the microprocessor, ROM or EPROM, RAM together with I/O ports on a printed circuit board.

In terms of component cost, the single-board computer is more expensive than its constituent parts. The saving on hardware development and production costs is, however, very significant. Particularly when production numbers are not large, a single-board computer can provide an economical and time-saving alternative to designing and developing a special-purpose CPU circuit. Figure 6.8 shows the configuration of a typical single-board computer in block diagram form. This is the SBC100 which is based on the Z80 microprocessor.

The single-board computer will include I/O ports for transferring digital data to and from the CPU. Where the system is designed from scratch, the I/O port components must be chosen by the designer. For simple 8-bit systems, a parallel digital output interface may consist of little more than an address decoder together with an 8-bit latch such as the 74LS373. Input ports can similarly be implemented with an address decoder and a set of three-state or open-collector buffers. Where more comprehensive I/O facilities are required, it may be more economical to use a special-purpose programmable interface device.

6.7 Partitioning of hardware and software

The system flowchart describes a variety of operations which must take place in a given sequence. In many cases, the designer can choose whether a particular operation is implemented by specially designed hardware or by the execution of a section of program by the micro-

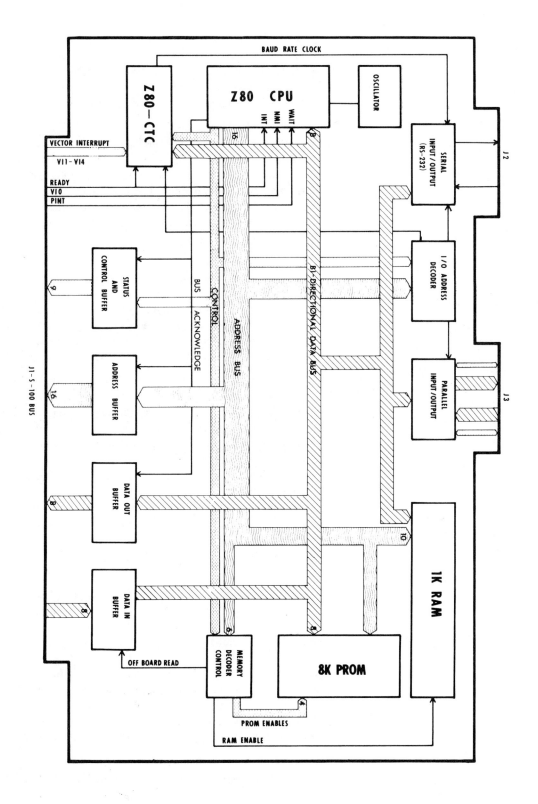

Figure 6.8 General configuration of SBC100 single-board computer

processor. Some operations allow no choice. The printing of results, for example, is obviously carried out by hardware consisting of the printer. The initial system flowcharts describe only the operations to be performed with no indication as to how they are performed. The flowchart can therefore describe a sequence of hardware operations, a computer program or a combination of both.

As with other design/development decisions, the two major factors in the hardware/software partition choice are performance and cost. The required speed of operation is important when considering performance. A given operation can almost always be performed more rapidly with special-purpose hardware than is possible with a program executed by a microprocessor. The designer may therefore be forced to employ hardware solutions for time-critical design problems.

As an example of the type of hardware/software choice in a practical situation, consider the timing of the data logging operation in the system introduced in Section 6.3. It will be recalled that temperatures are sampled and printed at intervals of one hour. Some means must be established therefore for fixing the time at which this logging operation takes place. Three possible methods are as follows:

1   Write a program that is executed in the interval between logging operations and generates exactly the required time delay.
2   Use a highly stable oscillator, normally crystal-controlled, whose output is sampled by the microprocessor or generates an interrupt. A program then counts cycles until the required time delay has occurred.
3   Use a highly stable oscillator with a frequency divider giving an output pulse every hour. After each logging operation, the output of the frequency divider is scanned until the next timing pulse is detected. Alternatively, the frequency-divider output can be used to generate an interrupt.

The approach varies from the totally software solution of (1) to the mainly hardware technique used in (3). The highly stable oscillator used in approach (2) and (3) is referred to as a 'real time clock'. A fourth alternative is to use the real time clock technique based on the mains supply frequency rather than the output of a crystal controlled oscillator. The short-term timing accuracy is reduced compared with the crystal-controlled oscillator method but would still meet the specification. The long-term accuracy of the mains supply frequency is very good and more than adequate for this purpose. Any one of the proposed solutions can satisfy the timing accuracy requirement. It is therefore the designer's task to choose the method that makes the smallest contribution to the cost of each system produced.

In terms of cost, the decision with regard to hardware or software timing of the interval between logging operations is probably not too

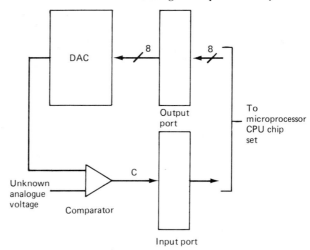

Figure 6.9 Analogue-to-digital conversion using DAC

important. This is because the required operation is relatively simple and implementation by hardware or software is a fairly cheap exercise. It does, however, provide a useful demonstration of the factors relating to hardware/software trade-off.

As a further example of the hardware/software decisions required we shall consider the implementation of AD conversion. In the data logging system, only four AD conversions are required every hour. The conversion speed is not critical. The designer therefore has the choice of using an off-the-shelf ADC module or connecting together a set of component parts. In the latter case, the microprocessor can be programmed to perform some parts of the AD conversion operation. Figure 6.9 shows the hardware for a scheme of this type. The scheme shown in Figure 6.9 results in long AD conversion times and is therefore not suitable when high-speed operation is required. In this case, no such restriction exists. Figure 6.10 shows the use of an off-the-shelf ADC module. The reason the system of Figure 6.9 might be preferred to that of Figure 6.10 in some cases is that Figure 6.9 may well have a lower component cost than Figure 6.10.

The AD conversion scheme shown in Figure 6.9 makes use of a low-cost DAC. The output of the DAC is compared with the unknown voltage using a comparator which is again a low-cost item. To perform the AD conversion, the microprocessor adjusts the input to the DAC until its output matches the unknown voltage. The digital input to the DAC is then a representation of the unknown analogue voltage.

The method by which the ADC input is adjusted until the two comparator inputs are equal depends on the program used to implement the conversion. A flowchart describing one possible

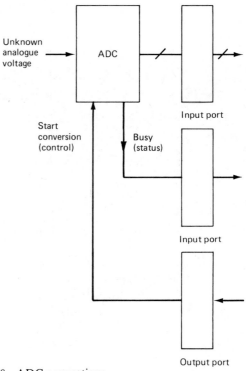

Figure 6.10 ADC connections

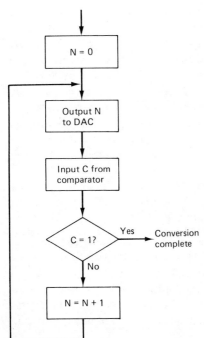

Figure 6.11 Simple counting algorithm for analogue-to-digital conversion

method is shown in Figure 6.11. This flowchart assumes that the comparator output changes from 0 to 1 when the input from the DAC becomes greater than the unknown voltage. The well known successive-approximation algorithm is more elegant and gives a faster conversion on average at the expense of greater program complexity. This is probably not justified in this case since the speed of the simple counting algorithm shown in Figure 6.11 is more than adequate for the proposed application.

When choosing between two alternative techniques, the total number of systems being produced is a crucial factor. This is discussed quantitatively in Section 6.4. The following worked example applies this quantitative approach to an analysis of the costs involved in the two methods of AD conversion.

6.8 Worked example

The leader of a design team is attempting to decide whether AD conversion is to be implemented:

1 Using an off-the-shelf ADC as shown in Figure 6.10; or
2 By means of a DAC and comparator as shown in Figure 6.9.

An initial estimate of components and software for each of the two schemes is made as follows

	Scheme 1	*Scheme 2*
Components	ADC + 1 IC	4 ICs
	Total cost £30	Total cost £8
Software	5 instructions	40 instructions
	occupying 8 bytes	occupying 60 bytes
	of memory	of memory

The firm concerned bases hardware design and production costs, excluding components, on the number of ICs or other modules used. Software design cost is based on the number of instructions. Software production cost is fixed by the number of memory locations occupied by the program. These costs are shown below:

Hardware design	£20 per IC or other module such as an ADC
Hardware production	£2 per IC
Software design	£5 per instruction
Software production	1p per byte

Calculate the cost of an ADC unit in each case when implemented by Scheme 1 and Scheme 2 for production runs of *(a)* 5 units and *(b)* 25 units.

Calculate the volume of production for which the cost of implementing AD conversion by Scheme 1 and Scheme 2 is approximately equal.

Solution

Let D be the total design cost, P the production cost per unit, C the component cost per unit and N the number of units produced. Then

$$\text{Cost per unit} = P + C + (D/N)$$

Scheme 1

Hardware design cost $= 2 \times £20 = £40$
Software design cost $= 5 \times £5 = £25$
Therefore $D = £40 + £25 = £65$
$\qquad C = £35$
Hardware production cost per unit $= 2 \times £2 = £4$
Software production cost per unit $= 8 \times 1p = £0.08$
Therefore $P = £4.08$
For 5 units the cost per unit is therefore

$$£4.08 + £30 + (£65/5) = £47.08$$

and for 25 units the cost per unit is therefore

$$£4.08 + £30 + (£65/25) = £36.68$$

Scheme 2

Hardware design cost $= 4 \times £20 = £80$

Software design cost $= 40 \times £5 = £200$

Therefore $D = £80 + £200 = £280$

$$C = £8$$

Hardware production cost per unit $= 4 \times £2 = £8$

Software production cost per unit $= 40 \times 1p = £0.40$

Therefore $P = £8.40$

For 5 units the cost per unit is therefore

$$£8.40 + £8 + (£280/5) = £72.40$$

and for 25 units the cost per unit is therefore

$$£8.40 + £8 + (£280/25) = £27.60$$

To determine the 'break even' production run:

$$£4.08 + £30 + (£65/N) = £8.40 + £8 + (£280/N)$$

Rearranging

$$£34.08 - £16.40 = (£280 - £65)/N$$

Therefore

$$N = (280 - 65)/(34.08 - 16.40)$$
$$= 12.16$$

It can be seen from this analysis that unless the number of systems produced is greater than 12, the low component cost of Scheme 2 does not compensate for the much higher design/development cost. The reader should not assume that cost figures used in this example are necessarily typical of actual component cost at any given point in time. Prices of such items as ADCs and DACs change as manufacturing technology advances. The long-term trend is for hardware component costs to decrease and design/development costs to increase, particularly for software. This reflects the labour-intensive nature of software design. The reader may care to speculate on the effect of this long-term trend on design decisions such as that considered in the above example.

Q6.6, 6.7

Questions

6.1 When developing a digital system which does not include a microprocessor, two important considerations are the choice of components and the design of the associated circuit. What additional factor must be considered when developing a microprocessor-based digital system?

6.2 Describe, by means of a flowchart, the various stages in the design/development cycle of a typical microprocessor-based system.

6.3 Explain why some parts of a microprocessor system's hardware cannot be tested separately from the associated software.

6.4 The output of a pressure transducer is a voltage which must be digitised by means of an ADC. The pressure varies between 0 and 100 N/m^2 and the user requires a resolution of 0.25 N/m^2. Calculate the minimum number of bits in the ADC output to give this resolution.

6.5 The input to an ADC varies between 0 and 10 V. Calculate the resolution in volts if the converter output is a 12-bit binary number.

6.6 A microprocessor system design specifies the use of a particular type of address decoder for which a suitable integrated circuit is available. It can also be implemented using separate logic gates, in which case three integrated circuits will be needed. The firm concerned estimates the cost of designing digital hardware as £30 per integrated circuit and the cost of production (excluding components) as £1 per integrated circuit. Component costs are as follows:

Single integrated circuit	£5
Circuit using separate gates	£2

Calculate the level of production at which the design involving separate gates becomes more cost-effective than the single integrated circuit.

6.7 A microcomputer system can be implemented in two ways, A and B, involving differing hardware and software costs as shown below:

	A, £	*B*, £
Hardware design/development cost	5,000	1,000
Hardware production cost per system (including components)	200	100
Software design/development cost	10,000	20,000
Software production cost/system	20	40

Calculate the number of systems that must be produced before B becomes more cost-effective than A.

Chapter 7 Microprocessor development systems

Objectives of this chapter. *When you have completed studying this chapter you should be able to:*

1 *Appreciate that a microprocessor development system is used in the following stages of a microprocessor system design/development cycle:*
   (a) Development and writing of the system program.
   (b) Testing of the system program.
   (c) Modification of the program where necessary.
   (d) Simulation/emulation of the system to integrate hardware and software.
2 *Appreciate that typical facilities within a development system can be:*
   (a) An operating program consisting of: operating system and monitor; editor; assembler; debugger; PROM programmer; loader; linker; locator; software trace.
   (b) Memory: for applications program development; for the operating system; for non-volatile bulk storage.
   (c) Console consisting of a VDT and keyboard together with a printer.
   (d) PROM programmer.
   (e) I/O facilities.
   (f) In-circuit emulator.

7.1 Hardware and software development

In Chapter 6 we considered the way that initial design decisions are made when developing a microprocessor system. Before proceeding to study the methods used in later stages of hardware and software design, it is useful to investigate the tools available to us. The most important of these tools, the microprocessor development system or MDS, has already been introduced briefly in Chapter 5. We shall now consider the facilities provided by a typical MDS in more detail.

The name 'Microprocessor development system' is used to describe a collection of items of equipment, i.e. hardware, and programs, i.e. software, which together provide the user with facilities which assist the design and development of microprocessor systems. Development systems of this kind vary greatly in complexity and cost depending on the facilities they offer. One essential feature however is some sort of computer which may be a microprocessor but could also be a minicomputer or even a large mainframe computer, shared with other users.

As we have seen in Chapter 6, to develop a microprocessor system requires the design of two components: hardware and software. Figure 6.1 shows that at least part of these hardware and software design processes can continue in parallel. A complete MDS will assist the design of both hardware and software and is particularly useful in the part of the development that involves the bringing together of these two elements. The term 'development system' is also sometimes used to describe a system that supports only the design and development of software. A name such as 'software development station' is, however, more appropriate in this case. However, whether we are using a software development station or a full-scale MDS, it should provide facilities to assist the writing, testing and modification of programs for the system being developed.

7.2   The development system configuration

The component parts of a typical MDS are described in Section 5.4 and Figure 5.4. For completeness, system components are again listed here. A typical full-scale development system will consist of:

1   A CPU with I/O interfaces to the other system components.
2   RAM to store applications programs developed by the user and support programs such as assemblers, compilers, etc., which are employed by the user. This type of data store is referred to as primary memory.
3   A bulk secondary store. This will be non-volatile and is most usually some form of magnetic disk system. It is used as a filing system to hold user and support programs when they are not required for execution. To execute a program, it must be transferred from secondary memory to primary RAM.
4   A console which will normally comprise a video display terminal (VDT) with a screen and typewriter-type keyboard. This is the means by which the user communicates with the development system and *vice versa*.
5   A printer to provide a permanent record of programs and data.

The facilities listed up to this point are essentially those of a software development station. A full-scale MDS would also include the following:

6   A unit that permits data or program code to be permanently stored in programmable read-only memory (PROM) chips. In practice, the programmer usually programs erasable PROMs (EPROMs) since these devices are more convenient for development purposes.

7   An in-circuit emulator (ICE). This is a very important unit for assisting hardware development and hardware/software integration. Its functions are described in Section 7.5.

8   Non-dedicated or 'spare' I/O ports. They may be employed by the user to attach any special-purpose peripheral devices required. These I/O ports may, for example, be used with peripheral devices from the system being developed, i.e. the 'target' system, to test I/O programs.

The components listed above constitute the MDS hardware. As with any computing system, however, this is only part of the story. Less **Q7.1–7.3**   visible is the other part of the system – the support software.

7.3   Support software

In this section we discuss programs that are provided for the user to assist him in developing other programs. The quality and extent of support software is usually more important than the hardware when choosing an MDS. This does not mean that it is not important to have well designed and reliable hardware. It is the support software, however, that governs the speed and ease with which the user can develop programs. Even components of the MDS that are provided to solve hardware problems, e.g. the in-circuit emulator, are dependent on the controlling support software.

Support software normally comes in the form of a number of separate programs or 'software packages', each of which has a well defined function. In the following sections we identify some of the standard software packages that will be provided with an MDS.

The operating system

As explained earlier, support for program development provided by a software development station or MDS will consist of a variety of different software packages. These will include an assembler, editor, monitor/debugger, compiler, etc. The software packages will be normally held in secondary memory such as a floppy disk store. When a particular package, such as an editor, is required, it must be transferred from secondary store to the primary RAM. Programs and data created by the user must also be transferred from primary to secondary store and *vice versa*.

To organise this transfer of data and programs between primary and secondary store, the software development station will be provided with an operating system. This system, sometimes called a disk operating system (DOS) is itself a program. It acts as an interface between the user and the development system hardware/software facilities. The user can issue commands to the operating system via the input keyboard. Messages from the operating system to the user are displayed on the screen of the system display console.

The text editor

To support both assembly and high-level language program development, some form of text editor is required. A text editor (or simply editor) is a program that allows the user to enter coded text into the system memory via the system keyboard. Once it has been entered, the text can be manipulated in various ways by operations such as deleting and inserting lines and characters. The stored text is viewed using the system VDT or printer. In a system that includes a secondary store the editor will allow commands to write coded text from RAM to a file in the secondary store and read from a secondary store file into RAM. This allows passages of text to be saved and recalled at will. Although we are describing the use of an editor to prepare high-level or assembly language programs, any text can be manipulated in the same way. The editor could be regarded as a primitive word processor.

Many would regard the text editor as the most important component of support software since it is the primary tool with which the programmer enters or modifies program code. The speed with which program modifications can be made obviously directly affects the productivity of a programmer and hence program development cost. Programmers will normally spend more time working with the text editor than with any other software support package, with the possible exception of the debugger.

Text editors are encountered in two forms. The more traditional kind operates in a line mode. In this case, the editor program maintains a pointer which identifies a current location in the coded text. This pointer can be moved about the text by issuing commands via the system console keyboard. A typical command of this kind is 'Move' which is implemented by typing 'nM' where 'n' is the number of character positions the pointer is to be moved. To clarify this, suppose that the character pointer is positioned as shown by the arrow in the line of text shown below:

```
THIS IS A XX FAULTY LINE
   ↑
```

Note that the pointer is always positioned between two character positions and that spaces must also be regarded as characters. To move the pointer to the beginning of the xx character pair, the command '8M' is entered which moves it 8 positions forward. The pointer is then positioned as shown below:

```
THIS IS A XX FAULTY LINE
          ↑
```

Another command 'nD' can then be entered to delete 'n' characters, starting at the pointer. In this case, the command 10D deletes 10 (decimal) characters leaving the line and character pointer as shown below:

```
THIS IS A LINE
             ↑
```

The example here is intended to give the reader a feel for the way a line editor is used. Obviously, the form of commands will differ with different editors. The commands described here are typical examples. Other commands allow the user to insert and change character strings. Some editors also allow blocks of text to be moved about.

Although some programmers can become highly skilled in the use of a line editor of the kind described above, there is no doubt that it is a relatively slow and tedious method of text manipulation. Virtually all of the newer microprocessor development systems will offer an alternative and superior type of editor based on the use of a controlled cursor. The cursor is usually in the form of a flashing or blinking line under a character position on the console video display as shown below:

THIS IS A XX FAULTY LINE
⎯⎯⎯⎯ Flashing cursor

Commands for inserting and deleting text are often similar to those of the line editor described above. The main advantages of the controlled cursor however are that its position is always immediately visible and it can be easily moved about the screen. Special keys are normally provided on the console keyboard for moving the cursor around the screen. Four such keys allowing up, down, right and left movement is the usual arrangement.

Q7.5, 7.6 To allow the use of a controlled-cursor type of text editor requires the availability of a special type of VDT. The most important feature of such a display device is that it must accept cursor-control signals from the computer system to which it is attached. These cursor-control signals are generated by the editor program in response to the commands issued by the user via the keyboard. The more simple type of VDT will not have this cursor-control capability and does not therefore allow the use of a controlled-cursor type editor.

The assembler

Assembly language and the characteristics of typical assemblers are discussed in detail in Chapter 1. In this section we shall remind the reader of the particular features of an assembler which are important to the designer of software for microprocessor systems. All assemblers offer the basic capability of converting text in the form of mnemonic instructions into machine code. An assembler which offered only this facility, however, would today be regarded as being of very limited use.

In Chapter 8 we shall see that, for a variety of reasons, modern program design methods require that large programs should be designed in the form of several sections or modules. These modules are then linked together to form the complete program. To do this conveniently with assembly language program requires a special assembler which can operate in conjunction with another software package called a linker. Linkers are discussed in the next section. Assemblers that allow module linkage almost always allow the production of relocatable programs. Relocatable programs are discussed in Chapter 1 and require the use of yet another special software package called a locator or relocator. Locators are described below. In many systems, the functions of the linker and locator are combined in a single software package.

Even if the bulk of software is to be written in a high-level language, it is still important to have an efficient assembler available when designing microprocessor systems. This is because it is almost always necessary to resort to assembly language for programs which interact directly with system hardware. Suppose, for example, you are designing a system whose main function is that of stock control. No experienced programmer would sensibly contemplate writing a stock control program using assembly language since it would be hopelessly uneconomic in the use of programming time compared with a high-level language. At some stage, however, the system must take in and put out data from and to the outside world. The input device may be a keyboard or VDT and the output device may well be a printer.

For programs that control and communicate with peripheral devices such as keyboards and printers, assembly language may well be the only possible choice. The suggested stock control system programs would therefore be implemented most efficiently using a high-level language with assembly-language-generated machine-code sections inserted wherever peripheral control is required. It is important therefore that MDS software should allow the implementation of 'hybrid' programs of this type.

Linkers

In Chapter 1 and the previous section, the importance of modular programming methods has been introduced. The linker is a software package that works with the assembler in making program module linking more convenient. Among other facilities, an efficient linker/assembler combination allows the declaration of labels as 'global'. This means that these labels can be used and have the same meaning in all linked modules. Thus, data created in one module can be used in another module. It is possible to write programs in modular form without a linker but the process is much less convenient.

Linkers sometimes operate at source program level which means that the original source code of the various modules is modified to produce a single linked program. It is more common for the linkage to take place at object-code level. If this is the case, the assembler will assemble the various source program modules separately, storing the resulting object-code modules in separate disk files. The linker then combines these object programs, making any modifications necessary to form the single linked object program.

Locators

As we have seen in Chapter 1, many assemblers allow a program to be declared as either absolute or relocatable. With a relocatable program, the position at which object code is to be stored in memory is not specified in the source program. Instead, the decision is deferred until the location (or relocation) process takes place. The locator program allows the user to enter the starting address of a relocatable program. Modifications are then made by the locator to the program object code to ensure that it will run successfully at the specified location. The procedure is described in more detail in Chapter 1.

Q7.7–7.9

High-level language

The alternative to assembly language is a high-level language such as PASCAL, CORAL, BASIC, etc. A single statement in one of these high-level languages converts into many machine-code instructions. This can effectively increase the productivity of the programmer. For this reason, high-level languages should be employed in preference to assembly language wherever possible.

A program that converts a sequence of high-level language statements such as

$$X = Y + Z$$

into a sequence of machine-code instructions which can be subsequently executed is called a compiler. Another type of high-level language to machine code translator is an interpreter. When writing programs for dedicated target systems, a compiled rather than an interpreted high-level language is normally necessary. This is because the internal operation of an interpreter usually differs from that of a compiler in such a way that it is unsuitable for producing machine-code programs which can be stored in ROM. There are ways of overcoming this, but it is normally more convenient to use a compiled rather than an interpreted high-level language.

The monitor/debugger

Facilities for program debugging are a fundamental requirement in any system that allows the user to create his own programs. This is true even when the computer is as simple as a microprocessor evaluation system with input/output restricted to a hexadecimal keyboard and display. Users of such systems will be familiar with the monitor which is often the only system software provided. With the assistance of a monitor, the user can enter the hexadecimal code for machine-code instructions which are then stored in memory. Commands entered via the hexadecimal keyboard allow breakpoints to be entered in a program and programs to be executed continuously or one instruction at a time. With these facilities, the user can debug simple programs.

Software development stations and MDSs usually provide monitor/debugging facilities which are rather more comprehensive than those described above. Commands entered via the system keyboard allow the usual capability of viewing and changing the contents of memory locations or working registers, program execution, single-step execution, etc. In addition it is normally possible to load data or programs into RAM from the secondary store by entering the appropriate command. Data or programs can similarly be written from RAM into a file held in the secondary store. The facilities offered by a typical monitor/debugger in a disk-based system are shown below. This particular monitor is called DDT (Dynamic Debugging Tool) and operates on 8080 programs. It is part of a set of software packages available with the popular CP/M disk operating system. The list of commands is not intended to serve as an instruction manual but is included to give the reader an idea of the facilities available with a typical disk-based monitor.

DDT commands

A (Assemble) Command 'As' directs DDT to start assembling mnemonic instructions and store the resulting machine instruction codes starting at the hexadecimal address 's'. After entering the command via the keyboard, DDT will prompt the user for the first mnemonic instruction, e.g. entering A1000 followed by MOV E,A will cause the code 5F to be stored in location 1000.

D (Display) Command 'D' allows the contents of memory to be viewed. There are three forms of the command:

D   memory contents are displayed from the current display address and continued for 16 display lines;

Ds   similar to 'D' but the area of memory displayed starts at location 's';

Ds,f   similar to 'Ds' but the area of memory displayed terminates at location 'f'.

F (Fill)   Command 'F' fills an area of memory with the same given number in every location. The general form is:

'Fs,f,c' where 's' is the starting address, 'f' the finishing address and 'c' the number to be stored. For example, entering F1000,1500,FF causes all locations between 1000 and 1500 to be filled with the number FF.

G (Go)   Command 'G' causes execution of a program to start. The general form has various options:

G   start execution at the current value of the program counter;
Gs   start execution with the program counter set to 's';
Gs,b   similar to 'Gs', but with a program breakpoint at location 'b';
Gs,b,c similar to 'Gs,b', but with a second breakpoint at location 'c';
G,b   start execution at the current value of the program counter with a breakpoint at 'b';
G,b,c   similar to 'G,b' with a second breakpoint at 'c'.

For example, G1000,1020 causes execution to start from 1000 with a breakpoint at 1020 and G,1000,1020 causes execution to start from the current value of the program counter with breakpoints set at 1000 and 1020.

L (List)   Command 'L' causes machine-code instructions in memory to be converted back to the corresponding mnemonics which are then displayed. This process is known as disassembly. The command comes in three forms:

L   display twelve lines of disassembled mnemonic instructions, starting at the current list address;
Ls   similar to 'L' with the list address set to 's';
Ls,f   similar to 'Ls' with disassembly terminating at location 'f'.

For example, suppose the contents of locations 1000–1004 are as follows:

Location	Contents
1000	FE
1001	FF
1002	D2
1003	00
1004	15

The command L1000,1000 would result in the following display

```
1000    CPI  FF
1002    JNC  15 00
```

M (Move)   Command 'M' causes a block of data to be moved from one area of memory to another. The general form is:

Ms,f,d   move the block of data contained in memory locations 's' to 'f' to an area starting at address 'd'.

For example, M1000,1FFF,3000 causes the contents of addresses 1000–1FFF to be copied in locations 3000–3FFF.

S (Set)   Command 'S' allows the contents of individual memory locations to be examined and changed if required.

Ss   the contents of location 's' are displayed. Entering a data byte overwrites the existing data in 's'. Entering a carriate return leaves the data unchanged. In either case, the contents of the next higher address are displayed in a similar fashion. Entering a full stop (.) terminates the command.

T (Trace)   Command 'T' causes execution of a program and displays the contents of all registers after each instruction is executed. The command allows two forms:

T   the current contents of all registers are displayed and one instruction is executed. This command allows single stepping through a program;

Tn   similar to 'T' but the trace operation continues for 'n' (hexadecimal) steps.

U (Untrace)   Command 'U' is identical to 'T' except that intermediate program steps are not displayed.

E (Examine)   Command 'E' allows the contents of the microprocessor registers to be displayed. The user also has the option of selectively changing the contents of registers. The command has two forms:

X   the contents of registers A,BC,DE,HL,S,P and F are displayed;

Xr   the contents of register 'r' are displayed. The user then has the option of entering new data via the keyboard.

For example KA followed by 3F causes register A to be loaded with 3F.

Other commands are I (input) and R (read) which interact with the operating system (CP/M).

7.4   Cross-software

When an organisation is setting up a facility to support the design and development of microprocessor-based systems, two options are available. One is to purchase hardware in the form of one or more MDSs specifically to support the particular microprocessors to be used. The other option is to use a powerful minicomputer or mainframe computer, which may already be available, with the assistance of special programs which go under the collective title of cross-software.

Cross-assemblers

We have described the function of an assembler as essentially to convert a program written in the microprocessor manufacturer's mnemonics to binary machine code. This is a data conversion process that can be performed by any computer given an appropriate program. When the computer performing the mnemonic-to-machine-code conversion is not of the same type in which the machine code will be executed, the process is called cross-assembly. With a suitable range of cross-assemblers, a programmer can write programs for a variety of microprocessors using only one computer.

Q7.10, 7.11

Simulators and emulators

The concept, implementation and use of a cross-assembler is little different to that of an assembler. Assembly of the machine-code program is, however, not the end of the programming process since the program must be tested and debugged. This presents a problem if a machine-code program for one computer is produced by a cross-assembler running on a different computer. We could, for example, use a PDP11 minicomputer with a cross-assembler to generate a machine-code program for a M6800 microprocessor. The M6800 machine-code program could not be immediately executed by the PDP11, however, since machine code for an M6800 is in no way identical to that for a PDP11.

To be absolutely certain that an M6800 machine-code program is correct, it must run and produce the correct results on an M6800. One way of partially overcoming this problem without resorting to the purchase of special M6800 hardware is to use a program called a simulator or emulator. The simulator or emulator will normally run on the same computer as the cross-assembler. It allows this computer to run programs for other processors such as the M6800. With the help of a simulator, a PDP11 can effectively 'pretend' to be an M6800, for example, and execute M6800 machine-code instructions.

The use of one computer that can support software development for a whole range of microprocessors is an attractive idea. There are problems inherent in this approach, however. These are concerned with program debugging and the use of simulators. Simulation of a microprocessor by another computer is not usually possible in real time. This means that executing a machine-code instruction for, say, an 8080 on a minicomputer which is simulating an 8080 will generally take longer than the same instruction executed by a real 8080. Any sections of a program that are time-critical cannot therefore be tested in this way.

Simulators also present problems when testing and debugging programs which are hardware-dependent. Routines involving I/O operations are an obvious example. For this type of program, there is little alternative to dedicated hardware involving the actual circuit for which the program is written.

In spite of the difficulties, the use of cross-software is a viable method of developing programs for microprocessor-based systems and is employed successfully by many design teams. The best way of using the technique is to generate machine-code programs using a cross-assembler. These programs are then transferred, either by down-loading or via EPROMs, to a dedicated hardware system for testing and debugging. The dedicated hardware system can be relatively simple and inexpensive in this case.

7.5 Hardware support facilities

Up to now, this chapter has concentrated on the facilities provided by an MDS to assist the design and development of software. It is right and proper that these software facilities should take pride of place since it is the production of programs that absorbs a major part of the development budget for most systems. However, support for hardware development is also important, and a true MDS should provide this.

When considering the support facilities available for microprocessor-based hardware, it is important to realise that much of the hardware can only be fully tested with the help of software. We can only test memory, for example, by writing data in and reading data out. The most natural way of doing this is to use the memory with a computer which performs these operations and checks the result. The facilities provided by an MDS should allow this sort of testing to be done quickly and conveniently.

In-circuit emulators (ICE)

An in-circuit emulator is probably the single most useful device for testing microprocessor-based circuits and for testing software which is directly concerned with the operation of hardware. Externally, the

ICE facility is seen as a multiway lead emerging from the main body of the MDS. The lead terminates in a header plug which has the same pin configuration as the microprocessor being emulated. To make use of the emulator, the user removes the microprocessor chip from its socket in the system under development and inserts the header plug in its place. The MDS is now called the 'host' and the system being developed is called the 'target'.

When the ICE is active, the host system generates on the pins of the probe header, exactly those signals which would be present on the pins of an operational microprocessor chip. When programs are executed in the host system, it appears to the target system that the program is being executed by a resident microprocessor. The difference is, of course, that the host system has full control of the program with all of the facilities offered by its debug/monitor program. Breakpoints can be inserted, registers examined, single-step execution implemented, etc. Even though the program is executed in the host system, however, signals are produced in the target system hardware which will, for example, implement input or output operations. This allows I/O circuits to be tested easily. Many ICEs allow timing of the computation to be controlled by either the host clock or the target clock. The non-viability of a target clock waveform can be detected by this since the computation will not proceed if this clock waveform is outside the required specification.

Memory substitution is the other major facility offered by an ICE. With memory substitution, addresses and control/status signals associated with memory read and write operations can be directed either to the target system or the host system. The user can therefore select a particular area of memory to be resident in the host or the target system. Using this facility, the user could, for example, run a program which is stored in area 2000–3000, say, in the host system, manipulating data which is stored in area 4000–5000 in the target system. Alternatively, the program could be stored in the target system with the host system storing data. This facility has obvious uses in checking the viability of memory in the target system.

When combined with an EPROM programmer as described in the next section, memory substitution can be of great assistance in the logical testing of system software in conjunction with hardware. This is most useful in the rather difficult phase of development which involves bringing together hardware and software which have been developed separately. When completing this part of the development cycle, it is common to operate the target system with a program running partially in the host system and partially in the target system.

The PROM programmer

An MDS is often used to assist the development of target systems in which the software is to be resident in some form of ROM. In the development of such systems, some form of ROM which can be programmed by the user is commonly employed. When the development is complete, the PROM can be replaced by a mask-programmed device.

In view of this need to support ROM-based systems, it is not surprising that most MDSs also include a method of programming some type of PROM. At the time of writing, by far the most common provision is a programmer for the ultra-violet erasable PROMs or EPROMs such as the 2708, 2716, 2732 range. Appendix N includes a data sheet for the 2716.

To clarify the function of an EPROM programmer, we shall describe briefly a typical hardware/software development cycle. After the planning phase, hardware/software partitions have been fixed and hardware and software design continues in parallel. Software is designed using a modular structure for the program. The hardware is designed and a prototype constructed. We now come to the point at which hardware and software are brought together. First, the hardware/software combination is tested using the ICE with memory substitution allowing the program to be stored entirely in the host system. Individual program modules are then tested. When a program module appears to be correct, the code is transferred to EPROM by means of the EPROM programmer.

The area of memory containing the module code in EPROM is then allocated to the target system. At this stage therefore, the program is stored partly in the host system and partly in the target system. As each program module tests out correctly, it is programmed into the EPROM. Bit by bit the program is therefore transferred from the host to the target system. Eventually, the program is completely contained in EPROM in the target system. At this point the ICE probe header is removed from the microprocessor socket in the host system and the microprocessor chip re-inserted. The target system should then be free-standing and independent of the MDS.

References and bibliography

7.1   B. E. Gladstone, 'Comparing microcomputer development systems', *Computer Design*, pp 83–90 (February 1979).
7.2   'Microcomputers, part 2: the development system', *Digital Design*, Vol. 8(1).

Questions

7.1   List the hardware components of a typical MDS.

7.2   What is the distinction between a software development station and a full-scale MDS?

7.3 What is the function of the secondary store in an MDS?

7.4 List the individual packages in the support software provided with a typical MDS.

7.5 Explain the function of a text editor.

7.6 What is the distinction between a line editor and a cursor-controlled editor? Which of these types of editor is normally regarded as the more convenient?

7.7 Explain the difference between absolute and relocatable assembly language programs.

7.8 Explain the difference between an assembly language pseudo-op and an executable instruction.

7.9 With the help of the Z80 instruction set given in Appendix D, state which of the following are pseudo-ops and which represent executable instructions:

```
PSECT
OUTD
RETI
EJECT
```

7.10 Explain the difference between an assembler and a cross-assembler.

7.11 What are the disadvantages of using a cross-assembler rather than an assembler for developing program for dedicated microprocessor systems?

Chapter 8 Software design methods

Objectives of this chapter *When you have completed studying this chapter you should be able to:*

1 Analyse the following stages in developing software for microprocessor systems as:
 (a) Development of the program flowchart.
 (b) Writing of the program.
 (c) Testing of the program.
 (d) Modification where necessary.
2 Describe the top-down, structured approach to the design of computer programs.

8.1 The importance of good software design methods

In Chapter 6 we have said that software typically absorbs over 50% of the total design/development budget for a microprocessor system. Indeed, it is not unusual for software to account for as much as 80–90% of the total development cost. Keeping software development costs down is therefore a highly effective way of producing a low-cost system. Writing, testing, debugging and documenting computer programs is by its very nature a labour-intensive procedure and therefore the key to reducing software costs is to improve the efficiency of the programmer. This means the adoption of methods that improve the ability of a programmer to generate as many lines of high-quality program code as possible in a given period of time. The methods advocated in this chapter have been developed with this aim in view.

Q8.1

Having emphasised the role of programmer productivity in keeping down system development costs, we now turn to the question of software quality. Poor-quality software can have a major influence on the extent to which the system meets the required specification. System reliability may also often be affected by poor-quality software. To the novice programmer, the concept of software quality is perhaps a little difficult to understand. In Section 8.2 therefore we discuss the characteristics of good-quality software.

The quality of a program depends, of course, on the basic ability of the programmer. Perhaps more important than this however is the method of approach adopted by the programmer. Beginners and those without formal training tend to adopt an intuitive approach which almost always results in a poor program. Good, formal program design methods, although sometimes tedious, are the only sure way of producing high-quality software.

8.2   Program characteristics

Section 8.1 introduced the concept of software quality. This would seem to imply that it is possible to identify certain characteristics which distinguish a high-quality program from one of low quality. Before going on to describe techniques for designing high-quality programs, it would therefore seem reasonable to define these desirable characteristics. As one might expect, there is some divergence of opinion among software designers as far as the desirability or otherwise of certain program features. Equally, there is general agreement concerning at least four features that are regarded as essential in a good program. These features are listed below.

(a) The program should be correct in that it meets the required specification. This feature must obviously take precedence over all others since a program that does not perform the specified computation is obviously of little use. To be absolutely sure that a program is correct does, however, imply that an accurate and unambiguous specification is available against which the performance of the program can be checked.

(b) The program should be adaptable and easily maintained.   Both of these requirements imply that modifications may be made to the program without the need for major structural changes. The importance of program maintenance is discussed in Section 8.3.

(c) The program should be well documented.   This goes hand in hand with *(b)* since it is very difficult to imagine a program that can be modified easily and is not at the same time well documented. It is important for the programmer to realise that he is not producing documentation solely or even mainly for his own benefit. More often than not, the task of modification falls on a programmer who is not the original author of the program.

(d) The program should be robust.   This means that it should be able to tolerate situations resulting from error conditions or simple mistakes by the operator. Consider a program that scans the switches of a control panel and implements a control operation. A robust program of this kind can cope with a situation in which the control switches are operated in an unexpected and perhaps incorrect manner as a result of human error. The program should be able to identify this as human error and maintain the safety and integrity of the

controlled system. Wherever possible, the program should communicate meaningful error messages to the operator. Thus, if a VDT is part of the system console, operation of the control panel in an unacceptable way should result in the display of an understand-able error message.

Q8.2

8.3 Program testing and maintenance

Many readers will be surprised by the idea that computer programs may need maintenance. This does not imply that a program can wear out in the sense that a mechanical system such as a car wears out. Program maintenance is usually required because very few, if any, software packages are totally error-free when they are first issued to the user. Repeatedly running a large program will reveal these hidden errors, which must then be corrected. It is this correction of initial program errors that is usually referred to as maintenance. The fact that large programs almost always contain undetected errors does not mean that all such programs have been written by incompetent programmers. Undoubtedly, a bad programmer will write programs containing more undetected errors than will a good programmer. It is a fact of life, however, that a large and complex program will contain undetected errors even when written by a good programmer. The main reason for this lies in the practical impossibility of exhaustively testing most large programs. If we assume that the purpose of a program is to start with some input data which is then processed to produce output data, a few simple calculations will illustrate the testing problem.

Consider a program designed to multiply two 16-bit binary numbers to give a 32-bit result. Now to be absolutely sure that the program contains no errors, it should be tested with every conceivable combination of input data which it might encounter when it is put into use. In this case, exhaustive testing should involve all possible pairs of 16-bit binary numbers. This requires a total of four thousand, two hundred and ninety-five million separate tests. If it is possible to make one test each second, the total test procedure would require over 136 years to complete. The program described is relatively simple. To exhaustively test a program of even moderate complexity can easily take many millions of years. This is an example of a programming difficulty that only becomes really visible when writing larger programs. With a small amount of practice, even a novice programmer can write programs of say ten or twenty instructions without error. It may even be possible to test small programs exhaustively. The impossibility of exhaustive testing of large programs has two implications for the program writer. Firstly, programs should be designed and implemented using formal methods which are known to minimise the occurrence of errors.

Secondly, programs should be organised in such a way that modification and the correction of errors is a straightforward procedure.

Another activity that is often described as maintenance is the modification of a program to make it more efficient or perhaps to provide additional facilities. This may be required even in the case of a dedicated system. Consider a consumer item such as the microprocessor-controlled washing machine described in Chapter 5. It is common for manufacturers of such products to periodically update them by providing additional features. In this case, it might be the inclusion of additional washing programs. This would, of course, be implemented by modifying the control program stored in ROM. Although this is perhaps a rather special case, it does emphasise the importance of designing software in such a way that it is easily maintained.

Q8.4

8.4   Large and small programs

In this section our main object is to emphasise the difference in approach required when we move from writing small programs to writing programs with a more practical application, which are usually much larger. In particular we wish to emphasise that the process of writing down a sequence of instructions constitutes an activity called program coding. Program coding is not the only, or even the most important, part of program writing.

The student of microprocessor software for engineering applications often starts by learning how to write simple programs in machine code. This can be a useful approach since it leads to a good understanding of the architecture and instruction set of the particular microprocessor used for programming exercises. However, it does have one disadvantage. The student may assume that program coding and program design are one and the same thing. This is because, for short programs, the program can often be produced by immediately writing down a sequence of machine-code instructions. Slightly longer programs, perhaps involving loops, may involve the use of a flowchart.

It is possible to become highly skilled at producing short programs in this informal manner. Some program writers become so familiar with a microprocessor instruction set and typical programming problems that they can write down a sequence of machine-code mnemonics directly from the program specification. Others take pleasure in programming tricks by which instructions employed in unusual or non-standard ways are used to reduce program memory space occupancy or allow the program to execute more rapidly. This is usually an unnecessary and undesirable practice.

The major difference between programs used as exercises during the learning process and programs designed for real engineering applications is usually that of size. It would be unusual for the program running in a microcomputer controlling an engineering system to consist of less than several hundred instructions. Several thousand instructions would be more typical. Attempting to produce large programs of this kind using *ad hoc* methods is to invite disaster. A proper approach to the design of program structure is absolutely essential. Programs of, say, twenty instructions can be written successfully with a casual approach to program planning. This is not the case for a program of one thousand instructions. Even small programs benefit from a formal approach to planning.

The ultimate object of any program design exercise is to generate a sequence of machine-code instructions which can be executed by the microprocessor concerned. This is true whatever programming language is used since the microprocessor operates fundamentally at machine-code level. Whatever language is used, however, program coding is a small and relatively minor part of the total program design procedure. The design of the program structure and completion of program documentation are both far more important and demanding tasks for the programmer. As a result, in the production of a successful and well designed program, much more time is devoted to planning and documentation than is occupied by the coding of the final program. In general, the more time spent on planning and documentation of a program, the less time is required for debugging and maintenance. Figure 8.1 shows how the total time spent developing a program is distributed between the various activities in a typical case (see Ref. 8.1).

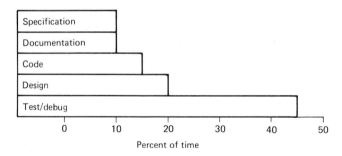

Figure 8.1 Percentage of time taken up by various activities during a typical
Q8.3 program development. Program maintenance is not included

8.5 Modular programs

When considering how large and complex microprocessor programs should be written, engineers often find it helpful to consider the analogous hardware design situation. Suppose, for example, that a design is required for a very special discrete component amplifier. It is estimated that the final circuit will contain, say, 40 transistors. One approach is to start from scratch, design the whole circuit, build it, switch on and hope that it meets the specification. When testing reveals that it does not, the design engineer commences debugging the circuit which means that he modifies it, hopefully to effect an improvement. The alternative approach is to examine the specification and decide on the number of stages of amplification required. The gains and other characteristics of each stage can then be specified. After this, the first stage is designed and constructed. It is then tested and modified if necessary until it meets the required specification. The second stage is designed and tested in the same way. When both stages meet their specifications, they are connected together and the two-stage combination is tested. Proceeding in this way, the amplifier is designed and tested stage-by-stage until the whole system is functioning in accordance with the specification. Engineers with any experience at all will recognise this approach as likely to produce a better design in a shorter time than the previous design method.

In the second design procedure for the amplifier outlined above, the overall design task is split down into a number of sub-tasks. These involve the design and testing of sub-sections of the amplifier. An important characteristic of the sub-sections is that they can be designed and tested independently. The relatively simple design problems associated with the individual stages of the amplifier can be handled with much more ease and confidence than is the case with a single, very large and complex circuit. This same principle of modularity should be applied to the writing of large computer programs, although the analogy should not be pushed too far. Modularisation is perhaps the single most important design technique for large programs.

The final program is visualised as being split into a number of sub-programs or program modules. Ideally, each module should consist of a sub-program that is totally independent of any other program module. This means that it can be written, tested and debugged in isolation in a way which does not depend on the correctness of another program module. In this way, inter-related program errors can be avoided. Total independence of program modules, although obviously desirable, cannot always be achieved completely. One difficulty is that some program modules will involve the processing of data generated by other modules. This can sometimes be overcome by testing the module with 'dummy' data generated with a specially written test program although this raises in turn the problem of interdependence between the testing program and the program being tested.

Some advantages of the modular approach to programming are as follows:

1   With modular methods, the time required to complete a large program is more or less linearly related to the number of instructions in the finished program. This means that a program of 4,000 instructions would take roughly twice as long to write as a program of 2,000 instructions. If no attempt is made to split the program into sub-programs, the time taken to complete a 4,000 instruction program can easily be much more than double that required for the 2,000 instruction program.

2   Most program errors can be isolated within single modules. This means that detection of errors is easier. Correction of errors often only affects the module in which the error occurs. This greatly assists program modification and maintenance.

3   Modules can be used many times in the same program. They can also be used in other programs.

4   Modular programs allow programming teams to be used more easily. Individual team members can be allocated different modules to develop.

Although modular methods of programming have many advantages and represent the only sensible way of writing large programs, it should be recognised that some penalties are involved and some special disciplines are required. Some of these are as follows:

a   The function of individual modules must be specified very precisely. A module may use data generated by one or more different modules. Its output data may in turn be used as inputs to yet other different modules. This implies that the formats of input and output data must be carefully defined, particularly if different modules are being developed by different members of a program development team. Many would regard this feature as an advantage rather than a disadvantage.

b   It may be necessary to write special programs to test modules.

c   Careful and comprehensive documentation is required for program modules. This discipline is not confined to modular programs. All programs should be adequately documented, whatever design methods are used.

d   Modular programs may require more memory space and execute more slowly than programs in non-modular form. This is not often a major disadvantage and is usually more than outweighed by the advantages of modularisation.

Q8.5

8.6   Decomposition

Having by now, hopefully, persuaded the reader that a modular approach is the only sensible way to design programs, we now consider the way in which the program modules are defined. The object of this part of the programming procedure is to specify a set of

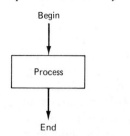

Figure 8.2 Symbolic description of computing process

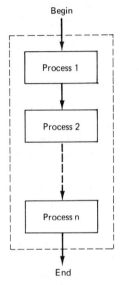

Figure 8.3 Linked computing process

modules that can be linked together to form a complete program to satisfy the required specification. One way of describing this in symbolic terms is to say that we are replacing the single computing process shown in Figure 8.2 by the linked processes shown in Figure 8.3. Each of the linked processes is implemented by a program module.

An important feature of program modules linked to form a complete program is that each module should have only one entry point and one exit point. The main reason for this is that debugging is assisted unmeasurably if it is known unequivocally that a particular junction between two processes can be reached by only one route through the program. The alternative to this results in the so-called *rats' nest* style of program in which no limit is placed on the number of module entry and exit points. The resulting multiple interlocking program loops will be familiar nightmares to readers who have used this method.

The procedure of defining the modules making up a complete program is known as *decomposition* and is normally carried out stage by stage. To describe the technique we shall start with a simple example. A program is required that starts with a list of 20 numbers stored in memory, finds the smallest number and multiplies it by a scaling constant. Figure 8.4 shows a symbolic description of the program. The data the program uses is the list of numbers and the scaling constant. The data the program generates is, of course, the smallest number in the list multiplied by the scaling constant. The picture of the program as a single block is called the Level 1 description.

Now suppose that we wish to write the program in assembly language for an 8-bit microprocessor such as the 8080, Z80 or 6800. Anyone with any programming experience will be aware that the program divides naturally into two well defined parts. The first part examines each number in the list to find the smallest. The second part multiplies this number by the scaling constant. Figure 8.5 shows this in symbolic form.

In Figure 8.5 we are defining 3 program modules. The Level 1 module makes use of two Level 2 modules. Alternatively we could say that the Level 1 module decomposes into two Level 2 modules. This does not eliminate the need for the Level 1 module, but it changes its nature dramatically. The Level 1 module can now consist of a simple program to link the two Level 2 modules.

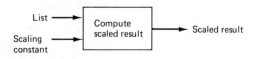

Figure 8.4   Level 1 description

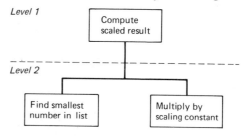

Figure 8.5 Level 2 decomposition

After splitting the total programming task by defining program modules as shown in Figures 8.4 and 8.5, the modules themselves can be broken down further if necessary. This process continues until the module specifications are simple enough to be implemented by sub-programs of manageable size. The reader might well enquire at this point as to how we might know when a program not yet written is of manageable size. The number of lines of program a programmer regards as manageable depends on the individual and his experience. Most programmers find modules of less than 50 assembly language instructions to be an acceptable size. The Level 2 modules defined in Figure 8.5 meet this criterion.

As an example of decomposition beyond Level 2, let us suppose that the program specification used in the above example has been modified. The program is still required to search through the list to find the smallest number N. Computation of the result now involves making the following calculation:

$$\text{Result} = (N + K)/(KN - 2)$$

where K is the scaling constant. This calculation is a good deal more complex than the simple multiplication of the previous example. Division is now also involved.

Figure 8.6 shows how the new specification leads to a further level of

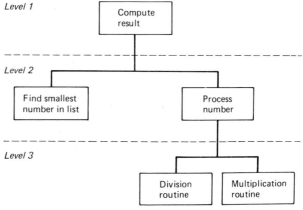

Figure 8.6 Level 3 decomposition

decomposition. The calculation of the result is now done by a 'process number' module which makes use of the lower-level multiplication and division modules. When a program is being defined in the form of linked modules, the program designer must estimate the number of instructions required to implement the various modules in order to determine whether the decomposition procedure has gone far enough. Experience will play a major part in this. Should a miscalculation be made and it becomes evident that a particular module involves a program module larger than can be handled conveniently, it is a straightforward matter to go back to the module definition and

Q8.9   break it down further.

8.7   Top-down methods

The process of decomposition leaves the program designer with a collection of boxes, each of which identifies a program module. If the designer has done his job properly, the particular computation implemented by each program module will be accurately defined. This is the point therefore at which the problem of designing individual program modules must be approached. As a first step we might consider which program module should be designed first. If the task is approached in a methodical way, there are two possibilities. The first takes the design of the lowest-level modules first and is called the bottom-up approach. The alternative method starts with the highest-level module and is called the top-down approach. Of the two methods, the top-down approach is favoured by most program designers and is the one advocated here.

In the case of assembly language programs, the most convenient form for program modules is that of a subroutine. Whatever form is used for the program modules, however, there will be many situations in which it is necessary to pass data from one module to another. With assembly language this is normally done by the data-generating program module placing it in one of the microprocessor registers or in a dedicated memory location before implementing the subroutine call, return or jump instruction to the data-receiving module.

An important part of the program design procedure is to define exactly how the data transfers described above will take place. Both the format of data and the means by which it is to be transferred should be clearly defined and specified in the program documentation. The need for planning of this kind is sometimes described as a disadvantage of the modular approach to programming. Others would see it more realistically as a desirable discipline which should be exercised whatever program design method is used.

One of the major disadvantages of the top-down approach is the difficulty of testing a module fully if it depends on results computed by a lower-level module. Consider the decomposition shown in Figure 8.6. Writing 'process number' routine will involve calls to multiplication and division subroutines. How, therefore, can we test the program before these multiplication and division subroutines have themselves been written? The normal method is to write dummy subroutines which simply return a known constant for the result of the multiplication. Properly used, this method of testing is highly reliable.

Q8.8

8.8 Structured programs

The structured approach

Having broken down the overall programming task into a number of sub-tasks by the process of decomposition, the program designer must then turn his attention to the design of the individual program modules. At this point, the urge to start program coding, i.e. writing down sequences of instructions, should be resisted. Before program coding commences, the structure of the program module must first be designed. The most widely accepted approach to program writing is based on the idea that all programs should be designed using certain standard building blocks or structures. It is asserted, in fact, that any program can be written using a combination of three fundamental structures. In this section, we shall use four such structures since this offers greater convenience when working with assembly language or machine code. One advantage of the structured approach to program design is that the internal structural features of a program are easily identified. This assists the reader in following the program flow which greatly eases the problems of debugging and maintenance. It also allows us to proceed in a logical and ordered manner.

Structured methods were originally developed to assist program design using high-level languages such as ALGOL, FORTRAN and COBOL, as shown in Ref. 8.3. The technique is general, however, and is used in this chapter to illustrate assembly language program development. Even when programming directly in machine code, structured methods can be used with advantage. It is true that some programming languages are more suited to structured programming than others. For example, PASCAL is currently regarded as being particularly convenient for the use of structured methods. This does not mean, however, that by using PASCAL we automatically write efficient structured programs. Good, structured programs can be written using 'unstructured' languages and, unfortunately, the reverse is also true.

The sequence structure

This is the simplest structure we shall identify. Each program module

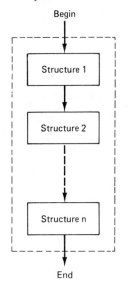

Figure 8.7 Sequence structure

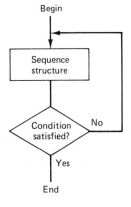

Figure 8.8 DO UNTIL flowchart

is regarded as implementing a process. In a sequence structure a process is replaced by a series of simpler processes. This is shown symbolically in Figure 8.7. The individual processes may themselves contain other structures.

The DO UNTIL structure

This structure formalises a program feature that the reader will have already encountered. Its function is to cause a sequence of instructions to be repeatedly executed until some condition is satisfied. This condition is often that a loop counter should contain zero. Figure 8.8 shows a flowchart for the structure. It should be noted that with this structure, the jump back condition is checked after the execution of the sequence structure. This means that the sequence is always executed at least once, even if the condition is satisfied on entry to the structure.

When writing assembly language programs many designers find it convenient to invent a formal way of describing the structural features of a program. The most common approach currently employed leads to a description which looks quite similar to a computer program written in a high-level language. It is referred to as pseudo-language or pseudo-code. We shall use pseudo-code in this way. Translation from pseudo-code to assembly language code is straightforward and conveniently done by hand. The pseudo-code is created by the programmer to suit his own purposes. However it is defined, it is important to ensure that it is used in a consistent manner. The pseudo-code used in this text for program description has many similarities to PASCAL. One advantage of pseudo-code is that the program description can be included as comments in the assembly listing whereas other types of descriptive material such as flowcharts must be prepared separately. Both flowcharts and pseudo-language have specific advantages and disadvantages. The programmer should choose whichever descriptive method seems best for the program structure concerned. A generalised description for the DO UNTIL structure is shown in Figure 8.9.

Figure 8.10 shows a description of a particular program using a flowchart. The same program is described in pseudo-code in Figure 8.11. Examination of the program description reveals that it is designed to multiply the unsigned binary number stored in memory location 0151 by 5. The result is stored in memory location 0151. A repeated addition algorithm is used and it is assumed that the result will not exceed 255 (decimal). It should be noted that at this stage the program description deals only with the logical structure and does not contain features that depend on the architecture of any specific microprocessor. Although it is not always possible, it is normally desirable at this stage to make the program description independent

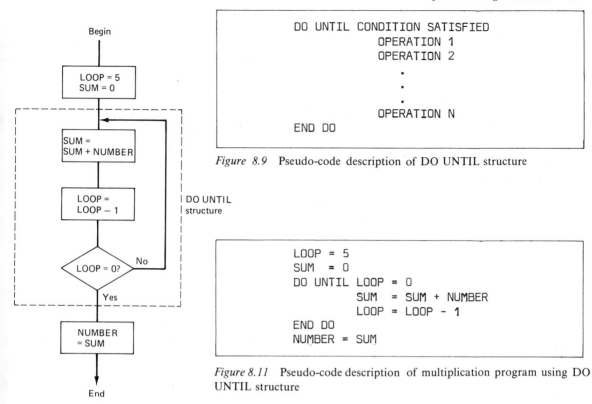

```
           DO UNTIL CONDITION SATISFIED
                OPERATION 1
                OPERATION 2
                     .
                     .
                     .
                OPERATION N
           END DO
```

Figure 8.9 Pseudo-code description of DO UNTIL structure

```
           LOOP = 5
           SUM  = 0
           DO UNTIL LOOP = 0
                SUM  = SUM + NUMBER
                LOOP = LOOP - 1
           END DO
           NUMBER = SUM
```

Figure 8.11 Pseudo-code description of multiplication program using DO UNTIL structure

Figure 8.10 Flowchart for multiplication program using DO UNTIL structure

of the processor, even for assembly language or machine-code programs.

An assembly listing for a program based on the structure of Figure 8.11 is shown in Figure 8.12. This listing includes comments describing the structure in pseudo-high-level-language form. Comments of this kind are an important feature of the assembly listing and should always be included. The program shown in Figure 8.12 is for the 8080 microprocessor. Figures 8.13 and 8.14 show programs, again based on the DO UNTIL structure of Figure 8.11, but this time for the Z80 and 6800 microprocessors, respectively. The descriptive comments shown in Figure 8.12 should be included in the listings of Figures 8.13 and 8.14, but are not repeated here for reasons of space.

The DO WHILE structure

This structure is also used when repeated execution of a sequence block is required. It differs from the DO UNTIL structure in that the condition check is made at the beginning of the structure as shown in the flowchart in Figure 8.15. A pseudo-code form of the structure is given in Figure 8.16. One consequence of the position of the

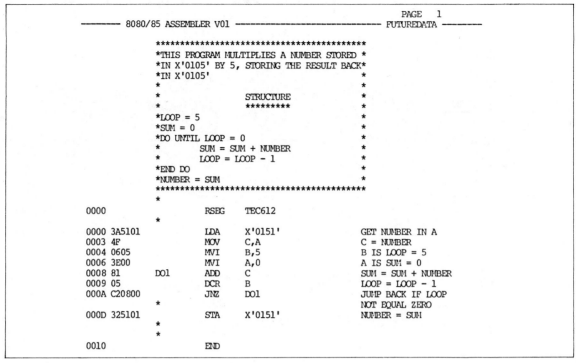

```
                                                        PAGE   1
     --------- 8080/85 ASSEMBLER V01 ------------------------- FUTUREDATA ---------

            ********************************************
            *THIS PROGRAM MULTIPLIES A NUMBER STORED *
            *IN X'0105' BY 5, STORING THE RESULT BACK*
            *IN X'0105'                              *
            *                                        *
            *                  STRUCTURE             *
            *                  *********             *
            *LOOP = 5                                *
            *SUM = 0                                 *
            *DO UNTIL LOOP = 0                       *
            *        SUM = SUM + NUMBER              *
            *        LOOP = LOOP - 1                 *
            *END DO                                  *
            *NUMBER = SUM                            *
            ********************************************
            *
     0000                 RSEG    TEC612
                  *
     0000 3A5101          LDA     X'0151'         GET NUMBER IN A
     0003 4F              MOV     C,A             C = NUMBER
     0004 0605            MVI     B,5             B IS LOOP = 5
     0006 3E00            MVI     A,0             A IS SUM = 0
     0008 81     DO1      ADD     C               SUM = SUM + NUMBER
     0009 05              DCR     B               LOOP = LOOP - 1
     000A C20800          JNZ     DO1             JUMP BACK IF LOOP
                  *                               NOT EQUAL ZERO
     000D 325101          STA     X'0151'         NUMBER = SUM
                  *
                  *
     0010                 END
```

Figure 8.12   8080 DO UNTIL program structure

```
                                                        PAGE   1
     --------- 6800/02 ASSEMBLER V01 ------------------------- FUTUREDATA ---------

     0000                 RSEG    TEC613
                  *
     0000 4F              CLRA                    A IS SUM = 0
     0001 C605            LDAB    #5              B IS LOOP = 5
     0003 BB0151 DO1      ADDA    X'0151'         SUM = SUM + NUMBER
     0006 5A              DECB                    LOOP = LOOP - 1
     0007 26FA            BNE     DO1
                  *
     0009 B70151          STAA    X'0151'         NUMBER = SUM
                  *
                  *
     000C                 END
```

Figure 8.13   M6800 DO UNTIL program structure

condition check in Figure 8.15 is that, if the condition is satisfied on entry, the sequence structure is never executed, unlike the situation with DO UNTIL in which the sequence structure is always executed at least once.

Figure 8.17 shows how the repeated addition program for multiplication by 5 could be implemented with a DO WHILE structure. A flowchart description of the program is given in Figure 8.18. Assembly language listings for 8080, Z80 and M6800 versions of the

```
                                                                PAGE   1
        -------- Z80 ASSEMBLER V01 ------------------------------- FUTUREDATA --------

        0000                    RSEG    TEC614
                    *
        0000 3A5101             LD      A,(X'0151')        GET NUMBER IN A
        0003 4F                 LD      C,A                C = NUMBER
        0004 0605               LD      B,5                B IS LOOP = 5
        0006 3E00               LD      A,0                A IS SUM = 0
        0008 81      DO1        ADD     A,C                SUM = SUM + NUMBER
        0009 10FD               DJNZ    DO1                LOOP = LOOP - 1
                    *                                      JUMP BACK IF NOT ZERO
        000B 325101             LD      (X'0151'),A        NUMBER = SUM
                    *
                    *
        000E                    END
```

Figure 8.14   Z80 DO UNTIL program structure

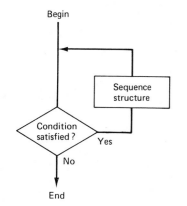

Figure 8.15   DO WHILE flowchart

```
DO WHILE CONDITION NOT SATISFIED
            OPERATION 1
            OPERATION 2
                 .
                 .
                 .
            OPERATION N
END DO
```

Figure 8.16   Pseudo-code description of DO WHILE structure

```
        LOOP = 5
        SUM  = 0
        DO WHILE LOOP ≠ 0
                LOOP = LOOP + 1
                SUM  = SUM + NUMBER
        END DO
        NUMBER = SUM
```

Figure 8.17   Pseudo-code description of multiplication program using DO WHILE structure

program are given in Figures 8.19, 8.20 and 8.21. When studying the three assembly language programs, the reader may note the relative inconvenience of implementing the DO WHILE structure with the 8080 and Z80. This is primarily a consequence of the register-oriented architecture of these microprocessors.

The IF THEN ELSE structure

Again, this structure formalises a programming technique that will be familiar to most readers, whatever their approach to program

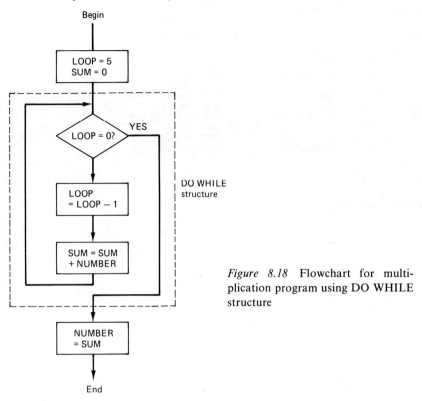

Figure 8.18 Flowchart for multiplication program using DO WHILE structure

```
                                                       PAGE    1
    --------- Z80 ASSEMBLER V01 ------------------------------- FUTUREDATA ---------

    0000                      RSEG     TEC620
                       *
    0000 3A5101          LD       A,(X'0151')         GET NUMBER IN A
    0003 4F              LD       C,A                 C = NUMBER
    0004 0605            LD       B,5                 B IS LOOP = 5
    0006 1600            LD       D,0                 D IS SUM = 0
    0008 78      DO1     LD       A,B                 GET LOOP IN A
    0009 FE00            CP       0                   LOOP = 0?
    000B CA1500          JP       Z,DO2               JUMP IF YES
    000E 05              DEC      B                   LOOP = LOOP - 1
    000F 7A              LD       A,D                 GET SUM IN A
    0010 81              ADD      A,C                 SUM = SUM + NUMBER
    0011 57              LD       D,A                 D IS SUM
    0012 C30800          JP       DO1
                       *
    0015 7A      DO2     LD       A,D                 GET SUM IN A
    0016 325101          LD       (X'0151'),A         NUMBER = SUM
                       *
                       *
    0019                     END
```

Figure 8.20 Z80 DO WHILE program structure

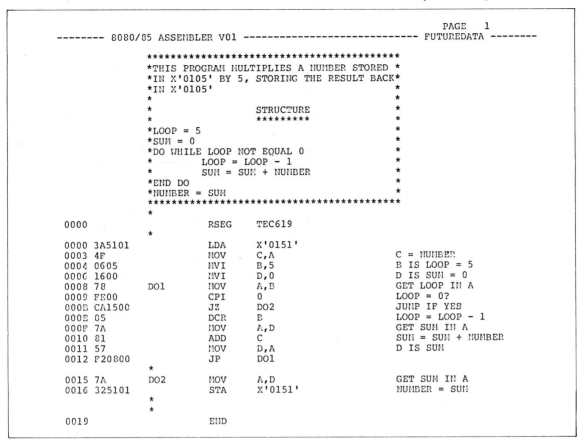

```
                                                        PAGE   1
-------- 8080/85 ASSEMBLER V01 ----------------------------- FUTUREDATA --------

                 **********************************************
                 *THIS PROGRAM MULTIPLIES A NUMBER STORED *
                 *IN X'0105' BY 5, STORING THE RESULT BACK*
                 *IN X'0105'                              *
                 *                                        *
                 *                  STRUCTURE             *
                 *                  ********              *
                 *LOOP = 5                                *
                 *SUM = 0                                 *
                 *DO WHILE LOOP NOT EQUAL 0               *
                 *        LOOP = LOOP - 1                 *
                 *        SUM = SUM + NUMBER              *
                 *END DO                                  *
                 *NUMBER = SUM                            *
                 **********************************************
                 *
     0000                      RSEG    TEC619
                 *
     0000 3A5101               LDA     X'0151'              C = NUMBER
     0003 4F                   MOV     C,A
     0004 0605                 MVI     B,5                  B IS LOOP = 5
     0006 1600                 MVI     D,0                  D IS SUM = 0
     0008 78       DO1         MOV     A,B                  GET LOOP IN A
     0009 FE00                 CPI     0                    LOOP = 0?
     000B CA1500               JZ      DO2                  JUMP IF YES
     000E 05                   DCR     B                    LOOP = LOOP - 1
     000F 7A                   MOV     A,D                  GET SUM IN A
     0010 81                   ADD     C                    SUM = SUM + NUMBER
     0011 57                   MOV     D,A                  D IS SUM
     0012 F20800               JP      DO1
                 *
     0015 7A       DO2         MOV     A,D                  GET SUM IN A
     0016 325101               STA     X'0151'              NUMBER = SUM
                 *
                 *
     0019                      END
```

Figure 8.19   8080 DO WHILE structure

```
                                                        PAGE   1
       -------- 6800/02 ASSEMBLER V01 ----------------------------- FUTUREDATA --------

     0000                      RSEG    TEC621
                 *
     0000 C605                 LDAB    #5                   B IS LOOP = 5
     0002 4F                   CLRA                         A IS SUM = 0
     0003 5D       DO1         TST     B                    LOOP = 0?
     0004 2706                 BEQ     DO2                  BRANCH IF YES
     0006 5A                   DECB                         LOOP = LOOP - 1
     0007 BB0151               ADDA    X'0151'              SUM = SUM + NUMBER
     000A 20F7                 BRA     DO1
                 *
     000C B70151   DO2         STAA    X'0151'              NUMBER = SUM
                 *
                 *
     000F                      END
```

Figure 8.21   M6800 DO WHILE program structure

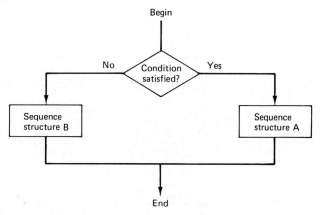

Figure 8.22   Flowchart for the IF THEN ELSE structure

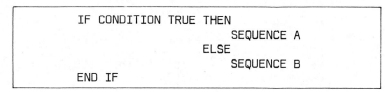

Figure 8.23   IF THEN ELSE pseudo-code

writing. As in the previous two structures, it involves testing a condition. In the IF THEN ELSE structure, two alternative courses of action are available. The operation actually carried out depends on whether or not the test condition is satisfied. Figures 8.22 and 8.23 show how the structure is described in flowchart and pseudo-code, respectively. Examples of programs including an IF THEN ELSE structure for the 8080, Z80 and M6800 are shown in Figures 8.24, 8.25 and 8.26, respectively. For reasons of space, full descriptive structural information is included only in the 8080 listing. The structure is identical for Figures 8.25 and 8.26.

A special case of the IF THEN ELSE structure occurs if a particular operation is required only when some condition is satisfied. If the condition is not satisfied, then no action is taken. Figure 8.27 shows a program including a structure of this kind. In the pseudo-code description, the CONTINUE statement implies that the program continues with no operation taking place.

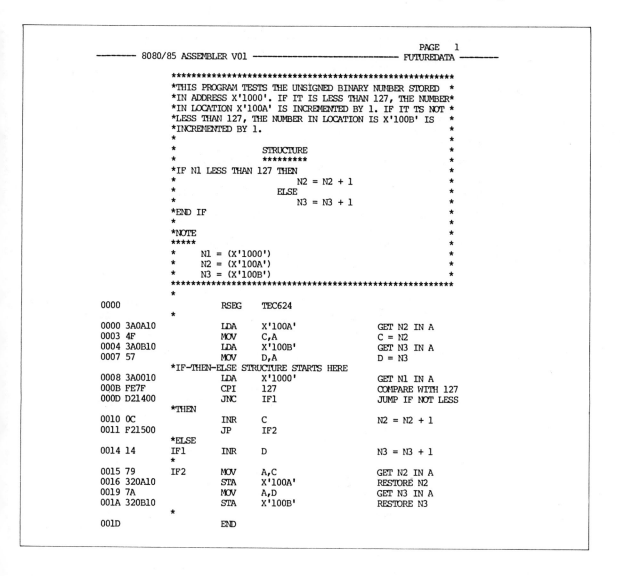

```
                                                           PAGE  1
--------- 8080/85 ASSEMBLER V01 ----------------------------- FUTUREDATA ---------

              *******************************************************
              *THIS PROGRAM TESTS THE UNSIGNED BINARY NUMBER STORED  *
              *IN ADDRESS X'1000'. IF IT IS LESS THAN 127, THE NUMBER*
              *IN LOCATION X'100A' IS INCREMENTED BY 1. IF IT TS NOT *
              *LESS THAN 127, THE NUMBER IN LOCATION IS X'100B' IS    *
              *INCREMENTED BY 1.                                      *
              *                                                       *
              *                    STRUCTURE                          *
              *                    *********                          *
              *IF N1 LESS THAN 127 THEN                               *
              *                         N2 = N2 + 1                   *
              *                    ELSE                               *
              *                         N3 = N3 + 1                   *
              *END IF                                                 *
              *                                                       *
              *NOTE                                                   *
              *****                                                   *
              *     N1 = (X'1000')                                    *
              *     N2 = (X'100A')                                    *
              *     N3 = (X'100B')                                    *
              *******************************************************
              *
0000                      RSEG    TEC624
                     *
0000 3A0A10               LDA     X'100A'           GET N2 IN A
0003 4F                   MOV     C,A               C = N2
0004 3A0B10               LDA     X'100B'           GET N3 IN A
0007 57                   MOV     D,A               D = N3
                *IF-THEN-ELSE STRUCTURE STARTS HERE
0008 3A0010               LDA     X'1000'           GET N1 IN A
000B FE7F                 CPI     127               COMPARE WITH 127
000D D21400               JNC     IF1               JUMP IF NOT LESS
                *THEN
0010 0C                   INR     C                 N2 = N2 + 1
0011 F21500               JP      IF2
                *ELSE
0014 14           IF1     INR     D                 N3 = N3 + 1
                     *
0015 79           IF2     MOV     A,C               GET N2 IN A
0016 320A10               STA     X'100A'           RESTORE N2
0019 7A                   MOV     A,D               GET N3 IN A
001A 320B10               STA     X'100B'           RESTORE N3
                     *
001D                      END
```

Figure 8.24   8080 IF THEN ELSE program structure

```
                                                          PAGE   1
 --------- Z80 ASSEMBLER V01 ----------------------------------- FUTUREDATA ---------

                    *Z80 IF-THEN-ELSE
    0000                    RSEG      TEC625
                    *
    0000 3A0A10             LD        A,(X'100A')          GET N2 IN A
    0003 4F                 LD        C,A                  C = N2
    0004 3A0B10             LD        A,(X'100B')          GET N3 IN A
    0007 57                 LD        D,A                  D = N3
                    *START OF IF-THEN-ELSE
    0008 3A0010             LD        A,(X'1000')          GET N1 IN A
    000B FE7F               CP        127                  COMPARE 127
    000D D21400             JP        NC,ELSE              JUMP IF NOT LESS
                    *THEN
    0010 0C                 INC       C                    N2 = N2 + 1
    0011 C31500             JP        ENDIF                JUMP TO ENDIF
                    *ELSE
    0014 14      ELSE       INC       D                    N3 = N3 + 1
                    *ENDIF
    0015 79      ENDIF      LD        A,C                  GET N2 IN A
    0016 320A10             LD        (X'100A'),A          RESTORE N2
    0019 7A                 LD        A,D                  GET N3 IN A
    001A 320B10             LD        (X'100B'),A          RESTORE N3
                    *
    001D                    END
```

Figure 8.25   Z80 IF THEN ELSE program structure

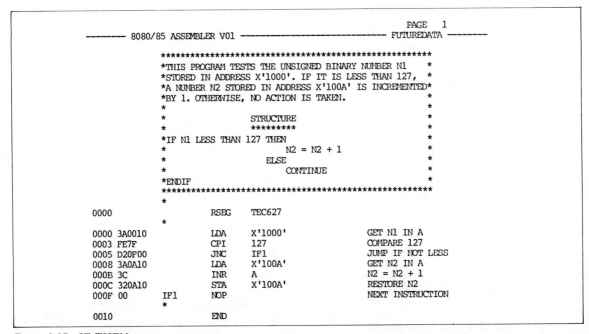

```
                                                          PAGE   1
 --------- 8080/85 ASSEMBLER V01 ------------------------------- FUTUREDATA ---------

                    ******************************************************
                    *THIS PROGRAM TESTS THE UNSIGNED BINARY NUMBER N1    *
                    *STORED IN ADDRESS X'1000'. IF IT IS LESS THAN 127,  *
                    *A NUMBER N2 STORED IN ADDRESS X'100A' IS INCREMENTED*
                    *BY 1. OTHERWISE, NO ACTION IS TAKEN.                *
                    *                                                    *
                    *                   STRUCTURE                        *
                    *                   *********                        *
                    *IF N1 LESS THAN 127 THEN                            *
                    *                        N2 = N2 + 1                 *
                    *                   ELSE                             *
                    *                        CONTINUE                    *
                    *ENDIF                                               *
                    ******************************************************
                    *
    0000                    RSEG      TEC627
                    *
    0000 3A0010             LDA       X'1000'              GET N1 IN A
    0003 FE7F               CPI       127                  COMPARE 127
    0005 D20F00             JNC       IF1                  JUMP IF NOT LESS
    0008 3A0A10             LDA       X'100A'              GET N2 IN A
    000B 3C                 INR       A                    N2 = N2 + 1
    000C 320A10             STA       X'100A'              RESTORE N2
    000F 00      IF1        NOP                            NEXT INSTRUCTION
                    *
    0010                    END
```

Figure 8.27   IF THEN program structure

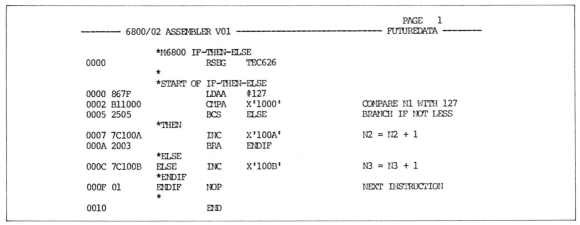

```
                                                    PAGE   1
        ———— 6800/02 ASSEMBLER V01 ———————————————————— FUTUREDATA ————

                   *M6800 IF-THEN-ELSE
        0000               RSEG    TEC626
                   *
                   *START OF IF-THEN-ELSE
        0000 867F          LDAA    #127
        0002 B11000        CMPA    X'1000'         COMPARE N1 WITH 127
        0005 2505          BCS     ELSE            BRANCH IF NOT LESS
                   *THEN
        0007 7C100A        INC     X'100A'         N2 = N2 + 1
        000A 2003          BRA     ENDIF
                   *ELSE
        000C 7C100B  ELSE  INC     X'100B'         N3 = N3 + 1
                   *ENDIF
        000F 01     ENDIF  NOP                     NEXT INSTRUCTION
                   *
        0010               END
```

Figure 8.26   M6800 IF THEN ELSE program structure

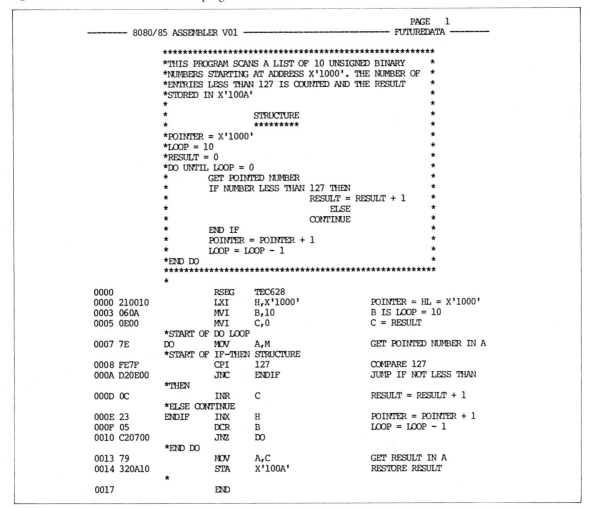

```
                                                    PAGE   1
        ———— 8080/85 ASSEMBLER V01 ———————————————————— FUTUREDATA ————

              ********************************************************
              *THIS PROGRAM SCANS A LIST OF 10 UNSIGNED BINARY      *
              *NUMBERS STARTING AT ADDRESS X'1000'. THE NUMBER OF   *
              *ENTRIES LESS THAN 127 IS COUNTED AND THE RESULT      *
              *STORED IN X'100A'                                    *
              *                                                     *
              *                    STRUCTURE                        *
              *                    *********                        *
              *POINTER = X'1000'                                    *
              *LOOP = 10                                            *
              *RESULT = 0                                           *
              *DO UNTIL LOOP = 0                                    *
              *       GET POINTED NUMBER                            *
              *       IF NUMBER LESS THAN 127 THEN                  *
              *                         RESULT = RESULT + 1         *
              *                                ELSE                 *
              *                             CONTINUE                *
              *       END IF                                        *
              *       POINTER = POINTER + 1                         *
              *       LOOP = LOOP - 1                               *
              *END DO                                               *
              ********************************************************
              *
        0000               RSEG    TEC628
        0000 210010        LXI     H,X'1000'       POINTER = HL = X'1000'
        0003 060A          MVI     B,10            B IS LOOP = 10
        0005 0E00          MVI     C,0             C = RESULT
                   *START OF DO LOOP
        0007 7E     DO     MOV     A,M             GET POINTED NUMBER IN A
                   *START OF IF-THEN STRUCTURE
        0008 FE7F          CPI     127             COMPARE 127
        000A D20E00        JNC     ENDIF           JUMP IF NOT LESS THAN
                   *THEN
        000D 0C            INR     C               RESULT = RESULT + 1
                   *ELSE CONTINUE
        000E 23     ENDIF  INX     H               POINTER = POINTER + 1
        000F 05            DCR     B               LOOP = LOOP - 1
        0010 C20700        JNZ     DO
                   *END DO
        0013 79            MOV     A,C             GET RESULT IN A
        0014 320A10        STA     X'100A'         RESTORE RESULT
                   *
        0017               END
```

Figure 8.28   IF THEN ELSE nested in a DO UNTIL loop

8.9   Structures within structures

So far, we have described programming structures only in isolation. In a complete program there will normally be many modules, each having its own structural features. In this case, a structure, such as IF THEN ELSE, can be regarded as a block of program which can then form part of another structure. Figure 8.28 shows the assembly listing for a program of this kind with an IF THEN ELSE structure embedded within a DO UNTIL loop. The program shown in Figure 8.27 could itself be regarded as a block which could then form part of yet another structure.

Q8.6, 8.7, 8.10–8.14

References and bibliography

8.1   M. V. Zelkowitz, 'Perspectives on software engineering', *ACM Computing Surveys*, p198 (June 1978).

8.2   A. D. Hearn, 'Top-down modular programming', *Byte*, Vol. 3 (7), (July 1978).

8.3   G. L. Richardson, C. W. Butler and J. D. Tomlinson, *A Primer on Structured Program Design*, Petrocelli Books (1980).

Questions

8.1   The total design/development budget for a microprocessor system can be divided into hardware and software development costs. Which component would normally be the greater?

8.2   Describe four characteristics you would expect to find in a well designed program.

8.3   Explain the distinction between programming and program coding.

8.4   Explain what is meant by program maintenance.

8.5   State four advantages and four disadvantages of the modular approach to program design.

8.6   Programming efficiency is generally defined in terms of the time taken to produce a debugged program to perform a given computing task. Using this definition, which would be more efficient, assembly language or a high-level language such as BASIC or PASCAL?

8.7   For what type of program must assembly language be used rather than a high-level language?

8.8   Explain what is meant by the top-down approach to program writing.

8.9   A microprocessor controls a drilling machine that drills holes at positions specified by co-ordinates entered via a keyboard. The programmer decides to split the drill control program into four sub-sections *(a)*, *(b)*, *(c)* and *(d)* as shown below:

(a) Keyboard data input.
(b) Position control of drill head.
(c) Implement drilling operation.
(d) System start-up and initialisation.

It is further decided that the program module controlling the position of the drill head must be split into two sub-sections as shown below:

(e) X axis drill head control.
(f) Y axis drill head control.

Describe the program using a hierarchical decomposition diagram.

8.10 By means of a flowchart and pseudo-code, describe a program which multiplies the contents of memory location 500 by 7 using the method of repeated addition. The result of the computation should be stored in address 600.

8.11 Design a program that adds 5 to each number in a list of fifty, starting at address 5000. The program should use a DO UNTIL loop. Flowchart and pseudo-code descriptions of the program should be given.

8.12 A program is required that determines how many of the numbers stored in memory area 1000–10FF are positive and how many are negative. Design a suitable program which uses an IF THEN ELSE structure nested in a DO UNTIL loop. Describe the program using *(a)* a flowchart and *(b)* pseudo-code.

8.13 Using the repeated addition algorithm of Question 8.10, design a program which multiplies by 5 each entry in a list of fifty numbers starting at address 1000. The program structure should be in the form of a DO UNTIL loop nested inside another DO UNTIL loop. Describe the program using pseudo-code.

8.14 A signed binary number is stored at address 1000. Design a program that tests the sign of the number. If the number is positive, the contents of a symbolic address POS are to be incremented. Otherwise, the contents of NEG are incremented. The program should be described using *(a)* a flowchart and *(b)* pseudo-code in the form of an IF THEN ELSE structure. [*Note:* Negative numbers have the most significant (sign) bit = 1.]

Chapter 9 Hardware development

Objectives of the chapter *After you have completed studying this chapter you should be able to:*

1 Analyse the following typical later stages in developing microprocessor systems:
  (a) Construction and testing of prototype hardware and firmware.
  (b) Simulation and emulation of system components to assist stage (a).
  (c) Modification of hardware and/or firmware as a result of stages (a) and (b)
2 Recognise that the ratio of the testing and debugging period to initial development rises significantly with the complexity of the system task.
3 Gain further insight into the use of microprocessor development systems as aids in the design and testing of hardware and software.

9.1 Hardware development

In this section we consider some of the later stages in the development of microprocessor system hardware. We assume that the system planning procedure has been correctly carried out and that major design decisions have been taken as described in Chapter 6. The task at this point is to then produce working prototype hardware from the initial circuit diagram. We shall describe the way in which a microprocessor development system with in-circuit emulation facilities can assist in the production and testing of this prototype.

9.2 Construction and testing of prototype hardware

Systems that are produced in quantity are normally constructed by mounting the various components, such as integrated circuits, capacitors and resistors, on specially designed printed circuit boards. Before the design of the printed circuit can proceed, however, the circuit design must be finalised and fully tested. This is the purpose of the hardware prototype.

Wire wrapping is the most popular construction method for a prototype circuit board. It is also widely used for constructing systems that are produced in very small numbers. Using this method, integrated circuits are fitted in sockets mounted on a proprietry prototyping board. These boards are drilled with holes in an 0.1-inch matrix, the same as the separation of pins on the standard dual in-line integrated circuit package. Integrated circuit sockets are provided with pins which can accept a wire-wrapped joint. Interconnections are therefore made using wires terminating in wrapped joints at the pins of integrated circuit sockets. Wire wrapping is a convenient way of making highly reliable connections yet allowing circuit modification where necessary. Figure 9.1 shows a typical wire-wrapped prototype board.

Careful consideration should be given to the positioning of integrated circuits on the prototyping board with the objective of keeping interconnections as short as possible. Experience plays a large part in obtaining a desirable circuit layout. Most prototyping boards will have d.c. power supply rails already printed and integrated circuits should be positioned so that connections to these supply lines are as short as possible. This is a good design practice which should be followed in all digital systems.

Adequate decoupling of power supply lines at regular intervals is also important. Disk ceramic capacitors of between 10 and 100 nF should be connected between positive supply and ground every two or three integrated circuits along the run of the supply rails. For wire-wrapped prototypes, decoupling at every integrated circuit package is by no

Figure 9.1   Wire-wrapped board

means unusual. Keeping decoupling capacitor lead lengths short is also important. Every unnecessary millimetre of wire increases the impedance of a capacitor and reduces its effectiveness in decoupling.

Q9.1

Some engineers choose to wire up the complete microprocessor system circuit and follow this with a systematic test and debug procedure. An alternative method is described here. It involves building the circuit in sections. Each section is tested and debugged before moving on to the next section. The approach avoids the possibility, however remote, of being faced with debugging a system containing several design and/or wiring faults.

9.3   A step-by-step approach to prototype construction

The order of construction described here is typical, although certain variations are possible. Testing is carried out at every stage using simple, special test programs running in the MDS. The aim should be to be sure that the system hardware and system software are functionally correct before bringing them together.

In describing this prototype construction/test sequence we shall assume that the system configuration is similar to that shown in Figure 4.30. The method is described in general terms. The construction and testing of a specific hardware prototype is described in more detail in Chapter 10. When describing the use of the in-circuit emulator (ICE) we shall refer to the prototype being tested as the target system. Some writers using this terminology also refer to the MDS itself as the host system. Construction/testing operations are as follows:

1   All integrated circuit sockets are mounted on the prototyping board and d.c. supply connections are made to the appropriate pins. Decoupling capacitors are also fitted at this stage.

2   The CPU chip set wiring is now completed. On connecting d.c. power supplies, it should be possible to observe a system clock waveform using an oscilloscope. The clock waveform can be checked to ensure that it falls within the required specification. At this stage, the CPU chip set may be operated in the free-run condition as described in Section 12.10. This will provide a further check as to its correct operation.

3   The wiring of the RAM can now be undertaken. If the RAM is of substantial size, this will be one of the major wiring tasks. To test the RAM, the ICE facility of the development system is brought into use. The CPU chip is first removed from its socket and the emulator probe inserted in its place. It will be recalled from Section 7.5 that the memory substitution facility of the ICE allows memory read/write

requests from the internal CPU to be directed either to the development system internal memory or to external memory. In this case, we specify that read/write operations to addresses in the target system RAM address space are directed to this external RAM. This method of memory substitution allows the MDS to write data to, and read data from, the target system RAM area.

With the help of the ICE, we can therefore manually load RAM addresses with data and read the contents of RAM addresses. A much more efficient way of testing the target system however is to use a memory test program. This program will run in the memory of the development system. An example will help to clarify this. Suppose the target system has RAM in the address space 4000–5000. We issue commands to the development system that all memory read/write

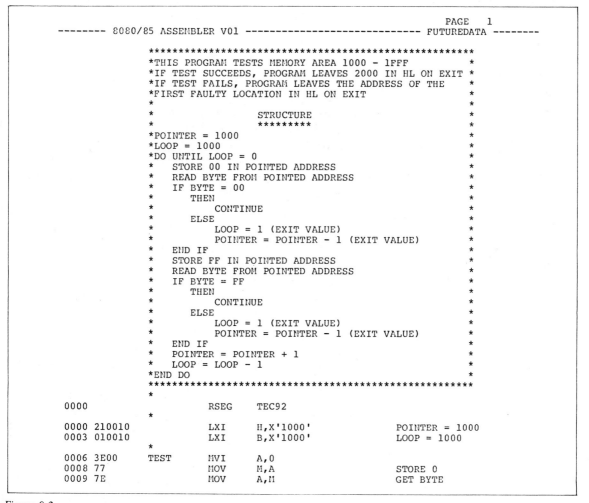

```
                                                      PAGE   1
-------- 8080/85 ASSEMBLER V01 --------------------------- FUTUREDATA --------

             ***********************************************************
             *THIS PROGRAM TESTS MEMORY AREA 1000 - 1FFF          *
             *IF TEST SUCCEEDS, PROGRAM LEAVES 2000 IN HL ON EXIT *
             *IF TEST FAILS, PROGRAM LEAVES THE ADDRESS OF THE    *
             *FIRST FAULTY LOCATION IN HL ON EXIT                 *
             *                                                    *
             *                    STRUCTURE                       *
             *                    ********                        *
             *POINTER = 1000                                      *
             *LOOP = 1000                                         *
             *DO UNTIL LOOP = 0                                   *
             *    STORE 00 IN POINTED ADDRESS                     *
             *    READ BYTE FROM POINTED ADDRESS                  *
             *    IF BYTE = 00                                    *
             *       THEN                                         *
             *           CONTINUE                                 *
             *       ELSE                                         *
             *           LOOP = 1 (EXIT VALUE)                    *
             *           POINTER = POINTER - 1 (EXIT VALUE)       *
             *    END IF                                          *
             *    STORE FF IN POINTED ADDRESS                     *
             *    READ BYTE FROM POINTED ADDRESS                  *
             *    IF BYTE = FF                                    *
             *       THEN                                         *
             *           CONTINUE                                 *
             *       ELSE                                         *
             *           LOOP = 1 (EXIT VALUE)                    *
             *           POINTER = POINTER - 1 (EXIT VALUE)       *
             *    END IF                                          *
             *    POINTER = POINTER + 1                           *
             *    LOOP = LOOP - 1                                 *
             *END DO                                              *
             ***********************************************************
             *
0000                     RSEG    TEC92
             *
0000 210010              LXI     H,X'1000'                POINTER = 1000
0003 010010              LXI     B,X'1000'                LOOP = 1000
             *
0006 3E00       TEST     MVI     A,0
0008 77                  MOV     M,A                      STORE 0
0009 7E                  MOV     A,M                      GET BYTE
```

Figure 9.2

```
                                                        PAGE    2
    -------- 8080/85 ASSEMBLER V01 --------------------------- FUTUREDATA --------

                    *IF THEN ELSE BEGINS
    000A FE00   IF1     CPI     0               BYTE = 0?
    000C CA1300         JZ      ENDIF1          JUMP IF YES
    000F 010100 ELSE1   LXI     B,1             LOOP = 1
    0012 2B             DCX     H               DECREMENT POINTER
    0013 3EFF   ENDIF1  MVI     A,X'FF'
    0015 77             MOV     M,A             STORE FF
    0016 7E             MOV     A,M             GET BYTE
                    *IF THEN ELSE BEGINS
    0017 FEFF          CPI     X'FF'            BYTE = FF?
    0019 CA2000         JZ      ENDIF2          JUMP IF YES
    001C 010100 ELSE2   LXI     B,1             LOOP = 1
    001F 2B             DCX     H               DEC POINTER
    0020 23     ENDIF2  INX     H               INC POINTER
    0021 0B             DCX     B               DEC LOOP
    0022 3E00           MVI     A,0
    0024 B9             CMP     C               C = 0?
    0025 C22D00         JNZ     AGAIN           JUMP IF NO
    0028 B8             CMP     B               B = 0?
    0029 C22D00         JNZ     AGAIN           JUMP IF NO
    002C C9             RET                     EXIT
    002D C30600 AGAIN   JMP     TEST            DO IT AGAIN
    0030               END
```

Figure 9.3

operations to this area of memory shall be directed to the target system. All other memory read/write operations are directed to the development system internal memory. Having established this, a memory test program is written and located at, say, 1000. This means that it can run in the development system internal memory. The program, however, tests the memory of the target system.

Figures 9.2 and 9.3 show a very simple memory test program, which simply writes fixed bytes, 00 and FF in this case, into each RAM address in turn. The contents of the address are then read to check if the correct byte is present. This is by no means a comprehensive memory test and merely illustrates the general principle. More effective memory test programs will write every possible 8-bit pattern into each RAM location with a read operation to check whether the correct byte is present.

Should a memory test fail, the fault must be cleared before further constructional work can proceed. Using the ICE, it is not difficult to detect data lines stuck permanently at 1 or 0. If one or more lines are stuck at 0, writing 00 into an address will apparently be successful. Attempting to write FF into the same address is not successful, leaving zeros in those bit positions corresponding to the faulty data lines.

Another fault that may be present at this stage is the absence of active chip enable signals at some or all of the RAM chips during memory read/write operations to the RAM address space. Here again, a test program running in the development system can help to locate the fault whether it results from faulty wiring or faulty address decoder design. A simple endless loop program is written which repeatedly writes and reads to and from RAM in the faulty area. A regular train of chip enable pulses should be observed using an oscilloscope if the chip address decoding circuit is functioning properly. The method is similar to that described later in this chapter and in Section 12.18 for locating faults in I/O ports.

4   With the RAM operational, the ROM may now be wired into the system. In this case, the 'write followed by read' type of test program cannot be used in view of the read-only nature of the memory devices. However, a specially programmed ROM containing known data can be used in conjunction with a suitable test program. The program simply reads the data in every ROM address and compares it with the known contents of the address. Stuck address and/or data lines and failure of chip enable decode circuits are among the more usual faults at this stage. Detection of these faults involves using the MDS ICE

Q9.3   facility as described for RAM debugging.

The ROM cannot be said to be fully tested until a program stored in ROM has been run successfully. Once again, a special ROM containing a suitable test program is required. It helps greatly if the ROM is programmable and preferably erasable. Test programs can then be simply stored and later erased if necessary. The actual function of the test program is not important provided that it can be demonstrated that the program runs successfully.

5   Input and output port circuits are now wired into the system, testing each port as it is completed. For the purpose of testing ports, it is usually necessary to simulate the I/O devices. If the system is controlling a 100-ton press for example, it would be foolhardy to use this device to make initial tests of the controlling system. Digital outputs are conveniently monitored using LEDs. Single digital inputs are easily simulated using switches. Analogue outputs can be monitored using test meters and analogue inputs simulated using potentiometers and voltage sources. Of course, tests will eventually take place with the real system peripherals connected, but not at this

Q9.4   early stage.

The MDS is again used to run programs to test I/O ports. With LEDs connected to the lines of an output port for example, the program need only output a byte of all zeros followed by a byte of all ones. Lines stuck at 0 or 1 are thereby easily detectable as is the total failure of the port to put out data. If this is the case, another test program is used which repeatedly attempts to output data from the port in an endless loop. The output of port address decoders should be observed with an oscilloscope while this program is running. A regular train of port enable pulses should be observed. This technique is also discussed in Section 12.8.

Lamps and switches do not always provide adequate substitutes for system elements for test purposes. To test serial I/O ports, it is necessary to employ a peripheral device which puts out and takes in compatible serial data. A VDT, for example, is a useful test peripheral for asynchronous I/O ports since it can receive and transmit asynchronous serial data. Test programs running in the MDS can take in characters when keys are depressed on the VDT keyboard. To test asynchronous output, a simple test program can display characters on the terminal screen.

On completion of I/O interface and port circuitry, the testing of hardware in isolation has probably gone as far as necessary. It is possible to use a special test program in ROM which exercises all hardware systems but it is probably more useful to move on to the next major development stage. This is the bringing together of system hardware and software.

9.4   Bringing together hardware and software/firmware

In this chapter and previous chapters we have described the way hardware and software development can proceed after the initial design planning stage. As we have said, much of this hardware and software development can take place in parallel. At some stage, therefore, the design/development team will arrive at a situation in which hardware and software have been developed and tested as far as is possible while they remain separate. This is the point at which they must be brought together and the system as a whole tested and debugged.

If the system is dedicated to a specific control or instrumentation function, the program will, of course, ultimately reside in some form of ROM. During system testing and debugging, however, it assists easy program modification if it resides in RAM. The use of the MDS ICE facility allows this. A ROM/PROM emulator can also assist in the final stages of testing.

The facility of system memory substitution by the MDS is used for initial hardware/software system testing. We have described memory substitution in Section 7.5. The complete target system software can now be run with simulated peripherals or, if it is physically possible, with the actual peripheral devices themselves connected. If the software has been properly designed in a modular form as described, it should be possible to test individual program modules with the target system hardware since I/O control programs for the individual peripheral devices will normally each consist of separate modules.

Testing of separate program modules may be followed by a run of the complete program using actual peripheral devices. This will first be done using the MDS ICE and memory substitution facility. If all is well, the program is transferred to ROM or, more specifically, to EPROM in most cases. The MDS should be capable of programming an EPROM directly with the tested target system program. Final testing can now be carried out with the program running in EPROM installed in the target system, but still controlled by the MDS ICE facility. If this test is successful, the ICE probe is removed and the microprocessor inserted in its place. The system performance can then be checked against the original specification.

9.5 The importance of testing and debugging

By now the reader will be aware that time spent in testing and debugging can form a very significant proportion of the total system development time. In Chapter 8 we emphasised that the proportion of time spent debugging software can rise in an uncontrolled way as the size and complexity of programs increases. To bring this phase of development under proper control, the use of proper top-down structured programming methods has been advocated. The object of this is, of course, to isolate design faults within small program modules, thus making their detection and elimination easier.

Testing and debugging large and complex hardware systems present many of the same problems as software. In a microprocessor system the consequences of a component or circuit element failing to function as designed are not usually localised in the region of the fault, but tend to propagate through the system. Other parts of the system may also not function correctly as a result. With multiple faults in a complete system, debugging time can therefore increase in an uncontrolled manner in the same way as software faults. The construction/testing procedure described in this chapter is advocated to allow debugging to be carried out in an orderly manner. A major objective is to isolate and identify component and circuit faults as they appear during construction of the prototype. Using these methods will allow the engineer or technician to produce a working

Q9.5 prototype in the shortest possible time.

Questions

9.1 What provision is made for power supply line decoupling on a typical wire-wrapped prototype board for a microprocessor system?

9.2 Describe how an in-circuit emulator can be used to test *(a)* an I/O port and *(b)* RAM during prototype construction.

9.3 Explain why the procedure for testing ROM or PROM must differ from that for testing RAM.

9.4 Describe two simple devices for simulating periphal devices for the purpose of system testing.

9.5 Explain why the ratio of the hardware testing and debugging period to initial development can rise significantly with the complexity of the system task.

Chapter 10 Microprocessor system design study

Objectives of this chapter *When you have completed studying this chapter and working through exercises you should be able to analyse the stages in the design/development of a typical, small, microprocessor-based sequential control system.*

10.1   The design/development programme

In this chapter we move from the more general aspects of micro-processor system design to consider a specific case. We shall examine the various stages in the design and development of the hardware and software for a fairly simple microprocessor-based process control system. Before proceeding with this, it is perhaps worth reminding ourselves of the typical stages used in developing microprocessor systems. These are:

1   Initial specification of the complete system.
2   Formulation of measures of cost-effectiveness, particularly the hardware/software partition.
3   Derivation of a system flowchart.
4   Selection of the necessary hardware devices: microprocessor, interfacing components, etc.
5   Definition of boundary constraints for the microcomputer program, e.g. timing and address space.
6   Decomposition of the program task into modular form. Possibly developing a program flowchart.
7   Designing module structure and program coding.
8   Program testing.
9   Marrying hardware and software. Modification where necessary.
10   Simulation/emulation of system.
11   Further modification where necessary.
12   Running hardware and firmware prototype.
13   Iteration of design/development/test cycle as necessary.

This list should not be interpreted as always defining the exact order in which the various activities occur. Many iterations will be necessary in a typical design/development programme. Thus, having reached stage (9), for example, when system hardware and software are brought together for the first time, it may then be necessary to revise some details of the program to remove some unforeseen **Q10.1**   difficulty.

The actual development sequence will also depend to a certain extent on the supporting hardware and software. In this case study we have assumed that the software support system provides us with a fully relocatable assembler with a linker which allows separate program modules to be combined in a single program.

10.2   System specification

Figure 10.1 shows a schematic diagram of the system for which a control system is required. Valves A and B when opened allow liquid to flow from the upper vessels into the lower vessel C. Opening valve C drains vessel C. This lower vessel is also provided with a heater and a temperature transducer. The system shown in Figure 10.1 is used to implement two chemical processes. Each process involves the mixing of two liquids and heating for various time intervals.

It will be recalled from Chapter 6 that it is important to establish a precise system specification at an early stage in the design process. In this case it will involve specifying the accuracy and resolution of the system variables: temperatures and times.

Although not strictly part of the system specification, further information is required at this point to ensure that the final design is cost-effective. Most important is the number of systems to be produced. In this case, only three systems are required. Equally important, as far as the choice of hardware components is concerned, is the support equipment available to the design team. We shall assume that the team has previous experience in the design of 8080-based systems and has a development system for the microprocessor available.

Another important aspect of the system specification, not so far considered, relates to the communication between the system and operator. The system specified is not completely automatic and will be controlled by an operator. Figure 10.2 shows the control buttons available. A normal mains supply on/off switch is provided. Two push-buttons are provided to select process 1 or process 2. These

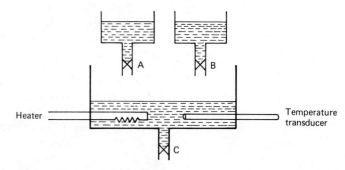

Figure 10.1   Chemical process plant

On/off	Process 1	Process 2	Run	Stop

Figure 10.2 Control switches

buttons are mechanically interlocked to prevent both processes being selected simultaneously. When the two upper vessels have been filled with the correct amount of liquid, the operator starts the chosen sequence by pressing the start button. In the event of malfunction, the process can be halted by pressing the stop button. Front panel controls are important in most systems. They may sometimes be specified in detail by the end-user but their function is quite often left to the system designer.

The presence of the on/off switch on the front panel identifies the need to consider the start-up condition. This is the condition we would wish the system to be in immediately after switch on and before the start button is operated. To ensure that the system is in a safe

---

The system is required to implement one of two control sequences associated with chemical processes 1 and 2. The two sequences are shown below.

Sequence 1

a Open valve A.
b Switch on heater, allow temperature to rise to 60°C.
c Maintain temperature at 60° ± 3°C for 30 ± 2 min.
d Open valve B.
e Switch on heater (if not already on) and allow temperature to rise to 80°C.
f Maintain temperature at 80° ± 3°C for 40 ± 2 min.
g Open valve C for at least 3 min.
h Close all valves.

Sequence 2

a Open valve A.
b Switch on heater, allow temperature to rise to 40°C.
c Maintain temperature at 40° ± 3°C for 50 ± 2 min.
d Open valve B.
e Switch on heater (if not already on) and allow temperature to rise to 70°C.
f Maintain temperature at 70° ± 3°C for 60 ± 2 min.
g Open valve C for at least 3 min.
h Close all valves.

Figure 10.3 Process control sequences

condition, we specify that the initial condition should be with valves A, B and C closed and the heater off. This should also be the condition after a sequence of operations has been completed.

10.3   System flowchart

Derivation of an initial system flowchart can usually follow the system specification. In this case, since the system behaves in relatively simple sequential manner, the flowchart shown in Figure 10.4 can be derived from the tabular description of system behaviour shown in Figure 10.3, with details of control panel functions added.

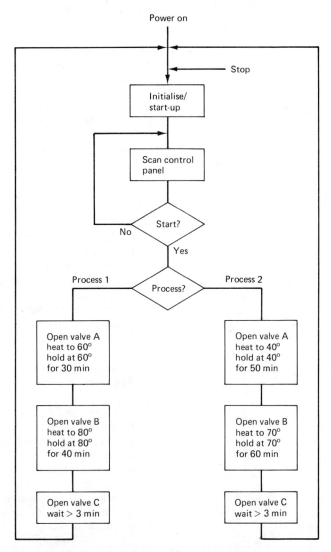

Figure 10.4   Chemical process control system flowchart

10.4 Formulation of measures of cost-effectiveness

At this point the individual stages in the development program become less clear. Initial decisions are made concerning the system configuration, hardware/software trade-offs, etc. These decisions may, in turn, affect the detailed operation of the system, which must then be described by a more comprehensive flowchart or in some other form.

```
SET SEQUENCE PARAMETERS
OPEN VALVE A
HEAT TO T1
HOLD AT T1 FOR P1 MINUTES
OPEN VALVE B
HEAT TO T2
HOLD AT T2 FOR P2 MINUTES
WAIT FOR 3 MINUTES
```

Figure 10.5 Main sequence control

One of the first points we note from Figure 10.3 is that, in general terms, the two processes do not differ. They do, however, differ in particulars such as temperatures and time intervals. It seems reasonable therefore to use one program which implements the general sequence, passing the appropriate time and temperature parameters to the program in an initialisation section. Figure 10.5 shows a description of this main cycle of operation, in general terms employing pseudo-code. This will also form the basis of the program module for implementing the main sequence.

Later in the design cycle, other aspects of cost-effectiveness will be considered. Not least of these will be the way the system tasks are partitioned between hardware and software. Again, this is not a simple decision and will be postponed until we have established the type of microprocessor to be used.

10.5 Selection of hardware devices

This is the stage in the design/development cycle at which we must make some initial decisions concerning the hardware configuration and the choice of hardware components. One of the more important of these decisions is the choice of microprocessor. We can estimate from the system specification that the computing power requirement is minimal to implement the simple sequential operation. The initial reaction might therefore be to choose an inexpensive 4-bit microprocessor, aiming at a system with a low chip count to minimise production cost. In this case, however, there are other more important factors. These are: the requirement for only three systems, the previous experience of the design team and the existing support for the 8080. These factors dominate any technical considerations.

With a production run of say 1,000 units, the cost of support for a new microprocessor and the perhaps extended development time due to lack of familiarity of the design team could be spread over the total number produced. This would possibly justify the use of a device other than the 8080. With a production run of three units, there can

Q10.2 be no argument; the 8080 is the only choice.

In the discussion of I/O requirements we shall concentrate on the microprocessor system itself. This means that we assume that valves

A, B and C are provided with solenoid driver units activated by logic signals. The heater can similarly be switched on and off by changing the controlling logic level.

The temperature transducer will generate an analogue output. Some form of AD conversion will therefore be required. We must also assume the existence of an amplifier to buffer the temperature transducer and provide an output voltage compatible with the chosen ADC.

The hardware/software partition in the case of AD conversion has been discussed at length in Chapter 6 and the conclusions reached there can be directly applied here. This results in a decision to use a self-contained ADC for the temperature measurement. The alternative partial software solution using a DAC/comparator combinations is ruled out by the requirement for only three systems. An 8-bit ADC is a reasonable choice in this case. The limited temperature resolution required would allow a converter with fewer bits but the cost advantage would be minimal. A wide variety of 8-bit SDCs is available in integrated circuit form, thus making the choice of a suitable unit easier. Figure 10.6 shows the configuration and timing characteristics of a typical converter of this kind. It will be seen that a negative-going pulse of at least 1 μs initiates conversion. While conversion is taking place the busy line is low, returning high when conversion is complete and the digital data are available at the output. The ADC shown in Figure 10.6 does not feature a three-state output, although this is a feature of some devices of this kind.

One feature of the system specification that affects both hardware and software is the need to establish timing intervals during the process. There are various ways of doing this, ranging from totally hardware to totally software methods as discussed in Section 6.7. The all-software method is well known and simply involves the execution of a delay loop program the appropriate number of times. This is simple to implement provided no other computation is required during the time interval. It is possible to design timing programs that

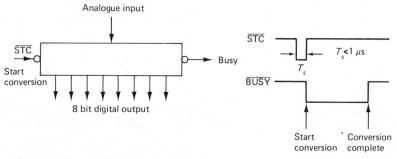

Figure 10.6 ADC characteristics

include other routines within the delay loop, but the complications can be considerable.

The all-hardware method of generating delays involves a programmable timer circuit external to the processor. When the delay is required, the processor initialises the timer to give the appropriate delay and issues a signal to start the timing process. At the completion of the time interval, the programmable timer generates a signal that can be scanned by the processor or alternatively generate a delay.

Q10.3

Both the all-software and all-hardware methods of generating timing intervals appear to have disadvantages for the system considered here. The method actually adopted is part-hardware and part-software and involves a real time clock. This is a very common technique when timing intervals are required. The real time clock generates pulses at fixed intervals. These pulses are counted by the processor until the desired time interval has elapsed. If, as is the case here, other computing activities will be taking place during the timing interval, it is usually more convenient to use the real time clock pulses as interrupts rather than scanning the clock signal line via an input port.

Adoption of the real time clock approach to timing has hardware implications in that a source of clock pulses is required. We must also consider the required frequency of these pulses. The upper limit frequency is theoretically limited by the speed with which the microprocessor can respond. If we choose too high a frequency, however, the program for counting pulses tends to become overlong, and the processor spends much of its time simply responding to interrupts. The lower limit is determined by the required time resolution, which in this case is very low. Three possibilities exist for the source of real time clock pulses:

1 A separate oscillator.
2 The microprocessor clock, suitably divided.
3 50 Hz mains frequency, possibly divided.

Examination of these three possibilities reveals that all are capable of providing a satisfactory real time clock and, perhaps surprisingly, the costs in terms of design and production are not greatly different. In this case, to simplify the specification of the counting program, we use method (3). A transformer reduces mains voltage to an appropriate level and the resulting 50 Hz waveform is clipped at 0 and +5 V. A frequency divider then divides by 50 to give pulses at 1 s intervals. The circuit is shown schematically in Figure 10.7.

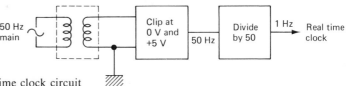

Figure 10.7 Real time clock circuit

Finally, in this section, we must consider the hardware requirement for providing safe start-up conditions as discussed in Section 10.2. Associated with this is the termination of a process in a safe manner when the STOP switch is operated on the control panel. Both problems can be solved in essentially the same way if we arrange for a RESET to occur at switch on or when the STOP switch is operated. Reset causes the 8080 to start executing instructions from address 0 onwards and this is where we must store the start-up program which **Q10.8** puts the system in a safe condition.

The requirement for this so-called 'power-on reset' is very common. Reset facilities are provided by the 8080 chip set, the 8224 clock generator in particular. Appendix F describes these reset facilities in detail and a suitable circuit is shown in Figure 10.8. When power is

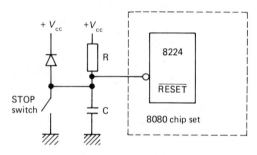

Figure 10.8 Power on RESET and STOP switch circuit

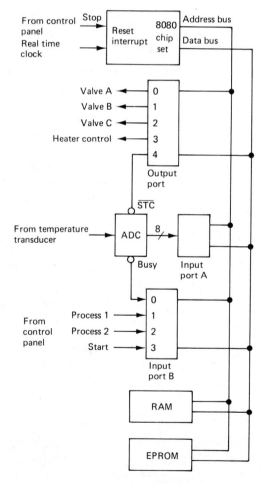

Figure 10.9 General system configuration

first switched on the capacitor C takes some time to charge. This holds the reset line low for a period after the microprocessor becomes active thus producing a reset condition. Operating of the stop switch **Q10.6** similarly generates a reset.

10.6 The system hardware configuration

Having established some of the more important measures of cost-effectiveness and hardware/software partitions, the system hardware configuration is beginning to emerge. In particular, the number and type of I/O lines are now defined as shown below:

Input lines

Control panel start	1 line
Control panel process 1 select	1 line
Control panel process 2 select	1 line
Control panel stop	1 line (reset)
ADC busy	1 line
ADC data	8 lines
Real time clock	1 line (interrupt)

Output lines

Valve A control	1 line
Valve B control	1 line
Valve C control	1 line
Heater control	1 line
ADC start conversion	1 line

From this, it can be seen that the system will have one reset and one interrupt input. In addition a total of 12 input lines and 5 output lines are required. We shall therefore require 2 input ports and 1 output port. Figure 10.9 shows a suitable configuration, excluding details of address decoding and control/status signals.

At this stage in our discussion we can say little about the size of the memory blocks shown in Figure 10.9. We can say, however, that part of the memory holding the program will be of the read-only variety. Some RAM will also be required to hold the microprocessor stack and for storage of program variables. Figure 10.9 specifies EPROM for the read-only part of memory since these devices offer much more flexibility in the design phase than do non-erasable varieties. When the design does become truly finalised, it is possible to replace the EPROMs with pin-compatible ROMs of other types if it is desired. For this design, the small numbers involved preclude the use of **Q10.7** mask-programmed ROM although programmable, fusible-link ROM could be used.

Some of the initial hardware decisions will affect the way the memory address space is allocated. We have seen that the system is reset at switch on and whenever the STOP switch is operated. With the 8080 microprocessor, this forces a jump to address 0. It is therefore essential that code for the start of the appropriate program module is present at this address. Program code will be held in EPROM and this therefore implies that the system EPROM must be allocated addresses at the bottom of memory space starting at 0. The 8080 interrupt service routine code will normally also be towards the bottom of memory, the actual starting address being determined by the interrupt hardware. This is discussed in Section 10.9.

Allocation of address space to RAM allows more flexibility since it will be used only for the 8080 stack and the storage of temporary data. However, by choosing the RAM address space carefully, the circuitry that generates chip enable signals for the memory chips can be made very simple. We shall allocate addresses to RAM starting at 8000. The reason for this particular choice will become apparent when we discuss the design of the memory in Section 10.8.

In a practical design situation, hardware and software design would proceed in parallel to some extent as shown in Figure 6.1. A software designer with some experience would probably have a reasonably accurate idea, therefore, of the amount of memory required at this stage. For prototype purposes this is not, however, absolutely necessary as the memory specification can be deferred until later, allowing the design of I/O hardware to proceed.

10.7 I/O port design

The design process so far reveals no unusual requirements for the I/O ports. Very simple circuits based on the use of three-state buffers and latches can therefore be employed. The question of port address decoding is, however, worth considering in detail since significant savings can be made in hardware by choosing port addresses carefully. We might first note, for example, that the system requires only one output port. This means that no address decoding whatsoever is required. The port is enabled simply by the $\overline{\text{IOWR}}$ signal from the 8080 chip set. Any OUT operation, whatever the address, will transfer data to this port. For programming convenience, we will allocate address 0 to the port, but this will have no significance as far as the hardware is concerned. Figure 10.10 shows the output port circuit.

Since more than one input port is required, some port address decoding is required for IN operations. Here again, hardware can be minimised by the choice of address. In the input ports circuit shown in Figure 10.11, port A is energised by any IN operation with a port

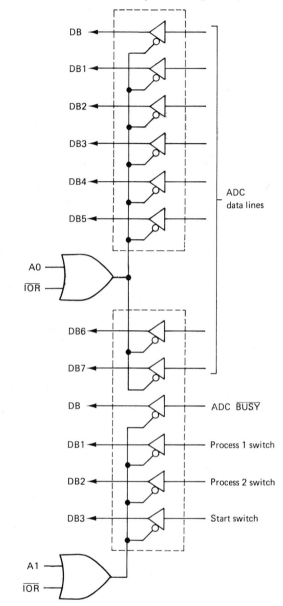

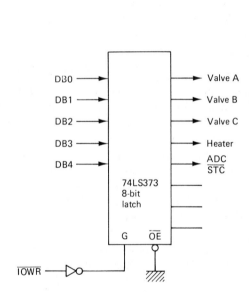

Figure 10.10 Output port

Figure 10.11 Input ports 0 and 1

address in which bit 0 is 0. Similarly, port B is energised by IN operations with port addresses in which bit 1 is 0. Again, for convenience, we shall use FE and FD as the addresses for the two input ports although, of course, many other addresses could also be used.

10.8 Memory design

Under normal circumstances, the design of memory circuitry is one of the later activities in the hardware design process. This is because it is necessary for the design of software to have progressed at least part of the way to completion before a realistic estimate can be made of the size of RAM and ROM/PROM necessary. For convenience, we deal with the topic at this point, making the assumption that software developed to the stage at which a ROM/PROM of less than 2 Kbytes and a RAM of not more than 256 bytes is indicated.

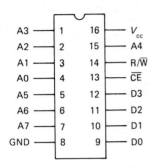

Figure 10.12 Type 2112, 256 × 4 static RAM chip pin connections

As we have discussed in Section 10.6, EPROM is the most convenient form of memory for the storage of program code in this case. An obvious choice would be a single 2716, a 2,048 × 8-bit EPROM whose characteristics are given in Appendix N. The choice of RAM is slightly less well defined. The modest size of RAM and the lack of automatic refresh facilities with the 8080 indicate the choice of static devices. A wide range of static RAM chips is available. In this case, we chose to employ two 2112 chips. Pin connections are given in Figure 10.12. Among the advantages of this device are the simple chip select control, low cost 16-pin package and the need for a single supply voltage only. This latter feature is not of great importance in the design of the system here since the 8080 CPU chip set itself will require three voltage supplies.

We come now to the allocation of addresses to RAM and ROM. In systems with only small amounts of memory, the need for complete decoding of the most significant bits of addresses to generate chip selects can be avoided. As we have said in Section 10.6, start-up and interrupt response requires the presence of EPROM with addresses starting from 0. There are no such restrictions on RAM addresses apart from the need to avoid conflicts with EPROM. We therefore distinguish between EPROM and RAM memory areas in the simplest possible way by a single bit of the total address. Addresses with the most significant bit 0 are allocated to EPROM with all other addresses allocated to RAM. Only bit 15 of the address is involved in the generation of chip selects as shown in the memory circuit diagram in Figure 10.13. Of course, this leads to ambiguity of addresses in that, for example, addresses 8000, 8100, 8200, . . . , FF00 will all access the same location in RAM. However, provided the programmer is aware of the memory configuration, this should cause no conflicts.

10.9 Interrupt handling

In Section 10.5 we have discussed the provision of the real time clock which is used by the system software to generate the various timing intervals required by the two processes. The decision to use the clock

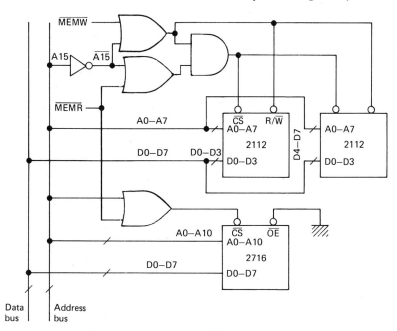

Figure 10.13   System RAM and EPROM

to generate interrupts has been taken to simplify the associated software. As a consequence, however, it is necessary to incorporate interrupt handling circuitry in the system hardware.

Section 3.3 described the way the 8080 responds to an interrupt. Figure 10.14 shows a circuit that is compatible with this response. When a low–high transition occurs on the RTC line, a '1' is latched into the bistable. This latching action is important, particularly if the interrupt is only present for a short time. It will be recalled from Section 3.3 that the interrupt line is only sampled by the 8080 during the final clock cycle of each instruction cycle. A brief pulse on the INT line might not, therefore, be detected if it occurred between one sample point and the next. Latching ensures that the interrupt is always recognised, no matter how short.

Q10.9

The 8080 responds to the interrupt by first disabling the interrupt and taking the interrupt enable line INTE low. This occurs during clock cycle T1 of machine cycle M1 as shown in Figure 2.8 of Appendix A. During clock cycle T2, the status information appears on the data bus and the interrupt acknowledge signal $\overline{\text{INTA}}$ is generated by the 8080 CPU chip set as shown in Figure 4.13. At this point, the interrupting device must 'jam' or force, on the data bus, the code for the next instruction to be executed.

The circuit shown in Figure 10.14 uses the INTE signal to reset the interrupt bistable. So long as INTE is low, the bistable cannot

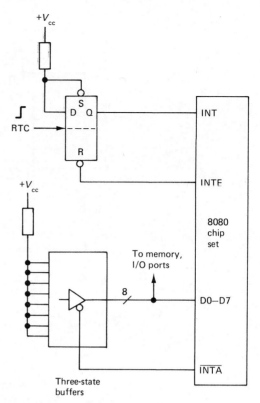

Figure 10.14   Interrupt circuit

respond to a further interrupt. The 8080 CPU also cannot respond to an interrupt during this time. It is the programmer's responsibility to ensure that the interrupt is re-enabled at the appropriate point by including an enable interrupt, EI, instruction in the program. This allows the 8080 to respond to interrupts again and takes line INTE high, thus permitting the next RTC low–high transition to latch '1' in the bistable.

Figure 10.14 also shows that the interrupt acknowledge signal is used to enable the three-state buffers which jam the next instruction code. In this case, the code is FF, which corresponds to an RST 38 instruction. The first instruction of the real time clock interrupt service routine must therefore be located at address 0038. This is compatible with the address space allocated to the 2716 EPROM in the system.

10.10   Software design

In terms of development cost, we now enter the most significant part of the design/development cycle. The cost implications of software development are particularly important in this case because of the

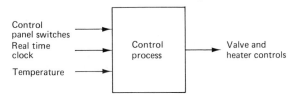

Figure 10.15 Level 1 specification

small production run. To keep the design process as efficient as possible, the top-down structured approach described in Chapter 6 will be used.

Figure 10.15 shows the level 1 description of the program. The decomposition to level 2 is well defined in this case since routines to handle the start-up/reset condition and interrupts must be quite distinct from the main sequence control program. Control can pass asynchronously from the main sequence to the interrupt service or reset service only as the result of the external event. This external event is the pressing of the STOP switch or the arrival of a real time clock pulse. Both interrupt service and reset service therefore constitute well defined level 2 program modules. Decomposition to level 2 is shown in Figure 10.16.

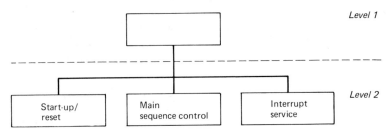

Figure 10.16 Decomposition to level 2

Main sequence control is by far the most complex level 2 module and will almost certainly require further decomposition. We note first that two distinct processes are implemented using the one sequence control program. It will therefore be necessary at the start of the program to pass the appropriate time and temperature parameters to the program. This requires a level 3 module to scan the control switches and detect whether the process 1 or process 2 select switch has been operated. The appropriate time and temperature parameters are then passed back to the main level 2 module.

As part of the process sequence it is necessary at times to raise the temperature to some predetermined level. We identify the program which performs this function as a level 3 module. Similarly, the program that maintains the temperature at a given level constitutes another level 3 module. In heating to a given target temperature, or

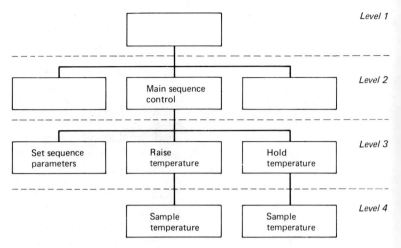

Figure 10.17   Decomposition to level 4

maintaining a temperature, it will be necessary to sample the actual temperature in vessel C. This will involve the initiation of an AD conversion and the taking in of the resulting data byte. A level 4 module is identified as performing this operation.

The decomposition diagram shown in Figure 10.17 should not be regarded as unchangeable. As the program design proceeds, it is quite possible that further decomposition may be necessary. When this occurs, a new decomposition diagram should be produced since it forms a valuable record of the program structure.

10.11   Data transfers between modules

Having carried the process of decomposition as far as is considered necessary, it is a useful exercise to specify the way in which data will be conveyed between program modules. With assembly language programs the most common method of transferring data is to use specified registers or dedicated memory locations. We shall use both methods in this case.

Let us consider the data transfers necessary between the modules identified in the decomposition diagram of Figure 10.17. One fairly obvious transfer is the temperature measurement from the level 4 module to one of the temperature-controlling level 3 modules. We specify here that the 8-bit temperature measurement shall be transferred via register A. This means that on exit from the 'sample temperature' module, the temperature measurement must be in register A.

Numbers relating to temperatures and timing intervals must also be transferred to the level 3 modules which heat the liquid to a given temperature and hold at a temperature for a given period. In this case we specify that temperature is transferred via register B and period via register C.

The other major data transfer is that of the process time and temperature parameters from the module in which they are generated back to the main sequence control module. There are four parameters to be transferred: two time values and two temperature values. Times are in the range 30–60 min and temperatures in the range of 40–80°C. A single byte will therefore suffice for each parameter, making a total of 4 bytes to transfer. With this number of bytes, the use of dedicated memory locations is indicated and we therefore store the temperatures in symbolic addresses T1 and T2, and the time intervals in addresses P1 and P2.

As a final point concerning the representation and transfer of data within the program, we note that it will be necessary as part of the control process to change individual lines of the output port without affecting the other lines. This is a common requirement where valves, relays, etc., are to be controlled. A simple way of doing this is to maintain a memory location whose contents are a record of the current state of the individual output port lines. We allocate the symbolic name OPSTAT to this location. If OPSTAT contains 3 therefore, this means that lines 0 and 1 of the output port are at 1 with all other lines at 1.

To change the state of an individual ouput line, it is necessary to use logical AND and OR operations. Suppose we wish to make line 2 of port 0 a logical 1 without changing any of the other lines. A logical OR operation is performed between the contents of OPSTAT and 02. To force line 2 to a logical 0, a logical AND is performed between the contents of OPSTAT and FB. In each case, the resulting byte is then output to the port and also stored as the current state in OPSTAT.

10.12 Module structure

Turning now to the design of the structure of individual modules, we commence with the level 1 module as is normal with the top-down approach. The structure in this case is so simple as to be almost trivial. It must be remembered, however, that the interrupt and reset service routines are important in determining the way the system operates, although interrupt service is not included as such in the level 1 structure. This is a situation in which the standard methods of describing high-level language program structures are not entirely satisfactory for assembly language programs. Figure 10.18 is an attempt to show the relationship between the level 1 module and the interrupt/reset activity. The formal module structure is shown in Figure 10.19. The assembly language source code for the level 1 module is shown in Figure 10.20. Note the necessity for setting the

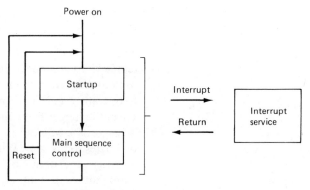

Figure 10.18   Main program flow

stack pointer and disabling the interrupt before calling the start-up routine. This is because the CALL instruction and the response to an interrupt both make use of the stack. The disable interrupt operation is a precaution rather than a necessity since the 8080 will start up with the interrupt disabled.

Structures for level 2 modules are shown in Figures 10.5, 10.21 and 10.22. They can all be coded and, at least partially, tested at this stage. Complete testing of the main sequence control and start-up modules is only possible in conjunction with the system I/O hardware. Figure 10.22 reveals the method used for counting the 1-s real time clock pulses. For reasons of space, assembly language listings for all modules will not be given. Listings of representative modules at all

```
DISABLE INTERRUPT
SET STACK POINTER
DO INDEFINITELY
    START-UP SEQUENCE
    MAIN SEQUENCE
END DO
```

Figure 10.19   Level 1 module structure

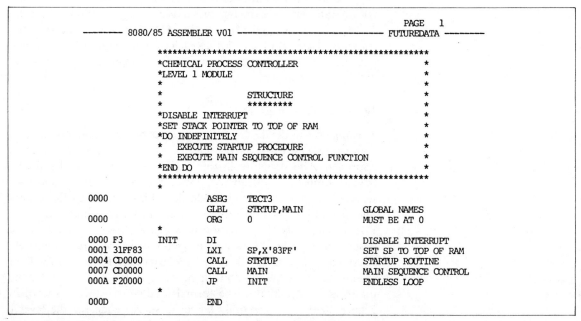

```
                                                    PAGE   1
      -------- 8080/85 ASSEMBLER V01 ---------------------- FUTUREDATA --------

            ***************************************************
            *CHEMICAL PROCESS CONTROLLER                     *
            *LEVEL 1 MODULE                                  *
            *                                                *
            *                 STRUCTURE                      *
            *                 *********                      *
            *DISABLE INTERRUPT                               *
            *SET STACK POINTER TO TOP OF RAM                 *
            *DO INDEFINITELY                                 *
            *   EXECUTE STARTUP PROCEDURE                    *
            *   EXECUTE MAIN SEQUENCE CONTROL FUNCTION       *
            *END DO                                          *
            ***************************************************
            *
0000                   ASEG      TECT3
                       GLBL      STRTUP,MAIN        GLOBAL NAMES
0000                   ORG       0                  MUST BE AT 0
            *
0000 F3     INIT       DI                           DISABLE INTERRUPT
0001 31FF83            LXI       SP,X'83FF'         SET SP TO TOP OF RAM
0004 CD0000            CALL      STRTUP             STARTUP ROUTINE
0007 CD0000            CALL      MAIN               MAIN SEQUENCE CONTROL
000A F20000            JP        INIT               ENDLESS LOOP
            *
000D                   END
```

Figure 10.20   Level 1 module program code

```
DISABLE INTERRUPT
HEATER OFF
CLOSE VALVE A
CLOSE VALVE C
DO UNTIL START = 1
    SCAN START
END DO
```

Figure 10.21 Start-up/reset routine

```
SAVE WORKING REGISTERS
SEC = SEC + 1
IF SEC = 60
    THEN
            SEC = 0
            MIN = MIN + 1
    ELSE
            CONTINUE
END IF
RESTORE WORKING REGISTERS
ENABLE INTERRUPT
RETURN FROM INTERRUPT
```

Figure 10.22 Interrupt service routine

levels are, however, included. Figures 10.23–10.26 show listings for the start-up/reset, interrupt service and main sequence control routines, respectively.

Moving down the hierarchy, consider Figure 10.25 which shows pseudo-code describing the module that heats the liquid until the temperature reaches TX. Whilst the structure appears satisfactory on the surface, it lacks the property of robustness discussed in Section 8.2. Robustness is a measure of the ability of the program to deal with the unexpected. Consider what would happen, if we employ the structure of Figure 10.27, if the temperature somehow exceeded TX. The heater would remain on with the liquid getting hotter and hotter since the program would never find the T = TX condition to be true. Figure 10.26 shows an alternative structure which provides additional robustness for safe operation. Pseudo-code for the remaining level 3 modules is shown in Figures 10.29 and 10.30.

10.13 Hardware prototype construction, testing and debugging

When the hardware design has been finalised as described in Sections 10.6–10.9, a wire-wrapped prototype can be constructed. The step-by-step methods described in Chapter 9 can be used with advantage. Power supply rails (d.c.) are first connected to appropriate pins of

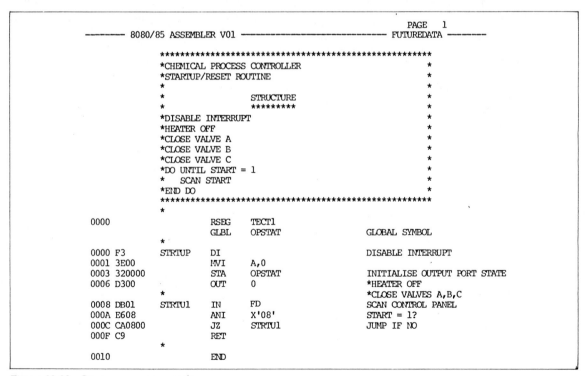

```
                                                           PAGE   1
        --------  8080/85 ASSEMBLER V01  -------------------------------  FUTUREDATA  --------

                 *****************************************************
                 *CHEMICAL PROCESS CONTROLLER                       *
                 *STARTUP/RESET ROUTINE                             *
                 *                                                  *
                 *                       STRUCTURE                  *
                 *                       *********                  *
                 *DISABLE INTERRUPT                                 *
                 *HEATER OFF                                        *
                 *CLOSE VALVE A                                     *
                 *CLOSE VALVE B                                     *
                 *CLOSE VALVE C                                     *
                 *DO UNTIL START = 1                                *
                 *    SCAN START                                    *
                 *END DO                                            *
                 *****************************************************
                 *
    0000                  RSEG     TECT1
                          GLBL     OPSTAT           GLOBAL SYMBOL
                 *
    0000 F3      STRTUP   DI                        DISABLE INTERRUPT
    0001 3E00             MVI      A,0
    0003 320000           STA      OPSTAT           INITIALISE OUTPUT PORT STATE
    0006 D300             OUT      0                *HEATER OFF
                 *                                  *CLOSE VALVES A,B,C
    0008 DB01    STRTU1   IN       FD               SCAN CONTROL PANEL
    000A E608             ANI      X'08'            START = 1?
    000C CA0800           JZ       STRTU1           JUMP IF NO
    000F C9               RET
                 *
    0010                  END
```

Figure 10.23 Start-up program code

```
                                                          PAGE   1
      -------- 8080/85 ASSEMBLER V01 --------------------------- FUTUREDATA -

                  *****************************************************
                  *CHEMICAL PROCESS CONTROLLER                       *
                  *INTERRUPT SERVICE ROUTINE                         *
                  *                                                  *
                  *                  STRUCTURE                       *
                  *                  ********                        *
                  *SAVE WORKING REGISTERS                            *
                  *SEC = SEC + 1                                     *
                  *IF SEC = 60                                       *
                  *    THEN                                          *
                  *          SEC = 0                                 *
                  *          MIN = MIN + 1                           *
                  *    ELSE                                          *
                  *          CONTINUE                                *
                  *END IF                                            *
                  *RESTORE WORKING REGISTERS                         *
                  *ENABLE INTERRUPT                                  *
                  *RETURN                                            *
                  *****************************************************
                  *
      0000               ASEC     TECT2
                         GLBL     SEC,MIN              GLOBAL NAMES
      0000               ORG      X'0038'
                  *
                  *SAVE REGISTERS*
      0038 F5             PUSH     PSW
      0039 E5             PUSH     H
      003A D5             PUSH     D
      003B C5             PUSH     B
                  *REGISTERS SAVED*
                  *
      003C 3A0000         LDA      SEC                 GET SECONDS
      003F 3C             INR      A                   SEC = SEC + 1
      0040 320000         STA      SEC                 SAVE SECONDS
                  *START OF IF-THEN STRUCTURE
      0043 FE3C           CPI      60                  SEC = 60?
      0045 C25400         JNZ      INT1                JUMP IF NO
                  *THEN
      0048 3E00           MVI      A,0
      004A 320000         STA      SEC                 SECONDS = 0
      004D 3A0000         LDA      MIN                 GET MINUTES
      0050 3C             INR      A                   MIN = MIN + 1
      0051 320000         STA MIN                      SAVE MINUTES
                  *END IF
                  *
                  *NOW RESTORE REGISTERS*
      0054 C1     INT1    POP      B
      0055 D1             POP      D
      0056 E1             POP      H
      0057 F1             POP      PSW
                  *REGISTERS RESTORED*
                  *
      0058 FB             EI       ENABLE INTERRUPT
      0059 C9             RET
                  *
      005A               END
```

Figure 10.24

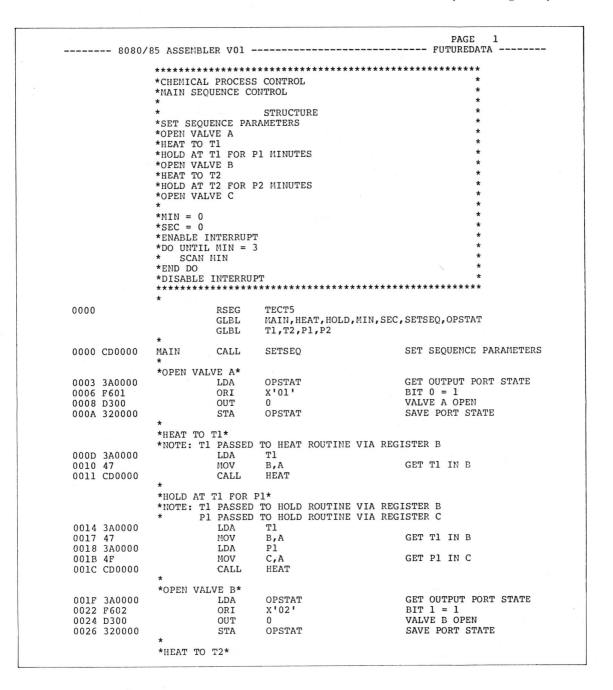

```
                                                      PAGE   1
   -------- 8080/85 ASSEMBLER V01 ----------------------------- FUTUREDATA --------

               ********************************************************
               *CHEMICAL PROCESS CONTROL                             *
               *MAIN SEQUENCE CONTROL                                *
               *                                                     *
               *                STRUCTURE                            *
               *SET SEQUENCE PARAMETERS                              *
               *OPEN VALVE A                                         *
               *HEAT TO T1                                           *
               *HOLD AT T1 FOR P1 MINUTES                            *
               *OPEN VALVE B                                         *
               *HEAT TO T2                                           *
               *HOLD AT T2 FOR P2 MINUTES                            *
               *OPEN VALVE C                                         *
               *                                                     *
               *MIN = 0                                              *
               *SEC = 0                                              *
               *ENABLE INTERRUPT                                     *
               *DO UNTIL MIN = 3                                     *
               *    SCAN MIN                                         *
               *END DO                                               *
               *DISABLE INTERRUPT                                    *
               ********************************************************
               *
   0000                        RSEG    TECT5
                               GLBL    MAIN,HEAT,HOLD,MIN,SEC,SETSEQ,OPSTAT
                               GLBL    T1,T2,P1,P2
               *
   0000 CD0000  MAIN           CALL    SETSEQ                SET SEQUENCE PARAMETERS
               *
               *OPEN VALVE A*
   0003 3A0000                 LDA     OPSTAT                GET OUTPUT PORT STATE
   0006 F601                   ORI     X'01'                 BIT 0 = 1
   0008 D300                   OUT     0                     VALVE A OPEN
   000A 320000                 STA     OPSTAT                SAVE PORT STATE
               *
               *HEAT TO T1*
               *NOTE: T1 PASSED TO HEAT ROUTINE VIA REGISTER B
   000D 3A0000                 LDA     T1
   0010 47                     MOV     B,A                   GET T1 IN B
   0011 CD0000                 CALL    HEAT
               *
               *HOLD AT T1 FOR P1*
               *NOTE: T1 PASSED TO HOLD ROUTINE VIA REGISTER B
               *      P1 PASSED TO HOLD ROUTINE VIA REGISTER C
   0014 3A0000                 LDA     T1
   0017 47                     MOV     B,A                   GET T1 IN B
   0018 3A0000                 LDA     P1
   001B 4F                     MOV     C,A                   GET P1 IN C
   001C CD0000                 CALL    HEAT
               *
               *OPEN VALVE B*
   001F 3A0000                 LDA     OPSTAT                GET OUTPUT PORT STATE
   0022 F602                   ORI     X'02'                 BIT 1 = 1
   0024 D300                   OUT     0                     VALVE B OPEN
   0026 320000                 STA     OPSTAT                SAVE PORT STATE
               *
               *HEAT TO T2*
```

Figure 10.25

```
                                                              PAGE   2
        -------- 8080/85 ASSEMBLER V01 ---------------------------- FUTUREDATA --------

                        *NOTE: T2 PASSED TO HEAT ROUTINE VIA REGISTER B
        0029 3A0000     LDA     T2
        002C 47         MOV     B,A                   GET T2 IN B
        002D CD0000     CALL    HEAT
                        *
                        *HOLD AT T2 FOR P2 MINUTES*
                        *NOTE: T2 PASSED TO HOLD ROUTINE VIA REGISTER B
                        *      P2 PASSED TO HOLD ROUTINE VIA REGISTER C
        0030 3A0000     LDA     T2
        0033 47         MOV     B,A                   GET T2 IN B
        0034 3A0000     LDA     P2
        0037 4F         MOV     C,A                   GET P2 IN C
        0038 CD0000     CALL    HOLD
                        *
                        *OPEN VALVE C*
        003B 3A0000     LDA     OPSTAT                GET OUTPUT PORT STATE
        003E F604       ORI     X'04'                 BIT 2 = 0
        0040 D300       OUT     0                     VALVE C OPEN
        0042 320000     STA     OPSTAT                SAVE PORT STATE
                        *
                        *WAIT 3 MINUTES*
        0045 3E00       MVI     A,0
        0047 320000     STA     MIN                   MIN = 0
        004A 320000     STA     SEC                   SEC = 0
        004D FB         EI                            ENABLE INTERRUPT
                        *DO UNTIL MIN = 3
        004E 3A0000 SCANM LDA   MIN                   SCAN MIN
        0051 FE03       CPI     3                     MIN = 3?
        0053 C24E00     JNZ     SCANM                 JUMP IF NO
                        *END DO
                        *
        0056 F3         DI                            DISABLE INTERRUPT
        0057 C9         RET
                        *
        0058            END
```

Figure 10.26

```
SEC = 0
MIN = 0
ENABLE INTERRUPT
DO UNTIL MIN = PX
    SAMPLE T
    IF T LESS THAN TX
        THEN
                HEATER ON
        ELSE
            IF T GREATER THAN TX
                THEN
                    HEATER OFF
                ELSE
                    CONTINUE
            END IF
    END IF
END DO
DISABLE INTERRUPT
:NOTE PX IN REGISTER C ON ENTRY
      TX IN REGISTER B ON ENTRY
```

```
HEATER ON
DO UNTIL T = TX
    SAMPLE T
END DO
```

Figure 10.27 Heat to TX using DO UNTIL

```
SAMPLE T
DO WHILE T LESS THAN TX
    HEATER ON
    SAMPLE T
END DO
```

Figure 10.28 Heat to TX using DO WHILE

Figure 10.29 Hold at TX for PX minutes

```
            SCAN PROCESS 1 CONTROL SWITCH
            IF PROCESS 1 = 1
                THEN
                        P1 = 30
                        P2 = 40
                        T1 = 60
                        T2 = 80
                ELSE
                        P1 = 50
                        P2 = 60
                        T1 = 40
                        T2 = 70
            END IF
```

Q10.10 *Figure 10.30* Set sequence parameters

integrated circuit sockets with decoupling capacitors at appropriate points. The CPU chip set consists of the 8080 CPU, 8228 bus controller and 8224 clock generator together with a suitable crystal. This chip set is connected as shown in Figure 4.13. Testing of the chip set is described in Section 9.3.

The next stage of construction involves wiring the two 2112 memory chips, as shown in Figure 10.13, to provide the system RAM. This is then tested as described in Section 9.3. The 2716 EPROM is similarly wired and first tested using an ICE to read data from a test EPROM programmed with known data. Code for simple test programs can then be programmed in the 2716 and executed under control of the ICE. Input and output ports can then be wired and tested one at a time using lamps and switches as indicators and digital data sources. Test programs running in the MDS with the ICE probe connected are used for this purpose.

After testing of the I/O ports associated with the ADC, the ADC itself should be wired into the circuit. A variable voltage source can be used as an input for the purposes of testing. Again, a test program executed by the MDS is employed. This test program must initiate an AD conversion by generating a 'start conversion' pulse, STC, as shown in Figure 10.6. This must appear on line 4 of the output port as shown in Figure 10.9. The busy signal is then scanned on line 0 of input port B until a high level indicates that the conversion is complete. A byte of data is then taken in via port B. Figure 10.31 describes the test program in pseudo-code form.

```
OUTPUT 1 TO S̅T̅C̅
OUTPUT 0 TO S̅T̅C̅
OUTPUT 1 TO S̅T̅C̅
DO UNTIL B̅U̅S̅Y̅ = 1
    INPUT B̅U̅S̅Y̅
END DO
```

Figure 10.31 Program to test ADC and input port

A further stage of hardware development involves wiring up and testing the interrupt circuit shown in Figure 10.4. For testing purposes a switch is used to implement the 0 to 1 transition required by this circuit to initiate an interrupt. The test program which will run at any convenient location in the MDS consists of the two instructions shown below:

```
INTEST  NOP
        JP    INTEST
```

This program is, of course, an endless loop. Now, remember that the circuit shown in Figure 10.14 jams the code FF on to the data bus when the 8080 acknowledges the interrupt. This is a restart instruction which causes a jump to occur to address 0038. To test the interrupt circuit, we therefore place a breakpoint at 0038 and execute the program shown above. When the test switch is operated generating an interrupt, the jump to 0038 should take place and the program breakpoint will become effective.

After wiring the real time clock circuit shown in Figure 10.7, it may be tested by applying a.c. mains input and checking the output of the clipping circuit with an oscilloscope. The output of the divider may also be checked using an oscilloscope, although a pulse counter may be more convenient.

10.14   Final testing

On completion of prototype testing and construction, the final stage in development proceeds. This involves testing the developed programs in conjunction with the hardware prototype. For the system considered here, the initial test might take place with the control panel and valves connected, but with a simulated load for the heater and a voltage source simulating the temperature transducer. As we have described in Section 9.4, the MDS ICE facility plays an important role in this test procedure since it allows system programs to run under full monitor control.

Assuming that the initial system test is satisfactory, a further test can be undertaken with the real heater and temperature transducer connected. In this case, vessels A and B must contain liquid. This is a critical stage in the test procedure since it is the first time that the complete hardware/software system has been operated as a single unit. During this test, the accuracy of time intervals and temperatures may be checked. Finally, the program is transferred from the MDS RAM to EPROM. This may be carried out as a single operation or could be done in stages as described in Section 7.5.

Questions

10.1   List the various stages in the design/development procedure for a typical microprocessor system.

10.2   In the case study described in this chapter, what are the two main reasons for choosing the 8080 microprocessor?

10.3 What reasons are given for employing the real time clock as a source of interrupts instead of simply scanning the clock via an input port?

10.4 What is the reason for using an external real time clock rather than a program timing loop for generating the time intervals required by the system?

10.5 What limits the lowest frequency of usable real time clock pulses?

10.6 Explain how a 'power-on reset' can be implemented.

10.7 What is the function of RAM in a dedicated microprocessor system?

10.8 State the address of the first instruction to be executed after a reset operation on the 8080 microprocessor.

10.9 Explain why it is important to use a latching circuit in the 8080 interrupt interface if the interrupt source generates very wide or very narrow pulses.

10.10 Code the program modules described in Figures 10.29 and 10.30 using the instruction set of any microprocessor with which you are familiar and any assembler to which you have access.

Chapter 11 Practical aspects of programmable memory

Objectives of this chapter *When you have completed studying this chapter and have performed the recommended practical work you should be able to:*

1 *Use manufacturers' data to select programmable memory devices.*
2 *Use manufacturers' data to define operating conditions for programmable memory devices.*
3 *Use EPROM to store a development program.*
4 *Program a programmable memory device.*
5 *State the procedure for erasing EPROM.*

11.1 The role of EPROM in microprocessor system development

At various points in the text up to this point, the particular role of EPROM in the hardware/software development cycle has been emphasised. Indeed, Chapter 7 described in some detail how the provision of an EPROM programmer allows a program to be transferred module-by-module from the host system RAM into the target system EPROM until the target system is completely free-standing.

Because EPROM is so useful in the development of microprocessor systems, TEC standard unit U80/674, which this text is intended to support, requires that the student should have practical experience in certain aspects of the use of EPROM. In this chapter, we describe various EPROM devices currently available and suggest practical exercises in their use which may be undertaken by the reader. Of course, the facilities available to the reader will determine the extent to which the reader can carry out these exercises exactly as specified. As with exercises suggested in other chapters, it is assumed that the reader has access to at least a software development station which supports assembly language. In addition to this, to complete the exercises in this chapter, an EPROM programmer is required which allows object programs in the development station RAM to be transferred to an EPROM. Devices of this kind also allow data to be read from a programmed EPROM. Figure 11.1 shows a suitable system.

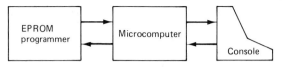

Figure 11.1 Software development station with EPROM programmer

11.2 Choosing programmable memory devices

When developing a microprocessor system that includes non-volatile programmable memory, one of the planning decisions is the choice of the number and type of the memory devices to be used. In this section we consider the factors affecting this choice. We must first of all be quite clear as to the type of device to which we are referring. Many microprocessor systems incorporate more than one type of non-volatile memory. Magnetic surface stores, e.g. in the form of floppy or hard disks, tapes or drums, are widely used for secondary stores in general-purpose microprocessor systems. This is not the type of memory we are considering here. In this chapter we are concerned with high-speed non-volatile monolithic memory which occupies part of the system memory address space in the same way as RAM. It is used to hold program code and permanent data and is commonly referred to as EPROM.

The term EPROM means 'erasable programmable read-only memory'. EPROMs are therefore devices which can be made to store data or program code.

The process of storing this data or program code is described as programming the EPROM. As the name implies, these devices are erasable which means that the stored data can be removed, a process sometimes described as 'washing' the EPROM. After washing, the EPROM can be reprogrammed with different data.

When choosing a programmable memory device, the amount of data to be stored will be an important consideration. If the EPROM is to store program code, the total number of bytes may not be known accurately until program development is complete. This could delay hardware design decisions in some cases. An experienced programmer can, however, usually estimate the approximate size of a program quite early in the design process. Therefore, provided the hardware designer allows a generous margin of error, this problem need not necessarily hold up hardware design. The more popular types of EPROM are low-cost devices and over-provision is not therefore normally a serious constraint.

Other factors affecting the choice of EPROM are primarily concerned with operating characteristics. The more important of these factors are listed below. The consideration of memory size, although dealt with above, is included for completeness.

Factors affecting EPROM choice

1   *Size of memory required*, i.e. number and size of words to be stored.

2   *Programming method*   Programming almost always requires a special-purpose programming unit which is not the same for different types of EPROM. The cost and availability of a suitable programmer will obviously affect the choice of EPROM. If a programmer is available for a particular type of EPROM, it will obviously be desirable to use this type wherever possible.

3   *Erasing method*   Erasing or washing an EPROM will also require special-purpose equipment. This will affect the choice of EPROM, the considerations being the same as those for programming.

4   *Access time*   Many EPROMs have quite long access times compared with, say, monolithic RAM devices. For the slower EPROMs therefore, it may be necessary to incorporate wait states in memory read and write operations. This complicates the system hardware.

Q11.7

5   *Speed of programming*   Although the time required to program data in an EPROM memory location is quite long compared with a RAM write operation, this is not often an important factor in the choice of EPROM. Programming an EPROM is not likely to be part of the normal system operation, only being required when the data or program stored in the EPROM is modified.

6   *Speed of erasure*   For some EPROMs, washing is a long process, 30 or 60 min in some cases. This is much longer than the time required for programming. Although washing will not occur in a completed system which includes an EPROM, the length of time required can be important during system development where it is necessary during a frequently iterated part of the development cycle. For this reason the majority of development should normally be undertaken with the program in RAM, transferring the code to EPROM only in the very final stages.

A further inconvenience which exists with some types of EPROM is that only complete erasure of data is possible. It is not, for example, possible to erase the contents of individual addresses or groups of addresses. The most common types of EPROM which are UV-erasable (as described in Section 11.3) fall into this category. After washing, therefore, the complete EPROM must be reprogrammed. Some of the so-called 'electrically erasable' EPROMs allow selective erasure of individual locations but, at the time of writing, they are less versatile and more costly than the UV-erasable variety.

Q11.1

11.3   Non-volatile monolithic memory devices

For most engineers, the ideal monolithic memory device would combine the speed and convenience of currently available static RAM chips with the ability to retain stored data indefinitely when the power is removed. Perhaps the semiconductor manufacturers will achieve this within the publishing lifetime of this text. At the time of writing, however, a variety of non-volatile programmable memory devices is available, each of which offers some, but not all, of the characteristics of the ideal memory device described above. In this section we describe a representative selection of these programmable memory chips.

UVEPROMs

These are programmable devices which store bits of data as 'packets' of charge on capacitors within the integrated circuit. Although the stored charge will leak away with time, the process is very slow. Typical examples of this type of memory will retain data for 10 years or more. The UVEPROM package is fitted with a transparent window immediately above the integrated circuit which forms the memory. Exposing the circuit to high-energy ultra-violet light causes a photocurrent to flow from the capacitors storing charge. The **Q11.2** discharge of these capacitors therefore erases the stored data.

A typical example of a UVEPROM, the 2716, is described by the data sheet in Appendex N, from which it will be seen that to erase data, the 2716 must be placed about 1 inch from an ultra-violet lamp with an intensity of 120 mW/m^2. During normal use, the stored data may be protected by covering the transparent window with opaque material.

The more recently introduced EPROMs all have similar programming requirements. This will typically involve applying a programming pulse to one of the chip input lines while the address and data are also present on the appropriate lines. It may be necessary in addition to increase the supply voltage from the value used when reading data. The programming procedure for the 2716 is taken as typical and described in more detail in Appendix P and later in this section. A brief description of the more common UVEPROM types is given below:

1702 This was the first popular UVEPROM. Organised as 256×8 bits, it represented a significant advance on previous non-volatile programmable memory devices. The main disadvantages of the 1702 are the relatively slow speed, complex programming requirements and the need for multiple voltage supplies. One of the programming difficulties is the need for fast rise-time programming pulses with an amplitude of around 30 V. This makes the circuitry required for the programmer quite complex and therefore expensive.

The 1702 has largely been superceded by the more convenient

UVEPROMs listed below. It would not normally be considered economic to incorporate the 1702 in new designs.

2708 The organisation of this device is 1,024 × 8 bits. Currently, probably the most popular UVEPROM, it provides economical non-volatile memory in a wide variety of systems. Most varieties of the 2708 require multiple voltage supplies although single supply types can be found. One disadvantage of the 2708 is that the required programming pulse amplitude is typically 26 V. This again makes the design of the programmer more complex than is the case with some other UVEPROMs.

2716, 2732 and 2764 These UVEPROMs, organised as 2,048 × 8 4,096 × 8 and 8,192 × 8 bits, respectively, have similar operating characteristics and can be dealt with at the same time. One of the major advantages of the 2716, 2732 and 2764 compared with earlier EPROMs such as the 2708 and 1702 is the relative ease with which they may be programmed. This is demonstrated by Figure 11.2 which is a simplfied version of the programming timing diagram. The 2716 is activated in the programming mode by taking $\overline{OE}$ high and connecting the V_{pp} line to +25V. The address to be programmed is applied to the address lines and the desired data byte is applied to the data lines. A period t_s of at least 2 μs must then elapse to allow address and data to become established. After this, $\overline{CE/PGM}$ is taken high for between 45 and 55 ms. At the end of this period, data must remain stable on the data lines for a further 2μs $= t_h$ after $\overline{CE/PGM}$ has returned to the low state. It is important to ensure that $\overline{CE/PGM}$ is pulsed in this way and not allowed to remain permanently high. Note that the programming pulse requires only standard TTL logic levels.

Q11.5

A wide range of EPROM programmers are commercially available. The facilities vary greatly depending on the price. The simplest type provide a hexadecimal keyboard for setting up the address and data. Programming is essentially manual, to one address at a time. More sophisticated and costly devices include a memory which can hold data before it is programmed into the EPROM. This allows the user to check the correctness of the data. All programmers will also allow data to be read from programmed EPROMs.

The most useful EPROM programmers form part of an MDS. In this case, programs are developed and debugged using the powerful software support facilities. Hardware and software is then integrated with the help of the ICE and the memory substitution facility. When the program is completely checked, the machine code can be programmed directly and automatically into an EPROM.

If a commercial EPROM programmer is not available, it is a straight-forward matter to implement the simple timing for programming shown in Figure 11.2. The most obvious method is to make use of an

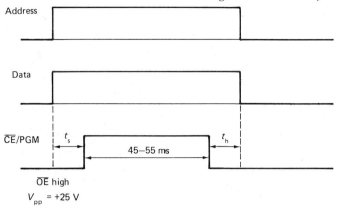

Figure 11.2 Programming waveforms for 2716 EPROM

existing microprocessor system, driving address, data and $\overline{\text{CE}}$/PGM lines directly via output ports. An input port can similarly be used to read data from the EPROM. Figure 11.3 shows how two 8-bit output ports and one bidirectional I/O port could provide the necessary facilities for programming and reading from 2716 EPROMs. It should be noted that when using a very simple approach to EPROM programming such as that shown in Figure 11.3, it is necessary to provide a manual switch to maintain V_{pp} at +25 V when in the programming mode. Particular care must also be taken when initialising the system to ensure that $\overline{\text{CE}}$/PGM does not become permanently high.

A program to implement the following sequence of operations would

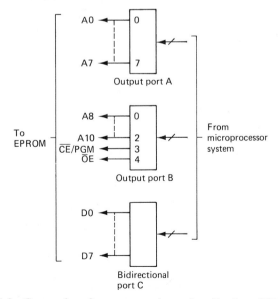

Figure 11.3 Connections for programming and reading from 2716 EPROM

program one location of the EPROM when connected as shown in Figure 11.3 with $V_{pp} = +25$ V:

1   Output address bits A0–A7 on lines 0–7 of port A.
2   Output address bits A8–A10 on lines 0–2 of port B with line 3 at 0 and line 4 at 1.
3   Output data byte via port C.
4   Wait at least 2 μs. Normal delay resulting from instruction execution times may be sufficient to ensure this. Alternatively, execution of one or more NOP instructions will provide the required delay.
5   Output 1 on line 3 of port B keeping all other lines unchanged.
6   Wait 45 ms. A delay loop should be used for this purpose.
7   Output 0 on line 3 of port B, keeping all other lines unchanged.
8   Wait at least 2 μs.

Normally, the instruction to program one EPROM location would form part of a larger routine which programs part or whole of the 2716. This in turn would be followed by a routine which reads the programmed EPROM to check whether the programming has been successful.

One problem with the 2716 programming method outlined above is that hardware or software malfunctions could leave $\overline{\text{CE}}$/PGM in the permanently high state. An alternative approach therefore uses a monostable to drive the $\overline{\text{CE}}$/PGM line. The monostable is triggered by a change of state on the microprocessor output line. This arrangement ensures that the $\overline{\text{CE}}$/PGM line does not remain at the high level for longer than the monostable period. Reference 11.4 describes a slightly different approach to the design of a 2716 programmer; this also uses a monostable to generate the programming pulse. Reference 11.1 describes a 2708 programmer in some detail.

Fusible-link PROMs

These are devices in which each bit store circuit is manufactured with a fusible link. Programming is accomplished by selectively applying a suitably high voltage to melt or 'blow' these links. Fusible link PROMs come in various types ranging from high-speed bipolar devices with access times of less than 50 ns to lower-power CMOS devices. The usual rule applies in that the higher the speed, the greater the power consumption.

In many ways, the operating characteristics of fusible-link PROMs correspond to those of the ideal, non-volatile memory devices described earlier. Unfortunately, they have the major disadvantage that they cannot be erased and reprogrammed. The melting of fusible links is an irreversible process; therefore, although useful for storing fully debugged program code, fusible-link PROMs do not normally play a large part in the design/development cycle.

As an example of a fusible-link PROM, Figure 11.4 shows pin connections and a block diagram for the Am27S15 which is a 4,096-bit bipolar PROM with an access time better than 60 ns. Data are organised in the PROM as 512×8 bits. Output data from the memory can be latched into a register which itself has three-state outputs. When the strobe line ST is high, the 8-bit output register is transparent. The three-state output gates are enabled when $\overline{E1}$ is low and E2 is high. Taking ST low latches the data in the output register and no further change in the output then takes place until ST goes high, even if the address changes. In the unprogrammed state, the PROM contains all zeros. Blowing a link programs a 1 in the bit position. Reference 11.5 describes a programmer for a popular range of fusible-link PROMs.

EAROMs

Figure 11.5 shows details of an electrically erasable PROM. This device is attractive since its pin configuration is similar to the popular 2716 UVEPROM with the added advantage that it can be quickly and conveniently erased by applying an appropriate erasure voltage. The maximum access time for this device is 450 ns.

A slightly different device is shown in Figure 11.6. This device stores 256 bits of data which is written in and read out in serial form. Like the device shown in Figure 11.5, the MCM2801 is electrically erasable. In this case, however, individual words can be erased and rewritten, unlike the MCM2816 which erases all addresses when the erasure voltage is applied.

11.4   EPROM programming

By this time the student should have a general understanding of the use of EPROMs to store program code and data during the later stages in the development of a microprocessor system. To consolidate this understanding it is important to gain practical experience in the use of a programmer to program a suitable EPROM. As we said at the beginning of this chapter, this requires that the student has access to an EPROM programmer. Ideally, this should be associated with an MDS or software development station. This then allows program code in the system RAM to be transferred directly into the EPROM. Facilities will also be available to check that the EPROM has been correctly programmed by reading data back.

By far the most convenient devices for the student to use for

DISTINCTIVE CHARACTERISTICS

- On-chip data latches
- Latched true and complemented output enables for easy word expansion
- Predetermined OFF outputs on power-up
- Plug-in replacement for the 82S115
- Fast access time – 60ns commercial and 90ns military maximum
- Performance pretested with N^2 patterns
- Highly reliable, ultra-fast programming Platinum-Silicide fuses – High programming yield
- Low current PNP inputs
- High current three-state outputs
- Common Generic PROM Series characteristics and programming procedures

LOGIC SYMBOL

21 22 23 1 2 3 4 5 6

A_0 A_1 A_2 A_3 A_4 A_5 A_6 A_7 A_8

20 — E_1

19 — E_2 **Am27S15**
4K LATCHED PROM
18 — ST

Q_0 Q_1 Q_2 Q_3 Q_4 Q_5 Q_6 Q_7

7 8 9 10 14 15 16 17

V_{CC} = Pin 24
GND = Pin 12
(Pins 11 and 13 open)

BPM-010

CONNECTION DIAGRAM
Top View

V_{CC} A_2 A_1 A_0 $\bar{E}_1$ E_2 ST Q_7 Q_6 Q_5 Q_4 NC

24 23 22 21 20 19 18 17 16 15 14 13

Am27S15

1 2 3 4 5 6 7 8 9 10 11 12

A_3 A_4 A_5 A_6 A_7 A_8 Q_0 Q_1 Q_2 Q_3 NC GND

Note: Pin 1 is marked for orientation.
NC = No connection.

BPM-011

ORDERING INFORMATION

Package Type	Temperature Range	Order Number
Hermetic DIP	0°C to +75°C	Am27S15DC
Hermetic DIP	−55°C to +125°C	Am27S15DM

FUNCTIONAL DESCRIPTION

The Am27S15 is an electrically programmable Schottky read only memory incorporating on-chip data and enable latches. The device is organized as 512 words of 8 bits and features three-state outputs with full 16mA drive capability.

When in the transparent mode, with the strobe (ST) input HIGH, reading stored data is accomplished by enabling the chip ($\bar{E}_1$ LOW and E_2 HIGH) and applying the binary word address to the address inputs, A_0-A_8. In this mode, changes of the address inputs cause the outputs, Q_0-Q_7, to read a different stored word; changes of either enable input level disable the outputs, causing them to go to the high impedance state.

Dropping the strobe input to the LOW level places the device in the latched mode of operation. The output condition present (reading a word of stored data or disabled) when the strobe goes LOW remains at the outputs, regardless of further address or enable transitions, until a positive (LOW to HIGH) strobe transition occurs. With the strobe HIGH, Q_0-Q_7 again respond to the address and enable input conditions.

If the strobe is LOW (latched mode) when V_{CC} power is first applied, the outputs will be in the disabled state, eliminating the need for special "power-up" design precautions.

BLOCK DIAGRAM

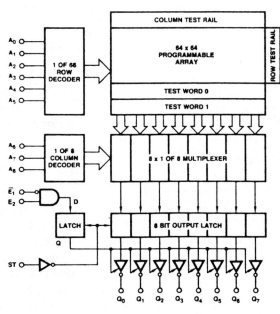

BPM-012

Figure 11.4

MCM2816

2048 × 8-BIT ELECTRICALLY ERASABLE PROM

The MCM2816 is a 16,384-bit Electrically Erasable Programmable Read Only Memory designed for handling data in applications requiring both nonvolatile memory and in-system reprogramming. The industry standard pinout in a 24-pin dual-in-line package makes the MCM2816 EEPROM compatible with the popular MCM2716 EPROM.

The MCM2816 saves time and money because of the in-system erase and reprogram capability. While V_{PP} is at 25 V and $\overline{G}$ is at V_{IL}, a 100 ms active high TTL erase pulse applied to the $\overline{E}$/Progr pin allows the entire memory to be erased to the "1" state. In addition to in-system programmability, this new-generation PROM is programmable on the standard EPROM programmer.

For ease of use, the device operates in the read mode from a single power supply and has a static power-down mode. The MCM2816 is fabricated in floating gate technology for high reliablity and producibility.

- Single + 5 V Power Supply
- Automatic Power-Down Mode (Standby)
- Single + 25 V Power Supply for Erase and Program
- Organized as 2048 Bytes of 8 Bits
- Maximum Access Time = 450 ns MCM2816
- Pin Compatible to MCM68316E and MCM2716
- In-System Program/Erase Capability
- Chip Erase Time of 10 ms

MOS
(N-CHANNEL, SILICON GATE)

2048 × 8-BIT ELECTRICALLY ERASABLE PROGRAMMABLE READ ONLY MEMORY

C SUFFIX
FRIT-SEAL CERAMIC PACKAGE
CASE 623-05

L SUFFIX CERAMIC PACKAGE ALSO AVAILABLE — CASE 716-06

PIN ASSIGNMENT

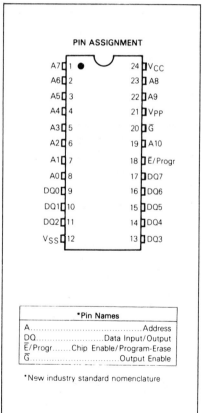

*Pin Names	
A	Address
DQ	Data Input/Output
$\overline{E}$/Progr	Chip Enable/Program-Erase
$\overline{G}$	Output Enable

*New industry standard nomenclature

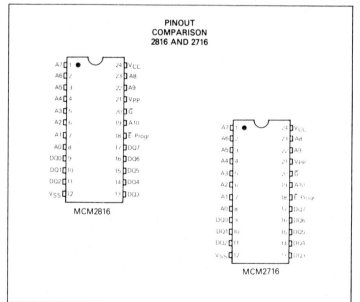

PINOUT
COMPARISON
2816 AND 2716

MCM2816

MCM2716

©MOTOROLA INC., 1981

ADI-862
(Replaces NP-332)

Figure 11.5

MCM2801

16 × 16-BIT SERIAL ELECTRICALLY ERASABLE PROM

The MCM2801 is a 256-bit serial Electrically Erasable PROM designed for handling small amounts of data in applications requiring both non-volatile memory and in-system information updates.

The MCM2801 saves time and money because of the in-system erase and reprogram capability. It has external control of timing functions and serial format for data and address. The MCM2801 is fabricated in floating gate technology for high reliability and producibility.

- Single +5 V Power Supply
- Organized as 16 Words of 16 Bits
- Fully TTL Compatible
- Single +25 V Power Supply for Erase and Program
- In-System Program/Erase Capability

MOS
(N-CHANNEL, SILICON GATE)

16 × 16 BIT
ELECTRICALLY ERASABLE PROM

CERDIP PACKAGE
CASE 632-06

PLASTIC PACKAGE ALSO AVAILABLE —
CASE 646-05

PIN ASSIGNMENT

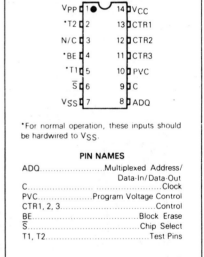

V_{PP} [1   14] V_{CC}
*T2 [2   13] CTR1
N/C [3   12] CTR2
*BE [4   11] CTR3
*T1 [5   10] PVC
$\overline{S}$ [6   9] C
V_{SS} [7   8] ADQ

*For normal operation, these inputs should be hardwired to V_{SS}.

PIN NAMES

ADQ	Multiplexed Address/Data-In/Data-Out
C	Clock
PVC	Program Voltage Control
CTR1, 2, 3	Control
BE	Block Erase
$\overline{S}$	Chip Select
T1, T2	Test Pins

BLOCK DIAGRAM

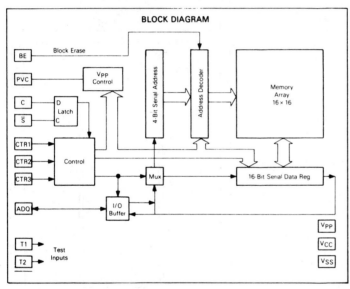

FIGURE 1 — V_{PP} CONTROL

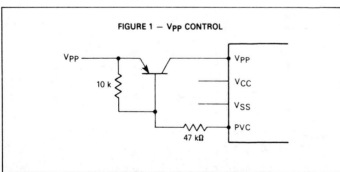

This device contains circuitry to protect the inputs against damage due to high static voltages or electric fields; however, it is advised that normal precautions be taken to avoid application of any voltage higher than maximum rated voltages to this high-impedance circuit.

This is advance information and specifications are subject to change without notice.

ADI-841

Figure 11.6

practical work are the UVERPROMs. Unless the equipment is very specialised, commercial EPROM programmers are designed specifically for one or more of the UVEPROMs. As a first experiment, therefore, the student should program a small area of an EPROM with some easily identifiable data. Storing 00 to 0F in the lowest 16 (decimal) locations would be a suitable start. Assuming that the EPROM programmer is attached to an MDS or software development station, the steps will be as follows:

1 Check that the EPROM is empty in the area you wish to program. Empty locations in UVEPROMs normally contain FF. The system you are using may be provided with a software package which can automatically check whether or not an EPROM is empty.
2 Store the data bytes in successive locations of a suitable area of the system RAM. This can be done using the monitor/debugger, provided with the system, which will allow the user to change the contents of memory locations.
3 Transfer the data from RAM to the EPROM. The EPROM programmer software will provide a command for this purpose.

As an example of the software provided with an EPROM programmer, we take the Futuredata universal MDS. Programmers for the 2704, 2708, 2758 and 2716 UVEPROMs are available with this system. The software support package provides the following commands:

C   Check if EPROM is empty.
P,nn   Program 'nn' bytes of EPROM starting at location 0. The system is displaying the contents of any desired area of RAM when it is in the EPROM programming mode. Data are transferred from RAM to the EPROM, starting at the address indicated by the display cursor.
I,nn   Transfer 'nn' bytes of data from the EPROM to the system RAM, starting at the address indicated by the display cursor.
V,nn   Data in the EPROM are verified against data in the development system RAM.

Should the programmer available to the student not form part of a development system, the EPROM programming exercise should still be carried out using a manual programmer. After successfully programming the EPROM it may then be erased and reprogrammed. The student should perform the washing operation, by exposing the UVEPROM chip to a suitable UV light source for the appropriate length of time. It is recommended that a commercial UVEPROM eraser is employed since these items of equipment should be provided with adequate screening of the UV light source to avoid inadvertent damage to the eyes.

The procedure described above provides useful experience in the programming and erasing of an EPROM. Wherever possible, this should be followed by a further practical exercise involving the use of an EPROM to store program code. This requires the availability of a microprocessor system with sockets that accept the appropriate type of EPROM. Many single-board computers suitable for this purpose are available at relatively low cost. The SBC100 described in Section 6.6 is a typical example.

The exercise consists essentially of storing the code for a program in EPROM, inserting the EPROM in the experimental system and checking whether the program will execute correctly. At this stage, the operations performed by the test program are not important, provided that its correct execution can be checked. If the student has access an MDS with ICE facilities, checking the test program presents no problem. The experimental system is run under the control of the development system with the ICE probe in place of the micro-processor as described in Section 7.5. Memory substitution allows the EPROM-resident program to be run under full control.

As an alternative to the use of an ICE facility to run the program resident in EPROM, an experimental system incorporating a resident monitor/debugger may be used. A simple microprocessor evaluation system is suitable if it has provision for accepting the appropriate type of EPROM. With such a system, the experimental system monitor/debugger (itself usually resident in ROM or EPROM) controls the execution of the test program in the usual way. When testing EPROM-resident programs in this way it should be noted that most monitor/debuggers will not allow the use of breakpoints in the program. This is because the monitor implements the breakpoint by changing the instruction at which the break is to occur. With a program permanently stored in EPROM, this is obviously not possible. The solution here is to terminate the EPROM-resident program with a jump instruction to an address in RAM at which a breakpoint can be set.

11.5   ROM simulation

One of the problems arising from the use of EPROMs to hold programs under development or temporary test programs is the time involved in making program changes. Popular types of UVEPROMs such as the 2708, 2716 and 2732 range may take as long as 30 min for erasure and several more minutes to reprogram. If we consider a typical member of the family, the 2716, the specification reveals that it can store 2 Kbytes of program code. Multiplying the EPROM erasure plus reprogramming time of, say, 35 min by the number of changes made during the development of a typical 2-Kbyte program gives some idea of the time added to the product development phase.

Of course, the situation is not always as bad as this but, even so, simply using EPROMs as a temporary program store during development almost always involves a time penalty.

In the absence of ICE facilities, a ROM simulator can provide a low-cost means of speeding up program development time. We shall use the term ROM simulator to refer to a device which simulates any type of ROM, including PROM and EPROM, since the principle is the same in each case. A ROM simulator is essentially a RAM having the same configuration as the ROM being simulated. Thus, to simulate a type 2716 EPROM, a RAM storing 2,048 $\times$ 8 bits is required since this is the storage capacity of the 2716. Emerging from the ROM simulator is a flexible lead terminating in a DIL header having the same number of pins as the simulated ROM.

To use the ROM simulator, the real ROM is removed from its socket in the system under test and the simulator header is inserted in its place. Of course, some means must be provided to store program code and data in the simulator RAM. The facilities for doing this will depend on the degree of sophistication of the simulator.

The control circuitry for the simulator again depends on the level of sophistication. Many ROM simulators contain a dedicated microprocessor to control the user read/write facilities. The output to the header probe will, however, be taken directly from the RAM, possibly via buffers since the simulator has to behave as nearly like the simulated ROM as possible. The header probe pin connections must also conform with those of the simulated ROM. This means that a separate simulator must be provided for each ROM simulated. An alternative approach is to have a common RAM with a number of 'personality' plug in modules for the different ROMs to be simulated. A circuit description of an EPROM simulator is given in Ref. 11.6.

Practical exercises

Note: the following exercises may be carried out using 2708, 2716, 2732 or 2764 UVEPROMs, depending on the programming facilities and experimental system available:

1   Erase a UVEPROM by exposing it to UV light for the appropriate period. Read and record the contents of addresses 0 to F after erasure. Now program address 0 with 00, address 1 with 01 and so on to address F with 0F. Read the contents of these addresses after to check that the data is present. Erase the EPROM and repeat the programming operation with different data.

2   Write down the program code appropriate to the microprocessor used in your experimental system for the operations listed below:

Load register A with 0F
Load register B with F0
Jump to a suitable RAM address

The final operation is necessary only if you are not using in-circuit emulation. Program the code into an EPROM which can be installed in your experimental system. Run the program under the control of the system monitor debugger. Check that, after executing the program, register A contains 0F and register B contains F0.

References and bibliography

11.1   J.W. Coffron, *Practical hardware details for 8080, 8085, Z80 and 6800 microprocessor systems*, Chapters 7 and 8, Prentice Hall (1981).

11.2   *Electrically alterable memory reliability*, Application report, NCR Corporation, Dayton, Ohio, USA.

11.3   *How to survive in the bipolar PROM, FPLA, PAL, MOSEPROM, diode matrix, PMUX and gate array programming jungle*, Application report, Data I/O Corporation, PO Box 308, 1297 NW Mall, Issaquah, Washington, USA.

11.4   'EPROMs survey', *Systems International (GB)*, Vol. 8(10), pp 35–39 (October 1980).

11.5   'Bench programmer for Fairchild TTL PROMs', *Electron Product Design (GB)*, Vol. 1(8), p 26 (November 1980).

11.6   S.K. Roberts, 'Simulating microcomputer software development by simulating an EPROM', *Electronic Design News (USA)*, pp 171–8 (20 April 1979).

Questions

11.1   State the major factors to be considered when choosing an EPROM for a particular application.

11.2   State the time during which stored data will remain valid in a typical UVEPROM.

11.3   Describe the procedure for erasing the 2716 EPROM.

11.4   State the power dissipated by a 2716 EPROM in the data read mode.

11.5   State the maximum and minimum permissible duration of the pulse applied to pin 18 of the 2716 EPROM during programming.

11.6   State the voltage that must be applied to pin 21 of the 2716, *(a)* during programming, *(b)* during a data read operation.

11.7 How does the access time of a typical EPROM such as the 2716 compare with that of a common static RAM device such as the 2114?

11.8 A microprocessor system is required to print pamphlets from time to time. It is proposed to hold the text for these pamphlets in the form of ASCII code stored in 2716 EPROMs. A pamphlet consists of 50 (decimal) lines of 60 (decimal) characters per line. How many 2716 EPROMs are required to store the text for three different pamphlets?

11.9 What is the major disadvantage of a PROM such as the Am27S15 compared with an EPROM when used to assist the development of microprocessor-based systems?

11.10 State two disadvantages of UVEPROMs such as the 2716 compared with EAROMs such as the 2811.

Chapter 12 Microprocessor fault-finding

Objectives of this chapter *When you have completed studying this chapter you should be able to:*

1 *List typical faults that can occur in microprocessor systems as:*
   (a) component failure;
   (b) open-circuit interconnection;
   (c) bridging or short-circuit interconnection;
   (d) externally induced interference;
   (e) original software design faults.
2 *Explain the use of conventional techniques for fault-finding as:*
   (a) d.c. test;
   (b) use of logic probe;
   (c) use of CRO;
   (d) visual inspection.
3 *Explain the use of software diagnostic programs to assist fault-finding with conventional test instruments.*

12.1 Instruments for fault-finding

We have seen that the incorporation of one or more microprocessors in an electronic systems radically affects the skills required at the design/development stage. Hardware fault-finding is another area in which the microprocessor demands new approaches and specialised skills. The presence of microprocessors in a system will also influence the choice of test equipment used for fault-finding.

The electronic service engineer traditionally relies heavily on instruments such as the multimeter, cathode ray oscilloscope and logic probe. These instruments can also be used to perform some of the tests required in microprocessor system fault diagnosis. In addition, however, the emergence of microprocessors has resulted in the availability of a new generation of test instruments such as the logic analyser and signature analyser. In-circuit emulation, a feature of some microprocessor development systems, is also a powerful tool for fault diagnosis. This chapter investigates the use of traditional fault-finding instruments and methods applied to microprocessor-based systems. Chapter 13 will describe the more specialised testing techniques using the logic analyser and signature analyser.

12.2 When do faults occur?

The need to diagnose faults in a microprocessor system can arise at various stages in the design/development/production cycle. Some of the more common situations are listed below:

1 Fault diagnosis on a newly constructed prototype breadboard. The system failure may be associated with faulty hardware design, faulty software design, faulty hardware wiring, component failure or any combination of the four. At this stage, the design/development engineer will often also diagnose and correct prototype faults.

2 Fault-finding on a newly constructed circuit board of proven design. This situation is likely to be encountered during product testing. The test engineer will normally be able to compare faulty boards with good examples. The majority of problems will be associated with component failure and short or open circuits caused by faulty soldering during production.

3 Diagnosing and correcting faults in equipment which has, at some time, operated correctly. The field service engineer is most likely to encounter this situation. The majority of such faults are likely to be the result of component failure. Replacement of faulty boards is probably the most common method of correcting faults in the field. Given the appropriate equipment, however, fault-finding at component level is possible and may also be cost-effective.

12.3 Typical faults

Many causes of failure in microprocessor systems are identical to those arising in other types of electronic system. Among the faults are:

(a) *Component failure* Microprocessor systems will usually include passive components such as resistors and capacitors, a few discrete semiconductor devices (such as transistors and diodes) and the integrated circuits which perform the computing tasks. Failure of any of these components can cause system malfunction.

(b) *Open-circuit* between points on a circuit board which should be connected.

(c) *Short-circuit* between points on a circuit board which should not be connected. This problem usually arises with adjacent tracks on a printed circuit.

(d) *Externally introduced interference* Mains-borne interference is probably the most common manifestation of this problem. Systems sharing the same mains circuit and switching inductive circuits often give rise to this type of interference. Although a difficult problem to solve, its effects can be minimised by careful attention to the supply and distribution of d.c. power in the microprocessor system.

(e) *Software faults* It is not uncommon for microprocessor systems to be delivered to customers with undetected faults in the software. Such software faults may only cause malfunction in fairly rare situations, such as an unusual combination of inputs to the system.

Q12.1

12.4   Visual inspection

When carried out with care, visual inspection is easily the most cost-effective of all fault-finding techniques. Twenty or thirty minutes devoted to a meticulous inspection of a printed circuit board with the help of a magnifier can often save many hours tracing faults. This is particularly true of faults on printed circuit boards of known good design.

Q12.3

One of the more common problems with printed circuit boards can be the presence of whiskers. These are minute strands of wire or possibly solder left over after components have been installed. On most printed boards used for microprocessor circuits, tracks run very close together and are easily bridged by whiskers resulting in short-circuits. Scrubbing the board (non-component side, of course) with a toothbrush dipped in alcohol is quite an effective remedy for this fault.

'Bridges' of solder between tracks of a printed circuit are similar in effect to whiskers, although more easily seen. They result from the over-enthusiastic application of solder when inserting components. A common location for solder bridges is between the pins of dual in-line integrated circuits. Unlike whiskers, bridges are not normally removed by scrubbing.

Q12.2

'Dry' joints are part of the folklore of electronic service engineers. They are solder joints which, as a result of faulty soldering technique, are mechanically sound but electrically open-circuit. Although not completely mythical, joints of this kind are much less common than is popularly believed. One reason for their long-lasting popularity in description of servicing problems is that they provide a convenient blanket explanation for more obscure faults. Much more common are joints which are deficient both mechanically and electrically as a result of insufficient solder or solder applied at too low a temperature. Suspect joints of this kind can usually be spotted by careful visual inspection.

During a visual inspection, components should be checked carefully. Apart from broken component leads, incorrect connection of transistors, reversed polarities of electrolytic and tantalum capacitors, incorrect diode polarity, etc., can all be detected at this stage. A common fault, not always detectable visually, is incorrect insertion of dual in-line integrated circuits in sockets. When carrying out this operation it is not difficult to allow one or more pins to bend under and fail to enter the socket. The fault may be invisible when viewed externally. Removal and re-insertion of all socketed integrated circuits is a convenient way of detecting this fault.

12.5   The multimeter

The traditional type of multimeter, analogue or digital, is a widely used test instrument for analogue and conventional digital circuits. Its usefulness is rather limited in microprocessor systems. It might be thought that the multimeter would be an obvious choice for checking static logic levels and integrated circuit supply voltages, etc. In fact, an oscilloscope is a much more satisfactory instrument in most cases. The amount of ripple and the presence of unwanted pulses or glitches on power supply rails can be of crucial importance when fault-finding. Standard d.c. measurements will not provide information of this kind. The same is true when measuring static logic levels.

Q12.4

Static logic levels are not a very common occurrence in microprocessor systems. Engineers whose experience has been concerned with sequential logic systems using, say, TTL logic, often forget this. One of the standard methods of testing 'conventional' sequential logic systems is to disconnect any continuous clocks and operate in 'single-shot' mode by applying separate pulses to the clock line. The logic levels at important nodes can be checked after each step and correct circuit operation verified or not as the case may be. Multimeters are quite satisfactory for this purpose.

The single-shot technique described above cannot, unfortunately, be applied to most microprocessors. This is because they are dynamic devices which have a minimum allowed clock frequency. If the clock does drop below this minimum frequency, the microprocessor ceases to function effectively. So-called single-shot operation can be achieved, but this does not imply single clock pulses and the processor still runs continuously.

A useful function which can be performed by a multimeter in testing microprocessor systems is checking for continuity. Short- and open-circuits can also be detected with the instrument operating in resistance measuring mode. The measurement of average d.c. supply current is also sometimes required since an excessive reading can indicate circuit malfunction.

12.6   The logic probe

Logic probes were initially introduced to indicate static logic levels. They are normally slender pencil-like devices with a tip which can

Figure 12.1   Logic probe. (*Courtesy:* Hewlett Packard Ltd)

make contact with circuit nodes. One or more indicator lamps are provided. The usual scheme is that a light is illuminated when the tip is connected to logic '1' and off otherwise. A better alternative is the provision of two lights, one indicating logic 0, the other logic 1. Points in the circuit which are floating are then detected by neither lamp being illuminated. Figure 12.1 shows a typical logic probe.

Most logic probes currently available also offer some pulse detection capability. The detection of continuous pulse trains is one possibility. An indicator is illuminated when the probe tip is in contact with a circuit mode whose voltage waveform is a continuous pulse train.

Pulse stretching is also a common capability in logic probes. With this mode of operation a single pulse detected by the probe is stretched to illuminate a light for an observable period, typically 1 s. This can be a useful provision when searching for spurious pulses or 'glitches' on lines which should be at a constant level. Another situation in which pulse stretching could be useful is a check on the presence of a pulse on the output of, say, an I/O port address decoder during the execution of an input or output instruction.

Q12.5, 12.6   Logic probes can provide useful information for diagnosing faults in microprocessor systems and conventional logic circuits. They are of relatively low cost when compared with most other items of test equipment, and can therefore be regarded as a cost-effective addition to the facilities available to the test or service engineer.

12.7   The oscilloscope

For fault-finding in the majority of traditional analogue and digital electronic systems, the cathode ray oscilloscope is by far the most useful instrument. Many engineers are surprised to discover that this is not always the case for microprocessor-based systems. There are two reasons for this. The first relates to the number of waveforms that need to be observed simultaneously. The second is connected with the character of the waveforms.

When testing a unit of an analogue system, observation of the input and output waveforms is usually sufficient to establish whether the unit is functioning properly. This can be done using a double trace oscilloscope. Even for quite complex test problems, four traces are adequate for most analogue systems. The situation is quite different when we come to test a microprocessor system.

A typical 'middle of the road' 8-bit microprocessor has an 8-line data bus and 16-line address bus. To follow data transactions in the system accurately, we need to simultaneously observe logic levels on all 24 lines. Ideally, we should also like to see what is happening on other control and status lines at the same time. The conventional double trace oscilloscope cannot help us much in this situation.

Analogue electronic systems are commonly tested using repetetive signals, often sinusoidal. The regularity of these signals allows the oscilloscope display to be triggered at one point in the cycle, thus giving a stable picture. Compare this with the normal situation in a microprocessor system. If we examine one line of the address or data bus, we shall see a voltage changing between the two logic levels. The changes are synchronous in that they occur at a given point in the system clock cycle. The pattern of changes is not necessarily regular however. The waveform may therefore be non-repetitive. Even if it is repetitive, the period may easily extend over several hundred or several thousand clock cycles. An oscilloscope cannot be synchronised in the normal way to obtain a steady picture. The oscilloscope will reveal that some activity is occurring on a bus line in that the voltage is changing between the two levels. It will not be possible to see any specific detail of the timing of these changes

Q12.7   however.

Despite the shortcomings outlined above, there are applications in which an oscilloscope can serve a useful purpose in the testing of microprocessors. The most obvious is in the examination of the system clock waveform. Figure 12.2 shows as an example the clock specification for the M6800 microprocessor reproduced from Appendix D. Some clock parameters, such as rise and fall times, may be quite critical. A good-quality oscilloscope is usually the best instrument for measuring the values of these parameters. The same is indeed true for any 'real time' measurement. Instruments such as logic analysers (discussed in Section 13.2) indicate voltages as high or low depending on whether they are above or below some threshold level. This makes them unsuitable for measuring quantities such as

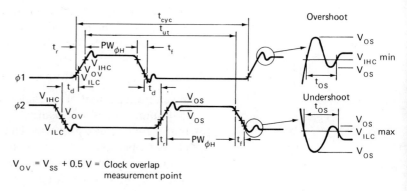

$V_{OV} = V_{SS} + 0.5$ V = Clock overlap
measurement point

Figure 12.2   M6800 clock waveform specification

waveform rise time and fall time. An oscilloscope is also the best instrument for observing transient oscillation at the leading and trailing edges of pulses, a phenomenon commonly referred to as ringing.

As we have said in Section 12.5, the measurement of a nominally constant voltage is another task in which the oscilloscope can perform a useful role. Of course, the same degree of accuracy is not possible as with, say, a digital voltmeter. In microprocessor systems, however, the important feature of a 'constant' voltage is often whether it has any imposed variations. Spurious pulses of as little as a few nanoseconds width can easily cause system malfunctions. It is therefore important that oscilloscopes used for observing d.c. voltage levels in microprocessor systems should also be capable of detecting

Q12.8   these very narrow pulses.

12.8   Generating repetitive test waveforms

The usefulness of the oscilloscope for diagnosing faults in microprocessor systems can be greatly extended if a test procedure can be devised that involves repetitive waveforms. It is often possible, by means of special test programs, to force a microprocessor to generate waveforms that are observable on an oscilloscope. These programs will involve loops of fairly short duration.

Figure 12.3 shows part of system which includes a Z80 microprocessor. Suppose that one task of the Z80 is to update an external display at one-minute intervals by latching two 4-bit BCD numbers into a shift register. We assume that a hardware fault exists resulting in an incorrect display. Apart from this incorrect display the system is operating normally.

When the system is running with the normal working program, an output to the display port occurs once each minute. This could possibly be investigated by observing waveforms with the help of a

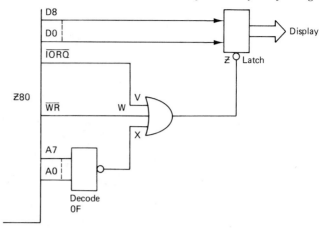

Figure 12.3

storage oscilloscope triggered when an output operation occurs. A better method is to use a special test program which executes output operations much more frequently. This will produce repetitive waveforms with periods short enough to allow observation using a normal oscilloscope.

In Figure 12.5, reproduced from Appendix F, it will be seen that when

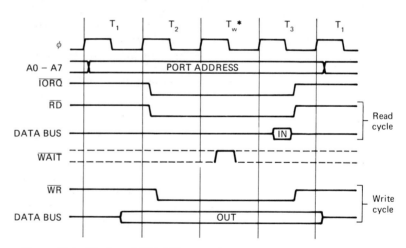

Figure 12.4 Timing of Z80 I/O operations

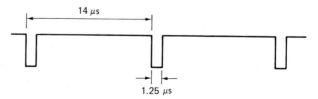

Figure 12.5 Waveform at point Z

an OUT 0F is executed by a Z80 microprocessor, lines $\overline{\text{IORQ}}$ and $\overline{\text{WR}}$ go low during the instruction execution cycle. The port address 0F also appears on A0–A7, the eight least significant lines of the address bus and the output data appears on the data bus. In Figure 12.4, the decoded port address, together with $\overline{\text{IORQ}}$ and $\overline{\text{WR}}$, generates a pulse that clocks the data on the address bus into the 8-bit latch.

As an initial assessment of the situation we note that, since the system appears to be working normally (apart from the display), it is unlikely that any of the data or address bus lines have shorts to earth or positive supply. The same is true of $\overline{\text{WR}}$ since this signal is also involved in memory write operations.

Before proceeding further, it is necessary to check that a fault does in fact exist. To do this, a test program consisting of the following two instructions is executed:

```
LD    A,xx
OUT   (0F),A
```

This program loads register A with the hexadecimal number 'xx' and puts out this number to port 0F. The program is executed five times with 'xx' = 00, 11, 22, 44 and 88. Using these values for 'xx' exercises every line of the latch input and output with both 0 and 1.

Each time the program is run, the number displayed and the logic levels at the latch outputs are checked. This will reveal whether or not a fault exists. If a fault is present, it will also determine whether the fault lies in the display itself.

Assuming that the fault does not lie in the display, the other main possibilities for the location of the fault are:

1 The latch and associated lines.
2 The three input OR gate and associated lines.
3 The port address decoder and associated lines.

In each case the method of testing is to check input and outputs to the component concerned. To make this possible using a normal oscilloscope, the following special test program is used:

```
AGAIN   LD    A,xx
        OUT   (0F),A
        JP    AGAIN
```

Now every time the OUT (0F),A instruction is executed, a pulse should appear at the output of the three-input OR gate to clock the data on the data bus into the 8-bit register. In the program shown, if we assume the Z80 clock has a frequency of 2 MHz, instruction execution times are as shown below:

```
AGAIN   LD    A,xx      3.5 µs
        OUT   (0F),A     5.5 µs
        JP    AGAIN      5.0 µs    Total   14.0 µs
```

If we look at the timing diagram for Z80 I/O instruction execution given in Figure 12.4 it can be seen that in executing the OUT instruction, $\overline{WR}$ and $\overline{IDRQ}$ go low for approximately 2.5 clock cycles or 1.25 μs. The program should therefore produce a latch clocking pulse at point Z of 1.25 μs width repeating every 14 μs as shown in Figure 12.5. A repetitive pulse train of this kind is easily observed using a normal oscilloscope.

The presence of a normal pulse train at point Z indicates a fault associated with the register. This could be a faulty chip or possibly an open-circuit on one of the data lines resulting from a 'dry' joint. We have already indicated that a short on a data bus is unlikely in view of the satisfactory system operation, apart from this output port.

If the pulse train is not present at point Z, the three inputs to the OR gate are examined using the oscilloscope. This should establish whether the fault lies in the OR gate or one of the input lines. The port
Q12.9 address decoder can be checked in a similar way.

12.9 Test and self-test program

In Section 12.8 we saw how special test programs could generate repetitive waveforms in a microprocessor system to allow an oscilloscope to be used for fault-finding. The use of test programs is much more general than this restricted example might indicate. A standard test and fault-finding procedure is to run a special test program whose purpose is to exercise the various parts of the system. Test programs of this kind may be stored in PROM and EPROM. The test engineer can then insert the test program ROM or EPROM in a socket in place of the ROM containing the normal system software. Alternatively a spare vacant socket may be provided in the system for this purpose.

In systems designed with a more sophisticated approach to testing and fault-finding, special test programs are incorporated in the system software as a matter of course. A service engineer or even the system user can then simply run the test routines whenever a fault is suspected. Printers provide good examples of this philosophy. Virtually all printers currently available incorporate a micro-processor as part of the control circuit. In most cases, the control program stored in ROM also includes test routines.

A typical small matrix printer, the EPSON MX80, allows the user to run a test routine by switching power on while the line feed control switch is depressed. The test program generates a printout which includes all printable characters. Figure 12.6 shows part of this test printout.

As we shall see in Chapter 13, the use of special test programs is an

Figure 12.6   Printer self-test

essential feature of the use of certain special fault-finding instruments such as the signature analyser. Fault-finding with logic analysers is also greatly assisted by the availability of test programs.

At an even higher level of sophistication, systems are now being designed that perform their own routine testing. This is not too difficult to implement provided it is introduced into the design exercise at the beginning. At regular intervals, the system software causes test routines to be executed. The results of the routines are checked by the program and a fault condition message is printed if they are not as expected. We may expect to see such self-testing capability become a common feature of microprocessor systems in the future.

In systems that have been designed without the provision of fault-finding facilities, running test programs may not always be convenient. We have described how special ROMs containing test programs can be inserted in place of system ROMs. This does not, however, provide any control over the running of the program. The best that we can do in a situation like this is to run a test program which is entered on power-up or reset. It is also unlikely that a dedicated microprocessor system will have facilities such as a keyboard and display by which the test engineer can communicate with the system. To overcome these problems, special test equipment is required. Some of the available instruments for this purpose are described in the next chapter.

12.10   Free-run testing   *under heading of more sophisticated methods of testing.*

The technique of employing test programs for generating repetitive waveforms (described in Sections 12.8 and 12.9) is useful when a fault is confined to, say, a peripheral interface circuit or an I/O port. Its success presupposes that the microprocessor itself is operating correctly. This is obvious since the generation of the repetitive waveform depends on the proper execution of the instructions of the test program. In this section we describe a test procedure that can be used when a more fundamental fault apparently prevents a microprocessor from executing instructions. This type of fault must be cleared before we can make use of any special test programs.

Assuming that the faulty system has been inspected visually as described in Section 12.4, some initial tests can be made. A multimeter or, preferably, an oscilloscope may be used to check that the correct static voltages are present at the appropriate pins of all integrated circuits. The system clock should also be examined using an oscilloscope of adequate bandwidth. Important parameters of the clock waveform such as rise time, fall time and pulse width should be checked against the microprocessor manufacturer's specification. When using an oscilloscope to examine the clock or any other waveform in a microprocessor system, a high-impedance probe should be employed to avoid capacitive loading which may distort the signal being observed.

Having completed the initial checks, if all is found to be satisfactory, the next stage is to force the microprocessor into a 'free run' condition. To demonstrate this technique, we use as an example the system shown in Figure 12.7. It will be seen that the system includes two ROMs holding the program and fixed data, two RAM chips, one input port and one output port. We shall assume that the system is faulty and the program is not apparently being executed.

To put the microprocessor in a free-run condition, it is necessary to break the data bus at a point near the microprocessor, shown as 'X' in Figure 12.7. The microprocessor data lines must then be held at logic levels which represent the code for an instruction which does not involve an address bus transaction. This implies an instruction which does not require a memory read/write operation or an I/O operation. Most microprocessor instruction sets include a 'no operation' (NOP) instruction which is highly suitable for this purpose. Other instructions are also suitable, however.

To break the data bus and force an instruction code on the microprocessor lines requires the use of a special test card. This card carries

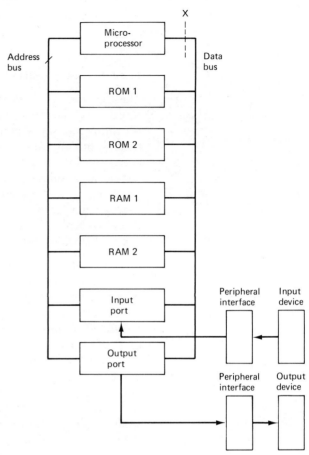

Figure 12.7

a socket to hold a microprocessor and has a header plug brought out on a flying lead and having the same pins configuration as the micro-processor. The data lines of the microprocessor socket on this test card are taken to logic levels which represent an NOP or other suitable instruction. Figure 12.8 shows a circuit for a test card for testing 8080-based systems. The 8080 NOP instruction has an opcode 00. Data lines in Figure 12.8 are therefore taken to ground. Figure 12.9 shows a test card for the 6800 microprocessor which has a NOP code of 01.

To use the test card, the microprocessor chip is removed from its socket in the system shown in Figure 12.8 and inserted into the socket on the test card. The 40-pin header plug on the test card flying lead is then inserted into the system microprocessor socket. All integrated circuits in the system which connect in any way to the address bus are also removed.

When the system being tested is switched on, the 8080 start-up

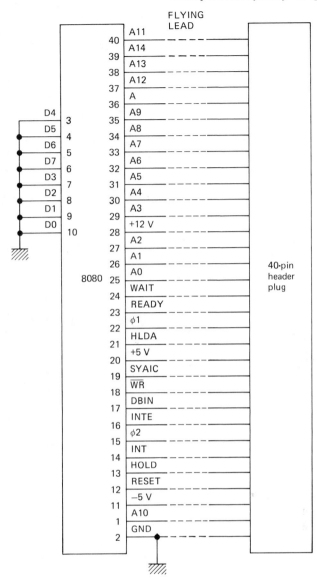

Figure 12.8

routine should commence with the contents of the program counter reset to 0000. The instruction is then normally fetched from this location and executed. With the test card in use, a NOP instruction will be executed and the contents of the program counter incremented to 0001. Another NOP instruction is then executed, the contents of the program counter incremented again and so on. The fetch phase of each instruction cycle causes the contents of the program counter to be placed on the address bus. As all this activity continues, the contents of the program counter will cycle through the values shown

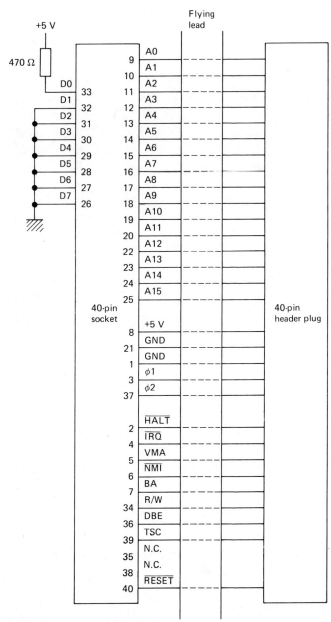

Figure 12.9   Test card for M6800

in Figure 12.10 and these addresses will duly appear in sequence on the lines of the address bus.

If we now concentrate our attention on any one address line, it is evident that on examination with an oscilloscope, we should see a square wave. Furthermore, the square wave on address line An will be at exactly twice the frequency of that on address line A(n+1). This

A15	A14	A13	A12	A11	A10	A9	A8	A7	A6	A5	A4	A3	A2	A1	A0	Hex
0	0	0	0	0	0	0	0	0	0	0	0	0	0	0	0	0 0 0 0
0	0	0	0	0	0	0	0	0	0	0	0	0	0	0	1	0 0 0 1
0	0	0	0	0	0	0	0	0	0	0	0	0	0	1	0	0 0 0 2
0	0	0	0	0	0	0	0	0	0	0	0	0	0	1	1	0 0 0 3
0	0	0	0	0	0	0	0	0	0	0	0	0	1	0	0	0 0 0 4
0	0	0	0	0	0	0	0	0	0	0	0	0	1	0	1	0 0 0 5
0	0	0	0	0	0	0	0	0	0	0	0	0	1	1	0	0 0 0 6
0	0	0	0	0	0	0	0	0	0	0	0	0	1	1	1	0 0 0 7
0	0	0	0	0	0	0	0	0	0	0	0	1	0	0	0	0 0 0 8
1	1	1	1	1	1	1	1	1	1	1	1	1	1	1	0	F F F E
1	1	1	1	1	1	1	1	1	1	1	1	1	1	1	1	F F F F
0	0	0	0	0	0	0	0	0	0	0	0	0	0	0	0	0 0 0 0
0	0	0	0	0	0	0	0	0	0	0	0	0	0	0	1	0 0 0 1

etc.

Figure 12.10 Address bus logic levels with free-running microprocessor (8080)

provides us with an easy way of checking all address lines. The signals at the pins of the microprocessor chip should first be checked. If none of the address lines are active, this points to a faulty microprocessor chip or perhaps a fault on one of the control lines. A short-circuit between the reset line and ground would produce this effect for example. If only one of the address lines is at an unchanging logic level, this indicates a short-circuit to supply or ground somewhere along the line.

Assuming that correct signals are found on all the address bus pins of the microprocessor, the signals on the address lines should be checked at various points on the bus. The address lines at the sockets of integrated circuits such as RAMs and ROMs are obvious points. If a signal disappears as we move along an address line, an open-circuit is indicated. Should all appear to be well, integrated circuits can now be re-inserted one at a time, starting with the program ROMs. Address lines are checked as before after insertion of each integrated circuit. If address line signals are still present when all integrated circuits have been inserted, it can be assumed that the fault is not associated with the address bus. Any integrated circuits with shorts on address lines will, of course, be detected by this procedure.

When the first program ROM is inserted, data will appear on the system data bus since instruction fetch cycles are being executed which cause data to be read from the ROMs at least part of the time. The data on the system data bus is not reaching the microprocessor owing to the artificial break we have inserted in the bus by using the test card. It is worth looking at each data line using the oscilloscope as each ROM is inserted separately. Although the oscilloscope cannot resolve details of the data waveform for reasons discussed in Section 12.7, lines permanently at logic 1 or 0 can be detected. This indicates a short to supply or ground or perhaps a faulty ROM. Total absence of data on the data bus after insertion of a ROM also indicates a faulty ROM chip. RAMs will normally contain random data after switch-on and should therefore also generate data on the data bus as the address bus cycles through the memory space allocated to a RAM chip. This again allows faulty RAM chips to be detected. Total absence of data on the data bus after insertion of a single ROM or RAM indicates either a faulty memory chip or failure to energise the chip enable line. This can again be confirmed by examination using an oscilloscope.

As the addresses cycle through all possible values when the microprocessor is free-running, all memory chip selects will be energised for part of the time. Should this not be the case for any or all of the chips, the fault may lie in a 'stuck' control line from the microprocessor or possibly a fault in an address decoding circuit. Obvious lines to check at this point are $\overline{WR}$ and SYNC, together with signals at intermediate points in the address decoders which generate the chip selects.

Interpretation of the waveforms displayed by an oscilloscope during the test procedure described here will depend on the microprocessor involved. The 8080 is fairly straightforward since address lines carry a square wave when the microprocessor is free-running. With the Z80, the situation is complicated by the facility for refreshing dynamic memory. This only involves lines A0–A6 of the address bus. As will be seen from Appendix B, during each instruction cycle, a refresh address will appear on these lines for part of the time. When the Z80 is free-running, this refresh address will cycle up through all possible values in exactly the same way as the address which appears on the bus as a result of the incrementing of the program counter during each instruction cycle. Thus the refresh address and instruction fetch address are aexactly the same for lines A0–A6.

Figure 12.11 shows the waveforms appearing on lines A2 and A7 during the two execution cycles during which the contents of the program counter are 007F and 0080. Bit 2 of the program counter therefore changes from 1 to 0 and bit 7 changes from 0 to 1. From Figure 12.11 it will be seen that whereas the A2 waveform always follows the logic level of bit 2 of the program counter, A7 is always low during the refresh period. The effect described here will be

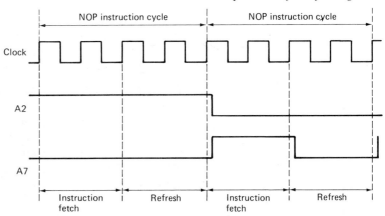

Figure 12.11 Z80 free-run address line waveforms

observed with a normal oscilloscope. A dual time-base instrument will, however, be necessary to see the sort of detail shown in Figure 12.11. Alternatively, a storage oscilloscope operating in single-shot mode might be suitable.

Other complications arise with other microprocessors. Some devices such as the 8085 employ part of the address bus in a dual role. For part of the 8085 instruction cycle, lines AD0–AD7 carry an address. For the remaining part of the cycle, however, they perform as a data bus. This must obviously be taken into account when interpreting the address bus observations in the free-run condition. The test card employed with the 8085 includes additional buffers to accommodate the dual role of lines AD0–AD7.

The approach to fault diagnosis described here is based on the use of conventional, general-purpose test equipment. Special-purpose instruments such as the logic analyser and particularly the signature analyser can also be applied in a free-running microprocessor test. These instruments will generally speed up the process of fault diagnosis which is obviously important for field maintenance. Chapter 13 includes a full description of the use of logic and signature analysis.

Q12.10

12.11 Software faults

Faults in software are essentially program design errors. They are not therefore directly comparable with hardware faults resulting from, say, component failure. Nevertheless, the effect may be the same in that the system becomes unavailable to the user.

No sensible manufacturer will deliver a microprocessor-based system with obvious software faults. A much more likely situation is the delivery of a system including software which is apparently

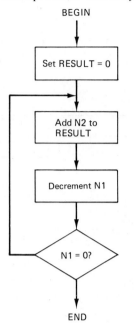

BEGIN

Set RESULT = 0

Add N2 to RESULT

Decrement N1

N1 = 0?

END

Figure 12.12   Flowchart for program containing data-dependent error

satisfactory but inadequately tested. Some software faults only become apparent with a particular combination of data. It is possible therefore for a program to perform in a satisfactory manner for quite some time before a combination of data triggers the fault.

Figure 12.12 shows a flowchart for a program containing an error of this kind. The same program is described using a pseudo-high-level language in Figure 12.13 and an assembly listing of the program coded for the 8080 microprocessor is shown in Figure 12.14. The program multiplies two 8-bit numbers stored in symbolic addresses N1 and N2, leaving the result in register pair H,L. A repeated addition algorithm is employed. It is perhaps worth saying that the reader should not use this example as a model of good programming practice.

Now the program shown in Figure 12.14 works perfectly well for most of the time. A brief check reveals, however, that whenever N2 is

```
RESULT = 0
DO UNTIL N1 = 0
            RESULT = RESULT + N2
            N1 = N1 - 1
END DO
END
```

Figure 12.13   Pseudo-code for data-dependent error program

```
                                                    PAGE   1
    -------- 8080/85 ASSEMBLER V01 ---------------------------- FUTUREDATA ----

                ***********************************************************
                *MULTIPLICATION BY REPEATED ADDITION                      *
                *N1,N2 ARE THE SYMBOLIC ADDRESSES OF THE TWO OPERANDS      *
                *THE RESULT IS LEFT IN REGISTER PAIR HL                    *
                *                                                          *
                *THIS PROGRAM CONTAINS A DATA DEPENDENT ERROR              *
                *THE RESULT IS INCORRECT WHEN N2 = 0                       *
                ***********************************************************
                *
    0000                    RSEG    TEC9
    0000 210000             LXI     H,0             RESULT = 0
    0003 3A1100             LDA     N1
    0006 4F                 MOV     C,A             C HOLDS N1
    0007 0600               MVI     B,0             B HOLDS 0
    0009 3A1200             LDA     N2              A HOLDS N2
    000C 09       AGAIN     DAD     B               ADD N2 TO RESULT
    000D 3D                 DCR     A               DECREMENT N2
    000E C20C00             JNZ     AGAIN
                *
                *
    0011         N1         DS      1               OPERAND N1
    0012         N2         DS      1               OPERAND N2
    0013                    END
```

Figure 12.14

equal to zero, an incorrect answer results. If this program is installed as part of the software in a dedicated microprocessor system, the error might even never emerge. Most users will not be so lucky and will obtain incorrect results from time to time.

Whenever software faults are identified, the program must be modified. The error in the program described above could be corrected with the help of a software development station supporting 8080 assembly language. For errors in programs which are hardware-dependent, an MDS equipped with in-circuit emulation is the more appropriate tool.

References and bibliography

12.1   J.D. Lenk, *How to Troubleshoot and Repair Microcomputers,* Reston Publishing Co., Inc., USA (1980).

12.2   *Using Delayed Sweep in Measuring Digital Word Trains,* Tektronix T900 Application note 41G1.0 (1976).

Questions

12.1   List five possible causes of failure of a microprocessor system.

12.2   Explain how solder bridges and whiskers can cause malfunction in a microprocessor system.

12.3   What is usually the most cost-effective way of detecting solder bridges?

12.4   Explain why an oscilloscope is often more satisfactory than a test meter for testing static voltages in a microprocessor system.

12.5   Describe the function of a logic probe.

12.6   Describe one example of a test which could be performed on a microprocessor system using the pulse-stretching facility of a logic probe.

12.7   Explain why a conventional oscilloscope is generally less useful for testing microprocessor systems than for testing other analogue and digital electronic systems.

12.8   Explain why an oscilloscope is a more suitable instrument than, say, a logic analyser for checking the clock waveform in a microprocessor system.

12.9   In the system described in Chapter 10, it is suspected that a fault exists in the RAM which is shown in Figure 10.13. Explain how a test program could be used to check whether the $\overline{\text{CS}}$ and R/$\overline{\text{W}}$ signals are reaching the two 2112 RAM chips, assuming the use of a conventional oscilloscope as the test instrument.

12.10   Explain what is meant by free-run testing of a microprocessor system.

Chapter 13 Specialised test equipment

Objectives of this chapter *When you have completed studying this chapter you should be able to:*

1 *Explain the use of logic and signature analysers and diagnostic programs for fault-finding.*
2 *Compare traditional and specialised methods for locating faults in microprocessor systems.*

13.1 Introduction

Chapter 12 reviewed the way in which general-purpose test equipment such as multimeters and cathode ray oscilloscopes can be used for fault diagnosis in microprocessor systems. In this chapter we shall discuss the principles of operation and methods of use of some special-purpose test instruments. These items of equipment, notably the logic analyser and signature analyser, have appeared relatively recently to meet an increasing demand from development and service engineers working with microprocessors.

13.2 The logic analyser

The logic analyser is an instrument which was introduced primarily to allow the observation of data flow in systems organised around buses. They are most commonly stand-alone instruments. A typical example is shown in Figure 13.1. An alternative approach in Figure 13.2 shows a normal oscilloscope fitted with a special logic analyser plug in unit. We have already discussed, in Chapter 12, the difficulties associated with the use of oscilloscopes in making such observations. Unlike the oscilloscope, the logic analyser is essentially a recording device which samples the signals being observed at regular intervals and stores the samples. The stored samples can then be displayed in various convenient formats.

Although logic analysers offer many advantages over oscilloscopes for observing events in microprocessor systems, there are also some disadvantages. Because voltage levels are coarsely recorded as either 'high' or 'low', the fine detail of signal level variations is lost. For measuring such things as rise time and fall time, therefore, the oscilloscope is still the most suitable instrument.

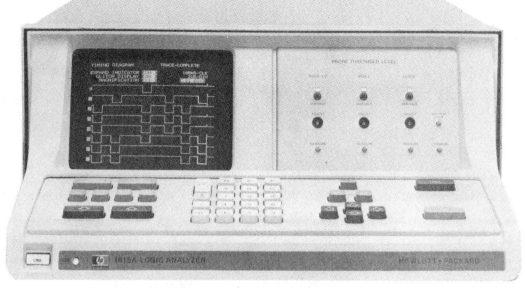

Figure 13.1   Hewlett Packard model 1615A stand-alone logic analyser

Figure 13.3 shows a schematic description of a logic analyser in block diagram form. At regular intervals, a clock initiates a sampling operation on each of n input lines. The voltage on each input line is then compared with a threshold level and classified as logic 0 or 1 depending on whether it is below or above this threshold. Figure 13.4 illustrates this process.

The threshold level used by the computer will depend on the type of logic devices generating the signals. If we take the popular 74LS range of TTL integrated circuits as an example, the specification states that when an output is at the low or logic 0 level, the maximum voltage is 0.5. When an output is at the high or logic 1 level, its minimum voltage is 2.7. A threshold midway between these two levels at 1.1 V would be appropriate in this case. Other types of logic elements will need different thresholds. CMOS operating with a supply of 15 V would require a threshold of 7.5 V for example.

The outputs of the n comparators in the logic analyser shown in Figure 13.3 constitute an n-bit binary word which is stored in location 0 of analyser M by n-bit memory. The previous contents of the memory are all shifted up one location also. Thus the previous contents of address 1 are now stored in address 0, the previous contents of address 1 in address 2 and so on. At the top of memory, the word which was previously stored in the highest address is pushed out and lost.

At any instant of time, the memory contains a record of the logic levels on the input lines over the previous M sampling periods. This

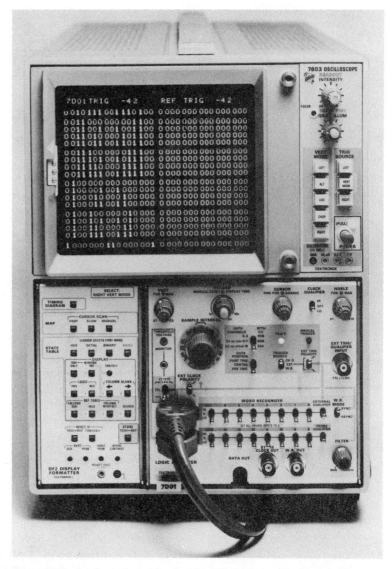

Figure 13.2 Logic analyser plug-in with Tektronics model 7603 oscilloscope

record is updated every time a new sample is taken. If the sampling process is stopped at any time, this effectively 'freezes' the record. The contents of the logic analyser memory then constitute a 'snapshot' of the changes in the logic levels on the input lines up to the time sampling stopped. Having obtained this record, the analyser can then display the data in various different formats.

Halting the sampling process can be effected in a variety of ways. The most direct method is by means of an externally generated trigger or synchronising signal. Most analysers have a trigger input which can

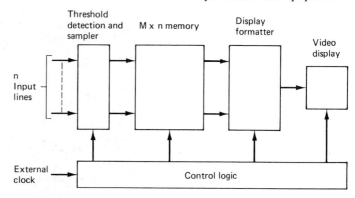

Figure 13.3 Logic analyser

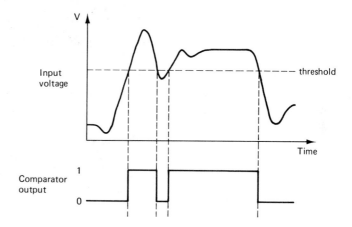

Figure 13.4 Threshold detection

be selected to operate on a high–low or low–high transition. However, the most useful triggering facility involves the recognition, by the analyser, of a triggering event. The user sets up an n-bit trigger pattern, usually by means of switches on the front panel of the analyser. At each sample time, the input data is compared with the trigger pattern. When a match is detected, the sampling process may be halted.

As an extension of triggering facilities, logic analysers can, if it is desired, allow the sampling process to continue for a period of time after a trigger event is detected. In this case, the stored data is a record of events leading up to and immediately following the trigger event. This, of course, provides data which could not be captured by a storage oscilloscope which only starts storing data after the occurrence of the trigger event. With the logic analyser, the user can also choose the number of samples which are taken after the trigger event.

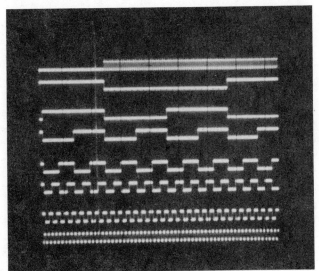

Figure 13.5   Logic analyser time domain display

Figure 13.5 shows one format for the display of stored data. This is the time domain display. The display looks similar to that of a multichannel oscilloscope. The reader should remember however that the logic analyser displays only 1 and 0 logic levels with none of the fine detail of voltage variations which would be seen with an oscilloscope. The display shown in Figure 13.5 was generated by a 16-channel logic analyser. To avoid overcrowding of the time domain display, the user can inhibit the traces associated with some channels. In the case of Figure 13.5, of the possible channels 1–16, only channels 8–16 are displayed with channel 16 at the bottom and channel 9 at the top. The

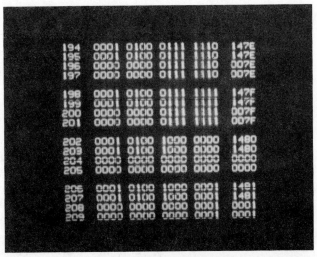

Figure 13.6   Logic analyser data domain display

vertical line towards the left of the display is a cursor whose function is described below.

Figure 13.6 shows a data domain display of part of the stored information which produced the time domain display shown in Figure 13.5. With the particular instrument used, the data domain always shows the full 16 channels with the right-hand columns giving the sample number and the left-hand columns the hexadecimal form of the 16-bit binary word. This instrument also offers the option of octal representation of the data word in place of the hexadecimal representation shown in Figure 13.6.

The data domain display in Figure 13.6 shows the logic levels on the 16 input lines of the analyser at 16 sample points numbered 194–209. The instrument concerned stores the data from a total of 512 sample points. A manual control on the front panel allows the user to step through the stored samples. The relationship between the time and data domain displays is established by the cursor of the time domain display. The position of this cursor corresponds to the sample at the top of the data domain display.

Two alternative mechanisms are possible for fixing the times at which the input lines are sampled. Synchronous sampling makes use of a synchronising signal from the system being tested. For a microprocessor system, this signal is often the system clock.

The data stored by the logic analyser will then be the logic levels on the analyser input lines during each clock cycle. Displays shown in Figures 13.5 and 13.6 were obtained in this way.

Some microprocessor manufacturers provide tables showing logic levels on data and address lines during each clock interval as the various instructions are executed. Therefore, with synchronous sampling, it is easy to see whether the logic levels on the address and data buses are behaving as expected. Some of the more sophisticated logic analysers extend this facility by converting the stored sample words into the mnemonics for machine-code instructions of a particular microprocessor. If the logic analyser is triggered to sample during the fetch phase of each instruction cycle, the successive instruction codes appearing on the data bus can be captured and displayed. As an example of this, we note from Figure 4.0-1 of Appendix B that the Z80 microprocessor has a line M1 which is active during each instruction fetch phase. Using the signal on this line to trigger a logic analyser allows the successive instruction codes to be sampled. Figure 13.7 shows a display obtained by a logic analyser offering this mnemonic decoding facility. The availability of mnemonic decoding does imply that the logic analyser is designed to operate with one type of microprocessor only. In practice, the instrument will consist of a general-purpose mainframe with a range of personality modules to accommodate different microprocessors.

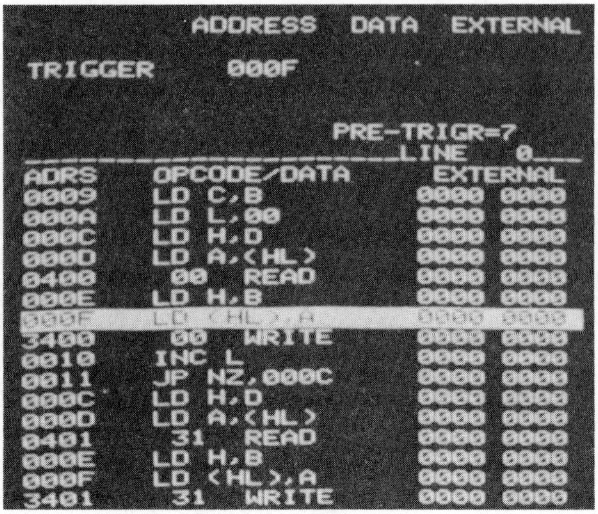

Figure 13.7   Inverse assembly of the data on the data buses is possible with the seven dedicated personality modules. This mnemonic display is in the familiar assembler format for easy interpretation

With synchronous operation of a logic analyser, the maximum sampling rate is one sample per clock cycle of the system being tested. If a fault condition exists in the system being tested, it may be suspected that changes in logic levels are taking place during the clock period. Short transitions of this kind are known as 'glitches'. To help identify glitches, asynchronous sampling may be employed.

With asynchronous sampling, an oscillator within the logic analyser fixes the sampling times. This allows the user to choose the sampling frequency which can be up to 100 MHz in the more sophisticated type of instrument. With a sampling rate which is higher than the clock frequency of the system under test, data and address lines can be sampled several times during each clock interval. Asynchronous sampling also allows the system clock waveform itself to be examined.

Q13.1

The most effective way to use the logic analyser is to identify the approximate locations of faults with synchronous sampling. The precise location of a glitch can then be located by operating asynchronously with a higher sampling rate.

Figure 13.8 shows how fast asynchronous sampling can reveal detail in waveforms which is invisible when sampling synchronously. Two channels of a logic analyser are used to examine the waveforms at the input and output of an inverting gate as shown in Figure 13.9. The actual waveforms concerned are shown in *(b)* and *(c)* of Figure 13.8. Synchronous sampling occurs on the high–low transition of the

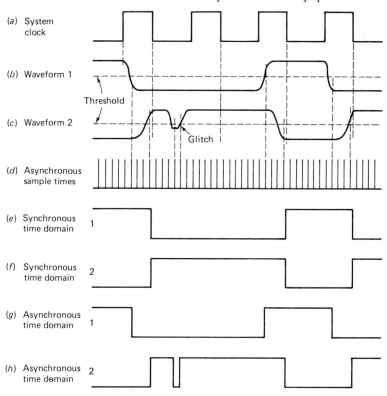

Figure 13.8 Logic analyser synchronous and asynchronous sampling

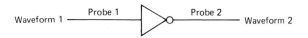

Figure 13.9 Logic analyser probe connections

system clock resulting in the time domain display of waveforms 1 and 2 shown in *(e)* and *(f)*.

The time domain display generated by fast asynchronous sampling is shown in *(g)* and *(h)*. It will be seen that the delay between the gate input and output waveforms is now revealed. Also evident is the glitch in waveform 2 which is completely invisible with synchronous sampling. Most analysers do, in fact, have other facilities for 'glitch catching' involving the use of a latch triggered by transitions of a signal. Even with synchronous operation, the use of the so-called latching mode would have detected the glitch in waveform 2 although with less precision as to its position.

Q13.3

The display shown in Figure 13.3 was generated by a 16-channel logic analyser. For clarity, only eight channels are activated. The eight traces display the activity on address lines A0–A7 of a Z80 microprocessor in the free-run mode. Address line A0 is at the bottom of the diagram with A7 at the top. The different character of the A7 waveform compared with A0–A6 will be noted. This results from the fact that A0–A6 carry a refresh address for part of each instruction execution cycle as discussed in section 12.10.

Various more sophisticated facilities are available with most logic analysers including the ability to expand a time domain display. In Figure 13.10, the cursor is seen as a vertical line. Figure 13.5 shows a display of the same data but with a five times expansion to the right of the cursor. The difference in character of the A7 waveform compared with A0–A7 can now be seen more clearly.

Having obtained the records of bus activity with the help of a logic analyser, the user is then faced with the problem of interpretation. Manufacturer's data for most microprocessors provides some information as to what we might expect to see on the data and address buses as each instruction is executed. The best example of this is provided by Table 9 of Appendix C. This shows the data and address bus activity during each clock cycle as each instruction in the instruction set is executed. Note that the 8-bit word on the data bus may not always be determined by the microprocessor and therefore for some instructions cannot always be predicted with certainty.

Figure 13.11 shows a logic analyser time domain display which might be expected after the execution of the two instructions given below. Synchronous sampling is assumed.

```
LDX   #X'1000'
STX   X'1027'
```

The two instructions are stored in memory starting at location 2000. The first instruction loads register X with the hexadecimal number 1000. The second instruction stores the 16-bit contents of register X in addresses 1027 and 1028. For convenience, timing data for these instructions is reproduced in Table 13.1 (taken from Table 9 of Appendix C).

The time domain display of Figure 13.11 is generated by a logic analyser with 16 input lines. Of these input lines, the eight least significant are connected to address bus lines A7–A0. The eight most significant input lines are connected to the data bus lines D7–D0. To ensure a readable hexadecimal representation of the data, the order of connection of input lines to bus lines is important. The display shown in Figure 13.11 is produced by triggering the logic analyser when the input word 2800 is detected. In Figure 13.11, therefore, the top line represents the most recent clock cycle with successively earlier clock cycles as we move down the display.

Starting at the bottom line of the display, A7–A0 = 00, which is, of course, the eight least significant bits 2000, the opcode address. Data

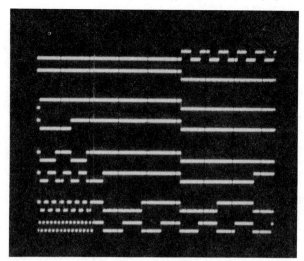

Figure 13.10 Logic analyser time domain display with trace expansion to the right of the cursor

Time domain display																Hex		
0	0	1	0	1	0	0	0	0	0	0	0	0	0	0	0	28	00	
0	0	1	0	0	1	1	1	0	0	0	1	0	0	0	0	27	10	
0	0	1	0	0	1	1	1	0	0	1	0	0	1	1	1	27	27	STX X'1027'
0	0	0	0	0	1	0	0	0	0	1	0	0	1	1	1	05	27	
0	0	0	0	0	1	0	0	0	0	0	1	0	0	0	0	04	10	
0	0	0	0	0	0	1	1	1	1	1	1	1	1	1	1	03	FF	LDX #X'1000'
0	0	0	0	0	0	1	0	0	0	0	0	0	0	0	0	02	00	
0	0	0	0	0	0	0	1	0	0	0	1	0	0	0	0	01	10	
0	0	0	0	0	0	0	0	1	1	0	0	1	1	1	0	00	CE	

A7–A0   D7–D0

Figure 13.11

Table 13.1 *M6800 instruction cycle summary for LDX and STX instructions*

Instruction	Cycle	Address bus	Data bus
LDX	1	Opcode address	Opcode
(immediate	2	Opcode address + 1	Operand data MSB
addressing)	3	Opcode address + 2	Operand data LSB
STX	1	Opcode address	Opcode
(extended	2	Opcode address + 1	Address of operand MSB
addressing)	3	Opcode address + 2	Address of operand LSB
	4	Address of operand	Irrelevant data
	5	Address of operand	Operand data MSB
	6	Address of operand + 1	Operand data LSB

lines D7–D0 carry CE which is the LDX opcode. During the next clock pulse, the next highest line of the display shows that A7–A0 carries 01 which is the eight least significant bits of 2001. Checking with Table 13.1 we can see that this is correct.

Table 13.1 also shows us that the data bus should carry the address of the operand's most significant byte at this time. Since the operand is 1027, the data bus therefore carries 10 as shown by the display. Therefore, by examining the display line-by-line, the correct operation of the system can be detected. Any deviation from the expected behaviour can be investigated more closely by running the program again, but sampling asynchronously at a higher rate in the region of the detected anomaly.

13.3   Signature analysers

Although the logic analyser is one of the most powerful weapons available for fault diagnosis in a laboratory situation, it does have certain disadvantages for the field test engineer. One difficulty is the sheer volume of information that the instrument collects and presents to the user. If we take as an example a modest logic analyser with 16 input lines which can store a maximum of 512 samples, this may present as many as 8,192 bits of data for examination. Although the data are presented in a convenient form, they must still be analysed to identify a fault situation. It may be necessary to use the logic analyser to observe data flow at several points along the system address and data buses, thus giving an additional volume of data.

To illustrate the special problems confronting the field service engineer of microprocessor-based systems, we may compare his situation with that of an engineer servicing analogue electronic systems. With an analogue system, the standard fault location tools are a multimeter and oscilloscope. Using these instruments, the service engineer can trace signals through the circuit. Service manuals will often contain circuit diagrams showing the shapes and amplitudes of waveforms appearing at various nodes in the circuit when it is operating correctly. Figure 13.12 shows an example of this. To check whether that part of the system described by the circuit shown in Figure 13.12 is working properly is a straightforward matter. The service engineer observes the shape and size of input and output waveforms using an oscilloscope. If the input waveform is as expected and the output waveform is not, then a fault exists somewhere in the circuit shown. Even if the input waveform is not as expected, a test engineer can break the input line and excite the circuit with a test waveform of the correct shape and size by a signal generator. With these aids, it is not uncommon for the field service engineer to be able to locate faults down to component level.

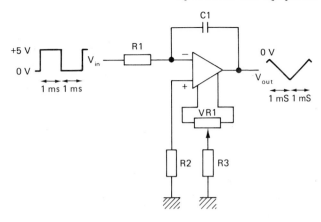

Figure 13.12   Waveform diagrams to assist fault-finding in analogue circuits

As we have seen, the problem with microprocessor-based systems is that waveforms at circuit nodes tend to be complex trains of pulses which can only be examined in detail using special instruments such as the logic analyser. These pulse trains cannot generally be described by simple amplitude/shape diagrams of the type found in analogue circuit service information. Finding faults at component level thus makes increased demands on the field service engineer and requires a much deeper understanding of the circuit operation than is the case with analogue systems. One consequence of this is the widespread use of board exchange as a means of servicing microprocessor equipment.

Signature analysers are instruments designed specifically to alleviate the difficulties involved in the field servicing of microprocessor systems. The technique of signature analysis allows us to characterise a complex pulse train by one simple parameter or 'signature' in much the same way that an analogue waveform is characterised by its shape and size.

Signature analysers operate synchronously with the clock of the system being tested. The single data probe of the analyser is placed on the test node or point in the circuit being checked. Once during each system clock cycle, the voltage at the probe is sampled and classified as logic 1 or 0 using a threshold detection technique similar to that used in a logic analyser and shown in Figure 13.4. The signature analyser will obviously need a second input consisting of the system clock waveform.

At the probe output, we therefore have a waveform which changes between the two logic levels. The changes will be synchronous in that a change will always occur at the same point in the clock cycle. They are not necessarily repetitive in the accepted sense however. The measurement made by the signature analyser takes place within a

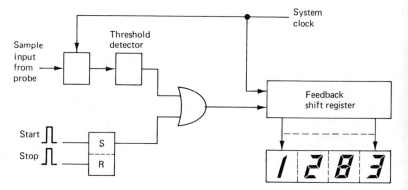

Figure 13.13 Simplified schematic layout of signature analyser

time interval defined by start and stop pulses, which must be generated by the system under test. Figure 13.13 shows a simplified schematic diagram of a signature analyser. When the RS bistable is set by the edge of the start pulse, the data samples are clocked into a special circuit known as a feedback shift register. Successive samples are clocked into the feedback shift register in this way until the RS bistable is reset by the stop pulse. Figure 13.14 shows the timing relationships for a typical data waveform in a signature analyser in which the RS bistable is triggered by the high–low transitions of start/stop pulses. Data are clocked into the feedback shift register on high–low transitions of the system clock.

Figure 13.15 shows an example of a 16-bit feedback register. It will be seen that the outputs from stages 16, 12, 9 and 7 are combined with the input bit stream in a modulo-2 adder to provide the next input to stage 1 of the register. A modulo-2 adder is a logic element whose

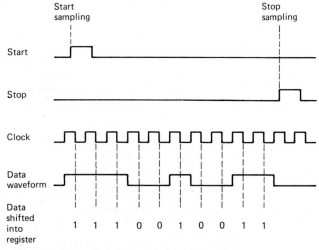

Figure 13.14 Signature analyser timing diagram

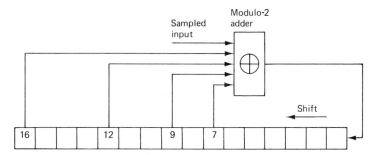

Figure 13.15 Sixteen-stage feedback shift register

output is logic 1 if any even number of outputs is at logic 1. For the purpose of this definition, zero is regarded as an even number. In the circuit shown in Figure 13.6 for example, if $Q16, Q12, Q9, Q7 = 1101$ and the input bit is 1, the output of the modulo-2 adder is zero since four of the inputs are at logic 1. Similarly if $Q16, Q12, Q9, Q7 = 0010$ and the input bit is 0, the output of the modulo-2 adder will be 1 since only one input (an odd number) is at logic 1.

The input bit stream is fed into the feedback shift register after the start pulse. Shifting is terminated by the stop pulse and the shift register contents then constitute the signature for the pulse train between start and stop. In most commercial signature analysers the contents of the shift register are decoded and displayed in hexadecimal or similar format. At this point, the reader may legitimately enquire as to the reason for the choice of a feedback shift register to generate the signature of the input waveform. Other methods are possible. One technique that has been used is to count the number of high–low and low–high transitions in the test wave-form between the start and stop pulses. This number can then certainly be used as a signature for the pulse train. What therefore is so special about the signature generated by the feedback shift register?

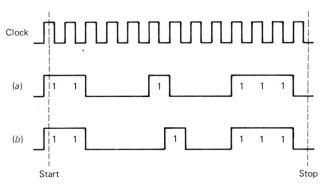

Figure 13.16 Signature analyser test waveform

To answer this question we must first realise that the usefulness of a signature analyser is determined by its ability to detect differences between correct and incorrect pulse trains. If an incorrect pulse train can generate a signature identical to that for the correct signal then the instrument has failed in its purpose. One feature of the feedback shift register logic analysers described here is their ability to generate different signatures from pulse trains which differ only slightly.

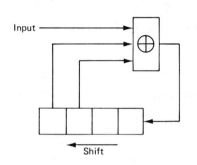

Figure 13.16 shows two pulse trains, *(a)* being correct and *(b)* being found in a faulty system. It will be seen that the only difference between *(a)* and *(b)* lies in the displacement of the narrow pulse in the centre of the train. Using level transitions as a signature reveals no error since both *(a)* and *(b)* have five such transitions. Now consider the use of a signature analyser based on the very simple four-stage feedback shift register shown in Figure 13.17. Figures 13.18 and 13.19 show how the contents of the register change as successive digits of the sampled input are clocked in. The correct waveform generates a signature of 0010 whereas the incorrect pulse train leaves a signature of 1001.

Figure 13.17 Four-stage feedback shift register

The above example simply demonstrates the superiority of the feedback shift register over transition counting as a means of error detection in one particular situation. It is, however, possible to prove the general superiority of feedback shift register methods mathematically.

Q13.6

Choice of feedback connections in the shift register is important in this application. References 13.1 and 13.3 give background theory and information concerning suitable feedback connections.

When using a signature analyser for fault location, a service engineer will check the signature at various test points or 'nodes' in the faulty circuit. These signatures are compared with those found at similar nodes in a circuit which is operating correctly. For this procedure to be successful, some means must be available for generating suitable pulse trains at the various nodes. What is needed is the equivalent of a signal generator which stimulates the nodes of an analogue circuit.

A very convenient way of stimulating many of the nodes of most microprocessor systems is to place the system in the free-run condition. This procedure (described in Section 12.10) causes the address on the address bus to continuously cycle through all possible values. As these addresses cycle through 0000–FFFF in a system with a 16-line address bus, the most significant line A15 will make one transition from 0 to 1. This will occur in the address transition 7FFF–8000. With most commercial signature analysers, the signal on A15 can be supplied to both the start and stop control lines. The first 0–1 transition then starts the signature analysis which is then terminated by the second transition. Reference 13.12 describes the technique in more detail.

State				Next input	Next input to shift register
0	0	0	0	1	1
0	0	0	1	1	1
0	0	1	1	0	0
0	1	1	0	0	1
1	1	0	1	0	0
1	0	1	0	1	0
0	1	0	0	0	1
1	0	0	1	0	1
0	0	1	1	0	0
0	1	1	0	1	0
1	1	0	0	1	1
1	0	0	1	1	0
0	0	1	0	0	

Figure 13.8 Feedback shift register state sequence for the correct waveform *(a)*

State				Next input	Next input to shift register
0	0	0	0	1	1
0	0	0	1	1	1
0	0	1	1	0	0
0	1	1	0	0	1
1	1	0	1	0	0
1	0	1	0	0	1
0	1	0	1	1	0
1	0	1	0	0	1
0	1	0	1	0	1
1	0	1	1	1	0
0	1	1	0	1	0
1	1	0	0	1	1
1	0	0	1	0	

Figure 13.19 Feedback shift register state sequence for faulty waveform *(b)*

Employing A15 as a means of opening and closing the signature analysis 'window' allows the signature on address lines A0–A14 to be checked as the addresses cycle through all possible values. For an 8080-based system, each cycle of 65,536 addresses will require 262,144 clock pulses since each NOP instruction requires four clock cycles for execution. Signatures should be checked at various points along the address bus.

As addresses cycle through all possible values with the microprocessor in the free-run mode, the outputs of address decoders will become active when the appropriate address appears, then inputs. The signatures at address decoder outputs can therefore indicate whether or not the circuit is functioning correctly. If address decoders are enabled by signals such as the 8080 $\overline{\text{MEMRD}}$ or $\overline{\text{IOWR}}$, it may be necessary to hold these lines at logical 0 to allow the signature to be generated. In all cases, signatures are compared with those found under similar test conditions in a system which is functioning **Q13.5** correctly.

References and bibliography

13.1   C.H. House, 'Engineering in the time domain calls for a new kind of digital instrument', *Electronics*, pp 75–81 (1 May 1975).

13.2   W.A. Farnbach, 'Systematic turn-on of microprocessor systems using logic state analysers', *Electronic Design*, p 15 (19 July 1976).

13.3   W.A. Farnbach, 'Logic state analysers – a new instrument for analysing sequential digital processes', *IEEE Transactions on instrumentation and measurement*, Vol.IM 24(4), pp 353–6 (December 1975).

13.4   C.T. Small and J.S. Morrill, Jr, 'The logic state analyser, a viewing port for the data domain', *Hewlett-Packard Journal*, pp 2–10 (August 1975).

13.5   W.A. Farnbach, 'Troubleshooting in the data domain is simplified by logic analysers', *Electronics*, pp 103–105 (15 May 1975).

13.6   R.L. Down, 'Understanding logic analysers', *Computer design*, Vol. 16(6), pp 188–91 (June 1977).

13.7   T. Clark, 'Troubleshooting microprocessor-based systems' *Digital Design*, pp 56–66 (February 1978).

13.8   G. Gordon and H. Nadig, 'Hexadecimal signatures identify troublespots in microprocessor systems', *Electronics* (3 March 1977).

13.9   R.A. Frohwerk, 'Signature analysis: a new digital field service method', *Hewlett-Packard Journal* (May 1977).

13.10 D.A. Sharrit, 'Designing serviceability into the Model 8568A spectrum analyser', *ibid.* (June 1978).

13.11 D.A. Sharrit, 'Team up a μP with signature analysis and ease troubleshooting in the field', *Electronic Design*, (4 January 1979).

13.12 A. Stefanski, 'Free-running signature analysis simplifies troubleshooting', *Electronic Design News* (5 February 1979).

Questions

13.1   Explain the distinction between synchronous and asynchronous sampling by a logic analyser.

13.2   With the help of a simple block diagram, describe the internal operation of a logic analyser.

13.3   Explain why synchronous sampling is better than asynchronous sampling when a logic analyser is used for glitch detection.

13.4   With the help of sketches, describe the time domain and data domain of display available with a logic analyser.

13.5   Explain the basic principle of signature analysis.

13.6   Determine the contents of the feedback shift register shown in Figure 13.17 if the sequence 11001111000 is shifted in synchronously. You may assume that the register initially contains 0000.

This is not true. A synchronous sampling is better than sychronous sampling when trying to detect glitches.

i.e.

Synchronous mode is set to the clock rate of the system being tested — this is no good as you may miss glitches.
Asynchronous — you are able to be running at a faster clock rate than the system under test ∴ there is more chance of detecting glitches.

15/3/87

Note:

The following Appendices contain examples of manufacturer's product information, reproduced by kind permission of the various companies. It is intended that this information should only serve as an example of the literature and product comparisons that are available. *They should not be used as a primary source for your design information.* Owing to the rapid advance of microelectronics, more up-to-date information will probably be available by the time you read this book.

Appendix A The Intel 8080 central processing unit

THE 8080 CENTRAL PROCESSING UNIT

The 8080 is a complete 8-bit parallel, central processor unit (CPU) for use in general purpose digital computer systems. It is fabricated on a single LSI chip (see Figure 3-1). using Intel's n-channel silicon gate MOS process. The 8080 transfers data and internal state information via an 8-bit, bidirectional 3-state Data Bus (D_0-D_7). Memory and peripheral device addresses are transmitted over a separate 16-bit 3-state Address Bus (A_0-A_{15}). Six timing and control outputs (SYNC, DBIN, WAIT, $\overline{WR}$, HLDA and INTE) emanate from the 8080, while four control inputs (READY, HOLD, INT and RESET), four power inputs (+12v, +5v, -5v, and GND) and two clock inputs (ϕ_1 and ϕ_2) are accepted by the 8080.

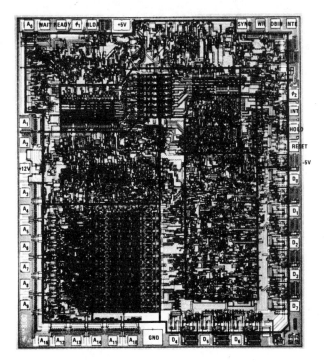

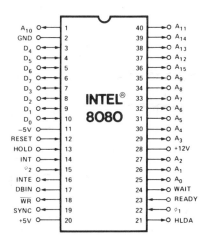

Figure 2-1. 8080 Photomicrograph With Pin Designations

ARCHITECTURE OF THE 8080 CPU

The 8080 CPU consists of the following functional units:

- Register array and address logic
- Arithmetic and logic unit (ALU)
- Instruction register and control section
- Bi-directional, 3-state data bus buffer

Figure 2-2 illustrates the functional blocks within the 8080 CPU.

Registers:

The register section consists of a static RAM array organized into six 16-bit registers:

- Program counter (PC)
- Stack pointer (SP)
- Six 8-bit general purpose registers arranged in pairs, referred to as B,C; D,E; and H,L
- A temporary register pair called W,Z

The program counter maintains the memory address of the current program instruction and is incremented auto-matically during every instruction fetch. The stack pointer maintains the address of the next available stack location in memory. The stack pointer can be initialized to use any portion of read-write memory as a stack. The stack pointer is decremented when data is "pushed" onto the stack and incremented when data is "popped" off the stack (i.e., the stack grows "downward").

The six general purpose registers can be used either as single registers (8-bit) or as register pairs (16-bit). The temporary register pair, W,Z, is not program addressable and is only used for the internal execution of instructions.

Eight-bit data bytes can be transferred between the internal bus and the register array via the register-select multiplexer. Sixteen-bit transfers can proceed between the register array and the address latch or the incrementer/decrementer circuit. The address latch receives data from any of the three register pairs and drives the 16 address output buffers (A_0-A_{15}), as well as the incrementer/decrementer circuit. The incrementer/decrementer circuit receives data from the address latch and sends it to the register array. The 16-bit data can be incremented or decremented or simply transferred between registers.

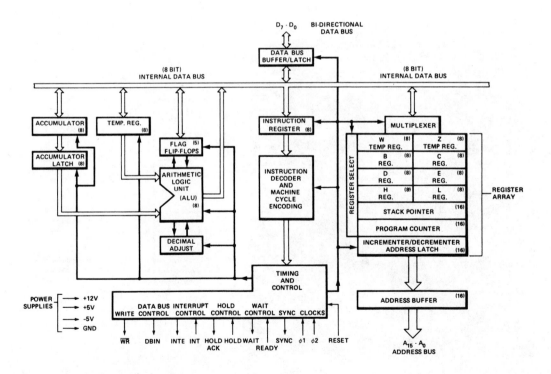

Figure 2-2. 8080 CPU Functional Block Diagram

Arithmetic and Logic Unit (ALU):

The ALU contains the following registers:

- An 8-bit accumulator

- An 8-bit temporary accumulator (ACT)

- A 5-bit flag register: zero, carry, sign, parity and auxiliary carry

- An 8-bit temporary register (TMP)

Arithmetic, logical and rotate operations are performed in the ALU. The ALU is fed by the temporary register (TMP) and the temporary accumulator (ACT) and carry flip-flop. The result of the operation can be transferred to the internal bus or to the accumulator; the ALU also feeds the flag register.

The temporary register (TMP) receives information from the internal bus and can send all or portions of it to the ALU, the flag register and the internal bus.

The accumulator (ACC) can be loaded from the ALU and the internal bus and can transfer data to the temporary accumulator (ACT) and the internal bus. The contents of the accumulator (ACC) and the auxiliary carry flip-flop can be tested for decimal correction during the execution of the DAA instruction (see Chapter 4).

Instruction Register and Control:

During an instruction fetch, the first byte of an instruction (containing the OP code) is transferred from the internal bus to the 8-bit instruction register.

The contents of the instruction register are, in turn, available to the instruction decoder. The output of the decoder, combined with various timing signals, provides the control signals for the register array, ALU and data buffer blocks. In addition, the outputs from the instruction decoder and external control signals feed the timing and state control section which generates the state and cycle timing signals.

Data Bus Buffer:

This 8-bit bidirectional 3-state buffer is used to isolate the CPU's internal bus from the external data bus (D_0 through D_7). In the output mode, the internal bus content is loaded into an 8-bit latch that, in turn, drives the data bus output buffers. The output buffers are switched off during input or non-transfer operations.

During the input mode, data from the external data bus is transferred to the internal bus. The internal bus is precharged at the beginning of each internal state, except for the transfer state (T_3—described later in this chapter).

THE PROCESSOR CYCLE

An **instruction cycle** is defined as the time required to fetch and execute an instruction. During the fetch, a selected instruction (one, two or three bytes) is extracted from memory and deposited in the CPU's instruction register. During the execution phase, the instruction is decoded and translated into specific processing activities.

Every instruction cycle consists of one, two, three, four or five machine cycles. A **machine cycle** is required each time the CPU accesses memory or an I/O port. The fetch portion of an instruction cycle requires one machine cycle for each byte to be fetched. The duration of the execution portion of the instruction cycle depends on the kind of instruction that has been fetched. Some instructions do not require any machine cycles other than those necessary to fetch the instruction; other instructions, however, require additional machine cycles to write or read data to/from memory or I/O devices. The DAD instruction is an exception in that it requires two additional machine cycles to complete an internal register-pair add (see Chapter 4).

Each machine cycle consists of three, four or five states. A state is the smallest unit of processing activity and is defined as the interval between two successive positive-going transitions of the ϕ_1 driven clock pulse. The 8080 is driven by a two-phase clock oscillator. All processing activities are referred to the period of this clock. The two non-overlapping clock pulses, labeled ϕ_1 and ϕ_2, are furnished by external circuitry. It is the ϕ_1 clock pulse which divides each machine cycle into states. Timing logic within the 8080 uses the clock inputs to produce a SYNC pulse, which identifies the beginning of every machine cycle. The SYNC pulse is triggered by the low-to-high transition of ϕ_2, as shown in Figure 2-3.

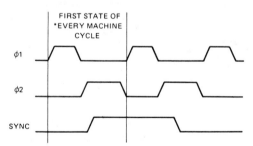

*SYNC DOES NOT OCCUR IN THE SECOND AND THIRD MACHINE CYCLES OF A DAD INSTRUCTION SINCE THESE MACHINE CYCLES ARE USED FOR AN INTERNAL REGISTER-PAIR ADD.

Figure 2-3. ϕ_1, ϕ_2 And SYNC Timing

There are three exceptions to the defined duration of a state. They are the WAIT state, the hold (HLDA) state and the halt (HLTA) state, described later in this chapter. Because the WAIT, the HLDA, and the HLTA states depend upon external events, they are by their nature of indeterminate length. Even these exceptional states, however, must be synchronized with the pulses of the driving clock. Thus, the duration of all states are integral multiples of the clock period.

To summarize then, each **clock period** marks a **state;** three to five states constitute a machine cycle; and one to five **machine cycles** comprise an **instruction cycle.** A full instruction cycle requires anywhere from four to eight-teen states for its completion, depending on the kind of instruction involved.

Machine Cycle Identification:

With the exception of the DAD instruction, there is just one consideration that determines how many machine cycles are required in any given instruction cycle: the number of times that the processor must reference a memory address or an addressable peripheral device, in order to fetch and execute the instruction. Like many processors, the 8080 is so constructed that it can transmit only one address per machine cycle. Thus, if the fetch and execution of an instruction requires two memory references, then the instruction cycle associated with that instruction consists of two machine cycles. If five such references are called for, then the instruction cycle contains five machine cycles.

Every instruction cycle has at least one reference to memory, during which the instruction is fetched. An instruction cycle must always have a fetch, even if the execution of the instruction requires no further references to memory. The first machine cycle in every instruction cycle is therefore a FETCH. Beyond that, there are no fast rules. It depends on the kind of instruction that is fetched.

Consider some examples. The add-register (ADD r) instruction is an instruction that requires only a single machine cycle (FETCH) for its completion. In this one-byte instruction, the contents of one of the CPU's six general purpose registers is added to the existing contents of the accumulator. Since all the information necessary to execute the command is contained in the eight bits of the instruction code, only one memory reference is necessary. Three states are used to extract the instruction from memory, and one additional state is used to accomplish the desired addition. The entire instruction cycle thus requires only one machine cycle that consists of four states, or four periods of the external clock.

Suppose now, however, that we wish to add the contents of a specific memory location to the existing contents of the accumulator (ADD M). Although this is quite similar in principle to the example just cited, several additional steps will be used. An extra machine cycle will be used, in order to address the desired memory location.

The actual sequence is as follows. First the processor extracts from memory the one-byte instruction word addressed by its program counter. This takes three states. The eight-bit instruction word obtained during the FETCH machine cycle is deposited in the CPU's instruction register and used to direct activities during the remainder of the instruction cycle. Next, the processor sends out, as an address,

the contents of its H and L registers. The eight-bit data word returned during this MEMORY READ machine cycle is placed in a temporary register inside the 8080 CPU. By now three more clock periods (states) have elapsed. In the seventh and final state, the contents of the temporary register are added to those of the accumulator. Two machine cycles, consisting of seven states in all, complete the "ADD M" instruction cycle.

At the opposite extreme is the save H and L registers (SHLD) instruction, which requires five machine cycles. During an "SHLD" instruction cycle, the contents of the processor's H and L registers are deposited in two sequentially adjacent memory locations; the destination is indicated by two address bytes which are stored in the two memory locations immediately following the operation code byte. The following sequence of events occurs:

(1) A FETCH machine cycle, consisting of four states. During the first three states of this machine cycle, the processor fetches the instruction indicated by its program counter. The program counter is then incremented. The fourth state is used for internal instruction decoding.

(2) A MEMORY READ machine cycle, consisting of three states. During this machine cycle, the byte indicated by the program counter is read from memory and placed in the processor's Z register. The program counter is incremented again.

(3) Another MEMORY READ machine cycle, consisting of three states, in which the byte indicated by the processor's program counter is read from memory and placed in the W register. The program counter is incremented, in anticipation of the next instruction fetch.

(4) A MEMORY WRITE machine cycle, of three states, in which the contents of the L register are transferred to the memory location pointed to by the present contents of the W and Z registers. The state following the transfer is used to increment the W,Z register pair so that it indicates the next memory location to receive data.

(5) A MEMORY WRITE machine cycle, of three states, in which the contents of the H register are transferred to the new memory location pointed to by the W,Z register pair.

In summary, the "SHLD" instruction cycle contains five machine cycles and takes 16 states to execute.

Most instructions fall somewhere between the extremes typified by the "ADD r" and the "SHLD" instructions. The input (INP) and the output (OUT) instructions, for example, require three machine cycles: a FETCH, to obtain the instruction; a MEMORY READ, to obtain the address of the object peripheral; and an INPUT or an OUTPUT machine cycle, to complete the transfer.

While no one instruction cycle will consist of more then five machine cycles, the following ten different types of machine cycles may occur within an instruction cycle:

(1) FETCH (M1)

(2) MEMORY READ

(3) MEMORY WRITE

(4) STACK READ

(5) STACK WRITE

(6) INPUT

(7) OUTPUT

(8) INTERRUPT

(9) HALT

(10) HALT • INTERRUPT

The machine cycles that actually do occur in a particular instruction cycle depend upon the kind of instruction, with the overriding stipulation that the first machine cycle in any instruction cycle is always a FETCH.

The processor identifies the machine cycle in progress by transmitting an eight-bit status word during the first state of every machine cycle. Updated status information is presented on the 8080's data lines (D_0-D_7), during the SYNC interval. This data should be saved in latches, and used to develop control signals for external circuitry. Table 2-1 shows how the positive-true status information is distributed on the processor's data bus.

Status signals are provided principally for the control of external circuitry. Simplicity of interface, rather than machine cycle identification, dictates the logical definition of individual status bits. You will therefore observe that certain processor machine cycles are uniquely identified by a single status bit, but that others are not. The M_1 status bit (D_6), for example, unambiguously identifies a FETCH machine cycle. A STACK READ, on the other hand, is indicated by the coincidence of STACK and MEMR signals. Machine cycle identification data is also valuable in the test and de-bugging phases of system development. Table 2-1 lists the status bit outputs for each type of machine cycle.

State Transition Sequence:

Every machine cycle within an instruction cycle consists of three to five active states (referred to as T_1, T_2, T_3, T_4, T_5 or T_W). The actual number of states depends upon the instruction being executed, and on the particular machine cycle within the greater instruction cycle. The state transition diagram in Figure 2-4 shows how the 8080 proceeds from state to state in the course of a machine cycle. The diagram also shows how the READY, HOLD, and INTERRUPT lines are sampled during the machine cycle, and how the conditions on these lines may modify the

basic transition sequence. In the present discussion, we are concerned only with the basic sequence and with the READY function. The HOLD and INTERRUPT functions will be discussed later.

The 8080 CPU does not directly indicate its internal state by transmitting a "state control" output during each state; instead, the 8080 supplies direct control output (INTE, HLDA, DBIN, $\overline{WR}$ and WAIT) for use by external circuitry.

Recall that the 8080 passes through at least three states in every machine cycle, with each state defined by successive low-to-high transitions of the ϕ_1 clock. Figure 2-5 shows the timing relationships in a typical FETCH machine cycle. Events that occur in each state are referenced to transitions of the ϕ_1 and ϕ_2 clock pulses.

The SYNC signal identifies the first state (T_1) in every machine cycle. As shown in Figure 2-5, the SYNC signal is related to the leading edge of the ϕ_2 clock. There is a delay (t_{DC}) between the low-to-high transition of ϕ_2 and the positive-going edge of the SYNC pulse. There also is a corresponding delay (also t_{DC}) between the next ϕ_2 pulse and the falling edge of the SYNC signal. Status information is displayed on D_0-D_7 during the same ϕ_2 to ϕ_2 interval. Switching of the status signals is likewise controlled by ϕ_2.

The rising edge of ϕ_2 during T_1 also loads the processor's address lines (A_0-A_{15}). These lines become stable within a brief delay (t_{DA}) of the ϕ_2 clocking pulse, and they remain stable until the first ϕ_2 pulse after state T_3. This gives the processor ample time to read the data returned from memory.

Once the processor has sent an address to memory, there is an opportunity for the memory to request a WAIT. This it does by pulling the processor's READY line low, prior to the "Ready set-up" interval (t_{RS}) which occurs during the ϕ_2 pulse within state T_2 or T_W. As long as the READY line remains low, the processor will idle, giving the memory time to respond to the addressed data request. Refer to Figure 2-5.

The processor responds to a wait request by entering an alternative state (T_W) at the end of T_2, rather than proceeding directly to the T_3 state. Entry into the T_W state is indicated by a WAIT signal from the processor, acknowledging the memory's request. A low-to-high transition on the WAIT line is triggered by the rising edge of the ϕ_1 clock and occurs within a brief delay (t_{DC}) of the actual entry into the T_W state.

A wait period may be of indefinite duration. The processor remains in the waiting condition until its READY line again goes high. A READY indication **must** precede the falling edge of the ϕ_2 clock by a specified interval (t_{RS}), in order to guarantee an exit from the T_W state. The cycle may then proceed, beginning with the rising edge of the next ϕ_1 clock. A WAIT interval will therefore consist of an integral number of T_W states and will always be a multiple of the clock period.

Instructions for the 8080 require from one to five machine cycles for complete execution. The 8080 sends out 8 bit of status information on the data bus at the beginning of each machine cycle (during SYNC time). The following table defines the status information.

STATUS INFORMATION DEFINITION

Symbols	Data Bus Bit	Definition
INTA*	D_0	Acknowledge signal for INTERRUPT request. Signal should be used to gate a restart instruction onto the data bus when DBIN is active.
$\overline{WO}$	D_1	Indicates that the operation in the current machine cycle will be a WRITE memory or OUTPUT function ($\overline{WO}$ = 0). Otherwise, a READ memory or INPUT operation will be executed.
STACK	D_2	Indicates that the address bus holds the pushdown stack address from the Stack Pointer.
HLTA	D_3	Acknowledge signal for HALT instruction.
OUT	D_4	Indicates that the address bus contains the address of an output device and the data bus will contain the output data when $\overline{WR}$ is active.
M_1	D_5	Provides a signal to indicate that the CPU is in the fetch cycle for the first byte of an instruction.
INP*	D_6	Indicates that the address bus contains the address of an input device and the input data should be placed on the data bus when DBIN is active.
MEMR*	D_7	Designates that the data bus will be used for memory read data.

*These three status bits can be used to control the flow of data onto the 8080 data bus.

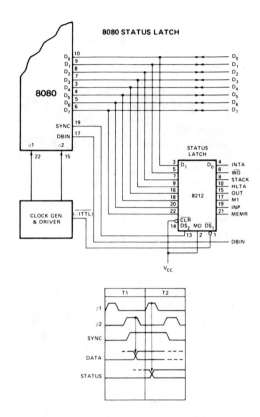

STATUS WORD CHART

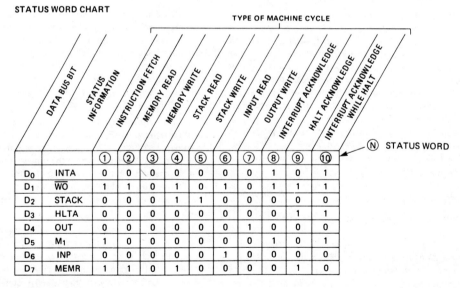

DATA BUS BIT	STATUS INFORMATION	INSTRUCTION FETCH ①	MEMORY READ ②	MEMORY WRITE ③	STACK READ ④	STACK WRITE ⑤	INPUT READ ⑥	OUTPUT WRITE ⑦	INTERRUPT ACKNOWLEDGE ⑧	HALT ACKNOWLEDGE ⑨	INTERRUPT ACKNOWLEDGE WHILE HALT ⑩
D_0	INTA	0	0	0	0	0	0	0	1	0	1
D_1	$\overline{WO}$	1	1	0	1	0	1	0	1	1	1
D_2	STACK	0	0	0	1	1	0	0	0	0	0
D_3	HLTA	0	0	0	0	0	0	0	0	1	1
D_4	OUT	0	0	0	0	0	0	1	0	0	0
D_5	M_1	1	0	0	0	0	0	0	1	0	1
D_6	INP	0	0	0	0	0	1	0	0	0	0
D_7	MEMR	1	1	0	1	0	0	0	0	1	0

Table 2-1. 8080 Status Bit Definitions

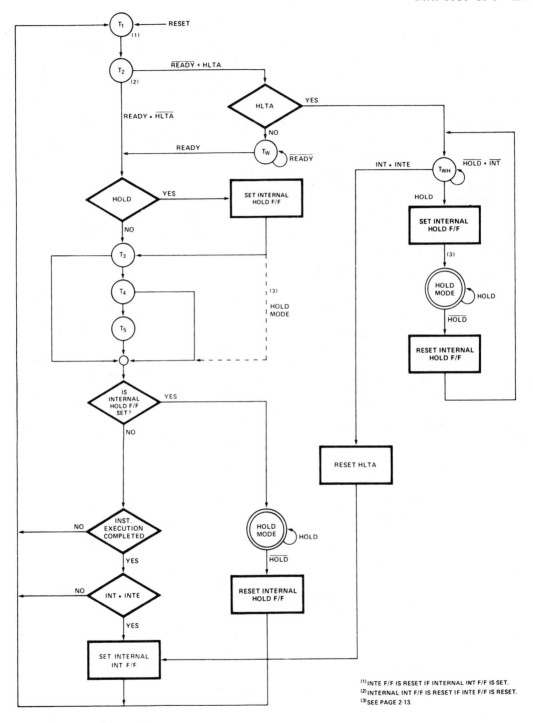

Figure 2-4. CPU State Transition Diagram

The events that take place during the T_3 state are determined by the kind of machine cycle in progress. In a FETCH machine cycle, the processor interprets the data on its data bus as an instruction. During a MEMORY READ or a STACK READ, data on this bus is interpreted as a data word. The processor outputs data on this bus during a MEMORY WRITE machine cycle. During I/O operations, the processor may either transmit or receive data, depending on whether an OUTPUT or an INPUT operation is involved.

Figure 2-6 illustrates the timing that is characteristic of a data input operation. As shown, the low-to-high transition of ϕ_2 during T_2 clears status information from the processor's data lines, preparing these lines for the receipt of incoming data. The data presented to the processor must have stabilized prior to both the "ϕ_1—data set-up" interval (t_{DS1}), that precedes the falling edge of the ϕ_1 pulse defining state T_3, and the "ϕ_2—data set-up" interval (t_{DS2}), that precedes the rising edge of ϕ_2 in state T_3. This same data must remain stable during the "data hold" interval (t_{DH}) that occurs following the rising edge of the ϕ_2 pulse. Data placed on these lines by memory or by other external devices will be sampled during T_3.

During the input of data to the processor, the 8080 generates a DBIN signal which should be used externally to enable the transfer. Machine cycles in which DBIN is available include: FETCH, MEMORY READ, STACK READ, and INTERRUPT. DBIN is initiated by the rising edge of ϕ_2 during state T_2 and terminated by the corresponding edge of ϕ_2 during T_3. Any T_W phases intervening between T_2 and T_3 will therefore extend DBIN by one or more clock periods.

Figure 2-7 shows the timing of a machine cycle in which the processor outputs data. Output data may be destined either for memory or for peripherals. The rising edge of ϕ_2 within state T_2 clears status information from the CPU's data lines, and loads in the data which is to be output to external devices. This substitution takes place within the

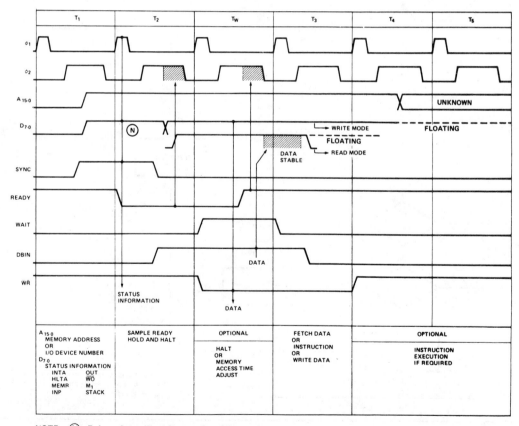

NOTE: (N) Refer to Status Word Chart on Page 2-6.

Figure 2-5. Basic 8080 Instruction Cycle

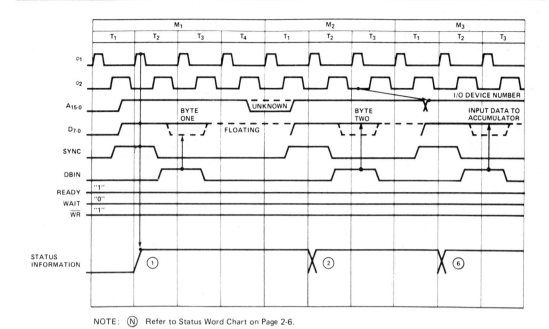

NOTE: (N) Refer to Status Word Chart on Page 2-6.

Figure 2-6. Input Instruction Cycle

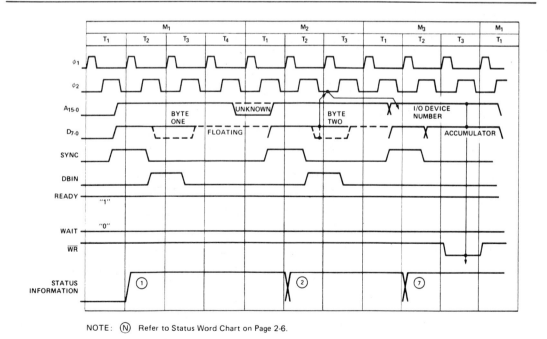

NOTE: (N) Refer to Status Word Chart on Page 2-6.

Figure 2-7. Output Instruction Cycle

"data output delay" interval (t_{DD}) following the ϕ_2 clock's leading edge. Data on the bus remains stable throughout the remainder of the machine cycle, until replaced by updated status information in the subsequent T$_1$ state. Observe that a READY signal is necessary for completion of an OUTPUT machine cycle. Unless such an indication is present, the processor enters the T$_W$ state, following the T$_2$ state. Data on the output lines remains stable in the interim, and the processing cycle will not proceed until the READY line again goes high.

The 8080 CPU generates a $\overline{WR}$ output for the synchronization of external transfers, during those machine cycles in which the processor outputs data. These include MEMORY WRITE, STACK WRITE, and OUTPUT. The negative-going leading edge of $\overline{WR}$ is referenced to the rising edge of the first ϕ_1 clock pulse following T$_2$, and occurs within a brief delay (t_{DC}) of that event. $\overline{WR}$ remains low until re-triggered by the leading edge of ϕ_1 during the state following T$_3$. Note that any T$_W$ states intervening between T$_2$ and T$_3$ of the output machine cycle will necessarily extend $\overline{WR}$, in much the same way that DBIN is affected during data input operations.

All processor machine cycles consist of at least three states: T$_1$, T$_2$, and T$_3$ as just described. If the processor has to wait for a response from the peripheral or memory with which it is communicating, then the machine cycle may also contain one or more T$_W$ states. During the three basic states, data is transferred to or from the processor.

After the T$_3$ state, however, it becomes difficult to generalize. T$_4$ and T$_5$ states are available, if the execution of a particular instruction requires them. But not all machine cycles make use of these states. It depends upon the kind of instruction being executed, and on the particular machine cycle within the instruction cycle. The processor will terminate any machine cycle as soon as its processing activities are completed, rather than proceeding through the T$_4$ and T$_5$ states every time. Thus the 8080 may exit a machine cycle following the T$_3$, the T$_4$, or the T$_5$ state and proceed directly to the T$_1$ state of the next machine cycle.

STATE	ASSOCIATED ACTIVITIES
T$_1$	A memory address or I/O device number is placed on the Address Bus (A$_{15-0}$); status information is placed on Data Bus (D$_{7-0}$).
T$_2$	The CPU samples the READY and HOLD inputs and checks for halt instruction.
TW (optional)	Processor enters wait state if READY is low or if HALT instruction has been executed.
T3	An instruction byte (FETCH machine cycle), data byte (MEMORY READ, STACK READ) or interrupt instruction (INTERRUPT machine cycle) is input to the CPU from the Data Bus; or a data byte (MEMORY WRITE, STACK WRITE or OUTPUT machine cycle) is output onto the data bus.
T4 T5 (optional)	States T$_4$ and T$_5$ are available if the execution of a particular instruction requires them; if not, the CPU may skip one or both of them. T$_4$ and T$_5$ are only used for internal processor operations.

Table 2-2. State Definitions

INTERRUPT SEQUENCES

The 8080 has the built-in capacity to handle external interrupt requests. A peripheral device can initiate an interrupt simply by driving the processor's interrupt (INT) line high.

The interrupt (INT) input is asynchronous, and a request may therefore originate at any time during any instruction cycle. Internal logic re-clocks the external request, so that a proper correspondence with the driving clock is established. As Figure 2-8 shows, an interrupt request (INT) arriving during the time that the interrupt enable line (INTE) is high, acts in coincidence with the ϕ_2 clock to set the internal interrupt latch. This event takes place during the last state of the instruction cycle in which the request occurs, thus ensuring that any instruction in progress is completed before the interrupt can be processed.

The INTERRUPT machine cycle which follows the arrival of an enabled interrupt request resembles an ordinary FETCH machine cycle in most respects. The M_1 status bit is transmitted as usual during the SYNC interval. It is accompanied, however, by an INTA status bit (D_0) which acknowledges the external request. The contents of the program counter are latched onto the CPU's address lines during T_1, but the counter itself is not incremented during the INTERRUPT machine cycle, as it otherwise would be.

In this way, the pre-interrupt status of the program counter is preserved, so that data in the counter may be restored by the interrupted program after the interrupt request has been processed.

The interrupt cycle is otherwise indistinguishable from an ordinary FETCH machine cycle. The processor itself takes no further special action. It is the responsibility of the peripheral logic to see that an eight-bit interrupt instruction is "jammed" onto the processor's data bus during state T_3. In a typical system, this means that the data-in bus from memory must be temporarily disconnected from the processor's main data bus, so that the interrupting device can command the main bus without interference.

The 8080's instruction set provides a special one-byte call which facilitates the processing of interrupts (the ordinary program Call takes three bytes). This is the RESTART instruction (RST). A variable three-bit field embedded in the eight-bit field of the RST enables the interrupting device to direct a Call to one of eight fixed memory locations. The decimal addresses of these dedicated locations are: 0, 8, 16, 24, 32, 40, 48, and 56. Any of these addresses may be used to store the first instruction(s) of a routine designed to service the requirements of an interrupting device. Since the (RST) is a call, completion of the instruction also stores the old program counter contents on the STACK.

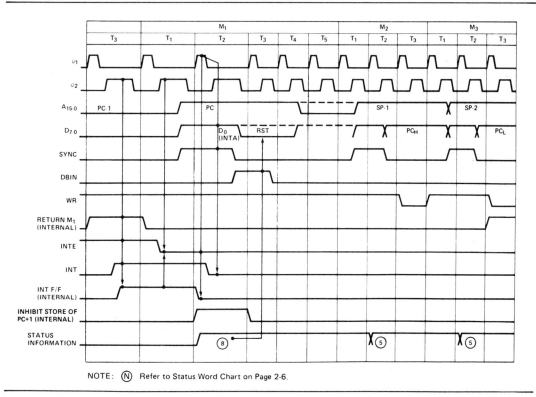

NOTE: (N) Refer to Status Word Chart on Page 2-6.

Figure 2-8. Interrupt Timing

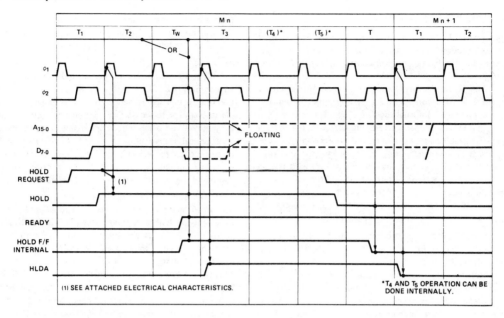

Figure 2-9. HOLD Operation (Read Mode)

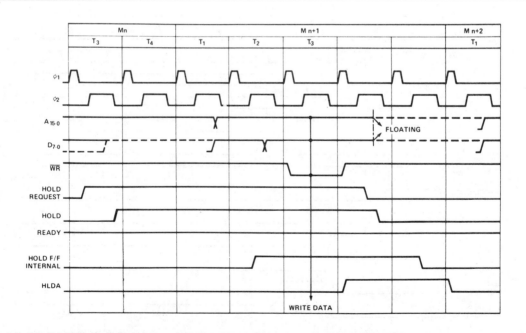

Figure 2-10. HOLD Operation (Write Mode)

HOLD SEQUENCES

The 8080A CPU contains provisions for Direct Memory Access (DMA) operations. By applying a HOLD to the appropriate control pin on the processor, an external device can cause the CPU to suspend its normal operations and relinquish control of the address and data busses. The processor responds to a request of this kind by floating its address to other devices sharing the busses. At the same time, the processor acknowledges the HOLD by placing a high on its HLDA outpin pin. During an acknowledged HOLD, the address and data busses are under control of the peripheral which originated the request, enabling it to conduct memory transfers without processor intervention.

Like the interrupt, the HOLD input is synchronized internally. A HOLD signal must be stable prior to the "Hold set-up" interval (t_{HS}), that precedes the rising edge of ϕ_2.

Figures 2-9 and 2-10 illustrate the timing involved in HOLD operations. Note the delay between the asynchronous HOLD REQUEST and the re-clocked HOLD. As shown in the diagram, a coincidence of the READY, the HOLD, and the ϕ_2 clocks sets the internal hold latch. Setting the latch enables the subsequent rising edge of the ϕ_1 clock pulse to trigger the HLDA output.

Acknowledgement of the HOLD REQUEST precedes slightly the actual floating of the processor's address and data lines. The processor acknowledges a HOLD at the beginning of T_3, if a read or an input machine cycle is in progress (see Figure 2-9). Otherwise, acknowledgement is deferred until the beginning of the state following T_3 (see Figure 2-10). In both cases, however, the HLDA goes high within a specified delay (t_{DC}) of the rising edge of the selected ϕ_1 clock pulse. Address and data lines are floated within a brief delay after the rising edge of the next ϕ_2 clock pulse. This relationship is also shown in the diagrams.

To all outward appearances, the processor has suspended its operations once the address and data busses are floated. Internally, however, certain functions may continue. If a HOLD REQUEST is acknowledged at T_3, and if the processor is in the middle of a machine cycle which requires four or more states to complete, the CPU proceeds through T_4 and T_5 before coming to a rest. Not until the end of the machine cycle is reached will processing activities cease. Internal processing is thus permitted to overlap the external DMA transfer, improving both the efficiency and the speed of the entire system.

The processor exits the holding state through a sequence similar to that by which it entered. A HOLD REQUEST is terminated asynchronously when the external device has completed its data transfer. The HLDA output returns to a low level following the leading edge of the next ϕ_1 clock pulse. Normal processing resumes with the machine cycle following the last cycle that was executed.

HALT SEQUENCES

When a halt instruction (HLT) is executed, the CPU enters the halt state (T_{WH}) after state T_2 of the next machine cycle, as shown in Figure 2-11. There are only three ways in which the 8080 can exit the halt state:

- A high on the RESET line will always reset the 8080 to state T_1; RESET also clears the program counter.
- A HOLD input will cause the 8080 to enter the hold state, as previously described. When the HOLD line goes low, the 8080 re-enters the halt state on the rising edge of the next ϕ_1 clock pulse.
- An interrupt (i.e., INT goes high while INTE is enabled) will cause the 8080 to exit the Halt state and enter state T_1 on the rising edge of the next ϕ_1 clock pulse. NOTE: The interrupt enable (INTE) flag **must** be set when the halt state is entered; otherwise, the 8080 will only be able to exit via a RESET signal.

Figure 2-12 illustrates halt sequencing in flow chart form.

START-UP OF THE 8080 CPU

When power is applied initially to the 8080, the processor begins operating immediately. The contents of its program counter, stack pointer, and the other working registers are naturally subject to random factors and cannot be specified. For this reason, it will be necessary to begin the power-up sequence with RESET.

An external RESET signal of three clock period duration (minimum) restores the processor's internal program counter to zero. Program execution thus begins with memory location zero, following a RESET. Systems which require the processor to wait for an explicit start-up signal will store a halt instruction (EI, HLT) in the first two locations. A manual or an automatic INTERRUPT will be used for starting. In other systems, the processor may begin executing its stored program immediately. Note, however, that the RESET has no effect on status flags, or on any of the processor's working registers (accumulator, registers, or stack pointer). The contents of these registers remain indeterminate, until initialized explicitly by the program.

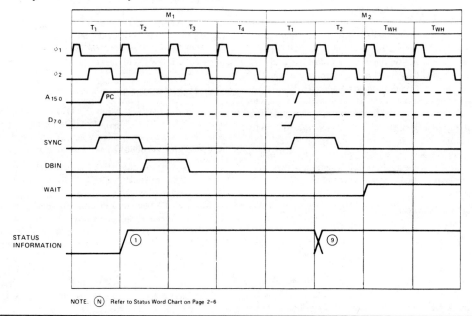

NOTE. (N)   Refer to Status Word Chart on Page 2-6

Figure 2-11. HALT Timing

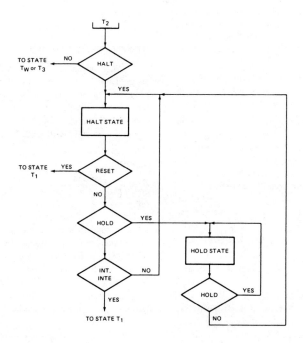

Figure 2-12. HALT Sequence Flow Chart.

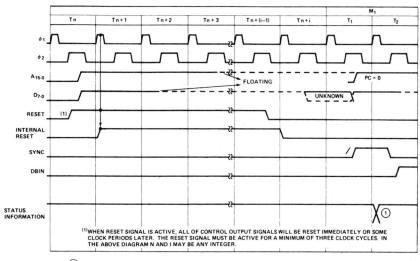

Figure 2-13. Reset.

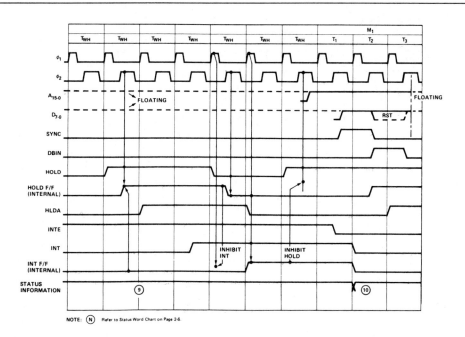

Figure 2-14. Relation between HOLD and INT in the HALT State.

MNEMONIC	OP CODE		M1[1]					M2		
	D7 D6 D5 D4	D3 D2 D1 D0	T1	T2[2]	T3	T4	T5	T1	T2[2]	T3
MOV r1,r2	0 1 D D	D S S S	PC OUT STATUS	PC = PC +1	INST→TMP/IR	(SSS)→TMP	(TMP)→DDD			
MOV r, M	0 1 D D	D 1 1 0				X[3]		HL OUT STATUS[6]	DATA→DDD	
MOV M, r	0 1 1 1	0 S S S				(SSS)→TMP		HL OUT STATUS[7]	(TMP)→DATA BUS	
SPHL	1 1 1 1	1 0 0 1				(HL)————→SP				
MVI r, data	0 0 D D	D 1 1 0				X		PC OUT STATUS[6]	B2→DDDD	
MVI M, data	0 0 1 1	0 1 1 0				X			B2→TMP	
LXI rp, data	0 0 R P	0 0 0 1				X			PC = PC + 1 B2→r1	
LDA addr	0 0 1 1	1 0 1 0				X			PC = PC + 1 B2→Z	
STA addr	0 0 1 1	0 0 1 0				X			PC = PC + 1 B2→Z	
LHLD addr	0 0 1 0	1 0 1 0				X			PC = PC + 1 B2→Z	
SHLD addr	0 0 1 0	0 0 1 0				X		PC OUT STATUS[6]	PC = PC + 1 B2→Z	
LDAX rp[4]	0 0 R P	1 0 1 0				X		rp OUT STATUS[6]	DATA→A	
STAX rp[4]	0 0 R P	0 0 1 0				X		rp OUT STATUS[7]	(A)→DATA BUS	
XCHG	1 1 1 0	1 0 1 1				(HL)←→(DE)				
ADD r	1 0 0 0	0 S S S				(SSS)→TMP (A)→ACT		[9]	(ACT)+(TMP)→A	
ADD M	1 0 0 0	0 1 1 0				(A)→ACT		HL OUT STATUS[6]	DATA→TMP	
ADI data	1 1 0 0	0 1 1 0				(A)→ACT		PC OUT STATUS[6]	PC = PC + 1 B2→TMP	
ADC r	1 0 0 0	1 S S S				(SSS)→TMP (A)→ACT		[9]	(ACT)+(TMP)+CY→A	
ADC M	1 0 0 0	1 1 1 0				(A)→ACT		HL OUT STATUS[6]	DATA→TMP	
ACI data	1 1 0 0	1 1 1 0				(A)→ACT		PC OUT STATUS[6]	PC = PC + 1 B2→TMP	
SUB r	1 0 0 1	0 S S S				(SSS)→TMP (A)→ACT		[9]	(ACT)-(TMP)→A	
SUB M	1 0 0 1	0 1 1 0				(A)→ACT		HL OUT STATUS[6]	DATA→TMP	
SUI data	1 1 0 1	0 1 1 0				(A)→ACT		PC OUT STATUS[6]	PC = PC + 1 B2→TMP	
SBB r	1 0 0 1	1 S S S				(SSS)→TMP (A)→ACT		[9]	(ACT)-(TMP)-CY→A	
SBB M	1 0 0 1	1 1 1 0				(A)→ACT		HL OUT STATUS[6]	DATA→TMP	
SBI data	1 1 0 1	1 1 1 0				(A)→ACT		PC OUT STATUS[6]	PC = PC + 1 B2→TMP	
INR r	0 0 D D	D 1 0 0				(DDD)→TMP (TMP) + 1→ALU	ALU→DDD			
INR M	0 0 1 1	0 1 0 0				X		HL OUT STATUS[6]	DATA→TMP (TMP)+1→ALU	
DCR r	0 0 D D	D 1 0 1				(DDD)→TMP (TMP)+1→ALU	ALU→DDD			
DCR M	0 0 1 1	0 1 0 1				X		HL OUT STATUS[6]	DATA→TMP (TMP)-1→ALU	
INX rp	0 0 R P	0 0 1 1				(RP) + 1————→RP				
DCX rp	0 0 R P	1 0 1 1				(RP) - 1————→RP				
DAD rp[8]	0 0 R P	1 0 0 1				X		(ri)→ACT	(L)→TMP, (ACT)+(TMP)→ALU	ALU→L, CY
DAA	0 0 1 0	0 1 1 1				DAA→A, FLAGS[10]				
ANA r	1 0 1 0	0 S S S				(SSS)→TMP (A)→ACT		[9]	(ACT)+(TMP)→A	
ANA M	1 0 1 0	0 1 1 0	PC OUT STATUS	PC = PC + 1	INST→TMP/IR	(A)→ACT		HL OUT STATUS[6]	DATA→TMP	

M3			M4			M5				
T1	T2[2]	T3	T1	T2[2]	T3	T1	T2[2]	T3	T4	T5
HL OUT STATUS[7]	(TMP) → DATA BUS									
PC OUT STATUS[6]	PC = PC + 1	B3 → rh								
	PC = PC + 1	B3 → W	WZ OUT STATUS[6]	DATA → A						
	PC = PC + 1	B3 → W	WZ OUT STATUS[7]	(A) → DATA BUS						
	PC = PC + 1	B3 → W	WZ OUT STATUS[6]	DATA → L, WZ = WZ + 1		WZ OUT STATUS[6]	DATA → H			
PC OUT STATUS[6]	PC = PC + 1	B3 → W	WZ OUT STATUS[7]	(L) → DATA BUS, WZ = WZ + 1		WZ OUT STATUS[7]	(H) → DATA BUS			
[9]	(ACT)+(TMP)→A									
[9]	(ACT)+(TMP)→A									
[9]	(ACT)+(TMP)+CY→A									
[9]	(ACT)+(TMP)+CY→A									
[9]	(ACT)-(TMP)→A									
[9]	(ACT)-(TMP)→A									
[9]	(ACT)-(TMP)-CY→A									
[9]	(ACT)-(TMP)-CY→A									
HL OUT STATUS[7]	ALU → DATA BUS									
HL OUT STATUS[7]	ALU → DATA BUS									
(rh)→ACT	(H)→TMP (ACT)+(TMP)+CY→ALU	ALU→H, CY								
[9]	(ACT)+(TMP)→A									

MNEMONIC	OP CODE		M1[1]					M2		
	D7 D6 D5 D4	D3 D2 D1 D0	T1	T2[2]	T3	T4	T5	T1	T2[2]	T3
ANI data	1 1 1 0	0 1 1 0	PC OUT STATUS	PC = PC + 1	INST→TMP/IR	(A)→ACT		PC OUT STATUS[6]	PC = PC + 1 B2	→TMP
XRA r	1 0 1 0	1 S S S				(A)→ACT (SSS)→TMP		[9]	(ACT)+(TPM)→A	
XRA M	1 0 1 0	1 1 1 0				(A)→ACT		HL OUT STATUS[6]	DATA	→TMP
XRI data	1 1 1 0	1 1 1 0				(A)→ACT		PC OUT STATUS[6]	PC = PC + 1 B2	→TMP
ORA r	1 0 1 1	0 S S S				(A)→ACT (SSS)→TMP		[9]	(ACT)+(TMP)→A	
ORA M	1 0 1 1	0 1 1 0				(A)→ACT		HL OUT STATUS[6]	DATA	→TMP
ORI data	1 1 1 1	0 1 1 0				(A)→ACT		PC OUT STATUS[6]	PC = PC + 1 B2	→TMP
CMP r	1 0 1 1	1 S S S				(A)→ACT (SSS)→TMP		[9]	(ACT)-(TMP), FLAGS	
CMP M	1 0 1 1	1 1 1 0				(A)→ACT		HL OUT STATUS[6]	DATA	→TMP
CPI data	1 1 1 1	1 1 1 0				(A)→ACT		PC OUT STATUS[6]	PC = PC + 1 B2	→TMP
RLC	0 0 0 0	0 1 1 1				(A)→ALU ROTATE		[9]	ALU→A, CY	
RRC	0 0 0 0	1 1 1 1				(A)→ALU ROTATE		[9]	ALU→A, CY	
RAL	0 0 0 1	0 1 1 1				(A), CY→ALU ROTATE		[9]	ALU→A, CY	
RAR	0 0 0 1	1 1 1 1				(A), CY→ALU ROTATE		[9]	ALU→A, CY	
CMA	0 0 1 0	1 1 1 1				$(\bar{A})$→A				
CMC	0 0 1 1	1 1 1 1				$\overline{CY}$→CY				
STC	0 0 1 1	0 1 1 1				1→CY				
JMP addr	1 1 0 0	0 0 1 1				X		PC OUT STATUS[6]	PC = PC + 1 B2	→Z
J cond addr[17]	1 1 C C	C 0 1 0				JUDGE CONDITION		PC OUT STATUS[6]	PC = PC + 1 B2	→Z
CALL addr	1 1 0 0	1 1 0 1				SP = SP - 1		PC OUT STATUS[6]	PC = PC + 1 B2	→Z
C cond addr[17]	1 1 C C	C 1 0 0				JUDGE CONDITION IF TRUE, SP = SP - 1		PC OUT STATUS[6]	PC = PC + 1 B2	→Z
RET	1 1 0 0	1 0 0 1				X		SP OUT STATUS[15]	SP = SP + 1 DATA	→Z
R cond addr[17]	1 1 C C	C 0 0 0			INST→TMP/IR	JUDGE CONDITION[14]		SP OUT STATUS[15]	SP = SP + 1 DATA	→Z
RST n	1 1 N N	N 1 1 1			φ→W INST→TMP/IR	SP = SP - 1		SP OUT STATUS[16]	SP = SP - 1 (PCH)	→DATA BUS
PCHL	1 1 1 0	1 0 0 1			INST→TMP/IR	(HL) ——— PC				
PUSH rp	1 1 R P	0 1 0 1				SP = SP - 1		SP OUT STATUS[16]	SP = SP - 1 (rh)	→DATA BUS
PUSH PSW	1 1 1 1	0 1 0 1				SP = SP - 1		SP OUT STATUS[16]	SP = SP - 1 (A)	→DATA BUS
POP rp	1 1 R P	0 0 0 1				X		SP OUT STATUS[15]	SP = SP + 1 DATA	→r1
POP PSW	1 1 1 1	0 0 0 1				X		SP OUT STATUS[15]	SP = SP + 1 DATA	→FLAGS
XTHL	1 1 1 0	0 0 1 1				X		SP OUT STATUS[15]	SP = SP + 1 DATA	→Z
IN port	1 1 0 1	1 0 1 1				X		PC OUT STATUS[6]	PC = PC + 1 B2	→Z, W
OUT port	1 1 0 1	0 0 1 1				X		PC OUT STATUS[6]	PC = PC + 1 B2	→Z, W
EI	1 1 1 1	1 0 1 1				SET INTE F/F				
DI	1 1 1 1	0 0 1 1				RESET INTE F/F				
HLT	0 1 1 1	0 1 1 0				X		PC OUT STATUS	HALT MODE[20]	
NOP	0 0 0 0	0 0 0 0	PC OUT STATUS	PC = PC + 1	INST→TMP/IR	X				

M3			M4			M5				
T1	T2[2]	T3	T1	T2[2]	T3	T1	T2[2]	T3	T4	T5
[9]	(ACT)+(TMP)→A									
[9]	(ACT)+(TMP)→A									
[9]	(ACT)+(TMP)→A									
[9]	(ACT)+(TMP)→A									
[9]	(ACT)+(TMP)→A									
[9]	(ACT)-(TMP); FLAGS									
[9]	(ACT)-(TMP); FLAGS									
PC OUT STATUS[6]	PC = PC + 1 B3 →W								WZ OUT STATUS[11]	(WZ) + 1 → PC
PC OUT STATUS[6]	PC = PC + 1 B3 →W								WZ OUT STATUS[11,12]	(WZ) + 1 → PC
PC OUT STATUS[6]	PC = PC + 1 B3 →W		SP OUT STATUS[16]	(PCH) →DATA BUS SP = SP - 1		SP OUT STATUS[16]	(PCL)→ DATA BUS		WZ OUT STATUS[11]	(WZ) + 1 → PC
PC OUT STATUS[6]	PC = PC + 1 B3 →W[13]		SP OUT STATUS[16]	(PCH) →DATA BUS SP = SP - 1		SP OUT STATUS[16]	(PCL)→ DATA BUS		WZ OUT STATUS[11,12]	(WZ) + 1 → PC
SP OUT STATUS[15]	SP = SP + 1 DATA →W								WZ OUT STATUS[11]	(WZ) + 1 → PC
SP OUT STATUS[15]	SP = SP + 1 DATA →W								WZ OUT STATUS[11,12]	(WZ) + 1 → PC
SP OUT STATUS[16]	(TMP = 00NNN000) →Z (PCL) →DATA BUS								WZ OUT STATUS[11]	(WZ) + 1 → PC
SP OUT STATUS[16]	(rl) →DATA BUS									
SP OUT STATUS[16]	FLAGS →DATA BUS									
SP OUT STATUS[15]	SP = SP + 1 DATA →rh									
SP OUT STATUS[15]	SP = SP + 1 DATA →A									
SP OUT STATUS[15]	DATA →W		SP OUT STATUS[16]	(H) →DATA BUS		SP OUT STATUS[16]	(L)→ DATA BUS	(WZ) →HL		
WZ OUT STATUS[18]	DATA →A									
WZ OUT STATUS[18]	(A) →DATA BUS									

NOTES:

1. The first memory cycle (M1) is always an instruction fetch; the first (or only) byte, containing the op code, is fetched during this cycle.

2. If the READY input from memory is not high during T2 of each memory cycle, the processor will enter a wait state (TW) until READY is sampled as high.

3. States T4 and T5 are present, as required, for operations which are completely internal to the CPU. The contents of the internal bus during T4 and T5 are available at the data bus; this is designed for testing purposes only. An "X" denotes that the state is present, but is only used for such internal operations as instruction decoding.

4. Only register pairs rp = B (registers B and C) or rp = D (registers D and E) may be specified.

5. These states are skipped.

6. Memory read sub-cycles; an instruction or data word will be read.

7. Memory write sub-cycle.

8. The READY signal is not required during the second and third sub-cycles (M2 and M3). The HOLD signal is accepted during M2 and M3. The SYNC signal is not generated during M2 and M3. During the execution of DAD, M2 and M3 are required for an internal register-pair add; memory is not referenced.

9. The results of these arithmetic, logical or rotate instructions are not moved into the accumulator (A) until state T2 of the next instruction cycle. That is, A is loaded while the next instruction is being fetched; this overlapping of operations allows for faster processing.

10. If the value of the least significant 4-bits of the accumulator is greater than 9 or if the auxiliary carry bit is set, 6 is added to the accumulator. If the value of the most significant 4-bits of the accumulator is now greater than 9, or if the carry bit is set, 6 is added to the most significant 4-bits of the accumulator.

11. This represents the first sub-cycle (the instruction fetch) of the next instruction cycle.

12. If the condition was met, the contents of the register pair WZ are output on the address lines (A_{0-15}) instead of the contents of the program counter (PC).

13. If the condition was not met, sub-cycles M4 and M5 are skipped; the processor instead proceeds immediately to the instruction fetch (M1) of the next instruction cycle.

14. If the condition was not met, sub-cycles M2 and M3 are skipped; the processor instead proceeds immediately to the instruction fetch (M1) of the next instruction cycle.

15. Stack read sub-cycle.

16. Stack write sub-cycle.

17.
CONDITION		CCC
NZ —	not zero (Z = 0)	000
Z —	zero (Z = 1)	001
NC —	no carry (CY = 0)	010
C —	carry (CY = 1)	011
PO —	parity odd (P = 0)	100
PE —	parity even (P = 1)	101
P —	plus (S = 0)	110
M —	minus (S = 1)	111

18. I/O sub-cycle: the I/O port's 8-bit select code is duplicated on address lines 0-7 (A_{0-7}) and 8-15 (A_{8-15}).

19. Output sub-cycle.

20. The processor will remain idle in the halt state until an interrupt, a reset or a hold is accepted. When a hold request is accepted, the CPU enters the hold mode; after the hold mode is terminated, the processor returns to the halt state. After a reset is accepted, the processor begins execution at memory location zero. After an interrupt is accepted, the processor executes the instruction forced onto the data bus (usually a restart instruction).

SSS or DDD	Value	rp	Value
A	111	B	00
B	000	D	01
C	001	H	10
D	010	SP	11
E	011		
H	100		
L	101		

8080 INSTRUCTION SET

Summary of Processor Instructions

Mnemonic	Description	D7	D6	D5	D4	D3	D2	D1	D0	Cycles
MOVE, LOAD, AND STORE										
MOVr1,r2	Move register to register	0	1	D	D	D	S	S	S	5
MOV M,r	Move register to memory	0	1	1	1	0	S	S	S	7
MOV r,M	Move memory to register	0	1	D	D	D	1	1	0	7
MVI r	Move immediate register	0	0	D	D	D	1	1	0	7
MVI M	Move immediate memory	0	0	1	1	0	1	1	0	10
LXI B	Load immediate register Pair B & C	0	0	0	0	0	0	0	1	10
LXI D	Load immediate register Pair D & E	0	0	0	1	0	0	0	1	10
LXI H	Load immediate register Pair H & L	0	0	1	0	0	0	0	1	10
STAX B	Store A indirect	0	0	0	0	0	0	1	0	7
STAX D	Store A indirect	0	0	0	1	0	0	1	0	7
LDAX B	Load A indirect	0	0	0	0	1	0	1	0	7
LDAX D	Load A indirect	0	0	0	1	1	0	1	0	7
STA	Store A direct	0	0	1	1	0	0	1	0	13
LDA	Load A direct	0	0	1	1	1	0	1	0	13
SHLD	Store H & L direct	0	0	1	0	0	0	1	0	16
LHLD	Load H & L direct	0	0	1	0	1	0	1	0	16
XCHG	Exchange D & E H & L Registers	1	1	1	0	1	0	1	1	4
STACK OPS										
PUSH B	Push register Pair B & C on stack	1	1	0	0	0	1	0	1	11
PUSH D	Push register Pair D & E on stack	1	1	0	1	0	1	0	1	11
PUSH H	Push register Pair H & L on stack	1	1	1	0	0	1	0	1	11
PUSH PSW	Push A and Flags on stack	1	1	1	1	0	1	0	1	11
POP B	Pop register Pair B & C off stack	1	1	0	0	0	0	0	1	10
POP D	Pop register Pair D & E off stack	1	1	0	1	0	0	0	1	10
POP H	Pop register Pair H & L off stack	1	1	1	0	0	0	0	1	10
POP PSW	Pop A and Flags off stack	1	1	1	1	0	0	0	1	10
XTHL	Exchange top of stack. H & L	1	1	1	0	0	0	1	1	18
SPHL	H & L to stack pointer	1	1	1	1	1	0	0	1	5
LXI SP	Load immediate stack pointer	0	0	1	1	0	0	0	1	10
INX SP	Increment stack pointer	0	0	1	1	0	0	1	1	5
DCX SP	Decrement stack pointer	0	0	1	1	1	0	1	1	5
JUMP										
JMP	Jump unconditional	1	1	0	0	0	0	1	1	10
JC	Jump on carry	1	1	0	1	1	0	1	0	10
JNC	Jump on no carry	1	1	0	1	0	0	1	0	10
JZ	Jump on zero	1	1	0	0	1	0	1	0	10
JNZ	Jump on no zero	1	1	0	0	0	0	1	0	10
JP	Jump on positive	1	1	1	1	0	0	1	0	10
JM	Jump on minus	1	1	1	1	1	0	1	0	10
JPE	Jump on parity even	1	1	1	0	1	0	1	0	10

Mnemonic	Description	D7	D6	D5	D4	D3	D2	D1	D0	Cycles
JPO	Jump on parity odd	1	1	1	0	0	0	1	0	10
PCHL	H & L to program counter	1	1	1	0	1	0	0	1	5
CALL										
CALL	Call unconditional	1	1	0	0	1	1	0	1	17
CC	Call on carry	1	1	0	1	1	1	0	0	11/17
CNC	Call on no carry	1	1	0	1	0	1	0	0	11/17
CZ	Call on zero	1	1	0	0	1	1	0	0	11/17
CNZ	Call on no zero	1	1	0	0	0	1	0	0	11/17
CP	Call on positive	1	1	1	1	0	1	0	0	11/17
CM	Call on minus	1	1	1	1	1	1	0	0	11/17
CPE	Call on parity even	1	1	1	0	1	1	0	0	11/17
CPO	Call on parity odd	1	1	1	0	0	1	0	0	11/17
RETURN										
RET	Return	1	1	0	0	1	0	0	1	10
RC	Return on carry	1	1	0	1	1	0	0	0	5/11
RNC	Return on no carry	1	1	0	1	0	0	0	0	5/11
RZ	Return on zero	1	1	0	0	1	0	0	0	5/11
RNZ	Return on no zero	1	1	0	0	0	0	0	0	5/11
RP	Return on positive	1	1	1	1	0	0	0	0	5/11
RM	Return on minus	1	1	1	1	1	0	0	0	5/11
RPE	Return on parity even	1	1	1	0	1	0	0	0	5/11
RPO	Return on parity odd	1	1	1	0	0	0	0	0	5/11
RESTART										
RST	Restart	1	1	A	A	A	1	1	1	11
INCREMENT AND DECREMENT										
INR r	Increment register	0	0	D	D	D	1	0	0	5
DCR r	Decrement register	0	0	D	D	D	1	0	1	5
INR M	Increment memory	0	0	1	1	0	1	0	0	10
DCR M	Decrement memory	0	0	1	1	0	1	0	1	10
INX B	Increment B & C registers	0	0	0	0	0	0	1	1	5
INX D	Increment D & E registers	0	0	0	1	0	0	1	1	5
INX H	Increment H & L registers	0	0	1	0	0	0	1	1	5
DCX B	Decrement B & C	0	0	0	0	1	0	1	1	5
DCX D	Decrement D & E	0	0	0	1	1	0	1	1	5
DCX H	Decrement H & L	0	0	1	0	1	0	1	1	5
ADD										
ADD r	Add register to A	1	0	0	0	0	S	S	S	4
ADC r	Add register to A with carry	1	0	0	0	1	S	S	S	4
ADD M	Add memory to A	1	0	0	0	0	1	1	0	7
ADC M	Add memory to A with carry	1	0	0	0	1	1	1	0	7
ADI	Add immediate to A	1	1	0	0	0	1	1	0	7
ACI	Add immediate to A with carry	1	1	0	0	1	1	1	0	7
DAD B	Add B & C to H & L	0	0	0	0	1	0	0	1	10
DAD D	Add D & E to H & L	0	0	0	1	1	0	0	1	10
DAD H	Add H & L to H & L	0	0	1	0	1	0	0	1	10
DAD SP	Add stack pointer to H & L	0	0	1	1	1	0	0	1	10

NOTES: 1. DDD or SSS: B 000. C 001. D 010. E 011. H 100. L 101. Memory 110. A 111.

2. Two possible cycle times. (6/12) indicate instruction cycles dependent on condition flags.

8080 INSTRUCTION SET

Summary of Processor Instructions (Cont.)

Mnemonic	Description	D_7	D_6	D_5	D_4	D_3	D_2	D_1	D_0	Clock[2] Cycles
SUBTRACT										
SUB r	Subtract register from A	1	0	0	1	0	S	S	S	4
SBB r	Subtract register from A with borrow	1	0	0	1	1	S	S	S	4
SUB M	Subtract memory from A	1	0	0	1	0	1	1	0	7
SBB M	Subtract memory from A with borrow	1	0	0	1	1	1	1	0	7
SUI	Subtract immediate from A	1	1	0	1	0	1	1	0	7
SBI	Subtract immediate from A with borrow	1	1	0	1	1	1	1	0	7
LOGICAL										
ANA r	And register with A	1	0	1	0	0	S	S	S	4
XRA r	Exclusive Or register with A	1	0	1	0	1	S	S	S	4
ORA r	Or register with A	1	0	1	1	0	S	S	S	4
CMP r	Compare register with A	1	0	1	1	1	S	S	S	4
ANA M	And memory with A	1	0	1	0	0	1	1	0	7
XRA M	Exclusive Or memory with A	1	0	1	0	1	1	1	0	7
ORA M	Or memory with A	1	0	1	1	0	1	1	0	7
CMP M	Compare memory with A	1	0	1	1	1	1	1	0	7
ANI	And immediate with A	1	1	1	0	0	1	1	0	7
XRI	Exclusive Or immediate with A	1	1	1	0	1	1	1	0	7
ORI	Or immediate with A	1	1	1	0	1	1	1	0	7
CPI	Compare immediate with A	1	1	1	1	1	1	1	0	7
ROTATE										
RLC	Rotate A left	0	0	0	0	0	1	1	1	4
RRC	Rotate A right	0	0	0	0	1	1	1	1	4
RAL	Rotate A left through carry	0	0	0	1	0	1	1	1	4
RAR	Rotate A right through carry	0	0	0	1	1	1	1	1	4
SPECIALS										
CMA	Complement A	0	0	1	0	1	1	1	1	4
STC	Set carry	0	0	1	1	0	1	1	1	4
CMC	Complement carry	0	0	1	1	1	1	1	1	4
DAA	Decimal adjust A	0	0	1	0	0	1	1	1	4
INPUT/OUTPUT										
IN	Input	1	1	0	1	1	0	1	1	10
OUT	Output	1	1	0	1	0	0	1	1	10
CONTROL										
EI	Enable Interrupts	1	1	1	1	1	0	1	1	4
DI	Disable Interrupt	1	1	1	1	0	0	1	1	4
NOP	No-operation	0	0	0	0	0	0	0	0	4
HLT	Halt	0	1	1	1	0	1	1	0	7

NOTES: 1. DDD or SSS: B=000, C=001, D=010, E=011, H=100, L=101, Memory=110, A=111.
2. Two possible cycle times, (6/12) indicate instruction cycles dependent on condition flags.

*All mnemonics copyright
ⓒ Intel Corporation 1977

Appendix B The Zilog Z80

2.0 Z80-CPU ARCHITECHURE

A block diagram of the internal architecture of the Z80-CPU is shown in Figure 2.0-1 The diagram shows all of the major elements in the CPU and it should be referred to throughout the following description.

Z80-CPU BLOCK DIAGRAM

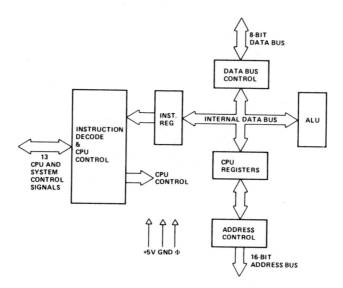

FIGURE 2.0-1

2.1 CPU REGISTERS

The Z80-CPU contains 208 bits of R/W memory that are accessible to the programmer. Figure 2.0-2 illustrates how this memory is configured into eighteen 8-bit registers and four 16-bit registers. All Z80 registers are implemented using static RAM. The registers include two sets of six general purpose registers that may be used individually as 8-bit registers or in pairs as 16-bit registers. There are also two sets of accumulator and flag registers.

Special Purpose Registers

1. **Program Counter (PC).** The program counter holds the 16-bit address of the current instruction being fetched from memory. The PC is automatically incremented after its contents have been transferred to the address lines. When a program jump occurs the new value is automatically placed in the PC, overriding the incrementer.

2. **Stack Pointer (SP).** The stack pointer holds the 16-bit address of the current top of a stack located anywhere in external system RAM memory. The external stack memory is organized as a last-in first-out (LIFO) file. Data can be pushed onto the stack from specific CPU registers or popped off of the stack into specific CPU registers through the execution of PUSH and POP instructions. The data popped from the stack is always the last data pushed onto it. The stack allows simple implementation of multiple level interrupts, unlimited subroutine nesting and simplification of many types of data manipulation.

Z80-CPU REGISTER CONFIGURATION

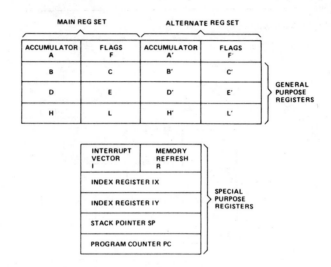

FIGURE 2.0-2

3. **Two Index Registers (IX & IY).** The two independent index registers hold a 16-bit base address that is used in indexed addressing modes. In this mode, an index register is used as a base to point to a region in memory from which data is to be stored or retrieved. An additional byte is included in indexed instructions to specify a displacement from this base. This displacement is specified as a two's complement signed integer. This mode of addressing greatly simplifies many types of programs, especially where tables of data are used.

4. **Interrupt Page Address Register (I).** The Z80-CPU can be operated in a mode where an indirect call to any memory location can be achieved in response to an interrupt. The I Register is used for this purpose to store the high order 8-bits of the indirect address while the interrupting device provides the lower 8-bits of the address. This feature allows interrupt routines to be dynamically located anywhere in memory with absolute minimal access time to the routine.

5. **Memory Refresh Register (R).** The Z80-CPU contains a memory refresh counter to enable dynamic memories to be used with the same ease as static memories. This 7-bit register is automatically incremented after each instruction fetch. The data in the refresh counter is sent out on the lower portion of the address bus along with a

refresh control signal while the CPU is decoding and executing the fetched instruction. This mode of refresh is totally transparent to the programmer and does not slow down the CPU operation. The programmer can load the R register for testing purposes, but this register is normally not used by the programmer.

Accumulator and Flag Registers

The CPU includes two independent 8-bit accumulators and associated 8-bit flag registers. The accumulator holds the results of 8-bit arithmetic or logical operations while the flag register indicates specific conditions for 8 or 16-bit operations, such as indicating whether or not the result of an operation is equal to zero. The programmer selects the accumulator and flag pair that he wishes to work with with a single exchange instruction so that he may easily work with either pair.

General Purpose Registers

There are two matched sets of general purpose registers, each set containing six 8-bit registers that may be used individually as 8-bit registers or as 16-bit register pairs by the programmer. One set is called BC, DE, and HL while the complementary set is called BD', DE' and HL'. At any one time the programmer can select either set of registers to work with through a single exchange command for the entire set. In systems where fast interrupt response is required, one set of general purpose registers and an accumulator/flag register may be reserved for handling this very fast routine. Only a simple exchange command need be executed to go between the routines. This greatly reduces interrupt service time by eliminating the requirement for saving and retrieving register contents in the external stack during interrupt or subroutine processing. These general purpose registers are used for a wide range of applications by the programmer. They also simplify programming, especially in ROM based systems where little external read/write memory is available.

2.2 ARITHMETIC & LOGIC UNIT (ALU)

The 8-bit arithmetic and logical instructions of the CPU are executed in the ALU. Internally the ALU communicates with the registers and the external data bus on the internal data bus. The type of functions performed by the ALU include:

Add	Left or right shifts or rotates (arithmetic and logical)
Subtract	Increment
Logical AND	Decrement
Logical OR	Set bit
Logical Exclusive OR	Reset bit
Compare	Test bit

2.3 INSTRUCTION REGISTER AND CPU CONTROL

As each instruction is fetched from memory, it is placed in the instruction register and decoded. The control section performs this function and then generates and supplies all of the control signals necessary to read or write data from or to the registers, controls the ALU and provides all required external control signals.

3.0 Z80-CPU PIN DESCRIPTION

The Z80–CPU is packaged in an industry standard 40 pin Dual In-Line Package. The I/O pins are shown in Figure 3.0-1 and the function of each is described below.

Z80 PIN CONFIGURATION

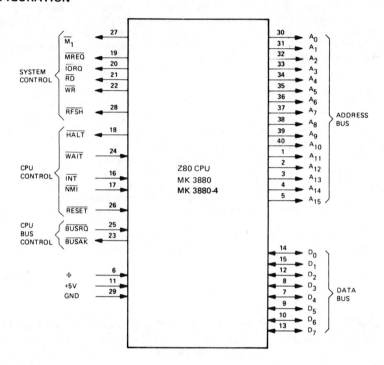

FIGURE 3.0-1

A_0-A_{15} (Address Bus)	Tri-state output, active high. A_0-A_{15} constitute a 16-bit address bus. The address bus provides the address for memory (up to 64K bytes) data exchanges and for I/O device data exchanges. I/O addressing uses the 8 lower address bits to allow the user to directly select up to 256 input or 256 output ports. A_0 is the least significant address bit. During refresh time, the lower 7 bits contain a valid refresh address.
D_0-D_7 (Data Bus)	Tri-state input/output, active high. D_0-D_7 constitute an 8-bit bidirectional data bus. The data bus is used for data exchanges with memory and I/O devices.
$\overline{M_1}$ (Machine Cycle one)	Output, active low. $\overline{M_1}$ indicates that the current machine cycle is the OP code fetch cycle of an instruction execution. Note that during execution of 2-byte op-codes, $\overline{M_1}$ is generated as each op code byte is fetched. These two byte op-codes always begin with CBH, DDH, EDH, or FDH. $\overline{M_1}$ also occurs with $\overline{IORQ}$ to indicate an interrupt acknowledge cycle.
$\overline{MREQ}$ (Memory Request)	Tri-state output, active low. The memory request signal indicates that the address bus holds a valid address for a memory read or memory write operation.

$\overline{\text{IORQ}}$
(Input/Output Request)

Tri-state output, active low. The $\overline{\text{IORQ}}$ signal indicates that the lower half of the address bus holds a valid I/O address for a I/O read or write operation. An $\overline{\text{IORQ}}$ signal is also generated with an $\overline{\text{M}_1}$ signal when an interrupt is being acknowledged to indicate that an interrupt response vector can be placed on the data bus. Interrupt Acknowledge operations occur during M_1 time while I/O operations never occur during M_1 time.

$\overline{\text{RD}}$
(Memory Read)

Tri-state output, active low. $\overline{\text{RD}}$ indicates that the CPU wants to read data from memory or an I/O device. The addressed I/O device or memory should use this signal to gate data onto the CPU data bus.

$\overline{\text{WR}}$
(Memory Write)

Tri-state output, active low. $\overline{\text{WR}}$ indicates that the CPU data bus holds valid data to be stored in the addressed memory or I/O device.

$\overline{\text{RFSH}}$
(Refresh)

Output, active low. $\overline{\text{RFSH}}$ indicates that the lower 7 bits of the address bus contain a refresh address for dynamic memories and current $\overline{\text{MREQ}}$ signal should be used to do a refresh read to all dynamic memories. A_7 is a logic zero and the upper 8 bits of the Address Bus contains the I Register.

$\overline{\text{HALT}}$
(Halt state)

Output, active low. $\overline{\text{HALT}}$ indicates that the CPU has executed a HALT software instruction and is awaiting either a non maskable or a maskable interrupt (with the mask enabled) before operation can resume. While halted, the CPU executes NOP's to maintain memory refresh activity.

$\overline{\text{WAIT}}$*
(Wait)

Input, active low. $\overline{\text{WAIT}}$ indicates to the Z80-CPU that the addressed memory or I/O devices are not ready for a data transfer. The CPU continues to enter wait states for as long as this signal is active. This signal allows memory or I/O devices of any speed to be synchronized to the CPU.

$\overline{\text{INT}}$
(Interrupt Request)

Input, active low. The Interrupt Request signal is generated by I/O devices. A request will be honored at the end of the current instruction if the internal software controlled interrupt enable flip-flop (IFF) is enabled and if the $\overline{\text{BUSRQ}}$ signal is not active. When the CPU accepts the interrupt, an acknowledge signal ($\overline{\text{IORQ}}$ during M_1 time) is sent out at the beginning of the next instruction cycle. The CPU can respond to an interrupt in three different modes that are described in detail in section 8.

$\overline{\text{NMI}}$

Input, negative edge triggered. The non maskable interrupt request line has a higher priority than $\overline{\text{INT}}$ and is always recognized at the end of the current instruction, independent of the status of the interrupt enable flip-flop. $\overline{\text{NMI}}$ automatically forces the Z80-CPU to restart to location 0066_H. The program counter is automatically saved in the external stack so that the user can return to the program that was interrupted. Note that continuous WAIT cycles can prevent the current instruction from ending, and that a $\overline{\text{BUSRQ}}$ will override a $\overline{\text{NMI}}$.

RESET

Input, active low. RESET forces the program counter to zero and initializes the CPU. The CPU initialization includes:

1) Disable the interrupt enable flip-flop
2) Set Register I = 00$_H$
3) Set Register R = 00$_H$
4) Set Interrupt Mode 0

During reset time, the address bus and data bus go to a high impedance state and all control output signals go to the inactive state. No refresh occurs.

BUSRQ
(Bus Request)

Input, active low. The bus request signal is used to request the CPU address bus, data bus and tri-state output control signals to go to a high impedance state so that other devices can control these buses. When BUSRQ is activated, the CPU will set these buses to a high impedance state as soon as the current CPU machine cycle is terminated.

BUSAK*
(Bus Acknowledge)

Output, active low. Bus acknowledge is used to indicate to the requesting device that the CPU address bus, data bus and tri-state control bus signals have been set to their high impedance state and the external device can now control these signals.

Φ

Single phase system clock.

*While the Z80-CPU is in either a WAIT state or a Bus Acknowledge condition, Dynamic Memory Refresh will not occur.

4.0 CPU TIMING

The Z80-CPU executes instructions by stepping through a very precise set of a few basic operations. These include:

Memory read or write

I/O device read or write

Interrupt acknowledge

All instructions are merely a series of these basic operations. Each of these basic operations can take from three to six clock periods to complete or they can be lengthened to synchronize the CPU to the speed of external devices. The basic clock periods are referred to as T states and the basic operations are referred to as M (for machine) cycles. Figure 4.0-0 illustrates how a typical instruction will be merely a series of specific M and T cycles. Notice that this instruction consists of three machine cycles (M1, M2 and M3). The first machine cycle of any instruction is a fetch cycle which is four, five or six T states long (unless lengthened by the wait signal which will be fully described in the next section). The fetch cycle (M1) is used to fetch the OP code of the next instruction to be executed. Subsequent machine cycles move data between the CPU and memory or I/O devices and they may have anywhere from three to five T cycles (again they may be lengthened by wait states to synchronize the external devices to the CPU). The following paragraphs describe the timing which occurs within any of the basic machine cycles. In section 7, the exact timing for each instruction is specified.

BASIC CPU TIMING EXAMPLE

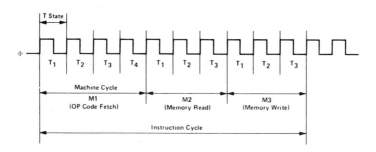

FIGURE 4.0-0

All CPU timing can be broken down into a few very simple timing diagrams as shown in Figure 4.0-1 through 4.0-7. These diagrams show the following basic operations with and without wait states (wait states are added to synchronize the CPU to slow memory or I/O devices).

4.0-1. Instruction OP code fetch (M1 cycle)

4.0-2. Memory data read or write cycles

4.0-3. I/O read or write cycles

4.0-4. Bus Request/Acknowledge Cycle

4.0-5. Interrupt Request/Acknowledge Cycle

4.0-6. Non maskable Interrupt Request/Acknowledge Cycle

4.0-7. Exit from a HALT instruction

INSTRUCTION FETCH

Figure 4.0-1 shows the timing during an M1 cycle (OP code fetch). Notice that the PC is placed on the address bus at the beginning of the M1 cycle. One half clock time later the $\overline{MREQ}$ signal goes active. At this time the address to the memory has had time to stabilize so that the falling edge of $\overline{MREQ}$ can be used directly as a chip enable clock to dynamic memories. The $\overline{RD}$ line also goes active to indicate that the memory read data should be enabled onto the CPU data bus. The CPU samples the data from the memory on the data bus with the rising edge of the clock of state T3 and this same edge is used by the CPU to turn off the $\overline{RD}$ and $\overline{MREQ}$ signals. Thus the data has already been sampled by the CPU before the $\overline{RD}$ signal becomes inactive. Clock state T3 and T4 of a fetch cycle are used to refresh dynamic memories. (The CPU uses this time to decode and execute the fetched instruction so that no other operation could be performed at this time). During T3 and T4 the lower 7 bits of the address bus contain a memory refresh address and the $\overline{RFSH}$ signal becomes active to indicate that a refresh read of all dynamic memories should be accomplished. Notice that a $\overline{RD}$ signal is not generated during refresh time to prevent data from different memory segments from being gated onto the data bus. The $\overline{MREQ}$ signal during refresh time should be used to perform a refresh read of all memory elements. The refresh signal can not be used by itself since the refresh address is only guaranteed to be stable during $\overline{MREQ}$ time.

INSTRUCTION OP CODE FETCH

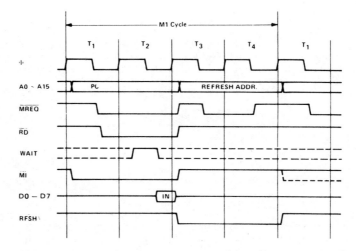

FIGURE 4.0-1

Figure 4.0-1A illustrates how the fetch cycle is delayed if the memory activates the $\overline{WAIT}$ line. During T2 and every subsequent Tw, the CPU samples the $\overline{WAIT}$ line with the falling edge of Φ. If the $\overline{WAIT}$ line is active at this time, another wait state will be entered during the following cycle. Using this technique the read cycle can be lengthened to match the access time of any type of memory device.

INSTRUCTION OP CODE FETCH WITH WAIT STATES

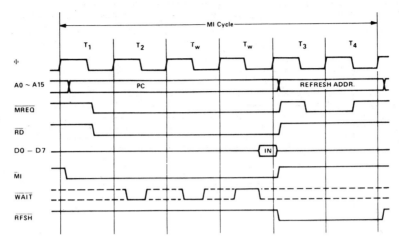

FIGURE 4.0-1A

MEMORY READ OR WRITE

Figure 4.0-2 illustrates the timing of memory read or write cycles other than an OP code fetch (M1 cycle). These cycles are generally three clock periods long unless wait states are requested by the memory via the $\overline{WAIT}$ signal. The $\overline{MREQ}$ signal and the $\overline{RD}$ signal are used the same as in the fetch cycle. In the case of a memory write cycle, the $\overline{MREQ}$ also becomes active when the address bus is stable so that it can be used directly as a chip enable for dynamic memories. The $\overline{WR}$ line is active when data on the data bus is stable so that it can be used directly as a R/W pulse to virtually any type of semiconductor memory. Furthermore the $\overline{WR}$ signal goes inactive one half T state before the address and data bus contents are changed so that the overlap requirements for virtually any type of semiconductor memory type will be met.

MEMORY READ OR WRITE CYCLES

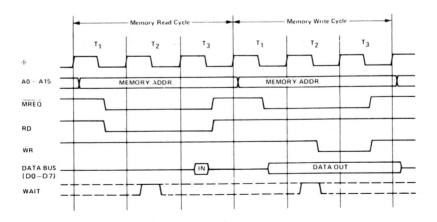

FIGURE 4.0-2

Figure 4.0-2A illustrates how a $\overline{\text{WAIT}}$ request signal will lengthen any memory read or write operation. This operation is identical to that previously described for a fetch cycle. Notice in this figure that a separate read and a separate write cycle are shown in the same figure although read and write cycles can never occur simultaneously.

MEMORY READ OR WRITE CYCLES WITH WAIT STATES

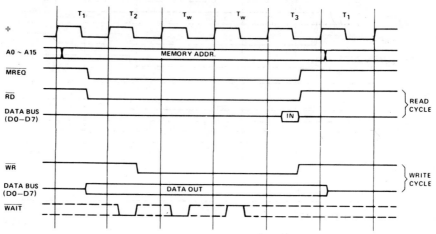

FIGURE 4.0-2A

INPUT OR OUTPUT CYCLES

Figure 4.0-3 illustrates an I/O read or I/O write operation. Notice that during I/O operations a single wait state is automatically inserted. The reason for this is that during I/O operations, the time from when the $\overline{\text{IORQ}}$ signal goes active until the CPU must sample the $\overline{\text{WAIT}}$ line is very short and without this extra state sufficient time does not exist for an I/O port to decode its address and activate the $\overline{\text{WAIT}}$ line if a wait is required. Also, without this wait state it is difficult to design MOS I/O devices that can operate at full CPU speed. During this wait state time the $\overline{\text{WAIT}}$ request signal is sampled. During a read I/O operation, the $\overline{\text{RD}}$ line is used to enable the addressed port onto the data bus just as in the case of a memory read. For I/O write operations, the $\overline{\text{WR}}$ line is used as a clock to the I/O port, again with sufficient overlap timing automatically provided so that the rising edge may be used as a data clock.

Figure 4.0-3A illustrates how additional wait states may be added with the $\overline{\text{WAIT}}$ line. The operation is identical to that previously described.

BUS REQUEST/ACKNOWLEDGE CYCLE

Figure 4.0-4 illustrates the timing for a Bus Request/Acknowledge cycle. The $\overline{\text{BUSRQ}}$ signal is sampled by the CPU with the rising edge of the last clock period of any machine cycle. If the $\overline{\text{BUSRQ}}$ signal is active, the CPU will set its address, data and tri-state control signals to the high impedance state with the rising edge of the next clock pulse. At that time any external device can control the buses to transfer data between memory and I/O devices. (This is generally known as Direct Memory Access [DMA] using cycle stealing). The maximum time for the CPU to respond to a bus request is the length of a machine cycle and the external controller can maintain control of the bus for as many clock cycles as is desired. Note, however, that if very long DMA cycles are used, and dynamic memories are being used, the external controller must also perform the refresh function. This situation only occurs if very large blocks of data are transferred under DMA control. Also note that during a bus request cycle, the CPU cannot be interrupted by either a $\overline{\text{NMI}}$ or an $\overline{\text{INT}}$ signal.

INPUT OR OUTPUT CYCLES

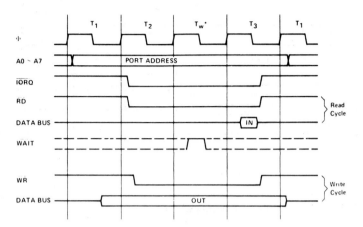

FIGURE 4.0-3

INPUT OR OUTPUT CYCLES WITH WAIT STATES

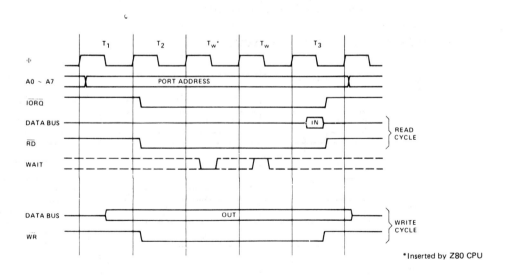

FIGURE 4.0-3A

BUS REQUEST/ACKNOWLEDGE CYCLE

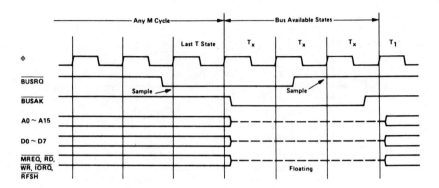

FIGURE 4.0-4

INTERRUPT REQUEST/ ACKNOWLEDGE CYCLE

Figure 4.0-5 illustrates the timing associated with an interrupt cycle. The interrupt signal (INT) is sampled by the CPU with the rising edge of the last clock at the end of any instruction. The signal will not be accepted if the internal CPU software controlled interrupt enable flip-flop is not set or if the BUSRQ signal is active. When the signal is accepted a special M1 cycle is generated. During this special M1 cycle the IORQ signal becomes active (instead of the normal MREQ) to indicate that the interrupting device can place an 8-bit vector on the data bus. Notice that two wait states are automatically added to this cycle. These states are added so that a ripple priority interrupt scheme can be easily implemented. The two wait states allow sufficient time for the ripple signals to stablilize and identify which I/O device must insert the response vector. Refer to section 8.0 for details on how the interrupt response vector is utilized by the CPU.

INTERRUPT REQUEST/ACKNOWLEDGE CYCLE

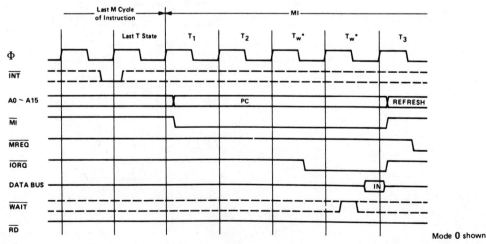

Mode 0 shown

FIGURE 4.0-5

Figure 4.0-5A illustrates how additional wait states can be added to the interrupt response cycle. Again the operation is identical to that previously described.

INTERRUPT REQUEST/ACKNOWLEDGE WITH WAIT STATES

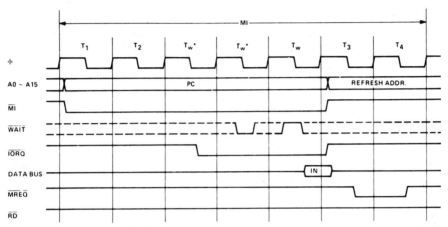

Mode **0** shown

FIGURE 4.0-5A

NON MASKABLE INTERRUPT RESPONSE

Figure 4.0-6 illustrates the request/acknowledge cycle for the non-maskable interrupt. A pulse on the $\overline{\text{NMI}}$ input sets an internal NMI latch which is tested by the CPU at the end of every instruction. This NMI latch is sampled at the same time as the interrupt line, but this line has priority over the normal interrupt and it can not be disabled under software control. Its usual function is to provide immediate response to important signals such as an impending power failure. The CPU response to a non maskable interrupt is similar to a normal memory read operation. The only difference being that the content of the data bus is ignored while the processor automatically stores the PC in the external stack and jumps to location 0066$_H$. The service routine for the non maskable interrupt must begin at this location if this interrupt is used.

HALT EXIT

Whenever a software halt instruction is executed the CPU begins executing NOP's until an interrupt is received (either a non-maskable or a maskable interrupt while the interrupt flip flop is enabled). The two interrupt lines are sampled with the rising clock edge during each T4 state as shown in Figure 4.0-7. If a non-maskable interrupt has been received or a maskable interrupt has been received and the interrupt enable flip-flop is set, then the halt state will be exited on the next rising clock edge. The following cycle will then be an interrupt acknowledge cycle corresponding to the type of interrupt that was received. If both are received at this time, then the non maskable one will be acknowledged since it was highest priority. The purpose of executing NOP instructions while in the halt state is to keep the memory refresh signals active. Each cycle in the halt state is a normal M1 (fetch) cycle except that the data received from the memory is ignored and a NOP instruction is forced internally to the CPU. The halt acknowledge signal is active during this time to indicate that the processor is in the halt state.

NON MASKABLE INTERRUPT REQUEST OPERATION

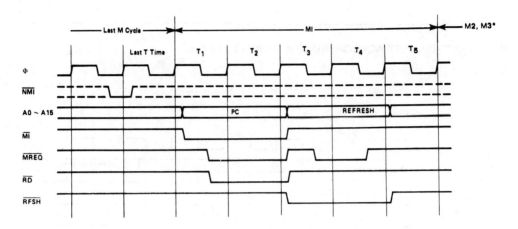

*M2 and M3 are stack write operations

FIGURE 4.0-6

HALT EXIT

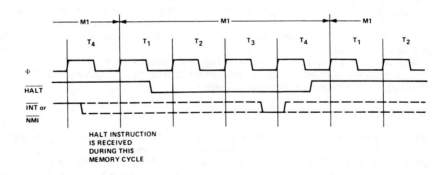

FIGURE 4.0-7

6.0 FLAGS

Each of the two Z80-CPU Flag registers contains six bits of information which are set or reset by various CPU operations. Four of these bits are testable; that is, they are used as conditions for jump, call or return instructions. For example a jump may be desired only if a specific bit in the flag register is set. The four testable flag bits are:

1) Carry Flag (C) — This flag is the carry from the highest order bit of the accumulator. For example, the carry flag will be set during an add instruction where a carry from the highest bit of the accumulator is generated. This flag is also set if a borrow is generated during a subtraction instruction. The shift and rotate instructions also affect this bit.

2) Zero Flag (Z) — This flag is set if the result of the operation loaded a zero into the accumulator. Otherwise it is reset.

3) Sign Flag(S) — This flag is intended to be used with signed numbers and it is set if the result of the operation was negative. Since bit 7 (MSB) represents the sign of the number (A negative number has a 1 in bit 7), this flag stores the state of bit 7 in the accumulator.

4) Parity/Overflow Flag(P/V) — This dual purpose flag indicates the parity of the result in the accumulator when logical operations are performed (such as AND A, B) and it represents overflow when signed two's complement arithmetic operations are performed. The Z80 overflow flag indicates that the two's complement number in the accumulator is in error since it has exceeded the maximum possible (+127) or is less than the minimum possible (−128) number that can be represented two's complement notation. For example consider adding:

$$
\begin{array}{rl}
+120 = & 0111\ 1000 \\
+105 = & \underline{0110\ 1001} \\
C = 0 & 1110\ 0001 = \text{-95 (wrong) Overflow has occurred;}
\end{array}
$$

Here the result is incorrect. Overflow has occurred and yet there is no carry to indicate an error. For this case the overflow flag would be set. Also consider the addition of two negative numbers:

$$
\begin{array}{rl}
\text{-5} = & 1111\ 1011 \\
\text{-16} = & \underline{1111\ 0000} \\
C = 1 & 1110\ 1011 = \text{-21 correct}
\end{array}
$$

Notice that the answer is correct but the carry is set so that this flag can not be used as an overflow indicator. In this case the overflow would not be set.

For logical operations (AND, OR, XOR) this flag is set if the parity of the result is even and it is reset if it is odd.

There are also two non-testable bits in the flag register. Both of these are used for BCD arithmetic. They are:

1) Half carry(H) — This is the BCD carry or borrow result from the least significant four bits of operation. When using the DAA (Decimal Adjust Instruction) this flag is used to correct the result of a previous packed decimal add or subtract.

2) Add/Subtract Flag (N) — Since the agorithim for correcting BCD operations is different for addition or subtraction, this flag is used to specify what type of instruction was executed last so that the DAA operation will be correct for either addition or subtraction.

The Flag register can be accessed by the programmer and its format is as follows:

```
D7                          DØ
┌───┬───┬───┬───┬───┬─────┬───┬───┐
│ S │ Z │ X │ H │ X │ P/V │ N │ C │
└───┴───┴───┴───┴───┴─────┴───┴───┘
```

X means flag is indeterminate.

Table 6.0-1 lists how each flag bit is affected by various CPU instructions. In this table a '·' indicates that the instruction does not change the flag, an 'X' means that the flag goes to an indeterminate state, an '0' means that it is reset, a '1' means that it is set and the symbol ‡ indicates that it is set or reset according to the previous discussion. Note that any instruction not appearing in this table does not affect any of the flags.

Table 6.0-1 includes a few special cases that must be described for clarity. Notice that the block search instruction sets the Z flag if the last compare operation indicated a match between the source and the accumulator data. Also, the parity flag is set if the byte counter (register pair BC) is not equal to zero. This same use of the parity flag is made with the block move instructions. Another special case is during block input or output instructions, here the Z flag is used to indicate the state of register B which is used as a byte counter. Notice that when the I/O block transfer is complete, the zero flag will be reset to a zero (i.e. B=0) while in the case of a block move command the parity flag is reset when the operation is complete. A final case is when the refresh or I register is loaded into the accumulator, the interrupt enable flip flop is loaded into the parity flag so that the complete state of the CPU can be saved at any time.

7.0 SUMMARY OF OP CODES AND EXECUTION TIMES

The following section gives a summary of the Z80 instruction set. The instructions are logically arranged into groups as shown on Tables 7.0-1 through 7.0-11. Each table shows the assembly language mnemonic OP code, the actual OP code, the symbolic operation, the content of the flag register following the execution of each instruction, the number of bytes required for each instruction as well as the number of memory cycles and the total number of T states (external clock periods) required for the fetching and execution of each instruction. Care has been taken to make each table self-explanatory without requiring any cross reference with the text or other tables.

SUMMARY OF FLAG OPERATION

Instruction	S	Z		H		P/V	N	C	Comments
	D7							D0	
ADD A,s; ADC A,s	↕	↕	X	↕	X	V	0	↕	8-bit add or add with carry
SUB s; SBCA,s; CP,s; NEG	↕	↕	X	↕	X	V	1	↕	8-bit subtract, subtract with carry, compare and negate accumulator
AND s	↕	↕	X	1	X	P	0	0	} Logical operations
OR s; XOR s	↕	↕	X	0	X	P	0	0	
INC s	↕	↕	X	↕	X	V	0	•	8-bit increment
DEC s	↕	↕	X	↕	X	V	1	•	8-bit decrement
ADD DD, SS	•	•	X	X	X	•	0	↕	16-bit add
ADC HL, SS	↕	↕	X	X	X	V	0	↕	16-bit add with carry
SBC HL, SS	↕	↕	X	X	X	V	1	↕	16-bit subtract with carry
RLA; RLCA; RRA; RRCA	•	•	X	0	X	•	0	↕	Rotate accumulator
RL s; RLC s; RR s; RRC s; SLA s; SRA s; SRL s	↕	↕	X	0	X	P	0	↕	Rotate and shift locations
RLD; RRD	↕	↕	X	0	X	P	0	•	Rotate digit left and right
DAA	↕	↕	X	↕	X	P	•	↕	Decimal adjust accumulator
CPL	•	•	X	1	X	•	1	•	Complement accumulator
SCF	•	•	X	0	X	•	0	1	Set carry
CCF	•	•	X	X	X	•	0	↕	Complement carry
IN r, (C)	↕	↕	X	0	X	P	0	•	Input register indirect
INI; IND; OUTI; OUTD	X	↕	X	X	X	X	1	•	} Block input and output
INIR; INDR; OTIR; OTDR	X	1	X	X	X	X	1	•	} Z = 0 if B ≠ 0 otherwise Z = 1
LDI; LDD	X	X	X	0	X	↕	0	•	} Block transfer instructions
LDIR; LDDR	X	X	X	0	X	0	0	•	} P/V = 1 if BC ≠ 0, otherwise P/V = 0
CPI; CPIR; CPD; CPDR	X	↕	X	X	X	↕	1	•	Block search instructions Z = 1 if A = (HL), otherwise Z = 0 P/V = 1 if BC ≠ 0, otherwise P/V = 0
LD A, I; LD A, R	↕	↕	X	0	X	IFF	0	•	The content of the interrupt enable flip-flop (IFF) is copied into the P/V flag
BIT b, s	X	↕	X	1	X	X	0	•	The state of bit b of location s is copied into the Z flag

The following notation is used in this table:

SYMBOL	OPERATION
C	Carry/link flag. C=1 if the operation produced a carry from the MSB of the operand or result.
Z	Zero flag. Z=1 if the result of the operation is zero.
S	Sign flag. S=1 if the MSB of the result is one.
P/V	Parity or overflow flag. Parity (P) and overflow (V) share the same flag. Logical operations affect this flag with the parity of the result while arithmetic operations affect this flag with the overflow of the result. If P/V holds parity, P/V=1 if the result of the operation is even, P/V=0 if result is odd. If P/V holds overflow, P/V=1 if the result of the operation produced an overflow.
H	Half-carry flag. H=1 if the add or subtract operation produced a carry into or borrow from bit 4 of the accumulator.
N	Add/Subtract flag. N=1 if the previous operation was a subtract.
	H and N flags are used in conjunction with the decimal adjust instruction (DAA) to properly correct the result into packed BCD format following addition or subtraction using operands with packed BCD format.
	The flag is affected according to the result of the operation.
•	The flag is unchanged by the operation.
0	The flag is reset by the operation.
1	The flag is set by the operation.
X	The flag is a "don't care".
V	P/V flag affected according to the overflow result of the operation.
P	P/V flag affected according to the parity result of the operation.
r	Any one of the CPU registers A, B, C, D, E, H, L.
s	Any 8-bit location for all the addressing modes allowed for the particular instruction.
ss	Any 16-bit location for all the addressing modes allowed for that instruction.
ii	Any one of the two index registers IX or IY.
R	Refresh counter.
n	8-bit value in range <0, 255>
nn	16-bit value in range <0, 65535>

TABLE 6.0-1

8-BIT LOAD GROUP

Mnemonic	Symbolic Operation	S	Z		H		P/V	N	C	Op-Code 76 543 210	Hex	No. of Bytes	No. of M Cycles	No. of T States	Comments
LD r, s	r ← s	●	●	X	●	X	●	●	●	01 r s		1	1	4	r, s Reg.
LD r, n	r ← n	●	●	X	●	X	●	●	●	00 r 110		2	2	7	000 B
										← n →					001 C
LD r, (HL)	r ← (HL)	●	●	X	●	X	●	●	●	01 r 110		1	2	7	010 D
LD r, (IX+d)	r ← (IX+d)	●	●	X	●	X	●	●	●	11 011 101	DD	3	5	19	011 E
										01 r 110					100 H
										← d →					101 L
LD r, (IY+d)	r ← (IY+d)	●	●	X	●	X	●	●	●	11 111 101	FD	3	5	19	111 A
										01 r 110					
										← d →					
LD (HL), r	(HL) ← r	●	●	X	●	X	●	●	●	01 110 r		1	2	7	
LD (IX+d), r	(IX+d) ← r	●	●	X	●	X	●	●	●	11 011 101	DD	3	5	19	
										01 110 r					
										← d →					
LD (IY+d), r	(IY+d) ← r	●	●	X	●	X	●	●	●	11 111 101	FD	3	5	19	
										01 110 r					
										← d →					
LD (HL), n	(HL) ← n	●	●	X	●	X	●	●	●	00 110 110	36	2	3	10	
LD (IX+d), n	(IX+d) ← n	●	●	X	●	X	●	●	●	11 011 101	DD	4	5	19	
										00 110 110	36				
										← d →					
										← n →					
LD (IY+d), n	(IY+d) ← n	●	●	X	●	X	●	●	●	11 111 101	FD	4	5	19	
										00 110 110	36				
										← d →					
										← n →					
LD A, (BC)	A ← (BC)	●	●	X	●	X	●	●	●	00 001 010	0A	1	2	7	
LD A, (DE)	A ← (DE)	●	●	X	●	X	●	●	●	00 011 010	1A	1	2	7	
LD A, (nn)	A ← (nn)	●	●	X	●	X	●	●	●	00 111 010	3A	3	4	13	
										← n →					
										← n →					
LD (BC), A	(BC) ← A	●	●	X	●	X	●	●	●	00 000 010	02	1	2	7	
LD (DE), A	(DE) ← A	●	●	X	●	X	●	●	●	00 010 010	12	1	2	7	
LD (nn), A	(nn) ← A	●	●	X	●	X	●	●	●	00 110 010	32	3	4	13	
										← n →					
										← n →					
LD A, I	A ← I	↕	↕	X	0	X	IFF	0	●	11 101 101	ED	2	2	9	
										01 010 111	57				
LD A, R	A ← R	↕	↕	X	0	X	IFF	0	●	11 101 101	ED	2	2	9	
										01 011 111	5F				
LD I, A	I ← A	●	●	X	●	X	●	●	●	11 101 101	ED	2	2	9	
										01 000 111	47				
LD R, A	R ← A	●	●	X	●	X	●	●	●	11 101 101	ED	2	2	9	
										01 001 111	4F				

Notes: r, s means any of the registers A, B, C, D, E, H, L
   IFF the content of the interrupt enable flip-flop (IFF) is copied into the P/V flag

Flag Notation: ● = flag not affected, 0 = flag reset, 1 = flag set, X = flag is unknown,
   ↕ = flag is affected according to the result of the operation.

Table 7.0-1

16-BIT LOAD GROUP

Mnemonic	Symbolic Operation	S	Z		H		P/V	N	C	76 543 210	Hex	No. of Bytes	No. of M Cycles	No. of T States	Comments
LD dd, nn	dd ← nn	•	•	X	•	X	•	•	•	00 dd0 001 ← n → ← n →		3	3	10	dd Pair 00 BC 01 DE
LD IX, nn	IX ← nn	•	•	X	•	X	•	•	•	11 011 101 00 100 001 ← n → ← n →	DD 21	4	4	14	10 HL 11 SP
LD IY, nn	IY ← nn	•	•	X	•	X	•	•	•	11 111 101 00 100 001 ← n → ← n →	FD 21	4	4	14	
LD HL, (nn)	H ← (nn+1) L ← (nn)	•	•	X	•	X	•	•	•	00 101 010 ← n → ← n →	2A	3	5	16	
LD dd, (nn)	dd_H ← (nn+1) dd_L ← (nn)	•	•	X	•	X	•	•	•	11 101 101 01 dd1 011 ← n → ← n →	ED	4	6	20	
LD IX, (nn)	IX_H ← (nn+1) IX_L ← (nn)	•	•	X	•	X	•	•	•	11 011 101 00 101 010 ← n → ← n →	DD 2A	4	6	20	
LD IY, (nn)	IY_H ← (nn+1) IY_L ← (nn)	•	•	X	•	X	•	•	•	11 111 101 00 101 010 ← n → ← n →	FD 2A	4	6	20	
LD (nn), HL	(nn+1) ← H (nn) ← L	•	•	X	•	X	•	•	•	00 100 010 ← n → ← n →	22	3	5	16	
LD (nn), dd	(nn+1) ← dd_H (nn) ← dd_L	•	•	X	•	X	•	•	•	11 101 101 01 dd0 011 ← n → ← n →	ED	4	6	20	
LD (nn), IX	(nn+1) ← IX_H (nn) ← IX_L	•	•	X	•	X	•	•	•	11 011 101 00 100 010 ← n → ← n →	DD 22	4	6	20	
LD (nn), IY	(nn+1) ← IY_H (nn) ← IY_L	•	•	X	•	X	•	•	•	11 111 101 00 100 010 ← n → ← n →	FD 22	4	6	20	
LD SP, HL	SP ← HL	•	•	X	•	X	•	•	•	11 111 001	F9	1	1	6	
LD SP, IX	SP ← IX	•	•	X	•	X	•	•	•	11 011 101 11 111 001	DD F9	2	2	10	
LD SP, IY	SP ← IY	•	•	X	•	X	•	•	•	11 111 101 11 111 001	FD F9	2	2	10	qq Pair 00 BC
PUSH qq	(SP-2) ← qq_L (SP-1) ← qq_H	•	•	X	•	X	•	•	•	11 qq0 101		1	3	11	01 DE 10 HL
PUSH IX	(SP-2) ← IX_L (SP-1) ← IX_H	•	•	X	•	X	•	•	•	11 011 101 11 100 101	DD E5	2	4	15	11 AF
PUSH IY	(SP-2) ← IY_L (SP-1) ← IY_H	•	•	X	•	X	•	•	•	11 111 101 11 100 101	FD E5	2	4	15	
POP qq	qq_H ← (SP+1) qq_L ← (SP)	•	•	X	•	X	•	•	•	11 qq0 001		1	3	10	
POP IX	IX_H ← (SP+1) IX_L ← (SP)	•	•	X	•	X	•	•	•	11 011 101 11 100 001	DD E1	2	4	14	
POP IY	IY_H ← (SP+1) IY_L ← (SP)	•	•	X	•	X	•	•	•	11 111 101 11 100 001	FD E1	2	4	14	

Notes: dd is any of the register pairs BC, DE, HL, SP
qq is any of the register pairs AF, BC, DE, HL
$(PAIR)_H$, $(PAIR)_L$ refer to high order and low order eight bits of the register pair respectively.
e.g. BC_L = C, AF_H = A

Flag Notation: • = flag not affected, 0 = flag reset, 1 = flag set, X = flag is unknown,
‡ flag is affected according to the result of the operation.

Table 7.0-2

EXCHANGE GROUP AND BLOCK TRANSFER AND SEARCH GROUP

Mnemonic	Symbolic Operation	S	Z		H		P/V	N	C	76 543 210	Hex	No. of Bytes	No.of M Cycles	No.of T States	Comments
EX DE, HL	DE↔HL	•	•	X	•	X	•	•	•	11 101 011	EB	1	1	4	
EX AF, AF'	AF↔AF'	•	•	X	•	X	•	•	•	00 001 000	08	1	1	4	
EXX	BC↔BC' DE↔DE' HL↔HL'	•	•	X	•	X	•	•	•	11 011 001	D9	1	1	4	Register bank and auxiliary register bank exchange
EX (SP), HL	H↔(SP+1) L↔(SP)	•	•	X	•	X	•	•	•	11 100 011	E3	1	5	19	
EX (SP), IX	IX_H↔(SP+1) IX_L↔(SP)	•	•	X	•	X	•	•	•	11 011 101 11 100 011	DD E3	2	6	23	
EX (SP), IY	IY_H↔(SP+1) IY_L↔(SP)	•	•	X	•	X	•	•	•	11 111 101 11 100 011	FD E3	2	6	23	
LDI	(DE)←(HL) DE ← DE+1 HL ← HL+1 BC ← BC-1	•	•	X	0	X	↕ ①	0	•	11 101 101 10 100 000	ED A0	2	4	16	Load (HL) into (DE), increment the pointers and decrement the byte counter (BC)
LDIR	(DE)←(HL) DE ← DE+1 HL ← HL+1 BC ← BC-1 Repeat until BC = 0	•	•	X	0	X	0	0	•	11 101 101 10 110 000	ED B0	2 2	5 4	21 16	If BC ≠ 0 If BC = 0
LDD	(DE)←(HL) DE ← DE-1 HL ← HL-1 BC ← BC-1	•	•	X	0	X	↕ ①	0	•	11 101 101 10 101 000	ED A8	2	4	16	
LDDR	(DE)←(HL) DE ← DE-1 HL ← HL-1 BC ← BC-1 Repeat until BC = 0	•	•	X	0	X	0	0	•	11 101 101 10 111 000	ED B8	2 2	5 4	21 16	If BC ≠ 0 If BC = 0
CPI	A − (HL) HL ← HL+1 BC ← BC-1	↕	↕ ②	X	↕	X	↕ ①	1	•	11 101 101 10 100 001	ED A1	2	4	16	
CPIR	A − (HL) HL ← HL+1 BC ← BC-1 Repeat until A = (HL) or BC = 0	↕	↕ ②	X	↕	X	↕ ①	1	•	11 101 101 10 110 001	ED B1	2 2	5 4	21 16	If BC ≠ 0 and A ≠ (HL) If BC = 0 or A = (HL)
CPD	A − (HL) HL ← HL-1 BC ← BC-1	↕	↕ ②	X	↕	X	↕ ①	1	•	11 101 101 10 101 001	ED A9	2	4	16	
CPDR	A − (HL) HL ← HL-1 BC ← BC-1 Repeat until A = (HL) or BC = 0	↕	↕ ②	X	↕	X	↕ ①	1	•	11 101 101 10 111 001	ED B9	2 2	5 4	21 16	If BC ≠ 0 and A ≠ (HL) If BC = 0 or A = (HL)

Notes: ① P/V flag is 0 if the result of BC-1 = 0, otherwise P/V = 1
② Z flag is 1 if A = (HL), otherwise Z = 0.

Flag Notation: • = flag not affected, 0 = flag reset, 1 = flag set, X = flag is unknown,
↕ = flag is affected according to the result of the operation.

Table 7.0-3

8-BIT ARITHMETIC AND LOGICAL GROUP

Mnemonic	Symbolic Operation	S	Z		H		P/V	N	C	76 543 210	Hex	No. of Bytes	No.of M Cycles	No.of T States	Comments	
ADD A, r	A ← A + r	↕	↕	X	↕	X	V	0	↕	10 000 r		1	1	4	r	Reg.
ADD A, n	A ← A + n	↕	↕	X	↕	X	V	0	↕	11 000 110		2	2	7	000	B
										← n →					001	C
															010	D
ADD A, (HL)	A ← A+(HL)	↕	↕	X	↕	X	V	0	↕	10 000 110		1	2	7	011	E
ADD A, (IX+d)	A←A+(IX+d)	↕	↕	X	↕	X	V	0	↕	11 011 101	DD	3	5	19	100	H
										10 000 110					101	L
										← d →					111	A
ADD A, (IY+d)	A←A+(IY+d)	↕	↕	X	↕	X	V	0	↕	11 111 101	FD	3	5	19		
										10 000 110						
										← d →						
ADC A, s	A ← A+s+CY	↕	↕	X	↕	X	V	0	↕	001					s is any of r, n,	
SUB s	A ← A - s	↕	↕	X	↕	X	V	1	↕	010					(HL), (IX+d),	
SBC A, s	A ← A - s - CY	↕	↕	X	↕	X	V	1	↕	011					(IY+d) as shown for	
AND s	A ← A ∧ s	↕	↕	X	1	X	P	0	0	100					ADD instruction.	
OR s	A ← A ∨ s	↕	↕	X	0	X	P	0	0	110					The indicated bits	
XOR s	A ← A ⊕ s	↕	↕	X	0	X	P	0	0	101					replace the 000 in	
CP s	A - s	↕	↕	X	↕	X	V	1	↕	111					the ADD set above.	
INC r	r ← r + 1	↕	↕	X	↕	X	V	0	●	00 r 100		1	1	4		
INC (HL)	(HL)←(HL)+1	↕	↕	X	↕	X	V	0	●	00 110 100		1	3	11		
INC (IX+d)	(IX+d) ← (IX+d)+1	↕	↕	X	↕	X	V	0	●	11 011 101	DD	3	6	23		
										00 110 100						
										← d →						
INC (IY+d)	(IY+d) ← (IY+d)+1	↕	↕	X	↕	X	V	0	●	11 111 101	FD	3	6	23		
										00 110 100						
										← d →						
DEC s	s ← s - 1	↕	↕	X	↕	X	V	1	●	101					s is any of r, (HL), (IX+d), (IY+d) as shown for INC. DEC same format and states as INC. Replace 100 with 101 in OP Code.	

Notes: The V symbol in the P/V flag column indicates that the P/V flag contains the overflow of the result of the operation. Similarly the P symbol indicates parity. V = 1 means overflow, V = 0 means not overflow, P = 1 means parity of the result is even, P = 0 means parity of the result is odd.

Flag Notation: ● = flag not affected, 0 = flag reset, 1 = flag set, X = flag is unknown.
↕ = flag is affected according to the result of the operation.

Table 7.0-4

GENERAL PURPOSE ARITHMETIC AND CPU CONTROL GROUPS

Mnemonic	Symbolic Operation	Flags								Op-Code		No. of Bytes	No. of M Cycles	No. of T States	Comments
		S	Z		H		P/V	N	C	76 543 210	Hex				
DAA	Converts acc, content into packed BCD following add or subtract with packed BCD operands	‡	‡	X	‡	X	P	•	‡	00 100 111	27	1	1	4	Decimal adjust accumulator
CPL	A → $\overline{A}$	•	•	X	1	X	•	1	•	00 101 111	2F	1	1	4	Complement accumulator (One's complement)
NEG	A → $\overline{A}$ + 1	‡	‡	X	‡	X	V	1	‡	11 101 101 / 01 000 100	ED / 44	2	2	8	Negate acc, (two's complement)
CCF	CY → $\overline{CY}$	•	•	X	X	X	•	0	‡	00 111 111	3F	1	1	4	Complement carry flag
SCF	CY → 1	•	•	X	0	X	•	0	1	00 110 111	37	1	1	4	Set carry flag
NOP	No operation	•	•	X	•	X	•	•	•	00 000 000	00	1	1	4	
HALT	CPU halted	•	•	X	•	X	•	•	•	01 110 110	76	1	1	4	
DI *	IFF → 0	•	•	X	•	X	•	•	•	11 110 011	F3	1	1	4	
EI *	IFF → 1	•	•	X	•	X	•	•	•	11 111 011	FB	1	1	4	
IM 0	Set interrupt mode 0	•	•	X	•	X	•	•	•	11 101 101 / 01 000 110	ED / 46	2	2	8	
IM 1	Set interrupt mode 1	•	•	X	•	X	•	•	•	11 101 101 / 01 010 110	ED / 56	2	2	8	
IM 2	Set interrupt mode 2	•	•	X	•	X	•	•	•	11 101 101 / 01 011 110	ED / 5E	2	2	8	

Notes: IFF indicates the interrupt enable flip-flop
CY indicates the carry flip-flop.

Flag Notation: • = flag not affected, 0 = flag reset, 1 = flag set, X = flag is unknown,
‡ = flag is affected according to the result of the operation.

*Interrupts are not sampled at the end of EI or DI

Table 7.0-5

16-BIT ARITHMETIC GROUP

Mnemonic	Symbolic Operation	Flags								Op-Code		No. of Bytes	No.of M Cycles	No.of T States	Comments	
		S	Z		H		P/V	N	C	76 543 210	Hex					
ADD HL, ss	HL ← HL+ss	•	•	X	X	X	•	0	$\updownarrow$	00 ss1 001		1	3	11	ss	Reg.
															00	BC
ADC HL, ss	HL ← HL+ss+CY	$\updownarrow$	$\updownarrow$	X	X	X	V	0	$\updownarrow$	11 101 101	ED	2	4	15	01	DE
										01 ss1 010					10	HL
															11	SP
SBC HL, ss	HL ← HL-ss-CY	$\updownarrow$	$\updownarrow$	X	X	X	V	1	$\updownarrow$	11 101 101	ED	2	4	15		
										01 ss0 010						
ADD IX, pp	IX ← IX + pp	•	•	X	X	X	•	0	$\updownarrow$	11 011 101	DD	2	4	15	pp	Reg.
										00 pp1 001					00	BC
															01	DE
															10	IX
															11	SP
ADD IY, rr	IY ← IY + rr	•	•	X	X	X	•	0	$\updownarrow$	11 111 101	FD	2	4	15	rr	Reg.
										00 rr1 001					00	BC
															01	DE
															10	IY
															11	SP
INC ss	ss ← ss + 1	•	•	X	•	X	•	•	•	00 ss0 011		1	1	6		
INC IX	IX ← IX + 1	•	•	X	•	X	•	•	•	11 011 101	DD	2	2	10		
										00 100 011	23					
INC IY	IY ← IY + 1	•	•	X	•	X	•	•	•	11 111 101	FD	2	2	10		
										00 100 011	23					
DEC ss	ss ← ss - 1	•	•	X	•	X	•	•	•	00 ss1 011		1	1	6		
DEC IX	IX ← IX - 1	•	•	X	•	X	•	•	•	11 011 101	DD	2	2	10		
										00 101 011	2B					
DEC IY	IY ← IY - 1	•	•	X	•	X	•	•	•	11 111 101	FD	2	2	10		
										00 101 011	2B					

Notes: ss is any of the register pairs BC, DE, HL, SP
              pp is any of the register pairs BC, DE, IX, SP
              rr is any of the register pairs BC, DE, IY, SP.

Flag Notation: • = flag not affected, 0 = flag reset, 1 = flag set, X = flag is unknown.
                   $\updownarrow$ = flag is affected according to the result of the operation.

Table 7.0-6

ROTATE AND SHIFT GROUP

Mnemonic	Operation	S	Z	H	P/V	N	C	Op-Code 76 543 210	Hex	No.of Bytes	No.of M Cycles	No.of T States	Comments
RLCA	CY ← [7 ← 0] A	•	•	0	•	0	↕	00 000 111	07	1	1	4	Rotate left circular accumulator
RLA	CY ← [7 ← 0] A	•	•	0	•	0	↕	00 010 111	17	1	1	4	Rotate left accumulator
RRCA	[7 → 0] → CY A	•	•	0	•	0	↕	00 001 111	0F	1	1	4	Rotate right circular accumulator
RRA	[7 → 0] → CY A	•	•	0	•	0	↕	00 011 111	1F	1	1	4	Rotate right accumulator
RLC r		↕	↕	0	P	0	↕	11 001 011 00 [000] r	CB	2	2	8	Rotate left circular register r
RLC (HL)		↕	↕	0	P	0	↕	11 001 011 00 [000] 110	CB	2	4	15	r = Reg.
RLC (IX+d)	CY ← [7 ← 0] r,(HL),(IX+d),(IY+d)	↕	↕	0	P	0	↕	11 011 101 11 001 011 ← d → 00 [000] 110	DD CB	4	6	23	000 B 001 C 010 D 011 E 100 H 101 L 111 A
RLC (IY+d)		↕	↕	0	P	0	↕	11 111 101 11 001 011 ← d → 00 [000] 110	FD CB	4	6	23	
RL s	CY ← [7 ← 0] s ≡ r,(HL),(IX+d),(IY+d)	↕	↕	0	P	0	↕	[010]					Instruction format and states are as shown for RLC's. To form new Op-Code replace [000] of RLC's with shown code
RRC s	[7 → 0] → CY s ≡ r,(HL),(IX+d),(IY+d)	↕	↕	0	P	0	↕	[001]					
RR s	[7 → 0] → CY s ≡ r,(HL),(IX+d),(IY+d)	↕	↕	0	P	0	↕	[011]					
SLA s	CY ← [7 ← 0] ← 0 s ≡ r,(HL),(IX+d),(IY+d)	↕	↕	0	P	0	↕	[100]					
SRA s	[7 → 0] → CY s ≡ r,(HL),(IX+d),(IY+d)	↕	↕	0	P	0	↕	[101]					
SRL s	0 → [7 → 0] → CY s ≡ r,(HL),(IX+d),(IY+d)	↕	↕	0	P	0	↕	[111]					
RLD	A [7-4 3-0] [7-4 3-0](HL)	↕	↕	0	P	0	•	11 101 101 01 101 111	ED 6F	2	5	18	Rotate digit left and right between the accumulator and location (HL). The content of the upper half of the accumulator is unaffected
RRD	A [7-4 3-0] [7-4 3-0](HL)	↕	↕	0	P	0	•	11 101 101 01 100 111	ED 67	2	5	18	

Flag Notation:　• = flag not affected, 0 = flag reset, 1 = flag set, X = flag is unknown,
　　　　　　　↕ = flag is affected according to the result of the operation.

Table 7.0-7

BIT SET, RESET AND TEST GROUP

Mnemonic	Symbolic Operation	S	Z		H		P/V	N	C	Op-Code 76 543 210	Hex	No. of Bytes	No.of M Cycles	No.of T States
BIT b, r	$Z \leftarrow \bar{r}_b$	X	↕	X	1	X	X	0	•	11 001 011 / 01 b r	CB	2	2	8
BIT b, (HL)	$Z \leftarrow \overline{(HL)}_b$	X	↕	X	1	X	X	0	•	11 001 011 / 01 b 110	CB	2	3	12
BIT b, (IX+d)$_b$	$Z \leftarrow \overline{(IX+d)}_b$	X	↕	X	1	X	X	0	•	11 011 101 DD / 11 001 011 CB / ← d → / 01 b 110		4	5	20
BIT b, (IY+d)$_b$	$Z \leftarrow \overline{(IY+d)}_b$	X	↕	X	1	X	X	0	•	11 111 101 FD / 11 001 011 CB / ← d → / 01 b 110		4	5	20
SET b, r	$r_b \leftarrow 1$	•	•	X	•	X	•	•	•	11 001 011 CB / [11] b r		2	2	8
SET b, (HL)	$(HL)_b \leftarrow 1$	•	•	X	•	X	•	•	•	11 001 011 CB / [11] b 110		2	4	15
SET b, (IX+d)	$(IX+d)_b \leftarrow 1$	•	•	X	•	X	•	•	•	11 011 101 DD / 11 001 011 CB / ← d → / [11] b 110		4	6	23
SET b, (IY+d)	$(IY+d)_b \leftarrow 1$	•	•	X	•	X	•	•	•	11 111 101 FD / 11 001 011 CB / ← d → / [11] b 110		4	6	23
RES b, s	$s_b \leftarrow 0$ $s \equiv r, (HL), (IX+d), (IY+d)$	•	•	X	•	X	•	•	•	[10]				

Comments:

r	Reg.
000	B
001	C
010	D
011	E
100	H
101	L
111	A

b	Bit Tested
000	0
001	1
010	2
011	3
100	4
101	5
110	6
111	7

RES b, s: To form new Op-Code replace [11] of SET b, s with [10]. Flags and time states for SET instruction.

Notes: The notation s$_b$ indicates bit b (0 to 7) or location s.

Flag Notation: • = flag not affected, 0 = flag reset, 1 = flag set, X = flag is unknown,
↕ = flag is affected according to the result of the operation.

Table 7.0-8

JUMP GROUP

Mnemonic	Symbolic Operation	S	Z		H		P/V	N	C	76 543 210	Hex	No. of Bytes	No.of M Cycles	No.of T States	Comments
JP nn	PC ← nn	•	•	X	•	X	•	•	•	11 000 011 ← n → ← n →	C3	3	3	10	
JP cc, nn	If condition cc is true PC ← nn, otherwise continue	•	•	X	•	X	•	•	•	11 cc 010 ← n → ← n →		3	3	10	
JR e	PC ← PC + e	•	•	X	•	X	•	•	•	00 011 000 ← e-2 →	18	2	3	12	
JR C, e	If C = 0, continue	•	•	X	•	X	•	•	•	00 111 000 ← e-2 →	38	2	2	7	If condition not met
	If C = 1, PC ← PC+e											2	3	12	If condition is met
JR NC, e	If C = 1, continue	•	•	X	•	X	•	•	•	00 110 000 ← e-2 →	30	2	2	7	If condition not met
	If C = 0, PC ← PC+e											2	3	12	If condition is met
JR Z, e	If Z = 0 continue	•	•	X	•	X	•	•	•	00 101 000 ← e-2 →	28	2	2	7	If condition not met
	If Z = 1, PC ← PC+e											2	3	12	If condition is met
JR NZ, e	If Z = 1, continue	•	•	X	•	X	•	•	•	00 100 000 ← e-2 →	20	2	2	7	If condition not met
	If Z = 0, PC ← PC+e											2	3	12	If condition is met
JP (HL)	PC ← HL	•	•	X	•	X	•	•	•	11 101 001	E9	1	1	4	
JP (IX)	PC ← IX	•	•	X	•	X	•	•	•	11 011 101 11 101 001	DD E9	2	2	8	
JP (IY)	PC ← IY	•	•	X	•	X	•	•	•	11 111 101 11 101 001	FD E9	2	2	8	
DJNZ, e	B ← B-1 If B = 0, continue	•	•	X	•	X	•	•	•	00 010 000 ← e-2 →	10	2	2	8	If B = 0
	If B ≠ 0, PC ← PC+e											2	3	13	If B ≠ 0

cc	Condition
000	NZ non zero
001	Z zero
010	NC non carry
011	C carry
100	PO parity odd
101	PE parity even
110	P sign positive
111	M sign negative

Notes: e represents the extension in the relative addressing mode.

e is a signed two's complement number in the range <126, 129>

e-2 in the op-code provides an effective address of pc+e as PC is incremented by 2 prior to the addition of e.

Flag Notation: • = flag not affected, 0 = flag reset, 1 = flag set, X = flag is unknown,
‡ = flag is affected according to the result of the operation.

Table 7.0-9

CALL AND RETURN GROUP

Mnemonic	Symbolic Operation	Flags								Op-Code			No. of Bytes	No.of M Cycles	No.of T States	Comments
		S	Z		H		P/V	N	C	76 543 210	Hex					
CALL nn	(SP-1) ← PC_H	•	•	X	•	X	•	•	•	11 001 101	CD	3	5	17		
	(SP-2) ← PC_L									← n →						
	PC ← nn									← n →						
CALL cc, nn	If condition	•	•	X	•	X	•	•	•	11 cc 100		3	3	10	If cc is false
	cc is false									← n →						
	continue,									← n →		3	5	17	If cc is true
	otherwise															
	same as															
	CALL nn															
RET	PC_L ← (SP)	•	•	X	•	X	•	•	•	11 001 001	C9	1	3	10	
	PC_H ← (SP+1)															
RET cc	If condition	•	•	X	•	X	•	•	•	11 cc 000		1	1	5	If cc is false
	cc is false															
	continue,											1	3	11	If cc is true
	otherwise															
	same as															
	RET															
RETI	Return from	•	•	X	•	X	•	•	•	11 101 101	ED	2	4	14	
	interrupt									01 001 101	4D				
RETN[1]	Return from	•	•	X	•	X	•	•	•	11 101 101	ED	2	4	14	
	non maskable									01 000 101	45				
	interrupt															
RST p	(SP-1) ← PC_H	•	•	X	•	X	•	•	•	11 t 111		1	3	11	
	(SP-2) ← PC_L															
	PC_H ← 0															
	PC_L ← p															

cc		Condition
000	NZ	non zero
001	Z	zero
010	NC	non carry
011	C	carry
100	PO	parity odd
101	PE	parity even
110	P	sign positive
111	M	sign negative

t	p
000	00H
001	08H
010	10H
011	18H
100	20H
101	28H
110	30H
111	38H

[1] RETN loads IFF_2 ← IFF_1

Flag Notation: • = flag not affected, 0 = flag reset, 1 = flag set, X = flag is unknown,
$\updownarrow$ = flag is affected according to the result of the operation.

Table 7.0-10

INPUT AND OUTPUT GROUP

Mnemonic	Symbolic Operation	S	Z	H	P/V	N	C	76 543 210	Hex	No. of Bytes	No. of M Cycles	No. of T States	Comments
IN A, (n)	$A \leftarrow (n)$	•	•	X	X	•	•	11 011 011	DB	2	3	11	n to $A_0 \sim A_7$
								← n →					Acc to $A_8 \sim A_{15}$
IN r, (C)	$r \leftarrow (C)$	↕	↕	X	P	0	•	11 101 101	ED	2	3	12	C to $A_0 \sim A_7$
	if r = 110 only the flags will be affected							01 r 000					B to $A_8 \sim A_{15}$
INI	$(HL) \leftarrow (C)$	X	①↕	X	X	X	1	•	11 101 101	ED	2	4	16	C to $A_0 \sim A_7$
	$B \leftarrow B-1$							10 100 010	A2				B to $A_8 \sim A_{15}$
	$HL \leftarrow HL+1$												
INIR	$(HL) \leftarrow (C)$	X	1	X	X	X	1	•	11 101 101	ED	2	5	21	C to $A_0 \sim A_7$
	$B \leftarrow B-1$							10 110 010	B2		(If B ≠ 0)		B to $A_8 \sim A_{15}$
	$HL \leftarrow HL+1$									2	4	16	
	Repeat until B = 0										(If B = 0)		
IND	$(HL) \leftarrow (C)$	X	①↕	X	X	X	1	•	11 101 101	ED	2	4	16	C to $A_0 \sim A_7$
	$B \leftarrow B-1$							10 101 010	AA				B to $A_8 \sim A_{15}$
	$HL \leftarrow HL-1$												
INDR	$(HL) \leftarrow (C)$	X	1	X	X	X	1	•	11 101 101	ED	2	5	21	C to $A_0 \sim A_7$
	$B \leftarrow B-1$							10 111 010	BA		(If B ≠ 0)		B to $A_8 \sim A_{15}$
	$HL \leftarrow HL-1$									2	4	16	
	Repeat until B = 0										(If B = 0)		
OUT (n), A	$(n) \leftarrow A$	•	•	X	•	X	•	•	11 010 011	D3	2	3	11	n to $A_0 \sim A_7$
													Acc to $A_8 \sim A_{15}$
OUT (C), r	$(C) \leftarrow r$	•	•	X	•	X	•	•	11 101 101	ED	2	3	12	C to $A_0 \sim A_7$
								01 r 001					B to $A_8 \sim A_{15}$
OUTI	$(C) \leftarrow (HL)$	X	①↕	X	X	X	1	•	11 101 101	ED	2	4	16	C to $A_0 \sim A_7$
	$B \leftarrow B-1$							10 100 011	A3				B to $A_8 \sim A_{15}$
	$HL \leftarrow HL+1$												
OTIR	$(C) \leftarrow (HL)$	X	1	X	X	X	1	•	11 101 101	ED	2	5	21	C to $A_0 \sim A_7$
	$B \leftarrow B-1$							10 110 011	B3		(If B ≠ 0)		B to $A_8 \sim A_{15}$
	$HL \leftarrow HL+1$									2	4	16	
	Repeat until B = 0										(If B = 0)		
OUTD	$(C) \leftarrow (HL)$	X	①↕	X	X	X	1	•	11 101 101	ED	2	4	16	C to $A_0 \sim A_7$
	$B \leftarrow B-1$							10 101 011	AB				B to $A_8 \sim A_{15}$
	$HL \leftarrow HL-1$												
OTDR	$(C) \leftarrow (HL)$	X	1	X	X	X	1	•	11 101 101	ED	2	5	21	C to $A_0 \sim A_7$
	$B \leftarrow B-1$							10 111 011	BB		(If B ≠ 0)		B to $A_8 \sim A_{15}$
	$HL \leftarrow HL-1$									2	4	16	
	Repeat until B = 0										(If B = 0)		

Notes: ① If the result of B - 1 is zero the Z flag is set, otherwise it is reset.

Flag Notation: • = flag not affected, 0 = flag reset, 1 = flag set, X = flag is unknown,
↕ = flag is affected according to the result of the operation.

Table 7.0-11

Appendix C The Motorola 6800

MICROPROCESSING UNIT (MPU)

The MC6800 is a monolithic 8-bit microprocessor forming the central control function for Motorola's M6800 family. Compatible with TTL, the MC6800, as with all M6800 system parts, requires only one +5.0-volt power supply, and no external TTL devices for bus interface.

The MC6800 is capable of addressing 65K bytes of memory with its 16-bit address lines. The 8-bit data bus is bidirectional as well as 3-state, making direct memory addressing and multiprocessing applications realizable.

- Eight-Bit Parallel Processing
- Bi-Directional Data Bus
- Sixteen-Bit Address Bus — 65K Bytes of Addressing
- 72 Instructions — Variable Length
- Seven Addressing Modes — Direct, Relative, Immediate, Indexed, Extended, Implied and Accumulator
- Variable Length Stack
- Vectored Restart
- Maskable Interrupt Vector
- Separate Non-Maskable Interrupt — Internal Registers Saved In Stack
- Six Internal Registers — Two Accumulators, Index Register, Program Counter, Stack Pointer and Condition Code Register
- Direct Memory Addressing (DMA) and Multiple Processor Capability
- Clock Rates as High as 1 MHz
- Simple Bus Interface Without TTL
- Halt and Single Instruction Execution Capability

MOS

(N-CHANNEL, SILICON-GATE)

MICROPROCESSOR

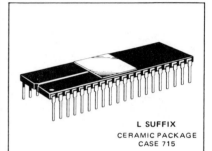

L SUFFIX
CERAMIC PACKAGE
CASE 715

NOT SHOWN: **P SUFFIX**
PLASTIC PACKAGE
CASE 711

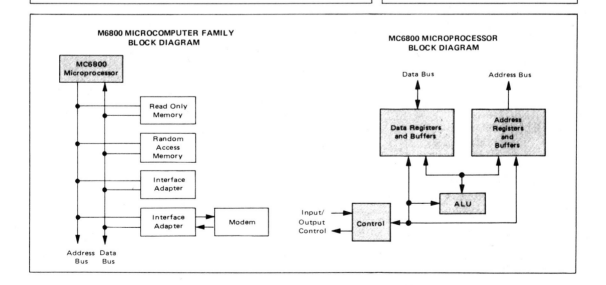

M6800 MICROCOMPUTER FAMILY
BLOCK DIAGRAM

MC6800 MICROPROCESSOR
BLOCK DIAGRAM

ELECTRICAL CHARACTERISTICS (V_{CC} = 5.0 V ± 5%, V_{SS} = 0, T_A = 0 to 70°C unless otherwise noted.)

Characteristic		Symbol	Min	Typ	Max	Unit
Input High Voltage	Logic	V_{IH}	V_{SS} + 2.0	—	V_{CC}	Vdc
	$\phi1,\phi2$	V_{IHC}	V_{CC} − 0.3	—	V_{CC} + 0.1	
Input Low Voltage	Logic	V_{IL}	V_{SS} − 0.3	—	V_{SS} + 0.8	Vdc
	$\phi1,\phi2$	V_{ILC}	V_{SS} − 0.1	—	V_{SS} + 0.3	
Clock Overshoot/Undershoot − Input High Level		V_{OS}	V_{CC} − 0.5	—	V_{CC} + 0.5	Vdc
− Input Low Level			V_{SS} − 0.5	—	V_{SS} + 0.5	
Input Leakage Current		I_{in}				µAdc
(V_{in} = 0 to 5.25 V, V_{CC} = max)	Logic*		—	1.0	2.5	
(V_{in} = 0 to 5.25 V, V_{CC} = 0.0 V)	$\phi1,\phi2$		—	—	100	
Three-State (Off State) Input Current	D0-D7	I_{TSI}	—	2.0	10	µAdc
(V_{in} 0.4 to 2.4 V, V_{CC} = max)	A0-A15,R/W		—	—	100	
Output High Voltage		V_{OH}				Vdc
(I_{Load} = −205 µAdc, V_{CC} = min)	D0-D7		V_{SS} + 2.4	—	—	
(I_{Load} = −145 µAdc, V_{CC} = min)	A0-A15,R/W,VMA		V_{SS} + 2.4	—	—	
(I_{Load} = −100 µAdc, V_{CC} = min)	BA		V_{SS} + 2.4	—	—	
Output Low Voltage		V_{OL}	—	—	V_{SS} + 0.4	Vdc
(I_{Load} = 1.6 mAdc, V_{CC} = min)						
Power Dissipation		P_D	—	0.600	1.2	W
Capacitance #	$\phi1,\phi2$	C_{in}	80	120	160	pF
(V_{in} = 0, T_A = 25°C, f = 1.0 MHz)	TSC		—	—	15	
	DBE		—	7.0	10	
	D0-D7		—	10	12.5	
	Logic Inputs		—	6.5	8.5	
	A0-A15,R/W,VMA	C_{out}	—	—	12	pF
Frequency of Operation		f	0.1	—	1.0	MHz
Clock Timing (Figure 1)						
Cycle Time		t_{cyc}	1.0	—	10	µs
Clock Pulse Width		$PW_{\phi H}$				ns
(Measured at V_{CC} − 0.3 V)	$\phi1$		430	—	4500	
	$\phi2$		450	—	4500	
Total $\phi1$ and $\phi2$ Up Time		t_{ut}	940	—	—	ns
Rise and Fall Times	$\phi1,\phi2$	$t_{\phi r}, t_{\phi f}$	5.0	—	50	ns
(Measured between V_{SS} + 0.3 V and V_{CC} − 0.3 V)						
Delay Time or Clock Separation		t_d	0	—	9100	ns
(Measured at V_{OV} = V_{SS} + 0.5 V)						
Overshoot Duration		t_{OS}	0	—	40	ns

*Except $\overline{IRQ}$ and $\overline{NMI}$, which require 3 kΩ pullup load resistors for wire-OR capability at optimum operation.
#Capacitances are periodically sampled rather than 100% tested.

FIGURE 1 − CLOCK TIMING WAVEFORM

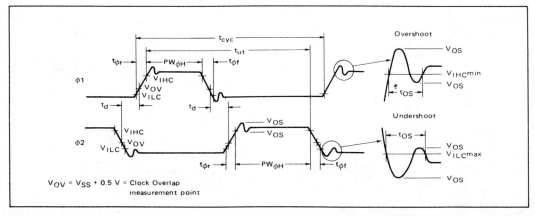

MAXIMUM RATINGS

Rating	Symbol	Value	Unit
Supply Voltage	V_{CC}	−0.3 to +7.0	Vdc
Input Voltage	V_{in}	−0.3 to +7.0	Vdc
Operating Temperature Range	T_A	0 to +70	°C
Storage Temperature Range	T_{stg}	−55 to +150	°C
Thermal Resistance	θ_{JA}	70	°C/W

This device contains circuitry to protect the inputs against damage due to high static voltages or electric fields; however, it is advised that normal precautions be taken to avoid application of any voltage higher than maximum rated voltages to this high impedance circuit.

READ/WRITE TIMING Figures 2 and 3, f = 1.0 MHz, Load Circuit of Figure 6.

Characteristic	Symbol	Min	Typ	Max	Unit
Address Delay	t_{AD}	−	220	300	ns
Peripheral Read Access Time $t_{acc} = t_{ut} - (t_{AD} + t_{DSR})$	t_{acc}	−	−	540	ns
Data Setup Time (Read)	t_{DSR}	100	−	−	ns
Input Data Hold Time	t_H	10	−	−	ns
Output Data Hold Time	t_H	10	25	−	ns
Address Hold Time (Address, R/W, VMA)	t_{AH}	50	75	−	ns
Enable High Time for DBE Input	t_{EH}	450	−	−	ns
Data Delay Time (Write)	t_{DDW}	−	165	225	ns
Processor Controls*					
Processor Control Setup Time	t_{PCS}	200	−	−	ns
Processor Control Rise and Fall Time	t_{PCr}, t_{PCf}	−	−	100	ns
Bus Available Delay	t_{BA}	−	−	300	ns
Three State Enable	t_{TSE}	−	−	40	ns
Three State Delay	t_{TSD}	−	−	700	ns
Data Bus Enable Down Time During φ1 Up Time (Figure 3)	$t_{\overline{DBE}}$	150	−	−	ns
Data Bus Enable Delay (Figure 3)	t_{DBED}	300	−	−	ns
Data Bus Enable Rise and Fall Times (Figure 3)	t_{DBEr}, t_{DBEf}	−	−	25	ns

*Additional information is given in Figures 12 through 16 of the Family Characteristics — see pages 17 through 20.

FIGURE 2 – READ DATA FROM MEMORY OR PERIPHERALS

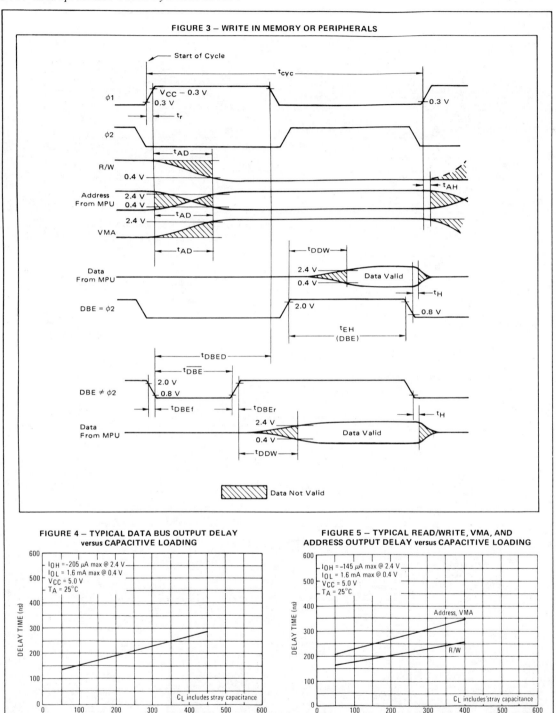

FIGURE 3 — WRITE IN MEMORY OR PERIPHERALS

FIGURE 4 — TYPICAL DATA BUS OUTPUT DELAY versus CAPACITIVE LOADING

FIGURE 5 — TYPICAL READ/WRITE, VMA, AND ADDRESS OUTPUT DELAY versus CAPACITIVE LOADING

MOTOROLA *Semiconductor Products Inc.*

FIGURE 6 – BUS TIMING TEST LOAD

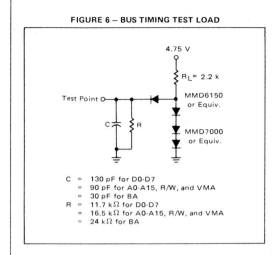

C = 130 pF for D0-D7
= 90 pF for A0-A15, R/W, and VMA
= 30 pF for BA
R = 11.7 kΩ for D0-D7
= 16.5 kΩ for A0-A15, R/W, and VMA
= 24 kΩ for BA

TYPICAL POWER SUPPLY CURRENT

FIGURE 7 – VARIATIONS WITH FREQUENCY

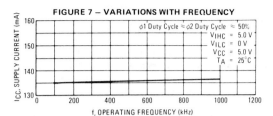

FIGURE 8 – VARIATIONS WITH TEMPERATURE

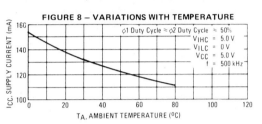

EXPANDED BLOCK DIAGRAM

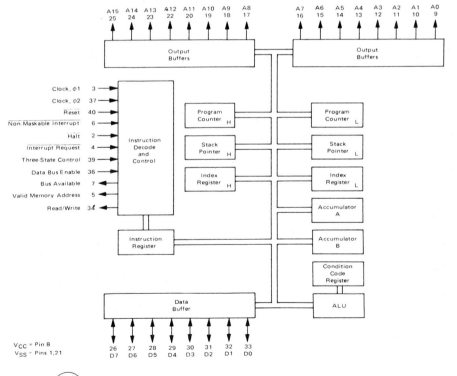

V_{CC} = Pin 8
V_{SS} = Pins 1,21

MOTOROLA *Semiconductor Products Inc.*

MPU SIGNAL DESCRIPTION

Proper operation of the MPU requires that certain control and timing signals be provided to accomplish specific functions and that other signal lines be monitored to determine the state of the processor.

Clocks Phase One and Phase Two ($\phi 1$, $\phi 2$) — Two pins are used for a two-phase non-overlapping clock that runs at the V_{CC} voltage level.

Address Bus (A0-A15) — Sixteen pins are used for the address bus. The outputs are three-state bus drivers capable of driving one standard TTL load and 130 pF. When the output is turned off, it is essentially an open circuit. This permits the MPU to be used in DMA applications.

Data Bus (D0-D7) — Eight pins are used for the data bus. It is bi-directional, transferring data to and from the memory and peripheral devices. It also has three-state output buffers capable of driving one standard TTL load and 130 pF.

Halt — When this input is in the low state, all activity in the machine will be halted. This input is level sensitive. In the halt mode, the machine will stop at the end of an instruction, Bus Available will be at a one level, Valid Memory Address will be at a zero, and all other three-state lines will be in the three-state mode.

Transition of the Halt line must not occur during the last 250 ns of phase one. To insure single instruction operation, the Halt line must go high for one Clock cycle.

Three-State Control (TSC) — This input causes all of the address lines and the Read/Write line to go into the off or high impedance state. This state will occur 700 ns after TSC = 2.0 V. The Valid Memory Address and Bus Available signals will be forced low. The data bus is not affected by TSC and has its own enable (Data Bus Enable). In DMA applications, the Three-State Control line should be brought high on the leading edge of the Phase One Clock. The $\phi 1$ clock must be held in the high state and the $\phi 2$ in the low state for this function to operate properly. The address bus will then be available for other devices to directly address memory. Since the MPU is a dynamic device, it can be held in this state for only 4.5 μs or destruction of data will occur in the MPU.

Read/Write (R/W) — This TTL compatible output signals the peripherals and memory devices whether the MPU is in a Read (high) or Write (low) state. The normal standby state of this signal is Read (high). Three-State Control going high will turn Read/Write to the off (high impedance) state. Also, when the processor is halted, it will be in the off state. This output is capable of driving one standard TTL load and 90 pF.

Valid Memory Address (VMA) — This output indicates to peripheral devices that there is a valid address on the address bus. In normal operation, this signal should be utilized for enabling peripheral interfaces such as the PIA and ACIA. This signal is not three-state. One standard TTL load and 90 pF may be directly driven by this active high signal.

Data Bus Enable (DBE) — This input is the three-state control signal for the MPU data bus and will enable the bus drivers when in the high state. This input is TTL compatible; however in normal operation, it would be driven by the phase two clock. During an MPU read cycle, the data bus drivers will be disabled internally. When it is desired that another device control the data bus such as in Direct Memory Access (DMA) applications, DBE should be held low.

Bus Available (BA) — The Bus Available signal will normally be in the low state; when activated, it will go to the high state indicating that the microprocessor has stopped and that the address bus is available. This will occur if the Halt line is in the low state or the processor is in the WAIT state as a result of the execution of a WAIT instruction. At such time, all three-state output drivers will go to their off state and other outputs to their normally inactive level. The processor is removed from the WAIT state by the occurrence of a maskable (mask bit I = 0) or nonmaskable interrupt. This output is capable of driving one standard TTL load and 30 pF.

Interrupt Request (IRQ) — This level sensitive input requests that an interrupt sequence be generated within the machine. The processor will wait until it completes the current instruction that is being executed before it recognizes the request. At that time, if the interrupt mask bit in the Condition Code Register is not set, the machine will begin an interrupt sequence. The Index Register, Program Counter, Accumulators, and Condition Code Register are stored away on the stack. Next the MPU will respond to the interrupt request by setting the interrupt mask bit high so that no further interrupts may occur. At the end of the cycle, a 16-bit address will be loaded that points to a vectoring address which is located in memory locations FFF8 and FFF9. An address loaded at these locations causes the MPU to branch to an interrupt routine in memory.

The Halt line must be in the high state for interrupts to be serviced. Interrupts will be latched internally while Halt is low.

The IRQ has a high impedance pullup device internal to the chip; however a 3 kΩ external resistor to V_{CC} should be used for wire-OR and optimum control of interrupts.

Reset — This input is used to reset and start the MPU from a power down condition, resulting from a power failure or an initial start-up of the processor. If a high level is detected on the input, this will signal the MPU to begin the restart sequence. This will start execution of a routine to initialize the processor from its reset condition. All the higher order address lines will be forced high. For the restart, the last two (FFFE, FFFF) locations in memory will be used to load the program that is addressed by the program counter. During the restart routine, the interrupt mask bit is set and must be reset before the MPU can be interrupted by IRQ.

 MOTOROLA *Semiconductor Products Inc.*

Figure 9 shows the initialization of the microprocessor after restart. Reset must be held low for at least eight clock periods after V_{CC} reaches 4.75 volts. If Reset goes high prior to the leading edge of $\phi2$, on the next $\phi1$ the first restart memory vector address (FFFE) will appear on the address lines. This location should contain the higher order eight bits to be stored into the program counter. Following, the next address FFFF should contain the lower order eight bits to be stored into the program counter.

Non-Maskable Interrupt (NMI) — A low-going edge on this input requests that a non-mask-interrupt sequence be generated within the processor. As with the Interrupt Request signal, the processor will complete the current instruction that is being executed before it recognizes the NMI signal. The interrupt mask bit in the Condition Code Register has no effect on NMI.

The Index Register, Program Counter, Accumulators, and Condition Code Register are stored away on the stack. At the end of the cycle, a 16-bit address will be loaded that points to a vectoring address which is located in memory locations FFFC and FFFD. An address loaded at these locations causes the MPU to branch to a non-maskable interrupt routine in memory.

NMI has a high impedance pullup resistor internal to the chip; however a 3 kΩ external resistor to V_{CC} should be used for wire-OR and optimum control of interrupts.

Inputs IRQ and NMI are hardware interrupt lines that are sampled during $\phi2$ and will start the interrupt routine on the $\phi1$ following the completion of an instruction.

Figure 10 is a flow chart describing the major decision paths and interrupt vectors of the microprocessor. Table 1 gives the memory map for interrupt vectors.

FIGURE 9 — INITIALIZATION OF MPU AFTER RESTART

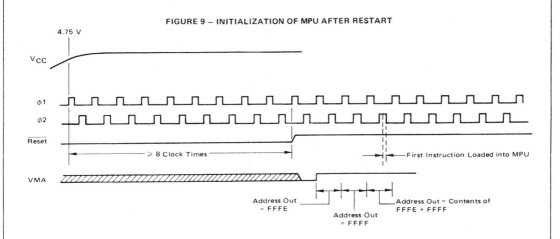

TABLE 1 — MEMORY MAP FOR INTERRUPT VECTORS

Vector MS	LS	Description
FFFE	FFFF	Restart
FFFC	FFFD	Non-maskable Interrupt
FFFA	FFFB	Software Interrupt
FFF8	FFF9	Interrupt Request

 MOTOROLA *Semiconductor Products Inc.*

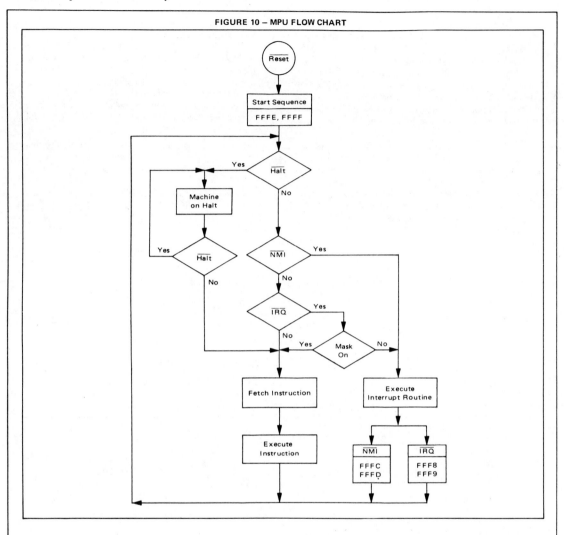

FIGURE 10 – MPU FLOW CHART

MPU REGISTERS

The MPU has three 16-bit registers and three 8-bit registers available for use by the programmer (Figure 11).

Program Counter – The program counter is a two byte (16-bits) register that points to the current program address.

Stack Pointer – The stack pointer is a two byte register that contains the address of the next available location in an external push-down/pop-up stack. This stack is normally a random access Read/Write memory that may

have any location (address) that is convenient. In those applications that require storage of information in the stack when power is lost, the stack must be non-volatile.

Index Register – The index register is a two byte register that is used to store data or a sixteen bit memory address for the Indexed mode of memory addressing.

Accumulators – The MPU contains two 8-bit accumulators that are used to hold operands and results from an arithmetic logic unit (ALU).

 MOTOROLA *Semiconductor Products Inc.*

FIGURE 11 – PROGRAMMING MODEL OF THE MICROPROCESSING UNIT

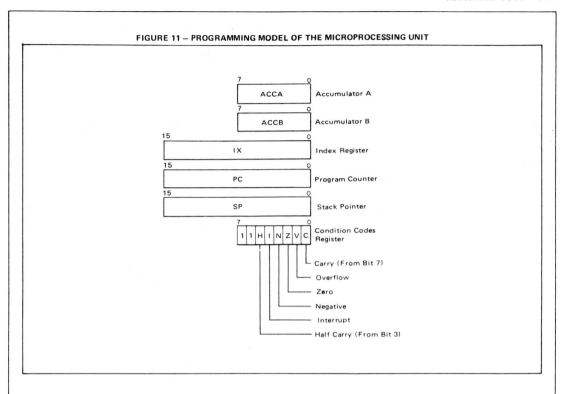

FIGURE 12 – SAVING THE STATUS OF THE MICROPROCESSOR IN THE STACK

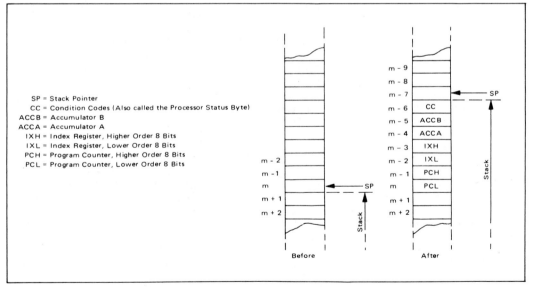

Condition Code Register – The condition code register indicates the results of an Arithmetic Logic Unit operation: Negative (N), Zero (Z), Overflow (V), Carry from bit 7 (C), and half carry from bit 3 (H). These bits of the Condition Code Register are used as testable conditions for the conditional branch instructions. Bit 4 is the interrupt mask bit (I). The unused bits of the Condition Code Register (b6 and b7) are ones.

Figure 12 shows the order of saving the microprocessor status within the stack.

MPU INSTRUCTION SET

The MC6800 has a set of 72 different instructions. Included are binary and decimal arithmetic, logical, shift, rotate, load, store, conditional or unconditional branch, interrupt and stack manipulation instructions (Tables 2 thru 6).

MPU ADDRESSING MODES

The MC6800 eight-bit microprocessing unit has seven address modes that can be used by a programmer, with the addressing mode a function of both the type of instruction and the coding within the instruction. A summary of the addressing modes for a particular instruction can be found in Table 7 along with the associated instruction execution time that is given in machine cycles. With a clock frequency of 1 MHz, these times would be microseconds.

Accumulator (ACCX) Addressing – In accumulator only addressing, either accumulator A or accumulator B is specified. These are one-byte instructions.

Immediate Addressing – In immediate addressing, the operand is contained in the second byte of the instruction except LDS and LDX which have the operand in the second and third bytes of the instruction. The MPU addresses

this location when it fetches the immediate instruction for execution. These are two or three-byte instructions.

Direct Addressing – In direct addressing, the address of the operand is contained in the second byte of the instruction. Direct addressing allows the user to directly address the lowest 256 bytes in the machine i.e., locations zero through 255. Enhanced execution times are achieved by storing data in these locations. In most configurations, it should be a random access memory. These are two-byte instructions.

Extended Addressing – In extended addressing, the address contained in the second byte of the instruction is used as the higher eight-bits of the address of the operand. The third byte of the instruction is used as the lower eight-bits of the address for the operand. This is an absolute address in memory. These are three-byte instructions.

Indexed Addressing – In indexed addressing, the address contained in the second byte of the instruction is added to the index register's lowest eight bits in the MPU. The carry is then added to the higher order eight bits of the index register. This result is then used to address memory. The modified address is held in a temporary address register so there is no change to the index register. These are two-byte instructions.

Implied Addressing – In the implied addressing mode the instruction gives the address (i.e., stack pointer, index register, etc.). These are one-byte instructions.

Relative Addressing – In relative addressing, the address contained in the second byte of the instruction is added to the program counter's lowest eight bits plus two. The carry or borrow is then added to the high eight bits. This allows the user to address data within a range of –125 to +129 bytes of the present instruction. These are two-byte instructions.

TABLE 2 – MICROPROCESSOR INSTRUCTION SET – ALPHABETIC SEQUENCE

ABA	Add Accumulators	CLR	Clear	PUL	Pull Data
ADC	Add with Carry	CLV	Clear Overflow	ROL	Rotate Left
ADD	Add	CMP	Compare	ROR	Rotate Right
AND	Logical And	COM	Complement	RTI	Return from Interrupt
ASL	Arithmetic Shift Left	CPX	Compare Index Register	RTS	Return from Subroutine
ASR	Arithmetic Shift Right	DAA	Decimal Adjust		
BCC	Branch if Carry Clear	DEC	Decrement	SBA	Subtract Accumulators
BCS	Branch if Carry Set	DES	Decrement Stack Pointer	SBC	Subtract with Carry
BEQ	Branch if Equal to Zero	DEX	Decrement Index Register	SEC	Set Carry
BGE	Branch if Greater or Equal Zero	EOR	Exclusive OR	SEI	Set Interrupt Mask
BGT	Branch if Greater than Zero	INC	Increment	SEV	Set Overflow
BHI	Branch if Higher	INS	Increment Stack Pointer	STA	Store Accumulator
BIT	Bit Test	INX	Increment Index Register	STS	Store Stack Register
BLE	Branch if Less or Equal	JMP	Jump	STX	Store Index Register
BLS	Branch if Lower or Same	JSR	Jump to Subroutine	SUB	Subtract
BLT	Branch if Less than Zero	LDA	Load Accumulator	SWI	Software Interrupt
BMI	Branch if Minus	LDS	Load Stack Pointer	TAB	Transfer Accumulators
BNE	Branch if Not Equal to Zero	LDX	Load Index Register	TAP	Transfer Accumulators to Condition Code Reg.
BPL	Branch if Plus	LSR	Logical Shift Right	TBA	Transfer Accumulators
BRA	Branch Always	NEG	Negate	TPA	Transfer Condition Code Reg. to Accumulator
BSR	Branch to Subroutine	NOP	No Operation	TST	Test
BVC	Branch if Overflow Clear	ORA	Inclusive OR Accumulator	TSX	Transfer Stack Pointer to Index Register
BVS	Branch if Overflow Set	PSH	Push Data	TXS	Transfer Index Register to Stack Pointer
CBA	Compare Accumulators			WAI	Wait for Interrupt
CLC	Clear Carry				
CLI	Clear Interrupt Mask				

TABLE 3 – ACCUMULATOR AND MEMORY INSTRUCTIONS

OPERATIONS	MNEMONIC	IMMED OP	~	=	DIRECT OP	~	=	INDEX OP	~	=	EXTND OP	~	=	IMPLIED OP	~	=	BOOLEAN/ARITHMETIC OPERATION (All register labels refer to contents)	H 5	I 4	N 3	Z 2	V 1	C 0
Add	ADDA	8B	2	2	9B	3	2	AB	5	2	BB	4	3				A + M · A	:	•	:	:	:	:
	ADDB	CB	2	2	DB	3	2	EB	5	2	FB	4	3				B + M · B	:	•	:	:	:	:
Add Acmltrs	ABA													1B	2	1	A + B · A	:	•	:	:	:	:
Add with Carry	ADCA	89	2	2	99	3	2	A9	5	2	B9	4	3				A + M + C · A	:	•	:	:	:	:
	ADCB	C9	2	2	D9	3	2	E9	5	2	F9	4	3				B + M + C · B	:	•	:	:	:	:
And	ANDA	84	2	2	94	3	2	A4	5	2	B4	4	3				A · M · A	•	•	:	:	R	•
	ANDB	C4	2	2	D4	3	2	E4	5	2	F4	4	3				B · M · B	•	•	:	:	R	•
Bit Test	BITA	85	2	2	95	3	2	A5	5	2	B5	4	3				A · M	•	•	:	:	R	•
	BITB	C5	2	2	D5	3	2	E5	5	2	F5	4	3				B · M	•	•	:	:	R	•
Clear	CLR							6F	7	2	7F	6	3				00 · M	•	•	R	S	R	R
	CLRA													4F	2	1	00 · A	•	•	R	S	R	R
	CLRB													5F	2	1	00 · B	•	•	R	S	R	R
Compare	CMPA	81	2	2	91	3	2	A1	5	2	B1	4	3				A − M	•	•	:	:	:	:
	CMPB	C1	2	2	D1	3	2	E1	5	2	F1	4	3				B − M	•	•	:	:	:	:
Compare Acmltrs	CBA													11	2	1	A − B	•	•	:	:	:	:
Complement, 1's	COM							63	7	2	73	6	3				M̄ · M	•	•	:	:	R	S
	COMA													43	2	1	Ā · A	•	•	:	:	R	S
	COMB													53	2	1	B̄ · B	•	•	:	:	R	S
Complement, 2's	NEG							60	7	2	70	6	3				00 − M · M	•	•	:	:	(1)	(2)
(Negate)	NEGA													40	2	1	00 − A · A	•	•	:	:	(1)	(2)
	NEGB													50	2	1	00 − B · B	•	•	:	:	(1)	(2)
Decimal Adjust, A	DAA													19	2	1	Converts Binary Add. of BCD Characters into BCD Format	•	•	:	:	:	(3)
Decrement	DEC							6A	7	2	7A	6	3				M − 1 · M	•	•	:	:	(4)	•
	DECA													4A	2	1	A − 1 · A	•	•	:	:	(4)	•
	DECB													5A	2	1	B − 1 · B	•	•	:	:	(4)	•
Exclusive OR	EORA	88	2	2	98	3	2	A8	5	2	B8	4	3				A ⊕ M · A	•	•	:	:	R	•
	EORB	C8	2	2	D8	3	2	E8	5	2	F8	4	3				B ⊕ M · B	•	•	:	:	R	•
Increment	INC							6C	7	2	7C	6	3				M + 1 · M	•	•	:	:	(5)	•
	INCA													4C	2	1	A + 1 · A	•	•	:	:	(5)	•
	INCB													5C	2	1	B + 1 · B	•	•	:	:	(5)	•
Load Acmltr	LDAA	86	2	2	96	3	2	A6	5	2	B6	4	3				M · A	•	•	:	:	R	•
	LDAB	C6	2	2	D6	3	2	E6	5	2	F6	4	3				M · B	•	•	:	:	R	•
Or, Inclusive	ORAA	8A	2	2	9A	3	2	AA	5	2	BA	4	3				A + M · A	•	•	:	:	R	•
	ORAB	CA	2	2	DA	3	2	EA	5	2	FA	4	3				B + M · B	•	•	:	:	R	•
Push Data	PSHA													36	4	1	A · M$_{SP}$, SP − 1 · SP	•	•	•	•	•	•
	PSHB													37	4	1	B · M$_{SP}$, SP − 1 · SP	•	•	•	•	•	•
Pull Data	PULA													32	4	1	SP + 1 · SP, M$_{SP}$ · A	•	•	•	•	•	•
	PULB													33	4	1	SP + 1 · SP, M$_{SP}$ · B	•	•	•	•	•	•
Rotate Left	ROL							69	7	2	79	6	3				M }	•	•	:	:	(6)	:
	ROLA													49	2	1	A } □ ← [b7 ...... b0] C	•	•	:	:	(6)	:
	ROLB													59	2	1	B }	•	•	:	:	(6)	:
Rotate Right	ROR							66	7	2	76	6	3				M }	•	•	:	:	(6)	:
	RORA													46	2	1	A } □ → [b7 ...... b0] C	•	•	:	:	(6)	:
	RORB													56	2	1	B }	•	•	:	:	(6)	:
Shift Left, Arithmetic	ASL							68	7	2	78	6	3				M }	•	•	:	:	(6)	:
	ASLA													48	2	1	A } □ ← [b7 ...... b0] ← 0 C	•	•	:	:	(6)	:
	ASLB													58	2	1	B }	•	•	:	:	(6)	:
Shift Right, Arithmetic	ASR							67	7	2	77	6	3				M }	•	•	:	:	(6)	:
	ASRA													47	2	1	A } [b7 ...... b0] → □ C	•	•	:	:	(6)	:
	ASRB													57	2	1	B }	•	•	:	:	(6)	:
Shift Right, Logic	LSR							64	7	2	74	6	3				M }	•	•	R	:	(6)	:
	LSRA													44	2	1	A } 0 → [b7 ...... b0] → □ C	•	•	R	:	(6)	:
	LSRB													54	2	1	B }	•	•	R	:	(6)	:
Store Acmltr.	STAA				97	4	2	A7	6	2	B7	5	3				A · M	•	•	:	:	R	•
	STAB				D7	4	2	E7	6	2	F7	5	3				B · M	•	•	:	:	R	•
Subtract	SUBA	80	2	2	90	3	2	A0	5	2	B0	4	3				A − M · A	•	•	:	:	:	:
	SUBB	C0	2	2	D0	3	2	E0	5	2	F0	4	3				B − M · B	•	•	:	:	:	:
Subtract Acmltrs.	SBA													10	2	1	A − B · A	•	•	:	:	:	:
Subtr. with Carry	SBCA	82	2	2	92	3	2	A2	5	2	B2	4	3				A − M − C · A	•	•	:	:	:	:
	SBCB	C2	2	2	D2	3	2	E2	5	2	F2	4	3				B − M − C · B	•	•	:	:	:	:
Transfer Acmltrs	TAB													16	2	1	A · B	•	•	:	:	R	•
	TBA													17	2	1	B · A	•	•	:	:	R	•
Test, Zero or Minus	TST							6D	7	2	7D	6	3				M − 00	•	•	:	:	R	R
	TSTA													4D	2	1	A − 00	•	•	:	:	R	R
	TSTB													5D	2	1	B − 00	•	•	:	:	R	R
																		H	I	N	Z	V	C

LEGEND:

- OP   Operation Code (Hexadecimal);
- ~   Number of MPU Cycles;
- =   Number of Program Bytes;
- +   Arithmetic Plus;
- −   Arithmetic Minus;
- ·   Boolean AND;
- M$_{SP}$ Contents of memory location pointed to be Stack Pointer;

- +   Boolean Inclusive OR;
- ⊙   Boolean Exclusive OR;
- M̄   Complement of M;
- ·   Transfer Into;
- 0   Bit = Zero;
- 00   Byte = Zero;

Note - Accumulator addressing mode instructions are included in the column for IMPLIED addressing

CONDITION CODE SYMBOLS:

- H   Half carry from bit 3;
- I   Interrupt mask
- N   Negative (sign bit)
- Z   Zero (byte)
- V   Overflow, 2's complement
- C   Carry from bit 7
- R   Reset Always
- S   Set Always
- :   Test and set if true, cleared otherwise
- •   Not Affected

TABLE 4 — INDEX REGISTER AND STACK MANIPULATION INSTRUCTIONS

POINTER OPERATIONS	MNEMONIC	IMMED OP	~	#	DIRECT OP	~	#	INDEX OP	~	#	EXTND OP	~	#	IMPLIED OP	~	#	BOOLEAN/ARITHMETIC OPERATION	H	I	N	Z	V	C
Compare Index Reg	CPX	8C	3	3	9C	4	2	AC	6	2	BC	5	3				$X_H - M, X_L - (M+1)$	•	•	⑦	↕	⑧	•
Decrement Index Reg	DEX													09	4	1	$X - 1 \rightarrow X$	•	•	•	↕	•	•
Decrement Stack Pntr	DES													34	4	1	$SP - 1 \rightarrow SP$	•	•	•	•	•	•
Increment Index Reg	INX													08	4	1	$X + 1 \rightarrow X$	•	•	•	↕	•	•
Increment Stack Pntr	INS													31	4	1	$SP + 1 \rightarrow SP$	•	•	•	•	•	•
Load Index Reg	LDX	CE	3	3	DE	4	2	EE	6	2	FE	5	3				$M \rightarrow X_H, (M+1) \rightarrow X_L$	•	•	⑨	↕	R	•
Load Stack Pntr	LDS	8E	3	3	9E	4	2	AE	6	2	BE	5	3				$M \rightarrow SP_H, (M+1) \rightarrow SP_L$	•	•	⑨	↕	R	•
Store Index Reg	STX				DF	5	2	EF	7	2	FF	6	3				$X_H \rightarrow M, X_L \rightarrow (M+1)$	•	•	⑨	↕	R	•
Store Stack Pntr	STS				9F	5	2	AF	7	2	BF	6	3				$SP_H \rightarrow M, SP_L \rightarrow (M+1)$	•	•	⑨	↕	R	•
Indx Reg → Stack Pntr	TXS													35	4	1	$X - 1 \rightarrow SP$	•	•	•	•	•	•
Stack Pntr → Indx Reg	TSX													30	4	1	$SP + 1 \rightarrow X$	•	•	•	•	•	•

TABLE 5 — JUMP AND BRANCH INSTRUCTIONS

OPERATIONS	MNEMONIC	RELATIVE OP	~	#	INDEX OP	~	#	EXTND OP	~	#	IMPLIED OP	~	#	BRANCH TEST	H	I	N	Z	V	C
Branch Always	BRA	20	4	2										None	•	•	•	•	•	•
Branch If Carry Clear	BCC	24	4	2										C = 0	•	•	•	•	•	•
Branch If Carry Set	BCS	25	4	2										C = 1	•	•	•	•	•	•
Branch If = Zero	BEQ	27	4	2										Z = 1	•	•	•	•	•	•
Branch If ≥ Zero	BGE	2C	4	2										N ⊕ V = 0	•	•	•	•	•	•
Branch If > Zero	BGT	2E	4	2										Z + (N ⊕ V) = 0	•	•	•	•	•	•
Branch If Higher	BHI	22	4	2										C + Z = 0	•	•	•	•	•	•
Branch If ≤ Zero	BLE	2F	4	2										Z + (N ⊕ V) = 1	•	•	•	•	•	•
Branch If Lower Or Same	BLS	23	4	2										C + Z = 1	•	•	•	•	•	•
Branch If < Zero	BLT	2D	4	2										N ⊕ V = 1	•	•	•	•	•	•
Branch If Minus	BMI	2B	4	2										N = 1	•	•	•	•	•	•
Branch If Not Equal Zero	BNE	26	4	2										Z = 0	•	•	•	•	•	•
Branch If Overflow Clear	BVC	28	4	2										V = 0	•	•	•	•	•	•
Branch If Overflow Set	BVS	29	4	2										V = 1	•	•	•	•	•	•
Branch If Plus	BPL	2A	4	2										N = 0	•	•	•	•	•	•
Branch To Subroutine	BSR	8D	8	2											•	•	•	•	•	•
Jump	JMP				6E	4	2	7E	3	3				See Special Operations	•	•	•	•	•	•
Jump To Subroutine	JSR				AD	8	2	BD	9	3					•	•	•	•	•	•
No Operation	NOP										01	2	1	Advances Prog. Cntr. Only	•	•	•	•	•	•
Return From Interrupt	RTI										3B	10	1		⑩					
Return From Subroutine	RTS										39	5	1	See Special Operations	•	•	•	•	•	•
Software Interrupt	SWI										3F	12	1		•	•	•	•	•	•
Wait for Interrupt*	WAI										3E	9	1		•	⑪	•	•	•	•

*WAI puts Address Bus, R/W, and Data Bus in the three-state mode while VMA is held low.

SPECIAL OPERATIONS

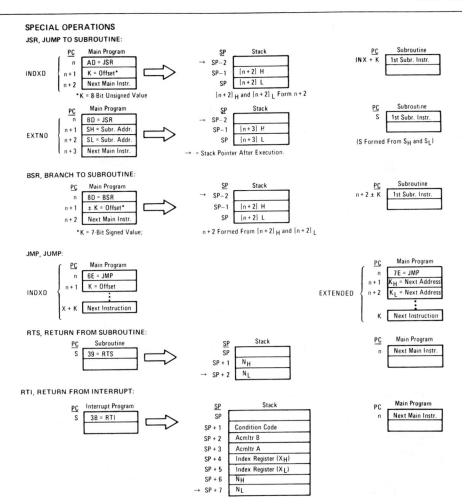

JSR, JUMP TO SUBROUTINE:

INDXD

PC	Main Program
n	AD = JSR
n + 1	K = Offset*
n + 2	Next Main Instr.

*K = 8-Bit Unsigned Value

SP	Stack
→ SP–2	
SP–1	[n + 2] H
SP	[n + 2] L

[n + 2] H and [n + 2] L Form n + 2

PC	Subroutine
INX + K	1st Subr. Instr.

EXTND

PC	Main Program
n	BD = JSR
n + 1	SH = Subr. Addr.
n + 2	SL = Subr. Addr.
n + 3	Next Main Instr.

SP	Stack
→ SP–2	
SP–1	[n + 3] H
SP	[n + 3] L

→ = Stack Pointer After Execution.

PC	Subroutine
S	1st Subr. Instr.

(S Formed From S_H and S_L)

BSR, BRANCH TO SUBROUTINE:

PC	Main Program
n	8D = BSR
n + 1	± K = Offset*
n + 2	Next Main Instr.

*K = 7-Bit Signed Value;

SP	Stack
→ SP–2	
SP–1	[n + 2] H
SP	[n + 2] L

n + 2 Formed From [n + 2] H and [n + 2] L

PC	Subroutine
n + 2 ± K	1st Subr. Instr.

JMP, JUMP:

INDXD

PC	Main Program
n	6E = JMP
n + 1	K = Offset
⋮	
X + K	Next Instruction

EXTENDED

PC	Main Program
n	7E = JMP
n + 1	K_H = Next Address
n + 2	K_L = Next Address
⋮	
K	Next Instruction

RTS, RETURN FROM SUBROUTINE:

PC	Subroutine
S	39 = RTS

SP	Stack
SP	
SP + 1	N_H
→ SP + 2	N_L

PC	Main Program
n	Next Main Instr.

RTI, RETURN FROM INTERRUPT:

PC	Interrupt Program
S	3B = RTI

SP	Stack
SP	
SP + 1	Condition Code
SP + 2	Acmltr B
SP + 3	Acmltr A
SP + 4	Index Register (X_H)
SP + 5	Index Register (X_L)
SP + 6	N_H
→ SP + 7	N_L

PC	Main Program
n	Next Main Instr.

TABLE 6 – CONDITION CODE REGISTER MANIPULATION INSTRUCTIONS

OPERATIONS	MNEMONIC	IMPLIED OP	IMPLIED ~	IMPLIED ≠	BOOLEAN OPERATION	5 H	4 I	3 N	2 Z	1 V	0 C
Clear Carry	CLC	0C	2	1	0 → C	●	●	●	●	●	R
Clear Interrupt Mask	CLI	0E	2	1	0 → I	●	R	●	●	●	●
Clear Overflow	CLV	0A	2	1	0 → V	●	●	●	●	R	●
Set Carry	SEC	0D	2	1	1 → C	●	●	●	●	●	S
Set Interrupt Mask	SEI	0F	2	1	1 → I	●	S	●	●	●	●
Set Overflow	SEV	0B	2	1	1 → V	●	●	●	●	S	●
Acmltr A → CCR	TAP	06	2	1	A → CCR	⎯⎯⎯⎯⎯⎯⎯ (12) ⎯⎯⎯⎯⎯⎯⎯					
CCR → Acmltr A	TPA	07	2	1	CCR → A	●	●	●	●	●	●

COND. CODE REG.

CONDITION CODE REGISTER NOTES: (Bit set if test is true and cleared otherwise)

1 (Bit V) Test: Result = 10000000?
2 (Bit C) Test: Result = 00000000?
3 (Bit C) Test: Decimal value of most significant BCD Character greater than nine? (Not cleared if previously set.)
4 (Bit V) Test: Operand = 10000000 prior to execution?
5 (Bit V) Test: Operand = 01111111 prior to execution?
6 (Bit V) Test: Set equal to result of N⊕C after shift has occurred.

7 (Bit N) Test: Sign bit of most significant (MS) byte = 1?
8 (Bit V) Test: 2's complement overflow from subtraction of MS bytes?
9 (Bit N) Test: Result less than zero? (Bit 15 = 1)
10 (All) Load Condition Code Register from Stack. (See Special Operations)
11 (Bit I) Set when interrupt occurs. If previously set, a Non-Maskable Interrupt is required to exit the wait state.
12 (All) Set according to the contents of Accumulator A.

TABLE 7 – INSTRUCTION ADDRESSING MODES AND ASSOCIATED EXECUTION TIMES
(Times in Machine Cycles)

	(Dual Operand) ACCX	Immediate	Direct	Extended	Indexed	Implied	Relative
ABA	•	•	•	•	•	2	•
ADC	x	2	3	4	5	•	•
ADD	x	2	3	4	5	•	•
AND	x	2	3	4	5	•	•
ASL	2	•	•	6	7	•	•
ASR	2	•	•	6	7	•	•
BCC	•	•	•	•	•	•	4
BCS	•	•	•	•	•	•	4
BEA	•	•	•	•	•	•	4
BGE	•	•	•	•	•	•	4
BGT	•	•	•	•	•	•	4
BHI	•	•	•	•	•	•	4
BIT	x	2	3	4	5	•	•
BLE	•	•	•	•	•	•	4
BLS	•	•	•	•	•	•	4
BLT	•	•	•	•	•	•	4
BMI	•	•	•	•	•	•	4
BNE	•	•	•	•	•	•	4
BPL	•	•	•	•	•	•	4
BRA	•	•	•	•	•	•	4
BSR	•	•	•	•	•	•	8
BVC	•	•	•	•	•	•	4
BVS	•	•	•	•	•	•	4
CBA	•	•	•	•	•	2	•
CLC	•	•	•	•	•	2	•
CLI	•	•	•	•	•	2	•
CLR	2	•	•	6	7	•	•
CLV	•	•	•	•	•	2	•
CMP	x	2	3	4	5	•	•
COM	2	•	•	6	7	•	•
CPX	•	3	4	5	6	•	•
DAA	•	•	•	•	•	2	•
DEC	2	•	•	6	7	•	•
DES	•	•	•	•	•	4	•
DEX	•	•	•	•	•	4	•
EOR	x	2	3	4	5	•	•

	(Dual Operand) ACCX	Immediate	Direct	Extended	Indexed	Implied
INC	2	•	•	6	7	•
INS	•	•	•	•	•	4
INX	•	•	•	•	•	4
JMP	•	•	•	3	4	•
JSR	•	•	•	9	8	•
LDA	x	2	3	4	5	•
LDS	•	3	4	5	6	•
LDX	•	3	4	5	6	•
LSR	2	•	•	6	7	•
NEG	2	•	•	6	7	•
NOP	•	•	•	•	•	2
ORA	x	2	3	4	5	•
PSH	•	•	•	•	•	4
PUL	•	•	•	•	•	4
ROL	2	•	•	6	7	•
ROR	2	•	•	6	7	•
RTI	•	•	•	•	•	10
RTS	•	•	•	•	•	5
SBA	•	•	•	•	•	2
SBC	x	2	3	4	5	•
SEC	•	•	•	•	•	2
SEI	•	•	•	•	•	2
SEV	•	•	•	•	•	2
STA	x	•	4	5	6	•
STS	•	•	5	6	7	•
STX	•	•	5	6	7	•
SUB	x	2	3	4	5	•
SWI	•	•	•	•	•	12
TAB	•	•	•	•	•	2
TAP	•	•	•	•	•	2
TBA	•	•	•	•	•	2
TPA	•	•	•	•	•	2
TST	2	•	•	6	7	•
TSX	•	•	•	•	•	4
TSX	•	•	•	•	•	4
WAI	•	•	•	•	•	9

NOTE: Interrupt time is 12 cycles from the end of the instruction being executed, except following a WAI instruction. Then it is 4 cycles.

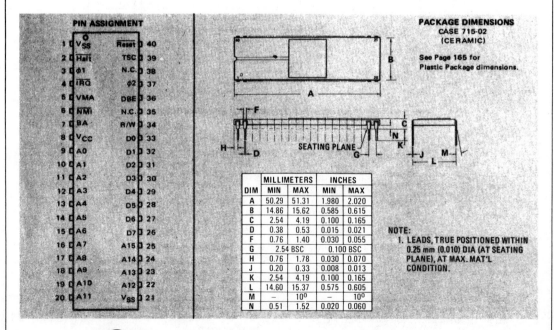

PIN ASSIGNMENT

1	V_SS	Reset	40
2	Halt	TSC	39
3	φ1	N.C.	38
4	IRQ	φ2	37
5	VMA	DBE	36
6	NMI	N.C.	35
7	BA	R/W	34
8	V_CC	D0	33
9	A0	D1	32
10	A1	D2	31
11	A2	D3	30
12	A3	D4	29
13	A4	D5	28
14	A5	D6	27
15	A6	D7	26
16	A7	A15	25
17	A8	A14	24
18	A9	A13	23
19	A10	A12	22
20	A11	V_SS	21

PACKAGE DIMENSIONS
CASE 715-02
(CERAMIC)

See Page 165 for Plastic Package dimensions.

DIM	MILLIMETERS		INCHES	
	MIN	MAX	MIN	MAX
A	50.29	51.31	1.980	2.020
B	14.86	15.62	0.585	0.615
C	2.54	4.19	0.100	0.165
D	0.38	0.53	0.015	0.021
F	0.76	1.40	0.030	0.055
G	2.54 BSC		0.100 BSC	
H	0.76	1.78	0.030	0.070
J	0.20	0.33	0.008	0.013
K	2.54	4.19	0.100	0.165
L	14.60	15.37	0.575	0.605
M	—	10°	—	10°
N	0.51	1.52	0.020	0.060

NOTE:
1. LEADS, TRUE POSITIONED WITHIN 0.25 mm (0.010) DIA (AT SEATING PLANE), AT MAX. MAT'L CONDITION.

 MOTOROLA *Semiconductor Products Inc.*

SUMMARY OF CYCLE BY CYCLE OPERATION

Table 8 provides a detailed description of the information present on the Address Bus, Data Bus, Valid Memory Address line (VMA), and the Read/Write line (R/W) during each cycle for each instruction.

This information is useful in comparing actual with expected results during debug of both software and hardware as the control program is executed. The information is categorized in groups according to Addressing Mode and Number of Cycles per instruction. (In general, instructions with the same Addressing Mode and Number of Cycles execute in the same manner; exceptions are indicated in the table.)

TABLE 8 – OPERATION SUMMARY

Address Mode and Instructions	Cycles	Cycle #	VMA Line	Address Bus	R/W Line	Data Bus
IMMEDIATE						
ADC EOR ADD LDA AND ORA BIT SBC CMP SUB	2	1	1	Op Code Address	1	Op Code
		2	1	Op Code Address + 1	1	Operand Data
CPX LDS LDX	3	1	1	Op Code Address	1	Op Code
		2	1	Op Code Address + 1	1	Operand Data (High Order Byte)
		3	1	Op Code Address + 2	1	Operand Data (Low Order Byte)
DIRECT						
ADC EOR ADD LDA AND ORA BIT SBC CMP SUB	3	1	1	Op Code Address	1	Op Code
		2	1	Op Code Address + 1	1	Address of Operand
		3	1	Address of Operand	1	Operand Data
CPX LDS LDX	4	1	1	Op Code Address	1	Op Code
		2	1	Op Code Address + 1	1	Address of Operand
		3	1	Address of Operand	1	Operand Data (High Order Byte)
		4	1	Operand Address + 1	1	Operand Data (Low Order Byte)
STA	4	1	1	Op Code Address	1	Op Code
		2	1	Op Code Address + 1	1	Destination Address
		3	0	Destination Address	1	Irrelevant Data (Note 1)
		4	1	Destination Address	0	Data from Accumulator
STS STX	5	1	1	Op Code Address	1	Op Code
		2	1	Op Code Address + 1	1	Address of Operand
		3	0	Address of Operand	1	Irrelevant Data (Note 1)
		4	1	Address of Operand	0	Register Data (High Order Byte)
		5	1	Address of Operand + 1	0	Register Data (Low Order Byte)
INDEXED						
JMP	4	1	1	Op Code Address	1	Op Code
		2	1	Op Code Address + 1	1	Offset
		3	0	Index Register	1	Irrelevant Data (Note 1)
		4	0	Index Register Plus Offset (w/o Carry)	1	Irrelevant Data (Note 1)
ADC EOR ADD LDA AND ORA BIT SBC CMP SUB	5	1	1	Op Code Address	1	Op Code
		2	1	Op Code Address + 1	1	Offset
		3	0	Index Register	1	Irrelevant Data (Note 1)
		4	0	Index Register Plus Offset (w/o Carry)	1	Irrelevant Data (Note 1)
		5	1	Index Register Plus Offset	1	Operand Data
CPX LDS LDX	6	1	1	Op Code Address	1	Op Code
		2	1	Op Code Address + 1	1	Offset
		3	0	Index Register	1	Irrelevant Data (Note 1)
		4	0	Index Register Plus Offset (w/o Carry)	1	Irrelevant Data (Note 1)
		5	1	Index Register Plus Offset	1	Operand Data (High Order Byte)
		6	1	Index Register Plus Offset + 1	1	Operand Data (Low Order Byte)

 MOTOROLA *Semiconductor Products Inc.*

Address Mode and Instructions	Cycles	Cycle #	VMA Line	Address Bus	R/W Line	Data Bus
INDEXED (Continued)						
STA	6	1	1	Op Code Address	1	Op Code
		2	1	Op Code Address + 1	1	Offset
		3	0	Index Register	1	Irrelevant Data (Note 1)
		4	0	Index Register Plus Offset (w/o Carry)	1	Irrelevant Data (Note 1)
		5	0	Index Register Plus Offset	1	Irrelevant Data (Note 1)
		6	1	Index Register Plus Offset	0	Operand Data
ASL LSR ASR NEG CLR ROL COM ROR DEC TST INC	7	1	1	Op Code Address	1	Op Code
		2	1	Op Code Address + 1	1	Offset
		3	0	Index Register	1	Irrelevant Data (Note 1)
		4	0	Index Register Plus Offset (w/o Carry)	1	Irrelevant Data (Note 1)
		5	1	Index Register Plus Offset	1	Current Operand Data
		6	0	Index Register Plus Offset	1	Irrelevant Data (Note 1)
		7	1/0 (Note 3)	Index Register Plus Offset	0	New Operand Data (Note 3)
STS STX	7	1	1	Op Code Address	1	Op Code
		2	1	Op Code Address + 1	1	Offset
		3	0	Index Register	1	Irrelevant Data (Note 1)
		4	0	Index Register Plus Offset (w/o Carry)	1	Irrelevant Data (Note 1)
		5	0	Index Register Plus Offset	1	Irrelevant Data (Note 1)
		6	1	Index Register Plus Offset	0	Operand Data (High Order Byte)
		7	1	Index Register Plus Offset + 1	0	Operand Data (Low Order Byte)
JSR	8	1	1	Op Code Address	1	Op Code
		2	1	Op Code Address + 1	1	Offset
		3	0	Index Register	1	Irrelevant Data (Note 1)
		4	1	Stack Pointer	0	Return Address (Low Order Byte)
		5	1	Stack Pointer − 1	0	Return Address (High Order Byte)
		6	0	Stack Pointer − 2	1	Irrelevant Data (Note 1)
		7	0	Index Register	1	Irrelevant Data (Note 1)
		8	0	Index Register Plus Offset (w/o Carry)	1	Irrelevant Data (Note 1)
EXTENDED						
JMP	3	1	1	Op Code Address	1	Op Code
		2	1	Op Code Address + 1	1	Jump Address (High Order Byte)
		3	1	Op Code Address + 2	1	Jump Address (Low Order Byte)
ADC EOR ADD LDA AND ORA BIT SBC CMP SUB	4	1	1	Op Code Address	1	Op Code
		2	1	Op Code Address + 1	1	Address of Operand (High Order Byte)
		3	1	Op Code Address + 2	1	Address of Operand (Low Order Byte)
		4	1	Address of Operand	1	Operand Data
CPX LDS LDX	5	1	1	Op Code Address	1	Op Code
		2	1	Op Code Address + 1	1	Address of Operand (High Order Byte)
		3	1	Op Code Address + 2	1	Address of Operand (Low Order Byte)
		4	1	Address of Operand	1	Operand Data (High Order Byte)
		5	1	Address of Operand + 1	1	Operand Data (Low Order Byte)
STA A STA B	5	1	1	Op Code Address	1	Op Code
		2	1	Op Code Address + 1	1	Destination Address (High Order Byte)
		3	1	Op Code Address + 2	1	Destination Address (Low Order Byte)
		4	0	Operand Destination Address	1	Irrelevant Data (Note 1)
		5	1	Operand Destination Address	0	Data from Accumulator
ASL LSR ASR NEG CLR ROL COM ROR DEC TST INC	6	1	1	Op Code Address	1	Op Code
		2	1	Op Code Address + 1	1	Address of Operand (High Order Byte)
		3	1	Op Code Address + 2	1	Address of Operand (Low Order Byte)
		4	1	Address of Operand	1	Current Operand Data
		5	0	Address of Operand	1	Irrelevant Data (Note 1)
		6	1/0 (Note 3)	Address of Operand	0	New Operand Data (Note 3)

TABLE 8 — OPERATION SUMMARY (Continued)

Address Mode and Instructions	Cycles	Cycle #	VMA Line	Address Bus	R/W Line	Data Bus
TABLE 8 – OPERATION SUMMARY (Continued)						
EXTENDED (Continued)						
STS STX	6	1	1	Op Code Address	1	Op Code
		2	1	Op Code Address + 1	1	Address of Operand (High Order Byte)
		3	1	Op Code Address + 2	1	Address of Operand (Low Order Byte)
		4	0	Address of Operand	1	Irrelevant Data (Note 1)
		5	1	Address of Operand	0	Operand Data (High Order Byte)
		6	1	Address of Operand + 1	0	Operand Data (Low Order Byte)
JSR	9	1	1	Op Code Address	1	Op Code
		2	1	Op Code Address + 1	1	Address of Subroutine (High Order Byte)
		3	1	Op Code Address + 2	1	Address of Subroutine (Low Order Byte)
		4	1	Subroutine Starting Address	1	Op Code of Next Instruction
		5	1	Stack Pointer	0	Return Address (Low Order Byte)
		6	1	Stack Pointer − 1	0	Return Address (High Order Byte)
		7	0	Stack Pointer − 2	1	Irrelevant Data (Note 1)
		8	0	Op Code Address + 2	1	Irrelevant Data (Note 1)
		9	1	Op Code Address + 2	1	Address of Subroutine (Low Order Byte)
INHERENT						
ABA DAA SEC ASL DEC SEI ASR INC SEV CBA LSR TAB CLC NEG TAP CLI NOP TBA CLR ROL TPA CLV ROR TST COM SBA	2	1	1	Op Code Address	1	Op Code
		2	1	Op Code Address + 1	1	Op Code of Next Instruction
DES DEX INS INX	4	1	1	Op Code Address	1	Op Code
		2	1	Op Code Address + 1	1	Op Code of Next Instruction
		3	0	Previous Register Contents	1	Irrelevant Data (Note 1)
		4	0	New Register Contents	1	Irrelevant Data (Note 1)
PSH	4	1	1	Op Code Address	1	Op Code
		2	1	Op Code Address + 1	1	Op Code of Next Instruction
		3	1	Stack Pointer	0	Accumulator Data
		4	0	Stack Pointer − 1	1	Accumulator Data
PUL	4	1	1	Op Code Address	1	Op Code
		2	1	Op Code Address + 1	1	Op Code of Next Instruction
		3	0	Stack Pointer	1	Irrelevant Data (Note 1)
		4	1	Stack Pointer + 1	1	Operand Data from Stack
TSX	4	1	1	Op Code Address	1	Op Code
		2	1	Op Code Address + 1	1	Op Code of Next Instruction
		3	0	Stack Pointer	1	Irrelevant Data (Note 1)
		4	0	New Index Register	1	Irrelevant Data (Note 1)
TXS	4	1	1	Op Code Address	1	Op Code
		2	1	Op Code Address + 1	1	Op Code of Next Instruction
		3	0	Index Register	1	Irrelevant Data
		4	0	New Stack Pointer	1	Irrelevant Data
RTS	5	1	1	Op Code Address	1	Op Code
		2	1	Op Code Address + 1	1	Irrelevant Data (Note 2)
		3	0	Stack Pointer	1	Irrelevant Data (Note 1)
		4	1	Stack Pointer + 1	1	Address of Next Instruction (High Order Byte)
		5	1	Stack Pointer + 2	1	Address of Next Instruction (Low Order Byte)

 MOTOROLA *Semiconductor Products Inc.*

TABLE 8 – OPERATION SUMMARY (Continued)

Address Mode and Instructions	Cycles	Cycle #	VMA Line	Address Bus	R/W Line	Data Bus
INHERENT (Continued)						
WAI		1	1	Op Code Address	1	Op Code
		2	1	Op Code Address + 1	1	Op Code of Next Instruction
		3	1	Stack Pointer	0	Return Address (Low Order Byte)
		4	1	Stack Pointer − 1	0	Return Address (High Order Byte)
	9	5	1	Stack Pointer − 2	0	Index Register (Low Order Byte)
		6	1	Stack Pointer − 3	0	Index Register (High Order Byte)
		7	1	Stack Pointer − 4	0	Contents of Accumulator A
		8	1	Stack Pointer − 5	0	Contents of Accumulator B
		9	1	Stack Pointer − 6 (Note 4)	1	Contents of Cond. Code Register
RTI		1	1	Op Code Address	1	Op Code
		2	1	Op Code Address + 1	1	Irrelevant Data (Note 2)
		3	0	Stack Pointer	1	Irrelevant Data (Note 1)
		4	1	Stack Pointer + 1	1	Contents of Cond. Code Register from Stack
	10	5	1	Stack Pointer + 2	1	Contents of Accumulator B from Stack
		6	1	Stack Pointer + 3	1	Contents of Accumulator A from Stack
		7	1	Stack Pointer + 4	1	Index Register from Stack (High Order Byte)
		8	1	Stack Pointer + 5	1	Index Register from Stack (Low Order Byte)
		9	1	Stack Pointer + 6	1	Next Instruction Address from Stack (High Order Byte)
		10	1	Stack Pointer + 7	1	Next Instruction Address from Stack (Low Order Byte)
SWI		1	1	Op Code Address	1	Op Code
		2	1	Op Code Address + 1	1	Irrelevant Data (Note 1)
		3	1	Stack Pointer	0	Return Address (Low Order Byte)
		4	1	Stack Pointer − 1	0	Return Address (High Order Byte)
		5	1	Stack Pointer − 2	0	Index Register (Low Order Byte)
	12	6	1	Stack Pointer − 3	0	Index Register (High Order Byte)
		7	1	Stack Pointer − 4	0	Contents of Accumulator A
		8	1	Stack Pointer − 5	0	Contents of Accumulator B
		9	1	Stack Pointer − 6	0	Contents of Cond. Code Register
		10	0	Stack Pointer − 7	1	Irrelevant Data (Note 1)
		11	1	Vector Address FFFA (Hex)	1	Address of Subroutine (High Order Byte)
		12	1	Vector Address FFFB (Hex)	1	Address of Subroutine (Low Order Byte)
RELATIVE						
BCC BHI BNE BCS BLE BPL BEQ BLS BRA BGE BLT BVC BGT BMI BVS	4	1	1	Op Code Address	1	Op Code
		2	1	Op Code Address + 1	1	Branch Offset
		3	0	Op Code Address + 2	1	Irrelevant Data (Note 1)
		4	0	Branch Address	1	Irrelevant Data (Note 1)
BSR		1	1	Op Code Address	1	Op Code
		2	1	Op Code Address + 1	1	Branch Offset
		3	0	Return Address of Main Program	1	Irrelevant Data (Note 1)
	8	4	1	Stack Pointer	0	Return Address (Low Order Byte)
		5	1	Stack Pointer − 1	0	Return Address (High Order Byte)
		6	0	Stack Pointer − 2	1	Irrelevant Data (Note 1)
		7	0	Return Address of Main Program	1	Irrelevant Data (Note 1)
		8	0	Subroutine Address	1	Irrelevant Data (Note 1)

Note 1. If device which is addressed during this cycle uses VMA, then the Data Bus will go to the high impedance three-state condition. Depending on bus capacitance, data from the previous cycle may be retained on the Data Bus.
Note 2. Data is ignored by the MPU.
Note 3. For TST, VMA = 0 and Operand data does not change.
Note 4. While the MPU is waiting for the interrupt, Bus Available will go high indicating the following states of the control lines: VMA is low; Address Bus, R/W, and Data Bus are all in the high impedance state.

 MOTOROLA *Semiconductor Products Inc.*

Appendix D The Advanced Micro Devices AmZ8002 16-bit microprocessor

PRELIMINARY DATA

DISTINCTIVE CHARACTERISTICS

- Sixteen general purpose registers
- Direct addressing up to 64KB memory
- Software compatible with AmZ8001 microprocessor
- Powerful instructions with flexible addressing modes
- Privileged/Non-Privileged mode of operation
- Sophisticated interrupt structure
- On-chip memory refresh facility
- TTL compatible inputs and outputs
- Single phase clock
- Single +5V power supply
- 40-pin package

GENERAL DESCRIPTION

The AmZ8002 is a general-purpose 16-bit CPU belonging to the AmZ8000 family of microprocessors. Its architecture is centered around sixteen 16-bit general registers. The CPU deals with 16-bit address spaces and hence can address directly 64 Kilobytes of memory. Facilities are provided to maintain three distinct address spaces – code, data and stack. The AmZ8002 implements a powerful instruction set with flexible addressing modes. These instructions operate on several data types – bit, byte, word (16-bit), long word (32-bit), byte string and word string. The CPU can execute instructions in one of two modes – System and Normal. Sometimes these modes are also known as Privileged and Non-Privileged, respectively. The CPU also contains an on-chip memory refresh facility. The AmZ8002 is software compatible with the AmZ8001 microprocessor. The AmZ8002 is fabricated using silicon-gate N-MOS technology and is packaged in a 40-pin DIP. The AmZ8002 requires a single +5 power supply and a single phase clock for its operation.

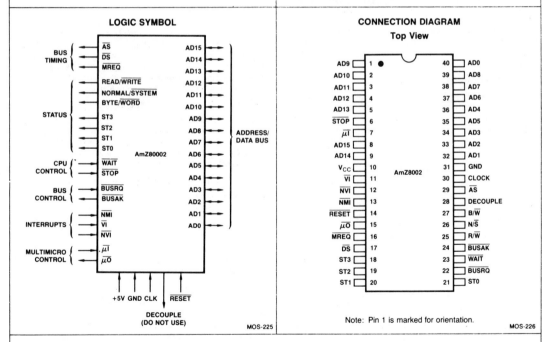

LOGIC SYMBOL

CONNECTION DIAGRAM
Top View

Note: Pin 1 is marked for orientation.

MOS-225

MOS-226

ORDERING INFORMATION

Package Type	Ambient Temperature	Maximum Clock Frequency
		4MHz
Hermetic DIP	0°C ≤ T_A ≤ 70°C	AmZ8002DC

INTERFACE SIGNAL DESCRIPTION

V_CC: +5V Power Supply

V_SS: Ground

AD0-AD15: Address/Data Bus (Bidirectional, 3-State)

This 16-bit multiplexed address/data bus is used for all I/O and memory transactions. HIGH on the bus corresponds to 1 and LOW corresponds to 0. AD0 is the least significant bit position with AD15 the most significant. The $\overline{AS}$ output and $\overline{DS}$ output will indicate whether the bus is used for address or data. The status output lines ST0-ST3 will indicate the type of transaction; memory or I/O.

$\overline{AS}$: Address Strobe (Output, 3-State)

LOW on this output indicates that the AD0-AD15 bus contains address information. The address information is stable by the time of the LOW-to-HIGH transition of the $\overline{AS}$ output (see timing diagrams). The status outputs ST0-ST3 indicate whether the bus contains a memory address or I/O address.

$\overline{DS}$: Data Strobe (Output, 3-State)

LOW on this output indicates that the AD0-AD15 bus is being used for data transfer. The R/$\overline{W}$ output indicates the direction of data transfer − read (or in) means data into the CPU and write (or out) means data from the CPU. During a read operation, data can be gated on to the bus when $\overline{DS}$ goes LOW. A LOW-to-HIGH transition on the $\overline{DS}$ output indicates that the CPU has accepted the data (see timing diagram). During a write operation, LOW on the $\overline{DS}$ output indicates that data is setup on the bus. Data will be removed sometime after the LOW-to-HIGH transition of the $\overline{DS}$ output (see timing diagram).

R/$\overline{W}$: Read/Write (Output, 3-State)

This output indicates the direction of data flow on the AD0-AD15 bus. HIGH indicates a read operation, i.e., data into the CPU and LOW indicates a write operation, i.e., data from the CPU. This output is activated at the same time as $\overline{AS}$ going LOW and remains stable for the duration of the whole transaction (see timing diagram).

B/$\overline{W}$: Byte/Word (Output, 3-State)

This output indicates the type of data transferred on the AD0-AD15 bus. HIGH indicates byte (8-bit) and LOW indicates word (16-bit) transfer. This output is activated at the same stage as $\overline{AS}$ going LOW and remains valid for the duration of the whole transaction (see timing diagram). The address generated by the CPU is always a byte address. However, the memory is organized as 16-bit words. All instructions and word operands are word aligned and are addressed by even addresses. Thus, for all word transactions with the memory the least significant address bit will be zero. When addressing the memory for byte transactions, the least significant address bit determines which byte of the memory word is needed; even address specifies the most significant byte and odd address specifies the least significant byte. In the case of I/O transactions, the address information on the AD0-AD15 bus refers to an I/O port and B/$\overline{W}$ determines whether a data word or data byte will be transacted. During I/O byte transactions, the least significant address bit A0 determines which half of the AD0-AD15 bus will be used for the I/O transactions. The ST0-ST3 outputs will indicate whether the current transaction is for memory, normal I/O or special I/O.

ST0-ST3: Status (Outputs, 3-State)

These four outputs contain information regarding the current transaction in a coded form. The status line codes are shown in the following table:

ST3	ST2	ST1	ST0	
L	L	L	L	Internal Operation
L	L	L	H	Memory Refresh
L	L	H	L	Normal I/O Transaction
L	L	H	H	Special I/O Transaction
L	H	L	L	Reserved
L	H	L	H	Non-Maskable Interrupt Acknowledge
L	H	H	L	Non-Vectored Interrupt Acknowledge
L	H	H	H	Vectored Interrupt Acknowledge
H	L	L	L	Memory Transaction for Operand
H	L	L	H	Memory Transaction for Stack
H	L	H	L	Reserved
H	L	H	H	Reserved
H	H	L	L	Memory Transaction for Instruction Fetch (Subsequent Word)
H	H	L	H	Memory Transaction for Instruction Fetch (First Word)
H	H	H	L	Reserved
H	H	H	H	Reserved

WAIT: Wait (Input)

LOW on this input indicates to the CPU that memory or I/O is not ready for the data transfer and hence the current transaction should be stretched. The $\overline{WAIT}$ input is sampled by the CPU at certain instances during the transaction (see timing diagram). If $\overline{WAIT}$ input is LOW at these instances, the CPU will go into wait state to prolong the transaction. The wait state will repeat until the $\overline{WAIT}$ input is HIGH at the sampling instant.

N/$\overline{S}$: Normal/System Mode (Output, 3-State)

HIGH on this output indicates that the CPU is operating in Normal Mode and LOW indicates operation in System Mode. This output is derived from the Flag Control Word (FCW) register. The FCW register is described under the program status information section of this document.

$\overline{MREQ}$: Memory Request (Output, 3-State)

LOW on this output indicates that a CPU transaction with memory is taking place.

$\overline{BUSRQ}$: Bus Request (Input)

LOW on this input indicates to the CPU that another device (such as DMA) is requesting to take control of the bus. The $\overline{BUSRQ}$ input can be driven LOW anytime. The CPU synchronizes this input internally. The CPU responds by activating $\overline{BUSAK}$ output LOW to indicate that the bus has been relinquished. Relinquishing the bus means that the AD0-AD15, $\overline{AS}$, $\overline{DS}$, B/$\overline{W}$, R/$\overline{W}$, N/$\overline{S}$, ST0-ST3 and $\overline{MREQ}$ outputs will be in the high impedance state. The requesting device should control these lines in an identical fashion to the CPU to accomplish transactions. The $\overline{BUSRQ}$ input must remain LOW as long as needed to perform all the transactions and the CPU will keep the $\overline{BUSAK}$ output LOW. After completing the transactions, the device must disable the AD0-AD15, $\overline{AS}$, $\overline{DS}$, B/$\overline{W}$, R/$\overline{W}$, N/$\overline{S}$, ST0-ST3 and $\overline{MREQ}$ into the high impedance state and stop driving the $\overline{BUSRQ}$ input LOW. The CPU will make $\overline{BUSAK}$ output HIGH sometime later and take back the bus control.

$\overline{BUSAK}$: Bus Acknowledge (Output)

LOW on this output indicates that the CPU has relinquished the bus in response to a bus request.

$\overline{\text{NMI}}$: Non-Maskable Interrupt (Input)

HIGH-to-LOW transition on this input constitutes non-maskable interrupt request. The CPU will respond with the non-maskable Interrupt Acknowledge on the ST0-ST3 outputs and will enter an interrupt sequence. The transition on the $\overline{\text{NMI}}$ can occur anytime. Of the three kinds of interrupts available, the non-maskable interrupt has the highest priority.

$\overline{\text{VI}}$: Vectored Interrupt (Input)

LOW on this input constitutes vectored interrupt request. Vectored interrupt is next lower to the non-maskable interrupt in priority. The VIE bit in the Flag and Control Word register must be* 1 for the vectored interrupt to be honored. The CPU will respond with Vectored Interrupt Acknowledge code on the ST0-ST3 outputs and will begin the interrupt sequence. The $\overline{\text{VI}}$ input can be driven LOW any time and should be held LOW until acknowledged.

$\overline{\text{NVI}}$: Non-Vectored Interrupt (Input)

LOW on this input constitutes non-vectored interrupt request. Non-vectored has the lowest priority of the three types of interrupts. The NVIE bit in the Flag and Control Word register must be 1 for this request to be honored. The CPU will respond with Non-Vectored Interrupt Acknowledge code on the ST0-ST3 outputs and will begin the interrupt sequence. The $\overline{\text{NVI}}$ input can be driven LOW anytime and should be held LOW until acknowledged.

$\overline{\mu\text{I}}$: Micro-In (Input)

This input participates in the resource request daisy chain. See the section on multimicroprocessor support facilities in this document.

μO: Micro-Out (Output)

This output participates in the resource request daisy chain. See the section on multimicroprocessor support facilities in this document.

$\overline{\text{RESET}}$: Reset (Input)

LOW on this input initiates a reset sequence in the CPU. See the section on Initialization for details on reset sequence.

CLK: Clock (Input)

All CPU operations are controlled from the signal fed into this input. See DC Characteristics for clock voltage level requirements.

DECOUPLE: (Output)

Output from the on-chip substrate bias generator. Do not use.

$\overline{\text{STOP}}$: Stop (Input)

This active LOW input facilitates one instruction at a time operation. See the section on single stepping.

PROCESSOR ORGANIZATION

The following is a brief discussion of the AmZ8002 CPU. For detailed information, see the AmZ8001/AmZ8002 Processor Instruction Set Manual (Publication No. AM-PUB086).

General Purpose Registers

The CPU is organized around sixteen 16-bit general purpose registers R0 through R15 as shown in Figure 1. For byte operations, the first eight registers (R0 through R7) can also be addressed as sixteen 8-bit registers designated as RL0, RH0 and so on to RL7 and RH7. The sixteen registers can also be grouped in pairs RR0, RR2 and so on to RR14 to form eight long

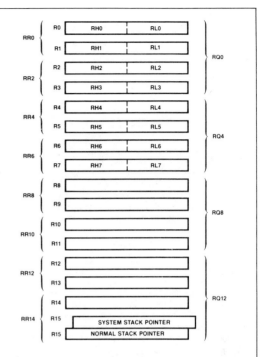

Figure 1. AmZ8002 Registers.

MOS-227

word (32-bit) registers. Similarly, the sixteen registers can be grouped in quadruples RQ0, RQ4, RQ8 and RQ12 to form four 64-bit registers.

STACK POINTER

The AmZ8002 architecture allows stacks to be maintained in the memory. Any general purpose register except R0 can be used as a stack pointer in stack manipulating instructions such as PUSH and POP. However, certain instructions such as subroutine call and return make implicit use of the register R15 as the stack pointer. Two implicit stacks are maintained – normal stack using R15 as the stack pointer and system stack using R15' as the system stack pointer (see Figure 1). If the CPU is operating in the Normal Mode, R15 is active, and if the CPU is in System Mode R15' will be used instead of R15. The implied stack pointer is a part of the general registers and hence can be manipulated using the instructions available for register operations.

PROCESSOR STATUS

The CPU status consists of the 16-bit Program Counter (PC) and the 16-bit Flag and Control Word (FCW) register (see Figure 2). The following is a brief description of the FCW bits.

S/$\overline{\text{N}}$: System/Normal – 1 indicates System Mode and 0 indicates Normal Mode.

VIE: Vectored Interrupt Enable – 1 indicates that Vectored Interrupt requests will be honored.

NVIE: Non-Vectored Interrupt Enable – 1 indicates that non-vectored interrupt requests will be honored.

C: Carry – 1 indicates that a carry has occurred from the most significant bit position when performing arithmetic operations.

Z: Zero – 1 indicates that the result of an operation is zero.

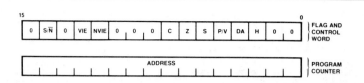

Figure 2. AmZ8002 Processor Status.

MOS-228

S: Sign – 1 indicates that the result of an operation is negative i.e., most significant bit is one.

P/V: Parity/Overflow – 1 indicates that there was an overflow during arithmetic operations. For logical operations this bit indicates parity of the result.

DA: Decimal Adjust – Records byte arithmetic operations.

H: Half Carry – 1 indicates that there was a carry from the most significant bit of the lower digit during byte arithmetic.

DATA TYPES

The AmZ8002 instructions operate on bits, digits (4 bits), bytes (8 bits), words (16 bits), long words (32 bits), byte strings and word strings type operands. Bits can be set, reset or tested. Digits are used to facilitate BCD arithmetic operations. Bytes are used for characters and small integers. Words are used for integer values and addresses while long words are used for large integer values. All operands except strings can reside either in memory or general registers. Strings can reside in memory only.

INTERRUPT AND TRAP STRUCTURE

Interrupt is defined as an external asynchronous event requiring program interruption. For example, interruption is caused by a peripheral needing service. Traps are synchronous events resulting from execution of certain instructions under some defined circumstances. Both interrupts and traps are handled in a similar manner by the AmZ8002.

The AmZ8002 supports three types of interrupts in order of descending priority – non-maskable, vectored and non-vectored. The vectored and non-vectored interrupts can be disabled by appropriate control bits in the FCW. The AmZ8002 has three traps – system call, unimplemented opcode and privileged instruction. The traps have higher priority than interrupts.

When an interrupt or trap occurs, the current program status is automatically pushed on to the system stack. The program status consists of processor status (i.e., PC and FCW) plus a 16-bit identifier. The identifier contains the reason, source and other coded information relating to the interrupt or trap.

After saving the current program status, the new processor status is automatically loaded from the new program status area located in the memory. This area is designated by the New Program Status Area Pointer (NPSAP) register. See AMPUB086 publication for further details.

ADDRESSING MODES

Information contained in the AmZ8002 instructions consists of the operation to be performed, the operand type and the location of the operands. Operand locations are designated by general register addresses, memory addresses or I/O addresses. The addressing mode of a given instruction defines the address space referenced and the method to compute the operand address. Addressing modes are explicitly specified or implied in an instruction. Figure 3 illustrates the eight explicit addressing modes: Register (R), Immediate (IM), Indirect Register (IR), Direct Address (DA), Indexed (X), Relative Address (RA), Base Address (BA) and Base Indexed (BX).

INPUT/OUTPUT

A set of I/O instructions are provided to accomplish byte or word transfers between the AmZ8002 and I/O devices. I/O devices are addressed using 16-bit I/O port addresses and I/O address space is not a part of the memory address space. Two types of I/O instructions are provided; each with its own 16-bit address space. I/O instructions include a comprehensive set of In, Out and Block transfers.

CPU TIMING

The AmZ8002 accomplishes instruction execution by stepping through a pre-determined sequence of machine cycles, such as memory read, memory write, etc. Each machine cycle requires between three and ten clock cycles. Bus Requests by DMA devices are granted at machine cycle boundaries. No machine cycle is longer than ten clock cycles; thus assuring fast response to a Bus Request (assuming no extra wait states). The start of a machine cycle is always marked by a LOW pulse on the $\overline{AS}$ output. The status output lines ST0-ST3 indicate the nature of the current cycle in a coded form.

STATUS LINE CODES

Status line coding was listed in the table shown under ST0-ST3 outputs in the Interface Signal Description. The following is a detailed description of the status codes.

Internal Operation:

This status code indicates that the AmZ8002 is going through a machine cycle for its internal operation. Figure 4 depicts an internal operation cycle. It consists of three clock periods identified as T1, T2 and T3. The $\overline{AS}$ output will be activated with a LOW pulse by the AmZ8002 to mark the start of a machine cycle. The ST0-ST3 will reflect the code for the internal operation. The $\overline{MREQ}$, $\overline{DS}$ and R/$\overline{W}$ outputs will be HIGH. The N/$\overline{S}$ output will remain at the same level as in the previous machine cycle. The AmZ8002 will ignore the $\overline{WAIT}$ input during the internal operation cycle. The CPU will drive the AD0-AD15 bus with unspecified information during T1. However, the bus will go into high impedance during T2 and remain in that state for the remainder of the cycle. The B/$\overline{W}$ output is also activated by the CPU with unspecified information.

Memory Refresh:

This status code indicates that AmZ8002 is accessing the memory to refresh. The refresh cycle consists of three clock periods as depicted in Figure 5. The CPU will activate the $\overline{AS}$ output with a LOW pulse to mark the beginning of a machine cycle and ST0-ST3 outputs will reflect the refresh cycle code. The least significant 9 lines of the AD0-AD15 bus contain the refresh address. Because the memory is word organized, the AD0 will always be LOW. The most significant 7 bus lines are not specified. The $\overline{DS}$ output will remain HIGH for the entire cycle while R/$\overline{W}$, B/$\overline{W}$ and N/$\overline{S}$ outputs will remain at the same level as in the machine cycle prior to refresh. The AD0-AD15 bus will go into high impedance state during T2 period and remain there for

Mode	Operand Addressing		Operand Value
	In the Instruction In a Register	In Memory	
Register	[REGISTER ADDRESS] → [OPERAND]		The content of the register.
Immediate	[OPERAND]		In the instruction
Indirect Register	[REGISTER ADDRESS] → [ADDRESS]	→ [OPERAND]	The content of the location whose address is in the register.
Direct Address	[ADDRESS]	→ [OPERAND]	The content of the location whose address is in the instruction.
Index	[REGISTER ADDRESS] → [DISPLACEMENT] / [BASE ADDRESS] → ⊕	→ [OPERAND]	The content of the location whose address is the address in the instruction, offset by the content of the working register.
Relative Address	[PC VALUE] / [DISPLACEMENT] → ⊕	→ [OPERAND]	The content of the location whose address is the content of the program counter, offset by the displacement in the instruction.
Base Address	[REGISTER ADDRESS] → [BASE ADDRESS] / [DISPLACEMENT] → ⊕	→ [OPERAND]	The content of the location whose address is the address in register, offset by the displacement in the instruction.
Base Index	[REGISTER ADDRESS] → [BASE ADDRESS] / [REGISTER ADDRESS] → [DISPLACEMENT] → ⊕	→ [OPERAND]	The content of the location whose address is the address in the register, offset by the displacement in the register.

Figure 3. Addressing Modes.

MOS-229

the remainder of the cycle. The AmZ8002 will activate the MREQ output LOW during the refresh cycle. It should be noted that WAIT input is ignored by the CPU for refresh operations.

I/O Transactions:

There are two status line codes used for I/O transaction cycles. The AmZ8002 provides two separate I/O spaces and two types of instructions called Normal I/O and Special I/O. Each I/O space is addressed by a 16-bit address called port address. The timing for both types of I/O transactions is essentially identical. A typical I/O cycle consists of four clock periods T1, T2, TWA and T3 as shown in Figure 6. The TWA is the wait state; insertion of one wait state for an I/O cycle is always automatic. Additional

wait cycles can be inserted by LOW on the WAIT input. The WAIT input is sampled during every TW state. If this input is LOW, one more wait state will be inserted. Insertion of wait states continues until WAIT input is HIGH. T3 state will follow the last wait state to complete the I/O cycle.

During I/O cycles the ST0-ST3 outputs will reflect appropriate code depending on the type of instruction being executed (Normal I/O or Special I/O). AS output will be pulsed LOW to mark the beginning of the cycle. The CPU drives the AD0-AD15 bus with the 16-bit port address specified by the current instruction. The N/S output will be LOW indicating that CPU is operating in the system mode. It should be recalled that the N/S output is derived from the appropriate bit in the FCW register. All I/O instructions are privileged instructions and will be allowed to

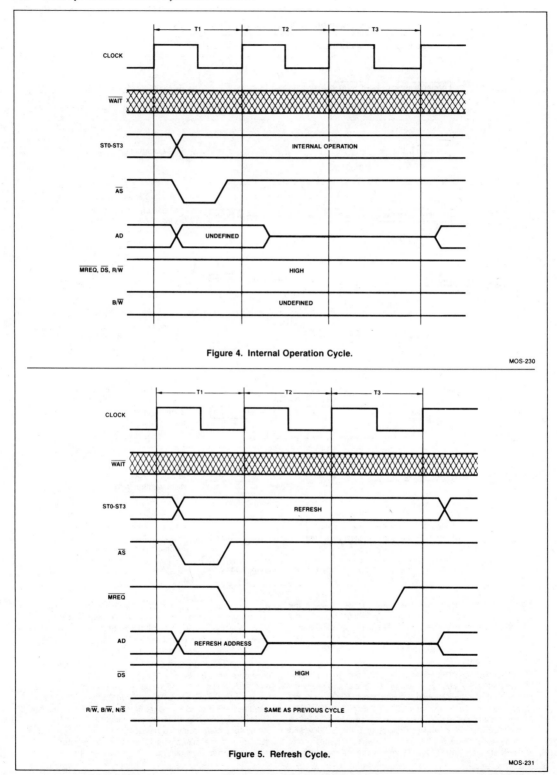

Figure 4. Internal Operation Cycle.

MOS-230

Figure 5. Refresh Cycle.

MOS-231

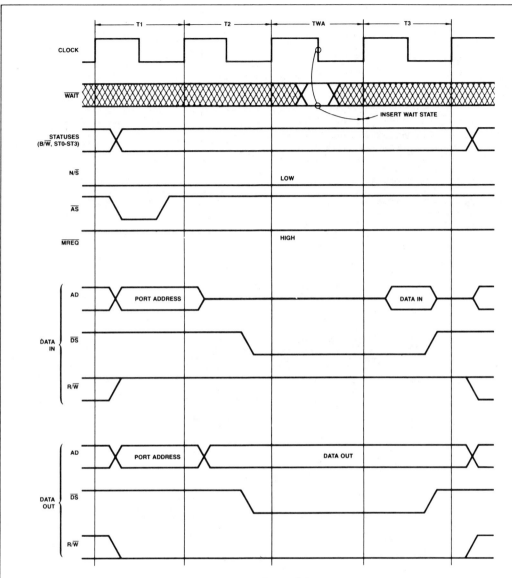

Figure 6. AmZ8002 I/O Cycle.

MOS-232

execute only if the FCW specifies system mode operation. The $\overline{\text{MREQ}}$ output will be HIGH. The AmZ8002 I/O instructions provide both word or byte transactions. The B/$\overline{\text{W}}$ output will be HIGH or LOW depending whether the instruction specifies a byte or word transfer.

Two kinds of I/O transfers should be considered: Data In means reading from the device and Data Out means writing into the device. For In operations, the R/$\overline{\text{W}}$ output will be HIGH. The AD0-AD15 bus will go into high impedance state during T2. During byte input instructions, the CPU reads either the even or odd half of the Data Bus, dependent upon the port address. If the port address is even, the most significant half of the Data Bus is read. If the port address is odd, the least significant half of

the Data Bus is read. During word input instructions, the CPU reads all 16 bits of the Data Bus. The AmZ8002 will drive the $\overline{\text{DS}}$ output LOW to signal to the device that data can be gated on to the bus. The CPU will accept the data during T3 and $\overline{\text{DS}}$ output will go HIGH signalling the end of an I/O transaction.

For Data Out, the R/$\overline{\text{W}}$ output will be LOW. The AmZ8002 will provide data on the AD0-AD15 bus and activates the $\overline{\text{DS}}$ output LOW during T2. During byte output instructions, the CPU duplicates the byte data onto both the high and low halves of the Data Bus and external logic, using A0, enables the appropriate byte port. During word output instructions the CPU outputs data onto all 16 bits of the Data Bus. The $\overline{\text{DS}}$ output goes HIGH during T3 and the cycle is complete.

Memory Transactions:

There are four status line codes that indicate a memory transaction:

a) Memory transaction to read or write an operand
b) Memory transaction to read from or write into the stack
c) Memory transaction to fetch the first word of an instruction (sometimes called IF1)
d) Memory transaction to fetch the subsequent word of an instruction (sometimes called IFN).

It can be appreciated that all the above transactions essentially fall into two categories: memory read and memory write. In the case of IF1 and IFN cycles, the memory will be read at the address supplied by the program counter. All AmZ8002 instructions are multiples of 16-bit words. Words are always addressed by an even address. Thus IF1 and IFN cycles involve performing a memory read for words. On the other hand, a memory transaction for operand and stack operation could be a read or write. Moreover, an operand could be a word or a byte. For stack operation involving the implied stack pointer the address will be supplied by the R15 (or R15'). For operand transactions, the

memory address will come from several sources depending on the instruction and the addressing mode. Memory transaction cycle timing is shown in Figure 7. It typically consists of three clock periods T1, T2 and T3. Wait states (TW) can be inserted between T2 and T3 by activating the $\overline{\text{WAIT}}$ input LOW. The $\overline{\text{WAIT}}$ input will be sampled during T2 and during every subsequent TW. The ST0-ST3 outputs will reflect the appropriate code for the current cycle early in T1 and the $\overline{\text{AS}}$ output will be pulsed LOW to mark the beginning of the cycle. The $\text{N}/\overline{\text{S}}$ output will indicate whether the normal or system address space will be used for the current cycle. As shown in the figure the $\overline{\text{MREQ}}$ output will go LOW during T1 to indicate a memory operation.

Consider a read operation first. The $\text{R}/\overline{\text{W}}$ output will be HIGH. The AmZ8002 will drive the AD0-AD15 with the appropriate address early in T1. During T2, the bus will go into high impedance state and $\overline{\text{DS}}$ output will be activated LOW by the CPU. The data can be gated on to the bus when $\overline{\text{DS}}$ is LOW. During T1 the $\text{B}/\overline{\text{W}}$ will also be activated to indicate byte or word will be transacted. The AmZ8002 memory is word organized and words are addressed by even addresses. However, when addressing bytes, the memory address may be odd or even; an even address for

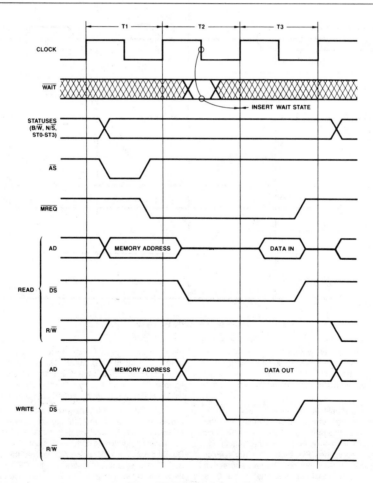

Figure 7. Memory Transactions.

MOS-233

most significant byte of a word and the next odd address for the least significant byte of that word. When reading a byte from the memory, the least significant address bit can be ignored and the whole word containing the desired byte is gated on to the bus. The CPU will pick the appropriate byte automatically. The AmZ8002 will drive the $\overline{DS}$ output HIGH indicating data acceptance.

Consider the write operation next. The R/$\overline{W}$ output will be LOW. The AmZ8002 removes the address and gates out the data to be written on the bus and activates the $\overline{DS}$ output LOW during T2. If the data to be written is a byte then the same byte will be on both halves of the bus. The $\overline{DS}$ output will go HIGH during T3 signifying completion of the cycle.

Interrupt Acknowledge:

There are three status line codes devoted to interrupt acknowledgement. These correspond to non-maskable, vectored and non-vectored interrupts. The Interrupt Acknowledge cycle is illustrated in Figure 8. The $\overline{NMI}$ input of the AmZ8002 is edge detected i.e., a HIGH to LOW input level change is stored in an internal latch. Similar internal storage is not provided for the $\overline{VI}$ and $\overline{NVI}$ inputs. For $\overline{VI}$ and $\overline{NVI}$ inputs to cause an interruption, the corresponding interrupt enable bits in the FCW must be 1. For the following discussion, both the VIE and NVIE bits in the FCW are assumed to be 1.

As shown in the figure, the $\overline{VI}$ input, $\overline{NVI}$ input and the internal $\overline{NMI}$ latch output are sampled during T3 of the last machine cycle of an instruction.

A LOW on these signals triggers the corresponding interrupt acknowledge sequence described below. The AmZ8002 executes a dummy IF1 cycle prior to entering the actual acknowledge cycle (see memory transactions for IF1 cycle description). During this dummy IF1 cycle, the program counter is not updated; instead the implied system stack pointer (R15') will be decremented. Following the dummy IF1 cycle is the actual interrupt acknowledge cycle.

The interrupt acknowledge cycle typically consists of 10 clock periods; T1 through T5 and five automatic TW (wait) states. As usual, the $\overline{AS}$ output will be pulsed LOW during T1 to mark the beginning of a cycle. The ST0-ST3 outputs will reflect the appropriate interrupt acknowledge code, the $\overline{MREQ}$ output will be HIGH, the N/$\overline{S}$ output remains the same as in the preceding cycle, the R/$\overline{W}$ output will be HIGH and the B/$\overline{W}$ output will be LOW. The AmZ8002 will drive the AD0-AD15 bus with unspecified information during T1 and the bus will go into the high impedance state during T2. Three TWA states will automatically follow T2. The WAIT input will be sampled during the third TWA state.

If LOW, an extra TW state will be inserted and the $\overline{WAIT}$ will be sampled again during TW. Such insertion of TW states continues until the $\overline{WAIT}$ input is HIGH. After the last TW state, the $\overline{DS}$ output will go LOW and two more automatic wait states follow. The interrupting device can gate up to a 16-bit identifier on to the bus when the $\overline{DS}$ output is LOW. The $\overline{WAIT}$ input will be sampled again during the last TWA state. If the $\overline{WAIT}$ input is LOW one TW state will be inserted and the $\overline{WAIT}$ will be sampled during TW. Such TW insertion continues until the $\overline{WAIT}$

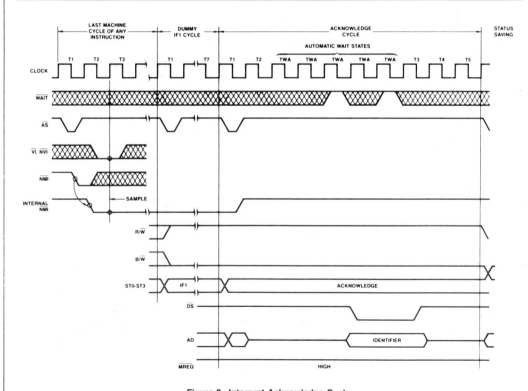

Figure 8. Interrupt Acknowledge Cycle.

MOS-234

input is HIGH. After completing the last TW state T3 will be entered and the $\overline{\text{DS}}$ output will go HIGH. The interrupting device should remove the identifier and cease driving the bus. T4 and T5 states will follow T3 to complete the cycle. Following the interrupt acknowledge cycle will be memory transaction cycles to save the status on the stack. Note that the N/$\overline{\text{S}}$ output will be automatically LOW during status saving.

The internal $\overline{\text{NMI}}$ latch will be reset to the initial state at $\overline{\text{AS}}$ going HIGH in the interrupt acknowledge cycle. The $\overline{\text{VI}}$ and $\overline{\text{NVI}}$ inputs should be kept LOW until this time also.

Status Saving Sequence:

The machine cycles following the interrupt acknowledge cycle push the old status information on the system stack in the following order: the 16-bit program counter; the flag and control word; and finally the interrupt/trap indentifier. Subsequent machine cycles fetch the new program status from the new program status area, and then branch to the interrupt/service routine.

BUS REQUEST/BUS ACKNOWLEDGE TIMING:

A LOW on the $\overline{\text{BUSRQ}}$ input is an indication to the AmZ8002 that another device (such as DMA) is requesting control of the bus. The $\overline{\text{BUSRQ}}$ input is synchronized internally at T1 of any machine cycle. (See below for exception.) The $\overline{\text{BUSAK}}$ will go LOW after the last clock period of the machine cycle. The LOW on the $\overline{\text{BUSAK}}$ output indicates acknowledgement. When $\overline{\text{BUSAK}}$ is LOW the following outputs will go into the high impedance state; AD0-AD15, $\overline{\text{AS}}$, $\overline{\text{DS}}$, $\overline{\text{MREQ}}$, ST0-ST3, B/$\overline{\text{W}}$, R/$\overline{\text{W}}$

and N/$\overline{\text{S}}$. The $\overline{\text{BUSRQ}}$ must be held LOW until all transactions are completed. When $\overline{\text{BUSRQ}}$ goes HIGH, it is synchronized internally, the $\overline{\text{BUSAK}}$ output will go HIGH and normal CPU operation will resume. Figure 9 illustrates the $\overline{\text{BUSRQ}}$/$\overline{\text{BUSAK}}$ timing.

It was mentioned that $\overline{\text{BUSRQ}}$ will be honored during any machine cycle with one exception. This exception is during the execution of TSET/TSETB instructions. $\overline{\text{BUSRQ}}$ will not be honored once execution of these instructions has started.

SINGLE STEPPING

The $\overline{\text{STOP}}$ input of the AmZ8002 facilitates one instruction at a time or single step operation. Figure 10 illustrates $\overline{\text{STOP}}$ input timing. The $\overline{\text{STOP}}$ input is sampled on the HIGH to LOW transition of the clock input that immediately precedes an IF1 cycle. If the $\overline{\text{STOP}}$ is found LOW, AmZ8002 introduces a memory refresh cycle after T3. Moreover, $\overline{\text{STOP}}$ input will be sampled again at T3. If $\overline{\text{STOP}}$ is LOW one more refresh cycle will follow the previous refresh cycle. The $\overline{\text{STOP}}$ will be sampled during T3 of the refresh cycle also. One additional refresh cycle will be added every time $\overline{\text{STOP}}$ input is sampled LOW. After completing the last refresh cycle which will occur after $\overline{\text{STOP}}$ is HIGH, the CPU will insert two dummy states T4 and T5 to complete the IF1 cycle and resume its normal operations for executing the instruction. See appropriate sections on memory transactions and memory refresh.

It should be noted that refresh cycles will occur in the stop mode even if the refresh facility is disabled in the refresh register.

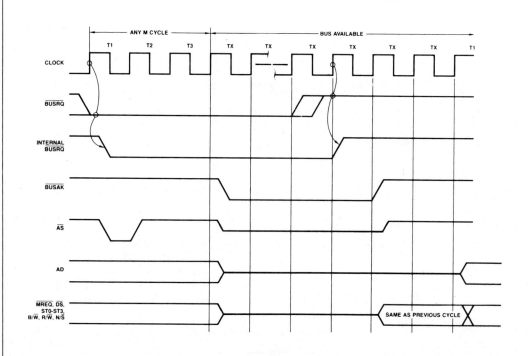

Figure 9. Bus Request/Acknowledge Cycle.

MOS-235

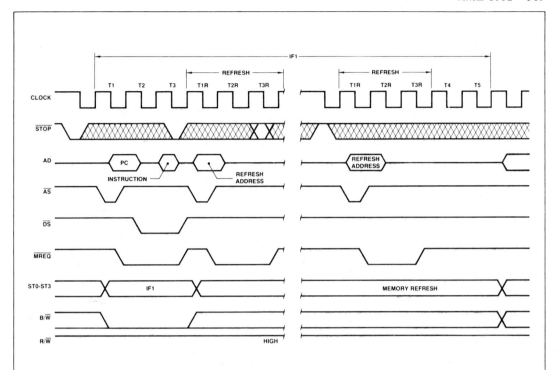

Figure 10. Single Step Timing.

MOS-236

MULTIMICROPROCESSOR FACILITIES

The AmZ8002 is provided with hardware and software facilities to support multiple microprocessor systems. The μO and μI signals of the AmZ8002 are used in conjunction with the MBIT, MREQ, MRES and MSET instructions for this purpose. The μO output can be activated LOW by using an appropriate instruction to signal a request from the AmZ8002 for a resource. The μI input is tested by the AmZ8002 before activating the μO output. LOW at the μI input at this time indicates that the resource is busy. The AmZ8002 can examine the μI input after activating the μO output LOW. The μI will be tested again to see if the requested resource became available. For detailed information on the Multimicroprocessor facilities the AmZ8001/AmZ8002 Processor Interface Manual (Publication No. AM-PUB089) should be consulted.

INITIALIZATION

A LOW on the $\overline{\text{Reset}}$ input starts the CPU initialization. The initialization sequence is shown in Figure 11. Within five clock periods after the HIGH to LOW level change of the $\overline{\text{Reset}}$ input the following will occur:

a) AD0-AD15 bus will be in the HIGH impedance state
b) $\overline{\text{AS}}$, $\overline{\text{DS}}$, $\overline{\text{MREQ}}$, $\overline{\text{BUSAK}}$ and $\overline{\mu O}$ outputs will be HIGH
c) ST0-ST3 outputs will be LOW
d) Refresh will be disabled
e) R/$\overline{\text{W}}$, B/$\overline{\text{W}}$ and N/$\overline{\text{S}}$ outputs are not affected. For a power on reset the state of these outputs is not specified.

After the $\overline{\text{Reset}}$ input returns HIGH and remains HIGH for three clock periods, two 16-bit memory read operations will be performed as follows. Note that the N/$\overline{\text{S}}$ output will be LOW and ST0-ST3 outputs will reflect IFN code.

a) The contents of the memory location 0002 will be read. This information will be loaded into the FCW of the AmZ8002.
b) The contents of the memory location 0004 will be read. This information will be loaded into the AmZ8002 program counter.

This completes initialization sequence and an IF1 cycle will follow to fetch the first instruction to begin program execution. See the section on memory transactions for timing.

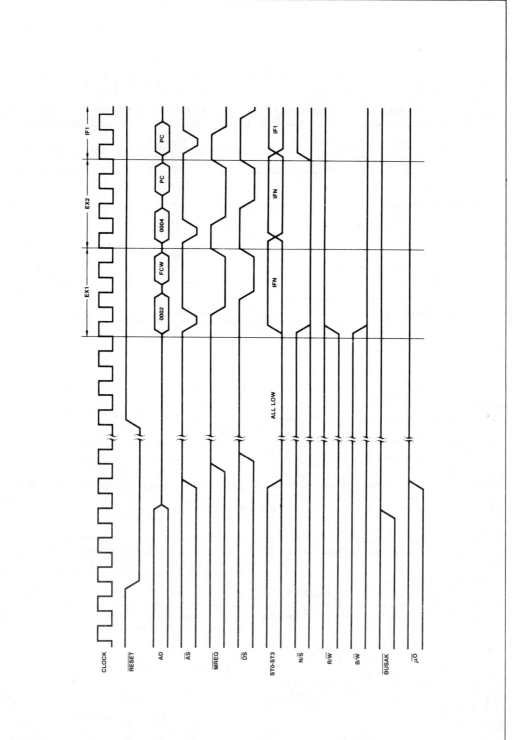

Figure 11. Reset Sequence.

MOS-237

AmZ8002 INSTRUCTION SET

LOAD AND EXCHANGE

Mne-monics	Operands	Addr. Modes	Operation
CLR CLRB	dst	R IR DA X	Clear dst ← 0
EX EXB	R, src	R IR DA X	Exchange R ← src
LD LDB LDL	R, src	R IM IM IR DA X BA BX	Load into Register R ← src
LD LDB LDL	dst, R	IR DA X BA BX	Load into Memory (Store) dst ← R
LD LDB	dst, IM	IR DA X	Load Immediate into Memory dst ← IM
LDA	R, src	DA X BA BX	Load Address R ← source address
LDAR	R, src	RA	Load Address Relative R ← source address
LDK	R, src	IM	Load Constant R ← n (n = 0 . . . 15)
LDM	R, src, n	IR DA X	Load Multiple R ← src (n consecutive words) (n = 1 . . . 16)
LDM	dst, R, n	IR DA X	Load Multiple (Store Multiple) dst ← R (n consecutive words) (n = 1 . . . 16)
LDR LDRB LDRL	R, src	RA	Load Relative R ← src (range −32768 . . . +32767)
LDR LDRB LDRL	dst, R	RA	Load Relative (Store Relative) dst ← R (range −32768 . . . +32767)
POP POPL	dst, R	R IR DA X	Pop dst ← IR Autoincrement contents of R
PUSH PUSHL	IR, src	R IM IR DA X	Push Autodecrement contents of R IR ← src

ARITHMETIC

Mne-monics	Operands	Addr. Modes	Operation
ADC ADCB	R, src	R	Add with Carry R ← R + src + carry
ADD ADDB ADDL	R, src	R IM IR DA X	Add R ← R + src
CP CPB CPL	R, src	R IM IR DA X	Compare with Register R − src
CP CPB	dst, IM	IR DA X	Compare with Immediate dst − IM
DAB	dst	R	Decimal Adjust
DEC DECB	dst, n	R IR DA X	Decrement by n dst ← dst − n (n = 1 . . . 16)
DIV DIVL	R, src	R IM IR DA X	Divide (signed) Word: $R_{n+1} ← R_{n,n+1} ÷ src$ $R_n ←$ remainder Long Word: $R_{n+2,n+3}$ $← R_{n...n+3} ÷ src$ $R_{n,n+1}$ ← remainder
EXTS EXTSB EXTSL	dst	R	Extend Sign Extend sign of low order half of st through high order half of dst
INC INCB	dst, n	R IR DA X	Increment by n dst ← dst + n (n = 1 . . . 16)
MULT MULTL	R, src	R IM IR DA X	Multiply (signed) Word: $R_{n,n+1} ← R_{n+1} • src$ Long Word: $R_{n...n+3}$ $← R_{n+2,n+3} • src$ *Plus seven cycles for each 1 in the multiplicand
NEG NEGB	dst	R IR DA X	Negate dst ← 0 − dst
SBC SBCB	R, src	R	Subtract with Carry R ← R − src − carry
SUB SUBB SUBL	R, src	R IM IR DA X	Subtract R ← R − src

LOGICAL

Mnemonics	Operands	Addr. Modes	Operation
AND ANDB	R, src	R IM IR DA X	AND R ← R AND src
COM COMB	dst	R IM IR DA X	Complement dst ← NOT dst
OR ORB	R, src	R IM IR DA X	OR R ← R OR src
TEST TESTB TESTL	dst	R IR DA X	TEST dst OR 0
TCC TCCB	cc, dst	R	Test Condition Code Set LSB if cc is true
XOR XORB	R, src	R IM IR DA X	Exclusive OR R ← R XOR src

BIT MANIPULATION

Mnemonics	Operand	Addr. Modes	Operation
BIT BITB	dst, b	R IR DA X	Test Bit Static Z flag ← NOT dst bit specified by b
BIT BITB	dst, R	R	Test Bit Dynamic Z flag ← NOT dst bit specified by contents of R
RES RESB	dst, b	R IR DA X	Reset Bit Static Reset dst bit specified by b
RES RESB	dst, R	R	Reset Bit Dynamic Reset dst bit specified by contents of R
SET SETB	dst, b	R IR DA X	Set Bit Static Set dst bit specified by b
SET SETB	dst, R	R	Set Bit Dynamic Set dst bit specified by contents of R
TSET TSETB	dst	R IR DA X	Test and Set S flag ← MSB of dst dst ← all 1s

PROGRAM CONTROL

Mnemonics	Operands	Addr. Modes	Operation
CALL	dst	IR DA X	Call Subroutine Autodecrement SP @ SP ← PC PC ← dst
CALR	dst	RA	Call Relative Autodecrement SP @ SP ← PC PC ← PC + dst (range −4094 to +4096)
DJNZ DBJNZ	R, dst	RA	Decrement and Jump if Non-Zero R ← R − 1 IF R = 0: PC ← PC + dst (range −254 to 0)
IRET*	−	−	Interrupt Return PS ← @ SP Autoincrement SP
JP	cc, dst	IR IR DA X	Jump Conditional If cc is true: PC ← dst
JR	cc, dst	RA	Jump Conditional Relative If cc is true: PC ← PC + dst (range −256 to +254)
RET	cc	−	Return Conditional If cc is true: PC ← @ SP Autodecrement SP
SC	src	IM	System Call Autodecrement SP @ SP ← old PS Push instruction PS ← System Call PS

*Privileged instructions. Executed in system mode only.

ROTATE AND SHIFT

Mnemonics	Operand	Addr. Modes	Operation
RLDB	R, src	R	Rotate Digit Left
RRDB	R, src	R	Rotate Digit Right
RL RLB	dst, n	R R	Rotate Left by n bits (n = 1, 2)
RLC RLCB	dst, n	R R	Rotate Left through Carry by n bits (n = 1, 2)
RR RRB	dst, n	R R	Rotate Right by n bits (n = 1, 2)
RRC RRCB	dst, n	R R	Rotate Right through Carry by n bits (n = 1, 2)
SDA SDAB SDAL	dst, R	R	Shift Dynamic Arithmetic Shift dst left or right by contents of R
SDL SDLB SDLL	dst, R	R	Shift Dynamic Logical Shift dst left or right by contents of R
SLA SLAB SLAL	dst, n	R	Shift Left Arithmetic by n bits
SLL SLLB SLLL	dst, n	R	Shift Left Logical by n bits
SRA SRAB SRAL	dst, n	R	Shift Right Arithmetic by n bits
SRL SRLB SRLL	dst, n	R	Shift Right Logical by n bits

BLOCK TRANSFER AND STRING MANIPULATION

Mne-monics	Operands	Addr. Modes	Operation
CPD CPDB	R_X, src, R_Y, cc	IR	Compare and Decrement R_X − src Autodecrement src address $R_Y \leftarrow R_Y - 1$
CPDR CPDRB	R_X, src, R_Y, cc	IR	Compare, Decrement and Repeat R_X − src Autodecrement src address $R_Y \leftarrow R_Y - 1$ Repeat until cc is true or $R_Y = 0$
CPI CPIB	R_X, src, R_Y, cc	IR	Compare and Increment R_X − src Autoincrement src address $R_Y \leftarrow R_Y - 1$
CPIR CPIRB	R_X, src, R_Y, cc	IR	Compare, Increment and Repeat R_X − src Autoincrement src address $R_Y \leftarrow R_Y - 1$ Repeat until cc is true or $R_Y = 0$
CPSD CPSDB	dst, src, R, cc	IR	Compare String and Decrement dst − src Autodecrement dst and src addresses $R \leftarrow R - 1$
CPSDR CPSDRB	dst, src, R, cc	IR	Compare String, Decr. and Repeat dst − src Autodecrement dst and src addresses $R \leftarrow R - 1$ Repeat until cc is true or $R = 0$
CPSI CPSIB	dst, src, R, cc	IR	Compare String and Increment dst − src Autoincrement dst and src addresses $R \leftarrow R - 1$
CPSIR CPSIRB	dst, src, R, cc	IR	Compare String, Incr. and Repeat dst − src Autoincrement dst and src addresses $R \leftarrow R - 1$ Repeat until cc is true or $R = 0$
LDD LDDB	dst, src, R	IR	Load and Decrement dst ← src Autodecrement dst and src addresses $R \leftarrow R - 1$
LDDR LDDRB	dst, src, R	IR	Load, Decrement and Repeat dst ← src Autodecrement dst and src addresses $R \leftarrow R - 1$ Repeat until $R = 0$

BLOCK TRANSFER AND STRING MANIPULATION (Cont.)

Mne-monics	Operands	Addr. Modes	Operation
LDI LDIB	dst, src, R	IR	Load and Increment dst ← src Autoincrement dst and src addresses $R \leftarrow R - 1$
LDIR LDIRB	dst, src, R	IR	Load, Increment and Repeat dst ← src Autoincrement dst and src addresses $R \leftarrow R - 1$ Repeat until $R = 0$
TRDB	dst, src, R	IR	Translate and Decrement dst ← src (dst) Autodecrement dst address $R \leftarrow R - 1$
TRDRB	dst, src, R	IR	Translate, Decrement and Repeat dst ← src (dst) Autodecrement dst address $R \leftarrow R - 1$ Repeat until $R = 0$
TRIB	dst, src, R	IR	Translate and Increment dst ← src (dst) Autoincrement dst address $R \leftarrow R - 1$
TRIRB	dst, src, R	IR	Translate, Increment and Repeat dst ← src (dst) Autoincrement dst address $R \leftarrow R - 1$ Repeat until $R = 0$
TRTDB	src 1, src 2, R	IR	Translate and Test, Decrement RH1 ← src 2 (src 1) Autodecrement src 1 address $R \leftarrow R - 1$
TRTDRB	src 1, src 2, R	IR	Translate and Test, Decrement and Repeat RH1 ← src 2 (src 1) Autodecrement src 1 address $R \leftarrow R - 1$ Repeat until $R = 0$ or RH1 = 0
TRTIB	src 1, src 2, R	IR	Translate and Test, Increment RH1 ← src 2 (src 1) Autoincrement src 1 address $R \leftarrow R - 1$
TRTIRB	src 1, src 2, R	IR	Translate and Test, Increment and Repeat RH1 ← src 2 (src 1) Autoincrement src 1 address $R \leftarrow R - 1$ Repeat until $R = 0$ or RH1 = 0

INPUT/OUTPUT

Mnemonics	Operands	Addr. Modes	Operation
IN* INB*	R, src	IR DA	Input R ← src
IND* INDB*	dst, src, R	IR	Input and Decrement dst ← src Autodecrement dst address R ← R − 1
INDR* INDRB*	dst, src, R	IR	Input, Decrement and Repeat dst ← src Autodecrement dst address R ← R − 1 Repeat until R = 0
INI* INIB*	dst, src, R	IR	Input and Increment dst ← src Autoincrement dst address R ← R − 1
INIR* INIRB*	dst, src, R	IR	Input, Increment and Repeat dst ← src Autoincrement dst address R ← R − 1 Repeat until R = 0
OUT* OUTB*	dst, R	IR DA	Output dst ← R
OUTD* OUTDB*	dst, src, R	IR	Output and Decrement dst ← src Autodecrement src address R ← R − 1
OTDR* OTDRB*	dst, src, R	IR	Output, Decrement and Repeat dst ← src Autodecrement src address R ← R − 1 Repeat until R = 0
OUTI* OUTIB*	dst, src, R	IR	Output and Increment dst ← src Autoincrement src address R ← R − 1
OTIR* OTIRB*	dst, src, R	IR	Ouput, Increment and Repeat dst ← src Autoincrement src address R ← R − 1 Repeat until R = 0
SIN* SINB*	R, src	DA	Special Input R ← src
SIND* SINDB*	dst, src, R	IR	Special Input and Decrement dst ← src Autodecrement dst address R ← R − 1
SINDR* SINDRB*	dst, src, R	IR	Special Input, Decr. and Repeat dst ← src Autodecrement dst address R ← R − 1 Repeat until R = 0
SINI* SINIB*	dst, src, R	IR	Special Input and Increment dst ← src Autoincrement dst address R ← R − 1
SINIR* SINIRB*	dst, src, R	IR	Special Input, Incr. and Repeat dst ← src Autoincrement dst address R ← R − 1 Repeat until R = 0

INPUT/OUTPUT (Cont.)

Mnemonics	Operands	Addr. Modes	Operation
SOUT* SOUTB*	dst, src	DA	Special Output dst ← src
SOUTD* SOUTDB*	dst, src, R	IR	Special Output and Decrement dst ← src Autodecrement src address R ← R − 1
SOTDR* SOTDRB*	dst, src, R	IR	Special Output, Decr. and Repeat dst ← src Autodecrement src address R ← R − 1 Repeat until R = 0
SOUTI* SOUTIB*	dst, src, R	IR	Special Output and Increment dst ← src Autoincrement src address R ← R − 1
SOTIR* SOTIRB*	dst, src, R	R	Special Output, Incr. and Repeat dst ← src Autoincrement src address R ← R − 1 Repeat until R = 0

CPU CONTROL

Mnemonics	Operands	Addr. Modes	Operation
COMFLG	flags	−	Complement Flag (Any combination of C, Z, S, P/V)
DI*	int	−	Disable Interrupt (Any combination of NVI, VI)
EI*	int	−	Enable Interrupt (Any combination of NVI, VI)
HALT*	−	−	HALT
LDCTL*	CTLR, src	R	Load into Control Register CTLR ← src
LDCTL*	dst, CTLR	R	Load from Control Register dst ← CTLR
LDCTLB	FLGR, src	R	Load into Flag Byte Register FLGR ← src
LDCTLB	dst, FLGR	R	Load from Flag Byte Register dst ← FLGR
LDPS*	src	IR DA X	Load Program Status PS ← src
MBIT*	−	−	Test Multi-Micro Bit Set S if μI is Low; reset S if μI is High.
MREQ*	dst	R	Multi-Micro Request
MRES*	−	−	Multi-Micro Reset
MSET*	−	−	Multi-Micro Set
NOP	−	−	No Operation
RESFLG	flag	−	Reset Flag (Any combination of C, Z, S, P/V)
SETFLG	flag	−	Set Flag (Any combination of C, Z, S, P/V)

*Privileged instructions. Executed in system mode only.

MAXIMUM RATINGS above which useful life may be impaired

Voltages on all inputs and outputs with respect to GND	−0.3 to +70V
Ambient Temperature under bias	0 to 70°C
Storage Temperature	−65 to +150°C

The products described by this specification include internal circuitry designed to protect input devices from damaging accumulations of static charge. It is suggested, nevertheless, that conventional precautions be observed during storage, handling and use in order to avoid exposure to excessive voltages.

ELECTRICAL CHARACTERISTICS over operating range (Note 1)

AmZ8002DC

Parameter	Description	Test Conditions	Min	Max	Units
V_{CH}	Clock Input High Voltage	Driven by External Clock Generator	$V_{CC}-0.4$	$V_{CC}+0.3$	Volts
V_{CL}	Clock Input Low Voltage	Driven by External Clock Generator	−0.3	0.45	Volts
V_{IH}	Input High Voltage		2.0	$V_{CC}+0.3$	Volts
V_{IL}	Input Low Voltage		−0.3	0.8	Volts
V_{OH}	Output High Voltage	$I_{OH} = -250\mu A$	2.4		Volts
V_{OL}	Output Low Voltage	$I_{OL} = +2.0mA$		0.4	Volts
I_{IL}	Input Leakage	$0.4 \leq V_{IN} \leq +2.4V$		±10	μA
I_{OL}	Output Leakage	$0.4 \leq V_{OUT} \leq +2.4V$		±10	μA
I_{CC}	V_{CC} Supply Current			300	mA

Note 1: Typical values are for $T_A = 25°C$, nominal supply voltages and nominal processing parameters.

Standard Test Conditions

The characteristics below apply for the following standard test conditions, unless otherwise noted. All voltages are referenced to GND. Positive current flows into the referenced pin. Standard conditions are as follows:

$$+4.75V \leq V_{CC} \leq +5.25V$$
$$GND = 0V$$
$$0°C \leq T_A \leq +70°C$$

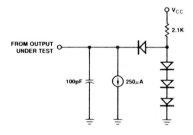

MOS-238

All AC parameters assume a load capacitance of 100pF max. Timing references between two output signals assume a load difference of 50pF max.

SWITCHING CHARACTERISTICS over operating range

AmZ8002DC

Number	Parameter	Description	Min	Max	Units
1	TcC	Clock Cycle Time	250	2000	ns
2	TwCh	Clock Width (High)	105	2000	ns
3	TwCl	Clock Width (Low)	105	2000	ns
4	TfC	Clock Fall Time		20	ns
5	TrC	Clock Rise Time		20	ns
6					
7					
8	TdC(Bz)	Clock ↑ to Bus Float		65	ns
9	TdC(A)	Clock ↑ to Address Valid		100	ns
10	TdC(Az)	Clock ↑ to Address Float		65	ns
11	TdA(DI)	Address Valid to Data In Required Valid	400		ns
12	TsDI(C)	Data In to Clock ↓ Set-up Time	70		ns
13	TdDS(A)	$\overline{DS}$ ↑ to Address Active	80		ns
14	TdC(DO)	Clock ↑ to Data Out Valid		100	ns
15	ThDI(DS)	Data In to $\overline{DS}$ ↑ Hold Time	0		ns
16	TdDO(DS)	Data Out Valid to $\overline{DS}$ ↑ Delay	230		ns
17	TdA(MR)	Address Valid to $\overline{MREQ}$ ↓ Delay	55		ns
18	TdC(MR)	Clock ↓ to $\overline{MREQ}$ ↓ Delay		80	ns
19	TwMRh	$\overline{MREQ}$ Width (High)	190		ns
20	TdMR(A)	$\overline{MREQ}$ ↓ to Address Not Active	70		ns
21	TdDO(DSW)	Data Out Valid to $\overline{DS}$ ↓ (Write) Delay	55		ns
22	TdMR(DI)	$\overline{MREQ}$ ↓ to Data In Required Valid	330		ns
23	TdC(MR)	Clock ↓ to $\overline{MREQ}$ ↑ Delay		80	ns
24	TdC(ASf)	Clock ↑ to $\overline{AS}$ ↓ Delay		80	ns
25	TdA(AS)	Address Valid to $\overline{AS}$ ↑ Delay	55		ns
26	TdC(ASr)	Clock ↓ to $\overline{AS}$ ↑ Delay		90	ns
27	TdAS(DI)	$\overline{AS}$ ↑ to Data In Required Valid	290		ns
28	TdDS(AS)	$\overline{DS}$ ↑ to $\overline{AS}$ ↓ Delay	70		ns
29	TwAS	$\overline{AS}$ Width (Low)	80		ns
30	TdAS(A)	$\overline{AS}$ ↑ to Address Not Active Delay	60		ns
31	TdAz(DSR)	Address Float to $\overline{DS}$ (Read) ↓ Delay	0		ns
32	TdAS(DSR)	$\overline{AS}$ ↑ to $\overline{DS}$ (Read) ↓ Delay	70		ns
33	TdDSR(DI)	$\overline{DS}$ (Read) ↓ to Data In Required Valid	155		ns
34	TdC(DSr)	Clock ↓ to $\overline{DS}$ ↑ Delay		70	ns
35	TdDS(DO)	$\overline{DS}$ ↑ to Data Out and STATUS Not Valid	80		ns
36	TdA(DSR)	Address Valid to $\overline{DS}$ (Read) ↓ Delay	120		ns
37	TdC(DSR)	Clock ↑ to $\overline{DS}$ (Read) ↓ Delay		120	ns
38	TwDSR	$\overline{DS}$ (Read) Width (Low)	275		ns
39	TdC(DSW)	Clock ↓ to $\overline{DS}$ (Write) ↓ Delay		95	ns
40	TwDSW	$\overline{DS}$ (Write) Width (Low)	160		ns
41	TdDSI(DI)	$\overline{DS}$ (Input) ↓ to Data In Required Valid	315		ns
42	TdC(DSf)	Clock ↓ to $\overline{DS}$ (I/O) ↓ Delay		120	ns
43	TwDS	$\overline{DS}$ (I/O) Width (Low)	400		ns
44	TdAS(DSA)	$\overline{AS}$ ↑ to $\overline{DS}$ (Acknowledge) ↓ Delay	960		ns
45	TdC(DSA)	Clock ↑ to $\overline{DS}$ (Acknowledge) ↓ Delay		120	ns
46	TdDSA(DI)	$\overline{DS}$ (Acknowledge) ↓ to Data In Required Delay	420		ns
47	TdC(S)	Clock ↑ to Status Valid Delay		110	ns
48	TdS(AS)	Status Valid to $\overline{AS}$ ↑ Delay	40		ns

SWITCHING CHARACTERISTICS (Cont.)

Number	Parameter	Description	AmZ8002DC Min	AmZ8002DC Max	Units
49	TsR(C)	$\overline{\text{RESET}}$ to Clock ↑ Set-up Time	180		ns
50	ThR(C)	$\overline{\text{RESET}}$ to Clock ↑ Hold Time	0		ns
51	TwNMI	$\overline{\text{NMI}}$ Width (Low)	100		ns
52	TsNMI(C)	$\overline{\text{NMI}}$ to Clock ↑ Set-up Time	140		ns
53	TsVI(C)	$\overline{\text{VI}}$, $\overline{\text{NVI}}$ to Clock ↑ Set-up Time	110		ns
54	ThVI(C)	$\overline{\text{VI}}$, $\overline{\text{NVI}}$ to Clock ↑ Hold Time	0		ns
55					
56					
57	Tsμi(C)	$\overline{\mu i}$ to Clock ↑ Set-up Time	180		ns
58	Thμi(C)	$\overline{\mu i}$ to Clock ↑ Hold Time	0		ns
59	TdC(μo)	Clock ↑ to $\overline{\mu o}$ Delay		120	ns
60	TsSTP(C)	$\overline{\text{STOP}}$ to Clock ↓ Set-up Time	140		ns
61	ThSTP(C)	$\overline{\text{STOP}}$ to Clock ↓ Hold Time	0		ns
62	TsWT(C)	$\overline{\text{WAIT}}$ to Clock ↓ Set-up Time	70		ns
63	ThWT(C)	$\overline{\text{WAIT}}$ to Clock ↓ Hold Time	0		ns
64	TsBRQ(C)	$\overline{\text{BUSRQ}}$ to Clock ↑ Set-up Time	90		ns
65	ThBRQ(C)	$\overline{\text{BUSRQ}}$ to Clock ↑ Hold Time	0		ns
66	TdC(BAKr)	Clock ↑ to $\overline{\text{BUSAK}}$ ↑ Delay		100	ns
67	TdC(BAKf)	Clock ↑ to $\overline{\text{BUSAK}}$ ↓ Delay		100	ns

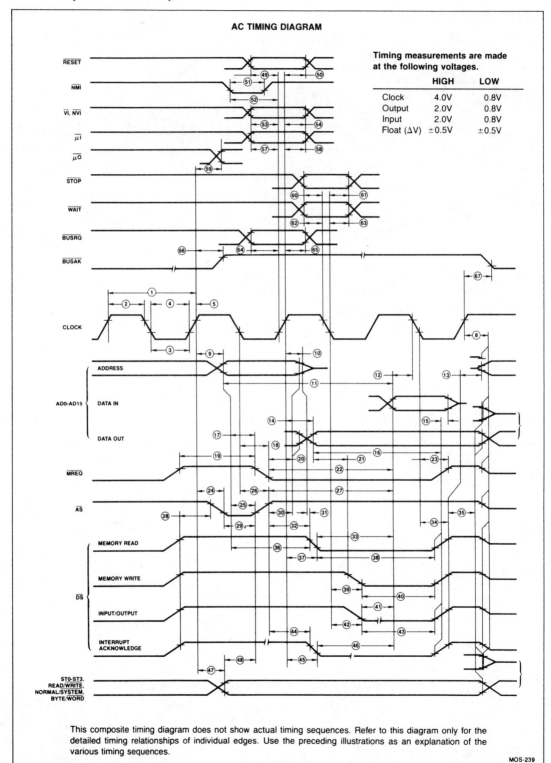

AC TIMING DIAGRAM

Timing measurements are made
at the following voltages.

	HIGH	LOW
Clock	4.0V	0.8V
Output	2.0V	0.8V
Input	2.0V	0.8V
Float (ΔV)	±0.5V	±0.5V

This composite timing diagram does not show actual timing sequences. Refer to this diagram only for the detailed timing relationships of individual edges. Use the preceding illustrations as an explanation of the various timing sequences.

MOS-239

PHYSICAL DIMENSIONS
Dual-In-Line

40-Pin Ceramic

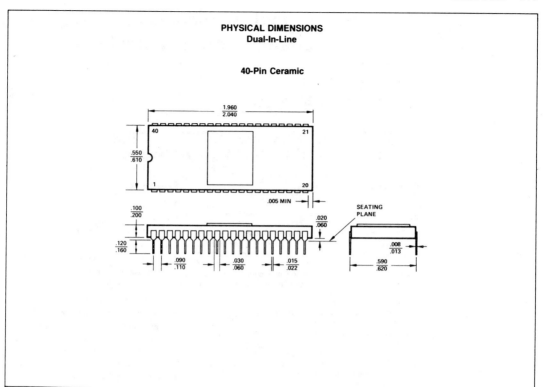

Appendix E National Semiconductor single-chip, N-channel microcontrollers

National Semiconductor

PRELIMINARY
AUGUST 1980

COP420L/COP421L and COP320L/COP321L Single-Chip N-Channel Microcontrollers

General Description

The COP420L, COP421L, COP320L, and COP321L Single-Chip N-Channel Microcontrollers are members of the COPS™ family, fabricated using N-channel, silicon gate MOS technology. These controller oriented processors are complete microcomputers containing all system timing, internal logic, ROM, RAM and I/O necessary to implement dedicated control functions in a variety of applications. Features include single supply operation, a variety of output configuration options, with an instruction set, internal architecture and I/O scheme designed to facilitate keyboard input, display output and BCD data manipulation. The COP421L is identical to the COP420L, but with 19 I/O lines instead of 23. They are an appropriate choice for use in numerous human interface control environments. Standard test procedures and reliable high-density fabrication techniques provide the medium to large volume customers with a customized controller oriented processor at a low end-product cost.

The COP320L is the extended temperature range version of the COP420L (likewise the COP321L is the extended temperature range version of the COP421L). The COP320L/COP321L are exact functional equivalents of the COP420L/COP421L.

Features

- Low cost
- Powerful instruction set
- 1k × 8 ROM, 64 × 4 RAM
- 23 I/O lines (COP420L)
- True vectored interrupt, plus restart
- Three-level subroutine stack
- 16 μs instruction time
- Single wide-range supply (4.5–9.5V)
- Low current drain (8 mA max @ 5V)
- Internal time-base counter for real-time processing
- Internal binary counter register with MICROWIRE™ compatible serial I/O
- General purpose and TRI-STATE® outputs
- LSTTL/CMOS compatible in and out
- Direct drive of LED digit and segment lines
- Software/hardware compatible with other members of COP400 family
- Extended temperature range device COP320L/COP321L (−40°C to +85°C)

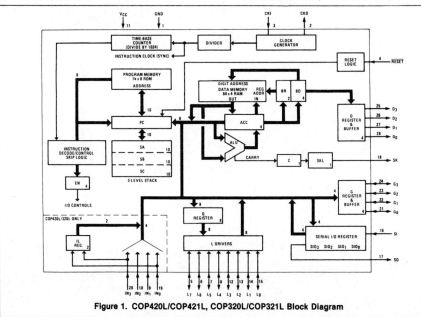

Figure 1. COP420L/COP421L, COP320L/COP321L Block Diagram

COP420L/COP421L

Absolute Maximum Ratings

Voltage at Any Pin Relative to GND	$-0.5V$ to $+10V$
Ambient Operating Temperature	$0\,°C$ to $+70\,°C$
Ambient Storage Temperature	$-65\,°C$ to $+150\,°C$
Lead Temperature (Soldering, 10 seconds)	$300\,°C$
Power Dissipation	0.75 Watt at $25\,°C$
	0.4 Watt at $70\,°C$

Absolute maximum ratings indicate limits beyond which damage to the device may occur. DC and AC electrical specifications are not ensured when operating the device at absolute maximum ratings.

DC Electrical Characteristics $0\,°C \leqslant T_A \leqslant +70\,°C$, $4.5V \leqslant V_{CC} \leqslant 9.5V$ unless otherwise noted.

Parameter	Conditions	Min.	Max.	Units
Standard Operating Voltage (V_{CC})	Note 1	4.5	6.3	V
Optional Operating Voltage (V_{CC})		4.5	9.5	V
Operating Supply Current	$V_{CC} = 5V$, (all inputs and outputs open)		8	mA
Input Voltage Levels				
CKI Input Levels				
Crystal Input				
Logic High (V_{IH})		2.0		V
Logic Low (V_{IL})		-0.3	0.4	V
Schmitt Trigger Input				
Logic High (V_{IH})		$0.7\ V_{CC}$		V
Logic Low (V_{IL})		-0.3	0.6	V
$\overline{RESET}$ Input Levels				
Logic High		$0.7\ V_{CC}$		V
Logic Low		-0.3	0.6	V
$\overline{RESET}$ Hysteresis		1.0		V
SO Input Level (Test mode)		2.0	3.0	V
All Other Inputs				
Logic High	$V_{CC} = MAX$	3.0		V
Logic High	with TTL trip level options	2.0		V
Logic Low	selected, $V_{CC} = 5V \pm 10\%$	-0.3	0.8	V
Logic High	with high trip level options	3.6		V
Logic Low	selected	-0.3	1.2	V
Input Capacitance			7	pF
Hi-Z Input Leakage		-1	$+1$	μA
Output Voltage Levels				
LSTTL Operation	$V_{CC} = 5V \pm 5\%$			
Logic High (V_{OH})	$I_{OH} = -25\mu A$	2.7		V
Logic Low (V_{OL})	$I_{OL} = 0.36\,mA$		0.4	V
CMOS Operation				
Logic High	$I_{OH} = -10\,\mu A$	$V_{CC} - 1$		V
Logic Low	$I_{OL} = +10\,\mu A$		0.2	V

Note 1: V_{CC} voltage change must be less than 0.5V/ms to maintain proper operation.

COP420L/COP421L

DC Electrical Characteristics (continued) 0°C ≤ T_A ≤ +70°C, 4.5V ≤ V_{CC} ≤ 9.5V unless otherwise noted.

Parameter	Conditions	Min.	Max.	Units
Output Current Levels				
Output Sink Current				
SO and SK Outputs (I_{OL})	V_{CC} = 9.5V, V_{OL} = 1.0V	4.5	22	mA
	V_{CC} = 4.5V, V_{OL} = 1.0V	2.2	11	mA
L_0-L_7 Outputs and Standard Size G_0-G_3 and D_0-D_3 Outputs (I_{OL})	V_{CC} = 9.5V, V_{OL} = 1.0V	2.0	9.0	mA
	V_{CC} = 4.5V, V_{OL} = 1.0V	1.0	4.5	mA
G_0-G_3 and D_0-D_3 Outputs with High Current Options (I_{OL})	V_{CC} = 9.5V, V_{OL} = 1.0V	15	75	mA
	V_{CC} = 4.5V, V_{OL} = 1.0V	7.0	35	mA
G_0-G_3 and D_0-D_3 Outputs with Very High Current Options (I_{OL})	V_{CC} = 9.5V, V_{OL} = 1.0V	30	150	mA
	V_{CC} = 4.5V, V_{OL} = 1.0V	15	75	mA
Output Source Current:				
Standard Configuration, All Outputs (I_{OH})	V_{CC} = 9.5V, V_{OH} = 4.75V	−70	−450	μA
	V_{CC} = 4.5V, V_{OH} = 2.25V	−26	−190	μA
Push-Pull Configuration, SO and SK Outputs (I_{OH})	V_{CC} = 9.5V, V_{OH} = 4.75V	−1.45	−15.5	mA
	V_{CC} = 4.5V, V_{OH} = 2.25V	−0.07	−2.8	mA
LED Configuration, L_0-L_7 Outputs, Low Current Driver Option (I_{OH})	V_{CC} = 9.5V, V_{OH} = 2.0V	−1.5	−15	mA
	V_{CC} = 6.0V, V_{OH} = 2.0V	−1.5	−9.0	mA
LED Configuration, L_0-L_7 Outputs, High Current Driver Option (I_{OH})	V_{CC} = 9.5V, V_{OH} = 2.0V	−3.0	−30	mA
	V_{CC} = 6.0V, V_{OH} = 2.0V	−3.0	−20	mA
TRI-STATE Configuration, L_0-L_7 Outputs, Low Current Driver Option (I_{OH})	V_{CC} = 9.5V, V_{OH} = 4.75V	−2.4	−24.5	mA
	V_{CC} = 4.5V, V_{OH} = 2.25V	−0.06	−3.8	mA
TRI-STATE Configuration, L_0-L_7 Outputs, High Current Driver Option (I_{OH})	V_{CC} = 9.5V, V_{OH} = 4.75V	−4.9	−47.5	mA
	V_{CC} = 4.5V, V_{OH} = 2.25V	−0.12	−8.1	mA
CKO Output				
RAM Power Supply Option Power Requirement	V_R = 3.3V		3.0	mA
TRI-STATE® Output Leakage Current		−10	+10	μA

COP420L/COP421L

AC Electrical Characteristics $0°C \leqslant T_A \leqslant +70°C$, $4.5V \leqslant V_{CC} \leqslant 9.5V$ unless otherwise noted.

Parameter	Conditions	Min.	Max.	Units
Instruction Cycle Time — t_C		15	40	μs
CKI				
Input Frequency — f_I	÷32 mode	0.8	2.0	MHz
	÷16 mode	0.4	1.0	MHz
	÷8 mode	0.2	0.5	MHz
	÷4 mode	0.1	0.25	MHz
Duty Cycle		30	60	%
Rise Time	$f_I = 2\,MHz$		120	ns
Fall Time			80	ns
CKI Using RC (÷4)	$R = 51\,k\Omega \pm 5\%$ $C = 100\,pF \pm 10\%$			
Instruction Cycle Time		15	25	μs
CKO as SYNC Input				
t_{SYNC}		400		ns
INPUTS:				
$IN_3 - IN_0$, $G_3 - G_0$, $L_7 - L_0$				
t_{SETUP}		8		μs
t_{HOLD}		600		ns
SI				
t_{SETUP}		2		μs
t_{HOLD}		600		ns
OUTPUTS:				
COP TO CMOS PROPAGATION DELAY	$V_{OH} = 0.7\,V_{CC}$, $V_{OL} = 0.3\,V_{CC}$, $C_L = 50\,pF$			
All Standard Output Configurations				
t_{PD1}			6.5	μs
SO, SK Outputs				
t_{PD1} (push-pull)			4.0	μs
t_{PD0}			1.2	μs
$D_3 - D_0$, $G_3 - G_0$				
t_{PD0}			2.7	μs
$L_7 - L_0$				
t_{PD0}			2.7	μs
t_{PD1} (standard size push-pull)			3.0	μs
t_{PD1} (high current push-pull)			2.5	μs
$L_7 - L_0$ LED Direct Drive Outputs	$6.0V \leqslant V_{CC} \leqslant 9.5V$, $V_{OH} = 2.0V$ $C_L = 50\,pF$			
t_{PD1} (standard size)			5.0	μs
t_{PD1} (high current)			4.5	μs
COP TO LSTTL PROPOGATION DELAY	$V_{CC} = 5V \pm 5\%$, $V_{OH} = 2.7V$ $V_{OL} = 0.4V$, $C_L = 50\,pF$			
SO, SK Outputs				
t_{PD1} (standard)			5	μs
t_{PD1} (push-pull)			3.5	μs
t_{PD0}			3	μs
$L_7 - L_0$ Outputs				
t_{PD1} (push-pull)			1.5	μs
$L_7 - L_0$, $G_3 - G_0$, $D_3 - D_0$ Outputs				
t_{PD1} (standard)			5.0	μs
t_{PD0}			2.0	μs
CKO (Figure 3b)				
t_{PD1}			0.4	μs
t_{PD0}			0.4	μs

COP320L/COP321L

Absolute Maximum Ratings

Voltage at Any Pin Relative to GND	−0.5V to +10V
Ambient Operating Temperature	−40°C to +85°C
Ambient Storage Temperature	−65°C to +150°C
Lead Temperature (Soldering, 10 seconds)	300°C
Power Dissipation	0.75 Watt at 25°C
	0.25 Watt at 85°C

Absolute maximum ratings indicate limits beyond which damage to the device may occur. DC and AC electrical specifications are not ensured when operating the device at absolute maximum ratings.

DC Electrical Characteristics   −40°C ≤ T_A ≤ +85°C, 4.5V ≤ V_{CC} ≤ 7.5V unless otherwise noted.

Parameter	Conditions	Min.	Max.	Units
Standard Operating Voltage (V_{CC})	Note 1	4.5	5.5	V
Optional Operating Voltage (V_{CC})		4.5	7.5	V
Operating Supply Current	V_{CC} = 5V, (all inputs and outputs open)		10	mA
Input Voltage Levels				
CKI Input Levels				
Crystal Input				
Logic High (V_{IH})		2.2		V
Logic Low (V_{IL})		−0.3	0.3	V
Schmitt Trigger Input				
Logic High (V_{CC})		0.7 V_{CC}		V
Logic Low (V_{IL})		−0.3	0.4	V
$\overline{RESET}$ Input Levels				
Logic High		0.7 V_{CC}		V
Logic Low		−0.3	0.4	V
$\overline{RESET}$ Hysteresis		1.0		V
SO Input Level (Test mode)		2.2	3.0	V
All Other Inputs				
Logic High	V_{CC} = MAX	3.0		V
Logic High	with TTL trip level options	2.2		V
Logic Low	selected, V_{CC} = 5V ± 10%	−0.3	0.4	V
Logic High	with high trip level options	3.6		V
Logic Low	selected	−0.3	1.2	V
Input Capacitance			7	pF
Hi-Z Input Leakage		−1	+1	μA
Output Voltage Levels				
LSTTL Operation	V_{CC} = 5V ± 5%			
Logic High (V_{OH})	I_{OH} = −20μA	2.7		V
Logic Low (V_{OL})	I_{OL} = 0.36mA		0.4	V
CMOS Operation				
Logic High	I_{OH} = −10μA	V_{CC} − 1		V
Logic Low	I_{OC} = +10μA		0.2	V

Note 1: V_{CC} voltage change must be less than 0.5V/ms to maintain proper operation.

COP320L/COP321L

DC Electrical Characteristics (continued) $-40°C \leqslant T_A \leqslant +85°C$, $4.5V \leqslant V_{CC} \leqslant 7.5V$ unless otherwise noted.

Parameter	Conditions	Min.	Max.	Units
Output Current Levels				
Output Sink Current				
SO and SK Outputs (I_{OL})	$V_{CC} = 7.5V$, $V_{OL} = 1.0V$	4.0	22	mA
	$V_{CC} = 4.5V$, $V_{OL} = 1.0V$	2.1	12	mA
L_0-L_7 Outputs and Standard Size G_0-G_3 and D_0-D_3 Outputs (I_{OL})	$V_{CC} = 7.5V$, $V_{OL} = 1.0V$	1.7	8.0	mA
	$V_{CC} = 4.5V$, $V_{OL} = 1.0V$	1.0	5.0	mA
G_0-G_3 and D_0-D_3 Outputs with High Current Options (I_{OL})	$V_{CC} = 7.5V$, $V_{OL} = 1.0V$	14	60	mA
	$V_{CC} = 4.5V$, $V_{OL} = 1.0V$	7.0	40	mA
G_0-G_3 and D_0-D_3 Outputs with Very High Current Options (I_{OL})	$V_{CC} = 7.5V$, $V_{OL} = 1.0V$	28	120	mA
	$V_{CC} = 4.5V$, $V_{OL} = 1.0V$	14	80	mA
Output Source Current:				
Standard Configuration, All Outputs (I_{OH})	$V_{CC} = 7.5V$, $V_{OH} = 3.75V$	-100	-500	μA
	$V_{CC} = 4.5V$, $V_{OH} = 2.25V$	-25	-250	μA
Push-Pull Configuration, SO and SK Outputs (I_{OH})	$V_{CC} = 7.5V$, $V_{OH} = 3.75V$	-1.3	-9.0	mA
	$V_{CC} = 4.5V$, $V_{OH} = 2.25V$	-0.06	-3.6	mA
LED Configuration, L_0-L_7 Outputs, Low Current Driver Option (I_{OH})	$V_{CC} = 7.5V$, $V_{OH} = 2.0V$	-1.4	-25	mA
	$V_{CC} = 6.0V$, $V_{OH} = 2.0V$	-1.4	-13.0	mA
LED Configuration, (Note 2) L_0-L_7 Outputs, High Current Driver Option (I_{OH})	$V_{CC} = 7.5V$, $V_{OH} = 2.0V$	-2.7	-51	mA
	$V_{CC} = 6.0V$, $V_{OH} = 2.0V$	-2.7	-26	mA
TRI-STATE Configuration, L_0-L_7 Outputs, Low Current Driver Option (I_{OH})	$V_{CC} = 7.5V$, $V_{OH} = 3.75V$	-1.3	-14.0	mA
	$V_{CC} = 4.5V$, $V_{OH} = 2.25V$	-0.05	-4.0	mA
TRI-STATE Configuration, L_0-L_7 Outputs, High Current Driver Option (I_{OH})	$V_{CC} = 7.5V$, $V_{OH} = 3.75V$	-2.5	-26.0	mA
	$V_{CC} = 4.5V$, $V_{OH} = 2.25V$	-0.1	-7.0	mA
CKO Output RAM Power Supply Option Power Requirement	$V_R = 3.3V$		4.0	mA
TRI-STATE® Output Leakage Current		-10	$+10$	μA

Note 2: Exercise great care not to exceed maximum device power dissipation limits when direct-driving LEDs (or sourcing similar loads) at high temperature.

COP320L/COP321L

AC Electrical Characteristics $-40°C \leqslant T_A \leqslant +85°C$, $4.5V \leqslant V_{CC} \leqslant 7.5V$ unless otherwise noted.

Parameter	Conditions	Min.	Max.	Units
Instruction Cycle Time — t_C		15	40	μs
CKI				
Input Frequency — f_I	÷32 mode	0.8	2.0	MHz
	÷16 mode	0.4	1.0	MHz
	÷8 mode	0.02	0.5	MHz
	÷4 mode	0.1	0.25	MHz
Duty Cycle		30	60	%
Rise Time	$f_I = 2\,MHz$		120	ns
Fall Time			80	ns
CKI Using RC (÷4)	$R = 51\,k\Omega \pm 5\%$ $C = 100\,pF \pm 10\%$			
Instruction Cycle Time		15	25	μs
CKO as SYNC Input				
t_{SYNC}		400		ns
INPUTS:				
$IN_3 - IN_0$, $G_3 - G_0$, $L_7 - L_0$				
t_{SETUP}		8		μs
t_{HOLD}		1		μs
SI				
t_{SETUP}		2		μs
t_{HOLD}		1		μs
OUTPUTS:				
COP TO CMOS PROPAGATION DELAY	$V_{OH} = 0.7\,V_{CC}$, $V_{OL} = 0.3\,V_{CC}$, $C_L = 50\,pF$			
All Standard Output Configurations				
t_{PD1}			7.0	μs
SO, SK Outputs				
t_{PD1} (push-pull)			4.5	μs
t_{PD0}			1.3	μs
$D_3 - D_0$, $G_3 - G_0$				
t_{PD0}			3.0	μs
$L_7 - L_0$				
t_{PD0}			3.0	μs
t_{PD1} (standard size push-pull)			3.3	μs
t_{PD1} (high current push-pull)			2.8	μs
$L_7 - L_0$ LED Direct Drive Outputs	$6.0V \leqslant V_{CC} \leqslant 7.5V$, $V_{OH} = 2.0V$			
t_{PD1} (standard size)	$C_L = 50\,pF$		5.5	μs
t_{PD1} (high current)			5.0	μs
COP TO LSTTL PROPOGATION DELAY	$V_{CC} = 5V \pm 5\%$, $V_{OH} = 2.7V$ $V_{OL} = 0.4V$, $C_L = 50\,pF$			
SO, SK Outputs				
t_{PD1} (standard)			5.5	μs
t_{PD1} (push-pull)			3.9	μs
t_{PD0}			3.3	μs
$L_7 - L_0$ Outputs				
t_{PD1} (push-pull)			1.7	μs
$L_7 - L_0$, $G_3 - G_0$, $D_3 - D_0$ Outputs				
t_{PD1} (standard)			5.5	μs
t_{PD0}			2.2	μs
CKO (Figure 3b)				
t_{PD1}			0.45	μs
t_{PD0}			0.45	μs

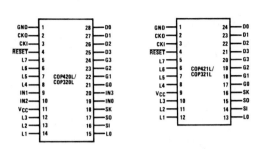

Figure 2. Connection Diagrams

Pin	Description	Pin	Description
$L_7 - L_0$	8 bidirectional I/O ports with TRI-STATE®	SK	Logic-controlled clock (or general purpose output)
$G_3 - G_0$	4 bidirectional I/O ports	CKI	System oscillator input
$D_3 - D_0$	4 general purpose outputs	CKO	System oscillator output (or general purpose input, RAM power supply or SYNC input)
$IN_3 - IN_0$	4 general purpose inputs (COP420L only)		
SI	Serial input (or counter input)	$\overline{\text{RESET}}$	System reset input
SO	Serial output (or general purpose output)	V_{CC}	Power supply
		GND	Ground

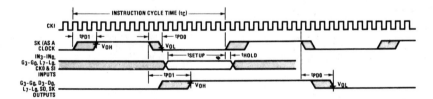

Figure 3. Input/Output Timing Diagrams (Crystal Divide-by-16 Mode)

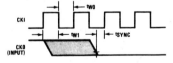

Figure 3a. Synchronization Timing

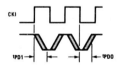

Figure 3b. CKO Output Timing

Functional Description

For ease of reading this description, only COP420L and/or COP421L are referenced; however, all such references apply equally to COP320L and/or COP321L, respectively.

A block diagram of the COP420L is given in Figure 1. Data paths are illustrated in simplified form to depict how the various logic elements communicate with each other in implementing the instruction set of the device. Positive logic is used. When a bit is set, it is a logic "1" (greater than 2 volts). When a bit is reset, it is a logic "0" (less than 0.8 volts).

Program Memory

Program Memory consists of a 1,024 byte ROM. As can be seen by an examination of the COP420L/421L instruction set, these words may be program instructions, program data or ROM addressing data. Because of the special characteristics associated with the JP, JSRP, JID and LQID instructions, ROM must often be thought of as being organized into 16 pages of 64 words each.

ROM addressing is accomplished by a 10-bit PC register. Its binary value selects one of the 1,024 8-bit words contained in ROM. A new address is loaded into the PC register during each instruction cycle. Unless the instruction is a transfer of control instruction, the PC register is loaded with the next sequential 10-bit binary count value. Three levels of subroutine nesting are implemented by the 10-bit subroutine save registers, SA, SB and SC, providing a last-in, first-out (LIFO) hardware subroutine stack.

ROM instruction words are fetched, decoded and executed by the Instruction Decode, Control and Skip Logic circuitry.

Data Memory

Data memory consists of a 256-bit RAM, organized as 4 data registers of 16 4-bit digits. RAM addressing is implemented by a 6-bit B register whose upper 2 bits (Br) select 1 of 4 data registers and lower 4 bits (Bd) select 1 of 16 4-bit digits in the selected data register. While the 4-bit contents of the selected RAM digit (M) is usually loaded into or from, or exchanged with, the A register (accumulator), it may also be loaded into or from the Q latches or loaded from the L ports. RAM addressing may also be performed directly by the LDD and XAD instructions based upon the 6-bit contents of the operand field of these instructions. The Bd register also serves as a source register for 4-bit data sent directly to the D outputs.

Internal Logic

The 4-bit A register (accumulator) is the source and destination register for most I/O, arithmetic, logic and data memory access operations. It can also be used to load the Br and Bd portions of the B register, to load and input 4 bits of the 8-bit Q latch data, to input 4 bits of the 8-bit L I/O port data and to perform data exchanges with the SIO register.

A 4-bit adder performs the arithmetic and logic functions of the COP420/421L, storing its results in A. It also outputs a carry bit to the 1-bit C register, most often employed to indicate arithmetic overflow. The C register, in conjunction with the XAS instruction and the EN register, also serves to control the SK output. C can be outputted directly to SK or can enable SK to be a sync clock each instruction cycle time. (See XAS instruction and EN register description, below.)

Four general-purpose inputs, $IN_3 - IN_0$, are provided.

The D register provides 4 general-purpose outputs and is used as the destination register for the 4-bit contents of Bd. The D outputs can be directly connected to the digits of a multiplexed LED display.

The G register contents are outputs to 4 general-purpose bidirectional I/O ports. G I/O ports can be directly connected to the digits of a multiplexed LED display.

The Q register is an internal, latched, 8-bit register, used to hold data loaded to or from M and A, as well as 8-bit data from ROM. Its contents are outputted to the L I/O ports when the L drivers are enabled under program control. (See LEI instruction.)

The 8 L drivers, when enabled, output the contents of latched Q data to the L I/O ports. Also, the contents of L may be read directly into A and M. L I/O ports can be directly connected to the segments of a multiplexed LED display (using the LED Direct Drive output configuration option) with Q data being outputted to the Sa – Sg and decimal point segments of the display.

The SIO register functions as a 4-bit serial-in/serial-out shift register or as a binary counter depending on the contents of the EN register. (See EN register description, below.) Its contents can be exchanged with A, allowing it to input or output a continuous serial data stream. SIO may also be used to provide additional parallel I/O by connecting SO to external serial-in/parallel-out shift registers. For example of additional parallel output capacity see Application #2.

The XAS instruction copies C into the **SKL latch**. In the counter mode, SK is the output of SKL; in the shift register mode, SK outputs SKL ANDed with the clock.

The EN register is an internal 4-bit register loaded under program control by the LEI instruction. The state of each bit of this register selects or deselects the particular feature associated with each bit of the EN register ($EN_3 - EN_0$).

1. The least significant bit of the enable register, EN_0, selects the SIO register as either a 4-bit shift register or a 4-bit binary counter. With EN_0 set, SIO is an asynchronous binary counter, *decrementing* its value by one upon each low-going pulse ("1" to "0") occurring on the SI input. Each pulse must be at least two instruction cycles wide. SK outputs the value of SKL. The SO output is equal to the value of EN_3. With EN_0 reset, SIO is a serial shift register shifting left each instruction cycle time. The data present at SI goes into the least significant bit of SIO. SO can be enabled to output the most significant bit of SIO each cycle time. (See 4 below.) The SK output becomes a logic-controlled clock.

2. With EN_1 set the IN_1 input is enabled as an interrupt input. Immediately following an interrupt, EN_1 is reset to disable further interrupts.

3. With EN_2 set, the L drivers are enabled to output the data in Q to the L I/O ports. Resetting EN_2 disables

the L drivers, placing the L I/O ports in a high-impedance input state.

4. EN_3, in conjunction with EN_0, affects the SO output. With EN_0 set (binary counter option selected) SO will output the value loaded into EN_3. With EN_0 reset (serial shift register option selected), setting EN_3 enables SO as the output of the SIO shift register,

outputting serial shifted data each instruction time. Resetting EN_3 with the serial shift register option selected disables SO as the shift register output; data continues to be shifted through SIO and can be exchanged with A via an XAS instruction but SO remains reset to "0." The table below provides a summary of the modes associated with EN_3 and EN_0.

Enable Register Modes — Bits EN_3 and EN_0

EN_3	EN_0	SIO	SI	SO	SK
0	0	Shift Register	Input to Shift Register	0	If SKL = 1, SK = Clock
					If SKL = 0, SK = 0
1	0	Shift Register	Input to Shift Register	Serial Out	If SKL = 1, SK = Clock
					If SKL = 0, SK = 0
0	1	Binary Counter	Input to Binary Counter	0	If SKL = 1, SK = 1
					If SKL = 0, SK = 0
1	1	Binary Counter	Input to Binary Counter	1	If SKL = 1, SK = 1
					If SKL = 0, SK = 0

Interrupt

The following features are associated with the IN_1 interrupt procedure and protocol and must be considered by the programmer when utilizing interrupts.

a. The interrupt, once acknowledged as explained below, pushes the next sequential program counter address (PC + 1) onto the stack, pushing in turn the contents of the other subroutine-save registers to the next lower level (PC + 1 → SA → SB → SC). Any previous contents of SC are lost. The program counter is set to hex address OFF (the last word of page 3) and EN_1 is reset.

b. An interrupt will be acknowledged only after the following conditions are met:
1. EN_1 has been set.
2. A low-going pulse ("1" to "0") at least two instruction cycles wide occurs on the IN_1 input.
3. A currently executing instruction has been completed.
4. All successive transfer of control instructions and successive LBIs have been completed (e.g., if the main program is executing a JP instruction which transfers program control to another JP instruction, the interrupt will not be acknowledged until the second JP instruction has been executed).

c. Upon acknowledgement of an interrupt, the skip logic status is saved and later restored upon popping of the stack. For example, if an interrupt occurs during the execution of ASC (Add with Carry, Skip on Carry) instruction which results in carry, the skip logic status is saved and program control is transferred to the interrupt servicing routine at hex address OFF. At the *end* of the interrupt routine, a RET instruction is executed to "pop" the stack and return program control to the instruction following the original ASC. *At this time*, the skip logic is enabled and skips this instruction because of the previous ASC carry. Subroutines and LQID instructions should not be nested

within the interrupt servicing routine since their popping the stack will enable any previously saved main program skips, interfering with the orderly execution of the interrupt routine.

d. The first instruction of the interrupt routine at hex address OFF must be a NOP.

e. A LEI instruction can be put immediately before the RET to re-enable interrupts.

Initialization

The Reset Logic will initialize (clear) the device upon power-up if the power supply rise time is less than 1 ms and greater than 1 μs. If the power supply rise time is greater than 1 ms, the user must provide an external RC network and diode to the RESET pin as shown below. The RESET pin is configured as a Schmitt trigger input. If not used it should be connected to V_{CC}. Initialization will occur whenever a logic "0" is applied to the RESET input, provided it stays low for at least three instruction cycle times.

Upon initialization, the PC register is cleared to 0 (ROM address 0) and the A, B, C, D, EN, and G registers are cleared. The SK output is enabled as a SYNC output, providing a pulse each instruction cycle time. *Data Memory (RAM) is not cleared upon initialization*. The first instruction at address 0 must be a CLRA.

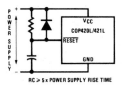

RC ≥ 5 x POWER SUPPLY RISE TIME

Power-Up Clear Circuit

Oscillator

There are four basic clock oscillator configurations available as shown by Figure 4.

a. Crystal Controlled Oscillator. CKI and CKO are connected to an external crystal. The instruction cycle time equals the crystal frequency divided by 32 (optional by 16 or 8).

b. External Oscillator. CKI is an external clock input signal. The external frequency is divided by 32 (optional by 16 or 8) to give the instruction cycle time. CKO is now available to be used as the RAM power supply (V_R), as a general purpose input, or as a SYNC input.

c. RC Controlled Oscillator. CKI is configured as a single pin RC controlled Schmitt trigger oscillator. The instruction cycle equals the oscillation frequency divided by 4. CKO is available as the RAM power supply (V_R) or as a general purpose input.

d. Externally Synchronized Oscillator. Intended for use in multi-COP systems, CKO is programmed to function as an input connected to the SK output of another COP chip operating at the same frequency (COP chip with L or C suffix) with CKI connected as shown. In this configuration, the SK output connected to CKO must provide a SYNC (instruction cycle) signal to CKO, thereby allowing synchronous data transfer between the COPs using only the SI and SO serial I/O pins in conjunction with the XAS instruction. Note that on power-up SK is automatically enabled as a

SYNC output (See Functional Description, Initialization, above).

CKO Pin Options

In a crystal controlled oscillator system, CKO is used as an output to the crystal network. As an option CKO can be a SYNC input as described above. As another option CKO can be a general purpose input, read into bit 2 of A (accumulator) upon execution of an INIL instruction. As another option, CKO can be a RAM power supply pin (V_R), allowing its connection to a standby/backup power supply to maintain the integrity of RAM data with minimum power drain when the main supply is inoperative or shut down to conserve power. Using either option is appropriate in applications where the COP420L/421L system timing configuration does not require use of the CKO pin.

RAM Keep-Alive Option

Selecting CKO as the RAM power supply (V_R) allows the user to shut off the chip power supply (V_{CC}) and maintain data in the RAM. To insure that RAM data integrity is maintained, the following conditions must be met:

1. $\overline{RESET}$ must go low before V_{CC} goes below spec during power-off; V_{CC} must be within spec before $\overline{RESET}$ goes high on power-up.

2. V_R must be within the operating range of the chip, and equal to $V_{CC} \pm 1V$ during normal operation.

3. V_R must be $\geqslant 3.3V$ with V_{CC} off.

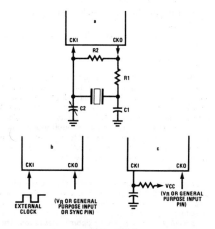

Crystal Oscillator

Crystal	Component Values			
Value	R1 (Ω)	R2 (Ω)	C1 (pF)	C2 (pF)
455 kHz	16k	1M	80	80
2.097 MHz	1k	1M	56	6–36

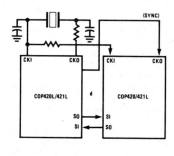

RC Controlled Oscillator

R (kΩ)	C (pF)	Instruction Cycle Time (μs)
51	100	19 $\pm$ 15%
82	56	19 $\pm$ 13%

Note: 200k $\geqslant$ R $\geqslant$ 25k
360 pF $\geqslant$ C $\geqslant$ 50 pF

Figure 4. COP420/421L Oscillator

I/O Options

COP420L/421L outputs have the following optional configurations, illustrated in Figure 5:

a. Standard — an enhancement mode device to ground in conjunction with a depletion-mode device to V_{CC}, compatible with LSTTL and CMOS input requirements. Available on SO, SK, and all D and G outputs.

b. Open-Drain — an enhancement-mode device to ground only, allowing external pull-up as required by the user's application. Available on SO, SK, and all D and G outputs.

c. Push-Pull — An enhancement-mode device to ground in conjunction with a depletion-mode device paralleled by an enhancement-mode device to V_{CC}. This configuration has been provided to allow for fast rise and fall times when driving capacitive loads. Available on SO and SK outputs only.

d. Standard L — same as **a.**, but may be disabled. Available on L outputs only.

e. Open Drain L — same as **b.**, but may be disabled. Available on L outputs only.

f. LED Direct Drive — an enhancement-mode device to ground and to V_{CC}, meeting the typical current sourcing requirements of the segments of an LED display. The sourcing device is clamped to limit current flow. These devices may be turned off under program control (See Functional Description, EN Register), placing the outputs in a high-impedance state to provide required LED segment blanking for a multiplexed display. Available on L outputs only.

g. TRI-STATE® Push-Pull — an enhancement-mode device to ground and V_{CC}. These outputs are TRI-STATE outputs, allowing for connection of these outputs to a data bus shared by other bus drivers. Available on L outputs only.

COP420L/COP421L inputs have the following optional configurations:

h. An on-chip depletion load device to V_{CC}.

i. A Hi-Z input which must be driven to a "1" or "0" by external components.

The above input and output configurations share common enhancement-mode and depletion-mode devices. Specifically, all configurations use one or more of six devices (numbered 1–6, respectively). Minimum and maximum current (I_{OUT} and V_{OUT}) curves are given in Figure 6 for each of these devices to allow the designer to effectively use these I/O configurations in designing a COP420L/421L system.

The SO, SK outputs can be configured as shown in **a.**, **b.**, or **c.** The D and G outputs can be configured as shown in **a.** or **b.** Note that when inputting data to the G ports, the G outputs should be set to "1." The L outputs can be configured as in **d.**, **e.**, **f.** or **g.**

An important point to remember if using configuration **d.** or **f.** with the L drivers is that even when the L drivers are disabled, the depletion load device will source a small amount of current (see Figure 6, device 2); however, when the L lines are used as inputs, the disabled depletion device *cannot* be relied on to source sufficient current to pull an input to a logic 1.

COP421L

If the COP420L is bonded as a 24-pin device, it becomes the COP421L, illustrated in Figure 2, COP420L/421L Connection Diagrams. Note that the COP421L does not contain the four general purpose IN inputs ($IN_3 - IN_0$). Use of this option precludes, of course, use of the IN options and the interrupt feature. All other options are available for the COP421L.

COP420L/COP421L Instruction Set

Table 1 is a symbol table providing internal architecture, instruction operand and operational symbols used in the instruction set table.

Table 2 provides the mnemonic, operand, machine code, data flow, skip conditions, and description associated with each instruction in the COP420L/421L instruction set.

Table 1. COP420L/421L Instruction Set Table Symbols

Symbol	Definition
INTERNAL ARCHITECTURE SYMBOLS	
A	4-bit Accumulator
B	6-bit RAM Address Register
Br	Upper 2 bits of B (register address)
Bd	Lower 4 bits of B (digit address)
C	1-bit Carry Register
D	4-bit Data Output Port
EN	4-bit Enable Register
G	4-bit Register to latch data for G I/O Port
IL	Two 1-bit Latches associated with the IN_3 or IN_0 Inputs
IN	4-bit Input Port
L	8-bit TRI-STATE I/O Port
M	4-bit contents of RAM Memory pointed to by B Register
PC	10-bit ROM Address Register (program counter)
Q	8-bit Register to latch data for L I/O Port
SA	10-bit Subroutine Save Register A
SB	10-bit Subroutine Save Register B
SC	10-bit Subroutine Save Register C
SIO	4-bit Shift Register and Counter
SK	Logic-Controlled Clock Output

Symbol	Definition
INSTRUCTION OPERAND SYMBOLS	
d	4-bit Operand Field, 0–15 binary (RAM Digit Select)
r	2-bit Operand Field, 0–3 binary (RAM Register Select)
a	10-bit Operand Field, 0–1023 binary (ROM Address)
y	4-bit Operand Field, 0–15 binary (Immediate Data)
RAM(s)	Contents of RAM location addressed by s
ROM(t)	Contents of ROM location addressed by t

Symbol	Definition
OPERATIONAL SYMBOLS	
+	Plus
–	Minus
→	Replaces
↔	Is exchanged with
=	Is equal to
$\overline{A}$	The ones complement of A
⊕	Exclusive-OR
:	Range of values

Table 2. COP420L/421L Instruction Set

Mnemonic Operand		Hex Code	Machine Language Code (Binary)	Data Flow	Skip Conditions	Description
ARITHMETIC INSTRUCTIONS						
ASC		30	$|0\ 0\ 1\ 1|0\ 0\ 0\ 0|$	$A + C + RAM(B) \rightarrow A$ $Carry \rightarrow C$	Carry	Add with Carry, Skip on Carry
ADD		31	$|0\ 0\ 1\ 1|0\ 0\ 0\ 1|$	$A + RAM(B) \rightarrow A$	None	Add RAM to A
ADT		4A	$|0\ 1\ 0\ 0|1\ 0\ 1\ 0|$	$A + 10_{10} \rightarrow A$	None	Add Ten to A
AISC	y	5-	$|0\ 1\ 0\ 1|\ \ y\ \ |$	$A + y \rightarrow A$	Carry	Add Immediate, Skip on Carry (y ≠ 0)
CASC		10	$|0\ 0\ 0\ 1|0\ 0\ 0\ 0|$	$\bar{A} + RAM(B) + C \rightarrow A$ $Carry \rightarrow C$	Carry	Complement and Add with Carry, Skip on Carry
CLRA		00	$|0\ 0\ 0\ 0|0\ 0\ 0\ 0|$	$0 \rightarrow A$	None	Clear A
COMP		40	$|0\ 1\ 0\ 0|0\ 0\ 0\ 0|$	$\bar{A} \rightarrow A$	None	Ones complement of A to A
NOP		44	$|0\ 1\ 0\ 0|0\ 1\ 0\ 0|$	None	None	No Operation
RC		32	$|0\ 0\ 1\ 1|0\ 0\ 1\ 0|$	"0" $\rightarrow$ C	None	Reset C
SC		22	$|0\ 0\ 1\ 0|0\ 0\ 1\ 0|$	"1" $\rightarrow$ C	None	Set C
XOR		02	$|0\ 0\ 0\ 0|0\ 0\ 1\ 0|$	$A \oplus RAM(B) \rightarrow A$	None	Exclusive-OR RAM with A
TRANSFER OF CONTROL INSTRUCTIONS						
JID		FF	$|1\ 1\ 1\ 1|1\ 1\ 1\ 1|$	$ROM(PC_{9:8}, A, M) \rightarrow PC_{7:0}$	None	Jump Indirect (Note 3)
JMP	a	6-	$|0\ 1\ 1\ 0\ 0\ 0|a_{9:8}|$ $|\quad a_{7:0}\quad|$	$a \rightarrow PC$	None	Jump
JP	a	--	$|1|\quad a_{6:0}\quad|$ (pages 2,3 only) or $|1\ 1|\quad a_{5:0}\quad|$ (all other pages)	$a \rightarrow PC_{6:0}$ $a \rightarrow PC_{5:0}$	None	Jump within Page (Note 4)
JSRP	a	--	$|1\ 0|\quad a_{5:0}\quad|$	$PC + 1 \rightarrow SA \rightarrow SB \rightarrow SC$ $0010 \rightarrow PC_{9:6}$ $a \rightarrow PC_{5:0}$	None	Jump to Subroutine Page (Note 5)
JSR	a	6- --	$|0\ 1\ 1\ 0\ 1\ 0|a_{9:8}|$ $|\quad a_{7:0}\quad|$	$PC + 1 \rightarrow SA \rightarrow SB \rightarrow SC$ $a \rightarrow PC$	None	Jump to Subroutine
RET		48	$|0\ 1\ 0\ 0|1\ 0\ 0\ 0|$	$SC \rightarrow SB \rightarrow SA \rightarrow PC$	None	Return from Subroutine
RETSK		49	$|0\ 1\ 0\ 0|1\ 0\ 0\ 1|$	$SC \rightarrow SB \rightarrow SA \rightarrow PC$	Always Skip on Return	Return from Subroutine then Skip

Table 2. COP420L/421L Instruction Set (continued)

Mnemonic	Operand	Hex Code	Machine Language Code (Binary)	Data Flow	Skip Conditions	Description
MEMORY REFERENCE INSTRUCTIONS						
CAMQ		33	0011|0011	$A \rightarrow Q_{7:4}$	None	Copy A, RAM to Q
		3C	0011|1100	$RAM(B) \rightarrow Q_{3:0}$		
CQMA		33	0011|0011	$Q_{7:4} \rightarrow RAM(B)$	None	Copy Q to RAM, A
		2C	0010|1100	$Q_{3:0} \rightarrow A$		
LD	r	–5	00|r|0101	$RAM(B) \rightarrow A$	None	Load RAM into A,
				$Br \oplus r \rightarrow Br$		Exclusive-OR Br with r
LDD	r,d	23	0010|0011	$RAM(r,d) \rightarrow A$	None	Load A with RAM pointed
		––	00|r|d			to directly by r,d
LQID		BF	1011|1111	$ROM(PC_{9:8},A,M) \rightarrow Q$	None	Load Q Indirect (Note 3)
				$SB \rightarrow SC$		
RMB	0	4C	0100|1100	$0 \rightarrow RAM(B)_0$	None	Reset RAM Bit
	1	45	0100|0101	$0 \rightarrow RAM(B)_1$		
	2	42	0100|0010	$0 \rightarrow RAM(B)_2$		
	3	43	0100|0011	$0 \rightarrow RAM(B)_3$		
SMB	0	4D	0100|1101	$1 \rightarrow RAM(B)_0$	None	Set RAM Bit
	1	47	0100|1101	$1 \rightarrow RAM(B)_1$		
	2	46	0100|0110	$1 \rightarrow RAM(B)_2$		
	3	4B	0100|1011	$1 \rightarrow RAM(B)_3$		
STII	y	7–	0111|y	$y \rightarrow RAM(B)$	None	Store Memory Immediate
				$Bd + 1 \rightarrow Bd$		and Increment Bd
X	r	–6	00|r|0110	$RAM(B) \leftrightarrow A$	None	Exchange RAM with A,
				$Br \oplus r \rightarrow Br$		Exclusive-OR Br with r
XAD	r,d	23	0010|0011	$RAM(r,d) \leftrightarrow A$	None	Exchange A with RAM
		––	10|r|d			pointed to directly by r,d
XDS	r	–7	00|r|0111	$RAM(B) \leftrightarrow A$	Bd decrements past 0	Exchange RAM with A
				$Bd - 1 \rightarrow Bd$		and Decrement Bd,
				$Br \oplus r \rightarrow Br$		Exclusive-OR Br with r
XIS	r	–4	00|r|0100	$RAM(B) \leftrightarrow A$	Bd increments past 15	Exchange RAM with A
				$Bd + 1 \rightarrow Bd$		and Increment Bd,
				$Br \oplus r \rightarrow Br$		Exclusive-OR Br with r
REGISTER REFERENCE INSTRUCTIONS						
CAB		50	0101|0000	$A \rightarrow Bd$	None	Copy A to Bd
CBA		4E	0100|1110	$Bd \rightarrow A$	None	Copy Bd to A
LBI	r,d	––	00|r|(d–1)	$r,d \rightarrow B$	Skip until not a LBI	Load B Immediate with r,d
			(d = 0, 9:15)			(Note 6)
			or			
		33	0011|0011			
		––	10|r|d			
			(any d)			
LEI	y	33	0011|0011	$y \rightarrow EN$	None	Load EN Immediate (Note 7)
		6–	0110|y			
XABR		12	0001|0010	$A \leftrightarrow Br\ (0,0 \rightarrow A_3, A_2)$	None	Exchange A with Br

Table 2. COP420L/421L Instruction Set (continued)

Mnemonic Operand		Hex Code	Machine Language Code (Binary)	Data Flow	Skip Conditions	Description
TEST INSTRUCTIONS						
SKC		20	0010 0000		C = "1"	Skip if C is True
SKE		21	0010 0001		A = RAM(B)	Skip if A Equals RAM
SKGZ		33	0011 0011		$G_{3:0} = 0$	Skip if G is Zero (all 4 bits)
		21	0010 0001			
SKGBZ		33	0011 0011	1st byte		Skip if G Bit is Zero
	0	01	0000 0001	⎫	$G_0 = 0$	
	1	11	0001 0001	⎪ 2nd byte	$G_1 = 0$	
	2	03	0000 0011	⎬	$G_2 = 0$	
	3	13	0001 0011	⎭	$G_3 = 0$	
SKMBZ	0	01	0000 0001		$RAM(B)_0 = 0$	Skip if RAM Bit is Zero
	1	11	0001 0001		$RAM(B)_1 = 0$	
	2	03	0000 0011		$RAM(B)_2 = 0$	
	3	13	0001 0011		$RAM(B)_3 = 0$	
SKT		41	0100 0001		A time-base counter carry has occurred since last test	Skip on Timer (Note 3)
INPUT/OUTPUT INSTRUCTIONS						
ING		33	0011 0011	G → A	None	Input G Ports to A
		2A	0010 1010			
ININ		33	0011 0011	IN → A	None	Input IN Inputs to A (Note 2)
		28	0010 1000			
INIL		33	0011 0011	IL_3, CKO, "0", IL_0 → A	None	Input IL Latches to A (Note 3)
		29	0010 1001			
INL		33	0011 0011	$L_{7:4}$ → RAM(B)	None	Input L Ports to RAM,A
		2E	0010 1110	$L_{3:0}$ → A		
OBD		33	0011 0011	Bd → D	None	Output Bd to D Outputs
		3E	0011 1110			
OGI	y	33	0011 0011	y → G	None	Output to G Ports Immediate
		5–	0101 y			
OMG		33	0011 0011	RAM(B) → G	None	Output RAM to G Ports
		3A	0011 1010			
XAS		4F	0100 1111	A ↔ SIO, C → SKL	None	Exchange A with SIO (Note 3)

Note 1: All subscripts for alphabetical symbols indicate bit numbers unless explicitly defined (e.g., Br and Bd are explicitly defined). Bits are numbered 0 to N where 0 signifies the least significant bit (low-order, right-most bit). For example, A_3 indicates the most significant (left-most) bit of the 4-bit A register.

Note 2: The INI instruction is not available on the 24-pin COP421L since this device does not contain the IN inputs.

Note 3: For additional information on the operation of the XAS, JID, LQID, INIL, and SKT instructions, see below.

Note 4: The JP instruction allows a jump, while in subroutine pages 2 or 3, to any ROM location within the two-page boundary of pages 2 or 3. The JP instruction, otherwise, permits a jump to a ROM location within the current 64-word page. JP may not jump to the last word of a page.

Note 5: A JSRP transfers program control to subroutine page 2 (0010 is loaded into the upper 4 bits of P). A JSRP may not be used when in pages 2 or 3. JSRP may not jump to the last word in page 2.

Note 6: LBI is a single-byte instruction if d = 0, 9, 10, 11, 12, 13, 14, or 15. The machine code for the lower 4 bits equals the binary value of the "d" data *minus 1*, e.g., to load the lower four bits of B (Bd) with the value 9 (1001_2), the lower 4 bits of the LBI instruction equal 8 (1000_2). To load 0, the lower 4 bits of the LBI instruction should equal 15 (1111_2).

Note 7: Machine code for operand field y for LEI instruction should equal the binary value to be latched into EN, where a "1" or "0" in each bit of EN corresponds with the selection or deselection of a particular function associated with each bit. (See Functional Description, EN Register.)

OPTION LIST

The COP420L/421L mask-programmable options are assigned numbers which correspond with the COP*420L* pins.

The following is a list of COP420L options. When specifying a COP421L chip, Options 9, 10, 19, and 20 must all be set to zero. The options are programmed at the same time as the ROM pattern to provide the user with the hardware flexibility to interface to various I/O components using little or no external circuitry.

Option 1 = 0: Ground Pin — no options available

Option 2: CKO Output
= 0: clock generator output to crystal/resonator (0 not allowable value if Option 3 = 3)
= 1: pin is RAM power supply (V_R) input
= 2: general purpose input with load device to V_{CC}
= 3: general purpose input, high-Z
= 4: multi-COP SYNC input (CKI ÷ 32, CKI ÷ 16)
= 5: multi-COP SYNC input (CKI ÷ 8)

Option 3: CKI Input
= 0: oscillator input divided by 32 (2 MHz max)
= 1: oscillator input divided by 16 (1 MHz max)
= 2: oscillator input divided by 8 (500 kHz max)
= 3: single-pin RC controlled oscillator (÷4)
= 4: Schmitt trigger clock input (÷4)

Option 4: RESET Input
= 0: load device to V_{CC}
= 1: Hi-Z input

Option 5: L_7 Driver
= 0: Standard output
= 1: Open-drain output
= 2: High current LED direct segment drive output
= 3: High current TRI-STATE® push-pull output
= 4: Low-current LED direct segment drive output
= 5: Low-current TRI-STATE® push-pull output

Option 6: L_6 Driver
same as Option 5

Option 7: L_5 Driver
same as Option 5

Option 8: L_4 Driver
same as Option 5

Option 9: IN_1 Input
= 0: load device to V_{CC}
= 1: Hi-Z input

Option 10: IN_2 Input
same as Option 9

Option 11: V_{CC} pin
= 0: Standard V_{CC}
= 1: Optional higher voltage V_{CC}

Option 12: L_3 Driver
same as Option 5

Option 13: L_2 Driver
same as Option 5

Option 14: L_1 Driver
same as Option 5

Option 15: L_0 Driver
same as Option 5

Option 16: SI Input
same as Option 9

Option 17: SO Driver
= 0: standard output
= 1: open-drain output
= 2: push-pull output

Option 18: SK Driver
same as Option 17

Option 19: IN_0 Input
same as Option 9

Option 20: IN_3 Input
same as Option 9

Option 21: G_0 I/O Port
= 0: very-high current standard output
= 1: very-high current open-drain output
= 2: high current standard output
= 3: high current open-drain output
= 4: standard LSTTL output (fanout = 1)
= 5: open-drain LSTTL output (fanout = 1)

Option 22: G_1 I/O Port
same as Option 21

Option 23: G_2 I/O Port
same as Option 21

Option 24: G_3 I/O Port
same as Option 21

Option 25: D_3 Output
same as Option 21

Option 26: D_2 Output
same as Option 21

Option 27: D_1 Output
same as Option 21

Option 28: D_0 Output
same as Option 21

Option 29: L Input Levels
= 0: standard TTL input levels ("0" = 0.8V, "1" = 2.0V)
= 1: higher voltage input levels ("0" = 1.2V, "1" = 3.6V)

Option 30: IN Input Levels
same as Option 29

Option 31: G Input Levels
same as Option 29

Option 32: SI Input Levels
same as Option 29

Option 33: RESET Input
= 0: Schmitt trigger input
= 1: standard TTL input levels
= 2: higher voltage input levels

Option 34: CKO Input Levels (CKO = input; Option 2 = 2,3) same as Option 29

Option 35 COP Bonding
= 0: COP420L (28-pin device)
= 1: COP421L (24-pin device)

TEST MODE (Non-Standard Operation)

The SO output has been configured to provide for standard test procedures for the custom-programmed COP420L. With SO forced to logic "1," two test modes are provided, depending upon the value of SI:

a. RAM and Internal Logic Test Mode (SI = 1)

b. ROM Test Mode (SI = 0)

These special test modes should not be employed by the user; they are intended for manufacturing test only.

APPLICATION #1: COP420L General Controller

Figure 9 shows an interconnect diagram for a COP420L used as a general controller. Operation of the system is as follows:

1. The $L_7 - L_0$ outputs are configured as LED Direct Drive outputs, allowing direct connection to the segments of the display.

2. The $D_3 - D_0$ outputs drive the digits of the multiplexed display directly and scan the columns of the 4×4 keyboard matrix.

3. The $IN_3 - IN_0$ inputs are used to input the 4 rows of the keyboard matrix. Reading the IN lines in conjunction with the current value of the D outputs allows detection, debouncing, and decoding of any one of the 16 keyswitches.

4. CKI is configured as a single-pin oscillator input allowing system timing to be controlled by a single-pin RC network. CKO is therefore available for use as a V_R RAM power supply pin. RAM data integrity is thereby assured when the main power supply is shut down (see RAM Keep-Alive option description).

5. SI is selected as the input to a binary counter input. With SIO used as a binary counter, SO and SK can be used as general purpose outputs.

6. The 4 bidirectional G I/O ports ($G_3 - G_0$) are available for use as required by the user's application.

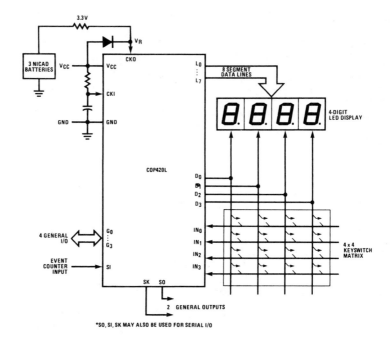

Figure 9. COP420L Keyboard/Display Interface

APPLICATION #2: Digitally Tuned Automotive Radio Controller and Clock

Figure 10 shows the COP420L interconnect diagram for a digitally tuned AM/FM car radio with digital clock LED display and 4×6 keyboard for storage and recall of station, search up and search down or scan up and scan down of stations, AM/FM select and time setting and display. Operation of the system is as follows:

1. The DS8907 uses a 4.0 MHz crystal to provide the time base for frequency synthesis and the 500 kHz time base for operation of the COP420L and the 50 Hz signal for the timekeeping function.

2. An unswitched 5V supply goes to the V_{CCM} pin of the DS8907 for the operation of the oscillator and divide-down for the 500 kHz and 50 Hz signals. It also provides V_{CC} for the COP420L so the time-keeping channel storage and last station selected data are not lost

when the ignition is turned off.

3. A switched 5V supply that goes high when the radio is turned on goes to the V_{CC} pin of the DS8907 for the frequency generating circuitry and to the G1 I/O pin of the COP420L.

4. L_1 through L_6 are outputs to the keyboard (push-pull options selected) and IN_0 through IN_3 are the keyboard inputs (pullup to V_{CC} and high trip levels selected.)

5. SK provides the clock and SO provides the data to the MM5450 display driver with serial input and to the DS8907 PLL synthesizer. L_7 is the enable pin for the MM5450 and G_0 (standard option selected) is the enable line for the DS8907.

6. In the search up and search down operations, G_2 informs the COP420L when a station has been detected.

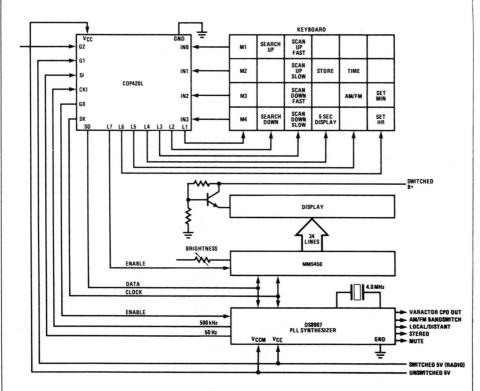

Figure 10. Electronically Tuned Radio System

Appendix F Clock generator and driver for Intel 8080A CPU

- **Single Chip Clock Generator/Driver for 8080A CPU**
- **Power-Up Reset for CPU**
- **Ready Synchronizing Flip-Flop**
- **Advanced Status Strobe**
- **Oscillator Output for External System Timing**
- **Crystal Controlled for Stable System Operation**
- **Reduces System Package Count**

The 8224 is a single chip clock generator/driver for the 8080A CPU. It is controlled by a crystal, selected by the designer, to meet a variety of system speed requirements.

Also included are circuits to provide power-up reset, advance status strobe and synchronization of ready.

The 8224 provides the designer with a significant reduction of packages used to generate clocks and timing for 8080A.

PIN CONFIGURATION

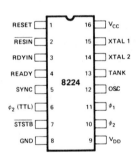

BLOCK DIAGRAM

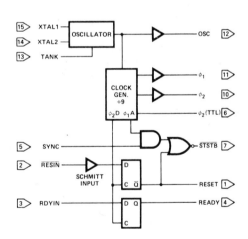

PIN NAMES

RESIN	RESET INPUT		XTAL 1	CONNECTIONS FOR CRYSTAL
RESET	RESET OUTPUT		XTAL 2	
RDYIN	READY INPUT		TANK	USED WITH OVERTONE XTAL
READY	READY OUTPUT		OSC	OSCILLATOR OUTPUT
SYNC	SYNC INPUT		ϕ_2 (TTL)	ϕ_2 CLK (TTL LEVEL)
STSTB	STATUS STB (ACTIVE LOW)		V_{CC}	+5V
			V_{DD}	+12V
ϕ_1	8080		GND	0V
ϕ_2	CLOCKS			

FUNCTIONAL DESCRIPTION

General

The 8224 is a single chip Clock Generator/Driver for the 8080A CPU. It contains a crystal-controlled oscillator, a "divide by nine" counter, two high-level drivers and several auxiliary logic functions.

Oscillator

The oscillator circuit derives its basic operating frequency from an external, series resonant, fundamental mode crystal. Two inputs are provided for the crystal connections (XTAL1, XTAL2).

The selection of the external crystal frequency depends mainly on the speed at which the 8080A is to be run at. Basically, the oscillator operates at 9 times the desired processor speed.

A simple formula to guide the crystal selection is:

$$\text{Crystal Frequency} = \frac{1}{t_{CY}} \text{ times } 9$$

Example 1: (500ns t_{CY})
2mHz times 9 = 18mHz*

Example 2: (800ns t_{CY})
1.25mHz times 9 = 11.25mHz

Another input to the oscillator is TANK. This input allows the use overtone mode crystals. This type of crystal generally has much lower "gain" than the fundamental type so an external LC network is necessary to provide the additional "gain" for proper oscillator operation. The external LC network is connected to the TANK input and is AC coupled to ground. See Figure 4.

The formula for the LC network is:

$$F = \frac{1}{2\pi \sqrt{LC}}$$

The output of the oscillator is buffered and brought out on ⊖SC (pin 12) so that other system timing signals can be derived from this stable, crystal-controlled source.

*When using crystals above 10mHz a small amount of frequency "trimming" may be necessary to produce the exact desired frequency. The addition of a small selected capacitance (3pF - 10pF) in series with the crystal will accomplish this function.

Clock Generator

The Clock Generator consists of a synchronous "divide by nine" counter and the associated decode gating to create the waveforms of the two 8080A clocks and auxiliary timing signals.

The waveforms generated by the decode gating follow a simple 2-5-2 digital pattern. See Figure 2. The clocks generated; phase 1 and phase 2, can best be thought of as consisting of "units" based on the oscillator frequency. Assume that one "unit" equals the period of the oscillator frequency. By multiplying the number of "units" that are contained in a pulse width or delay, times the period of the oscillator frequency, the approximate time in nanoseconds can be derived.

The outputs of the clock generator are connected to two high level drivers for direct interface to the 8080A CPU. A TTL level phase 2 is also brought out ϕ_2 (TTL) for external timing purposes. It is especially useful in DMA dependant activities. This signal is used to gate the requesting device onto the bus once the 8080A CPU issues the Hold Acknowledgement (HLDA).

Several other signals are also generated internally so that optimum timing of the auxiliary flip-flops and status strobe (STSTB) is achieved.

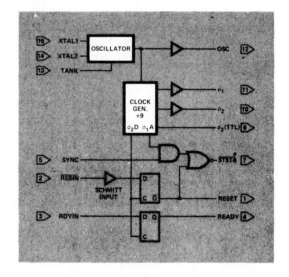

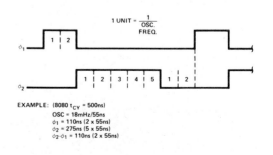

1 UNIT = $\frac{1}{\text{OSC. FREQ.}}$

EXAMPLE: (8080 t_{CY} = 500ns)
OSC = 18mHz/55ns
ϕ_1 = 110ns (2 x 55ns)
ϕ_2 = 275ns (5 x 55ns)
ϕ_2-ϕ_1 = 110ns (2 x 55ns)

STSTB (Status Strobe)

At the beginning of each machine cycle the 8080A CPU issues status information on its data bus. This information tells what type of action will take place during that machine cycle. By bringing in the SYNC signal from the CPU, and gating it with an internal timing signal (ϕ1A), an active low strobe can be derived that occurs at the start of each machine cycle at the earliest possible moment that status data is stable on the bus. The $\overline{\text{STSTB}}$ signal connects directly to the 8228 System Controller.

The power-on Reset also generates $\overline{\text{STSTB}}$, but of course, for a longer period of time. This feature allows the 8228 to be automatically reset without additional pins devoted for this function.

Power-On Reset and Ready Flip-Flops

A common function in 8080A Microcomputer systems is the generation of an automatic system reset and start-up upon initial power-on. The 8224 has a built in feature to accomplish this feature.

An external RC network is connected to the $\overline{\text{RESIN}}$ input. The slow transition of the power supply rise is sensed by an internal Schmitt Trigger. This circuit converts the slow transition into a clean, fast edge when its input level reaches a predetermined value. The output of the Schmitt Trigger is connected to a "D" type flip-flop that is clocked with ϕ2D (an internal timing signal). The flip-flop is synchronously reset and an active high level that complies with the 8080A input spec is generated. For manual switch type system Reset circuits, an active low switch closing can be connected to the $\overline{\text{RESIN}}$ input in addition to the power-on RC net-network.

The READY input to the 8080A CPU has certain timing specifications such as "set-up and hold" thus, an external synchronizing flip-flop is required. The 8224 has this feature built-in. The RDYIN input presents the asynchronous "wait request" to the "D" type flip-flop. By clocking the flip-flop with ϕ2D, a synchronized READY signal at the correct input level, can be connected directly to the 8080A.

The reason for requiring an external flip-flop to synchronize the "wait request" rather than internally in the 8080 CPU is that due to the relatively long delays of MOS logic such an implementation would "rob" the designer of about 200ns during the time his logic is determining if a "wait" is necessary. An external bipolar circuit built into the clock generator eliminates most of this delay and has no effect on component count.

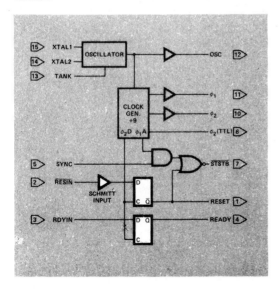

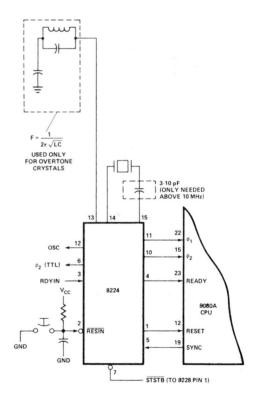

Appendix G System controller and bus driver for Intel 8080A CPU

- ■ Single Chip System Control for MCS-80™ Systems
- ■ Built-in Bi-Directional Bus Driver for Data Bus Isolation
- ■ Allows the Use of Multiple Byte Instructions (e.g. CALL) for Interrupt Acknowledge

- ■ User Selected Single Level Interrupt Vector (RST 7)
- ■ 28 Pin Dual In-Line Package
- ■ Reduces System Package Count
- ■ *8238 Has Advanced $\overline{\text{IOW}}$/$\overline{\text{MEMW}}$ for Large System Timing Control

The 8228 is a single chip system controller and bus driver for MCS-80. It generates all signals required to directly interface MCS-80 family RAM, ROM, and I/O components.

A bi-directional bus driver is included to provide high system TTL fan-out. It also provides isolation of the 8080 data bus from memory and I/O. This allows for the optimization of control signals, enabling the systems deisgner to use slower memory and I/O. The isolation of the bus driver also provides for enhanced system noise immunity.

A user selected single level interrupt vector (RST 7) is provided to simplify real time, interrupt driven, small system requirements. The 8228 also generates the correct control signals to allow the use of multiple byte instructions (e.g., CALL) in response to an INTERRUPT ACKNOWLEDGE by the 8080A. This feature permits large, interrupt driven systems to have an unlimited number of interrupt levels.

The 8228 is designed to support a wide variety of system bus structures and also reduce system package count for cost effective, reliable, design of the MCS-80 systems.

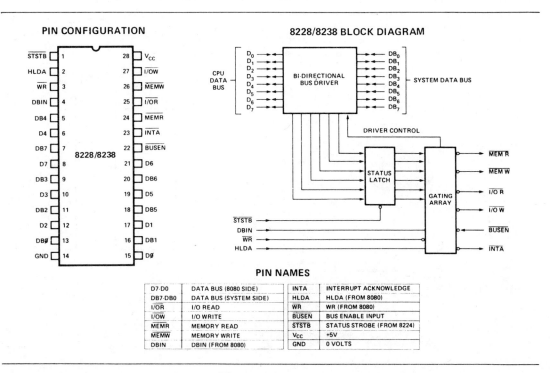

PIN CONFIGURATION

8228/8238 BLOCK DIAGRAM

PIN NAMES

D7-D0	DATA BUS (8080 SIDE)	INTA	INTERRUPT ACKNOWLEDGE
DB7-DB0	DATA BUS (SYSTEM SIDE)	HLDA	HLDA (FROM 8080)
I/OR	I/O READ	WR	WR (FROM 8080)
I/OW	I/O WRITE	BUSEN	BUS ENABLE INPUT
MEMR	MEMORY READ	STSTB	STATUS STROBE (FROM 8224)
MEMW	MEMORY WRITE	Vcc	+5V
DBIN	DBIN (FROM 8080)	GND	0 VOLTS

FUNCTIONAL DESCRIPTION

General

The 8228 and 8238 are single chip System Controllers and Data Bus drivers for the 8080 Microcomputer System. They generate all control signals required to directly interface MCS-80™ family RAM, ROM, and I/O components.

Schottky Bipolar technology is used to maintain low delay times and provide high output drive capability to support small to medium systems.

Bi-Directional Bus Driver

An eight bit, bi-directional bus driver is provided to buffer the 8080 data bus from Memory and I/O devices. The 8080A data bus has an input requirement of 3.3 volts (min) and can drive (sink) a maximum current of 1.9mA. The 8228/38 data bus driver assures that these input requirements will be not only met but exceeded for enhanced noise immunity. Also, on the system side of the driver adequate drive current is available (10mA Typ.) so that a large number of Memory and I/O devices can be directly connected to the bus.

The Bi-Directional Bus Driver is controlled by signals from the Gating Array so that proper bus flow is maintained and its outputs can be forced into their high impedance state (3–state) for DMA activities.

Status Latch

At the beginning of each machine cycle the 8080 CPU issues "status" information on its data bus that indicates the type of activity that will occur during the cycle. The 8228/38 stores this information in the Status Latch when the $\overline{STSTB}$ input goes "low". The output of the Status Latch is connected to the Gating Array and is part of the Control Signal generation.

Gating Array

The Gating Array generates control signals ($\overline{MEM\ R}$, $\overline{MEM\ W}$, $\overline{I/O\ R}$, $\overline{I/O\ W}$ and $\overline{INTA}$) by gating the outputs of the Status Latch with signals from the 8080 CPU (DBIN, $\overline{WR}$, and HLDA).

The "read" control signals ($\overline{MEM\ R}$, $\overline{I/O\ R}$ and $\overline{INTA}$) are derived from the logical combination of the appropriate Status Bit (or bits) and the DBIN input from the 8080 CPU.

The "write" control signals from the 8228 ($\overline{MEM\ W}$, $\overline{I/O\ W}$) are derived from the logical combination of the appropriate Status Bit (or bits) and the $\overline{WR}$ input from the 8080 CPU. The write signals coming from the 8238 are advanced for large system timing control.

All Control Signals are "active low" and directly interface to MCS-80 family RAM, ROM and I/O components.

The $\overline{INTA}$ control signal is normally used to gate the "interrupt instruction port" onto the bus. It also provides a special feature in the 8228/38. If only one basic vector is needed in the interrupt structure, such as in small systems, the 8228/38 can automatically insert a RST 7 instruction onto the bus at the proper time. To use this option, simply connect the $\overline{INTA}$ output of the 8228/38 (pin 23) to the +12 volt supply through a series resistor (1K ohms). The voltage is sensed internally by the 8228/38 and logic is "set-up" so that when the DBIN input is active a RST 7 instruction is gated on to the bus when an interrupt is acknowledged. This feature provides a single interrupt vector with no additional components, such as an interrupt instruction port.

When using CALL as an Interrupt instruction the 8228/38 will generate an $\overline{INTA}$ pulse for each of the three bytes.

The $\overline{BUSEN}$ (Bus Enable) input to the Gating Array is an asynchronous input that forces the data bus output buffers and control signal buffers into their high-impedance state if it is a "one". If $\overline{BUSEN}$ is a "zero" normal operation of the data buffer and control signals take place.

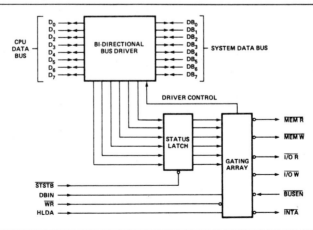

8228/38 BLOCK DIAGRAM

Appendix H Signetics high-speed hex tri-state buffers and inverters

DIGITAL 8T SERIES INTERFACE TTL/MSI
PRODUCT AVAILABLE IN 0°C TO 75°C
TEMP RANGE ONLY

8T95
8T96
8T97
8T98

DESCRIPTION

Each of the Tri-State Bus Interface Elements described herein has low current PNP inputs and is designed with Schottky TTL technology for ultra high speed. The devices are used to convert TTL/DTL or MOS/CMOS to tri-state TTL Bus levels. For maximum systems flexibility the 8T95 and 8T97 do so without logic inversion, whereas, the 8T96 and 8T98 provide the logical complement of the input. The 8T95 and 8T96 feature a common control line for all six devices, whereas, the 8T97 and 8T98 have control lines for four devices from one input and two from another input.

FEATURES

- LOW CURRENT PNP INPUTS (400μA)
- HIGH SPEED SHOTTKY TTL DESIGN (TYP. 8ns)
- TTL/DTL, MOS/CMOS COMPATIBLE
- LOW POWER DISSIPATION
  8T95/97 TYP. 325mW
  8T96/98 TYP. 295mW
- HIGH SPEED REPLACEMENTS FOR
  DM 8095 = 8T95
  DM 8096 = 8T96
  DM 8097 = 8T97
  DM 8098 = 8T98

PIN CONFIGURATIONS (Top View)

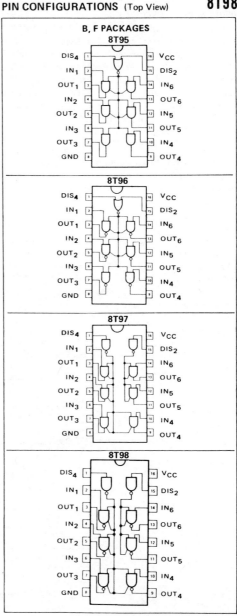

TRUTH TABLES

8T95			
DISABLE DIS_1	INPUT DIS_2	INPUT	OUTPUT
0	0	0	0
0	0	1	1
0	1	x	H-z
1	0	x	H-z
1	1	x	H-z

8T96			
DISABLE DIS_1	INPUT DIS_2	INPUT	OUTPUT
0	0	0	1
0	0	1	0
0	1	x	H-z
1	0	x	H-z
1	1	x	H-z

TRUTH TABLES (Cont'd)

8T97			
DISABLE DIS$_4$	INPUT DIS$_2$	INPUT	OUTPUT
0	0	0	0
0	0	1	1
x	1	x	H-z*
1	x	x	H-z**

8T98			
DISABLE DIS$_4$	INPUT DIS$_2$	INPUT	OUTPUT
0	0	0	1
0	0	1	0
x	1	x	H-z*
1	x	x	H-z**

*Output 5-6 only   **Output 1-4 only   x = Irrelevant

DC ELECTRICAL CHARACTERISTICS Over Recommended Voltage and Temperature Range

CHARACTERISTIC	LIMITS				TEST CONDITIONS		NOTES
	MIN.	TYP.	MAX.	UNITS			
Logical "1" Input Voltage	2.0			V	V_{CC} = Min T_A = 25°C		
Logical "0" Input Voltage			0.8	V	V_{CC} = Min T_A = 25°C		
Logical "1" Output Voltage	2.4			V	V_{CC} = Min I_0 = −5.2 mA		6
Logical "0" Output Voltage			0.5	V	I_{out} = 48 mA		7
Third State Input Current			−40	μA	V_{CC} = Max	V_{in} = 0.5V DIS = 2.0V	
Third State Output Current			40	μA	V_{CC} = Max	V_o = 2.4V	
			−40	μA		V_o = 0.5V	
Logical "1" Input Current			40	μA	V_{CC} = Max	V_{in} = 2.4V	
Logical "0" Input Current			−400	μA	V_{CC} = Max	V_{IN} = 0.5V DIS = 0.5V	
Output Short Circuit Current	−40	−80	−115	mA	V_{CC} = Max	V_o = 0V	9, 10
Supply Current 8T95/97 (each device) 8T96/98		65 59	98mA 89mA	mA	V_{CC} = Max		
Input Voltage Rating	5.5			V	I_{in} = 1 mA		
Input Clamp Voltage			−1.5	V	V_{CC} = Min	I_{in} = −12 mA	
Output V_{CC} Clamp Voltage			1.5	V	V_{CC} = 0V	I_0 = 12 mA	
Output Ground Clamp Voltage			−1.5	V	V_{CC} = 0V	I_0 = −12 mA	

Appendix I Octal transparent latch

54F/74F373

OCTAL TRANSPARENT LATCH
(With 3-State Outputs)

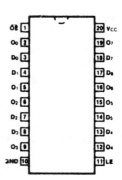

DESCRIPTION — The 'F373 consists of eight latches with 3-state outputs for bus organized system applications. The flip-flops appear transparent to the data when Latch Enable (LE) is HIGH. When LE is LOW, the data that meets the setup times is latched. Data appears on the bus when the Output Enable ($\overline{OE}$) is LOW. When $\overline{OE}$ is HIGH the bus output is in the high impedance state.

- **EIGHT LATCHES IN A SINGLE PACKAGE**
- **3-STATE OUTPUTS FOR BUS INTERFACING**

LOGIC SYMBOL

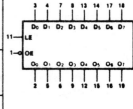

V_{CC} = Pin 20
GND = Pin 10

ORDERING CODE: See Section 5

PKGS	COMMERCIAL GRADE V_{CC} = +5.0 V ±5%, T_A = 0°C to +70°C	MILITARY GRADE V_{CC} = +5.0 V ±10%, T_A = -55°C to +125°C	PKG TYPE
Plastic DIP (P)	74F373PC		9Z
Ceramic DIP (D)	74F373DC	54F373DM	4E
Flatpak (F)	74F373FC	54F373FM	4F

INPUT LOADING/FAN-OUT: See Section 2 for U.L. definitions

PIN NAMES	DESCRIPTION	54F/74F (U.L.) HIGH/LOW
$D_0 - D_7$	Data Inputs	0.5/0.375
LE	Latch Enable Input (Active HIGH)	0.5/0.375
$\overline{OE}$	Output Enable Input (Active LOW)	0.5/0.375
$O_0 - O_7$	3-State Latch Outputs	25/12.5

FUNCTIONAL DESCRIPTION — The 'F373 contains eight D-type latches with 3-state output buffers. When the Latch Enable (LE) input is HIGH, data on the D_n inputs enters the latches. In this condition the latches are transparent, i.e., a latch output will change state each time its D input changes. When LE is LOW the latches store the information that was present on the D inputs a setup time preceding the HIGH-to-LOW transition of LE. The 3-state buffers are controlled by the Output Enable ($\overline{OE}$) input. When $\overline{OE}$ is LOW, the buffers are in the bi-state mode. When $\overline{OE}$ is HIGH the buffers are in the high impedance mode but this does not interfere with entering new data into the latches.

LOGIC DIAGRAM

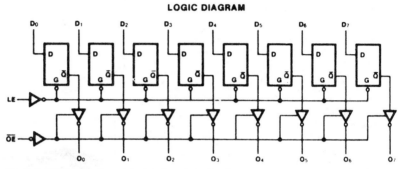

Please note that this diagram is provided only for the understanding of logic operations and should not be used to estimate propagation delays.

DC CHARACTERISTICS OVER OPERATING TEMPERATURE RANGE (unless otherwise specified)

SYMBOL	PARAMETER	54F/74F			UNITS	CONDITIONS
		Min	Typ	Max		
I_{CC}	Power Supply Current (All Outputs OFF)		35	55	mA	V_{CC} = Max, $\overline{OE}$ = 4.5 V D_n, LE = Gnd

AC CHARACTERISTICS: See Section 2 for waveforms and load configurations

SYMBOL	PARAMETER	54F/74F T_A = +25°C, V_{CC} = +5.0 V C_L = 50 pF			54F T_A, V_{CC} = MIL C_L = 50 pF		74F T_A, V_{CC} = COM C_L = 50 pF		UNITS	FIG. NO.
		Min	Typ	Max	Min	Max	Min	Max		
t_{PLH} t_{PHL}	Propagation Delay D_n to O_n	3.0 2.0	5.3 3.7	7.0 5.0			3.0 2.0	8.0 6.0	ns	2-17 2-19
t_{PLH} t_{PHL}	Propagation Delay LE to O_n	5.0 3.0	9.0 5.2	11.5 7.0			5.0 3.0	13.0 8.0	ns	2-17 2-21
t_{PZH} t_{PZL}	Output Enable Time	2.0 2.0	5.0 5.6	11.0 7.5			2.0 2.0	12.0 8.5	ns	2-25 2-26 2-27
t_{PHZ} t_{PLZ}	Output Disable Time*	2.0 2.0	4.5 3.8	6.5 5.0			2.0 2.0	7.5 6.0	ns	2-25 2-26 2-27

Appendix J Motorola MC6820 peripheral interface adapter

PERIPHERAL INTERFACE ADAPTER (PIA)

The MC6820 Peripheral Interface Adapter provides the universal means of interfacing peripheral equipment to the MC6800 Micro-processing Unit (MPU). This device is capable of interfacing the MPU to peripherals through two 8-bit bidirectional peripheral data buses and four control lines. No external logic is required for interfacing to most peripheral devices.

The functional configuration of the PIA is programmed by the MPU during system initialization. Each of the peripheral data lines can be programmed to act as an input or output, and each of the four control/interrupt lines may be programmed for one of several control modes. This allows a high degree of flexibility in the over-all operation of the interface.

- 8-Bit Bidirectional Data Bus for Communication with the MPU
- Two Bidirectional 8-Bit Buses for Interface to Peripherals
- Two Programmable Control Registers
- Two Programmable Data Direction Registers
- Four Individually-Controlled Interrupt Input Lines; Two Usable as Peripheral Control Outputs
- Handshake Control Logic for Input and Output Peripheral Operation
- High-Impedance 3-State and Direct Transistor Drive Peripheral Lines
- Program Controlled Interrupt and Interrupt Disable Capability
- CMOS Drive Capability on Side A Peripheral Lines

MOS

(N-CHANNEL, SILICON-GATE)

PERIPHERAL INTERFACE ADAPTER

L SUFFIX
CERAMIC PACKAGE
CASE 715

NOT SHOWN: **P SUFFIX**

PLASTIC PACKAGE
CASE 711

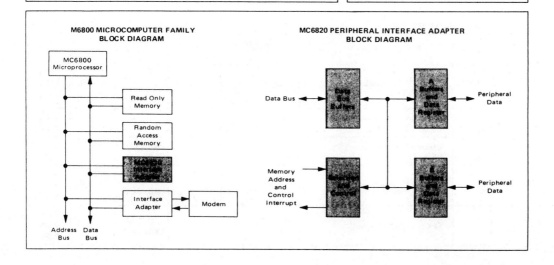

ELECTRICAL CHARACTERISTICS (V_{CC} = 5.0 V ±5%, V_{SS} = 0, T_A = 0 to 70°C unless otherwise noted.)

Characteristic		Symbol	Min	Typ	Max	Unit
Input High Voltage	Enable	V_{IH}	V_{SS} + 2.4	–	V_{CC}	Vdc
	Other Inputs		V_{SS} + 2.0	–	V_{CC}	
Input Low Voltage	Enable	V_{IL}	V_{SS} –0.3	–	V_{SS} + 0.4	Vdc
	Other Inputs		V_{SS} –0.3	–	V_{SS} + 0.8	
Input Leakage Current R/W, $\overline{Reset}$, RS0, RS1, CS0, CS1, $\overline{CS2}$, CA1,		I_{in}	–	1.0	2.5	μAdc
(V_{in} = 0 to 5.25 Vdc) CB1, Enable						
Three-State (Off State) Input Current D0-D7, PB0-PB7, CB2		I_{TSI}	–	2.0	10	μAdc
(V_{in} = 0.4 to 2.4 Vdc)						
Input High Current PA0-PA7, CA2		I_{IH}	–100	–250	–	μAdc
(V_{IH} = 2.4 Vdc)						
Input Low Current PA0-PA7, CA2		I_{IL}	–	–1.0	–1.6	mAdc
(V_{IL} = 0.4 Vdc)						
Output High Voltage		V_{OH}				Vdc
(I_{Load} = –205 μAdc, Enable Pulse Width < 25 μs) D0-D7			V_{SS} + 2.4	–	–	
(I_{Load} = –100 μAdc, Enable Pulse Width <25 μs) Other Outputs			V_{SS} + 2.4	–	–	
Output Low Voltage		V_{OL}	–	–	V_{SS} + 0.4	Vdc
(I_{Load} = 1.6 mAdc, Enable Pulse Width < 25 μs)						
Output High Current (Sourcing)		I_{OH}				
(V_{OH} = 2.4 Vdc) D0-D7			–205	–	–	μAdc
Other Outputs			–100	–	–	μAdc
(V_O = 1.5 Vdc, the current for driving other than TTL, e.g.,						
Darlington Base) PB0-PB7, CB2			–1.0	–2.5	–10	mAdc
Output Low Current (Sinking)		I_{OL}	1.6	–	–	mAdc
(V_{OL} = 0.4 Vdc)						
Output Leakage Current (Off State) $\overline{IRQA}$, $\overline{IRQB}$		I_{LOH}	–	1.0	10	μAdc
(V_{OH} = 2.4 Vdc)						
Power Dissipation		P_D	–	–	650	mW
Input Capacitance	Enable	C_{in}	–	–	20	pF
(V_{in} = 0, T_A = 25°C, f = 1.0 MHz) D0-D7			–	–	12.5	
PA0-PA7, PB0-PB7, CA2, CB2			–	–	10	
R/W, $\overline{Reset}$, RS0, RS1, CS0, CS1, $\overline{CS2}$, CA1, CB1			–	–	7.5	
Output Capacitance $\overline{IRQA}$, $\overline{IRQB}$		C_{out}	–	–	5.0	pF
(V_{in} = 0, T_A = 25°C, f = 1.0 MHz) PB0-PB7			–	–	10	
Peripheral Data Setup Time (Figure 1)		t_{PDSU}	200	–	–	ns
Delay Time, Enable negative transition to CA2 negative transition		t_{CA2}	–	–	1.0	μs
(Figure 2, 3)						
Delay Time, Enable negative transition to CA2 positive transition		t_{RS1}	–	–	1.0	μs
(Figure 2)						
Rise and Fall Times for CA1 and CA2 input signals (Figure 3)		t_r, t_f	–	–	1.0	μs
Delay Time from CA1 active transition to CA2 positive transition		t_{RS2}	–	–	2.0	μs
(Figure 3)						
Delay Time, Enable negative transition to Peripheral Data valid		t_{PDW}	–	–	1.0	μs
(Figures 4, 5)						
Delay Time, Enable negative transition to Peripheral CMOS Data Valid		t_{CMOS}	–	–	2.0	μs
(V_{CC} – 30% V_{CC}, Figure 4; Figure 12 Load C) PA0-PA7, CA2						
Delay Time, Enable positive transition to CB2 negative transition		t_{CB2}	–	–	1.0	μs
(Figure 6, 7)						
Delay Time, Peripheral Data valid to CB2 negative transition		t_{DC}	20	–	–	ns
(Figure 5)						
Delay Time, Enable positive transition to CB2 positive transition		t_{RS1}	–	–	1.0	μs
(Figure 6)						
Rise and Fall Time for CB1 and CB2 input signals (Figure 7)		t_r, t_f	–	–	1.0	μs
Delay Time, CB1 active transition to CB2 positive transition		t_{RS2}	–	–	2.0	μs
(Figure 7)						
Interrupt Release Time, $\overline{IRQA}$ and $\overline{IRQB}$ (Figure 8)		t_{IR}	–	–	1.6	μs
Reset Low Time* (Figure 9)		t_{RL}	2.0	–	–	μs

*The Reset line must be high a minimum of 1.0 μs before addressing the PIA.

 MOTOROLA *Semiconductor Products Inc.*

MAXIMUM RATINGS

Rating	Symbol	Value	Unit
Supply Voltage	V_{CC}	−0.3 to +7.0	Vdc
Input Voltage	V_{in}	−0.3 to +7.0	Vdc
Operating Temperature Range	T_A	0 to +70	°C
Storage Temperature Range	T_{stg}	−55 to +150	°C
Thermal Resistance	θ_{JA}	82.5	°C/W

This device contains circuitry to protect the inputs against damage due to high static voltages or electric fields; however, it is advised that normal precautions be taken to avoid application of any voltage higher than maximum rated voltages to this high impedance circuit.

BUS TIMING CHARACTERISTICS

READ (Figures 10 and 12)

Characteristic	Symbol	Min	Typ	Max	Unit
Enable Cycle Time	t_{cycE}	1.0	—	—	µs
Enable Pulse Width, High	PW_{EH}	0.45	—	25	µs
Enable Pulse Width, Low	PW_{EL}	0.43	—	—	µs
Setup Time, Address and R/W valid to Enable positive transition	t_{AS}	160	—	—	ns
Data Delay Time	t_{DDR}	—	—	320	ns
Data Hold Time	t_H	10	—	—	ns
Address Hold Time	t_{AH}	10	—	—	ns
Rise and Fall Time for Enable input	t_{Er}, t_{Ef}	—	—	25	ns

WRITE (Figures 11 and 12)

Characteristic	Symbol	Min	Typ	Max	Unit
Enable Cycle Time	t_{cycE}	1.0	—	—	µs
Enable Pulse Width, High	PW_{EH}	0.45	—	25	µs
Enable Pulse Width, Low	PW_{EL}	0.43	—	—	µs
Setup Time, Address and R/W valid to Enable positive transition	t_{AS}	160	—	—	ns
Data Setup Time	t_{DSW}	195	—	—	ns
Data Hold Time	t_H	10	—	—	ns
Address Hold Time	t_{AH}	10	—	—	ns
Rise and Fall Time for Enable input	t_{Er}, t_{Ef}	—	—	25	ns

FIGURE 1 – PERIPHERAL DATA SETUP TIME
(Read Mode)

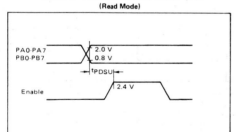

FIGURE 2 – CA2 DELAY TIME
(Read Mode; CRA-5 = CRA-3 = 1, CRA-4 = 0)

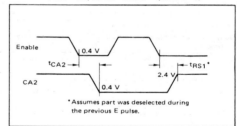

*Assumes part was deselected during the previous E pulse.

FIGURE 3 – CA2 DELAY TIME
(Read Mode; CRA-5 = 1, CRA-3 = CRA-4 = 0)

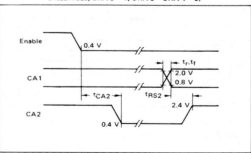

 MOTOROLA *Semiconductor Products Inc.*

FIGURE 4 – PERIPHERAL CMOS DATA DELAY TIMES
(Write Mode; CRA-5 = CRA-3 = 1, CRA-4 = 0)

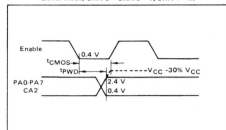

FIGURE 5 – PERIPHERAL DATA AND CB2 DELAY TIMES
(Write Mode; CRB-5 = CRB-3 = 1, CRB-4 = 0)

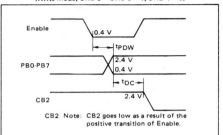

CB2 Note: CB2 goes low as a result of the positive transition of Enable.

FIGURE 6 – CB2 DELAY TIME
(Write Mode; CRB-5 = CRB-3 = 1, CRB-4 = 0)

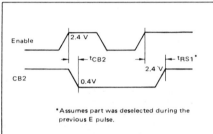

*Assumes part was deselected during the previous E pulse.

FIGURE 7 – CB2 DELAY TIME
(Write Mode; CRB-5 = 1, CRB-3 = CRB-4 = 0)

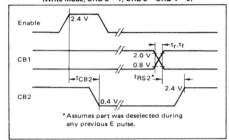

*Assumes part was deselected during any previous E pulse.

FIGURE 8 – IRQ RELEASE TIME

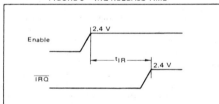

FIGURE 9 – RESET LOW TIME

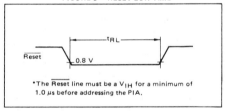

*The Reset line must be a V_{IH} for a minimum of 1.0 μs before addressing the PIA.

FIGURE 10 – BUS READ TIMING CHARACTERISTICS
(Read Information from PIA)

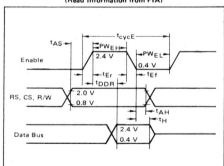

FIGURE 11 – BUS WRITE TIMING CHARACTERISTICS
(Write Information into PIA)

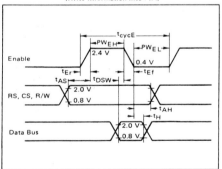

 MOTOROLA *Semiconductor Products Inc.*

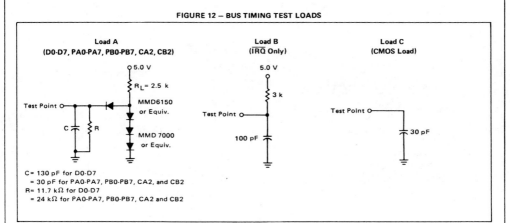

FIGURE 12 – BUS TIMING TEST LOADS

Load A
(D0-D7, PA0-PA7, PB0-PB7, CA2, CB2)

Load B
(IRQ Only)

Load C
(CMOS Load)

C= 130 pF for D0-D7
  = 30 pF for PA0-PA7, PB0-PB7, CA2, and CB2
R= 11.7 kΩ for D0-D7
  = 24 kΩ for PA0-PA7, PB0-PB7, CA2 and CB2

PIA INTERFACE SIGNALS FOR MPU

The PIA interfaces to the MC6800 MPU with an eight-bit bi-directional data bus, three chip select lines, two register select lines, two interrupt request lines, read/write line, enable line and reset line. These signals, in conjunction with the MC6800 VMA output, permit the MPU to have complete control over the PIA. VMA should be utilized in conjunction with an MPU address line into a chip select of the PIA.

PIA Bi-Directional Data (D0-D7) – The bi-directional data lines (D0-D7) allow the transfer of data between the MPU and the PIA. The data bus output drivers are three-state devices that remain in the high-impedance (off) state except when the MPU performs a PIA read operation. The Read/Write line is in the Read (high) state when the PIA is selected for a Read operation.

PIA Enable (E) – The enable pulse, E, is the only timing signal that is supplied to the PIA. Timing of all other signals is referenced to the leading and trailing edges of the E pulse. This signal will normally be a derivative of the MC6800 φ2 Clock.

PIA Read/Write (R/W) – This signal is generated by the MPU to control the direction of data transfers on the Data Bus. A low state on the PIA Read/Write line enables the input buffers and data is transferred from the MPU to the PIA on the E signal if the device has been selected. A high on the Read/Write line sets up the PIA for a transfer of data to the bus. The PIA output buffers are enabled when the proper address and the enable pulse E are present.

Reset – The active low Reset line is used to reset all register bits in the PIA to a logical zero (low). This line can be used as a power-on reset and as a master reset during system operation.

PIA Chip Select (CS0, CS1 and CS2) – These three input signals are used to select the PIA. CS0 and CS1 must be high and CS2 must be low for selection of the device. Data transfers are then performed under the control of the Enable and Read/Write signals. The chip select lines must be stable for the duration of the E pulse. The device is deselected when any of the chip selects are in the inactive state.

PIA Register Select (RS0 and RS1) – The two register select lines are used to select the various registers inside the PIA. These two lines are used in conjunction with internal Control Registers to select a particular register that is to be written or read.

The register and chip select lines should be stable for the duration of the E pulse while in the read or write cycle.

Interrupt Request (IRQA and IRQB) – The active low Interrupt Request lines (IRQA and IRQB) act to interrupt the MPU either directly or through interrupt priority circuitry. These lines are "open drain" (no load device on the chip). This permits all interrupt request lines to be tied together in a wire-OR configuration.

Each Interrupt Request line has two internal interrupt flag bits that can cause the Interrupt Request line to go low. Each flag bit is associated with a particular peripheral interrupt line. Also four interrupt enable bits are provided in the PIA which may be used to inhibit a particular interrupt from a peripheral device.

Servicing an interrupt by the MPU may be accomplished by a software routine that, on a prioritized basis, sequentially reads and tests the two control registers in each PIA for interrupt flag bits that are set.

The interrupt flags are cleared (zeroed) as a result of an

MOTOROLA *Semiconductor Products Inc.*

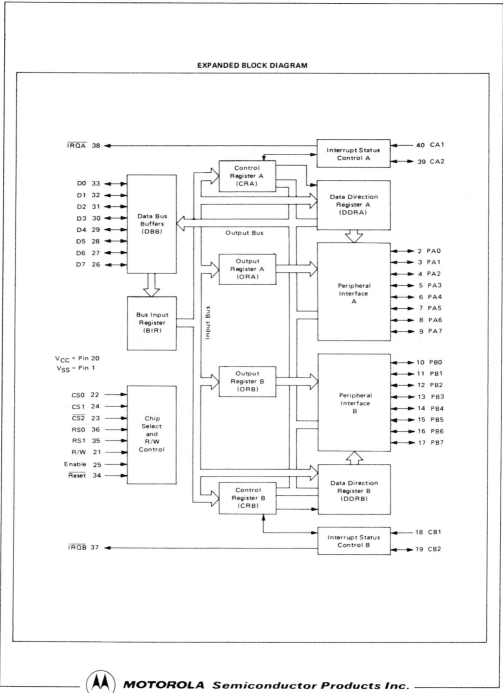

EXPANDED BLOCK DIAGRAM

MPU Read Peripheral Data Operation of the corresponding data register. After being cleared, the interrupt flag bit cannot be enabled to be set until the PIA is deselected during an E pulse. The E pulse is used to condition the interrupt control lines (CA1, CA2, CB1, CB2). When these lines are used as interrupt inputs at least one E pulse must occur from the inactive edge to the active edge of the interrupt input signal to condition the edge sense network. If the interrupt flag has been enabled and the edge sense circuit has been properly conditioned, the interrupt flag will be set on the next active transition of the interrupt input pin.

PIA PERIPHERAL INTERFACE LINES

The PIA provides two 8-bit bi-directional data buses and four interrupt/control lines for interfacing to peripheral devices.

Section A Peripheral Data (PA0-PA7) — Each of the peripheral data lines can be programmed to act as an input or output. This is accomplished by setting a "1" in the corresponding Data Direction Register bit for those lines which are to be outputs. A "0" in a bit of the Data Direction Register causes the corresponding peripheral data line to act as an input. During an MPU Read Peripheral Data Operation, the data on peripheral lines programmed to act as inputs appears directly on the corresponding MPU Data Bus lines. In the input mode the internal pullup resistor on these lines represents a maximum of one standard TTL load.

The data in Output Register A will appear on the data lines that are programmed to be outputs. A logical "1" written into the register will cause a "high" on the corresponding data line while a "0" results in a "low". Data in Output Register A may be read by an MPU "Read Peripheral Data A" operation when the corresponding lines are programmed as outputs. This data will be read properly if the voltage on the peripheral data lines is greater than 2.0 volts for a logic "1" output and less than 0.8 volt for a logic "0" output. Loading the output lines such that the voltage on these lines does not reach full voltage causes the data transferred into the MPU on a Read operation to differ from that contained in the respective bit of Output Register A.

Section B Peripheral Data (PB0-PB7) — The peripheral data lines in the B Section of the PIA can be programmed to act as either inputs or outputs in a similar manner to PA0-PA7. However, the output buffers driving these lines differ from those driving lines PA0-PA7. They have three-state capability, allowing them to enter a high impedance state when the peripheral data line is used as an input. In addition, data on the peripheral data lines PB0-PB7 will be read properly from those lines programmed as outputs even if the voltages are below 2.0 volts for a "high". As outputs, these lines are compatible with standard TTL and may also be used as a source of up to 1 milliampere at 1.5 volts to directly drive the base of a transistor switch.

Interrupt Input (CA1 and CB1) — Peripheral Input lines CA1 and CB1 are input only lines that set the interrupt flags of the control registers. The active transition for these signals is also programmed by the two control registers.

Peripheral Control (CA2) — The peripheral control line CA2 can be programmed to act as an interrupt input or as a peripheral control output. As an output, this line is compatible with standard TTL; as an input the internal pullup resistor on this line represents one standard TTL load. The function of this signal line is programmed with Control Register A.

Peripheral Control (CB2) — Peripheral Control line CB2 may also be programmed to act as an interrupt input or peripheral control output. As an input, this line has high input impedance and is compatible with standard TTL. As an output it is compatible with standard TTL and may also be used as a source of up to 1 milliampere at 1.5 volts to directly drive the base of a transistor switch. This line is programmed by Control Register B.

NOTE: It is recommended that the control lines (CA1, CA2, CB1, CB2) should be held in a logic 1 state when $\overline{\text{Reset}}$ is active to prevent setting of corresponding interrupt flags in the control register when $\overline{\text{Reset}}$ goes to an inactive state. Subsequent to $\overline{\text{Reset}}$ going inactive, a read of the data registers may be used to clear any undesired interrupt flags.

INTERNAL CONTROLS

There are six locations within the PIA accessible to the MPU data bus: two Peripheral Registers, two Data Direction Registers, and two Control Registers. Selection of these locations is controlled by the RS0 and RS1 inputs together with bit 2 in the Control Register, as shown in Table 1.

TABLE 1 – INTERNAL ADDRESSING

		Control Register Bit		
RS1	RS0	CRA-2	CRB-2	Location Selected
0	0	1	X	Peripheral Register A
0	0	0	X	Data Direction Register A
0	1	X	X	Control Register A
1	0	X	1	Peripheral Register B
1	0	X	0	Data Direction Register B
1	1	X	X	Control Register B

X = Don't Care

INITIALIZATION

A low reset line has the effect of zeroing all PIA registers. This will set PA0-PA7, PB0-PB7, CA2 and CB2 as inputs, and all interrupts disabled. The PIA must be configured during the restart program which follows the reset.

Details of possible configurations of the Data Direction and Control Register are as follows.

DATA DIRECTION REGISTERS (DDRA and DDRB)

The two Data Direction Registers allow the MPU to control the direction of data through each corresponding peripheral data line. A Data Direction Register bit set at "0" configures the corresponding peripheral data line as an input; a "1" results in an output.

CONTROL REGISTERS (CRA and CRB)

The two Control Registers (CRA and CRB) allow the MPU to control the operation of the four peripheral control lines CA1, CA2, CB1 and CB2. In addition they allow the MPU to enable the interrupt lines and monitor the status of the interrupt flags. Bits 0 through 5 of the two registers may be written or read by the MPU when the proper chip select and register select signals are applied. Bits 6 and 7 of the two registers are read only and are modified by external interrupts occurring on control lines CA1, CA2, CB1 or CB2. The format of the control words is shown in Table 2.

TABLE 2 – CONTROL WORD FORMAT

	7	6	5	4	3	2	1	0
CRA	IRQA1	IRQA2	CA2 Control			DDRA Access	CA1 Control	

	7	6	5	4	3	2	1	0
CRB	IRQB1	IRQB2	CB2 Control			DDRB Access	CB1 Control	

Data Direction Access Control Bit (CRA-2 and CRB-2) – Bit 2 in each Control register (CRA and CRB) allows selection of either a Peripheral Interface Register or the Data Direction Register when the proper register select signals are applied to RS0 and RS1.

Interrupt Flags (CRA-6, CRA-7, CRB-6, and CRB-7) – The four interrupt flag bits are set by active transitions of signals on the four Interrupt and Peripheral Control lines when those lines are programmed to be inputs. These bits cannot be set directly from the MPU Data Bus and are reset indirectly by a Read Peripheral Data Operation on the appropriate section.

TABLE 3 – CONTROL OF INTERRUPT INPUTS CA1 AND CB1

CRA-1 (CRB-1)	CRA-0 (CRB-0)	Interrupt Input CA1 (CB1)	Interrupt Flag CRA-7 (CRB-7)	MPU Interrupt Request IRQA (IRQB)
0	0	↓ Active	Set high on ↓ of CA1 (CB1)	Disabled — IRQ remains high
0	1	↓ Active	Set high on ↓ of CA1 (CB1)	Goes low when the interrupt flag bit CRA-7 (CRB-7) goes high
1	0	↑ Active	Set high on ↑ of CA1 (CB1)	Disabled — IRQ remains high
1	1	↑ Active	Set high on ↑ of CA1 (CB1)	Goes low when the interrupt flag bit CRA-7 (CRB-7) goes high

Notes: 1. ↑ indicates positive transition (low to high)

2. ↓ indicates negative transition (high to low)

3. The Interrupt flag bit CRA-7 is cleared by an MPU Read of the A Data Register, and CRB-7 is cleared by an MPU Read of the B Data Register.

4. If CRA-0 (CRB-0) is low when an interrupt occurs (Interrupt disabled) and is later brought high, IRQA (IRQB) occurs after CRA-0 (CRB-0) is written to a "one".

 MOTOROLA *Semiconductor Products Inc.*

Control of CA1 and CB1 Interrupt Input Lines (CRA-0, CRB-0, CRA-1, and CRB-1) — The two lowest order bits of the control registers are used to control the interrupt input lines CA1 and CB1. Bits CRA-0 and CRB-0 are used to enable the MPU interrupt signals $\overline{IRQA}$ and $\overline{IRQB}$, respectively. Bits CRA-1 and CRB-1 determine the active transition of the interrupt input signals CA1 and CB1 (Table 3).

TABLE 4 – CONTROL OF CA2 AND CB2 AS INTERRUPT INPUTS
CRA5 (CRB5) is low

CRA-5 (CRB-5)	CRA-4 (CRB-4)	CRA-3 (CRB-3)	Interrupt Input CA2 (CB2)	Interrupt Flag CRA-6 (CRB-6)	MPU Interrupt Request $\overline{IRQA}$ ($\overline{IRQB}$)
0	0	0	↓ Active	Set high on ↓ of CA2 (CB2)	Disabled — $\overline{IRQ}$ remains high
0	0	1	↓ Active	Set high on ↓ of CA2 (CB2)	Goes low when the interrupt flag bit CRA-6 (CRB-6) goes high
0	1	0	↑ Active	Set high on ↑ of CA2 (CB2)	Disabled — $\overline{IRQ}$ remains high
0	1	1	↑ Active	Set high on ↑ of CA2 (CB2)	Goes low when the interrupt flag bit CRA-6 (CRB-6) goes high

Notes: 1.   ↑ indicates positive transition (low to high)

2.   ↓ indicates negative transition (high to low)

3.   The Interrupt flag bit CRA-6 is cleared by an MPU Read of the A Data Register and CRB-6 is cleared by an MPU Read of the B Data Register.

4.   If CRA-3 (CRB-3) is low when an interrupt occurs (Interrupt disabled) and is later brought high, $\overline{IRQA}$ ($\overline{IRQB}$) occurs after CRA-3 (CRB-3) is written to a "one".

TABLE 5 – CONTROL OF CB2 AS AN OUTPUT
CRB-5 is high

CRB-5	CRB-4	CRB-3	CB2 Cleared	CB2 Set
1	0	0	Low on the positive transition of the first E pulse following an MPU Write "B" Data Register operation.	High when the interrupt flag bit CRB-7 is set by an active transition of the CB1 signal.
1	0	1	Low on the positive transition of the first E pulse after an MPU Write "B" Data Register operation.	High on the positive edge of the first "E" pulse following an "E" pulse which occurred while the part was deselected.
1	1	0	Low when CRB-3 goes low as a result of an MPU Write in Control Register "B".	Always low as long as CRB-3 is low. Will go high on an MPU Write in Control Register "B" that changes CRB-3 to "one".
1	1	1	Always high as long as CRB-3 is high. Will be cleared when an MPU Write Control Register "B" results in clearing CRB-3 to "zero".	High when CRB-3 goes high as a result of an MPU Write into Control Register "B".

 MOTOROLA *Semiconductor Products Inc.*

Control of CA2 and CB2 Peripheral Control Lines (CRA-3, CRA-4, CRA-5, CRB-3, CRB-4, and CRB-5) — Bits 3, 4, and 5 of the two control registers are used to control the CA2 and CB2 Peripheral Control lines. These bits determine if the control lines will be an interrupt input or an output control signal. If bit CRA-5 (CRB-5) is low, CA2 (CB2) is an interrupt input line similar to CA1 (CB1) (Table 4). When CRA-5 (CRB-5) is high, CA2 (CB2) becomes an output signal that may be used to control peripheral data transfers. When in the output mode, CA2 and CB2 have slightly different characteristics (Tables 5 and 6).

TABLE 6 — CONTROL OF CA-2 AS AN OUTPUT
CRA-5 is high

CRA-5	CRA-4	CRA-3	CA2	
			Cleared	Set
1	0	0	Low on negative transition of E after an MPU Read "A" Data operation.	High when the interrupt flag bit CRA-7 is set by an active transition of the CA1 signal.
1	0	1	Low on negative transition of E after an MPU Read "A" Data operation.	High on the negative edge of the first "E" pulse which occurs during a deselect.
1	1	0	Low when CRA-3 goes low as a result of an MPU Write to Control Register "A".	Always low as long as CRA-3 is low. Will go high on an MPU Write to Control Register "A" that changes CRA-3 to "one".
1	1	1	Always high as long as CRA-3 is high. Will be cleared on an MPU Write to Control Register "A" that clears CRA-3 to a "zero".	High when CRA-3 goes high as a result of an MPU Write to Control Register "A".

PIN ASSIGNMENT

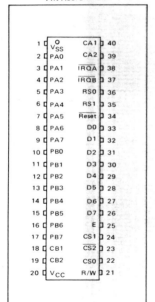

PACKAGE DIMENSIONS

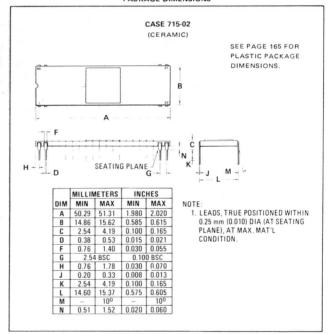

CASE 715-02
(CERAMIC)

SEE PAGE 165 FOR PLASTIC PACKAGE DIMENSIONS.

DIM	MILLIMETERS		INCHES	
	MIN	MAX	MIN	MAX
A	50.29	51.31	1.980	2.020
B	14.86	15.62	0.585	0.615
C	2.54	4.19	0.100	0.165
D	0.38	0.53	0.015	0.021
F	0.76	1.40	0.030	0.055
G	2.54 BSC		0.100 BSC	
H	0.76	1.78	0.030	0.070
J	0.20	0.33	0.008	0.013
K	2.54	4.19	0.100	0.165
L	14.60	15.37	0.575	0.605
M	–	10⁰	–	10⁰
N	0.51	1.52	0.020	0.060

NOTE:
1. LEADS, TRUE POSITIONED WITHIN 0.25 mm (0.010) DIA (AT SEATING PLANE), AT MAX. MAT'L CONDITION.

 MOTOROLA *Semiconductor Products Inc.*

Appendix K Intel 8251A programmable communication interface

8251A
PROGRAMMABLE COMMUNICATION INTERFACE

- **Synchronous and Asynchronous Operation**
  - **Synchronous:**
    5-8 Bit Characters
    Internal or External Character
    Synchronization
    Automatic Sync Insertion
  - **Asynchronous:**
    5-8 Bit Characters
    Clock Rate — 1,16 or 64 Times
    Baud Rate
    Break Character Generation
    1, 1½, or 2 Stop Bits
    False Start Bit Detection
    Automatic Break Detect
    and Handling

- **Baud Rate —DC to 64k Baud**
- **Full Duplex, Double Buffered, Transmitter and Receiver**
- **Error Detection — Parity, Overrun, and Framing**
- **Fully Compatible with 8080/8085 CPU**
- **28-Pin DIP Package**
- **All Inputs and Outputs Are TTL Compatible**
- **Single 5 Volt Supply**
- **Single TTL Clock**

The 8251A is the enhanced version of the industry standard, Intel® 8251 Universal Synchronous/Asynchronous Receiver/Transmitter (USART), designed for data communications with Intel's new high performance family of microprocessors such as the 8085. The 8251A is used as a peripheral device and is programmed by the CPU to operate using virtually any serial data transmission technique presently in use (including IBM Bi-Sync). The USART accepts data characters from the CPU in parallel format and then converts them into a continuous serial data stream for transmission. Simultaneously, it can receive serial data streams and convert them into parallel data characters for the CPU. The USART will signal the CPU whenever it can accept a new character for transmission or whenever it has received a character for the CPU. The CPU can read the complete status of the USART at any time. These include data transmission errors and control signals such as SYNDET, TxEMPTY. The chip is constructed using N-channel silicon gate technology.

PIN CONFIGURATION BLOCK DIAGRAM

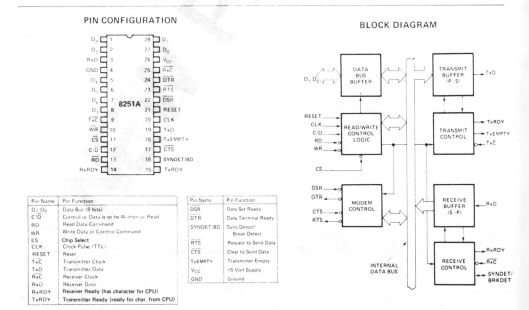

Pin Name	Pin Function
D₇ D₀	Data Bus (8 bits)
C/D̄	Control or Data is to be Written or Read
RD	Read Data Command
WR	Write Data or Control Command
CS	Chip Select
CLK	Clock Pulse (TTL)
RESET	Reset
T×C	Transmitter Clock
T×D	Transmitter Data
R×C	Receiver Clock
R×D	Receiver Data
R×RDY	Receiver Ready (has character for CPU)
T×RDY	Transmitter Ready (ready for char. from CPU)

Pin Name	Pin Function
DSR	Data Set Ready
DTR	Data Terminal Ready
SYNDET/BD	Sync Detect/ Break Detect
RTS	Request to Send Data
CTS	Clear to Send Data
T×EMPTY	Transmitter Empty
V_CC	+5 Volt Supply
GND	Ground

8251A

APPLICATIONS OF THE 8251A

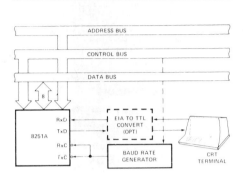

Asynchronous Serial Interface to CRT Terminal,
DC-9600 Baud

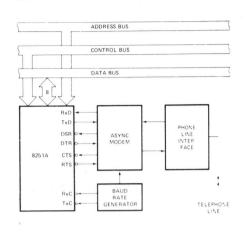

Asynchronous Interface to Telephone Lines

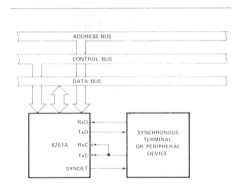

Synchronous Interface to Terminal or Peripheral Device

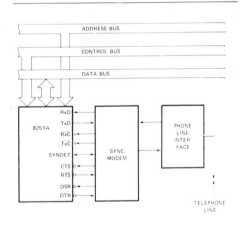

Synchronous Interface to Telephone Lines

Appendix L Intel 2114 1,024 × 4-bit static RAM

	2114-2	2114-3	2114	2114L3	2114L
Max. Access Time (ns)	200	300	450	300	450
Max. Power Dissipation (mw)	710mw	710mw	710mw	370mw	370mw

- **High Density 18 Pin Package**
- **Identical Cycle and Access Times**
- **Single +5V Supply**
- **No Clock or Timing Strobe Required**
- **Completely Static Memory**

- **Directly TTL Compatible: All Inputs and Outputs**
- **Common Data Input and Output Using Three-State Outputs**
- **Pin-Out Compatible with 3605 and 3625 Bipolar PROMs**

The Intel® 2114 is a 4096-bit static Random Access Memory organized as 1024 words by 4-bits using N-channel Silicon-Gate MOS technology. It uses fully DC stable (static) circuitry throughout — in both the array and the decoding — and therefore requires no clocks or refreshing to operate. Data access is particularly simple since address setup times are not required. The data is read out nondestructively and has the same polarity as the input data. Common input/output pins are provided.

The 2114 is designed for memory applications where high performance, low cost, large bit storage, and simple interfacing are important design objectives. The 2114 is placed in an 18-pin package for the highest possible density.

It is directly TTL compatible in all respects: inputs, outputs, and a single +5V supply. A separate Chip Select ($\overline{CS}$) lead allows easy selection of an individual package when outputs are or-tied.

The 2114 is fabricated with Intel's N-channel Silicon-Gate technology — a technology providing excellent protection against contamination permitting the use of low cost plastic packaging.

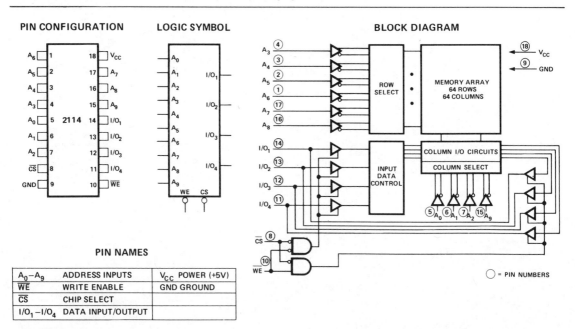

A_0–A_9	ADDRESS INPUTS	V_{CC} POWER (+5V)
$\overline{WE}$	WRITE ENABLE	GND GROUND
$\overline{CS}$	CHIP SELECT	
I/O_1–I/O_4	DATA INPUT/OUTPUT	

A.C. CHARACTERISTICS $T_A = 0°C$ to $70°C$, $V_{CC} = 5V \pm 5\%$, unless otherwise noted.

READ CYCLE [1]

SYMBOL	PARAMETER	2114-2 Min.	2114-2 Max.	2114-3, 2114L3 Min.	2114-3, 2114L3 Max.	2114, 2114L Min.	2114, 2114L Max.	UNIT
t_{RC}	Read Cycle Time	200		300		450		ns
t_A	Access Time		200		300		450	ns
t_{CO}	Chip Selection to Output Valid		70		100		100	ns
t_{CX}	Chip Selection to Output Active	0		0		0		ns
t_{OTD}	Output 3–state from Deselection	0	40	0	80	0	100	ns
t_{OHA}	Output Hold from Address Change	10		10		10		ns

WRITE CYCLE [2]

SYMBOL	PARAMETER	2114-2 Min.	2114-2 Max.	2114-3, 2114L3 Min.	2114-3, 2114L3 Max.	2114, 2114L Min.	2114, 2114L Max.	UNIT
t_{WC}	Write Cycle Time	200		300		450		ns
t_W	Write Time	100		150		200		ns
t_{WR}	Write Release Time	20		0		0		ns
t_{OTW}	Output 3-state from Write	0	40	0	80	0	100	ns
t_{DW}	Data to Write Time Overlap	100		150		200		ns
t_{DH}	Data Hold From Write Time	0		0		0		ns

NOTES: 1. A Read occurs during the overlap of a low $\overline{CS}$ and a high $\overline{WE}$.
2. A Write occurs during the overlap of a low $\overline{CS}$ and a low $\overline{WE}$.

A.C. CONDITIONS OF TEST

Input Pulse Levels . . . . 0.8 Volt to 2.4 Volt

Input Rise and Fall Times . . . . 10 nsec

Input and Output Timing Levels . . . . 1.5 Volts

Output Load . . . . 1 TTL Gate and C_L = 50 pF

Appendix M Texas Instruments dynamic RAM

TMS 4116-30 JDH, NH
16,384-BIT DYNAMIC RANDOM-ACCESS MEMORY

FEBRUARY 1979

- 16,384 X 1 Organization
- All Inputs Including Clocks TTL-Compatible
- Unlatched Three-State Fully TTL-Compatible Output
- Access Time . . . 300 ns
- Cycle Time . . . 560 ns
- Common I/O Capability with "Early Write" Feature
- Low-Power Dissipation
  — Operating . . . . 441 mW (max)
  — Standby . . . . . . 19 mW (max)
- 1-T Cell Design, N-Channel Silicon-Gate Technology
- 16-Pin 300-Mil Package Configuration

16-PIN CERAMIC AND PLASTIC DUAL-IN-LINE PACKAGE (TOP VIEW)

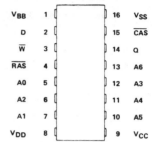

V_{BB}	1		16	V_{SS}
D	2		15	$\overline{CAS}$
$\overline{W}$	3		14	Q
$\overline{RAS}$	4		13	A6
A0	5		12	A3
A2	6		11	A4
A1	7		10	A5
V_{DD}	8		9	V_{CC}

PIN NOMENCLATURE			
A0-A6	Address Inputs	$\overline{W}$	Write Enable
$\overline{CAS}$	Column address strobe	V_{BB}	−5 V power supply
D	Data Input	V_{CC}	+5 V power supply
Q	Data Output	V_{DD}	+12 V power supply
$\overline{RAS}$	Row address strobe	V_{SS}	0 V ground

description

The TMS 4116-30 JH, NH is a monolithic high-speed dynamic 16,384-bit MOS random-access memory organized as 16,384 one-bit words. It employs single-transistor storage cells and N-channel silicon-gate technology.

All inputs and outputs are compatible with Series 74 TTL circuits including clocks: Row Address Strobe $\overline{RAS}$ (or $\overline{R}$) and Column Address Strobe $\overline{CAS}$ (or $\overline{C}$). All address lines (A0 through A6) and data-in (D) are latched on chip to simplify system design. Data out (Q) is unlatched to allow greater system flexibility.

Typical power dissipation is less than 350 milliwatts active and 6 milliwatts during standby (V_{CC} is not required during standby operation). To retain data, only 10 milliwatts average power is required which includes the power consumed to refresh the contents of the memory.

The TMS 4116-30 JDH, NH is offered in 16-pin dual-in-line sidebraze (JD) and plastic (N) packages and is guaranteed for operation from $0°C$ to $55°C$. The package is designed for insertion in mounting-hole rows on 300-mil centers.

operation

address (A0 through A6)

Fourteen address bits are required to decode 1 of 16,384 storage cell locations. Seven row-address bits are set up on pins A0 through A6 and latched onto the chip by the row-address strobe ($\overline{RAS}$). Then the seven column-address bits are set up on pins A0 through A6 and latched onto the chip by the column-address strobe ($\overline{CAS}$). All addresses must be stable on or before the falling edges of $\overline{RAS}$ and $\overline{CAS}$. $\overline{RAS}$ is similar to a chip enable in that it activates the sense amplifiers as well as the row decoder. $\overline{CAS}$ is used as a chip select activating the column decoder and the input and output buffers.

† The term "read-write cycle" is sometimes used as an alternative title to "read-modify-write cycle".

TMS 4116-30 JDH, NH
16,384-BIT DYNAMIC RANDOM-ACCESS MEMORY

write enable ($\overline{W}$)

The read or write mode is selected through the write enable ($\overline{W}$) input. A logic high on the $\overline{W}$ input selects the read mode and a logic low selects the write mode. The write enable terminal can be driven from standard TTL circuits without a pull-up resistor. The data input is disabled when the read mode is selected. When $\overline{W}$ goes low prior to $\overline{CAS}$, data-out will remain in the high-impedance state for the entire cycle permitting common I/O operation.

data-in (D)

Data is written during a write or read-modify-write cycle. The latter falling edge of $\overline{CAS}$ or $\overline{W}$ strobes data into the on-chip data latch. This latch can be driven from standard TTL circuits without a pull-up resistor. In an early write cycle $\overline{W}$ is brought low prior to $\overline{CAS}$ and the data is strobed in by $\overline{CAS}$ with setup and hold times referenced to this signal. In a delayed write or read-modify-write cycle, $\overline{CAS}$ will already be low, thus the data will be strobed in by $\overline{W}$ with setup and hold times referenced to this signal.

data-out (Q)

The three state output buffer provides direct TTL compatibility (no pull-up resistor required) with a fan-out of two Series 74 TTL loads. Data-out is the same polarity as data-in. The output is in the high-impedance (floating) state until $\overline{CAS}$ is brought low. In a read cycle the output goes active after the enable time interval $t_{a(C)}$ that begins with the negative transition of $\overline{CAS}$ as long as $t_{a(R)}$ is satisfied. The output becomes valid after the access time has elapsed and remains valid while $\overline{CAS}$ is low; $\overline{CAS}$ going high returns it to a high-impedance state. In an early write cycle, the output is always in the high-impedance state. In a delayed write or read-modify-write cycle, the output will follow the sequence for the read cycle.

refresh

A refresh operation must be performed at least every two milliseconds to retain data. Since the output buffer is in the high-impedance state unless $\overline{CAS}$ is applied, the $\overline{RAS}$ only refresh sequence avoids any output during refresh. Strobing each of the 128 row addresses (A0 through A6) with $\overline{RAS}$ causes all bits in each row to be refreshed. $\overline{CAS}$ remains high (inactive) for this refresh sequence, thus conserving power.

power-up

V_{BB} must be applied to the device either before or at the same time as the other supplies and removed last. Failure to observe this precaution will cause dissipation in excess of the absolute maximum ratings due to internal forward bias conditions. This also applies to system use, where failure of the V_{BB} supply must immediately shut down the other supplies. After power up, eight memory cycles must be performed to achieve proper device operation.

absolute maximum ratings over operating free-air temperature range (unless otherwise noted)*

Voltage on any pin (see Note 1) . . . . −0.5 to 20 V
Voltage on V_{CC}, V_{DD} supplies with respect to V_{SS} . . . . −1 to 15 V
Short circuit output current . . . . 50 mA
Power dissipation . . . . 1 W
Operating free-air temperature range . . . . 0°C to 55°C
Storage temperature range . . . . −65°C to 150°C

NOTE 1: Under absolute maximum ratings, voltage values are with respect to the most-negative supply voltage, V_{BB} (substrate), unless otherwise noted. Throughout the remainder of this data sheet, voltage values are with respect to V_{SS}.

*Stresses beyond those listed under "Absolute Maximum Ratings" may cause permanent damage to the device. This is a stress rating only and functional operation of the device at these or any other conditions beyond those indicated in the "Recommended Operating Conditions" section of this specification is not implied. Exposure to absolute-maximum-rated conditions for extended periods may affect device reliability.

TEXAS INSTRUMENTS
LIMITED

TMS 4116-30 JDH, NH
16,384-BIT DYNAMIC RANDOM-ACCESS MEMORY

functional block diagram

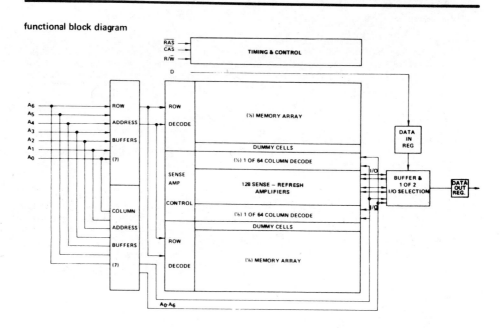

recommended operating conditions

PARAMETER		MIN	NOM	MAX	UNIT
Supply voltage, V_{BB}		−4.5	−5	−5.5	V
Supply voltage, V_{CC}		4.5	5	5.5	V
Supply voltage, V_{DD}		11.4	12	12.6	V
Supply voltage, V_{SS}			0		V
High-level input voltage, V_{IH}	All inputs except $\overline{RAS}$, $\overline{CAS}$, $\overline{WRITE}$	2.4		5.5	V
	$\overline{RAS}$, $\overline{CAS}$, $\overline{WRITE}$	2.7		5.5	
Low-level input voltage, V_{IL} (see Note 2)		−1	0	0.8	V
Refresh time interval, $t_{refresh}$				2	ms
Operating free-air temperature, T_A		0		55	°C

NOTE 2: The algebraic convention where the more positive (less negative) limit is designated as maximum is used in this data sheet for logic voltage levels only.

TEXAS INSTRUMENTS
LIMITED

TMS 4116-30 JDH, NH
16,384-BIT DYNAMIC RANDOM-ACCESS MEMORY

electrical characteristics over full ranges of recommended operating conditions (unless otherwise noted)

	PARAMETERS	TEST CONDITIONS	MIN	TYP[†]	MAX	UNIT
V_{OH}	High-level output voltage	$I_{OH} = -5$ mA	2.4			V
V_{OL}	Low-level output voltage	$I_{OL} = 4.2$ mA			0.4	V
I_I	Input current (leakage)	$V_I = 0$ V to 5.5 V All other pins = 0 V except $V_{BB} = -5$ V			±10	µA
I_O	Output current (leakage)	$V_O = 0$ to 5.5 V, $\overline{CAS}$ high			±10	µA
$I_{BB(1)}$	Average operating current			50	200	µA
$I_{CC(1)}$*	during read or write	Minimum cycle time			4**	mA
$I_{DD(1)}$	cycle			27	35	mA
$I_{BB(2)}$		After 1 memory cycle		10	100	µA
$I_{CC(2)}$	Standby current	$\overline{RAS}$ and $\overline{CAS}$			±10	µA
$I_{DD(2)}$		high		0.5	1.5	mA
$I_{BB(3)}$		Minimum cycle time		50	200	µA
$I_{CC(3)}$	Average refresh current	$\overline{RAS}$ cycling,			±10	µA
$I_{DD(3)}$		$\overline{CAS}$ high		20	27	mA

*V_{CC} is applied only to the output buffer, so I_{CC} depends on output loading.
**Output loading two standard TTL loads.

capacitance over recommended supply voltage range and operating free-air temperature range, f = 1 MHz

	PARAMETER	MIN	TYP[†]	MAX	UNIT
$C_{i(A)}$	Input capacitance, address inputs		4	5	pF
$C_{i(D)}$	Input capacitance, data input		4	5	pF
$C_{i(RC)}$	Input capacitance, strobe inputs		8	10	pF
$C_{i(W)}$	Input capacitance, write enable input		8	10	pF
C_O	Output capacitance		5	7	pF

[†]All typical values are at $T_A = 25°C$ and nominal supply voltages.

switching characteristics over recommended supply voltage range and operating free-air temperature range

	PARAMETER	TEST CONDITIONS	ALTERNATE SYMBOL	MIN	MAX	UNIT
$t_{a(C)}$	Access time from column address strobe	$C_L = 100$ pF, Load = 2 Series 74 TTL gates	t_{CAC}		190	ns
$t_{a(R)}$	Access time from row address strobe	t_{RLCL} = MAX, $C_L = 100$ pF Load = 2 Series 74 TTL gates	t_{RAC}		300	ns
t_{PXZ}	Output disable time	$C_L = 100$ pF, Load = 2 Series 74 TTL gates	t_{OFF}	0	60	ns

TEXAS INSTRUMENTS
LIMITED

**TMS 4116-30 JDH, NH
16,384-BIT DYNAMIC RANDOM-ACCESS MEMORY**

timing requirements over recommended supply voltage range and operating free-air temperature range

	PARAMETER	ALTERNATE SYMBOL	MIN	MAX	UNIT
$t_{c(rd)}$	Read cycle time	t_{RC}	560		ns
$t_{c(W)}$	Write cycle time	t_{WC}	560		ns
$t_{c(RW)}$	Read; modify-write cycle time	t_{RWC}	690		ns
$t_{w(CL)}$	Pulse width, column address strobe low	t_{CAS}	190	10,000	ns
$t_{w(RH)}$	Pulse width, row address strobe high (precharge time)	t_{RP}	250		ns
$t_{w(RL)}$	Pulse width, row address strobe low	t_{RAS}	300	10,000	ns
$t_{w(W)}$	Write pulse width	t_{WP}	100		ns
t_T	Transition times (rise and fall) for $\overline{RAS}$ and $\overline{CAS}$	t_T	3	50	ns
$t_{su(AC)}$	Column address setup time	t_{ASC}	0		ns
$t_{su(AR)}$	Row address setup time	t_{ASR}	0		ns
$t_{su(D)}$	Data setup time	t_{DS}	0		ns
$t_{su(rd)}$	Read command setup time	t_{RCS}	0		ns
$t_{su(WCH)}$	Write command setup time before $\overline{CAS}$ high	t_{CWL}	125		ns
$t_{su(WRH)}$	Write command setup time before $\overline{RAS}$ high	t_{RWL}	125		ns
$t_{h(ACL)}$	Column address hold time after $\overline{CAS}$ low		100		ns
$t_{h(AR)}$	Row address hold time	t_{RAH}	60		ns
$t_{h(ARL)}$	Column address hold time after $\overline{RAS}$ low	t_{AR}	210		ns
$t_{h(CRL)}$	$\overline{CAS}$ hold time after $\overline{RAS}$ low	t_{CSH}	300		ns
$t_{h(DCL)}$	Data hold time after $\overline{CAS}$ low	t_{DH}	100		ns
$t_{h(DRL)}$	Data hold time after $\overline{RAS}$ low	t_{DHR}	210		ns
$t_{h(DWL)}$	Data hold time after $\overline{W}$ low	t_{DH}	100		ns
$t_{h(rd)}$	Read command hold time	t_{RCH}	0		ns
$t_{h(WCL)}$	Write command hold time after $\overline{CAS}$ low	t_{WCH}	100		ns
$t_{h(WRL)}$	Write command hold time after $\overline{RAS}$ low	t_{WCR}	210		ns
t_{CHRL}	Delay time, column address strobe high to row address strobe low	t_{CRP}	0		ns
t_{CLRH}	Delay time, column address strobe low to row address strobe high	t_{RSH}	190		ns
t_{CLWL}	Delay time, column address strobe low to $\overline{W}$ low (read, modify-write cycle only)	t_{CWD}	200		ns
$t_{refresh}$	Refresh time interval	t_{REF}		2	ms
t_{RLCL}	Delay time, row address strobe low to column address strobe low (maximum value specified only to guarantee access time)	t_{RCD}	60	110	ns
t_{RLWL}	Delay time, row address strobe low to $\overline{W}$ low (read, modify-write cycle only)	t_{RWD}	300		ns
t_{WLCL}	Delay time, $\overline{W}$ low to column address strobe low (early write cycle)	t_{WCS}	0		ns

TEXAS INSTRUMENTS
LIMITED

TMS 4116-30 JDH, NH
16,384-BIT DYNAMIC RANDOM-ACCESS MEMORY

read cycle timing

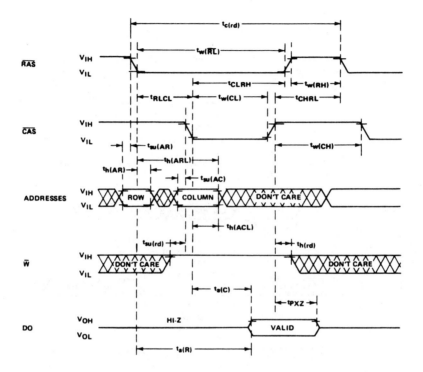

TMS 4116-30 JDH, NM
16,384-BIT DYNAMIC RANDOM-ACCESS MEMORY

early write cycle timing

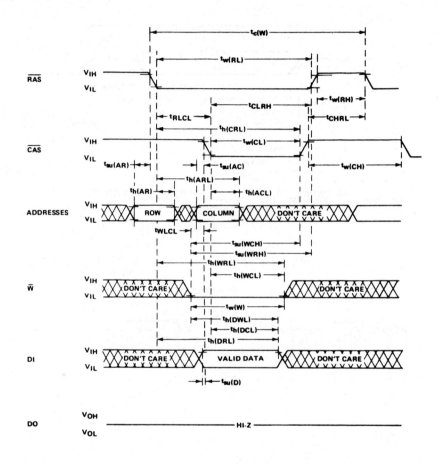

TMS 4116-30 JDH, NH
16,384-BIT DYNAMIC RANDOM-ACCESS MEMORY

write cycle timing

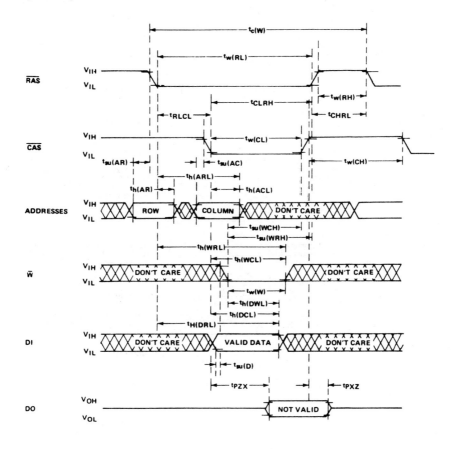

read-write/read-modify-write cycle timing

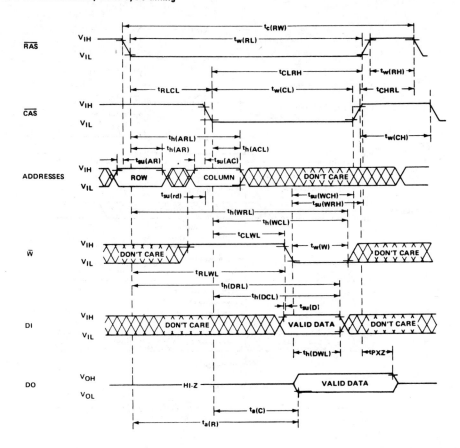

TMS 4116-30 JDH, NH
16,384-BIT DYNAMIC RANDOM-ACCESS MEMORY

$\overline{RAS}$-only refresh timing

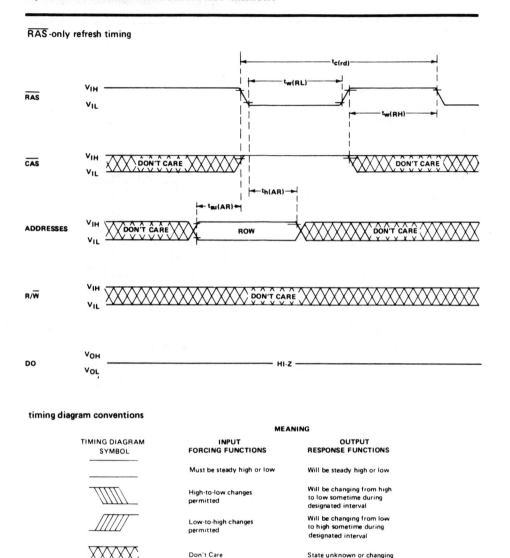

timing diagram conventions

TIMING DIAGRAM SYMBOL	MEANING	
	INPUT FORCING FUNCTIONS	OUTPUT RESPONSE FUNCTIONS
	Must be steady high or low	Will be steady high or low
	High-to-low changes permitted	Will be changing from high to low sometime during designated interval
	Low-to-high changes permitted	Will be changing from low to high sometime during designated interval
	Don't Care	State unknown or changing
	(Does not apply)	Center line is high-impedance off-state

TEXAS INSTRUMENTS
LIMITED

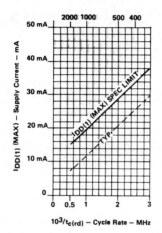

CYCLE RATE (& TIME) vs MAX SUPPLY
CURRENT, $I_{DD(1)}$

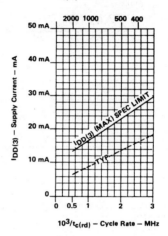

CYCLE RATE (& TIME) vs MAX SUPPLY
CURRENT, $I_{DD(3)}$

Appendix N Intel 2716 16K UVEPROM

- **Single +5V Power Supply**
- **Simple Programming Requirements Single Location Programming Programs With One 50ms Pulse**
- **Low Power Dissipation 525mW Max. Active Power 132mW Max. Standby Power**

- **Pin Compatible To Intel 2316E ROM**
- **Fast Access Time: 450ns Max.**
- **Inputs and Outputs TTL Compatible During Read And Program**

The Intel® 2716 is a 16,384-bit ultraviolet erasable and electrically programmable read-only memory (EPROM). The 2716 operates from a single 5-volt power supply, has a static power down mode, and features fast single address location programming. It makes designing with EPROMs faster, easier and more economical. For production quantities, the 2716 user can convert rapidly to Intel's new pin-for-pin compatible 16K ROM, the 2316E.

Since the 450-nsec 2716 operates from a single 5-volt supply, it is ideal for use with the newer high performance +5V microprocessors such as Intel's 8085 and 8048. The 2716 is also the first EPROM with a static power down mode which reduces the power dissipation without increasing access time. The maximum active power dissipation is 525 mW while the maximum standby power dissipation is only 132 mW, a 75% savings.

The 2716 has the simplest and fastest method yet devised for programming EPROMs — single pulse TTL level programming. No need for high voltage pulsing because all programming controls are handled by TTL signals. Now, it is possible to program on-board, in the system, in the field. Program any location at any time — either individually, sequentially or at random, with the 2716's single address location programming. Total programming time for all 16,384 bits is only 100 seconds.

PIN CONFIGURATION

```
A7   [ 1       24 ]  VCC
A6   [ 2       23 ]  A8
A5   [ 3       22 ]  A9
A4   [ 4       21 ]  VPP
A3   [ 5       20 ]  CS
A2   [ 6       19 ]  A10
A1   [ 7       18 ]  PD/PGM
A0   [ 8       17 ]  O7
O0   [ 9       16 ]  O6
O1   [ 10      15 ]  O5
O2   [ 11      14 ]  O4
GND  [ 12      13 ]  O3
```

PIN NAMES

A_0-A_{10}	ADDRESSES
PD/PGM	POWER DOWN/PROGRAM
$\overline{CS}$	CHIP SELECT
O_0-O_7	OUTPUTS

MODE SELECTION

MODE \ PINS	PD/PGM (18)	$\overline{CS}$ (20)	V_{PP} (21)	V_{CC} (24)	OUTPUTS (9-11, 13-17)
Read	V_{IL}	V_{IL}	+5	+5	D_{OUT}
Deselect	Don't Care	V_{IH}	+5	+5	High Z
Power Down	V_{IH}	Don't Care	+5	+5	High Z
Program	Pulsed V_{IL} to V_{IH}	V_{IH}	+25	+5	D_{IN}
Program Verify	V_{IL}	V_{IL}	+25	+5	D_{OUT}
Program Inhibit	V_{IL}	V_{IH}	+25	+5	High Z

BLOCK DIAGRAM

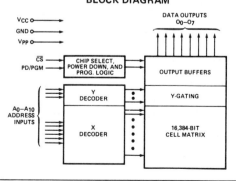

ERASURE CHARACTERISTICS

The erasure characteristics of the 2716 are such that erasure begins to occur when exposed to light with wavelengths shorter than approximately 4000 Angstroms (Å). It should be noted that sunlight and certain types of fluorescent lamps have wavelengths in the 3000–4000Å range. Data show that constant exposure to room level fluorescent lighting could erase the typical 2716 in approximately 3 years, while it would take approximatley 1 week to cause erasure when exposed to direct sunlight. If the 2716 is to be exposed to these types of lighting conditions for extended periods of time, opaque labels are available from Intel which should be placed over the 2716 window to prevent unintentional erasure.

The recommended erasure procedure (see page 3-55) for the 2716 is exposure to shortwave ultraviolet light which has a wavelength of 2537 Angstroms (Å). The integrated dose (i.e., UV intensity $\times$ exposure time) for erasure should be a minimum of 15 W-sec/cm^2. The erasure time with this dosage is approximately 15 to 20 minutes using an ultraviolet lamp with a 12000 μW/cm^2 power rating. The 2716 should be placed within 1 inch of the lamp tubes during erasure. Some lamps have a filter on their tubes which should be removed before erasure.

DEVICE OPERATION

The six modes of operation of the 2716 are listed in Table I. It should be noted that all inputs for the six modes are at TTL levels. The power supplies required are a +5V V_{CC} and a V_{PP}. The V_{PP} power supply must be at 25V during the three programming modes, and must be at 5V in the other three modes.

TABLE I. MODE SELECTION

MODE	PD/PGM (18)	$\overline{CS}$ (20)	V_{PP} (21)	V_{CC} (24)	OUTPUTS (9-11, 13-17)
Read	V_{IL}	V_{IL}	+5	+5	D_{OUT}
Deselect	Don't Care	V_{IH}	+5	+5	High Z
Power Down	V_{IH}	Don't Care	+5	+5	High Z
Program	Pulsed V_{IL} to V_{IH}	V_{IH}	+25	+5	D_{IN}
Program Verify	V_{IL}	V_{IL}	+25	+5	D_{OUT}
Program Inhibit	V_{IL}	V_{IH}	+25	+5	High Z

READ MODE

Data is available at the outputs in the read mode. Data is available 450 ns (t_{ACC}) from stable addresses with $\overline{CS}$ low or 120 ns (t_{CO}) from $\overline{CS}$ with addresses stable.

DESELECT MODE

The outputs of two or more 2716s may be OR-tied together on the same data bus. Only one 2716 should have its outputs selected ($\overline{CS}$ low) to prevent data bus contention between 2716s in this configuration. The outputs of the other 2716s should be deselected with the $\overline{CS}$ input at a high TTL level.

POWER DOWN MODE

The 2716 has a power down mode which reduces the active power dissipation by 75%, from 525 mW to 132 mW. Power down is achieved by applying a TTL high signal to the PD/PGM input. In power down the outputs are in a high impedance state, independent of the $\overline{CS}$ input.

PROGRAMMING

Initially, and after each erasure, all bits of the 2716 are in the "1" state. Data is introduced by selectively programming "0's" into the desired bit locations. Although only "0's" will be programmed, both "1's" and "0's" can be presented in the data word. The only way to change a "0" to a "1" is by ultraviolet light erasure.

The 2716 is in the programming mode when the V_{PP} power supply is at 25V and $\overline{CS}$ is at V_{IH}. The data to be programmed is applied 8 bits in parallel to the data output pins. The levels required for the address and data inputs are TTL.

When the addresses and data are stable, a 50 msec, active high, TTL program pulse is applied to the PD/PGM input. A program pulse must be applied at each address location to be programmed. You can program any location at any time — either individually, sequentially, or at random. The program pulse has a maximum width of 55 msec. The 2716 must not be programmed with a DC signal applied to the PD/PGM input.

Programming of multiple 2716s in parallel with the same data can be easily accomplished due to the simplicity of the programming requirements. Like inputs of the paralleled 2716s may be connected together when they are programmed with the same data. A high level TTL pulse applied to the PD/PGM input programs the paralleled 2716s.

PROGRAM INHIBIT

Programming of multiple 2716s in parallel with different data is also easily accomplished. Except for PD/PGM, all like inputs (including $\overline{CS}$) of the parallel 2716s may be common. A TTL level program pulse applied to a 2716's PD/PGM input with V_{PP} at 25V will program that 2716. A low level PD/PGM input inhibits the other 2716s from being programmed.

PROGRAM VERIFY

A verify should be performed on the programmed bits to determine that they were correctly programmed. The verify may be performed wth V_{PP} at 25V. Except during programming and program verify, V_{PP} must be at 5V.

Z80 COUNTER TIMER CIRCUIT MK 3882

FEATURES

☐ Each channel may be selected to operate in either a counter mode or timer mode.

☐ Programmable interrupts on counter or timer states.

☐ Readable down counter indicates number of counts-to-go until zero.

☐ Selectable 16 or 256 clock prescaler for each timer channel

☐ Selectable positive or negative trigger may initiate timer operation

☐ Three channels have zero count/timeout outputs capable of driving Darlington transistors

☐ Daisy chain priority interrupt logic included to provide for automatic interrupt vectoring without external logic.

☐ All inputs and outputs fully TTL compatible.

DESCRIPTION

The Mostek Z80 product line is a complete set of microcomputer components, development systems and support software. The Z80 microcomputer component set includes all of the circuits necessary to build high-performance microcomputer systems with virtually no other logic and a minimum number of low cost standard memory elements.

The Z80 Counter Timer Circuit (CTC) is a programmable, four channel device that provides counting and timing functions for the Z80 CPU. The Z80-CPU configures the Z80-CTC's four independent channels to operate under various modes and conditions as required.

STRUCTURE

● N−Channel Silicon Gate Depletion Load Technology

● 28 Pin DIP

● Single 5 volt supply

● Single phase 5 volt clock

● Four independent programmable 8-bit counter/16-bit timer channels

Z80 FAMILY

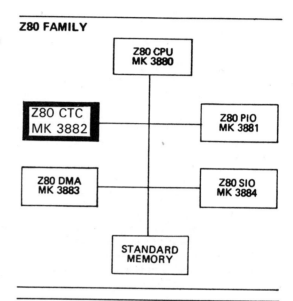

PIN CONNECTIONS

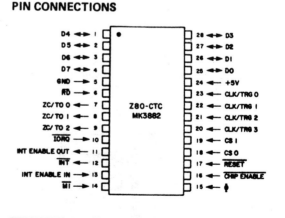

Appendix P Zilog Z6132 quasi-static RAM

Description

The Zilog Z6132 is a +5 V intelligent MOS dynamic RAM organized as 4096 words by eight bits. Although it uses single-transistor dynamic storage cells, the Z6132 effectively functions as a static RAM because it performs and controls its own refresh. This eliminates the need for external refresh circuitry and combines the convenience of a static RAM with the high density and low power consumption normally associated with a dynamic RAM.

The Z6132 is particularly suited for microprocessor and minicomputer applications where its byte-wide organization, transparent self-refresh and single supply voltage reduce the parts count and simplify the design.

The Z6132 uses high-performance depletion-load double-poly n-channel silicon-gate MOS technology with a mixture of static and dynamic circuitry that provides a small memory cell, fast access and low power consumption. The Z6132 has separate pins for addresses and bidirectional data I/O to provide maximum flexibility in its application.

The circuit is packaged in an industry-standard 28-pin DIP and pin compatible with the proposed JEDEC standard.

The Z6132 conforms with the Z-Bus specification used by the new generation of Zilog microprocessors, the Z8 and Z8000.

Features

- Byte-wide organization: 4096 words by eight bits

- Access and cycle times guaranteed over voltage and temperature range:

Part Number	Access Time	Cycle Time
Z6132-3	200 ns	350 ns
Z6132-4	250 ns	375 ns
Z6132-5	300 ns	425 ns

- Low power consumption: 200 mW active, 125 mW stand-by

- Industry-standard 28-pin DIP with JEDEC-recommended pinout

- ±10% tolerance on single +5 V supply voltage

- Automatic self-refresh scheme with slow-and fast-cycle modes

- All inputs and outputs are TTL compatible

- On-chip substrate bias generator

- Interfaces readily to Z8 and Z8000

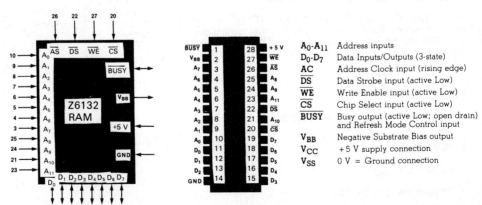

A_0-A_{11}	Address inputs
D_0-D_7	Data Inputs/Outputs (3-state)
AC	Address Clock input (rising edge)
$\overline{DS}$	Data Strobe input (active Low)
$\overline{WE}$	Write Enable input (active Low)
$\overline{CS}$	Chip Select input (active Low)
$\overline{BUSY}$	Busy output (active Low; open drain) and Refresh Mode Control input
V_{BB}	Negative Substrate Bias output
V_{CC}	+5 V supply connection
V_{SS}	0 V = Ground connection

Figure 1. Logic Symbol   **Figure 2. Pin Assignments**   **Pin Names**

Functional Description

The Z6132 4K x 8 quasi-static RAM is organized as two separate blocks, each having two sets of 64 rows on either side of the 128 sense amplifiers (Figure 3). Both blocks have separate and independent row address buffers and decoders, but they share the column decoder and the internal 8-bit wide data path. The two sets of row address decoders are addressed either by the address inputs A_1-A_7 or by the internal 7-bit refresh counter. The least significant address input (A_0) selects one of the two blocks for external access. While the selected block performs a read or write operation, the other memory block uses the refresh counter address to refresh one row. Details of the self-refresh mechanism are explained later.

A memory cycle starts when the rising edge of Address Clock (AC) clocks in Chip Select ($\overline{CS}$), A_0, and Write Enable ($\overline{WE}$). If the chip is not selected ($\overline{CS}$ = High), all other inputs are ignored for the rest of the cycle (that is, until the next rising edge of AC). Both memory blocks are self refreshed by the 7-bit refresh counter. If the chip is selected ($\overline{CS}$ = Low), the 12 address bits and the Write Enable bit are clocked into their registers. A_0 determines which block is addressed by A_1-A_{11}; the other block is refreshed by the 7-bit refresh counter.

The Chip Select and Address inputs must be valid only during a short hold time after the rising edge of AC. This allows address/data multiplexing, because data I/O is controlled by a separate control input Data Strobe ($\overline{DS}$).

Read Cycle

A read cycle is initiated by the rising edge of Address Clock (AC) while Chip Select ($\overline{CS}$) is Low and Write Enable ($\overline{WE}$) High. A Low level on the Data Strobe ($\overline{DS}$) input activates the Data outputs after a specified delay from the rising edge of AC as well as the falling edge of $\overline{DS}$, whichever comes later. During a read operation, $\overline{DS}$ is nothing but a static Output Enable signal.

Write Cycle

A write cycle is initiated by the rising edge of Address Clock (AC) while Chip Select ($\overline{CS}$) is Low and Write Enable ($\overline{WE}$) is Low.

The $\overline{WE}$ input is checked again at the beginning (falling edge) of Data Strobe ($\overline{DS}$).

If $\overline{WE}$ is still Low, this falling edge of $\overline{DS}$ edge-triggers the data on the D_0-D_7 inputs into the addressed memory location. Data must be valid only during a short hold time after the falling edge of $\overline{DS}$.

Write Inhibit Cycle

After a write cycle has been initiated, the actual write operation can still be aborted by pulling $\overline{WE}$ High again before the falling edge of $\overline{DS}$. This write inhibit cycle is a special feature that permits starting a write cycle early at AC time, but still allows the option of inhibiting the write operation later at $\overline{DS}$ time.

Note: *Whenever a write cycle has been initiated, it must be accompanied by a High-to-Low transition on the Data Strobe input.*

Maximum Cycle Time

The maximum read or write cycle time requirements (15,000 and 800 ns) do not apply to any individual cycle. They are specified to guarantee a complete refresh in a 2 ms period.

Appendix Q Texas Instruments decoders/demultiplexers

TTL
MSI

TYPES SN54154, SN54L154, SN74154, SN74L154
4-LINE-TO-16-LINE DECODERS/DEMULTIPLEXERS

BULLETIN NO. DL-S 7211805, DECEMBER 1972

- '154 is Ideal for High-Performance Memory Decoding
- 'L154 is Designed for Power-Critical Applications
- Decodes 4 Binary-Coded Inputs into One of 16 Mutually Exclusive Outputs
- Performs the Demultiplexing Function by Distributing Data From One Input Line to Any One of 16 Outputs
- Input Clamping Diodes Simplify System Design
- High Fan-Out, Low-Impedance, Totem-Pole Outputs
- Fully Compatible with Most TTL, DTL, and MSI Circuits

SN54154 . . . J OR W PACKAGE
SN54L154 . . . J PACKAGE
SN74154, SN74L154 . . . J OR N PACKAGE
(TOP VIEW)

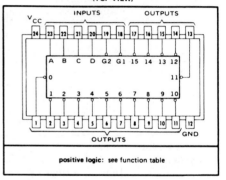

positive logic: see function table

TYPE	TYPICAL AVERAGE PROPAGATION DELAY		TYPICAL POWER DISSIPATION
	3 LEVELS OF LOGIC	STROBE	
'154	23 ns	19 ns	170 mW
'L154	46 ns	38 ns	85 mW

description

Each of these monolithic, 4-line-to-16-line decoders utilizes TTL circuitry to decode four binary-coded inputs into one of sixteen mutually exclusive outputs when both the strobe inputs, G1 and G2, are low. The demultiplexing function is performed by using the 4 input lines to address the output line, passing data from one of the strobe inputs with the other strobe input low. When either strobe input is high, all outputs are high. These demultiplexers are ideally suited for implementing high-performance memory decoders. For ultra-high-speed systems, SN54S138/SN74S138 and SN54S139/SN74S139 are recommended.

These circuits are fully compatible for use with most other TTL and DTL circuits. All inputs are buffered and input clamping diodes are provided to minimize transmission-line effects and thereby simplify system design.

Series 54 and 54L devices are characterized for operation over the full military temperature range of -55°C to 125°C; Series 74 and 74L devices are characterized for operation from 0°C to 70°C.

TEXAS INSTRUMENTS

TYPES SN54154, SN54L154, SN74154, SN74L154
4-LINE-TO-16-LINE DECODERS/DEMULTIPLEXERS

logic

FUNCTION TABLE

INPUTS						OUTPUTS															
G1	G2	D	C	B	A	0	1	2	3	4	5	6	7	8	9	10	11	12	13	14	15
L	L	L	L	L	L	L	H	H	H	H	H	H	H	H	H	H	H	H	H	H	H
L	L	L	L	L	H	H	L	H	H	H	H	H	H	H	H	H	H	H	H	H	H
L	L	L	L	H	L	H	H	L	H	H	H	H	H	H	H	H	H	H	H	H	H
L	L	L	L	H	H	H	H	H	L	H	H	H	H	H	H	H	H	H	H	H	H
L	L	L	H	L	L	H	H	H	H	L	H	H	H	H	H	H	H	H	H	H	H
L	L	L	H	L	H	H	H	H	H	H	L	H	H	H	H	H	H	H	H	H	H
L	L	L	H	H	L	H	H	H	H	H	H	L	H	H	H	H	H	H	H	H	H
L	L	L	H	H	H	H	H	H	H	H	H	H	L	H	H	H	H	H	H	H	H
L	L	H	L	L	L	H	H	H	H	H	H	H	H	L	H	H	H	H	H	H	H
L	L	H	L	L	H	H	H	H	H	H	H	H	H	H	L	H	H	H	H	H	H
L	L	H	L	H	L	H	H	H	H	H	H	H	H	H	H	L	H	H	H	H	H
L	L	H	L	H	H	H	H	H	H	H	H	H	H	H	H	H	L	H	H	H	H
L	L	H	H	L	L	H	H	H	H	H	H	H	H	H	H	H	H	L	H	H	H
L	L	H	H	L	H	H	H	H	H	H	H	H	H	H	H	H	H	H	L	H	H
L	L	H	H	H	L	H	H	H	H	H	H	H	H	H	H	H	H	H	H	L	H
L	L	H	H	H	H	H	H	H	H	H	H	H	H	H	H	H	H	H	H	H	L
L	H	X	X	X	X	H	H	H	H	H	H	H	H	H	H	H	H	H	H	H	H
H	L	X	X	X	X	H	H	H	H	H	H	H	H	H	H	H	H	H	H	H	H
H	H	X	X	X	X	H	H	H	H	H	H	H	H	H	H	H	H	H	H	H	H

H = high level, L = low level, X = irrelevant

functional block diagram and schematics of inputs and outputs

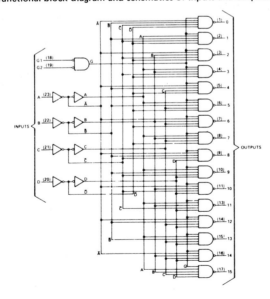

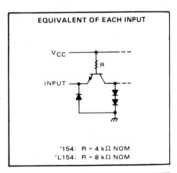

EQUIVALENT OF EACH INPUT

'154: R = 4 kΩ NOM
'L154: R = 8 kΩ NOM

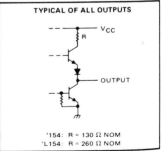

TYPICAL OF ALL OUTPUTS

'154: R = 130 Ω NOM
'L154: R = 260 Ω NOM

TEXAS INSTRUMENTS

Appendix R ASCII code

The table opposite lists the complete set of codes. Groups of letters are non-printing control characters and of particular interest are CR = carriage return, LF = line feed, SP = space and DEL = delete. The parity bit shown is the even parity bit which, together with the 7-bit code, produces the complete 8 bits for each character.

Even parity bit	7-bit octal code	Char.	Even parity bit	7-bit octal code	Char.	Even parity bit	7-bit octal code	Char.
0	000	NUL	0	053	+	0	126	V
1	001	SOH	1	054	,	1	127	W
1	002	STX	0	055	–	1	130	X
0	003	ETX	0	056	.	0	131	Y
1	004	EOT	1	057	/	0	132	Z
0	005	ENQ	0	060	Ø	1	133	[
0	006	ACK	1	061	1	0	134	\
1	007	BEL	1	062	2	1	135	]
1	010	BS	0	063	3	1	136	↑
0	011	HT	1	064	4	0	137	←
0	012	LF	0	065	5	0	140	`
1	013	VT	0	066	6	1	141	a
0	014	FF	1	067	7	1	142	b
1	015	CR	1	070	8	0	143	c
1	016	SO	0	071	9	1	144	d
0	017	SI	0	072	:	0	145	e
1	020	DLE	1	073	;	0	146	f
0	021	DC1	0	074	<	1	147	g
0	022	DC2	1	075	=	1	150	h
1	023	DC3	1	076	>	0	151	i
0	024	DC4	0	077	?	0	152	j
1	025	NAK	1	100	@	1	153	k
1	026	SYN	0	101	A	0	154	l
0	027	ETB	0	102	B	1	155	m
0	030	CAN	1	103	C	1	156	n
1	031	EM	0	104	D	0	157	o
1	032	SUB	1	105	E	1	160	p
0	033	ESC	1	106	F	0	161	q
1	034	FS	0	107	G	0	162	r
0	035	GS	0	110	H	1	163	s
0	036	RS	1	111	I	0	164	t
1	037	US	1	112	J	1	165	u
1	040	SP	0	113	K	1	166	v
0	041	!	1	114	L	0	167	w
0	042	"	0	115	M	0	170	x
1	043	#	0	116	N	1	171	y
0	044	$	1	117	O	1	172	z
1	045	%	0	120	P	0	173	{
1	046	&	1	121	Q	1	174	|
0	047	'	1	122	R	0	175	}
0	050	(	0	123	S	0	176	~
1	051	)	1	124	T	1	177	DEL
1	052	*	0	125	U			

Answers to Questions

1.1 In the form of code, representing characters of the source program text. See also Section 1.5.

1.2 To convert instruction mnemonics of the source program into the machine-code object program. See also Section 1.5.

1.3 Editor.

1.4 See Figure 1.2.

1.5 To allow the programmer to pass information to the assembler which directs the way the program is assembled. See also Section 1.10.

1.6 Pseudo-ops do not represent executable machine-code instructions.

1.7 GLBL, ORG, DS, END.

1.8 ORG.

1.9 In an absolute program, the programmer specifies the location at which the object code will ultimately be stored in memory by means of an ORG pseudo-op in the source program. With a relocatable program, the location of the object program is specified at a later stage using a locator or possibly a linker. See also Sections 1.12, 1.13 and 1.14.

1.10 To fix the address at which a relocatable program is to be stored in memory by modifying all position-dependent addresses in the object code. See also Section 1.14.

1.11 To link together separate program modules to form a single unified program. See also Section 1.15.

2.1 The COP420L is a single-chip microcomputer or microcontroller whereas the other devices could more properly be called CPU-type microprocessors. See also Section 2.3.

2.2 *(a)* Control; *(b)* status.

2.3 *(a)* 2; *(b)* 1; *(c)* 2; *(d)* 1.

2.4 To minimise the number of pins on the microprocessor package and thereby reduce production costs.

2.5 8080, Z8000 (other microprocessors also have this feature).

2.6   See Section 2.3, 'The Z8000'.

2.7   *(a)* 65,536; *(b)* 65,536; *(c)* 8,388,608.

2.8   INX B and PUSH B. (Many other instructions also operate on 16-bit words.) See Appendix A.

2.9   See Section 2.5.

2.11   See Section 2.6, 'Register- and memory-oriented processors'.

2.12   *(a)*   See Section 2.6, 'Register- and memory-oriented processors'.
      (b)   See Section 2.7, 'Direct addressing'.
      (c)   See Section 2.7, 'Immediate addressing'.
      (d)   See Section 2.7, 'Register indirect addressing'.
      (e)   See Section 2.7, 'Indexed addressing'.

2.13   *(a)* Indexed; *(b)* register indirect.

2.14   One or more common computing tasks which are carried out by two or more computers which are being compared. The efficiency with which the tasks are carried out by the various computers can be used as a guide to their suitability for a particular application.

2.15   *8080*

		Clock cycles	Bytes
LDA	NUMBR1	13	3
MOV	B,A	5	1
LDA	NUMBR2	13	3
ADD	B	4	1
STA	NUMBR3	13	3
		48	11

Execution time = 48 μs

Z80

LD	A,(NUMBR1)	13
LD	B,A	4
LD	A,(NUMBR2)	13
ADD	A,B	4
LD	(NUMBR3),A	13
		47

Execution time = 11.75 μs

M6800

LDAA	NUMBR1	4	3
ADDA	NUMBR2	4	3
STAA	NUMBR3	5	3
		13	9

Execution time $= 9$ μs
(Extended addressing is assumed. The use of direct addressing would reduce execution time and memory occupancy.)

Note: Other programs will perform the desired computing function.

3.1 See Section 3.2.

3.2 With interrupt-initiated I/O, the processor can perform other computing tasks between input or output operations. With busy scan, the processor is occupied 100% of the time in servicing the input or output device. See also Section 3.2.

3.3 See Figure 3.10.

3.4 See Figure 3.9.

3.5 A vectored interrupt provides the CPU with a code which identifies the source of the interrupt. With a non-vectored interrupt, the CPU must identify the source before it can be serviced. See also Section 3.3.

3.6 See Section 3.3.

3.7 *(a)* Single-chip microcomputers with built-in I/O ports.
(b) The separate I/O port approach.
(c) The memory-mapped approach.
See also Section 3.1.

3.8 Port I/O: 8080, Z80, Z8000 and others.
Memory-mapped: M6800, 6502 and others.
See also Section 3.1.

3.9 $\overline{\text{IORQ}}$ which goes low when an IN or OUT instruction is executed.

3.10 Code 0010 or 0011 appears on the status lines ST0–ST3 when an interrupt or output operation is taking place. See also Section 3.1.

3.11 *(a)* 256; *(b)* 256; *(c)* 65,536 (ROM and RAM memory space); *(d)* 131,072.

3.12 An interrupt which initiates a safety shut down of a system controlled by the microprocessor. This is only one example – others are possible.

3.13

8080	3
M6800	1
Z80	1
Z8000	1
COP420L	1

3.14 CMOS.

4.1 *Data bus* – carries data and instruction codes to and from the CPU during the execution of a program.
Address bus – carries the address of a memory location or other functional unit during a data transaction.
See also Section 4.1.

4.2 IORQ, RD. Many other answers are acceptable and may be obtained from Appendices A–F.

4.3 See Section 4.2.

4.4 The figure varies depending on the particular device, but a TTL gate can typically sink ten or twenty times as much current as an NMOS output line. See also Section 4.2.

4.5 See Section 4.2.

4.6 See Section 4.2.

4.7 High, low and high impedance. See also Section 4.2.

4.8 The diagram is similar to Figure 4.10 with one additional AND gate.

4.9 9 MHz.

4.10 *(a)* To generate a timing strobe for an 8228 bus controller.
(b) To generate a synchronised RESET signal for the 8080 CPU.
See also Section 4.3 and Appendix F.

4.11 The main function is to demultiplex data and status signals from the combined data/status bus. See also Section 4.3 and Appendix G.

4.12 See Figure 4.14.

4.13 To carry a strobe signal which indicates when the multiplexed address/data bus is carrying an address. See also Section 4.3.

4.14 The diagram is identical to Figure 4.17 with the four-input OR gate replaced by a four-input NAND gate. See also Section 4.4.

4.15 *(a)* Serial I/O; *(b)* memory-mapped parallel I/O. See also Section 4.5.

4.16 By storing an appropriate bit pattern in the data direction registers (DDRA and DDRB). See also Section 4.5 and Appendix J.

4.17 See Section 4.5.

4.18 The essential distinction is that with synchronous transmission, timing information in the form of a clock waveform is transmitted along with the data. With asynchronous transmission, timing information is contained within the data waveform. See also Section 4.5.

4.19 See Figures 4.22 and 4.23.

4.20 See Section 4.5.

4.21 *(a)* Parity check; *(b)* overrun error check; *(c)* framing error check. See also Section 4.5.

4.22   *Advantage* – static RAM does not require refreshing.
Disadvantage – amount of memory which can be packed in each integrated circuit chip is less with static RAM than with dynamic RAM.
See also Section 4.6.

4.23   See Section 4.6.

4.24   A large part of the circuitry required for refreshing dynamic RAM is contained within the CPU chip.

4.25   To minimise the number of pins on the IC package. See also Section 4.6.

5.1   *(a)*   The range of computing tasks justifies the description as general-purpose. A medium-size or large business-oriented, general-purpose computer is generally used for this type of application.
   (b)   Although the application is semi-dedicated, it would probably be implemented on a general-purpose computer.
   (c)   Dedicated.
   (d)   Dedicated.

5.2   *(a)*   In view of the small production run, development costs would be the more important.
   (b)   Consumer items are designed to be produced in large numbers. For a system such as this therefore, production costs would normally be more important than development costs.
   (c)   The answer to this problem is by no means clear-cut. With a production run of 5000 units, production costs would normally outweigh development costs. In this case however, complicating factors exist. The development and production costs of the controller will contribute only a small proportion to total development and production costs of the engine. The long time scale and competitive nature of the market also means that updating and possible redesign of the controller should be contemplated during the production life of the system. To give a firm answer to this question requires much more information about the project, its market and the costing of the other components of the engine.

5.3   In a dedicated system, the program is normally stored in ROM. In a general-purpose system, the program is stored in secondary memory and transferred to primary RAM before execution.

5.4   The number of integrated circuits in a dedicated system is usually smaller than the number in a general-purpose system of comparable computing power.

5.5   See Section 5.2.

5.6 See Section 5.3.

5.7 See Figure 5.3.

5.8 See Sections 5.2, 5.3 and 5.4.

6.1 The design of software. See also Section 6.1.

6.2 See Figure 6.1.

6.3 Part of the system software will be concerned with the control of physical devices such as printers, actuators, stepping motors, etc. This software cannot be fully tested unless the physical devices are connected to the system. See also Section 6.2.

6.4 9.

6.5 0.0024 V.

6.6 60 units.

6.7 75 systems.

7.1 See Section 7.2, Section 7.3 and Figure 5.4.

7.2 A software development station provides facilities for developing assembly or high-level language programs. A full-scale MDS will in addition support hardware development with in-circuit emulation, memory substitution, etc. See also Sections 7.1 and 7.5.

7.3 To provide non-volatile bulk storage for standard support programs such as assemblers, compilers, etc., and to store programs developed by the user. See also Section 7.2.

7.4 *(a)* Operating system and monitor.
(b) Editor.
(c) Assembler.
(d) Compiler(s).
(e) Debugger.
(f) Loader.
(g) Linker.
(h) Locator.
(i) Software trace.

7.5 See Section 7.3.

7.6 See Section 7.3.

7.7 See Section 7.3.

7.8 See Section 7.4.

7.9 See Section 7.4.

8.1 Software.

8.2 See Section 8.2.

8.3 Programming is a term used to describe the complete program design process. This consists of decomposition of the programming task to define program modules followed by the design of the module structure. The final phase, called program coding, involves writing down the assembly language or high-level language source code to implement the program structures.

8.4 See Section 8.3.

8.5 See Section 8.5.

8.6 High-level language.

8.7 Programs requiring close control of peripheral hardware, for example, printer driver routines. Assembly language may also be preferred when speed of execution is of major importance.

8.8 See Section 8.7.

8.9 See Figure A.

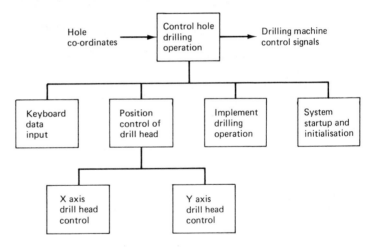

Figure A   Solution to Question 8.9

8.10 The program is similar to that shown in Figures 8.10 and 8.11 but with LOOP = 7.

8.11 See Figure B.

8.12 See Figure C.

8.13 See Figure D.

8.14 See Figure E. Note that by using the twos complement representation, negative numbers always have the least significant bit (LSB) equal to 1.

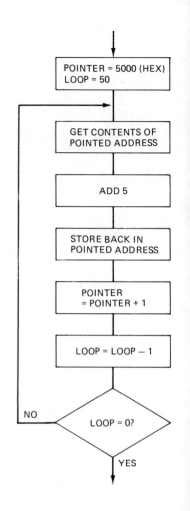

```
POINTER = 5000 (hex)
LOOP = 50
DO UNTIL LOOP = 0
        ITEM = CONTENTS OF POINTED ADDRESS
        ITEM = ITEM + 5
        STORE ITEM IN POINTED ADDRESS
        POINTER = POINTER + 1
        LOOP = LOOP - 1
END DO
```

Figure B   Solution to Question 8.11

```
NUMBER = CONTENTS OF ADDRESS 1000
IF MSB OF NUMBER = 0
    THEN
        POS = POS + 1
    ELSE
        NEG = NEG + 1
END IF
```

Figure C   Solution to Question 8.12

```
LOOP 1 = 50
POINTER = 1000 (hex)
DO UNTIL LOOP 1 = 0
        NUMBER = CONTENTS OF POINTED ADDRESS
        SUM = 0
        LOOP 2 = 5
        DO UNTIL LOOP 2 = 0
                SUM = SUM + NUMBER
                LOOP 2 = LOOP 2 - 1
        END DO
        STORE SUM IN POINTED ADDRESS
        POINTER = POINTER + 1
        LOOP = LOOP 1 - 1
END DO
```

Figure D Solution to Question 8.13

Figure E Solution to Question 8.14

```
POS = 0
NEG = 0
LOOP = 100 (hex)
POINTER = 1000 (hex)
DO UNTIL LOOP = 0
   NUMBER = CONTENTS OF POINTED ADDRESS
   IF MSB OF NUMBER = 0
      THEN
           POS = POS + 1
      ELSE
           NEG = NEG + 1
   END IF
   POINTER = POINTER + 1
   LOOP = LOOP - 1
END DO
```

9.1 Disk ceramic 10–100μF decoupling capacitors to at least every two or three integrated circuits. In addition, electrolytic or tantalum decoupling capacitors of 10–100 μF to every five or ten integrated circuits is desirable.

9.2 See Section 9.4.

9.3 For obvious reasons, a read/write testing cycle which is appropriate to RAM cannot be used with ROM. The test procedure for ROM therefore involves the read operation only on a ROM with known contents. See also Section 9.3.

9.4 LEDs for simulating data receiving devices (sinks). Switches for simulating data transmitting devices (sources).

9.5 The main reason is that increased complexity increases the possibility of multiple faults as a result of design or constructional errors. Finding one fault in the presence of others is always difficult and the level of difficulty increases at a rate related roughly exponentially to the number of faults present. The modular approach to both hardware and software attempts to avoid this problem by ensuring that not more than one fault is present at any one time in a module being tested.

10.1 See Section 10.1.

10.2 *(a)* Existing support for 8080.
       (b) Previous experience of design time and short production run of system to be designed.

10.3 The major reason is that some computation is required in the interval between clock pulses. See also Section 10.5.

10.4 Since data must be processed during the timing interval, a simple loop delay program cannot be used. It then becomes very difficult to predict and control time delays as the various possible computations take place. An external real time clock offers a much less complicated alternative in this case. See also Section 10.5.

10.5 The time resolution required. See Section 10.5.

10.6 See Section 10.5.

10.7 To provide a storage area for the stack and also to hold temporary variables generated during the execution of the program.

10.8 0000.

10.9 See Section 10.9.

11.1 See Section 11.2.

11.2 10 years.

11.3 See Appendix N.

11.4 525 mW. See also Appendix N.

11.5 Maximum 55 ms, minimum 45 ms.

11.6 *(a)* +25 V; *(b)* +5 V. See also Appendix N.

11.7 2716 access time is typically 300–500 ns.
2114 access time is typically 200–450 ns.
See also Appendices L and N.

11.8 5.

11.9 The PROM cannot be erased to make program modifications whereas an EPROM can be erased many times, thus avoiding the use of a new memory device every time the program is modified.

11.10 *(a)* UVEPROMs take longer to program than EAROMs.
(b) UVEPROMs take much longer to erase than EAROMs.
The overall result of both of these disadvantages is that the test–erase–reprogram cycle may take an unacceptably long time if UVEPROMs are the only way of supporting software development in dedicated systems. EAROMs reduce this time, but do not forget that they have their own problems as described in Section 11.4.

12.1 See Section 12.3.

12.2 See Section 12.4.

12.3 Visual inspection. See also Section 12.4.

12.4 The oscilloscope can detect rapid variations in d.c. voltage supply levels which may be important in microprocessor systems but which cannot be detected using a normal test meter. See also Section 12.7.

12.5 See Section 12.6.

12.6 See Section 12.6.

12.7 Apart from the system clock, repetitive waveforms which can be easily viewed with an oscilloscope do not occur very often in microprocessor systems. See also Section 12.7.

12.8 The oscilloscope can measure important parameters such as rise time and overshoot which the logic analyser is incapable of measuring.

12.9 $\overline{CS}$ should be activated when a memory read or write operation occurs with an address in which $A15 = 1$. Figure F shows the pseudo-code description of a program which repeatedly reads all such addresses, cycling through from 8000–FFFF. While this program is running, a regular train of $\overline{CS}$ pulses should be observed by means of

```
REPEAT = 1
DO UNTIL REPEAT = 0
               POINTER = 8000
               LOOP    = 8000
               DO UNTIL LOOP = 0
                         READ POINTED ADDRESS
                         POINTER = POINTER + 1
                         LOOP = LOOP - 1
               END DO
END DO
```

Figure F

an oscilloscope. The second beam of the oscilloscope can monitor R/$\overline{\text{W}}$ which should always be high when $\overline{\text{CS}}$ is low. A similar program with a write operation in place of read produces a train of $\overline{\text{CS}}$ pulses but in this case, R/$\overline{\text{W}}$ should be low when $\overline{\text{CS}}$ is low. See also Section 12.8.

12.10 See Section 12.10.

13.1 With synchronous sampling, the sampling times are fixed by the clock of the system under test. Asynchronous sampling uses a clock within the logic analyser to determine sampling times. See also Section 13.2.

13.2 See Section 13.2 and Figure 13.3.

13.3 See Section 13.2.

13.4 See Section 13.2 and Figures 13.5 and 13.6.

13.5 See Section 13.3.

13.6 1101.

Index